EDITED AND WITH CONTRIBUTIONS BY STEPHEN SWALES

Marketing Geography

THIRD EDITION

PEARSON

Custom
Publishing

Printed in Canada

10   9   8

ISBN 0-536-69374-9

2008420143

ED/MJ

Please visit our web site at *www.pearsoncustom.com*

PEARSON CUSTOM PUBLISHING
501 Boylston Street, Suite 900, Boston, MA 02116
A Pearson Education Company

Contents

Copyright Acknowledgments

Introduction

MARKETING GEOGRAPHY
Stephen Swales

Geography matters in the success of both public and private sector enterprises. At the very least services need to address the two major components of supply and demand both of which have "geographies" that can be very distinctive. The objective of service provision is to bring together supply and demand in an effective manner – see Table 1 for examples of supply and demand pairings.

Table 1: Supply and Demand

Supply	Demand
Store	Customers
Hospital	Patients
Library	Patrons
School	Students
Cinema	Patrons
Restaurant	Clientele

Each of these aspects of supply and demand has a geographical distribution and **location strategies** can play a role in effectively bringing supply and demand together. For example, if community services are responsible for providing language services for recent immigrants, it is useful to locate facilities relative to the target group. A retail chain is likely to have a target market in mind, where is this target market and how can the retail chain locate to appeal to them? As we will see, however, Marketing Geography is about much more than **location** of supply relative to market (demand). Retailing and other commercial activities have an important **global** context and retailing is increasingly a global enterprise. Aspects of consumer behaviour are distinctively **spatial** in character – for example, how are retailers responding to the increased **mobility** of consumers? Retail uses command the visible and accessible sites in urban places and as such dominate urban physical **landscapes**. For better or worse shopping activities are a preoccupation of North American society and reflect a cultural, social and lifestyle context where shopping is far from just economic exchange, for many shopping is genuine recreation and core to social interaction. The combination of entertainment and shopping has long been a successful commercial strategy.

It is evident that a geographical theme runs through retail strategies, what is the value of a geographical perspective?

The Value of the Geographical Perspective

We will briefly explore the value of the geographical perspective by reaching back to the nineteenth century followed by a contemporary retail example.

It may seem odd to go back to the middle of the nineteenth century to explore the value of Geography but the oft used study of cholera in Soho (see Figure 1) serves well to illustrate the power of the geographical perspective. Dr. John Snow, sometimes referred to as the father of epidemiology, was attempting to account

Figure 1: Snow's Cholera Map of Soho, London 1848

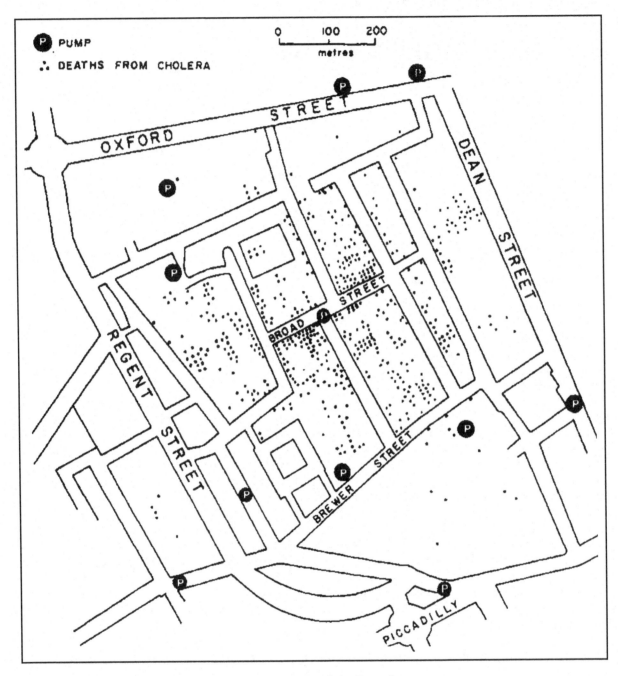

Source: D. Stamp (1964), reproduced in H.R. Jones (1981), *A Population Geography*

for a series of cholera outbreaks in central London. Contemporary wisdom of the time thought the disease was airborne. Snow mapped the incidence of cholera deaths together with water pumps and roads. The spatial pattern of the cholera deaths is very distinctive, strongly clustered around the Broad Street pump. Cholera showed a distance decay pattern from the pump – the greater distance from the pump, the fewer the deaths from cholera. Snow suggested there was something amiss with the water supply at Broad Street and tested his hypothesis by having the handle of the pump removed. The incidence of cholera plummeted. It was not for another fifty years that chemical analysis was sufficiently advanced to confirm such contamination; Snow had effectively identified the source of the problem using simple Geography.

A number of geographical concepts are important here. **Data are collected** on the addresses of deaths and locations of water pumps and these **data are mapped** to explore the distribution of the deaths. A distinctive **clustered pattern** is revealed suggesting a **distance decay relationship** between the incidence of cholera and a specific pump – the further from the pump the fewer the deaths. Note that the dataset alone is unlikely to reveal the pattern – the map is crucial to pick out the **spatial relationship**. People distant from the Broad Street pump are less likely to have cholera because other pumps – **intervening opportunities** – are available to these people. Although the overall pattern is obvious there are **anomalies** and Snow needed to account for these to be confident in his hypothesis and conclusion. Some areas neighbouring the pump did not have cholera and some distant areas did have cholera even when intervening opportunities (other pumps) were nearby (see Figure 1). The nearby sites without cholera included a convent which had its own water supply in a well and a brewery where the workers had a choice to drink beer! The distant cholera households likely included people who visited the Broad Street area for work, shopping or social activities and drank the water while in the vicinity. (This latter point relates to an important consideration in retail strategies – we may use residence based data such as customer addresses and the census to suggest journey-to-shop origins but many shoppers begin their shopping journey from work. This partly accounts for very healthy retail in the core of some Canadian cities which tap on a nearby sizeable work population.)

Data collection and mapping are central to simple retail applications. Home addresses, or often simply postal codes, are routinely collected by retailers and mapped relative to the store (see Figure 2). In some retail types, address data are collected as a matter of course, for example as in video rentals and banks, but other means of data collection include traditional competitions, surveys, credit cards and affinity (loyalty) cards. (The latter more comprehensive methods capture much more data than just addresses if combined with scanned point-of-sale data.)

If we consider the pattern of customers in Figure 2 it is evident that the customers are strongly clustered in the vicinity of the store (which is a video store) and there is a distance decay pattern with a decreasing number of customers with increasing distance from the store. This is a simple but important observation and is often lost on many businesses:

> "In spite of the intuitive nature of the model which shows that people are increasingly less likely to visit retail or service centres which are of greater distance from their residence or workplace, it nevertheless comes as a surprise to many on the marketing side of organizations that, rather than market share being evenly spread across a region, high levels of penetration are concentrated around branches." (Birkin et. al. 1996, p. 6)

The reason for this distance decay pattern is that there is a disincentive nature to covering distance - it costs in money and time to cover distance and the greater the distance the greater the cost. So this disincentive nature of distance is a real economic consideration in the relationship between customers and prospective supply destinations.

Although the distance decay pattern is evident in Figure 2 there are anomalies. Some areas in the immediate vicinity of the store do not have any customers and, although most customers are relatively close, some are very distant. A quick check of an aerial photograph would show that the nearby empty areas are non-residential areas such as industrial and parks. It is not to say that industrial and other commercial areas will not generate customers among the workers but theses customers would be identified by their home addresses. This might also explain some of the distant customers who use the store because it is near their workplace. These distant customers travel long distances and must be passing by other video stores – intervening opportunities – to reach this video store. This could perhaps be explained by the fact that the video store is a specialty video store providing specific language videos not available at the other video stores.

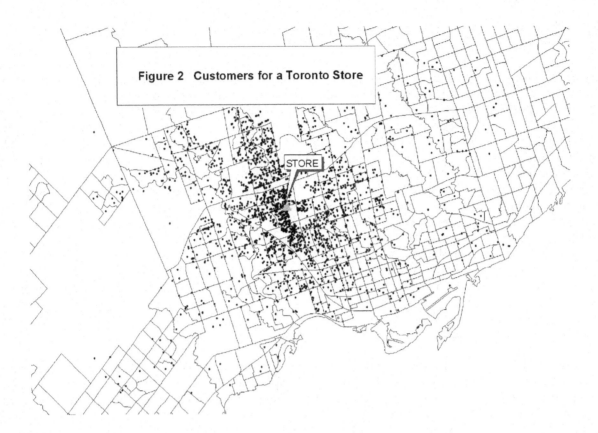

Figure 2   Customers for a Toronto Store

The Geography in Retail Analysis

Geographers bring to retail analysis a perspective that has much to do with the success of the retail enterprise in general and retail facilities in particular. Consider the following ideas:

- With increased **globalization** retail firms need to know the **geographical characteristics of different countries.**
- Firms seek out good **locations** for their facilities.
- Locations will be selected relative to the **spatial distribution of a target market.** Geographers are concerned with the **composition and spatial distribution of demographic groups.**
- Firms will also locate relative to the **spatial distribution of the competition**.
- **Accessibility of sites** is considered to be critical to success. Geographers have an intuitive and practical understanding of how locations vary in levels of accessibility. **Visibility of sites** is also an important characteristic for successful locations.
- **Trade area analysis** used by Geographers identifies the extent of service areas for stores or centres and the market composition within these areas.
- Geographers also have effective **site selection tools** to evaluate the characteristics and potential of prospective sites.
- Retail analysis benefits from a suite of **geotechnology tools** Geographers have at their disposal including Geographical Information Systems (GIS), aerial photography, remote sensing and GPS.
- **Spatial mobility** is a very important component of consumer behaviour. Geographers have both a theoretical and practical understanding of **spatial interaction.**

Box One

Distance Decay

Sometimes referred to as 'the first law of geography' the concept of distance decay suggests that all other things being equal nearer things are more likely to interact than distant things. Put in a different way, we would observe that interaction with a location declines with distance - this is the "decay" concept. The relationship is shown graphically in the figure below.

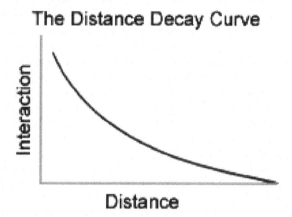

Examples of distance decay include the declining number of students with distance from the university, the declining number of commuters with distance from the downtown and the declining noise levels with distance from the soccer stadium. The most obvious business example of distance decay is the tendency for customers of a store to be more likely drawn from nearer areas rather than distant areas. The further an area from a store the fewer the customers for the store. This uneven spatial interaction is obviously of critical importance in understanding market composition and distribution and also consumer behaviour. Consider the example of a video store and customers in Figure 2.

- Retail firms **model** the likely impacts of different **locational scenarios**. Models are often used by Geographers in such analysis.

- Shopping areas try to appeal to customers with a **sense of place** and for better or worse retail functions dominate the impression of **urban landscapes** because they seek out **the most accessible and visible sites.** Geographers have a traditional concern with place and landscape.

- Geographers have good **fieldwork skills** with which they are able to observe commercial supply and local market. Prospective retail sites are typically evaluated on the ground as well as in the office.

- There is a traditional association between **Planning and Geography** and Geographers understand the processes of land use change and the procedures that bring them about. Retail change takes place within a planning arena.

At the very least Geographers have an understanding of the Geography of Demand and the Geography of Supply together with the processes that bring them together:

"To meet demand, suppliers usually establish a distribution channel for their products. Some of these channels involve locating outlets (shops, petrol stations, hospitals, etc.) in distinct physical locations as part of a supply network. Other channels, such as mail order, telephone banking and so on, have more flexible geographical characteristics. However, in all cases there is an interaction between demand and supply that involves the flow of something, whether this be money,

information, people, or goods. It is an understanding of the complex inter-relationship between demand and supply and the way this varies over space and time that is at the heart of many organizations' management responsibility." (Birkin et. al. 1996, p.2)

An Outline for Marketing Geography

Figure 3 provides a diagrammatic outline for the study of Marketing Geography.

We are concerned with the two major components of marketing, **Market** (or demand) and **Supply**, each of which has distinctive geographies. Of **Market** (demand) we could ask: what is the composition of market and where are different market groups found? How is population distributed across a country and within urban areas? Where are different socioeconomic, demographic (age and sex) and ethnic groups found? Where can we find combinations of characteristics that form important target markets, for example, upper income highly mobile baby boomers or middle income Italian families? What is the spatial extent of market areas presently? What processes, for example residential mobility, are responsible for change in market distribution? What will the composition and location of market be like in the future?

Figure 3   Marketing Geography

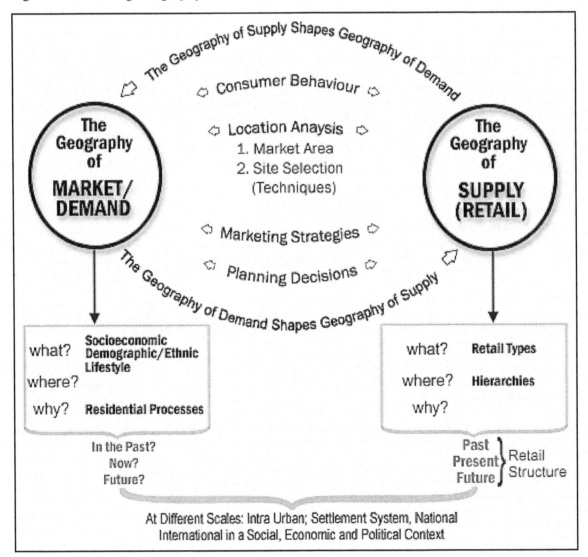

Of **Supply** we can ask: what are the different types of retail supply and where are they typically found? There is much diversity in retail supply including traditional retail strips, suburban retail strips, shopping centres (malls), ancillary retail[1] and recently, power retail[2]. What are the implications of non-store retailing such as the Internet? How has the spatial distribution of retailing changed as each new type of retailing has evolved? Why is retail structure distinctively hierarchical in nature? What new types of retailing will develop as the market continues to change? What type of supply will appeal to aging baby boomers?

Change in market clearly shapes retail supply, for example, when middle income populations began to suburbanize, shopping malls and more recently power retail followed. It is also true that supply shapes market, the massive advertising industry is testament to this. **Change in the retail landscape** is a function of the interplay of supply and market processes.

How are market and supply brought together? **Consumer behaviour** brings the components together. For example, many consumers have increased in their mobility and this has important consequences for retail location strategy as fewer larger facilities are built, increasing the average travel distance for consumers.

Techniques are also used to bring supply and demand together. **Trade area analysis** identifies the real extent of service areas through customer spotting and market penetration and also theoretical service areas using normative techniques that incorporate the spatial interaction of consumers with stores and centres. These techniques can be used to model the impact of different retail location scenarios.

More specific than trade areas are the actual sites of facilities and a suite of **site selection methods** are used, to varying degrees and with mixed results, to evaluate prospective sites.

Retail change is a function of **marketing strategies** but also takes place within a formal **planning** arena. Retail development proposals are usually evaluated at the municipal planning level.

The context for all this activity is economic, cultural and social, taking place at different scales: local (at the intra-urban scale), national (at the settlement scale) and increasingly global.

A Global Enterprise

Retailing is increasingly a global enterprise. There is nothing new about globalization which arguably goes back to the ancient Greeks and certainly to the European overseas exploits beginning in the 15th century, but the new globalization is quite different from anything that has gone before.

North Americans have access to an immense variety of products from an increasing diversity of sources, products that are good quality and affordable. What makes this possible are recent changes that have taken place under a new, much more flexible, post-Fordist mode of production known as **advanced or disorganized capitalism**.

Characteristics of these changes include: less government involvement; the rise of transnational corporations (TNCs) that seek out best sites for production in multiple countries; a new international division of labour (NIDL) which enables producers to seek out labour efficiencies worldwide; freer trade brought about by trading blocs (such as the EU and NAFTA) and the World Trade Organization (WTO); the opening up of massive new markets in the old eastern bloc, India and China; the shift to service and consumer

---

[1] Retail found in some other predominant land use such as office towers, subway stations and airports.
[2] Big box retail found in clusters as power centres or, if more than one cluster, power nodes.

industries; and flexible production systems that can respond to changes quickly. Added to this are: logistical improvements in transportation (such as containerization, super cargo ships and GPS); better information collection and transfer (such as point-of-sale scanners, bar codes, RFIDs); new consumer technologies and services (e.g. laptop computers, computer software, digital music, MP3 players, iPods, iPhones, PDAs, CDs, DVDs, cell phones, Wii, video/computer games, flat screen TVs, online shopping, etc.); global branding (Just Do It!); and just-in-time (JIT) delivery systems. The results are not always good as producers exploit the cheapest sites for production, but retailers have access to much bigger global markets, a greater diversity of types of goods and a greater diversity of sources of goods. Consumers have access to a vast array of affordable products. Opportunities for retailers to expand into new markets are substantial, for example, many big western retailers have expanded into China (Wang and Du consider this in Chapter 1).

A Big Industry

Retailing is a big industry in Canada. In 2006, 1,715,114 people were employed in retail trade - about 12.5% of the total labour force (see Table 2). An additional 820,194 were employed in food service and drinking places and 739,728 in wholesale trade. In 2007 about $412.2 billion was spent in retail (see Table 3). Of the non-automotive activities, food and beverage, general merchandise and clothing dominate in employment numbers (Table 2) and supermarkets and general merchandise in sales (Table 3).

Table 2 Retail Trade Employment					
	2002	**2003**	**2004**	**2005**	**2006**
			number		
Retail trade	**1,541,496**	**1,586,326**	**1,623,533**	**1,670,283**	**1,715,114**
Motor vehicle and parts dealers	160,440	167,451	170,129	172,104	177,772
Furniture and home furnishings stores	60,803	61,543	63,937	67,179	68,554
Electronics and appliance stores	57,963	58,023	57,921	60,623	61,750
Building material and garden equipment and supplies dealers	79,556	81,171	82,673	87,227	93,609
Food and beverage stores	398,254	418,541	442,183	459,304	471,391
Health and personal care stores	123,138	127,957	127,810	129,695	132,733
Gasoline stations	81,113	81,222	81,480	83,168	84,658
Clothing and clothing accessories stores	173,053	178,656	177,110	181,829	190,889
Sporting goods, hobby, book and music stores	75,812	74,717	75,842	79,795	82,009
General merchandise stores	207,024	210,731	218,748	223,597	224,988
Miscellaneous store retailers	84,321	87,199	88,040	88,988	89,426
Non-store retailers	40,018	39,113	37,661	36,773	37,335

Note: North American Industry Classification System (NAICS), 2002 - 44-45.
Source: Statistics Canada, CANSIM, table 281-0024 and Catalogue no. 72-002-X. Last modified: 2008-01-22.

Table 3: Retail trade, by industry, Canada					
	2003	2004	2005	2006	2007
			unadjusted		
			$ millions		
All retail trade groups	**331,143.4**	**346,721.5**	**366,170.7**	**389,567.4**	**412,207.0**
Total excluding new, used and recreational motor vehicle and parts dealers	248,565.9	264,021.2	279,353.7	297,523.7	316,227.7
New car dealers	68,183.6	68,141.1	71,515.6	74,663.2	77,197.0
Used and recreational motor vehicle & parts dealers	14,393.9	14,559.2	15,301.4	17,380.5	18,782.2
Gasoline stations	29,951.3	33,363.8	38,356.8	41,606.9	46,085.3
Furniture stores	7,923.8	8,506.5	8,914.4	9,585.5	10,130.7
Home furnishings stores	3,971.6	4,438.9	4,686.3	5,339.9	5,988.8
Computer and software stores	1,883.9	1,581.8	1,557.5	1,517.6	1,417.6
Home electronics and appliance stores	9,089.7	9,443.1	10,164.8	11,157.0	12,323.9
Home centres and hardware stores	14,595.2	16,597.8	18,220.7	20,126.5	21,541.2
Specialized building materials and garden stores	4,316.0	4,372.8	4,340.4	4,627.9	5,084.7
Supermarkets	56,874.1	59,760.9	62,196.3	63,512.5	65,291.8
Convenience and specialty food stores	8,371.4	8,806.9	9,128.6	9,356.4	10,123.8
Beer, wine and liquor stores	13,293.7	13,789.8	14,343.9	15,160.3	16,035.5
Pharmacies and personal care stores	21,266.6	22,769.3	23,642.7	26,070.3	28,357.6
Clothing stores	14,567.1	15,311.6	16,069.3	17,248.5	18,254.0
Shoe, clothing accessories and jewellery stores	4,903.8	4,876.8	4,981.3	5,400.3	5,585.8
General merchandise stores[1]	40,011.0	42,123.7	43,758.4	46,518.3	48,624.3
Department stores[1]	20,800.8	21,849.9	x	..	..
Other general merchandise stores[1]	19,210.2	20,273.8	x	..	..
Sporting goods, hobby, music and book stores	8,676.1	8,831.4	9,379.3	10,003.1	10,612.8
Miscellaneous store retailers	8,870.7	9,446.1	9,613.1	10,292.8	10,769.9

x: suppressed to meet the confidentiality requirements of the Statistics Act. .. : not available for a specific period of time.
Note: North American Industry Classification System (NAICS), 2002.
1. As of December 2005, Statistics Canada is no longer publishing separate figures for "Department stores" and "Other general merchandise stores" due to confidentiality constraints. Instead, "Department stores" sales are combined with "Other general merchandise stores" sales and are published under the grouping "General merchandise stores".
Source: Statistics Canada, CANSIM, table (for fee) 080-0014 and Catalogue no. 63-005-X. Last modified: 2008-02-22.

The Chapters of This Book

The following table identifies topics in Marketing Geography and related chapters in the book.

TOPIC	CHAPTER(S)
The Global Context of Retailing	Swales, Stephen, *Introduction*; Ch.1 Wang, S. and Du, P., *Foreign Retailers in China: Stories of Success and Setbacks*.
Overview of Canadian Retailing	Ch.2 Jones, K. and Hernandez, T., *Dynamics of the Canadian Retail Environment*.
Typology of Retailing	Ch. 2 Jones, K. and Hernandez, T., *Dynamics of the Canadian Retail Environment*. The evolution of retailing is considered in Ch.12 Hernandez, T., Helix, J. and Moore, P., *The Changing Character of Retail Strips in the City of Toronto: 1996-2005*
Spatial Concepts and Retailing	Swales, Stephen, *Introduction*; Ch.3 Wang, S., Gomez-Insausti, R., Barbiero, P. and McNally, B., *Entertainment Cross-Shopping*
Trade Area Analysis	Ch.4 Swales, Stephen, *Trade Area Analysis*
Site Selection	Ch.5 Swales, Stephen, *Site Selection and Evaluation*
Canadian Markets	Ch.6 Simmons, J. and Kamikihara, S., *The Canadian Market*
Urban Markets	Ch.7 Simmons, J. and Kamikihara, S., *Urban Markets*; Ch.8 Simmons, J. and Kamikihara, S., *Canada's Megamarkets*; Ch.9 Swales, Stephen, *Recent Canadian Urban Experience: Evidence from the 2006 Census*
Market Change	Ch.10 Simmons, J. and Kamikihara, S., and Hernandez, T., *Aging Consumers and the Commercial Structure*
Retail Supply	Ch.11 Daniel, C. and Hernandez, T. *Canada's Leading Retailers*
Retail Types and Change	Ch.12 Hernandez, T., Helix, J. and Moore, P., *The Changing Character of Retail Strips in the City of Toronto: 1996-2005*; Ch.13 Wrigley, N., and Lowe, M., *The Mall*; Ch.14 Hernandez, T., Erguden, T., and Svindal, M., *Power Retail Growth in Canada and the GTA: 2006*; Ch.15 Hernandez et. al. *Hot Spots in Canadian Retailing: 2002–2003*
Consumer Behaviour	Ch.16 Losch, B., *Consumer Behaviour and Power Retailing*; Ch.3 Wang et.al.; Ch.4 Swales
Planning Issues	Planning ideas are addressed in Ch.12 Hernandez, T., Helix, J. and Moore, P., *The Changing Character of Retail Strips in the City of Toronto: 1996-2005*
The Future?	Ch.17 Hernandez, T., *Lifestyle Centres in Canada: 2007*; Ch.18 Swales, Stephen, *Some Data and Observations on the Digital Divide and Internet Shopping*

The appendices and chapters 9, 11, and 18 contain data that could be used in student assignments.

" . . . not only is geography relevant and important, it can also be exciting in that it can sit comfortably within the heart of the business process that large organizations undertake" (Birkin et.al. 1996, p. 3)

" . . . these everyday practices of consumption have great significance, economically and culturally; and that they are fundamentally geographical, implicated in production of the 'global', 'local' and non-academic or 'lay' geographical knowledges. In sum, I argue that in significant part we both produce and understand our geographies through our everyday, mundane activities as consumers." (Crang, P. 2005 p.360)

Clearly Geography is relevant in corporate marketing strategies and in everyday consumption activities. If Marketing is about how to best reach consumers of goods and services then Marketing Geography is how to locate facilities to best reach the consumers of goods and services, but it is much more than this . . . as we will see.

References

Birkin, M., Clarke, G., Clarke, M., and Wilson, A. (1996) *Intelligent GIS: Location Decisions and Strategic Planning,* Cambridge: GeoInformation.

Crang, P. (2005), "Consumption and its geographies" in Daniels, P., Bradshaw, M., Shaw, D. and Sidway, J. (eds.), *An Introduction to Human Geography: Issues for the 21st Century,* Harlow: Pearson.

Jones, H. R. (1981) *A Population Geography,* London: Harper and Row.

Statistics Canada 2008, Catalogue no. 63-005-X.
http://www40.statcan.ca/l01/cst01/trad15a.htm

Statistics Canada 2008, Catalogue no. 72-002-X.
http://www40.statcan.ca/l01/cst01/labr71g.htm

Chapter 1

FOREIGN RETAILERS IN CHINA: STORIES OF SUCCESS AND SETBACKS

Shuguang Wang and Paul Du

Introduction

In the early 1990s, the orthodox retail geography was re-theorized by Wrigley, Lowe and a few other European economic geographers, and a new geography of retailing was advocated to reflect a series of important changes in the global economy (Lowe and Wrigley 1996). A number of retail corporations, mostly in Europe and North America, sought to acquire others in order to consolidate resources and markets. Through merger, they rose to the status of global corporations or Transnational Corporations (TNC). These retailers have become increasingly active in mediating producer-consumer relations (Currah and Wrigley, 2004; Coe and Hess, 2005), including the creation of new, and re-configuration of existing, retail spaces to induce consumption. As their home markets became saturated, these new global corporations were compelled to explore foreign markets, including the emerging markets of Asia and Latin America. Associated with this retail internationalization has been the migration of retail capital across national borders and the development of retail spaces in foreign consumer markets.

Unlike orthodox retail geography, which focused on the site selection of business locations and delimitation of trade areas in localized markets, the new geography of retailing takes both a political and economic approach, viewing retail capital as a component part of a larger system of production and consumption (Blomley, 1996). In other words, all consumer goods have surplus values locked up in them, and those surplus values are not realized until the consumer goods are purchased by consumers through one of many retail channels. The main concern of the new geography of retailing is the grounding of the global flow of retail capital (i.e., sinking of capital into physical assets in overseas markets) and its geographical expressions (or spatial outcomes). It also calls for much more serious treatment of regulations because they impact corporate strategies and geographical market structures.

The process involving retail internationalization is complex. Dawson (2003:4) proposes a four-phase model to describe the complex process: stability, consolidation, control, and dominance. Initially, there is considerable fluidity as the firm familiarizes itself with the new market. In the second phase, the firm adjusts to new conditions, consolidating its position. After that, it will attempt to exert control over vertical and horizontal channel relationships. Once the retailer becomes established in the new market, mature strategies seeking market dominance similar to those used in its home market, are applied.

Dawson (2003) also points out that few firms pass through the complete model as many fail to achieve their objectives and decide to withdraw from the market at some stage. The failures of four high-profile international retailers (namely, the USA's Home Depot and J.C. Penny, Carrefour of France, and Royal Ahold of Holland) in Chile and their subsequent withdrawal from that country are testimony of the challenges of retail internationalization (Globalization's Winners and Losers, 2006). The reasons for their failure vary, however, the "standardization versus adaptation" debate continues in international businesses.

With reference to another model developed by Vida and Fairhurst (1998), the direction and pace of the retail internationalization process is influenced by both firm characteristics and the external retail environment. The key characteristics internal to the firm are resource availability and commitment, and its differential advantages. The retail environment factors include market conditions, consumer affluence, cultural preference, competition, and regulation. Together, they influence a company's willingness to initiate international retail activities, maintain a constant level of involvement, increase or decrease its involvement, or completely withdraw from the international market (Vida and Fairhurst, 1998:145).

While there have been many studies regarding the 'direction of international retail expansion', such studies have tended to focus on market re-orientation from advanced (or core) markets in North America and Western Europe to emerging markets in Asia and Latin America; few have examined the direction of intra-national expansion within a host market.

Within the globalizing economy, China is the new frontier for many international businesses, and the country offers both a massive source of cheap labor and a market of mass consumption. Foreign retailers began to enter China in 1992. Since then, many of them have established a firm presence within the largest emerging market in the world. Nonetheless, China's market has not been an easy one to penetrate, and from the beginning, foreign retailers encountered a variety of difficulties. Indeed, when China first opened its consumer market to foreign retailers, there were high-threshold barriers to the inflow of foreign retail capital. Accordingly, persistent foreign retailers followed both conventional and unconventional paths to penetrate the Chinese market. The earlier patterns of entry and expansion by foreign retailers were documented by Wang (2003) who highlighted the various government restrictions and illustrated how foreign retailers bypassed regulatory barriers to enter the highly protected Chinese market. Wang (2003) also predicted that the winners would be European and American retailers, who possess the most resources and advanced information technologies and do business in new retail formats, and pointed out that cultural distance is a much less important factor for business success. Since then, significant changes have taken place in both the market conditions in China and its regulatory system including the elimination of trade barriers after China's admission to the World Trade Organization (WTO) in December 2001 (with the WTO agreeing that China completely eliminate trade barriers within three years). These market and policy shifts have afforded further opportunities for foreign retailers to enter and expand within China's emerging market of 1.3 billion consumers.

In the context of the new geography of retailing, this report revisits the foreign retailers in post-WTO China with two objectives: (1) to analyze the market penetration and performance of the major foreign retailers, i.e., to identify the winners and losers; and (2) to examine corporate strategies in relation to the variations in levels of market penetration and performance among the foreign retailers. This report begins with a brief review of the recent changes in market conditions and in the regulatory regime in order to provide context. As Myers and Alexander (2007:8) point out, the degree of regulatory control may make an international market either more or less attractive, and macro economic conditions can alter the direction of international retail expansion. The report then proceeds to analyze the growth patterns and market performance of the major foreign retailers, and to examine their corporate strategies. It concludes with a brief summary of the study and remarks on future trends. The study draws information and data from three types of sources: government statistics, corporate websites, and news reports. In importance, this study contributes to the conceptualization and generalization of the geographical and organizational characteristics of retail TNCs, called for by Wrigley and Currah (2006). Additionally the report adds to the knowledge of the direction of international retail expansion within a single country.

Recent Changes in Market Conditions and Elimination of Unconventional Trade Barriers

Two decades of economic reform have nurtured an affluent consumer market in China, and the size of this market has continued to grow in the last five years. As is shown in Table 1, per capita income increased by 136% and 28% in urban and rural areas respectively between 2000 and 2004; and per capita expenditure increased by 44% in urban areas and 31% in rural areas. In 2004, the rural population was 757.1 million, and the urban population was 542.8 million (National Bureau of Statistics of China, 2005). Measured by population size and per capita income – the two benchmark indicators of consumer market size – China's consumer market is estimated to be 8,556 billion yuan (US $1,070 billion) in 2004.

Changes in consumption patterns are reflected in an overall increase in per capita income. Detailed expenditure breakdowns are shown in Table 2. In both urban and rural areas, consumers still spend a larger proportion of their income on food products than on any other category of goods: 38% in urban areas and 47% in rural areas. Education, housing and transportation/communication have become large categories of expenditure, next only to food: they now account for 10 to 15% of total expenditure. Although spending on apparels, home furniture and durables has declined to less than 10%, total demand is still high and the market is huge. In the 1970s, consumers sought the so-called "three pieces" consiting of a watch, bicycle, and sewing machine. In recent years, other items have become popular including: LCD HDTVs, digital cameras, laptop computers, cell phones, air conditioners, water heaters, "smart" washer/microwave

---

TABLE 1. Increase in per capita income and expenditure in China, 2000-2004 (in Chinese yuan)

Income and Expenditure (urban vs. rural)		2000	2004	2000-2004 change
Income	Urban	4,288	10,128	136%
	Rural	3,146	4,039	28%
Expenditure	Urban	4,998	7,183	44%
	Rural	1,670	2,185	31%

Source: China Chain Store Association, 2005.

Consumption Category	Rural			Urban		
	Per Capita Expenditure (in yuan)	%	Estimated Total Expenditure (in million yuan)	Per Capita Expenditure (in yuan)	%	Estimated Total Expenditure (in million yuan)
Food	1,032	47.2	815.42	2,710	37.7	467.34
Apparels	120	5.5	94.82	687	9.6	118.47
Household furniture & durables	89	4.1	70.32	407	5.7	70.19
Health care	131	6.0	103.51	528	7.4	91.05
Transportation & communication	193	8.8	152.5	844	11.7	145.55
Education, recreation & entertainment	248	11.4	195.95	1,033	14.4	178.14
Housing & utilities	324	14.8	256.01	734	10.2	126.58
All others	48	2.2	37.93	240	3.3	41.39
Total	2,185	100	1,726.46	7,183.	100	1,238.71

TABLE 2. Consumption Patterns and Volumes in Rural and Urban China, 2004

Source: China Chain Store Association, 2005.

oven/dishwasher/refrigerators, and even automobiles. According to the National Bureau of Statistics (2005), the consumer market is far from being saturated with these products. Many families are replacing what they already have with new models, and foreign retailers are all competing with their Chinese counterparts, as well as among themselves, for a piece of the market.

Foreign retailers were allowed to enter China in 1992 to experiment, but their first stores did not open until 1995 due to a series of restrictions that were unconventional to the GATT/WTO member countries. In addition to limiting foreign retail operations to joint ventures, the Chinese government had only a very vague state spatial strategy, confining the experiment to 11 cities in the east coastal region (see Figure 1) (Wang, 2003; Wang and Zhang, 2006). In 2001, after 15 years of prolonged negotiations and numerous concessions, China was finally admitted to the WTO. This required that China remove all remaining trade barriers and open its retail market completely within a period of three years. To fulfill its obligations, the state government announced in April 2004 its latest policy changes with regard to Foreign Direct Investment (FDI) in commercial sectors including retailing, marking the end of the 12 year experiment. The latest policies, released by the Ministry of Commerce in Document No. 8 of 2004, lifted virtually all restrictions and promised a fully-open and fair market to international retailers (Ministry of Commerce, 2004). The key policies regarding retailing are highlighted as follows:

- As of December 11, 2004, foreign retailers may establish business operations, both retailing and wholesaling, anywhere in China.

- Also effective December 11, 2004, foreign retailers and investors may operate wholly-owned retail enterprises as well as joint ventures.

- In addition to in-store retailing, other forms of retailing are now permitted, including the selling of goods via TV, telephone, mail, internet, and vending machines.

- Provincial governments are granted the authority to approve future entrants or openings of new outlets in their respective jurisdictions, with the exception of wholly-owned and foreign-controlled large joint ventures.

While these policies were particularly welcomed by the big international retail chains, they also opened up new areas of business for smaller companies which did not qualify to compete under the 1999 laws. With the removal of the unconventional barriers, China shifted to regulating foreign retailers by legal means (mainly in the form of planning legislations) commonly acceptable to WTO members. For example, the Ministry of Commerce issued two related documents that same year. The first (Document No. 180 of 2004) requires that all municipalities make their own bylaws regarding commercial facility development, and that the bylaws be compatible with the respective municipal general plan. The second (Document No. 390 of 2004) provides standardized definitions of the various retail formats and facility types. Municipalities across the country are required to follow these standards in developing their own bylaws. The new policies stipulate that future retail establishments must conform to municipal plans and local land use bylaws. Land use rights must be publicly bid on. Large facilities that are 10,000 m² or more (most foreign operations are in this category), must also go through a public hearing process. At these hearings, pertinent government officials, industry leaders, interested retailers and representatives of the potentially affected communities are invited to comment on the business proposals. Foreign-invested enterprises must also accept and pass annual inspections with audited financial reports. Those

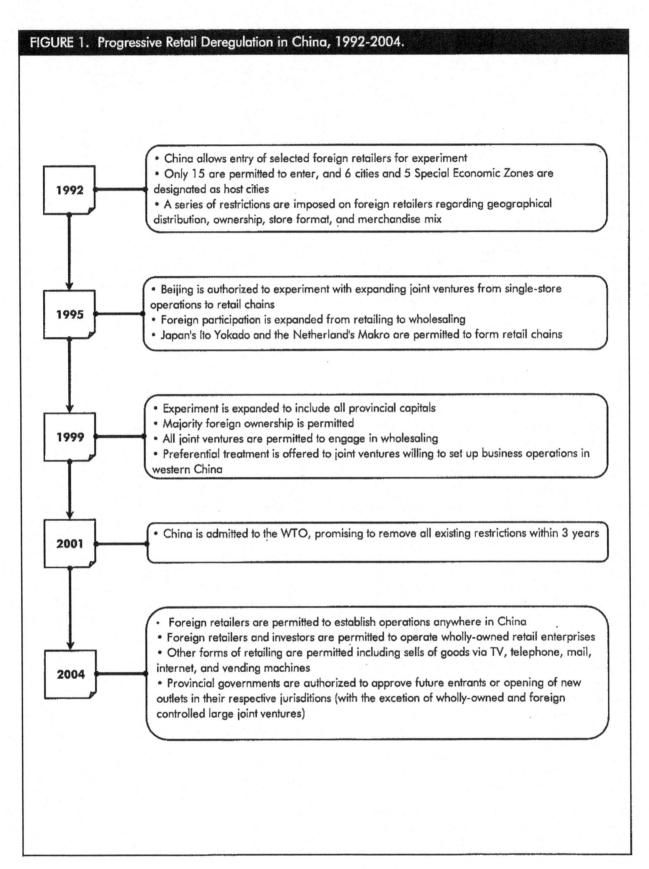

FIGURE 1. Progressive Retail Deregulation in China, 1992-2004.

1992
- China allows entry of selected foreign retailers for experiment
- Only 15 are permitted to enter, and 6 cities and 5 Special Economic Zones are designated as host cities
- A series of restrictions are imposed on foreign retailers regarding geographical distribution, ownership, store format, and merchandise mix

1995
- Beijing is authorized to experiment with expanding joint ventures from single-store operations to retail chains
- Foreign participation is expanded from retailing to wholesaling
- Japan's Ito Yokado and the Netherland's Makro are permitted to form retail chains

1999
- Experiment is expanded to include all provincial capitals
- Majority foreign ownership is permitted
- All joint ventures are permitted to engage in wholesaling
- Preferential treatment is offered to joint ventures willing to set up business operations in western China

2001
- China is admitted to the WTO, promising to remove all existing restrictions within 3 years

2004
- Foreign retailers are permitted to establish operations anywhere in China
- Foreign retailers and investors are permitted to operate wholly-owned retail enterprises
- Other forms of retailing are permitted including sells of goods via TV, telephone, mail, internet, and vending machines
- Provincial governments are authorized to approve future entrants or opening of new outlets in their respective jurisditions (with the excetion of wholly-owned and foreign controlled large joint ventures)

that fail to pass the annual inspections will not be allowed to open new stores, and may even be ordered to close their existing operations. Most significantly, the latest deregulation allows foreign retailers to "exploit the local economies of different places" (Currah and Wrigley, 2004:6) in China.

Market Penetration and Performance of Foreign Retailers

The success of foreign retailers is typically assessed with two indicators: the degree of market penetration, and the level of business performance. The former is measured not only by the number of stores but also by their geographic distribution, as a wider geographic distribution indicates success over local protectionism and cultural barriers. Performance is measured by retail sales and profit levels. Because data on profits is not readily available, retail sales figures are used as the sole indicator of performance, though retailers with high sales volumes may not yet be profitable. For convenience of analysis, the major foreign retailers are separated into three groups: Western retailers (which include both North American and European retailers), Japanese retailers, and those from Southeast Asia (see Table 3). Retailers from Taiwan are included in consistency with China's regulatory policies.

In general, Western retailers have achieved higher levels of market penetration in China than have other foreign retailers. By the end of 2006, Wal-Mart had opened 74 stores in 36 cities; Carrefour 91 stores in 33 cities; Metro 33 stores in 28 cities; Auchan 16 stores in 10 cities; and B&Q 58 stores in 26 cities (see Figures 2 to 6). It should be stressed that much of their expansion has been achieved since 2001, the year China was admitted to the WTO (see Table 4). Wal-Mart opened 63 stores since then, compared with 11 in the 5-year period between 1996 and 2001. Carrefour opened 64 outlets, more than twice as many as its openings between 1995 and 2001. Similarly, Metro opened 25 and B&Q 56, as opposed to 8 (1996-2001) and 2 (1999-2001) respectively. As exemplified by Wal-Mart and Carrefour, the market penetration of Western retailers has taken place in two directions simultaneously: from the eastern coastal region to the western interior, and from large urban centers (mainly provincial capitals) to second and even third-tier cities.

Ikea and Makro have had limited market penetration, with the former having only 4 stores in 4 cities and the latter having 5 stores in 2 cities. The first two Ikea stores were

opened in Shanghai (1998) and Beijing (1999), respectively. While both stores recently moved into new and larger facilities, Ikea did not add any new stores in these two largest urban centers. Instead, it opened its third store in Guangzhou in 2005 and its fourth store in Chengdu in 2006. Makro entered China in 1996, with its first two operations established in Guangzhou and Shantou in Guangdong Province. One year later, it moved to Beijing and opened two stores in the Capital (one in 1997 and the other in 1998). However, not until 2003 was it able to resume expansion and open new stores: one in each of Tianjin, Shijiazhuang and Shenyang. In 2004, when it obtained state approval to do business in wholesaling, it decided to sell its stakes in its Guangdong operations and to focus on expansion in Northern China. Unfortunately, its recent expansion has suffered serious setbacks with both its Shenyang and Shijiazhuang stores closing within a year due to heavy losses (Du, 2004). These losses forced Makro to retreat to Beijing and Tianjin, where it opened two new stores in 2006.

Japanese retailers are among the earliest foreign entrants to China's retail market. Of the first 15 foreign retailers approved by the Chinese government in 1992, four were Japanese. Yet, their expansion has been much slower and geographically limited when compared with their North American and European rivals. Jusco, which entered China in 1996, set up only 3 operations in its first five years: two department stores in Guangzhou and a shopping centre (anchored by a department store) in Qingdao (see Table 4). It once had a department store in Shanghai, but that store was closed in 2000 due to losses. Jusco also experimented with a supermarket in Qingdao, but that store did not survive for long either. While its expansion has accelerated since 2001 with seven new openings, most of the new Jusco stores are hypermarkets concentrated in Guangdong province. Isetan entered China even earlier in 1993. It has since opened only 5 stores in 4 cities: two in Shanghai, and one in each of Tianjin, Jinan and Chengdu. Ito Yokado and SOGO are two other slow starters. In the 9 years since its entry in 1997, Ito Yokado opened only 7 stores in two cities (5 in Beijing and 2 in Chengdu), but 6 of them were opened in the last five years. SOGO still has only 2 stores (one in Beijing and the other in Wuhan) despite having been in China for 8 years. While Daiei had more stores (12 in total), they were all located in one city. Daiei was never able to expand beyond Tianjin. In 2005, it sold its entire operation to a Beijing-based domestic retail chain – Wu-Mart, announcing its withdrawal from the Chinese market. Lawson, a CVS chain, suffered a similar fate. In 8 years between 1996 and 2004, Lawson opened 96 stores, all

TABLE 3. Major Foreign Retailers in China, 2006

Home Region/Country	Retailer	Year of 1st Store Opening	Category	Format	Penetration No. of Stores	Penetration No. of Cities	Performance Total sales* (million US$)	Performance Per store sales* (1,000 US$)
Western	Wal-Mart (U.S.)	1996	G. M.** & food	hypermarket	74	36	941.9	22,196
	Carrefour (France)	1995	G. M. & food	hypermarket	91	33	2,030.1	32,743
	Auchan (France)	1999	G. M. & food	hypermarket	16	10	439	39,907
	B&Q (U.K.)	1999	Home improvement	warehouse	58	26	251.3	11,964
	Metro (Germany)	1996	G. M. & food	warehouse/membership	33	28	807.4	35,103
	Ikea (Sweden)	1998	furniture	warehouse	4	4	100	50,000
	Makro (Netherlands)	1997	Food	warehouse/membership	5	2	187.5	31,250
Japan	Isetan	1993	G. M.	department store	5	4	n/a	n/a
	Ito Yokado	1998	G. M. & food	department store	7	2	362.5	72,500
	Jusco	1996	G. M. & food	department store	10	7	81.3	40,652
	Lawson	1996	Food	convenience	198	1	27.5	229
	Daiei	1995	Food	supermarket	12	1	56.3	4,688
	SOGO	1998	G. M.	department store	2	2	n/a	n/a
S. E. Asia	Lotus (Thailand)	1997	G. M. & food	hypermarket	75	31	924.3	22,543
	Parkson (Malaysia)	1994	G. M. & food	department store	37	26	925	30,833
	RT-Mart (Taiwan)	1997	G.M. & food	hypermarket	70	52	1,187.5	29,688
	Trust-Mart (Taiwan/U.K.)	1997	G. M. & food	hypermarket/superstore	101	34	1,500.00	17,046
	Hymart-Hymall (Taiwan)	1998	G. M. & food	hypermarket	45	19	875	28,226
	Pacific	1993	G.M.	department store	9	5	537.5	53,750
	E-Mart (S. Korea)	1997	G. M. & food	hypermarket	4	2	n/a	n/a

Sources: Various Corporate web sites and China Chain Store Association, 2005.

* 2004 data; ** G.M. = general merchandise

FIGURE 2.   Distribution of Wal-Mart Stores in China, before and after WTO

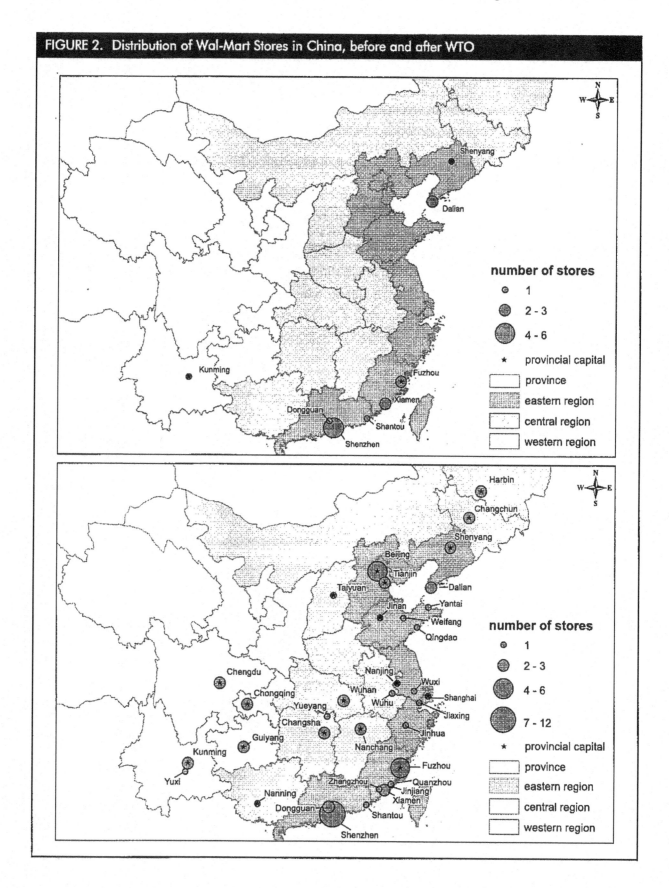

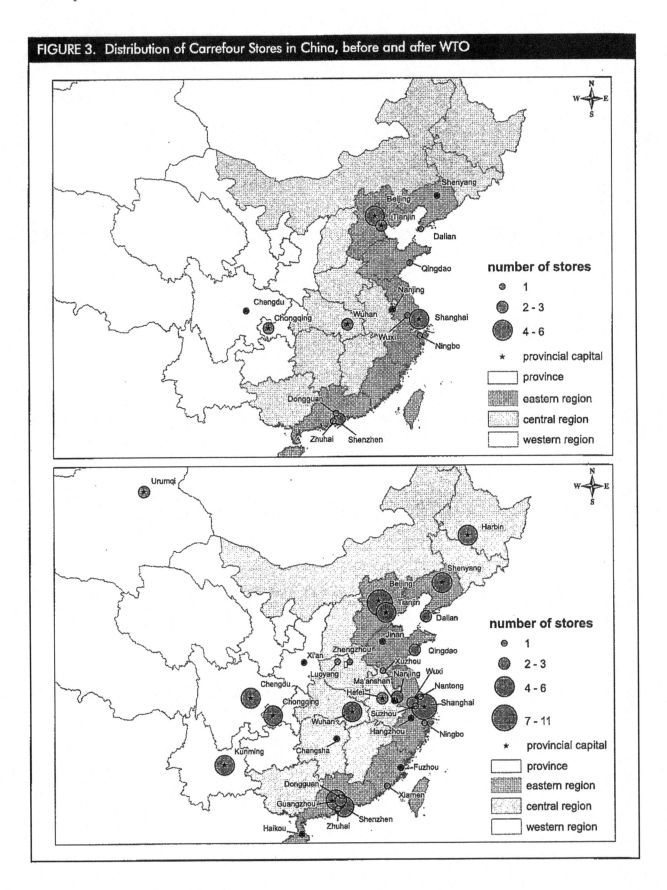

FIGURE 3. Distribution of Carrefour Stores in China, before and after WTO

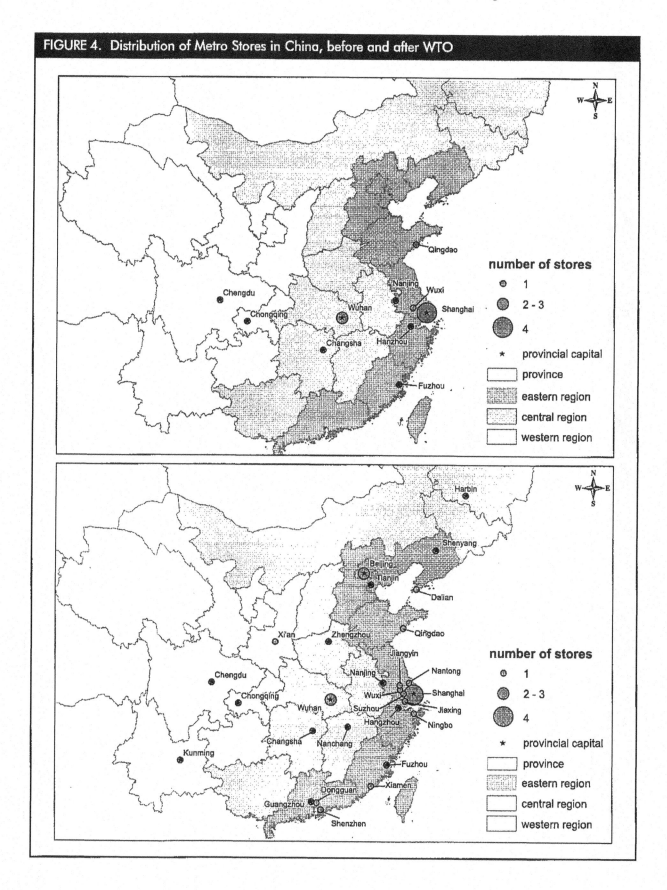

FIGURE 4. Distribution of Metro Stores in China, before and after WTO

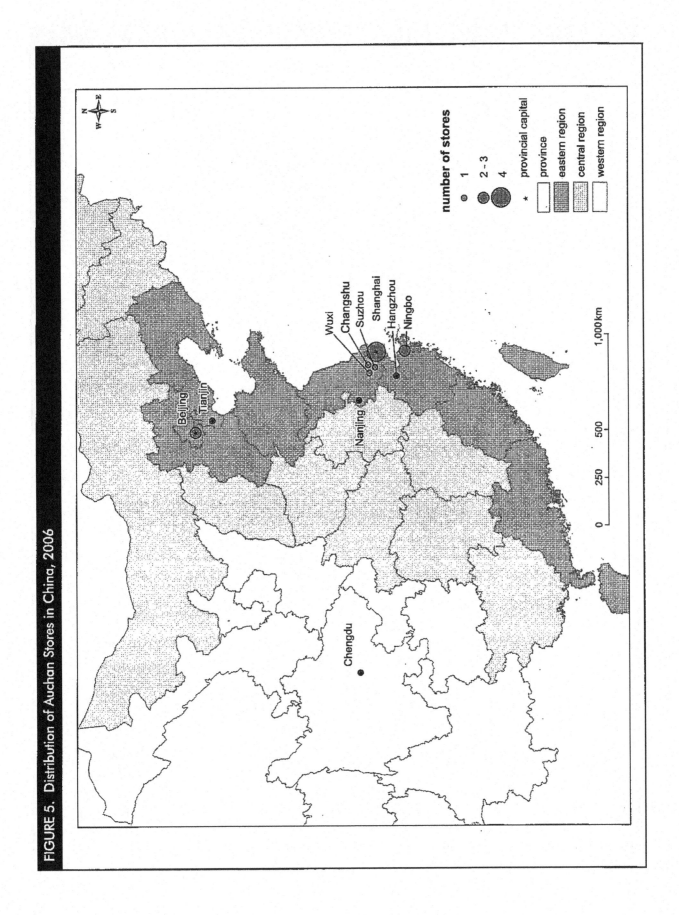

FIGURE 5. Distribution of Auchan Stores in China, 2006

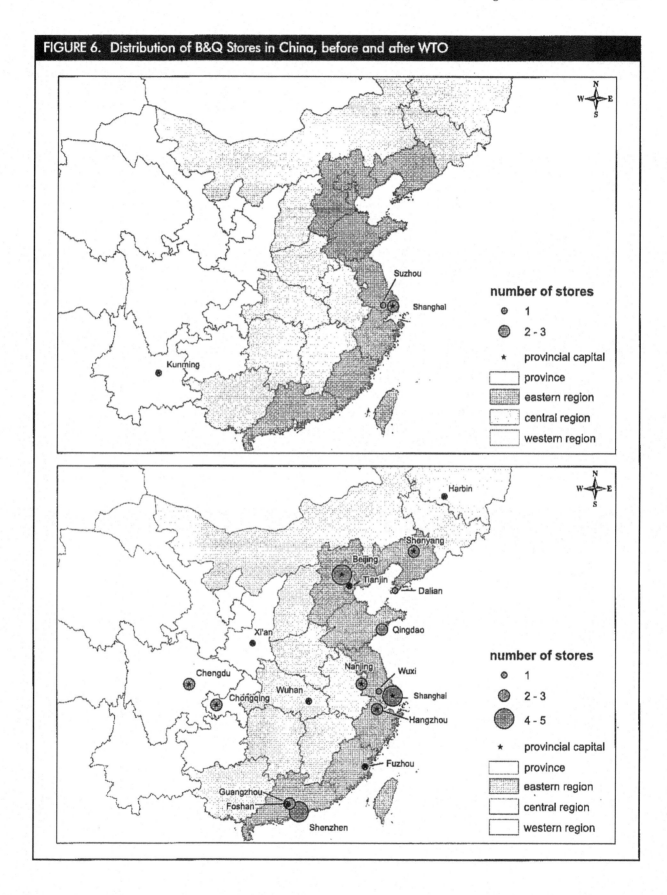

FIGURE 6. Distribution of B&Q Stores in China, before and after WTO

located in Shanghai. Unable to make a profit, Lawson conceded its controlling ownership in 2004 to its local partner – Lianhua Group. With the injection of additional capital, the transformed Lawson expanded by 100 additional stores in less than a year (Shanghai Lawson begins to make a profit, 2004).

Major players from Southeast Asia are represented by Trust-Mart, RT-Mart (see Figure 7), Hymart-Hymall (see Figure 8), Lotus (see Figure 9), and E-Mart – all hypermarket operators (see Table 3). Although they cannot compare with the retail superpowers of Wal-Mart, Carrefour and Metro in terms of capital and IT resources, they have been able to capture a much larger market share in China than the Japanese retailers. Since entering the mainland in 1999, Trust-Mart has opened 101 stores in 34 cities, more than any other discounter. RT-Mart and Hymart-Hymall now have 70 and 45 hypermarkets in 52 and 19 cities, respectively. The Thai-based Lotus is another early entrant and leader in setting up hypermarkets in China with impressive results. It now operates 75 stores in 31 cities, with a level of market penetration close to that of Carrefour, Wal-Mart and Metro. Compared with the other Southeast Asian retailers, the South Korea-based E-Mart is a much slower starter. In the 7 years after its first store opened in Shanghai in 1997, E-Mart was largely dormant with no expansion at all. It was not until 2004 when E-Mart began to expand by opening a second store in

Shanghai. One year later, it opened 2 more stores: one in Shanghai and the other in Tianjin. Both Parkson (see Figure 10) and Pacific also established a fair presence in China, but unlike the other Southeast Asian retailers, they focus on the department store format. Parkson now has 37 stores in 26 cities, and Pacific has 9 stores in 5 cities.

Naturally, total sales are related to the degree of market penetration. Overall, Western and Southeast Asian retailers sell much more than the Japanese retailers, as is shown in Table 3. According to the China Chain Store Association (2005), most of them are among China's Top 50 retail chains by sales: Carrefour (5th), Trust-Mart (13th), Wal-Mart (20th), Lotus (21st), Metro (24th), Auchan (36th), B&Q (48th). RT-Mart, Parkson and Hymart-Hymall should have also placed in the Top 25, as they all achieved total sales higher than that of Metro, but for unknown reasons, they are not included in the Association's official announcement. Of the Japanese retailers, only Ito Yokado achieved sales higher than those of Makro and Ikea. Since the number of stores varies among the foreign chains, per store annual sales are also compared. Surprisingly, the Japanese Ito Yokado tops all others, with US$72.5 million per store. The Jusco stores, with sales of US$40.6 million per store, also perform better than the stores operated by Western and Southeast Asian retailers (except Ikea). Daiei and Lawson have much lower sales because they are smaller supermarket and CVS operations.

TABLE 4. Store Openings of Major Foreign Retailers in China, before and after WTO

Home region/country	Retailer	Before 2002	2002 and After
Western	Wal-Mart	11	63
	Carrefour	27	64
	Auchan	1	15
	B&Q	2	56
	Metro	8	25
	Ikea	2	2
	Makro	4	5
Japan	Isetan	3	2
	Ito Yokado	1	6
	Jusco	3	7
	Lawson	-	-
	Daiei	12	0
	SOGO	1	1
S.E. Asia	Lotus	4	71
	Parkson	-	-
	RT-Mart	13	57
	Trust-Mart	-	-
	Hymart-Hymall	7	38
	E-Mart	1	3
	Pacific	-	-

Sources: Various Corporate Websites

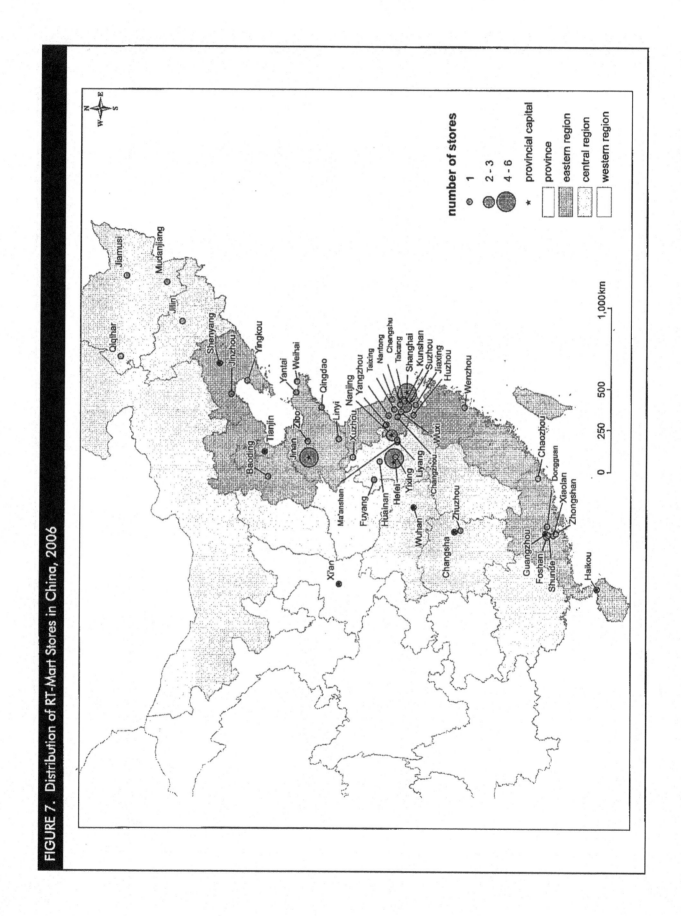

FIGURE 7. Distribution of RT-Mart Stores in China, 2006

25

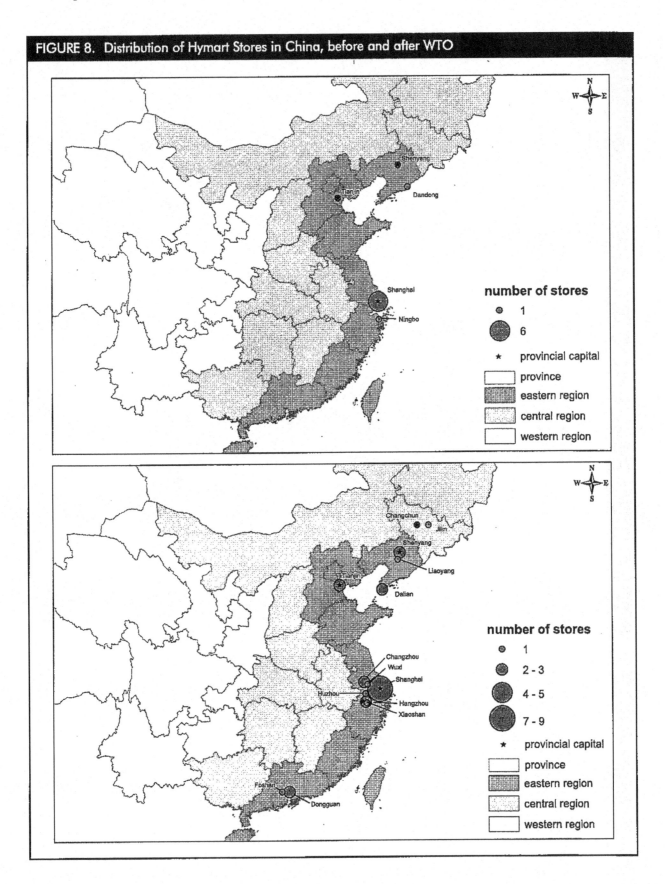

FIGURE 8.　Distribution of Hymart Stores in China, before and after WTO

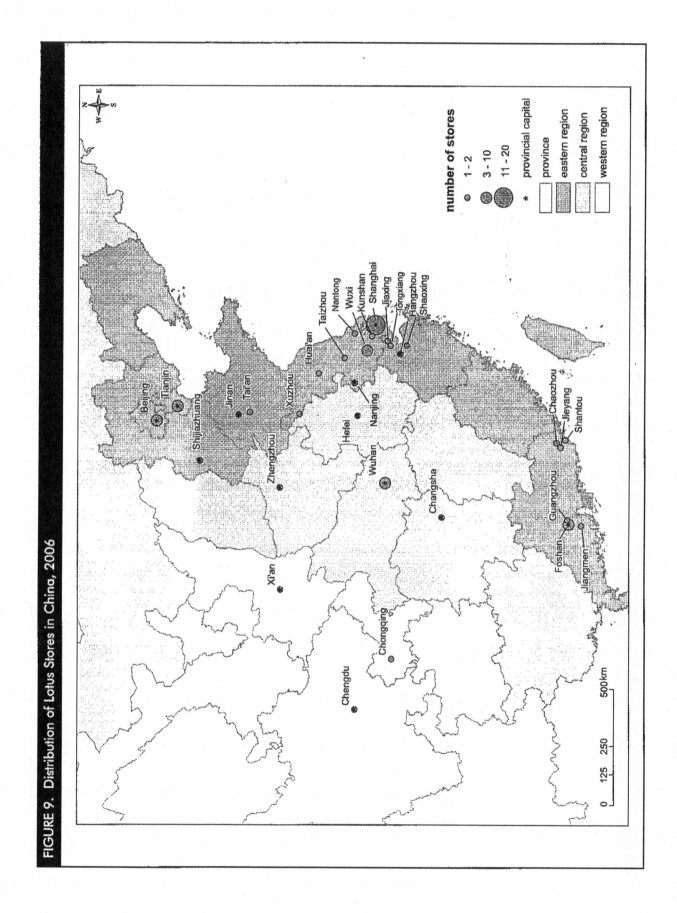

FIGURE 9. Distribution of Lotus Stores in China, 2006

number of stores

- 1 - 2
- 3 - 10
- 11 - 20

★ provincial capital

province

eastern region

central region

western region

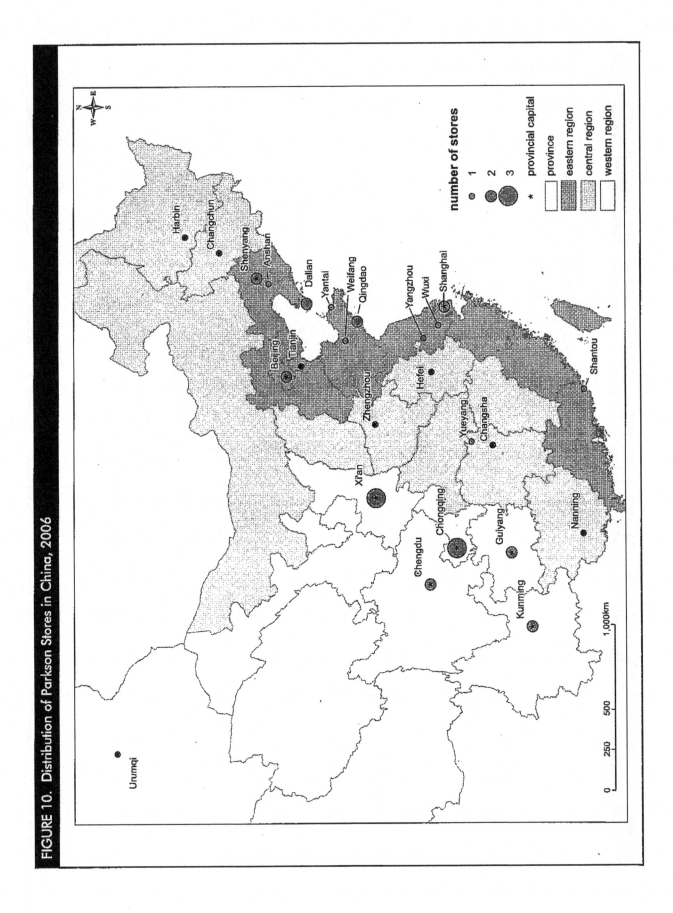

FIGURE 10. Distribution of Parkson Stores in China, 2006

Of the Western retailers, Ikea, Auchan, Metro, Carrefour and Makro all have higher per store sales than Southeast Asian retailers; only Wal-Mart and B&Q have lower sales. While Southeast Asian retailers have high total sales, they seem to be less efficient than their Western and Japanese counterparts, as indicated by per store sales, with the exception of Pacific (Table 3).

Examination of Corporate Strategies

There is no one single formula for success for all retailers. Each corporation devises its own strategies, which makes the study of organizational structures important (Wrigley and Currah, 2006). According to retail industry analysts (Koopman, 2000), every growth strategy must be built on the following pillars in order to maintain a competitive edge: (1) the retailer must offer a competitively superior product as defined by local consumers; (2) the retailer must be able to develop superior economics across the value chain that delivers the product to the local consumer; and (3) global retailers must be able to execute in the local environment. This section attempts to relate success and failure to the various corporate strategies with regard to format, merchandise sourcing, acquisition of real estate, and adaptation to local market conditions. Since this examination is based on secondary information, a systematic analysis is impractical and not attempted in this report.

Western Retailers

In general, Western retailers possess more capital resources than their Japanese and Southeast Asian counterparts to invest and expand in China. The examination here goes beyond this general factor and looks at other aspects of corporate strategies.

Evidently, all Western retailers choose the big box format to ground their retail capital and expand in China. This has allowed them to dominate specific retail sectors with little competition in the local market. It seems that the hypermarket, which offers a wide assortment of goods to mass consumers at competitive prices, proves to serve the local markets better than the competing formats such as the department store and the supermarket. Wal-Mart operates in China with three formats: supercenters (Wal-Mart's term for hypermarket), Sam's Club (warehouse membership clubs), and neighborhood centers (mini-supermarket). However, the majority of its outlets,

67 out of 74, are supercenters. Carrefour and Auchan also expanded in this format, with all stores under their respective banners being hypermarkets. These hypermarkets have been modified to adapt to the local geography where land is scarce, but the multi-level configuration has not deterred shoppers at all.

Metro and Makro focus exclusively on the warehouse membership club format, open only to registered members, who are mostly corporate consumers and small retailers. Yet, this format does not seem to serve the local market as well as the hypermarket. While each city has numerous small retailers, it is not clear whether these membership clubs are their preferred "suppliers" and if purchasing from these clubs would leave them with a reasonable profit margin, given that there exist numerous domestic wholesalers and suppliers in the country with a loosely regulated distribution system. For individual consumers, real savings from shopping at a membership club would be achieved by purchasing in bulk. Yet, due to the lack of private automobiles and shortage of living space, few shoppers can carry multiple bags, or have space at home for a second refrigerator or a freezer to store bulk groceries. There are already signs of a lack of consumer support for membership clubs, suggesting that this format may not be viable in the Chinese market, at least not yet. So far, Wal-Mart operates only four Sam's Clubs in the whole country. One of its three stores in the city of Kunming was launched as a Sam's Club, but had to be converted to a supercenter shortly thereafter. Makro (Dutch) also has had great difficulty expanding with this format. It entered Beijing in 1997, but has been able to expand with only two additional stores in this city of 13 million consumers. It opened a store in Shenyang in May 2004 and another one in Shijiazhuang, but both stores shut down in less than a year (Du, 2004). The only membership club chain that seems to be still expanding is Metro (German).

The supermarket does not seem to be a competitive format either. Ahold (Dutch) established a supermarket chain, 'The Tops' in 1996 in Shanghai and later expanded to 40 stores. However, it failed miserably due to fierce competition from local supermarket chains and had to withdraw from the country completely after five years in the market. Carrefour introduced 8 supermarkets in Beijing in 2004 under a different banner, 'Champion Supermarket', but they were never able to become profitable. In June 2006, Carrefour sold them off to focus on hypermarkets (Li, 2006a).

Unlike the food and general merchandise retailers, Ikea and B&Q specialize in furniture and home improvement products. They focus on promoting high-quality, Western lifestyle products, including garden decor, sunrooms, patio furniture, and barbeque ovens. While their products are popular among certain consumers, they are also too expensive for most ordinary citizens. This is the main reason for Ikea's slow expansion and the demise of OBI in China - The German OBI sold all of its 13 stores to B&Q in 2005. It will take quite some time to nurture the market for consumption of these higher-end lifestyle products.

A particular format must be supported not only by the right location but also by available and affordable real estate. As well, it depends on the settlement patterns of the local market and the imbedded transportation system. Together, they manifest the spatial outcomes of retail capital flow. In general, retailers employ one or both of the following approaches to acquiring business premises: constructing self-owned stores, and leasing space from other developers. At home in the U.S., Wal-Mart customarily acquires land at strategically selected locations and builds its own stores (Simmons and Graff 1998). In China, it chose to lease properties from either local retailers or domestic real estate developers, to minimize sunk costs. Wal-Mart has formed strategic alliances with two major Chinese developers: Shenzhen International Trust & Investment Corporation (SZITIC) and Wanda Group. SZITIC is Wal-Mart's long-time partner in China. Most supercenters in Shenzhen are constructed and owned by SZITIC, but are leased to Wal-Mart. To facilitate Wal-Mart expanding further and faster, SZITIC in 2002 created a subsidiary named SZITIC Commercial Property Development Ltd., whose main purpose is to search for sites, obtain land use rights, and develop retail premises in different cities to meet the needs of Wal-Mart expansion. In 2004, it broke ground in Shenzhen to build a new 200,000 m² facility to house Wal-Mart's Asia and China HQ Offices and a new Sam's Club (Wal-Mart's Asia HQ Office will have a new home in Shenzhen, 2004). To augment its financial capability, SZITIC Commercial Property Development Ltd, in late 2004, entered into a joint venture with Singapore's largest real estate corporation – Capital Land Group. The two parties announced plans to raise new capital through Hong Kong's Stock Exchange.

Wanda Group, whose core business is in property development, is based in Dalian of Liaoning Province in northeast China. In addition to commercial properties, Wanda develops large-scale housing projects, and often combines the two types of development on the same tract of land. Wal-Mart has entered into agreements with Wanda to lease commercial spaces from its properties. At present, 10 Wal-Mart supercenters are operated in Wanda-built shopping centers, with six more to open in the near future (Wanda Group, 2007).

Metro employs a different approach from that of Wal-Mart. To control leasing costs and reduce reliance on Chinese developers, Metro created its own property development arm. This subsidiary is responsible for locating sites, negotiating land leases, and building stores (Lu 2000). It is possible that Metro made this decision due to its difficulties in obtaining suitable premises from local developers. Its warehouse-style retail outlets typically require a one-floor configuration surrounded by spacious parking lots. Perhaps few Chinese developers are willing to invest in this exclusive type of structure in fear of heavy sunk costs. Since construction of self-owned stores requires large sums of investment, it certainly affects the speed of expansion. In 2005, Metro began to lease spaces from Chinese developers and opened its first store in Shenzhen. It recently announced plans to open its second store in Beijing, also by leasing retail space (Li, 2006b).

All other Western retailers also rely on their local partners or domestic developers for business premises. In recent years, some of them began to expand through the path of acquisition. Auchan acquired one third of RT-Mart's stakes in its China operations in 2001. Tesco purchased 50% of Hymart-Hymall's ownership in 2004. As already noted, B&Q acquired German OBI's entire Chinese operation in 2005 and renamed all 13 OBI stores. Wal-Mart in 2007 obtained 35% of Trust-Mart's total shares. Carrefour is currently in negotiation with Le-ke-duo – a domestic hypermarket chain – to purchase its existing stores. According to Alexander (1997), international retailers sometimes acquire a minor interest in a retail operation in order to monitor the performance of that company. If operations proceed favourably, minority interests may lead to outright acquisition. It is reported that Wal-Mart plans to control Trust-Mart by 2010 (Wal-Mart aims to control Trust-Mart, 2007)

For international retailers, another daunting task is to secure supplies of merchandise and distribute them to their local stores. For both economic and cultural reasons, foreign retailers purchase almost all of their products from local suppliers. After moving its Global Purchasing Center from Hong Kong to Shenzhen in 2001, Wal-Mart has established three branches in Dongguan, Fuzhou, and

Shanghai, respectively. Presently, Wal-Mart deals with over 15,000 Chinese suppliers (Wal-Mart China, 2007). Besides its purchasing centers, Wal-Mart has built three distribution centers, one in each of Shenzhen, Tianjin and Shanghai, to supply its stores in China. However, because its stores are located in 34 cities, with 13 cities having only one store, the three distribution centers are hardly operated to their full capacity, and the economies of scale (Amin, 2003) have not been full realized in China. Most merchandise is still shipped to its stores directly from suppliers, which contributes to higher merchandise costs.

This problem is not unique to Wal-Mart. All other Western retailers face the same difficulties in China, where they have not been able to replicate their efficient distribution systems. To compensate for the "lost profits" in merchandise distribution, almost all foreign retailers turned to squeezing suppliers by imposing a variety of fees including store entrance and promotion fees. Carrefour is the most notorious such retailer. In 2006, the Shanghai Commerce Information Center, together with FMCG Research Center, conducted a survey of suppliers for their experiences in dealing with retailers, both domestic and foreign. Ninety-eight suppliers participated in the survey rating 51 retailers, both foreign and domestic. The foreign retailers rated are listed in Table 5. Wal-Mart received the highest rating in all three categories: general satisfaction, cost of doing business with, and level of trust. Carrefour was rated as the most expensive retailer to do business with, and it does not have a good relationship with the surveyed suppliers.

At the European Day of Commerce conference in 2001, the President and CEO of Ahold stressed the importance of social reputations of companies with the following remarks: "We see consumers and consumer groups who increasingly make their choices, positively and negatively, based on the social reputations of companies. And we see governments looking to hold companies accountable for their behaviors everywhere in the world" (Crawford 2001). The senior executives of the Western retailers certainly know very well the importance of developing and maintaining good relations with the various levels of government in China. They have been making concerted efforts to foster a positive corporate image as "outstanding corporate citizens." Since becoming Wal-Mart CEO in 2000, Lee Scott has paid five visits to China to meet with high-ranking officials including the Head of State (Che, 2002). At every occasion, Scott repeats the message that Wal-Mart contributes to China's economic development in five significant ways: (1) it

purchases large quantities of goods from local producers and supports export; (2) it creates jobs and pays corporate taxes to the government; (3) it shares consumer feedback information with producers and helps them develop new products and improve product quality; (4) it introduces advanced retail techniques and experience to promote the Chinese retail industry standards and development; and, (5) it will contribute to the development of China's western region through investment in new stores. Wal-Mart plays a corporate slogan for the same purpose: "work with the community; pay back to the community." Each time it opens a new store, Wal-Mart announces at the grand opening ceremony a donation to charitable organizations or communities to "help the neighborhood, support education of children, and protect the environment" (Wal-Mart China, 2007). Between 1996 and 2003, it donated a total of US $1.2 million to such initiatives. In November 2004, it made another donation of US $1 million to China's Tsinghua University to help establish a Center for the Study of Retailing, with Lee Scott presenting the cheque to the university in person (Ma, 2004). Wal-Mart even relaxed its global non-union policy in China, allowing unions to be formed in its Chinese stores. In November 2005, it invited all 120 employees who had worked for Wal-Mart for 10 years, together with their families, to Shenzhen to honour them for their loyalty.

Apparently, its public relations efforts have worked in its favor, and possibly contributed to its sales performance as well. In 2003, Wal-Mart was selected by the consumers in Shenzhen as the most favored retail store. In the same year, it was rated one of the most respected enterprises in a national survey conducted jointly by Peking University and the Economic Observer newspaper. In June 2004, Wal-Mart was elected by another national newspaper – Guangming Daily – to receive the Best Community Services of Guangming Charity Award (Wal-Mart China 2007). Despite the fact that Wal-Mart had always maintained majority ownership in its joint ventures before China's admission to the WTO, it was never admonished by the Chinese government, as was Carrefour (Wang, 2003).

Western retailers often also took advantage of local government officials who pursue political credits measured by the amount of FDI that they attract to their cities. These officials often courted Western retailers and offered them land and sites at premium locations with deep discounts. It is reported that the government of Hangzhou posted for public bidding a piece of land zoned for commercial use, as is now required by the state government, but it attached the stringent condition that the successful bidder must bring in one of the Top 100 retailers in the world (Zhou, 2006). In the end, only SZITIC Commercial Property Development Ltd., the Wal-Mart partner, qualified for the bidding and subsequently obtained the associated land use right at a price even lower than residential land. Similar deals have happened in other cities.

Japanese Retailers

The expansion of Japanese retailers was seriously affected by a combination of three factors: the formats they chose to penetrate the Chinese market, the financial difficulties of their parent companies at home, and the rigidity of their business decision-making.

Unlike their Western counterparts, the Japanese retailers entered the Chinese market with conventional department store formats (Yaohan, Jusco, Ito Yokado, Isetan, and SOGO), supermarkets (Daiei), and CVS (Lawson). They also focused on high-end consumers and targeted wealthy families. As has been mentioned earlier, these formats have proven less competitive than the hypermarket format. The department store was the dominant retail format in China until the mid 1990s. In the late 1980s and the early 1990s, there was massive construction of glamorous department stores in all urban centers. By the time Japanese department stores arrived, this sector of the retail market was already saturated. Their department stores suffered further in the late 1990s when faced with competition from more

specialized stores. Supermarkets encountered similar circumstances. In the late 1980s and the 1990s, numerous state-owned grocery stores were converted into low-quality supermarkets and convenience stores. In Shanghai alone, there existed 1,743 supermarkets and 4,267 convenience stores in 2005 (Shanghai Economic Commission, 2005). Besides, outdoor markets are abundant and are still popular among many urban consumers.

Shortly after their entry in the mid and late 1990s, most Japanese retail corporations encountered financial crises in their home country, partly triggered by the infamous East Asian Financial Crisis. Yaohan, one of the first 15 foreign retailers approved by the Chinese government in 1992, entered China in 1995 and built two large department stores in Shanghai. In 1997 its parent company went bankrupt and its operations were handed to its Chinese partner – Shanghai No. 1 Department Store Group. SOGO, also a department store chain with stores in a number of Southeast Asian countries, entered Beijing in 1998. Three years later in 2001, it opened its second China store in the City of Wuhan (Liang and Liu, 2001). In the same year, its debt-laden parent company applied for bankruptcy in Japan and the expansion of its Chinese operations have been stalled ever since. Daiei was the first foreign retailer to open supermarkets in China. In the 10 years after its entry in 1995, it was able to expand to 12 stores, but all of them were confined to Tianjin. In 2004, its parent company, under pressure from its creditors, sought restructuring help from a state-backed corporate turnaround body – the Industrial Revitalization Corp. of

Retailer	General Satisfaction	Cost of Doing Business With	Level of Trust
Wal-Mart	3.78	2.82	4.19
Metro	3.51	3.31	3.94
Lawson	3.41	3.37	3.69
E-Mart	3.23	3.32	3.54
Auchan	3.21	3.68	3.73
Carrefour	2.96	4.04	3.75
Lotus	2.96	3.44	3.13
RT-Mart	2.83	3.72	3.26
Hymart-Hymall	2.79	4.00	3.31
Trust-Mart	2.53	3.40	2.50

TABLE 5. Rating of Foreign Retailers by Chinese Suppliers, 2006*

Source: Shanghai Commerce Information Center and FMCG Research Center, 2006.

* scores range from 1 to 5, with 1 being the lowest and 5 being the highest.

Japan. They chose Marubeni and Advantage Partners (a buyout firm) to sponsor Daiei's revival (Reuters, 2006). Part of the restructuring plan was to sell some of its operations (including those in China) and use the proceeds to repay debts. In 2005, Daiei sold its entire operation in Tianjin to a Beijing-based retail chain (Wu-Mart Group), and withdrew from China completely (Beijing Wu-Mart acquires Tianjin Daiei, 2005). Jusco, Ito Yokado and Lawson encountered similar difficulties, and the investments needed for expansion were not forthcoming. Lawson relinquished its controlling stakes to its local partner – Lianhua Group, which now owns 51% of Lawson. Within one year of the ownership restructuring, the chain was able to expand from 96 stores to 198.

Another factor that has affected their expansion is lack of flexibility in business-decision making. To use what has become a classic example, every new store location that Lawson chose in Shanghai had to be approved by the headquarters office in Japan. As well, Lawson was permitted to open stores only in areas west of Shanghai Railway Station, but not in areas east of the station (Shanghai Lawson begins to make a profit, 2004). While many Western and Asian retailers were aggressively seeking entry approval from local governments and bypassing the state government, the Japanese retailers were largely following the rules to the letter and patiently awaiting deregulation. While the Japanese retailers are law-abiding corporate citizens and never got into trouble with the Chinese government, they lost first-mover advantages to their competitors in many cities and have paid high prices in a market where regulation is far from being perfect and 'under-the-table' deals are rampant.

Compared with their Western and Southeast Asian competitors, Japanese retailers have also been slow in consolidating their operations in China. Practically, Jusco has two separate operations: one is a joint venture between Avon (Hong Kong) and Guangdong Tianhe (Group) Ltd. based in Guangzhou, and the other is a joint-venture between Avon (Japan) and Qingdao Materials Cooperatives based in Qingdao. Ito Yokado started with two separate enterprises: one is Chengdu-Ito Yokado created in 1996; the other is Huatang-Ito Yokado in Beijing registered in 1997. In 2004, Ito Yokado established two more joint ventures in Beijing: Wangfujing-Ito Yokado Commerce Ltd., and 7-Eleven (Beijing) Ltd. The former focuses on the development of supermarkets, and the latter on convenience stores. While most Western retailers are moving towards consolidation, Ito Yokado apparently has no plans to do the same. Due to the fragmented nature of its operations, it is very difficult for Ito Yokado to set up and operate distributions centers. Instead, it relies on an intermediate distributor – Pacific Merchandise Distribution (Wang, 2004).

Despite their slow growth, the Japanese stores perform relatively well (see Table 3). Although only Lawson is included in the survey (see Table 5), Chinese suppliers seem to be satisfied with the way Japanese retailers do business with them. It should be noted that while the Japanese department store chains are still expanding, they have recently modified the format by adding either a food department or a supermarket. Two years ago, Jusco expanded its shopping center in Qingdao by adding more floor space to the supermarket as well as to the department store. Its new Jusco stores in Shenzhen and Guangzhou are all more like hypermarkets.

Southeast Asian Retailers

Information about the corporate strategies of the Southeast Asian retailers is scant. Particularly, very little is known about Parkson and E-Mart. As is shown in Table 3, most Southeast Asian retailers mimic the Western retailers by using the hypermarket as the leading format to penetrate the Chinese market. The fact that they are able to expand with impressive results proves once again that, by far, the hypermarket competes better than other formats in China. Except Hymart-Hymall, all the Southeast Asian retailers rely on their local partners or local developers for business premises. In recent years, Hymart-Hymall began to develop a chain of community shopping centres with its hypermarket as the anchor store. So far, three such shopping centers have been built in Shanghai (Wang, Zhang and Wang, 2006)

The Taiwanese retailers have benefited from two major factors: preferential government policies and their cultural and ethnic affinity with the mainland. In June 1988, the State Council announced the provision of major preferential policies that both encourage and protect business investment from Taiwan. This has given Taiwanese investors a competitive edge over other Southeast Asian retailers. Trust-Mart, the Taiwanese retail chain with most stores in China, was established by Winston Wong, the son of the founder of Formosa Plastics. Both father and son enjoy good business relations with the mainland. Further, the Taiwanese retailers are more familiar with consumer tastes and preferences due to cultural similarity.

Despite these advantages, the Taiwanese retailers reportedly played with government rules, as did Carrefour. When restrictions were still in place limiting foreign retailers to joint ventures in a handful of cities and provincial capitals, RT-Mart aggressively opened stores in various cities with different names to disguise itself (Gu, 2006). In 2005, when restrictions were lifted, it quickly flipped the store signs to RT-Mart and the number of stores increased instantly.

It is also widely reported that the expansion of Taiwanese retailers has been achieved at the expense of their suppliers, and that delay in payment is a common occurrence (Ai, 2005). This practice is confirmed by the results of the survey of suppliers conducted by Shanghai Commerce Information Center and FMCG Research Center (see Table 5). Not surprisingly, the three major Taiwanese retailers received the lowest ratings in the survey: the least satisfied by the Chinese suppliers, the most expensive to do business with, and the least trusted by suppliers. This could be a serious factor affecting future expansions.

To overcome their limitations in capital resources and their lack of competency in management of large-scale retail/logistics operations, Taiwanese retailers all sought partnerships with the Western retail giants. As described earlier, RT-Mart (China) teamed up with Auchan by exchanging one third of ownership in their respective China operations in 2000 (Gu, 2006); Hymart-Hymall entered a joint venture agreement with Tesco in 2004 by relinquishing 50% of its ownership to the resource-rich British retailer (British supermarket giant Tesco lands in China, 2004); and more recently, Trust-Mart conceded 35% of its ownership to Wal-Mart. It seems that the Taiwanese retailers do not intend to run hypermarket as their core business. They know they cannot compete with the Western retail heavyweights in a long battle and perhaps will eventually sell their entire operations to the global retailers.

The ten Pacific department stores were developed by the Taiwanese Pacific SOGO, which was once a subsidiary of Taiwan's Pacific Building Group. In 2002, due to SOGO's economic difficulties in Japan, Pacific Building sold the subsidiary to Far East Group – another Taiwanese corporation. As a result, all the department stores under the Pacific banner changed hands (Bai, 2006).

Parkson worked with its local partners to secure business real estate in the early stages. In 2004, it also entered a long-term agreement with Wanda Group, as did Wal-Mart, for the provision of retail sites. With this agreement, Parkson's new stores are located in Wanda shopping centers, with Wal-Mart as co-tenant (Chen, 2004). Since then, five Parkson stores have opened in Wanda shopping centers respectively in Tianjin, Shenyang, Nanjing, Harbin, and Dalian (Wanda Group, 2007).

Summary and Concluding Remarks

International retailers have been "the movers and shapers" of the global economy (Dicken, 2003:3), and they often facilitate changes in market structures. Growing levels of retail internationalization are mainly driven by the growing size and sophistication of retail businesses, but the trend is also a response to changing consumer demand and affluence (Myers and Alexander, 2007). In the last 15 years, over 300 foreign retailers have established a business presence in China, many of which are among the Top 100 in the world. With the continued growth of the consumer market and the elimination of the unconventional trade barriers in China, their expansion has accelerated steadily. All the major retail corporations have their own geostrategy, but these have largely been dictated by the state spatial strategies of the Chinese government. That is, expansion into interior and secondary cities did not happen until the Chinese government revised its state spatial strategy after admission to the WTO. Their presence and expansion in the form of retail chains has helped consolidate the long-fragmented local markets, and an integrated national market is in the making.

While none of the foreign retailers in China has passed through the complete model described by Dawson (2003), their levels of market penetration and performance vary, indicating that they are in different phases of the model. Clearly, the Western retailers, which possess the most resources and advanced information technologies and conduct their business in new retail formats, are taking the lead in penetrating the Chinese market. Wal-Mart and Carrefour can both be said to have completed the consolidation (the second) phase. They have both just begun to exert control over vertical and horizontal channel relationships. Western retailers are also moving from organic growth, defined as new store development (Alexander, 1997), towards acquisition. Their success tends to suggest that cultural proximity is much less important than corporate strength of TNCs, that is, resource availability/commitment, and differential advantages (Vida and Fairhurst, 1998). The Southeast

Asian retailers, which mimic Western retailers by copying the hypermarket format, have also expanded their operations with impressive results, but their staying power is unclear. Instead of aiming to gain market control and dominance, they began to relinquish a significant part of their business interests to Western retail superpowers. Although the Japanese retailers received the least negative publicity, they have made the least inroads in penetrating the Chinese market due mainly to the economic difficulties of their parent companies and the less competitive format that they adopted to expand in China. They are only in the early stages of consolidation. Over time, as China's regulatory environment improves further, the Japanese retailers should fare significantly better.

The battle among foreign retailers for a share of the Chinese market will become more intense. Carrefour has already withdrawn from Japan (2005) and South Korea (2006) to focus on expansion in China (Chen, 2006). Wal-Mart has recently given up its operations in South Korea (2006) to also concentrate on the Chinese market. As well, a number of foreign retailers are moving towards "independence" in an effort to consolidate their power in decision making (Zhen et al., 2005; Ma, 2006). In 2005, Carrefour formed a wholly-owned subsidiary in Haikou of Hainan Province, and bought out its Chinese partners in Kunming, Urumqi, and Changsha. In the same year, Metro increased its China ownership from 60% to 90%. Similarly, Lotus opened its first wholly-owned store in Jinan, and bought out its Chinese partners in Beijing, Tianjin and Shanghai. In the meantime, the American Best Buy, Home Depot, and Business Depot (all big box retailers), have firm plans to enter in the imminent future through the path of acquisition. It is anticipated that a wave of merger/acquisition-driven consolidation in the retail market will take place in China in the next 10 to 15 years, a phenomenon that happened in the late 1990s across the world (Currah and Wrigley, 2004). Foreign retailers, and especially Western retailers, will become powerful players, reshaping the corporate and physical landscape of retailing in China.

While China is embracing global liberalism, the future expansion of foreign retailers is not without new roadblocks. China is nurturing its own retail heavyweights to combat foreign competition and defend the national market. In July 2004, the Ministry of Commerce announced the selection of 20 domestic retailers to form the "national team", to which the Chinese government will provide special assistance if needed. On the top of the list is the Shanghai-based Brilliance Group, which was created by the Shanghai Municipal Government in 2003 through the merger of four stated-owned corporations. As the country's largest distribution conglomerate, the group owns over 7,000 retail outlets across the country, ranging from convenience stores and supermarkets to hypermarkets and shopping centers. The existence and strengthening of the national team will force foreign retailers to focus on second- or third- tier cities in the next round of expansion.

As the process of retail internationalization deepens in China, its regulatory system is facing new challenges: that is, how to best balance the need to maintain national economic sovereignty and security, whilst simultaneously providing international retailers with national-level rights of establishment so that they are not subject to discriminatory domestic policies (Rugman and Gestrin, 1997).

References

Ai, Y. (2005) Six potential crises will hurt Trust-Mart's operations in China, *Fortune Times*, December 21. (Haoyouduo fengguang beihou de anshang, liu da weiji zhide fansi, *Caifu Shibao*, December 21.)

Alexander, N. (1997) *International Retailing*, Oxford (UK): Blackwell Publishers Ltd.

Amin, A. (2003) Spaces of corporate learning. In J. Peck and H. W. Yeung (eds.), *Remaking the Global Economy*, London: Sage Publications, pp114-129.

Bai, S. (2006) Dispute resurfaces over the right of using the Pacific Department Store brand, *Yipu* September 23. ("Taipingyang Baihuo" shiyong quan you qi zhengyi, *Yipu*, September 23.), www.yipu.com.cn.

Beijing Wu-mart acquires Tianjin Daiei (2005) *Daily Economic News*, February 5. Retrieved from http://finance.sina.com.cn. (Beijing Wumei lakai shougou Tianjin Dairong chaoshi xumu (2005), *Meiri Jingji Xinwen*, February 5.)

Blomley, N. (1996) 'I'd like to dress her all over': masculinity, power and retail space. In N. Wrigley and M. Lowe (eds), *Retailing, Consumption and Capital: toward the New Retail Geography*, Essex (London): Longman Group Ltd., pp238-256.

British supermarket giant Tesco lands in China (2004) http://news.bbc.co.uk/chinese/simp/hi/newsid_3890000 / 2004-07-14.

Che, Y. (2002) President Jiang Zemin receives Wal-Mart CEO, *People's Daily (overseas edition)*, October 9: p1. (Jiang Zemin huijian Woerma gongsi zongcai, *Renmin Ribao (Haiwaiban)*.)

Chen, B. (2004). Parkson joins forces with Wanda Group to speed up expansion in China, *Chongqing Evening News*, April 30 . (Baisheng Baihuo qianshou Wanda Mall, quansu kuozhang. *Chongqing Wanbao*, April 30.)

Chen, H. (2006) The myths of Carrefour and Wal-Mart withdraw from South Korea. Linkshop, (http://www.linkshop.com.cn/web/Article1.aspx?ArticleId=59951&ClassID=21) retrieved on June 30, 2006. (Jialefu Woerma hanguo zaoyu "huatielu" zhimi. Shanglianwang.)

China Chain Store Association (2005) *China Chain Store Almanac 2005*, Beijing: China Commerce Publishing House.

Coe, N. and Hess, M. (2005) The internationalization of retailing: implications for supply network restructuring in East Asia and Eastern Europe, *Journal of Economic Geography* (advance access published April 11, 2005): pp1-25.

Crawford, F. (2001) Business without borders, *Chain Store Age*, 12: pp86-96.

Currah, A. and Wrigley, N. (2004) Networks of organizational learning and adaptation in retail TNCs, *Global Networks*, 4(1): 1-23.

Dawson, J. (2003) Introduction. In J. Dawson, Masso Mukoyama, Sang Chul Choi and Roy Larke (eds), *The Internationalization of Retailing in Asia*, London and New York: RoutedgeCurzon, pp1-5.

Dicken, P. (2003) *Global Shift: Reshaping the Global Economic Map in the 21st Century* (4th ed.), London: Sage.

Du, C. (2004) Makro looks forward to the arrival of the Spring. *IT Manager's World*, retrieved from www2.ceocio.com.cn/issues/2004/5/text/t_5_16.asp. (Wankelong de chuntian. *IT Jingli Shijie*)

Globalization's winners and losers: lessens from retailers J. C. Penny, Home depot, Carrefour, Ikea and others (2006) *Strategic Direction*, 22(9): pp27-29.

Gu, B. (2006). The submarine emerges from under water, RT-Mart is to make another Wal-Mart in China, *Oriental Entrepreneur*, August 3. (Qianshuiting fuchu shuimian, Darunfa zai zao yige Woerma (2006) *Dongfang Qiyejia*, August 3.)

Koopman, J. C. (2000) Successful global retailers a rare bred, *Canadian Manager* (Spring Issue): pp22-28.

Li, W. (2006a) Carrefour adjusts its China business strategy, Champion Supermarket changes hands, *First Financial Post*, April 11. Retrieved from http://finance.qq.com/a /20060411/000368.htm. (Jialefu tiaozheng Zhongguo zhanlüo, Guanjun Chaoshi yishou (2006), *Diyi Caijing Ribao*, April 11.)

Li, W. (2006b) Metro modifies its growth pattern and plans to open a second store in Beijing by leasing property, *New Capital Times*, October 5. (Mai-de-long tiaozheng "maidi jingying" moshi, Beijing dier dian xuanze zulin (2005), *Xinjingbao*, October 5.)

Liang, C. and Liu, Q. (2001) Japanese SOGO applies for bankruptcy protection; Wuhan SOGO has a spectacular grand opening, *Changjiang Daily*, January 2. Retrieved from www.cnhan.com/gb/content/2002-01/02/content_42410.htm. (Riben SOGO pochan baohu, Wuhan SOGO renqi gaozhang (2001), *Changjiang Ribao*, January 2.)

Lowe, M. and Wrigley, N. (1996) Towards the new retail geography. In N. Wrigley and M. Lowe (eds), *Retailing, Consumption and Capital: toward the New Retail Geography*, Essex (London): Longman Group Ltd.: pp3-30.

Lu, G. (2000) Speech at the Forum on Retail Chain Development, *Supplementary Papers Presented at the Second Forum on Chain Store Development in China*, Beijing: China Chain Store Association. (Zai Zhongguo liansuoye huiyi shang de zuotan fayan, *Dier Jie Zhongguo Liansuoye Huiyi Buchong Lunwenji*, Beijing: Zhongguo Liansuo Jingying Xiehui).

Ma, X. (2004) Lee Scott: Wal-Mart will not operate wholly-owned stores in China, *Beijing Morning News*, November 3. (Woerma buhui zai Zhongguo gao duzi, *Beijing Chenbao*, November 3.)

Ma, Y. (2006) Expansion trajectories of foreign retailers in China. Retrieved from http://www.linkshop.com.cn. (Waizi lingshou liansuo jutou Zhongguo fazhan luxiantu.)

Ministry of Commerce (2004) *Policies Governing Foreign Investment in the Commercial Sector*. Beijing: Ministry of Commerce. (Shangwubu (2004) Waishang Touzi Shangye Lingyu Guanli Banfa.)

Myers, H. and Alexander, N. (2007) The role of retail internationalization in the establishment of a European retail structure, *International Journal of Retail & Distribution Management*, 35 (1): pp6-19.

National Bureau of Statistics of China (2005) *2005 Statistics Yearbook*. Beijing.

Reuters (2006) Japan's Daiei to sell 39 outlets to cut debts. Retrieved on September 1 from http://today.reuters.com/news/articleinvesting.aspx?type=bondsNews&storyID=2006-09-02t024824z_01_t15725_rtridst_0_retail-japan-daiei.xml.

Rugman, A. H. and Gestrin, M. (1997) New rules for multinational investment, *The International Executive*, 39 (1): 21-33.

Shanghai Commerce Information Center and FMCG Research Center (2006) *2006 Survey of Merchandise Suppliers for Retailer Satisfaction*. Shanghai.

Shanghai Economic Commission (2005) *Shanghai Commercial Activity Development Report*. Shanghai: Shanghai Science and Technology Literature Publication House.

Shanghai Lawson begins to make a profit (2004) *East Morning News*, December 19. Retrieved from www.yipu.com.cn. (Shanghai Laosen bianlidian kaishi yingli (2004) *Dongfang Zaobao*, December 19.)

Simmons, J. and Graff, T. (1998) *Wal-Mart comes to Canada* (Research Report 9). Toronto: Centre for the Study of Commercial Activity, Ryerson Polytechnic University.

Vida, R. and Fairhurst, A. (1998) International expansion of retail firms: a theoretical approach for future investigations, *Journal of Retailing and Consumer Services*, 5 (3): 143-151.

Wal-Mart aims to control Trust-Mart by 2010 (2007) Retrieved on March 16 from http://www.linkshop.com.cn/web/archives/2007/69237.shtml. (Wo-er-ma gao cong: 2010 nian konggu Hao-you-do, chigu bili wei ding.)

Wal-Mart's Asia HQ Office will have a new home in Shenzhen (2004) *Shenzhen Economic Daily*, October 27. (Touzi qiye yuan, Woerma zai Shenzhen xingjian yazhou zongbu (2004) *Shenzhen Shangbao*, October 27.)

Wal-Mart China (2007). http://www.wal-martchina.com.

Wanda Group (2007). http://www.wanda.com.cn.

Wang, H. (2004) Ito Yokado contracts merchandise distribution to a 3rd party, http://finance.tom.news.tom.com/1001/1006/20041115-113805.html.

Wang, S. (2003). Internationalization of retailing in China. In J. Dawson, Masso Mukoyama, Sang Chul Choi and Roy Larke (eds), *The Internationalization of Retailing in Asia*, London and New York: RoutedgeCurzon, pp114-135.

Wang, S. and Zhang, Y. (2006) Penetrating the Great Wall and conquering the Middle Kingdom: Wal-Mart in China. In Stanley Brunn (ed), *Wal-Mart World: The World's Biggest Corporation in the Global Economy*, New York: Routledge, pp293-314.

Wang, S., Y. Zhang and Y. Wang (2006) Opportunities and challenges of shopping centre development in China: a case study of Shanghai, *Journal of Shopping Center Research*, 13 (1): pp19-55.

Wrigley, N. and Currah, A. (2006) Globalizing retail and the 'new e-conomy': the organizational challenge of e-commerce for the retail TNCs, *Geoforum*, 37: pp340-351.

Zhen, D., Wei, Y., Zhang, Y., and Qi, Y. (2005) End-of-2005 review: be aware of foreign retailers quietly transforming China's retail sector, *Supermarket Weekly*, December 23. (2005 nianzhong pandian: jingti waizi shentou "yanbian" Zhongguo lingshou (2005) *Chaoshi Zhoukan*, December 23)

Zhou, Y. (2006) Wal-Mart accelerates acquisition of land and property in China for speedy expansion, *21st Century Economic News*, August 20. (Wo-er-ma Zhongguo daju quandi kuozhang: di chengbe? Ling chengbe? *Ershi Yi Shiji Jingji Baodao*, August 20.)

Chapter 2

DYNAMICS OF THE CANADIAN RETAIL ENVIRONMENT

Ken Jones and Tony Hernandez

The retail landscapes of urban Canada reflect the immense diversity of social classes, incomes, ethnicity, lifestyles, and business formats that comprise our cities. Strips, neighbourhood streets, suburban plazas, power centres, downtowns, and revitalized boutique districts are some of the most visible elements of the metropolitan landscape. Names like The Bay, Wal-Mart, Canadian Tire, Club Monaco, Harry Rosen, and HMV are instantly recognized by most Canadians.

Retailing is a major component of the Canadian economy. In 2004, total retail sales (including automotive) measured $346.7 billion or 25.7 per cent of the gross domestic product (Statistics Canada, 2005d). Thirteen per cent of the Canadian workforce, 1,754,885 persons, are employed in the retail sector (Statistics Canada, 2001a). In our society, retailing is pervasive. For many, shopping is a major leisure activity. Retail sales absorb approximately one-third of our disposable income and the image of our cities is shaped in large part by the nature and vibrancy of their retail environments.

This chapter will describe and interpret the various elements that comprise and shape our urban retail system, stressing geographical, locational dimensions. First, we will briefly review the literature associated with intra-urban retailing. Second, we examine the evolution of the Canadian intra-urban retail system, focusing on the development of the shopping centre, the rebirth of the central city, the growth of the big-box and power retailers, and the role of the specialty retail area. Next, a general morphology of the contemporary urban retail structure will be introduced. The chapter concludes by presenting an integrated framework for evaluating the intra-urban retail system and outlining a series of trends related to the future of retailing in Canada.

Intra-Urban Retailing: A Review

The literature in geography on urban retailing can be grouped into four research perspectives: (1) the identification and classification of various structural elements of the retail landscape; (2) the spatial dynamics of retail change; (3) the development and operation of various retail structures—shopping centres, central area retail districts, retail strips, and specialty retail areas; (4) applied research investigations. In applied research, geographers assess new retail locations for major retail firms and use various spatial models to analyze shopping centre impacts.

The development of a systematic classification of retail structures is based to a large extent on the pioneering works of Proudfoot (1937) and Berry (1963). These studies differentiated shopping environments on the basis of their locational and functional characteristics. The literature related to urban retail change can be traced back to the empirical work of Simmons (1966). Simmons's conceptual model of retail change examined how socioeconomic conditions and elements of urban growth influence the development of the intra-urban retail system. In this model, temporal and spatial variations in income, technological development, and urban demographic growth and change affect consumer mobility and preferences, and eventually cause an adjustment in the nature and distribution of retail structures. In this and related, more recent analyses, the final disposition of the retail system is viewed as the outcome of the spatial strategies of, and interplay between, developers, retailers, and planners—the actors who ultimately shape the future form of the urban retail landscape.

Retail structural analysis has had a long tradition in urban geography. In the 1950s and 1960s, North

American studies of retail structure dominated the literature. These studies explored suburban retail strip development, retail mix and usage patterns, inner-city retail decline, the emergence of the shopping centre, and the specialty retail phenomenon. More recently, applied studies have tended to focus on particular elements or projects associated with the retail system. Because of their nature, most of these studies adopt a micro-based, case study approach. Typically, these analyses are undertaken to provide advice to retail corporations concerning the investment potential of particular locations or to aid government agencies in assessing the social, economic, or environmental impact of a specific development. In the literature, the works of Applebaum (1968), Davies and Rogers (1984), and Lea (1989) illustrate these forms of study.

Evolution of the Canadian Urban Retail System

The contemporary retail landscape of urban Canada is the product of a series of complex structural changes. Retail structure is perhaps the most responsive element in the urban landscape. A high degree of volatility was confirmed by an analysis of aggregate failure rate of retail enterprises along 175 major retail streets in Metropolitan Toronto, 1994–6—a staggering 33 per cent (CSCA, 1998). In some categories, such as fashion, the failure rates over the three-year period were in the 40–4 per cent range, while the lowest turnover rates were experienced by pharmacies (24.5 per cent) and laundries (19.7 per cent). Very minor shifts in the income, demographic, lifestyle, and/or competitive characteristics of an area will lead to quite rapid changes in both form and structure of the retail environment. Conceptually, the retail fabric of our cities has been created in response to the dynamic interplay of demographic, technological, behavioural, and entrepreneurial change (Figure 1).

The spatial pattern of retail groupings relates to the technology of the time. When mobility is low, retail activities concentrate; when mobility increases, retail activities disperse. At a finer level, consumer and entrepreneurial decisions can determine which retail areas grow and which areas decline. Consumer preferences for both retail goods and destinations can reflect a whole set of considerations that can be broadly defined as lifestyle-related. Certain urban shopping areas move in and out of fashion for particular consumer groups. On the supply side, investment decisions are based on the entrepreneur's

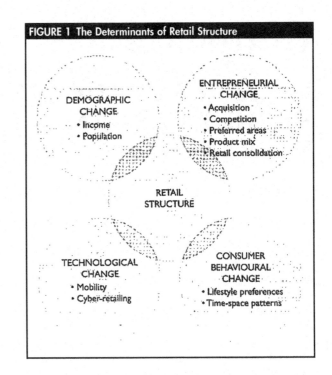

FIGURE 1 The Determinants of Retail Structure

assessment of the future disposition of the retail system. Will a certain downtown redevelopment project be successful? How will the competition react? What will be the demographic composition and demands of a community in 10 years? What demographic cohorts will experience growth, and what demographic cohorts will experience decline?

The Pre-World War II System

The intra-urban retail system has experienced several transformations in the last 60 years. These transformations were tied to successions in types of urban structure and transportation: the compact pre-automobile city; the dispersed automobile city; and the emerging information city.

In the pre-war city, both aggregate consumer mobility and car ownership were low. In response, many consumers shopped daily for food and going downtown to shop was viewed as a normal activity. An examination of the pattern of retail activities in urban Canada prior to 1950 reflected this reality. Nearby corner stores were a necessity and downtown retailing flourished. It was the age of the department store. To illustrate, in 1930 all divisions of the T. Eaton and Robert Simpson companies controlled an impressive 10.5 per cent of total retail sales in Canada (Royal Commission on Price Spreads, 1935). Because of the reliance on public transit along major arterials, inner-city retail strips were a significant element in the retail landscape. These strips extended into the residential portions of the city and consisted of almost continuous rows of shops that served essentially local convenience-oriented needs.

Relatively low mobility in the pre-war city explains retail location patterns. Day-to-day shopping was carried out close to the home. High-order goods were typically purchased downtown, the uncontested public transit accessibility hub at a time when transit was the dominant form of transportation (Jones and Simmons, 1993).

The Emergence of the Shopping Centre

In 1950, the next era of retail development began with the opening of Park Royal Shopping Centre in Vancouver. For the next 40 years, the planned shopping centre, the automobile, and suburbanization were the major forces shaping retail structure. By 2003, shopping centre sales accounted for approximately 60 per cent of non-automotive retail sales in the country (ICSC, 2005a) and for almost all the growth in shopping goods activity.

Shopping centre development in Canada has undergone four periods of evolution since its inception. In the 1950s, shopping centre developers adopted a *consequent* development strategy where the shopping centre was constructed after the housing stock in a given area and the details of the market were known. Most were small, unenclosed 'plazas' that

were automobile-oriented, and developed independently to serve community convenience needs. During this period, retail planning controls were in most cases non-existent and often a form of uncontrolled retail sprawl resulted. The major Canadian department store chains were reluctant to move to the suburbs. Both Eaton's and Simpsons adopted a wait-and-see attitude and were content to remain securely located in the downtown cores of Canadian cities.

The 1960s saw a shift with the emergence of *simultaneous* shopping centre development where both the centre and the housing stock were built at the same time, with the shopping centre viewed as the centre of the 'planned' community. In Canada, the first development to adopt this approach was Don Mills Plaza in Toronto (1959). This linkage between residential and commercial land uses helped to foster the emergence of several large development companies. These included Cadillac Fairview, Bramalea, and Trizec. The philosophy of simultaneous development became accepted at all levels, from the large regional complexes (e.g., Fairview Mall, Bramalea City Centre, and Scarborough Town Centre in Toronto) to the neighbourhood plazas that form the centre of small residential communities.

By the end of the 1960s, the shopping centre industry in Canada was well established and a level of corporate control over the prime shopping centre locations in Canada had been assured. Table 1 lists

Table 1 Selected Major Canadian Shopping/Power Centre Owners and Management Companies, 2004–5			
Owner/Management Co.	Headquarters	Total # Centres/ Properties	Total Gross Leasable Area (sq.ft.)
Ivanhoe-Cambridge	Toronto	50	31,486,055
First Professional	Toronto	132	29,420,465
RioCan	Toronto	190	24,189,987
Cadillac Fairview Corp.	Toronto	31	21,569,000
Oxford Properties Group	Toronto	32	13,564,798
20 Vic Management Inc.	Toronto	22	13,174,816
First Capital Realty	Toronto	103	12,700,000
Crombie Properties	Stellarton, NS	78	9,722,944
Trinity Dvlp. Group Inc.	Toronto	33	9,300,000
Calloway REIT	Calgary	56	8,302,376
Canadian Real Est. Inv. Trust	Toronto	24	5,695,428

Source: Maclean-Hunter Web site (2005).

selected major shopping centre and power centre developers in Canada, most of which are a legacy of this period. These developers are arguably the most important players in determining the spatial structure of the retail distribution system in Canada. It is important to note that the shopping centre system that emerged from the 1960s was essentially homogeneous in nature. One shopping centre at any one level of the hierarchy looked much the same as the next, with the same layout and design, and the same range of goods, services, and tenants in the same standardized environment—a style of development very much in keeping with the meta-narrative of rational comprehensive planning.

In large part, this sameness was the product of the corporatization of the shopping centre based on synergy between corporate, chain retailers and shopping centre developers that continues to the present. Throughout North America, the planned shopping centre provided the principal vehicle for the entry of and ultimate dominance of the retail chain in the urban marketplace (Doucet et al., 1988). By 1986, slightly more than half of all retail chains and department stores in Canada were located in shopping centres—51.7 per cent or 17,795 outlets. Certain types of retail chains were disproportionately shopping centre-oriented. In terms of total sales, women's clothing (91 per cent), luggage and leather goods (89 per cent), children's clothing (87 per cent), jewellery stores (85 per cent), and shoe stores (83 per cent) were the retail activities that showed the greatest propensity for shopping centre locations.

The relationship between the retail chain and the shopping centre is reflected in the redistribution of retail space in many metropolitan environments. For example, in Metropolitan Toronto (since 1998, the City of Toronto), which has kept an inventory of retail space since 1953, the share of the total retail space found in planned shopping facilities rose from 2.4 per cent in 1953 to 40.8 per cent in 1971, 54.5 per cent in 1986, and 55.3 per cent in 1994 (Simmons et al., 1996).

The early 1970s saw a gradual shift to a third stage in some larger metropolitan markets—the 'catalytic' shopping centre. In this case, the shopping centre was viewed as a growth pole that would stimulate future development. Typically, a super-regional shopping centre built in a 'greenfield' at the intersection of two major expressways would precede residential development by three to five years.

Scarborough Town Centre and Mississauga's Square One are prime examples of this trend in the Toronto region. In part, these developments were in keeping with the 'bigger is better' philosophy that permeated North American business decision-making in this period. The success of these centres was also contingent on both the presence of large development companies with extensive land banks and the willingness and ability of national chains to enter a location and wait for the market to develop.

The 1960s and 1970s were also characterized by the commercial revitalization of central cores. In Canada, the first attempt at a downtown shopping centre was in London, Ontario (Wellington Square, 1960). By the end of the 1970s, most major cities in Canada had an enclosed downtown shopping facility. Most were joint ventures that involved the developer, a major department store (often Eaton's), and an important financial institution. Over 30 city centres in Canada experienced this form of development, which reshaped the retail form of Canada's downtowns (see Table 2 for a list of the major shopping centres in Canada).

The end of the 1970s saw market saturation of the suburban shopping centre in Canada. Developers pursued a series of alternative growth strategies. First, a number of selected shopping centres were rejuvenated. This process generally involved the enclosing and 'remixing' (i.e., changing the store types to accommodate new trends in consumption) of first-generation regional shopping centres constructed in the 1960–5 period. Second, through a strategy termed 'infilling' a number of smaller towns became targets for enclosed regional or community malls on their periphery. (As a consequence, a number of downtown cores in these smaller communities experienced severe decline.) A third option adopted by major developers such as Cadillac Fairview, Olympia and York, Bramalea, Oxford, Cambridge, Trizec, and Daon was to become active in the high-growth markets of the United States— Canadian retail-commercial developers became major players in Los Angeles, New York City, Dallas, Minneapolis, and Denver.

The 1980s saw the emergence of a fourth form of shopping centre development—the shopping centre as an *entertainment or tourist attraction*. The overt mixing of retailing and recreation in a major shopping centre is an innovation peculiar to Canada. The 350,000-square-metre (3,800,000-square-foot)

Table 2 Major Shopping Centres in Canada		
Centre/Node	Market	Gross Leasable Area
West Edmonton Mall	Edmonton	3,800,000 sq. ft.
Heartland Town Centre	Mississauga, Ont.	1,800,000 sq. ft.
Toronto Eaton Centre	Toronto	1,624,000 sq. ft.
Square One Shopping Centre	Mississauga, Ont.	1,600,000 sq. ft.
Yorkdale Shopping Centre	Toronto	1,544,165 sq. ft.
Les Galeries de la Capitale	Quebec City	1,400,000 sq. ft.
Pacific Centre	Vancouver	1,390,000 sq. ft.
Place Laurier	Ste-Foy, Que.	1,340,000 sq. ft.
Scarborough Town Centre	Scarborough, Ont.	1,313,137 sq. ft.
Le Carrefour Laval	Laval, Que.	1,243,000 sq. ft.
Polo Park Shopping Centre	Winnipeg	1,202,000 sq. ft.
Vaughan Mills	Vaughan, Ont.	1,200,000 sq. ft.
Chinook Centre	Calgary	1,175,000 sq. ft.
Bramalea City Centre	Brampton, Ont.	1,155,201 sq. ft.
Oshawa Centre	Oshawa, Ont.	1,120,800 sq. ft.
Les Promenades St-Bruno	St-Bruno-de-Mont., Que.	1,084,000 sq. ft.
St Laurent Centre	Ottawa	1,073,560 sq. ft.
Devonshire Mall	Windsor, Ont.	1,055,955 sq. ft.
Le Centre Fairview Pointe Claire	Pointe-Claire, Que.	1,020,000 sq. ft.
Les Galeries d'Anjou	Anjou, Que.	1,013,000 sq. ft.
Twin Oaks Town Centre	Windsor, Ont.	1,000,000 sq. ft.

Source: Rogers Media Publishing, 2005.

West Edmonton Mall is by far the most ambitious example of this type of megaproject, with dozens of tourist attractions including an ice skating rink, wave pool, submarine rides, marineland, aviary, Fantasyland Hotel, children's amusement park, and a mock 'Parisian' shopping boulevard.[1] In these environments retailing and entertainment go hand in hand. Also in the 1980s, many inner-city shopping centres and redeveloped waterfront properties have been targeted partly at tourists and recreational shoppers. Over the last decade, the entertainment component has become a more important component of many shopping destinations as multi-screen theatres or virtual-reality complexes become shopping centre anchors and key tenants within power centres.

By far the most active form of shopping centre development in Canada during the 1980s was the revitalization of existing properties. Developers have found that shopping centres have a distinct life cycle. After approximately 10–15 years, most centres are in need of renovation. Since their initial construction, the demography and income level of their trade area may have changed, their competitive environment altered, and their 'book value' depreciated to zero. Revitalization offers a number of advantages to the developer. Existing shopping centres are well situated in a known market, they experience fewer zoning or environmental regulatory problems, and renovation typically involves lower construction and financial costs than does the construction of new complexes. Most of these renewal projects involve the re-tenanting of the centre and result in an increase in the total number of retail units. Even if no additional retail space is added, because of the reduction in the space requirements of most retailers, the actual number of stores in a centre can increase dramatically. Revitalization has taken a number of forms. These include expansions, enclosures, re-tenanting, renovations, or various combinations of the above.

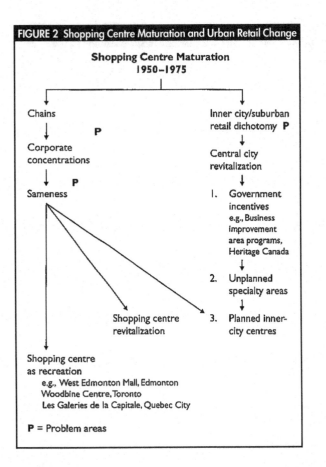

FIGURE 2 Shopping Centre Maturation and Urban Retail Change

Shopping Centre Maturation
1950–1975

Chains
↓ P
Corporate concentrations
↓ P
Sameness
↓
Shopping centre revitalization

Shopping centre as recreation
  e.g., West Edmonton Mall, Edmonton
  Woodbine Centre, Toronto
  Les Galeries de la Capitale, Quebec City

Inner city/suburban retail dichotomy P
↓
Central city revitalization
↓
1. Government incentives
   e.g., Business improvement area programs, Heritage Canada
↓
2. Unplanned specialty areas
↓
3. Planned inner-city centres

P = Problem areas

Figure 2 illustrates the process whereby shopping centre maturation contributed to major shifts in the growth of new retail forms. In essence, the intra-urban shopping centre hierarchy that was developed between 1950 and 1970 led to a dichotomous retail system. The new suburban system was planned, functionally homogeneous, and the domain of the retail chain. In contrast, the older inner-city areas remained unplanned and were dominated by independent merchants. By the mid-1970s, shopping centre developers recognized that they had created a series of standardized, often overly sanitized, shopping environments. Their response was threefold. First, through shopping centre renovation, they instituted new, upscale design features in many of their major centres. Second, they began to experiment with new marketing approaches such as the shopping centre as an entertainment vehicle. Third, they returned to the inner city, often with the assistance of local government authorities, to develop planned central city shopping centres (e.g., Pacific Centre, Vancouver), festival retail developments in waterfront locations (e.g., Market Square, Saint John), or historic properties (e.g., Le Vieux Port, Montreal; Warehouse District, Winnipeg).

Lately, in many cities across Canada, provincial authorities reinvested in old inner-city shopping districts through a variety of business improvement programs. Grant programs, often subsidized by a property tax levy, were used to upgrade the physical appearance of retail strips, improve public parking, and provide assistance for a wide range of business activities such as advertising, marketing, and financial management (Holdsworth, 1985). In part, these programs were used to offset some of the consequences of shopping centre competition on traditional retail areas. In other cases, inner-city areas rejuvenated 'naturally'. In this scenario, selected inner-city strips in major metropolitan areas developed a specialty focus. These areas provided an alternative shopping environment to the shopping centre. They stressed assortment and quality of merchandise and merchant expertise and offered the vitality of an uncontrolled shopping environment. In some districts, such as Toronto's Yorkville and Vancouver's Gastown, this process was initiated in the 1960s.

The Arrival of the Big-Box Retailers and Power Centres

The 1990s will be remembered as a decade where virtually no shopping centre growth took place in Canada (Doucet and Jones, 1997; ICSC, 1997). Indeed, Vaughan Mills Shopping Centre, opened in 2004, was the first major shopping centre built in Canada since 1989. Shopping centre sales decline stems from a variety of factors—recession in the early 1990s; high cross-border shopping, 1990–2; decline in consumer real incomes; aging of the Canadian population and corresponding shifts in retail expenditures (Foot and Stoffman, 1996)—have led to a downturn in consumer spending (Kidd, 1996). The introduction of major competition in big-box retailers and power centres and the arrival of Wal-Mart precipitated a consumer shift to the free-standing discount department store/superstore. In response, shopping centres' share of retail sales declined and some shopping centres have been closed and/or changed to other land uses. Table 3 provides a selected list of the store portfolios of major big-box retailers in Canada between 2001 and 2004.

Changes in the competitive environment have altered the tenant mix of the regional shopping centre. Hardware, food, sporting goods, toys, electronics, furniture, office supplies, arts and crafts, pet stores, and

Table 3 Big-Box Retailers in Canada, 2001–4		
Category	No. Units (2001)	No. Units (2004)
Discount Department		
Wal-Mart	196	234
Warehouse Clubs		
Price Club/Costco	60	62
Automotive		
Canadian Tire (not all big-box)	451	456
Home Improvement		
Home Depot	76	109
Rona Home & Garden	3	25
Office Products		
Business Depot/Staples	183	229
Office Depot/Office Place	37	33
Computers/Electronics		
Future Shop/Best Buy	91	130
Books		
Chapters	76	72
Indigo	9	12
Sporting Goods		
Sport Chek	91	113
Sportmart	46	99
Home Furnishings		
Brick	61	82
Ikea	9	12
Toys and Games		
Toys R Us	64	64
Arts and Crafts		
Michaels	24	34
Bedding Supplies		
Linens & Things	8	19
HomeSense	9	36
Home Outfitters	14	46

optical wear have been under the most pressure from the invasion of big-box retailers, mostly US-based (Hernandez, Jones, and Maze, 2003). Large retailers, such as Home Depot, Sports Authority, Toys R Us, Office Depot, Chapters, Business Depot,

Michaels, Lenscrafters, and PetStuff, which stress competitive pricing, assortment, and brand merchandise, increasingly dominate our retail markets (Jones et al., 1994). In the Greater Toronto Area (GTA), between 1995 and 2002, the number of big-box retailers increased from 267 to 695, accounting for approximately 33 million square feet of retail space (Hernandez, Birsiotto, and Jones, 2003). During the same period, shopping centres in the GTA grew by only approximately 90,000 square metres (one million square feet) (CSCA, 1998). Exacerbating the problem for the shopping centre is the higher sales productivity of the big-box retailer. In 2003, it has been estimated that big-box retailers control approximately 10 per cent of total retail selling area, but account for nearly 20 per cent of all non-automotive sales (Simmons and Hernandez, 2004a; 2004b). These big-box retailers have clustered into what have been termed power centres and power nodes (see Tables 4 and 5).

Table 4 Power Retail across Canada, 2003		
Measure	Total	Average
Power Centres	204	
Total stores	3,936	19.3
Big-box stores	1,465	7.2
Big-box share (%)	26.9	26.9
Total floor area (sq.ft.)	77,435,000	379,600
Big-box floor area (sq.ft.)	65,887,000	323,000
Big-box share (%)	85.1	85.1
Ancillary stores	2,471	30.6
Retail	1,530	19.0
Food	534	6.6
Services	407	5.0
*Power Nodes**	103	
Total stores	6,828	66.3
Big-box stores	1,541	22.6
Total floor area (sq. ft.)	93,991,000	912,500
Big-box floor area (sq. ft.)	74,240,000	720,800
Big-box share (%)	79.0	79.0
Power Centres in Power Nodes	162	1.57
Total floor area (sq. ft.)	55,274,000	536,600
Power centre share (%)	58.9	58.9

*Some power nodes also include conventional shopping centres not included in this database.

Source: CSCA (2004).

Defining Power Retail

Big box: Big-box outlets are typically three or more times larger than other comparable stores. The definition of 'big box' varies by sector and is determined by gross leasable area.

Power centre: Three or more big-box retailers with shared parking lot and, typically, ancillary commercial services.

Power node: One power centre with additional big boxes or other power centres/major malls within a one kilometre radius, typically centred on a major intersection.

In 2003, more than 200 power centres operated across Canada, mostly in the fastest-growing retail markets. Table 6 provides a list of the top 20 retail hotspots across Canada, based on the *Small Area Retail Trade Estimates* released by Statistics Canada. As a result of power retail, the regional shopping centre has become marginalized and increasingly dominated by fashion merchandisers and personal services. In response, in many shopping centres, rents have fallen, vacancies have increased, many shopping centre properties have become overvalued, and the ownership has changed hands.

Table 5 Major Power Nodes in Canada (over 1 million total store sq. ft.)

Power Node	Market	Total No. of Stores	Total Store Sq. Ft.	Total No. of Big Boxes	Total Big Box Sq. Ft.
Hwy 400 & Hwy 7	Vaughan, Ont.	163	2,744,354	74	2,309,559
Sunridge	Calgary	201	1,968,594	53	1,651,357
Langley	Langley, BC	194	1,924,244	58	1,625,232
Coquitlam	Coquitlam, BC	85	1,897,349	44	1,661,449
Stoney Plain/Terra Losa	Edmonton	201	1,704,123	48	1,331,740
Bayers Lake	Halifax	73	1,442,620	36	1,258,900
Westhills Town Centre	Calgary	145	1,366,360	35	1,032,133
Polo Park	Winnipeg	49	1,356,911	33	1,350,911
137th Ave. NW	Edmonton	135	1,354,897	39	1,104,013
Heartland Town Centre	Mississauga, Ont.	142	1,329,923	43	1,091,723
Quebec City	Quebec City	58	1,305,289	22	1,188,989
Shawnessy Town Centre	Calgary	127	1,276,765	29	966,560
Saint-Bruno	Saint-Bruno, Que.	42	1,269,000	24	1,170,900
Barrie 400	Barrie, Ont.	84	1,204,027	28	1,058,865
Hwy 2 & Harwood Ave.	Ajax, Ont.	72	1,189,508	33	1,067,356
Calgary Trail and 34th Ave.	Edmonton	94	1,159,677	38	979,570
Yonge St. and Davis Dr.	Newmarket, Ont.	71	1,151,252	35	1,011,553
Eglinton Ave. E. & Warden Ave.	Toronto	98	1,137,987	24	914,902
Regent Ave. & Lagimodiere Blvd	Winnipeg	41	1,136,305	21	1,073,855
Hwy 403 & Dundas St. E.	Oakville, Ont.	74	1,102,936	36	968,876
Trans-Canada Hwy and Victoria Ave. E.	Regina	53	1,056,900	27	1,002,800
Kanata	Ottawa	111	1,004,680	24	701,572

Source: CSCA National Power Centre Database, 2004.

Table 6 Retail Hotspots in Canada: 2001

Rank 2000	Rank 1999	FSA*	Market	Sales Score	Sales/Location ($000)**	Power Centre	Major Shopping Destination	#Shopping Centre	#Power Centre
1	2	T2H	MacLeod Trail, Calgary	11.29	4106.675	Heritage Towne Ctr/Chinook Crossing	Chinook S.C.	9	2
2	1	L3R	Markham/Unionville, Ont.	8.67	1761.110	Woodside Centre	Markville S.C.	19	1
3		S7K	Saskatoon, CBD	7.15	2445.530	River City Centre	Midtown S.C.	4	1
4	7	M6A	Toronto (North York)	5.68	2374.757		Yorkdale S.C.	4	
5	3	L4L	Woodbridge, Ont.	5.62	2388.820	Seven & 400 Power Ctr/Colossus Power Ent Ctr/Weston Rd. & Hwy 7	Woodbridge Town Centre	13	3
6	4	L4M	Barrie, Ont.	5.52	2751.654	Bayfield St & Livingstone St	Bayfield St./Georgian Mall	5	1
7	8	M5C, M5B	Toronto, CBD	5.43	2207.020		Eaton Centre/The Bay	5	
8	11	H9R	Pointe Claire, Que	5.30	2815.577	Trans-Canadienne & Blvd St-Jean Power Centre/Hwy 40 and Blvd Des Sources	Fairview Centre	6	2
9		N8X	Windsor, Ont.	5.15	3138.092	Devonshire Power Centre	Devonshire Mall	7	1
10	13	V5H	Burnaby, BC	5.15	2393.892		Metrotown	6	
11	6	MIP	Toronto (Scarborough)	5.03	2475.664	Kennedy Commons	Scarborough Town Centre	7	1

(continued)

Table 6 Retail Hotspots in Canada: 2001 (Continued)

Rank 2000	Rank 1999	FSA*	Market	Sales Score	Sales/Location ($000)***	Power Centre	Major Shopping Destination	#Shopping Centre	#Power Centre
12	9	H3B, H3A	Montreal, CBD	5.00	1421.243		Place Ville Marie/Eaton Centre	10	
13	10	V6X	Richmond, BC	4.71	1595.487	Hwy 99 & Bridgeport Rd	Lansdowne S.C.	11	1
14	14	T1Y	Calgary, Alta	4.54	3274.663	Sunridge Towne Centre	Sundridge S.C.	7	1
15		L5B	Mississauga City Centre	4.54	2290.726	Square One Power Ent. Ctr	Square One	8	1
16	15	T2E	Calgary	4.47	2213.750		Deerfoot Mall	4	
17		T5T	West Edmonton, Alta	4.36	1706.216	Terra Losa Power Centre	West Edmonton Mall	5	1
18		T3A	Calgary	4.34	2813.041	Dalhousie Station/ Country Hills Blvd NW & Sarcee Trail NW	Market Mall	5	2
19	18	M9W	Toronto (Etobicoke)	4.34	2808.752		Woodbine Shopping Centre	9	
20		T2J	Calgary	4.23	2137.998		Southcentre Mall	15	

*Forward sortation area, FSAs correspond to the areas covered by the first three characters of the postal code.
***Sales/Location calculated as retail sales in FSA/# of locations in FSA.

Source: Statistics Canada (2001b).

The Role and Positioning of Specialized Retail Areas

There have always been specialized retail clusters within metropolitan areas. It is the growth in the importance of these types of districts that is new. Several reasons account for this, including: general reaction to the sterility of suburban plazas; an expansion of consumer demand; and changes in demographics and lifestyles. Specialty retailing tends to be an inner-city phenomenon and is often spatially associated with gentrified residential areas or waterfronts.

The pattern of specialty retailing can be either dispersed or concentrated. The former includes merchants who offer a highly specialized product (e.g., model trains, comic books, historical documents) and who rely on consumer motivations that can be best described as esoteric. These retailers have no need to form specialty clusters since they offer one-of-a-kind merchandise and their customers will travel long distances to purchase the product. The other group of specialty retailers clusters in order to attract a certain set of consumers, e.g., antique and art dealers, furniture stores, high-fashion retailers, suppliers of electronic equipment, restaurants, and automobile showrooms.

Jones and Simmons (1993) have identified five distinct types of specialty clusters: specialty product areas; fashion centres; factory outlets/off-price centres; historic or theme developments; and ethnic strips. In addition to these five clusters, lifestyle centres geared to the higher-income shopper can be added as a new variant of specialty retail.

Specialty product areas provide an environment for comparison shopping, where choice offered by a group of stores selling similar goods attracts consumers. Some areas, such as Granville Island Market in Vancouver and Harbourfront Antiques in Toronto, serve the entire metropolitan market (and enjoy high tourist appeal); others serve a more limited market. Those areas that serve the whole metropolitan market tend to locate near the city centre, though automobiles and furniture districts, because of space requirements, locate at the periphery in low-rent areas. The neighbourhood specialty strip is typically found in older residential areas that have experienced gentrification (e.g., The Beaches, Toronto; Rue St-Denis, Montreal; Old Strathcona, Edmonton), providing quality food and fashion goods and new forms of personal services.

Fashion and factory outlet centres are on the opposite sides of the spectrum. Fashion outlet centres deliver designer products in an upscale environment (e.g., Bay-Bloor/Yorkville, Toronto; Sherbrooke West/Crescent, Montreal); factory outlets offer perhaps last year's styles or imitations in a low-overhead store. Both forms of retail development attract the recreational shopper. Fashion streets are often the most expensive and visible shopping locations within the metropolis (e.g., Fifth Avenue, New York City; North Michigan Avenue, Chicago), with close links to the high-income sectors and/or executive employment locations. These high-fashion streets have been particularly attractive to European chains and sometimes have been incorporated into mixed-use projects that integrate offices, hotels, and entertainment.

The factory outlet, or off-price centre, is a relatively recent variant of the suburban shopping centre. In these locations costs are reduced by strategies such as less glamorous mall design, reduced customer service, minimal mall/store fixtures, and a reliance on merchandise that is end-of-the-line, overruns, or seconds. The Cookstown Manufacturers' Outlet Mall located on the outskirts of Barrie, Ontario, provides an excellent example. The 200,000-square-foot mall located on the major highway linking Toronto to Barrie and surrounding 'cottage country' is positioned to capture tourist shoppers. It houses 57 tenants, including Tommy Hilfiger, Nike, Paderno, and the Cadbury Chocolate factory outlets. In Canada, these centres are not as prominent as in the United States.

Historic redeveloped properties or theme malls have become a feature of revitalization in older parts of the city, especially waterfront and warehouse districts. Historic Properties in Halifax, Quebec City's Lower Town, Toronto's Distillery District, and Winnipeg's Warehouse District suggest that a variety of developments are possible. Historic or architecturally important buildings provide the focus. In some developments existing building stock is used, and in others new structures are created. In either case, these environments take on the appearance and function of planned shopping centres.[2]

Specialized retailers capitalize on another amenity: small towns and villages in attractive rural settings. Unplanned versions of these recreational retailing clusters have also emerged in smaller communities near large metropolitan regions that provide close-by markets: Niagara-on-the-Lake, Elora, and St Jacobs in Ontario and Knowlton in Quebec are examples.

These retail environments are seasonal and are comprised of independent merchants, although in certain instances land costs/rental rates have put extreme pressure on the traditional character of these areas.

Ethnic strips are normally associated with the point of entry of an immigrant group in the city. At first, the retail component adjusts to serve the needs of the immediate neighbourhood. In this phase certain types of products dominate, in particular food and fashion retailers, restaurants and personal services linked to the community's cultural heritage. Eventually, the strip evolves to cater to members of the ethnic group throughout the metropolitan area, and over time these areas may also become tourist attractions, as is the case with Kensington Market and Chinatown in Toronto.

The rapid growth of specialty retailing areas has added a new aspect of competition within the urban retail system. The addition of a shopping goods function to the retail strip presents the consumer with an alternative to the conventional shopping centre. It also has generated a series of negative externalities based on the growing retail traffic in certain inner-city neighbourhoods. Independent merchants have normally satisfied specialty retail demands but more specialized chains now are taking aim at the market niches that such unplanned street environments and theme malls provide. In response, some conventional malls are attempting to develop more distinct images and in some of our major urban areas (e.g., Toronto and Vancouver) ethnic shopping centres are emerging (Wang, 1996).

Lifestyle centres have been a key element of new retail development in the US over the last decade. In Canada only a small number of centres can be identified as 'lifestyle-type' centres. According to the International Council of Shopping Centers, a lifestyle centre is:

> most often located near affluent residential neighborhoods . . . caters to the retail needs and 'lifestyle' pursuits of consumers in its trading area. It has an open-air configuration and typically includes at least 50,000 square feet of retail space occupied by upscale national chain specialty stores. Other elements differentiate the lifestyle center in its role as a multi-purpose leisure-time destination, including restaurants, entertainment, and design ambience and amenities such as fountains and street furniture that are conducive to casual browsing. These centers may be anchored by one or more conventional or fashion specialty department stores. (ICSC, 2005b)

The Village at Park Royal adjacent to the Park Royal Regional Shopping Mall on North Shore in Vancouver provides a Canadian example of a lifestyle centre. The 238,000-square-foot centre houses a number of major big-box stores including Home Depot, Urban Barn, Old Navy, and Michaels. Opened in 2004, the Village provides winding streetscapes in an architecturally themed environment. Parking is directly in front of stores and limited to one-hour only along the main street, which is lined with trees, street furniture, and ornate lighting. Located next to the 1.2 million-square-foot Park Royal Shopping Mall, the Village at Park Royal provides an up-market unenclosed retail spur to the existing mall, serving the relatively high-income demographic of North Shore, Vancouver.

Downtown

The downtown constitutes a distinct retail environment. Once the unchallenged centre of high-order retail activity, downtown has had to adapt to successive retail transitions over the past century. This area's high-density built environment distinguishes it from the remainder of the metropolitan region. The premium on downtown space forces all establishments, including retail, to be parsimonious with their use of land. Also, downtown's unparalleled transit access sets it apart from suburban locales, though the area is less accommodating to cars than suburbs where parking is free and plentiful.

The central business district of a city combines almost all the retail types described above: it is the highest-order unplanned centre serving the entire metropolitan region. Usually, it incorporates a series of diverse retail areas. These can include skid row that features bars, cheap restaurants, and adult entertainment; high-fashion streets; major inner-city shopping centres; entertainment districts; traditional shopping streets; underground retail concourses; ancillary malls associated with mixed-use developments; and historic redeveloped specialty retail areas.

In many major US cities, and in many smaller centres in Canada, the downtown retail environment has been threatened by the continued development of planned suburban shopping destinations within an essentially no-growth market. In other places, including most major Canadian metropolitan areas, the downtown has been viewed as a retail investment. In a retail context, the former T. Eaton Company was the major player in the redevelopment of over 20 Canadian cores. Yet despite these investments, the relative share of CBD retail sales is declining. In Toronto, the central core now accounts for 9.7 per cent of the retail floor space and 6.9 per cent of retail employment in the Greater Toronto Area (Simmons et al., 1996).

In both Canada and the US, the key to downtown survival is the vibrancy of the economic base of the community or region as a whole. The downtowns of blue-collar industrial cities, such as Hamilton, Sudbury, and Windsor, are most vulnerable. Downtowns are more successful in cities, like Halifax or Saskatoon, that act as regional service centres. Factors that contribute to the success of downtown retailing include a strong public transit system that focuses on the core, a concentration of office/government employment in the downtown area, inner-city high-rise apartment or condominium development, a safe, unthreatening inner-city environment, and the willingness of major retailers (normally department stores), developers, and financial institutions to invest in the central area.

Towards a Classification of the Urban Retail System

The retail landscape within metropolitan areas is difficult to categorize. Neighbourhoods change, access patterns evolve, consumer preferences are modified, and new retail forms are developed. New retail typologies emerge daily as retail stores and districts are continuously undergoing change. If a store does not work, the retailer can shift the product mix or alter the image or advertising. It is not uncommon for the same location to go through dozens of variations in function and/or form over a 20-year period.

Four different approaches have been taken to classify the urban retail structure. These relate to the *morphology* or spatial form, the *functional composition* of the business types, the composition of the *market* served, and *ownership*.

In this chapter, a revised version of the taxonomy developed by Jones and Simmons (1993) differentiates urban retailing according to morphology, location, and market size and type (Figure 3). Each urban retail area initially is defined as either a centre or a strip. Then, in sequential stages, all areas are placed into inner-city and suburban categories and centres are further subdivided into planned and unplanned classes. Each retail area is assigned a position in the intra-urban retail hierarchy reflecting the size of its market and is further classified as satisfying either spatial or specialized markets.

Inner-city retailing has been dominated historically by the unplanned shopping area. Three unplanned forms are possible—the CBD, specialty product areas, and larger retail clusters at major intersections served by public transit. The first two serve

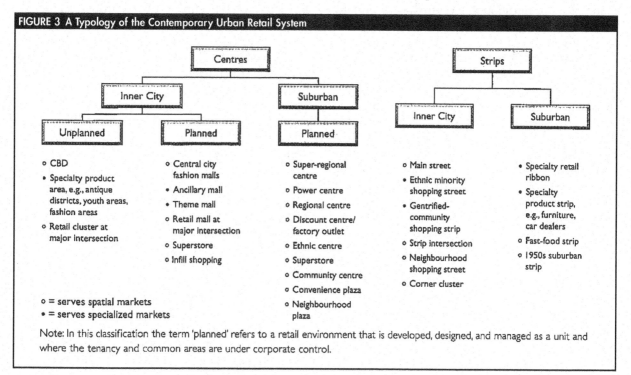

FIGURE 3 A Typology of the Contemporary Urban Retail System

Centres
- Inner City
  - Unplanned
    - ○ CBD
    - • Specialty product area, e.g., antique districts, youth areas, fashion areas
    - ○ Retail cluster at major intersection
  - Planned
    - ○ Central city fashion malls
    - • Ancillary mall
    - • Theme mall
    - ○ Retail mall at major intersection
    - ○ Superstore
    - ○ Infill shopping
- Suburban
  - Planned
    - ○ Super-regional centre
    - ○ Power centre
    - ○ Regional centre
    - ○ Discount centre/ factory outlet
    - ○ Ethnic centre
    - ○ Superstore
    - ○ Community centre
    - ○ Convenience plaza
    - ○ Neighbourhood plaza

Strips
- Inner City
  - • Main street
  - • Ethnic minority shopping street
  - • Gentrified-community shopping strip
  - ○ Strip intersection
  - ○ Neighbourhood shopping street
  - ○ Corner cluster
- Suburban
  - • Specialty retail ribbon
  - • Specialty product strip, e.g., furniture, car dealers
  - ○ Fast-food strip
  - ○ 1950s suburban strip

○ = serves spatial markets
• = serves specialized markets

Note: In this classification the term 'planned' refers to a retail environment that is developed, designed, and managed as a unit and where the tenancy and common areas are under corporate control.

metropolitan markets, the latter more community demands. Planned inner-city shopping areas, a recent phenomenon, have become a common feature in urban Canada since the mid-1970s. Downtown we find the central city fashion mall, which often has been the focus of major urban revitalization projects, and the ancillary retail complex that has become the normal underground use in major office, hotel, and condominium developments in Montreal and Toronto.

Since the 1970s, four inner-city planned centre types have emerged: theme malls, infill shopping centres, retail mall developments at major intersections, and superstores or hypermarkets. Theme malls are normally tourist-oriented, occupy waterfront locations, and promote a distinct specialty product theme and atmosphere. The infill centre is a typical suburban shopping centre transplanted to the city. The development of planned centres at major inner-city intersections represented a modernization of traditional retailing at these shopping nodes that took advantage of established public transit linkages and the traditional regional shopping focus. The superstore represents the return of the major supermarket chains to previously abandoned inner-city locations—typically, single retail units occupying a minimum of 4,500 square metres (50,000 square feet), offering discount prices and wide product assortment, and relying on extensive trading areas.

Planned suburban shopping centres are essentially hierarchical—ranging from neighbourhood plaza to super-regional shopping centre. They can be classified by several criteria such as number of stores, number of establishments, floor surface, total selling area, number of parking spaces, customer volumes, trade area size, rental rates, and sales per square foot values. Since the 1960s there have been three additions to the planned suburban retail system. First, during the late 1960s the super-regional shopping centre, anchored by a minimum of two major department stores, comprised over 90,000 square metres (a million square feet) of gross leasable area and served a market of approximately 500,000 customers. Next came the discount or off-price centre with 'no-frill' shopping catering to the bargain-oriented market. This discount trend is reflected in the growth of three other retail forms—the factory outlet, the flea market, and the warehouse/superstore. Other variants of the suburban shopping centre include the mega-mall/recreational complex (e.g., West Edmonton [Johnson, 1987]) and new suburban complexes that are increasingly directed towards market segments—the family, the young urban professional.

The retail strip is effectively differentiated according to location in the inner city or suburbs. In the inner city, six retail forms can be identified. Main streets (the downtown strip), strip intersections, neighbourhood shopping streets, and corner store clusters have served essentially the same functions since the early 1900s. The main street still remains the foremost focus of retail activity for most large Canadian cities, although its proportion of total urban retail sales has declined. In smaller metropolitan regions, high vacancy rates attest to both relative and absolute retail decline. Neighbourhood retail areas continue to serve the daily needs of local populations and reflect the cultural and lifestyle characteristics of the resident population of the areas they serve. These neighbourhood strips are some of the most volatile elements in the urban retail landscape. In ethnic and gentrified communities some serve specialized, metropolitan-wide markets, particularly with respect to restaurants, fashion goods, and specialized products (e.g., art and antiques).

In the suburbs, four distinct forms of strip retailing have evolved, all auto-dependent. The first comprises unplanned 1950s suburban strip shopping on major suburban arterials. Normally, they are characterized by a series of small centres, with limited parking abutting property fronts. Some suburban arterials have taken on a specialty focus. Typically, these specialized clusters include fast-food restaurants, automobile dealers, furniture warehouses, home improvement retailers, and discount merchandisers.

Since the late 1980s, big-box retailers (also known as category killers) and power centres have been added to the urban retail system. These can include a variety of retail forms, all based on low margins and high sales per square foot and supported by low land costs and labour inputs—hence high volumes and low unit prices. Typically, these retailers occupy industrial lands and prefer highly accessible, expressway/highway locations. In the typical power centre, one would find a free-standing Price Club/Costco and Home Depot, and a variety of other category killers (Chapters, Business Depot, HomeSense, and Michaels) (see Figure 4).

This classification provides a conceptual framework for understanding the complexity of the urban retail

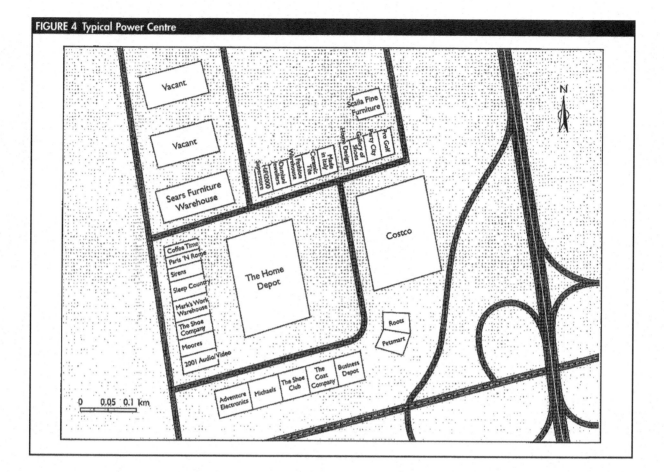

FIGURE 4 Typical Power Centre

environment. It should be remembered that the downtown makes up between 10 and 15 per cent of stores and the outlying shopping centres perhaps another 20 per cent, accounting for close to half the sales in the metropolitan region. However, approximately two-thirds of urban retailers operate in a variety of other shopping environments where they serve both specialized and convenience-oriented needs.

Conclusion

The urban retail system is structurally complex. In attempting to understand this environment, three distinct approaches should be integrated (Figure 5). First, it is necessary to describe, and develop an inventory of, the functional characteristics and spatial distribution patterns of the retail structure using basic dimensions such as retail type, number of stores, employment, ownership, and store turnover rates. The second and third approaches examine the retail system as demand and supply. Geographers have been more comfortable examining spatial aspects of demand—retail expenditure patterns, journey-to-shop,

distance decay relationships, and images of various retail environments with markets typically assessed in terms of location, areal extent, income level (market size), demographic composition, and lifestyle characteristics. The third component, retail supply, has been overlooked in most geographic appraisals of the urban retail landscape. Important questions to be addressed include: How do particular retailers react to specific market segments? How does the retail firm decide what retail merchandise to stock in a particular area? How are locational strategies formulated? What is the relationship between the retail chain and the shopping centre developer? What determines the retailer's ability to pay for a particular location? What is the role of retail planning control on investment activity?

This chapter concludes by speculating on some of the changes that most probably will impact the Canadian urban retailing system over the next decade. First, as our population ages, new retail types and forms will target increased convenience, new merchandising mixes, and the growth of new specialty chains that specifically cater to the 'greying' population (e.g., nutrition and health food stores). The 'baby-boomer' market seems likely to

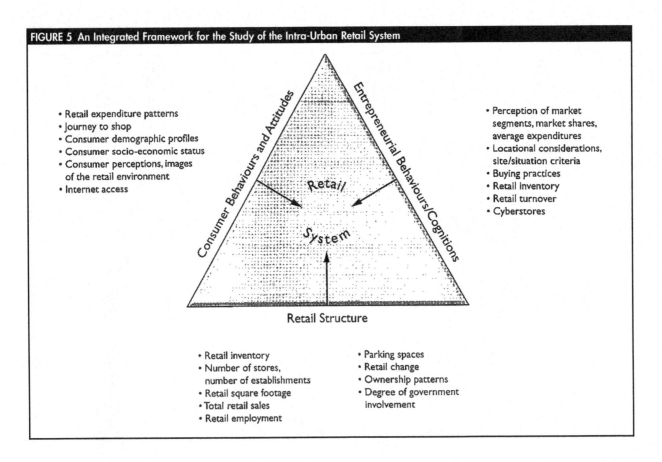

FIGURE 5 An Integrated Framework for the Study of the Intra-Urban Retail System

Consumer Behaviours and Attitudes

Entrepreneurial Behaviours/Cognitions

Retail System

- Retail expenditure patterns
- Journey to shop
- Consumer demographic profiles
- Consumer socio-economic status
- Consumer perceptions, images of the retail environment
- Internet access

- Perception of market segments, market shares, average expenditures
- Locational considerations, site/situation criteria
- Buying practices
- Retail inventory
- Retail turnover
- Cyberstores

Retail Structure

- Retail inventory
- Number of stores, number of establishments
- Retail square footage
- Total retail sales
- Retail employment

- Parking spaces
- Retail change
- Ownership patterns
- Degree of government involvement

demand higher-end retail venues (e.g., lifestyle centres) and generally to be less inclined to shop in 'big-box' formats. Second, corporate concentration throughout the Canadian retail system will continue to increase—two retailers tend to dominate each retail category. This retail consolidation will occur both through acquisition and by the arrival in Canada of major American and European retailers, reflecting growth of an international retail system (Yeates, 1998) and the realities of the North American Free Trade Agreement. (Most effected will be department stores and fashion retailers.) Third, the dichotomy between inner-city and suburban retailing will increase. Certain areas will cater exclusively to particular market segments, and shopping environments will be developed to serve distinct lifestyle groupings—normally the affluent. Structurally, either large power centres or free-standing destination retailers will continue to grow, as will small convenience centres (as witnessed by the growth in food-anchored shopping centres). The established enclosed mall environment will continue to be challenged by demands for large operating square footage. The demise of the traditional department store has raised issues relating to the definition

and operation of 'anchor' stores. Who are the new 'anchor' stores or 'anchor clusters'? As increasing numbers of malls integrate big-box format stores within and/or on their out-pads, how are consumer behaviours changing, and what does this mean in terms of retail lease rates? Finally, new issues will influence the operation of our retail system. These may include property rights and shopping centre access; the consequences of 'overstoring' on new retail development; the role of planning legislation on the final disposition of our urban retail future; the long-term impact of e-retailing; and privacy issues related to the proliferation of large databases that capture the purchasing patterns of the individual consumer.

The retail environment is continually washed by waves of innovation. New products, new store types, new technologies, new locations emerge, and new market segments are identified. There is constant interplay among categories of actors—retailers, consumers, developers, all levels of government, and, increasingly, technology providers. In this system winners and losers are quickly identified as the retail landscape constantly evolves.

Notes

1. The Eaton Centre, the most popular tourist destination in Toronto (Toronto, n.d.), further illustrates this phenomenon.

2. In the United States, these forms of inner-city shopping areas have become commonplace and have added a new, upscale dimension to the retail fabric of central cities. One developer, James Rouse, has been prominent in this form of retail renewal. Examples of the 'Rouse Model' include Faneuil Hall, Boston; The South Street Seaport, New York City; Harbor-Place, Baltimore; and The Gallery on Market Street East, Philadelphia. In other cases, a property of some importance is renovated as a specialty theme mall. Examples of these forms of development include Trolley Square, Salt Lake City; Union Station and Georgetown Park, Washington, DC; Jax's Brewery, New Orleans; Old Colony Mill, Keene, NH; and Ghirardelli Square, San Francisco.

Chapter 3

ENTERTAINMENT CROSS-SHOPPING: A COMPARATIVE ANALYSIS

Shuguang Wang, Ricardo Gomez-Insausti, Marco Biasiotto, Pina Barbiero and Bruce McNally

Summary

The idea of increasing marginal profits of shopping centers through cross-shopping in relation to entertainment has gained acceptance in the 1990s; however, this relationship has not been as strong as first anticipated. It appears that entertainment hardly produces the synergistic effects needed to encourage cross-shopping. This study was designed to examine and compare cross-shopping patterns related to retail-driven businesses in order to identify the factors that influence the specificity and intensity of cross-shopping within entertainment, and between entertainment and retailing categories in a power node and a regional mall. Findings showed that entertainment-related cross-shopping is more specific and less intense at the power node than at the mall. The power node facilitated 'delayed' cross-shopping while the mall encouraged more 'immediate' forms of cross-shopping. Types of entertainment cross-shopping proved to be associated with level of enjoyment only at the mall, and with cross-shopping intensity only at the power node. The mall exhibited several dominant types of entertainment cross-shoppers but mainly concentrated within a specific range of cross-shopping intensity, while the power node displayed a few dominant types widely dispersed across different levels of cross-shopping intensity.

Introduction

The consolidation of department stores and the competition from new retail formats such as superstores, membership clubs, discount outlets, catalogs and e-commerce has increasingly directed customer flows away from traditional shopping places. In order to revitalize shopping malls, attract customers back to them and even compete against e-commerce, retailers and developers alike have adopted entertainment as a 'drawing-card' (Cohen, 1999). However, new retail formats such as power centers have also developed entertainment facilities, increasing competition even more between shopping destinations and entertainment providers. In Canada, in the late 1990s, mega-theaters began to invade new shopping areas in the suburbs of major cities. However, the process appears to have reached a turning point, as mega-theaters are facing some problems of over-expansion (Potter, 1999). The overall experience has been fairly successful so far, but evidence from the US shows that mega-theaters may work well with shopping centers until marketplaces become oversaturated and unprofitable for movie exhibitors, or logistical expansions get too expensive for developers (Kenyon 1999).

The idea of increasing marginal profits through entertainment activities in shopping locations gained acceptance in the 1990s as people started spending more on entertainment. In Canada, the average expenditure on entertainment per household grew in real terms by almost 14% between 1992 and 1996 (Earl, 1999). Movie admissions rose strikingly at the end of the 1990s as mega-theaters flourished in the suburbs of major Canadian cities. Between 1998 and 1999 ticket sales were up by 6% at larger theaters (Doran, 1999) and about 220 new screens were added in Toronto alone (Potter, 1999).

Entertainment as a commercial activity has taken different forms such as retailer-driven businesses (e.g. theaters, restaurants, entertainment-based services and music/bookstores), and permanent and programmatic owner/developer-driven features (e.g. carousels, play areas and promotional shows) (de Barros Barreto & Konarski, 1999). Mega-theaters, themed restaurants, large music/bookstores, entertainment industry-related stores and play venues appear to attract more potential shoppers and enhance the whole shopping experience. The expected outcome from this type of investments has been higher levels of cross-shopping, particularly in closed environments such as shopping malls.

However, the relationship between entertainment and cross-shopping itself has not been as strong as first anticipated and has been questioned by many developers and researchers. Recent studies indicate that the entertainment-retail mix hardly produces the synergy needed to encourage cross-shopping in malls (Haynes & Talpade, 1996; Eastlick et al., 1998; Baker, 1999), and that entertainment can be actually a distracter and not a facilitator to shopping behavior (Christiansen et al., 1999).

Although the proportion of entertainment-related cross-shopping is relatively small in comparison to total retail cross-shopping, an enjoyable entertainment experience may have an overall positive impact on cross-shopping, specially within the entertainment category itself. As amusement is considered either an intrinsically or extrinsically motivated discretionary activity (Neulinger, 1981; Haywood, 1995), entertainment-related cross-shopping can be viewed as an extension of the experiences occurring in a leisure environment. This synergy likely encourages cross-shopping between complementary entertainment formats at a particular time. Cross-shopping within the entertainment category itself may be therefore higher than between categories (Eastlick et al., 1998). Customer motivations, times for leisure activities and retail shopping may differ over time generating, for instance, low or 'delayed' cross-shopping. For example, mall visitors drawn by family entertainment purposes are less likely to cross-shop, at that moment at least, than those going primarily for shopping (Haynes & Talpade, 1996).

The spatial organization of the shopping environment -distribution, size, compatibility and complementarity of the stores- also affects the level of cross-shopping. The large size and lack of compactness of power centers make it difficult for customers to shop the entire center, producing lower levels of cross-shopping (Lord & Bodkin, 1996: 54). However, a combination of factors such as car accessibility, customer job schedules and store hours likely produce a 'more flexible' and 'fragmented' type of cross-shopping due to more 'customized' use of power centers. Although previous evidence shows that the degree of cross-shopping differs between regional malls and power centers, the specificity and intensity of entertainment cross-shopping in each of these shopping environments remain unknown. Not only does the number of cross-shoppers matter, but also the specificity and intensity of their expenditure does. Regional malls may generate a higher degree of cross-shopping than power centers but they may also attract a functionally different crowd.

Research Objective

The goal of this research is to compare entertainment cross-shopping patterns at retailer-driven businesses (e.g. movie-theaters, restaurants, music/bookstores and play venues) in a power node and a regional mall in order to identify the factors that affect the specificity and intensity of cross-shopping within entertainment and between entertainment and retailing at both locations. Recent evidence suggests that lower levels of cross-shopping should be expected at a power center (Lord & Bodkin, 1996), different types and levels of cross-shopping should be expected for different shopping motivations (Eastlick et al., 1998), and cross-shopping levels might not necessarily related to customers' level of entertainment motivation or enjoyment (Kang & Kim, 1999).

Method and Data Analysis

Entertainment-related cross-shopping patterns are examined for two different and competing shopping environments: a power node (an open environment for shopping)[1]; and, a regional mall (a traditional enclosed shopping space). The former is a new regional retail space with up-to-date entertainment facilities while the latter is a traditional regional shopping center with typical mall entertainment facilities.

Sampling and Data Collection

Within the Greater Toronto Area (GTA), Canada, a power node (PN) and a regional mall (RM) with retail-driven entertainment businesses were chosen for this study (Figure 1). The PN is located in a part of the outer suburbs that grew very rapidly in the 1990s, about 2.8% per annum, while the RM is located in the inner suburbs (well connected to public transport),

Figure 1

Location of the Power Node (PN) and Regional Mall (RM) in the Greater Toronto Area, Canada

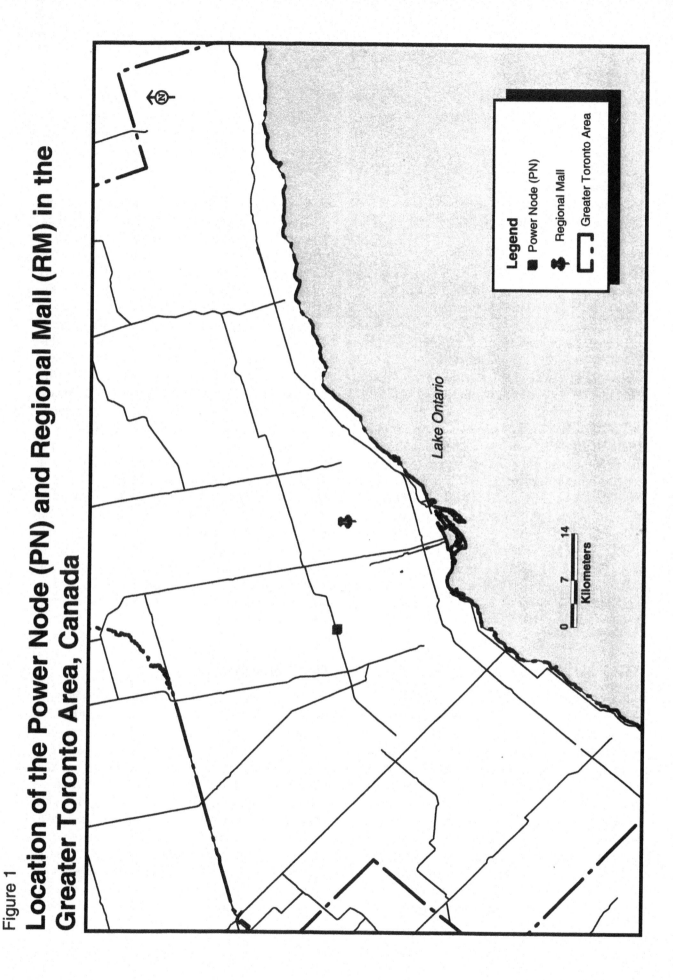

which grew moderately at an annual rate of 1.3% (Yeates, 2000). The selection of these two places guarantees some degree of generalization as they represent two of the major shopping formats with entertainment facilities that currently compete in suburban marketplaces. The PN is a regional shopping place that started developing in the 1990s while the RM is a traditional but renovated regional mall established in the early 1970s.

An inventory of all retail activities at both locations was done through fieldwork digitized in GIS format. The spatial organization of both places was analyzed in detail before intercept surveys of shoppers were conducted. Customers, age 13 and over[2], were intercepted by trained interviewers at the entrance of movie-theaters, music/bookstores, play venues and restaurants, from 1:00 to 10:00 p.m. during July 15-18, 1999 at the PN and August 5-8, 1999 at the RM[3]. The period Thursday-Sunday was chosen as typical 'entertainment' days in Toronto. Respondents who cooperated with the study got gift certificates to be used in a well-known chain of coffee shops. Interviewees were asked to supply specific information on their sociodemographics and the cross-shopping activities they performed before or after using an entertainment facility. The survey resulted in 1,250 valid questionnaires, 660 for the PN and 590 for the RM. This information was compiled and geo-coded to be used in the comparative analysis of entertainment cross-shopping patterns between both locations.

Survey and Operational Concepts

The survey had two sets of questions on customer cross-shopping behavior and sociodemographics. *Cross-shopping patterns* were obtained through the identification of the shopping activities (i.e. retailing, eating, entertaining and browsing) that the customer performed during a certain period around the specific moment of the interview (i.e. within two hours, between two and six hours, and between six and twenty-four hours). These time categories were intended to capture possible lags in cross-shopping. Subjects were also asked for the total amount of money and time spent on the above activities, form of payment, the total number of people in the entertain-

ment party by age group, frequency of the entertainment routine, level of enjoyment, reasons for place selection, reasons for not performing other activities in that place[4], mode of transportation and usual place of residence by postal code.

Sociodemographics were obtained through questions on gender, cultural background, occupation, current employment status, job schedule, and the total number of people and income in the economic family of the customer. Three of these operational definitions require some technical explanation. First, *gender* was identified based on customer appearance, i.e. masculine or feminine gender, as oppose to biological male or female sex. Customer behavior is likely more influenced by gender construction than by biological sex. Second, *cultural background* was determined by the interviewee based on his/her own identity construction. By so doing, it was intended to avoid the use of pre-established classifications that usually mix ethnic (e.g. Anglo-Saxon) and racial characteristics (e.g. black). Behavioral patterns are often more influenced by self-constructed identities than by inherited ethnic or racial characteristics. Third, the concept of *economic family* was used to grasp the total income and number of people that share wealth with the interviewee. Although *economic family* usually produces results similar to those for households, it facilitates the analysis of customers' lifestyles as it focuses on consumption by 'individuals' related rather than by 'place of living'.

Analytical Techniques

Since survey data were mostly categorical, comparative analyses were undertaken through crosstabulation techniques, chi-square tests and log-linear modeling. Differences in customer sociodemographics and cross-shopping patterns between the PN and the RM were assessed through chi-square tests. The identification of cross-shoppers' profiles by location was obtained through log-linear modeling that recognized significant interaction effects among customers' characteristics and behavior[5]. However, it was necessary sometimes to collapse some categories, because of low frequencies or sampling zeros, to run the models properly. Age, employment status, cross-shopping intensity, routine frequency, the number of people involved in the entertainment experience and reasons for place selection needed some regrouping for modeling purposes. Ending categories were the most frequently affected. All tests and parameters in this study were considered significant at $\alpha = .05$.

Results

Location Analysis and Market Penetration

The spatial organizations of the PN and the RM were analyzed to compare their shopping structures and their potential influence on cross-shopping. Long distances between stores in an open space like the PN appear to affect cross-shopping negatively. However, this influence may vary for different types of customers. The PN is a relatively new retail formation at the intersection of two major highways in the outer-suburbs of the GTA, i.e. north of metropolitan Toronto. It started with two big boxes in the early 1990s, expanded considerably with the establishment of a power center in the mid-1990s, and enhanced with the addition of two mega-theaters in the late 1990s (Jones & Doucet, 1998). The PN comprises a cluster of big boxes, some discount department stores, two mega-theaters, several restaurants and offices, surrounded by middle and upper-middle income neighborhoods. It is a 'hot' entertainment spot due to its novelty. The two mega-theaters are equipped with the latest technology and run simultaneously about 15-18 and 26-28 screens respectively. They belong to the first phase of the mega-theater expansion aimed at suburban marketplaces of major Canadian cities (Thoma, 1999). In addition to these two entertainment anchors, several full-licensed restaurants and two large music and bookstores contribute to the attractiveness of the PN as an entertainment destina-

tion. The restaurants, mega-theaters and music/bookstores are newly opened and perform rather well. During the survey period, for example, the average gross revenue per seat fluctuated from $4.0 to $12.0 and $2.0 to $7.0, for each cinema respectively[6]. Peaks in ticketing sales at both theaters were reached on Saturday, indicative of the 'entertaining destination' image the PN.

In contrast, the RM is a well-established shopping center that opened in the 1970s, expanded in the late 1980s, and was improving its accessibility at the time of the survey. It is an 'enclosed space' of about 800,000 sq. ft. that includes offices, two traditional department stores, a supermarket, a few full-licensed restaurants, some music/bookstores, some play venues and more than 200 other retailers. It is next to a main highway intersection in a typical middle-income inner suburb of the GTA, i.e. in the northern part of metropolitan Toronto. Although the mall has updated and continuously improved its facilities, it has not yet introduced any major transformation in terms of entertainment. The existing multiplex cinema has less than ten screens but performs relatively well. During the survey period the average gross revenue per seat varied from $2.5 to $5.25. Friday was the most important day for ticketing sales at the mall.

By mapping usual place of residence of surveyed customers, it was possible to assess the level of market penetration for the entertainment facilities at both locations. The maps show that the entertainment facilities of the PN have a much larger market area than those of the RM (Figures 2 & 3). The spatial distribution of entertainment customers at the PN shows that 25% of them come from within about 5.2 km (2.49 miles), 50% from 10.0 km (6.21 miles), and 75% from 18.0 km (11.18 miles) (Table 1). In contrast,

Proportion of Customers in Trade Area	n	Distance from the PN		n	Distance from the RM	
		km	(miles)		km	(miles)
25%	142	5.2	(3.23)	135	2.0	(1.24)
50%	287	10.0	(6.21)	269	4.0	(2.49)
75%	428	18.4	(11.43)	406	8.3	(5.16)

Table 1. Market Penetration by Location

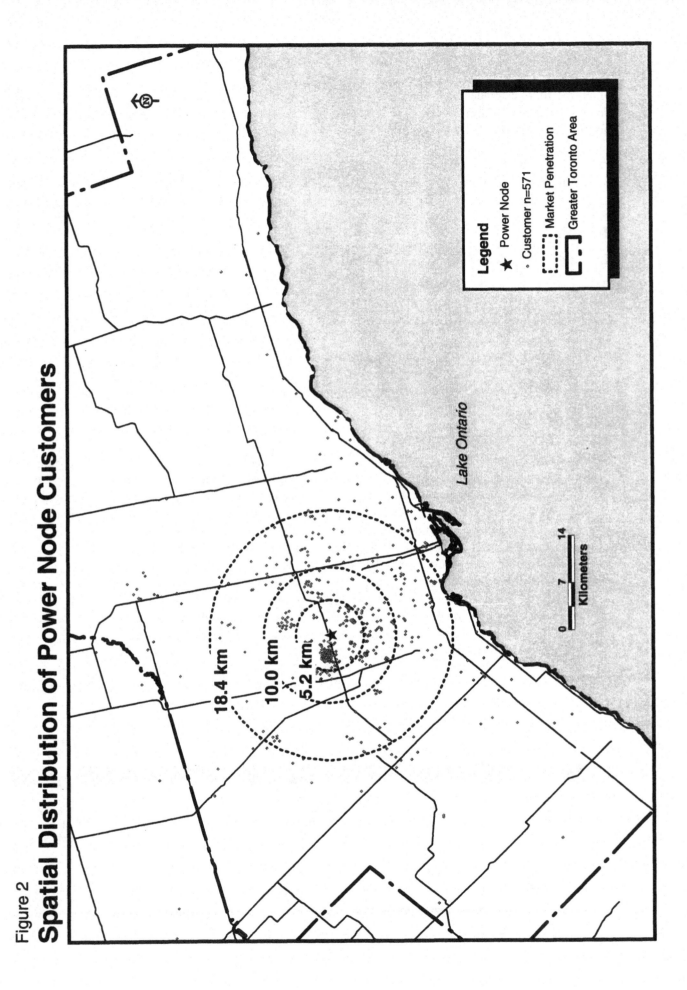

Figure 2
Spatial Distribution of Power Node Customers

Legend

★ Power Node
○ Customer n=571
Market Penetration
Greater Toronto Area

Lake Ontario

18.4 km
10.0 km
5.2 km

0   7   14
Kilometers

Figure 3

Spatial Distribution of Regional Mall Customers

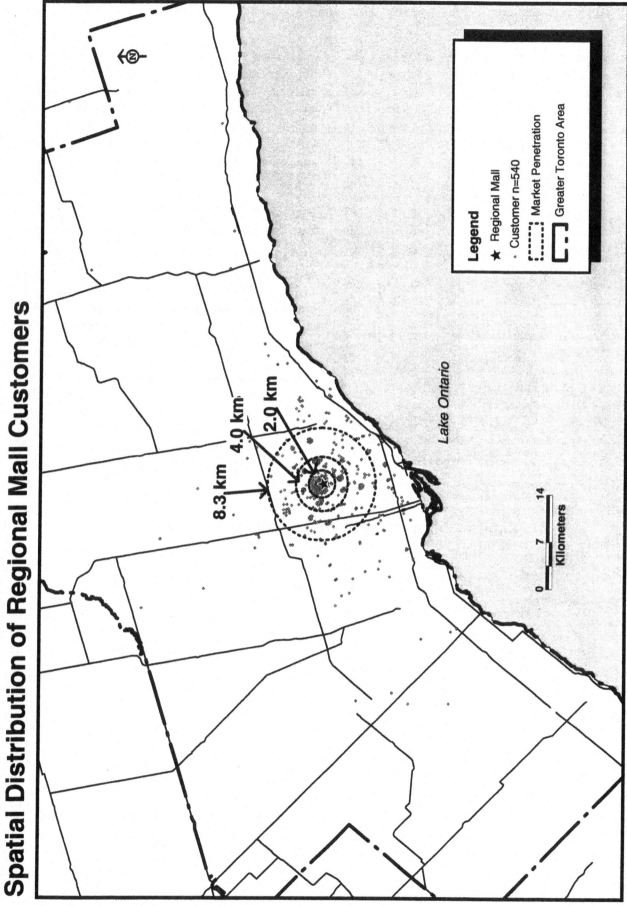

customers at the RM are more concentrated over space. Their distribution shows that 25% come to the mall from within about 2.0 km (1.24 miles), 50% from within 4.0 km (2.49 miles), and 75% from within 8.2 km (4.97 miles). The greater degree of attraction of the PN is noticeable due to its recently inaugurated facilities and privileged position in the highway system. The average distance that an entertainment customer travels to reach the PN is about 17.6 km (10.94 miles) while that for the RM is just 7.0km (4.35 miles). Customers from well beyond the surroundings of the PN patronize its entertainment facilities. Whether this phenomenon is related to the attractiveness of the PN itself or to that of its entertainment facilities remained to be discussed.

The RM exhibits a distance-decay curve for entertainment customers that declines continuously, and steeply after about 5km (3.11 miles) from the mall; 50% of the customers are within a radius of 4.0 km (Figure 4). In contrast, the curve for the PN increases considerably within the first 5 km up to reaching a turning point before 15km (9.32 miles) away from the node; 50% of the customers are within a 10.0 km

(6.21 miles) radius. The curves show that the RM shoppers are spatially concentrated around the mall, likely related to its location in the inner suburbs with higher population densities. The PN customers, by contrast, are more spread out and mainly coming from medium distances, likely in relation to the lower population density of the outer suburbs.

Sociodemographics of Entertainment Customers

The survey data supplied information on customer sociodemographics for both locations (Table 2). No significant difference was found in gender between the PN and the RM. However, both places differed significantly in customer age groups. The percentage of teenagers was higher at the mall (28.6%) because of the accessibility by public transport, while that of customers in their thirties and forties accounted for bigger proportions at the PN (46.3% combined). Cultural background also differed significantly between both locations. The RM displayed a fairly diverse crowd with some concentration of Chinese/Asian people. The PN accounted for a higher

Figure 4 Distance-Decay Curves for the PN and the RM

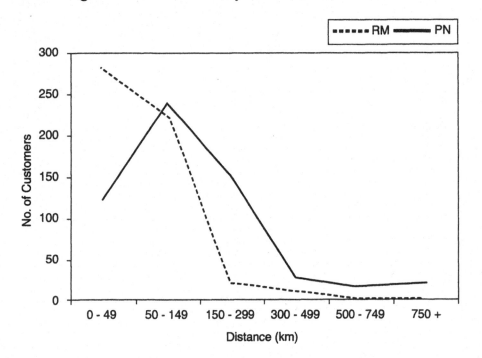

proportion of customers with Italian background (22.8%) as it is located close to some heavily populated Italian neighborhoods.

There was a significant difference in customers' occupation between both places. Professional and administrative/managerial shoppers were in higher proportions at the PN, 30.8% and 16.8% respectively, while students were well represented (27.5%) at the RM. In terms of employment status, customers at both places contrasted significantly. Full-time and self-employed were more frequently found at the PN

Table 2. Sociodemographics by Location

	PN %[a]	RM %[b]		PN %[a]	RM %[b]
Gender ($\chi^2 = 3.574$, p=.061)			**Cultural Background** ($\chi^2 = 214.148$, p=.000)		
Masculine	50.6	45.3	Canadian/N. American	34.9	25.5
Feminine	49.4	54.7	European[e]	12.7	14.3
			Italian	22.8	2.7
Age ($\chi^2 = 105.859$, p=.000)			Anglo-Saxon	11.1	8.0
13 – 19 years	8.4	28.6	Chinese/Asian	4.4	14.5
20 – 29 years	36.3	35.5	South Asian	2.5	6.0
30 – 39 years	26.7	18.0	Caribbean	2.2	8.0
40 – 49 years	19.6	10.2	African	1.0	4.2
50 – 64 years	7.1	4.4	East Indian	3.3	5.8
65 years and over	1.8	3.2	Arabic	0.8	7.8
			Other	4.3	3.3
Occupation ($\chi^2 = 95.896$, p=.000)			**Economic Family (E.F.) Income** ($\chi^2 = 31.448$, p=.000)[f]		
Clerical/Sales/Services	22.4	23.6	Under $30,000	7.7	14.7
Administrative/Managerial	16.8	9.1	$30,000 – 49,999	17.9	26.6
Techn./Machin./Craft/Constr.	11.8	7.1	$50,000 – 69,999	29.2	29.1
Professional	30.8	20.1	$70,000 and over	45.2	29.6
Student	9.3	27.5			
Other[c]	8.9	12.6			
Employment Status ($\chi^2 = 101.338$, p=.000)			**No. of People in Economic Family** ($\chi^2 = 18.776$, p=.001)		
Full-time	63.1	46.1	One	17.5	14.7
Non full-time	9.3	14.6	Two	27.5	19.7
Self-employed	11.8	5.1	Three	17.1	16.4
Unemployed	2.4	1.2	Four	21.4	26.8
Retired	2.9	3.1	Five or more	16.6	22.4
Other[d]	10.5	29.9			
Job Schedule ($\chi^2 = 68.658$, p=.000)			**No. of People in E.F. under 15 Years of Age**		
9:00-5:00	45.3	35.6	($\chi^2 = 1.154$, p=.764)		
Other day shift	7.5	7.7	One	54.1	55.5
Night shift	2.1	4.3	Two	31.2	27.7
Flexible	27.9	16.9	Three	12.8	13.5
Other (includes Students)	17.1	35.5	Four or more	1.8	3.2
			No. of People in E.F. 65 or more Years of Age		
			($\chi^2 = .764$, p=.382)		
			One	57.6	67.5
			Two	42.4	32.5

a n for the PN ranges from 651 to 658
b n for the RM ranges from 581 to 590
c 'Other' occupation comprises mainly homemakers and retired.
d 'Other' employment status includes mainly homemakers and students.
e Anglo-Saxon and Italians excluded.
f Figures are in Canadian dollars.

(74.9% combined) while the RM exhibited a higher proportion of people in category 'other' (29.9%) that included students. As for job schedule, the difference between both places was also significant. While the PN concentrated more customers with flexible schedules (27.9%), the RM displayed a higher proportion of customers in the 'other' category (35.5%) where students were classified.

Both places differed significantly in customer income. Higher proportions of customers with economic family income under $50,000 were found at the RM (41.3% combined). However, customers with economic family income of $70,000 and over accounted for a higher proportion at the PN (45.2%). Although entertainment customers at both locations were not from neighboring areas exclusively, as shown in Figures 2 & 3, a large proportion of them resided in the immediate neighborhoods. Findings from the survey match fairly well with estimations made by independent sources that classified neighborhoods around the PN as middle and upper-middle income, and those around the RM as middle-income (Feliciano & Assoc. 1999). The size of customers' economic families also contrasted significantly between both locations. Economic families of four and more were more frequently found at the RM (49.2% combined) while those of two people accounted for a higher proportion at the PN. Contrary to these findings, no significant differences were found in the number of youngsters and elders in customers' economic families.

In summary, regarding the most distinctive sociodemographic characteristics, it appears that the entertainment customers of the PN are older and less culturally diverse. They are mainly professionals and administrative/managerial workers, full-timers, self-employed and flexi-timers. They appear to have a relatively higher income and smaller economic families. By contrast, customers at the RM are identified as a younger and more culturally diverse crowd. They are mainly students, from relatively lower income and larger economic families.

Entertainment Customers' Behavior

Data from the survey provided specific information on cross-shopping behavior at the PN and the RM (Table 3). No significant difference was found in the time spent on eating-entertainment between both places; most food-entertainment cross-shopping (within category) occurred within a two-hour range in either location. However, retail- and browsing-entertainment cross-shopping (basically between categories) differed significantly between both places. The PN showed higher proportions of retail- and browsing-entertainment within the 6-24 hour range (i.e. 'delayed' cross-shopping), 21.2% and 17.8% respectively against 7.9% and 7.1% at the RM. These findings support the idea that shoppers might have a more customized use of the PN. They might visit the PN more frequently, for specific purposes and different lengths of time.

The frequency of the entertainment routine proved to differ significantly between both places. The RM exhibited higher proportions of customers that visited the mall more than once a week (18.7%) and in party groups of teenagers (24.9% combined). In contrast, the PN reported higher proportions of party groups of two and three or more adults, 36.2% and 13.2% respectively. The PN reported 48.2% of customers with high level of enjoyment during the entertainment routine, while 32.8% of customers at the RM accounted for medium level of enjoyment. In terms of total time spent on entertainment-related activities, there was no significant difference between both places. Most customers, 88.5% at the PN and 91.0% at the RM, spent up to four hours on the whole entertainment experience.

However, a significant difference was found in the amount of money spent on entertainment. The regional mall accounted for a higher proportion of spending under $20 (38.8%) while the power node exhibited a higher concentration of expenditures between $21 and $50 (34.2%). It is noteworthy that the proportion of customers spending over $100 was about the same, 10% at both locations. Cross-shopping intensity also proved to be significantly different between the PN and the RM. Spending between $21 and $50 per hour was more frequently found at the PN (34.2%) while under $10/hour was more common at the RM (21.0%). The form of payment showed no significant difference between the PN and the RM; cash was the method most frequently chosen in either location.

A significant difference was found in reasons for choosing entertainment destination. Novelty, good entertainment facilities and specialty services were

Table 3. Entertainment Cross-Shoppers' Behavior by Location

	PN %	RM %		PN %	RM %
Food-Entertainment Cross-Shopping ($\chi^2 = 2.021$, p=.364)			**Total Time Spent** ($\chi^2 = 4.176$, p=.124)		
Within 2 hours	77.1	80.9	Less than 2 hours	41.5	46.7
Between 2 & 6 hours	16.8	15.1	2 - 4 hours	47.0	44.3
Between 6 & 24 hours	6.1	4.0	More than 4 hours	11.5	9.0
Retail-Entertainment Cross-Shopping ($\chi^2 = 22.007$, p=.000)			**Money Spent** ($\chi^2 = 48.609$, p=.000)		
Within 2 hours	55.2	67.6	Up to $20	21.1	38.8
Between 2 & 6 hours	23.6	24.5	$21 – 50	45.1	31.1
Between 6 & 24 hours	21.2	7.9	$51 – 100	23.5	19.3
			Over $100	10.3	10.7
Browsing-Entertainment Cross-Shopping ($\chi^2 = 12.350$, p=.002)			**Intensity ($/hour)** ($\chi^2 = 17.177$, p=.002)		
Within 2 hours	58.6	64.5	Under $10/hour	14.9	21.0
Between 2 & 6 hours	23.6	25.3	$10 - 20/hour	34.8	36.9
Between 6 & 24 hours	17.8	7.1	$21 - 50/hour	34.2	24.1
			$51 - 100/hour	13.8	14.7
			Over $100/hour	2.3	3.3
Routine Frequency ($\chi^2 = 12.924$, p=.012)			**Form of Payment** ($\chi^2 = 5.028$, p=.081)		
More than once a week	11.9	18.7	Credit card	25.6	21.9
Weekly	27.1	23.8	Debit card	26.7	23.6
Twice a month	20.7	22.1	Cash	47.7	54.5
Monthly	23.4	20.7			
1 – 4 times yearly/first time	16.8	14.6			
Persons Involved in Routine ($\chi^2 = 102.419$, p=.000)			**Reasons for Place Selection** ($\chi^2 = 106.534$, p=.000)		
1- 2 teenagers	4.0	16.4	Novelty	12.9	4.6
3 teenagers or more	2.0	8.5	Proximity	32.2	51.4
1 adult	23.3	24.4	Easy to get	8.9	8.6
1 adult & minor(s)	9.9	9.2	Comfortable environment	7.7	5.1
2 adults	36.2	28.1	Good assortment of stores &services/		
2 adults & minor(s)	8.8	4.6	Extended hours	8.6	14.0
3 adults or more	13.2	6.8	Good entertain. facilities	13.0	6.3
3 adults or more & minor(s)	2.6	2.0	Meet/spend time w/friends	3.7	4.5
			Have a good time/Release stress	2.1	2.2
Level of Enjoyment ($\chi^2 = 36.263$, p=.000)			Affordability	1.5	0.3
None (0)	1.4	.9	Specialty services	6.6	1.0
Low (1)	2.8	6.3	Parking availability/Other	2.9	1.9
Medium (2)	47.6	60.0			
High (3)	48.2	32.8	**Mode of Transportation** ($\chi^2 = 234.852$, p=.000)		
			Car/Taxi	98.3	65.7
			Public	0.8	23.3
			Walk/Other	0.9	11.0

more frequently reported for the PN, 12.9%, 13.0% and 6.6% respectively. In contrast, proximity (51.4%) and a good assortment of stores and services (14.0%) were the responses associated with the regional the RM shoppers. There was also a significant difference in the mode of transportation that customers used to reach the PN and the RM. At the power node, 98.3% of the respondents were car/taxi users while the regional mall accounted for higher proportions of walkers/other (11.0%) and public transportation riders (23.3%).

In summary, food-entertainment cross-shoppers (within category) generally spend up to two hours on the whole cross-shopping experience in either place. Entertainment-shoppers at the power node are characterized by 'delayed' retail- and browsing- entertainment cross-shopping, party groups of two and more adults, high level of enjoyment, and expenditures between $21 and $50 per hour. Most of these customers tend to use cars/taxis and choose the place because of novelty, good entertainment facilities and specialty services. In contrast, the RM appears to have higher proportions of 'immediate' retail- and browsing-entertainment cross-shopping. The mall respondents tend to visit the mall more than once a week, and are more associated with groups of teenagers. Most customers enjoy the mall entertainment routine only moderately. The mall appears to concentrate more customers spending less than $10/hour. Proximity, good assortment of stores and services are

common reasons for choosing the mall. Customers that walk or take public transportation to reach the place are in higher proportions at the mall.

Entertainment Cross-Shopping Patterns

In order to identify specific patterns of cross-shopping undertaken by entertainment patrons, disaggregated information from the survey was classified according to specific objectives. By combining type of activity and store identity, responses were grouped regarding the type of cross-shopping: no cross-shopping; and cross-shopping 1) within entertainment; 2) between entertainment and retail, 3) between entertainment and browsing. A significant difference was found in the level of entertainment cross-shopping between the PN and the RM. However, a higher proportion of entertainment customers did not cross-shop at all in either place, 43.9% at the PN and 35.4% at the RM (Table 4). Respondents that did cross-shop behaved differently at the two locations. Cross-shopping within the entertainment category was higher at the PN (23.0%), while retail-based cross-shopping was proportionally higher at the RM (27.6%).

The RM reported higher proportions of cross-shopping in the apparel/home fashion and office/other specialty store categories, 25.1% and 22.4% respectively. The mall also showed a higher proportion of multiple-store cross-shopping (22.0%). This finding confirmed the regional position as a

Table 4. Entertainment Cross-Shopping Types by Location

	PN %	RM %		PN %	RM %
Cross-Shopping ($\chi^2 = 72.375$, p=.000)			**Food-Entertainment** ($\chi^2 = 65.622$, p=.000)		
No cross-shopping	43.9	35.4	Full licensed	54.6	12.0
Within entertainment	23.0	9.3	Fast food	45.4	88.0
Between categories	16.6	27.6			
Browsing	16.5	27.6			
Retail-Entertainment ($\chi^2 = 74.301$, p=.000)			**Browsing-Entertainment** ($\chi^2 = 53.339$, p=.000)		
Apparel & Home Stores	13.6	25.1	Apparel	41.3	78.2
Music/Bookstores	22.4	5.4	Home	39.2	10.9
Office/Other Spec. Stores	5.6	22.4	Office	14.7	3.1
Dept./Disc. Dept. Stores	38.3	22.0	Other	4.9	7.8
Food Market	6.5	3.1			
Multiple Stores	13.6	22.0			

primary destination for shopping. At the regional mall, department stores and brand-name clothing and other specialty stores were frequently visited. In contrast, the PN exhibited higher proportions of cross-shopping by big-box music/bookstores (entertainment-related stores) and discount department stores, 22.4% and 38.3% respectively. Eating-entertainment cross-shopping behavior was significantly different between the PN and the RM. Fast food accounted for 88.0% of the food-related cross-shopping at the RM while full-licensed restaurants were the most frequently reported form of food-related cross-shopping at the PN (54.6%). Some newly opened medium-price restaurants contributed positively to the attractiveness of the PN as an entertainment destination. Also a significant difference was found in browsing-entertainment cross-shopping between the PN and the RM. Entertainment customers browsing apparel stores were more frequently found at the RM (78.2%) while those looking for home and office products were more common at the PN, 39.2% and 14.7% respectively. The presence of two home and office big boxes is related to this pattern at the PN.

The association between entertainment cross-shopping types and the level of enjoyment in the entertainment experience proved to be significant at the RM ($\chi2 = 15.445$, p = .016) but not at the PN ($\chi2 = 2.445$, p = .875). The results for the RM show that medium and high levels of enjoyment concentrate higher proportions of entertainment cross-shoppers as long as browsing is a cross-shopping category. Browsing-entertainment cross-shopping is the category that concentrates most entertainment customers with medium and high levels of enjoyment at the mall. By contrast, the results for the PN indicate that, despite having high or medium level of enjoyment, entertainment customers at the PN that did not cross-shop, or cross-shopped within entertainment itself, or cross-shopped between categories do not differ significantly.

Types of entertainment cross-shopping proved to be associated with intensity of cross-shopping at the PN ($\chi2 = 27.102$, p = .001) but not at the RM ($\chi2 = 8.082$, p = .526). Entertainment customers that do not cross-shop at the PN tend to spend less intensively

because they spend more time on entertainment-based activities. This finding supports findings from previous studies (Haynes & Talpade, 1996; Eastlick et al., 1998). However, those that cross-shop are inclined to spend as much on within as on between categories. The RM shows that browsing entertainment cross-shoppers tend to spend more intensively ($20/hour or more) on entertainment cross-shopping.

It appears that entertainment-related cross-shopping is more focused at the PN than the RM. The PN tends to exhibit more cross-shopping within the entertainment category itself such as restaurants and music/bookstores. Nonetheless, between-category cross-shopping, either retailing- or browsing-entertainment, is also more specific. It is mostly directed towards discount department stores and big boxes such as home and office outlets. In contrast, the RM exhibits more cross-shopping between a variety of categories (e.g. more visits to apparel, home, and multiple stores). At the mall, within-category cross-shopping is virtually dominated by food (e.g. fast food) rather than by entertainment-related retail (e.g. music/bookstores). At the mall, apparel browsing seems to appeal to a considerable proportion of entertainment customers, indicating a wider concept of entertainment.

Entertainment Cross-Shopping by Customer Profile

The level of enjoyment in the entertainment routine showed no significant association with cross-shopping intensity at either location, ($\chi2 = 3.329$, p = .767 for the PN, and $\chi2 = 7.039$, p = .317 for the RM). Rather, the intensity of cross-shopping was better reflected by customer profile measured by age, occupation, employment status, and party group. Log-linear modeling helped produce a better understanding of cross-shoppers' behavior through the analysis of multi-way crosstabulations, and generated clearer results than those produced by the two-way crosstabulations. Significant parameters for interaction effects were used to identify dominant profiles of customers at each location . Occupation and age proved to influence significantly many categories of cross-shopping intensity (Table 5). At the PN, clerical/sales/service people between 30 and 49 years of age tended to spend between $21 and $50 per hour on entertainment-related activities. Professionals in their thirties and forties usually spent between $10 and $20 per hour as they used more time on the whole entertainment experience. Spending under $10/hour was dominant among clerical/sales/service workers in their teens and twenties, and teenager technician/machinist/craft/construction workers. Teenage students usually spend under $20 per hour.

At the RM, professionals in their thirties and forties were inclined to expend between $21 and $50 or even more than $50 per hour as they spent less time on the mall-based cross-shopping experience. Spending between $10 and $20 per hour was common among professionals in their twenties, administrative/managerial workers in their thirties and forties, and technician/machinist/craft/construction workers and students in their teens and twenties. The same spending pattern was identifiable among clerical/sales/service workers 20 and over, and among customers 50 and over classified in occupational category 'other' that mainly included housemakers or the retired. Cross-shopping intensity under $10/hour was only dominant among teenager technician/machinist/craft/construction workers.

The intensity of cross-shopping also proved to be influenced by the employment status and the number of people involved in the entertainment experience (Table 6). At the PN, two adults working full-time tended to expend between $21 and $50 per hour. Spending between $10 and $20 per hour was common in parties of three or more who were self-employed or non full-time workers, two adults working full-time, and one adult full-timer accompanied by minor(s). The same intensity of cross-shopping was found among customers in groups of three and more teenagers who were self-employed or non full-timers, and parties of up to two teenager students. Expenditure under $10/hour is typical of groups of three and more teenager students, and parties of one or two teenagers who are self-employed or non full-timers.

At the RM, groups of two adult customers that work full-time tended to spend between $21 and $50 and over $50 per hour. Parties of one and three or more

adults working full time usually spent between $10 and $20 per hour. The same cross-shopping intensity was also found among customers in parties of two and three or more adults, one and two adult with minor(s), and three or more teenagers who are self-employed or non full-timers. Groups of one, two and three or more adult full-timers accompanied by minor(s) generally expend between $10 and $20 per hour on what appears to be a typically family-oriented outing. One adult accompanied by a minor(s), and one or two adults mostly retired or unemployed, and teenager students also tend to spend between $10 and $20 per hour. Parties of two adult full-timers, and one or two teenagers self-employed or non full-timers tend to spend under $10/hour.

In summary, combining results from Tables 5 and 6, the PN shows only a few dominant profiles of cross-shoppers while the RM displays several types of cross-shoppers, particularly in the $10-$20/hour range. At the PN, three groups of customers were clearly identified: 1) middle-age people in clerical/sales/service jobs, working full-time, involved in parties of two people, and spending between $21 and $50 per hour; 2) students, in parties of one, two and three or more teenagers, and spending between $10 and $20 per hour; and 3) teenager clerical/sales/service workers or students, in parties of one, two and three or more people, and spending under $10 per hour.

The cross-shopping patterns for the RM are not as simple as for the PN. The RM displays several dominant profiles of cross-shoppers; however, three major groups can be recognized: 1) middle-age professionals, working full-time, in two-people parties, and spending between $21 and $50 or over $50/hour; 2) teenagers working in clerical/sales/service jobs, self-employed or non full-timers, in two-people parties, and spending under $10 per hour; and 3) students in their teens and twenties, in two-people parties, and spending between $10 and $20 per hour. In addition to these three major groups, two other ones can be identified: 4) one, two and three or more adults with minor(s), and spending between $10 and $20 per hour; and 5) customers in technician/machinist/craft/construction or clerical/sales/service jobs, in their teens or twenties, and spending between $10 and $20 per hour.

Table 5. Entertainment Cross-Shopping Intensity by Significant Interactions with Occupation and Age per Location ($\alpha = .05$)

Occupation	Age (years)	Entertainment Under $10/hour		$10 - $20/hour		Cross-Shopping $21 - 50/hour		Intensity Over $50/hour	
		PN	RM	PN	RM	PN	RM	PN	RM
Professional	30 – 49			25.751			8.102		17.040
	20 - 29				1.953				
Admin./Manag.	30 - 49				1.018				
Technician/Mach. Craft/ Construction	20 - 29				2.546				
	13 - 19	1.946			3.478				
Clerical/Sales/ Service	≥ 50				6.352				
	30 - 49				2.184	0.834			
	20 - 29	1.115			2.971				
	13 - 19	1.373	1.342						
Student	20 - 29	1.721			1.765				
	13 - 19	1.609		1.534	3.205				
Other[a]	≥ 50				1.344				

a Category 'other' includes mainly homemakers and retired.

Table 6. Entertainment Cross-Shopping Intensity by Significant Interactions with Number of Persons Involved in Routine and Employment Status per Location ($\alpha = .05$)

No. of Persons Involved in Routine	Employment Status	Entertainment Under $10/hour		$10 - $20/hour		Cross-Shopping $21 - 50/hour		Intensity Over $50/hour	
		PN	RM	PN	RM	PN	RM	PN	RM
≥ 3 adults	Full time				1.61				
	Non FT/Self-empl.			1.63	1.86				
≥ 3 ad. & minor(s)	Full time				4.06				
2 adults	Full time		6.67	7.71		10.35	13.20		13.31
	Non FT/Self-empl.				3.80				
	Other[a]				2.53				
2 adults & minor(s)	Full time				1.18				
	Non FT/Self-empl.				1.86				
1 adult	Full time				1.12				
	Other				1.07				
1 adult & minor(s)	Full time			2.48	2.60				
	Non FT/Self-empl.				5.62				
	Other				3.21				
1 – 2 teenagers	Non FT/Self-empl.	1.61	1.66						
	Other			1.20	3.71				
≥ 3 teenagers	Non FT/Self-empl.			3.15	1.91				
	Other	2.00			4.30				

a Category 'other' comprises mainly retired, unemployed and students.

Entertainment Cross-Shopping Frequency

The frequency of the entertainment cross-shopping proved to be influenced by the number of people involved in the party and customer job schedule (Table 7). Customers that visit the PN for the first time or go there just a few times a year are mostly in parties of three or more adults working day shifts other than 9:00-5:00, and two adults with minor(s) with flexible job schedule. Groups of two adults working 9:00-5:00 or in night shifts appear to visit the PN once or twice a month. One adult with flexible job schedule tends to visit the PN once or more weekly. At the RM, visits for the first time or a few times a year are mostly done people in parties of three or more adults working 9:00-5:00 or with other job schedule[8], two adults with minor(s) with flexible schedule, and one adult working day shifts other than 9:00-5:00. One or two visits a month are frequently done by people in parties of three or more adults working night shifts, two adults working 9:00-5:00, and two adults and minor(s) with other job schedule. One or more visits a week are basically performed by customers in parties of one adult and minor(s) with flexible job schedule, parties of up to two teenagers and one adult with other job schedule (many students).

In summary, the entertainment facilities of the PN usually receive one or more visits a week from one adult working flexible hours while those of the RM get frequent visit from parties of teenagers, one adult with minor(s), and one adult alone. Parties of three adults or more are more inclined to visit the mall once or twice a month. However, two-adult parties appear to visit either place only a few times a year.

Entertainment Place Selection

Reasons for choosing the entertainment destination proved to be influenced by customer occupation and the number of people involved in the entertainment trip. For proper modeling, original response categories were reduced to three broad classes: 1) physical/environmental features (i.e. novelty, proximity, easy to get to, comfortable environment and parking availability); 2) service characteristics (i.e. extended hours, good assortment of stores and services, good entertainment facilities, affordability and specialty service); and 3) personal/social reasons (i.e. meet and spend time with friends, have a good time, release stress, and other).

At the PN, physical/environmental reasons were important factors for customers in parties of two and three or more adult professionals, and one adult professional with minor(s). The service characteristics of the destination were mostly reported by customers in

Table 7. Frequency of Entertainment Cross-Shopping Routine by Significant Interactions with Number of Persons Involved in Routine and Job Schedule per Location ($\alpha = .05$)							
No. of Persons Involved in Routine	**Job Schedule**	**Entertainment Cross-Shopping Routine Frequency**					
		Once or more weekly		**1-2 times monthly**		**1-4 times yearly/1st time**	
		PN	RM	PN	RM	PN	RM
≥ 3 adults	9:00-5:00						1.530
	Other day shift					2.078	
	Night shift				1.006		
	Other[a]						1.731
2 adults	9:00-5:00			19.884	68.177		
	Night shift			1.442			
2 adults & minor(s)	Flexible					1.541	3.140
	Other				1.484		
1 adult	Other day shift						2.629
	Flexible	0.752					
	Other		1.128				
1 ad. & minor(s)	Flexible		1.621				
1 – 2 teenagers	Other		1.339				

a Category 'other' comprises house-keepers mainly.

groups of two adult professionals with minor(s), one adult professional or technician/machinist/craft/construction worker, and three or more teenagers in technician / machinist / craft / construction jobs. Personal/social reasons for choosing the entertainment destination were dominant among parties of three or more adults in administrative/managerial positions or students, and three or more teenagers in clerical/sales/service jobs. At the RM, physical/environmental characteristics were most cited by shoppers in parties of two adult professionals, and one adult professional with minor(s). The service characteristics of the place were most important for parties of two adults, mainly housemakers or retired (classified as 'other' occupation), and one adult professional with minor(s). Personal/social reasons tend to be more commonly chosen among people in parties of three or more adult professionals, and three or more teenager students. In summary, larger groups and teenagers and elders appear to select their entertainment destination mainly for personal and social reasons. Smaller groups and middle-age customers tend to choose the location based more on physical/environmental reasons. Family-oriented groups, those including minors, appear to frequently choose the entertainment location based on factors that related to the service characteristics of the entertainment destination.

Discussion and Conclusions

The market draw of the entertainment facilities at PN covers a much more extensive trade area than that of the RM. However, most of the entertainment cross-shoppers at the PN tend to do it within the entertainment category, which shows that the PN is a major regional entertainment destination. Many customers choose the PN because of its good entertainment facilities and novelty. In contrast, entertainment customers at the RM are more inclined to cross-shop and browse between variety of retail categories, which suggest that the mall is more a shopping destination offering a wider spectrum of entertainment options to satisfy a different crowd. Mall customers tend to choose the place for its proximity, and good assortment of stores and services.

Differences in the sociodemographics of entertainment customers at both locations suggest different lifestyles which influence a different set of entertainment objectives and shopping behaviors at each location. The PN is patronized by older entertainment

Table 8. Reasons for Place Selection by Significant Interactions with Number of People Involved in Routine and Occupation per Location ($\alpha = .05$)

No. of Persons Involved in Routine	Occupation	Reasons for Place Selection					
		Physical/Environment		Service		Personal/Social	
		PN	RM	PN	RM	PN	RM
≥ 3 adults	Professional	1.171					2.760
	Admin./Managerial					1.726	
	Student					1.785	
	Other	1.193					
2 adults	Professional	68.683	68.039				
	Other				1.234		
2 adults & minor(s)	Professional			1.238			
	Student				3.271		
1 adult	Professional			1.038			
	Techn./Craft/Constr.			1.047			
1 adult & minor(s)	Professional	1.421			1.944		
	Adm./Managerial		1.804				
≥ 3 teenagers	Clerical/Sales/Serv.					1.900	
	Techn./Craft/Constr.			3.084			
	Student						1.564

a Category 'other' comprises housemakers mainly.

customers with higher levels of income, while the RM attracts younger shoppers with relatively lower levels of income. Although a high proportion of entertainment customers do not cross-shop at either location, those that did exhibited more focused cross-shopping at the PN. The power node by its tenant mix encourages more cross-shopping within the entertainment category. The PN also appears to encourage more 'delayed' cross-shopping between categories. This suggests a more single-purpose and customized use of the power node, i.e. different visits for specific reasons at different times. At the mall, entertainment cross-shopping proves to have some association with customer level of enjoyment, as those enjoying the entertainment routine are also inclined to browse.

The intensity of cross-shopping shows that it is associated with types of cross-shopping. At the PN, entertainment customers that do not cross-shop usually spend less amount of money per hour as they use more time on the entire entertainment experience while those that cross-shop do it more intensively. However, entertainment customer profiles give a richer understanding of cross-shopping patterns by location. Typical entertainment customers at the PN can be characterized as middle-age clerical/sales/service full-time workers in two-people parties and spending between $21 and $50 per hour; teenager students in parties of one or more people spending between $10 and $20 per hour; and teenager clerical/sales/service workers or students in parties of one or more people spending under $10 per hour.

In contrast, typical entertainment shoppers at the RM can be described as middle-age full-time professionals in two-people parties, spending between $21 and $50 or over $50/hour; teenagers in clerical/sales/service jobs, self-employed or non full-timers, in two-people parties and spending under $10 per hour; students in their teens and twenties, in parties of two people that tend to spend between $10 and $20 per hour; parties of adults with minor(s) spending between $10 and $20 per hour; and technician/machinist/craft/construction and clerical/sales/service workers in their teens and twenties that spend between $10 and $20 per hour.

In methodological terms, a multi-way cross-tabulation analysis demonstrated to be useful in identifying and comparing shopper characteristics by location. The groups of entertainment customers that log-linear modeling uncovered match only partially with results from the two-way crosstabulations done to compare customer sociodemographics and cross-shopping behavior by location. The interactions among explanatory variables are necessarily missing in two-way crosstabulations.

Notes

1 A grouping (usually facing each other around a major highway intersection) of at least one power strip and one power centre, or at least two power centres (i.e. must involve at least one power centre) (Yeates, 2000: 45).

2 Consumers 18 and under cover about 20 per cent of the Canadian market and spend yearly around US$7 billion on entertainment, food and fashion (Financial Post, July 15, 1999).

3 Times and locations were adjusted properly regarding mall hours.

4 Many customers did not provide answers for this question; therefore, it was excluded from the analysis.

5 The parameters of log-linear models are the natural log-odds of the cell frequencies rather than the observed counts in a multi-way crosstabulation. The dependent variable is therefore the natural logarithm of the ratio of the probability of a dominant event to that of a subdominant event. All categorical variables that are used for the multi-way classification are the explanatory variables. The SPSS general log-linear command for saturated models was used to generate the parameters for main and interaction effects but only significant interaction effects were used in this analysis. In a three-way crosstabulation, as used in this study, the generic model is as follows:

$$\ln F_{ijk} = \mu + \lambda_i{}^A + \lambda_j{}^B + \lambda_k{}^C + \lambda_{ij}{}^{AB} + \lambda_{ik}{}^{AC} + \lambda_{jk}{}^{BC} + \lambda_{ijk}{}^{ABC}$$

6 Estimations by seat for each theatre result from dividing daily total sales by the average number of seats multiplied by the number of screens used in the day of reference.

7 Only the significance of the parameter matters, not its magnitude. The weight or size of the parameter does not have a clear explanatory power.

8 Category other comprises housekeepers mainly.

References

Baker, M. (1999), "Theatres in the Mall," *ICSC Research Quarterly*, 6 (3) Fall, 9-13.

Cohen, N. (1999), Industry sees entertainment as key to re-gaining sales lost to e-commerce, *Shopping Centres Today* 20 (7), 7 &16.

Christiansen, T., L. Comer, R. Feinberg and H. Rinne (1999), "The Effects of Mall Entertainment Value on Mall Profitability", *Journal of Shopping Centre Research* 6 (2), 7-71.

de Barros Barreto C. and J. Konarski III (1999), "Shopping Centres and Entertainment: A Typology," *ICSC Entertainment & Retail: Types and Profiles*, New York: ICSC, 1-23.

Doran, D. (1999), 'Megaplexes help to boost moviegoing,' *The Toronto Star*, (August 25, Section D).

Earl, L. (1999), 'Entertainment Services: A Growing Consumer Market', *Canadian Economic Observer*, Ottawa: Statistics Canada (Catalogue 11-010), (June): 3.1-3.11.

Eastlick, M. A., S. Lotz and S. Shim (1998), "Retail-tainment: Factors Impacting Cross-Shopping in Regional Malls," *Journal of Shopping Centre Research*, 5 (1), 7-31.

Feliciano, L.V. & Associates (1999), *Report on selected socio-economic variables for the trading areas of the Power Node and the Regional Mall specially done for this study*. Toronto: L.V. Feliciano & Assoc. Inc.

Financial Post (1999), "It's hard to ignore mall rats with $5.4 billion, no matter how annoying," (July 15, Section C).

Haynes, J. B. and S. Talpade (1996), "Does Entertainment Draw Shoppers? The Effects of Entertainment Centres on Shopping Behavior in Malls," *Journal of Shopping Centre Research*, 3(2), 29-48.

Haywood, L. (1995), *Understanding Leisure*, 2nd Ed. Cheltenham: Stanley Thornes.

Jones, K. & M. J. Doucet (1998), *The Big Box, the Big Screen, the Flagship, and Beyond: Impact and Trends in the Greater Toronto Area*. Toronto: Centre for the Study of the Commercial Activity, Ryerson Polytechnic University. Research Report 1998-7.

Kang, J. and Y. K. Kim (1999), "Role of Entertainment in Cross-Shopping and in the Revitalization of Regional Shopping Centres", *Journal of Shopping Centre Research*, 6(2), 41.-71.

Kenyon, K. (1999), "Megatheatre wars heating up", *Shopping Centres Today* 20 (4), 1 & 27-28.

Lord, J. D. and C. D. Bodkin (1996), "Cross-Shopping Patterns in Power Centres", *Journal of Shopping Centre Research*, 3(1), 33-57.

Neulinger, J. (1981), *The Psychology of Leisure*, 2nd Ed., Springfield: C. Thomas.

Potter, M. (1999), "Megaplex Mania: The Sequel", *The Toronto Star*, (July 9, Section D).

Thoma, P. (1999), "Invasion of the Mega-plex: Part III", *Real Estate Trends*, Toronto: PricewaterhouseCoopers. (Fall/Winter): 6-8.

Yeates, M. (2000), *The GTA @Y2K: The Dynamics of Change in the Commercial Structure of the Greater Toronto Area*, Toronto: Centre for the Study of the Commercial Activity, Ryerson Polytechnic University. Research Report 2000-1.

Chapter 4

TRADE AREA ANALYSIS
Stephen Swales

> ***Trade Area Delimitation***: *identifying the spatial limits of a market population served by a retail or commercial facility.*

Spatial Analysis: Public sector and private sector decisions

Trade area analysis draws from the spatial analysis tradition in Geography. Basic questions in the spatial analysis approach are: Where are land uses (such as retail facilities) located? Why are they where they are? Where should they be in the future? As such, spatial analysis can be very applied in its perspective. Consider the following spatial problems:

- A number of municipalities are to be amalgamated into a single "megacity", how should we locate fire halls to service the larger new city rather than the original individual municipalities? One key measure of efficiency of fire halls is average response time, obviously to a large degree determined by the *locations* of the fire halls.
- The government is to close a number of hospital emergency departments, which ones (locations) should be closed, keeping in mind that we wish to reduce the negative impacts of hospital closures on the populations they serve? Which locations have most populations at risk – the elderly and very young – within their service areas? One negative impact of closures is the increase in average travel time to hospitals, an obvious geographic factor.
- How do we delimit market areas around a set of shopping centres in a city?
- What is the best site to locate a new shopping centre keeping in mind we want to maximise the economic return of the new centre but at the same time minimise the impact of the new centre on existing centres?
- We are a major department-store chain faced with restructuring involving the closure of 31 of our 85 stores. Which 31 store locations should be closed?
- Did urban centres diffuse from a limited number of urban hearths over time?
- Was the spread of cholera in 19th century London associated with contaminated water pumps?

Although all these problems clearly benefit from spatial analysis, the first five examples are obviously of more contemporary applied relevance. The questions on fire halls and hospitals are questions about public service provision where *all* the population must be serviced to a minimum level, for example, in a city all addresses are within a maximum response time of fire halls and ambulance services. The questions on retail facilities, such as shopping centres, are mostly addressed by the private sector, but are also considered by the public sector in planning decisions. Unlike public sector services, shopping centre developers for example, seek out the most economically viable sites and do not have a mandate to service all the population to a minimum level. Both public and private sector problems benefit from the spatial techniques we will now discuss in more detail. Our emphasis, however, will be on private sector examples, more specifically retail locational analysis.

Normative and Behavioural Approaches in Retail Analysis

A central question in retail location analysis is how to define (or delimit) the market area of retail facilities. Two broad types of techniques are used to delimit trade areas: behavioural approaches and normative approaches.

> ***Behavioural Approaches***. "Customer spotting" or market penetration techniques are examples of behavioural approaches in retail locational analysis. In this approach retailers identify where the customers *actually* come from to delimit the trade area. The "behaviour" part is the consumer behaviour of the customers travelling to the store, shopping centre or town - whichever is our focus of study.

> ***Normative Approaches***. Normative approaches ask the question *what should be given certain assumptions*. An example of a "what should be question" in retail analysis is: where should the trade area boundaries of a shopping centre be given the assumption that shoppers are attracted to near, large centres rather than distant small centres?

CUSTOMER SPOTTING TECHNIQUES

To execute customer spotting and market penetration techniques we first need data on where the customers come from. In the past this was obtained mostly by the use of surveys, delivery addresses and competitions or by recording licence plates in parking lots. To enter the competition to win the barbecue at the supermarket you have to provide your address. How often have you been asked for your postal code at the check out of a store? In some cases you are *required* to give the retailer your address information as in the case of video rentals.

Once the data are obtained it is relatively easy to map the customer locations, see the example in Figure 1. Typical patterns that are observed include strong clustering around the store, as in this example. Note that the distance decay pattern can be examined further; in Figure 1 the customers within 2 miles of the store have been captured and they amount to almost 50% of the total. The map also shows income distribution and part of the postal code table that was used to "spot" the customers.

A much more comprehensive way of "spotting" customers is the use of affinity cards such as an Air Miles card or a store's own credit card. Such cards not only enable the

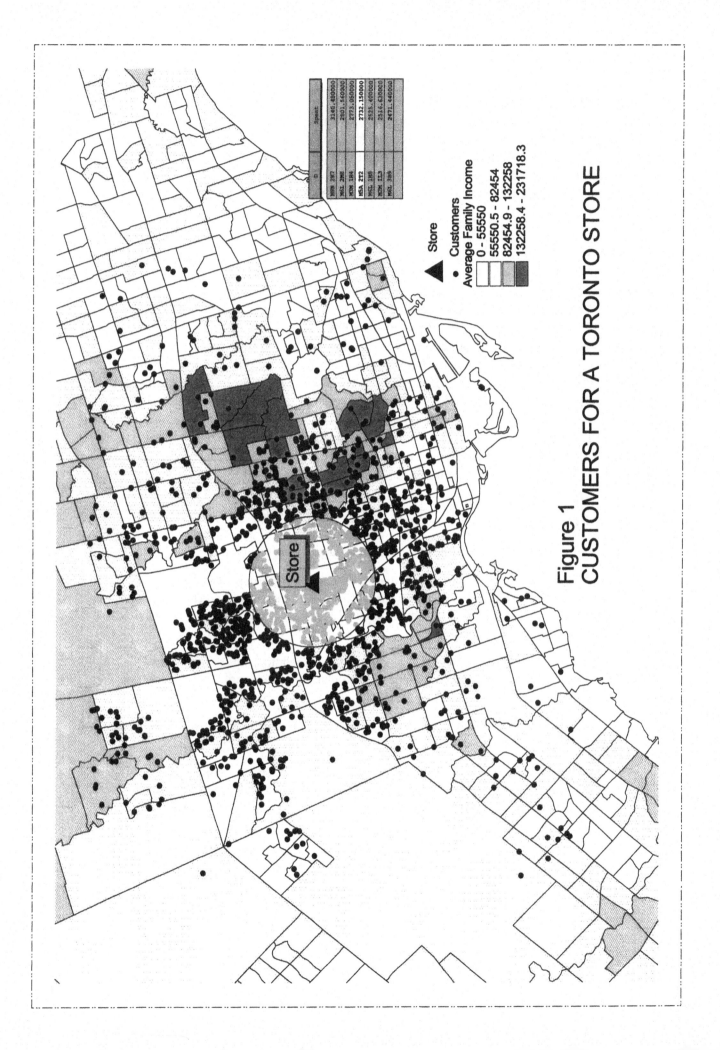

Figure 1
CUSTOMERS FOR A TORONTO STORE

identification of the customer, but also, because they are scanned with every purchase, have the potential to measure how often we shop, what we buy, how much we spend, and, if the card required a credit check, what we are able to spend! A vast amount of data is assembled in this way, such that a new skill has been developed called "data mining" whereby attempts are made to identify patterns in spending habits such as the combination of purchases. One celebrated association is the combined purchases of diapers and beer by men in U.S. stores.

Beer and Diapers

Data mining activity is said to have found an association between diaper and beer purchases by men in the US. It is not entirely clear which they pick up first; do they pick up the diapers, feel good about themselves and reward themselves by purchasing beer, or do they pick up the beer, feel guilty, then purchase the diapers? Quite apart from the interesting psychology of this pattern, how could this information be used in practice? Two strategies could be tried, put the beer and diapers closer together to increase the propensity to purchase each, or place them wide apart to increase mobility in the store and therefore exposure to more products. Further data analysis could reveal the relative success of each strategy. Monitoring vast amounts of data of this kind has much potential to reveal lifestyle and consumption patterns, but also has ethical concerns. Debates have arisen between retailers and credit card companies about the ownership of customer data; interestingly the customers themselves are not in this debate.

Data Mining Techniques

The association of purchases is one of a number of data mining techniques:

- **Classes**: Stored data is used to locate data in predetermined groups. For example, a restaurant chain could mine customer purchase data to determine when customers visit and what they typically order. This information could be used to increase traffic by having daily specials.

- **Clusters**: Data items are grouped according to logical relationships or consumer preferences. For example, data can be mined to identify market segments or consumer affinities.

- **Associations**: Data can be mined to identify associations. The beer-diaper example is an example of associative mining.

- **Sequential patterns**: Data is mined to anticipate behavior patterns and trends. For example, an outdoor equipment retailer could predict the likelihood of a backpack being purchased based on a consumer's purchase of sleeping bags and hiking shoes.

Note: WalMart is a leader in data mining, and captures point-of-sale transactions from over 2,900 stores in 6 countries and continuously transmits this data to its massive 7.5 terabyte Teradata data warehouse.

Source: http://www.anderson.ucla.edu/faculty/jason.frand/teacher/technologies/palace/datamining.htm

Market Penetration

By using the customer spotting data in conjunction with some measure of potential customers for areas around the store it is possible to estimate the level of penetration into each neighbourhood. The potential customers can be obtained from census data which can be combined with household spending data (see examples of each in the Appendix) to approximate how much potential expenditure is available in each neighbourhood. How many customers and what sales does the store actually get from each neighbourhood? Which neighbourhoods are they notably successful in? Are there similar neighbourhoods elsewhere which could serve as new store locations?

The basic address information enables the retailer to identify the location of their primary market area (usually the first 60% of their custom) and their secondary market area (the next 25% of custom). Thus, we can see the extent to which retailers have penetrated markets.

In summary, these approaches identify what the actual market area is through the identification of the actual customers. One disadvantage of such approaches compared to the normative approaches we are about to discuss is that they can be quite costly to administer.

NORMATIVE APPROACHES

In essence these approaches model consumer behaviour on the basis of assumptions. As such they are more theoretical in nature than the customer spotting approaches - they do not ask where the customers actually come from but rather predict where they should come from on the basis of the established assumptions. If the basic assumptions of the normative models are met, their predictions often match well the actual patterns of consumer behaviour. In some scenarios there is relatively little choice but to use normative approaches; for example, in the analysis of a *proposed* shopping centre there are not yet any customers available to be asked the customer spotting questions. Normative approaches can be applied relatively easily and cheaply since they do not require detailed and expensive surveys to identify the actual origin of customers.

Much of the remainder of our discussion will dwell on three normative techniques used in retail location analysis, but before we explore them in depth we need to revisit some key spatial concepts.

Relevant Spatial Concepts

The normative techniques we are to explore require an understanding of key spatial concepts which are reviewed here.

- *distance decay*: with increasing distance from a location interaction with that location will decrease. For example, a shopping centre will draw most of its shoppers from nearby, the number of shoppers for the centre will decrease with distance from the centre.
- *disincentive nature of distance*: one reason why interaction decreases with distance is that there is a very real economic cost, in time and money, to covering distance. The longer the distance, the greater the cost to cover it.
- *location and competition* Location decisions by retailers are not made in isolation, rather they have to be sensitive to the competition. For example, intervening opportunity strategies (as in retail interceptor rings) on the part of retailers involve a retail facility presenting itself to the customers as a closer retail opportunity than the competition.
- *gravity model*: spatial interaction is not just dependant on distance but also the relative attraction (size) of centres. A large centre can have the effect of reducing the friction of distance associated with it. For example, consumers are willing to travel further to a larger shopping centre than to a smaller shopping centre. This is sometimes referred to as "social physics".
- *utility*: the usefulness or attraction of a centre to the consumer. This can be related to distance from the centre and/or the size of the centre.
- *simplifying assumptions*: all models have unifying or simplifying assumptions that attempt to isolate the key factors thought to be relevant to the analysis and remove the many complexities of the real world thought not to be relevant in the application of the model. Such simplifying assumptions are evident in the normative models used in retail locational analysis. Unrealistic assumptions can be the source of weaknesses in models.

The Principles of Normative Retail Techniques

Our discussion will now focus on three normative techniques used in retail locational analysis:

- Thiessen polygon method - Key principle: distance (or proximity)

- Converse breakpoint method - Key principle: distance and size

- Huff model - Key principle: distance and size in a probability framework

Before we consider them in detail let us discuss the main principles of each.

Imagine that we have two competing retailers, retailer Y and retailer X, as in the diagram below (figure 2). Our objective is to divide up the market between them. A very simple way to do this is to draw a construction line between them and measure exactly halfway along it (bisect the line) and use this as our boundary line. This has been done in the diagram.

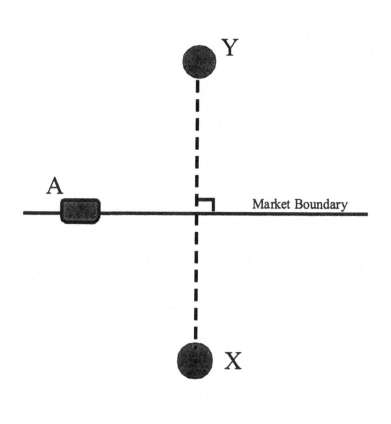

Figure 2

All consumers on Y's side of the line shop at Y and all consumers on X's side of the line shop at X. They shop at the nearest centre to them; *distance* alone determines where they shop. What if household "A" lives on the line, where do they shop? They are indifferent about which retailer they go to because they are exactly the same distance from each; in fact this line is known as the *line of spatial indifference* (or point of indifference) for this reason. The idea that distance (proximity) alone determines where we shop is the single principle of the first of our techniques - the *Thiessen polygon technique,* which we will explore in more detail in a moment. In order for this simple division of the market to work, a number of conditions must be assumed, some of these may have occurred to you already - and we will certainly consider them in detail later - but for the time being let us note what is probably the most obvious assumption: if the consumers base their decisions on distance alone then the two retailers must be *identical in every respect.*

Let us now introduce a complication to our original scenario. Rather than being identical, our two retailers vary in size; retailer Y is much larger than retailer X as in the diagram below (figure 3). Would this affect the location of the boundary line? Where would the boundary line likely move?

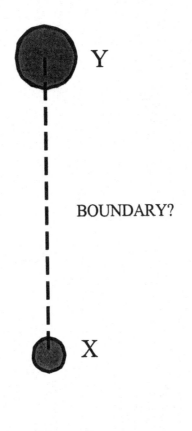

BOUNDARY?

Figure 3

The boundary would likely move *away from* the larger centre Y because its attraction (size) helps to overcome the friction of distance for consumers. So in our diagram below (figure 4), retailer Y captures more of the market because it is larger. Some consumers, such as "B" are closer to X but they shop at Y nonetheless because of it's larger size i.e. it's greater attraction. Again, if you are on the line you are spatially *indifferent*, this time on the basis of considering size as well as distance. By adding the size component to our basic distance model we have identified the main principle behind our second technique, the *Converse breakpoint method*, which is a simple gravity model. Consumers assess the utility of a centre to be a function of distance and size combined.

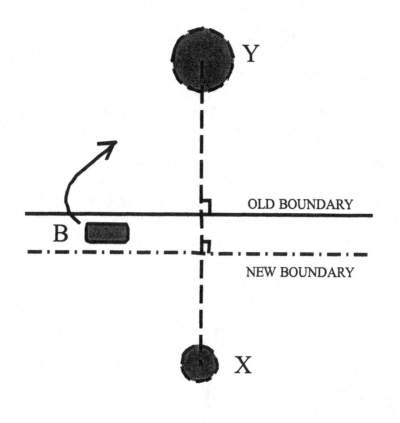

Figure 4

In both of our examples so far we have drawn a line that divides exclusive trading areas: everybody on Y's side of the line goes to Y, everybody on X's side of the line goes to X, and if they are *on* the line they are spatially indifferent. These exclusive market areas are known as *spatial monopoly areas*. In reality, although there is a high probability that you would go to a nearer centre, especially if it is larger, there is **not** a 100% probability. There is always some probability that you will shop at a distant smaller centre. In fact rather than spatial monopoly market areas we are more likely to see market areas that overlap. This addition of the probability concept that accommodates the likelihood of overlapping markets is the principle behind our third method: the *Huff model*.

Having established the basic principles behind each of our three techniques, let us now explore them in detail.

The Thiessen Polygon Technique

Thiessen Polygon Construction Technique

- Draw construction lines between a centre and all adjacent centres.
- Bisect each of the construction lines (i.e. measure exactly halfway along each line).
- Extend the bisectors at **right angles** (90 degrees) to the construction lines until they meet other extended bisecting lines. See the example below (figure5) which shows the boundaries between store Y and four competitors (X1, X2, X3 and X4).
- This produces spatial monopoly trade areas around each of the centres.

Figure 5

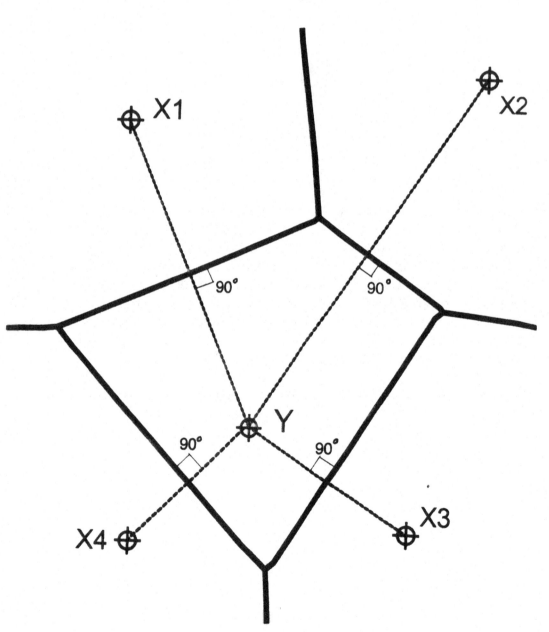

The trade areas will have been drawn on a base map that shows not only the location of the centres but also some source of market area data such as census tracts. The census tracts falling within the trade area can then be identified. The example above is redrawn below (figure 6) showing census tracts within the polygon-defined trade area. Census tracts are relatively small urban neighbourhoods of about 4,000 people; the census contains many relevant market variables (e.g. income, demographics, ethnicity, see the Appendix for examples).

In this example we are focussing on only one retail outlet; we could extend the polygon application to include the whole set of outlets in the chain, as shown in figure 7.

Figure 6

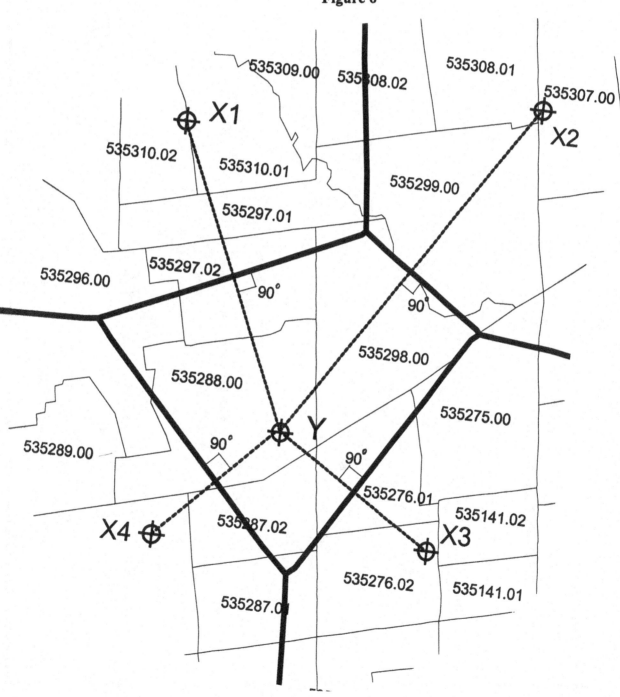

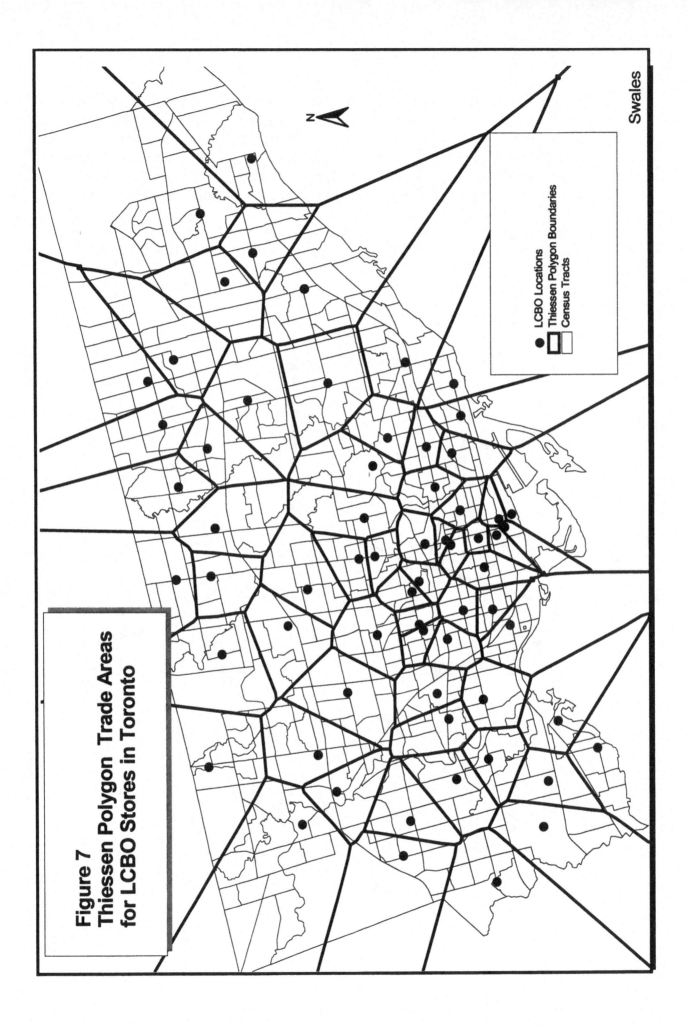

Figure 7
Thiessen Polygon Trade Areas
for LCBO Stores in Toronto

LCBO Locations
Thiessen Polygon Boundaries
Census Tracts

N

Swales

Assumptions

- Distance to the retail opportunity is the factor that determines <u>where</u> the consumer will shop, they will patronise the nearest store. This is because there is a disincentive nature to distance.
- If relative proximity is the only variable that differentiates the stores, then the stores are identical in all aspects of supply: goods, prices, service, etc.
- Retail centres service spatial monopoly trade areas i.e. markets do not overlap.
- All areas (space) is serviced.
- Consumers are fully informed, fully rational, decision makers. In this assumption about consumer behaviour we consider the consumers to be *economic operators*. They know all the locations, all the distances to them, and based on this full information they will make the most rational choice by travelling to the nearest centre.
- Uniform travel plain on an uninterrupted travel surface, i.e. it is equally easy to travel in any direction.

Applications

Examples. Given the substantial assumptions of the method it might seem doubtful that there are real world applications. In fact, the Thiessen method does work reasonably well as a broad indicator of locational strategy when the main assumptions are broadly met: i.e. that distance is the key decision-making factor and that the retail outlets are somewhat identical. Examples include beer stores, liquor stores, fast food chains, some other chains, shopping centres of similar size, and to some extent postal outlets. So, for example, the majority of beer stores in Ontario are identical - the same selection, pricing, bottle returns, level of service, and store design. For most consumers any beer store is much the same as another. Why then would they take the extra time and expense to travel to a more distant one? They are very likely to go to the beer store nearest to them (this is of course assuming that they *know where* the nearest one is and that they will respond to this knowledge rationally! - see the economic operator assumption above). Interestingly the map comparing theoretical (Thiessen) and actual (customer spotted) market areas of beer stores below (figure 8) shows that they are remarkably similar. What if you had to apply one of these methods at your own expense, which one would you choose? *You* could apply the Thiessen polygon technique (using the above directions) in a matter of minutes. To do the customer spotting you would have to design and apply a representative survey of customers at all the outlets to ascertain the origin of the customers. This would involve much time, effort and expense. If the result is much the same as the normative Thiessen polygon approach, why bother?

TRADE AREA FOR BREWERS' RETAIL STORES: OTTAWA

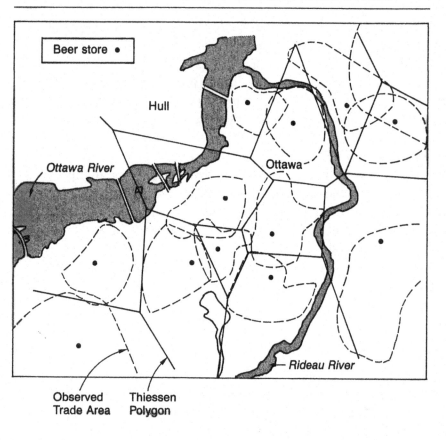

Figure 8

Source: K. Jones and J. Simmons (1993), *Location, Location, Location: Analyzing the Retail Environment*, Toronto: Nelson.

What is the market for each of our stores? We could use the polygons to capture the underlying market data from the census tracts and evaluate the theoretical amount of market for each trade area. Problems may arise when census tracts are only partially in the trade area (see the box below). If the census data are used in conjunction with household expenditure data (see examples in Appendix) which includes spending by family income groups on specific products (e.g. liquor) we could estimate the $ value available from each trade area. Which stores are performing above their theoretical amount, which below, do stores in each group have other notable characteristics which may explain their performance? Although this evaluation of the present theoretical market is useful, the real power of a normative model such as the Thiessen polygon is to explore changes in the system such as good locations for new outlets.

Partial Census Tracts in a Trade Area

How do we deal with the census tracts (c.t.'s) that are only partially inside the trade area (i.e. the ones that overlap the market boundaries)? Two methods can be considered: the *centroid method* and the *proportional grid method*. The centroid method draws the two longest diagonals within the census tract. The point where these diagonals cross is known as the centroid; if the centroid falls *outside* the trade area boundary then *all* the c.t. is excluded, if the centroid falls *inside* the trade area then *all* the c.t. is included. Do you see any problems in applying this rather crude method? It is somewhat problematic when applied to a relatively small number of large areas, as in our example. If you were to apply the centroid method to the partial c.t.'s in Figure 6 which c.t.'s would be included in the trade area and which would be excluded? Is it difficult to identify the longest diagonals in some of the irregularly shaped census tracts?

In the *proportional grid method* we overlay a transparency of fine grid squares over the census tract and count the total number of squares for that census tract. We then count the number of squares of the census tract that actually fall within the trade area and use this to work out the proportion of the census tract data to include in the trade area. So quite simply, if the census tract amounts to 100 grid squares in total and 20 of the grid squares are actually inside the trade area then we include 20% of the data from that census tract in our trade area analysis (this, of course, assumes that the population in the census tract is evenly distributed). This approach gives a reasonable measure of the proportion of each ct within the trade area without having to calculate the actual area of unusual shapes. It is a finer method than the centroid method.

What are the theoretically best sites for new outlets? In theory, the sites to consider for new outlets should be at least on the lines of indifference and at best at the vertices (junctions) of boundary lines (i.e the corners of the polygons). These are the locations that are presently poorly serviced, that is, people at these locations have to travel a relatively long distance to get to a retail outlet. Also these locations will provide less competition to other stores in the chain, they are less likely to "cannibalise" their neighbours. Of course, we use this as a broad indicator; if the vertices are in the middle of a river, as is the case in two of the instances in the beer store example above, we are not likely to locate new beer stores there - unless we have a barge handy!

Finding Gaps in the map. If we have applied the method to a set of centres (such as associate stores of a retail chain) rather than just one, then in theory *larger polygons* indicate large geographic areas (not necessarily large populations) that are relatively poorly serviced. Smaller polygons are relatively well serviced areas, i.e. consumers have to travel only a relatively short distance to the retail centre. The larger polygons are probably the first places we would look when considering locations for new retail outlets. This is assuming of course that there is any substantial population to service; the large polygons could be an indication of little population and non-residential uses (such as an airport). If we were closing one of the stores of the chain rather than opening new ones, then we would likely begin by looking at the relatively *small polygons*. The closure of a store in an area of relatively small polygons should not inconvenience the existing customers too much because the increased distance they would now need to travel should be relatively short. Keep in mind that the polygons are only the beginning of the analysis and point to likely strategies; much more thorough analysis of the sites in question would follow.

A fast-food restaurant example. The strategies above are, to some extent, seen in the example of the chain of fast-food restaurants shown in the map below (figure 9). The polygons are drawn on the original set of restaurants established from 1969-76, (shown in squares on the map). The locations of the restaurants in the next phase of expansion, 1977-80 (circles on the map), reveal a remarkable match to the Thiessen polygon approach. In the suburban areas the new outlets are mostly located on lines of indifference or vertices of polygons (downtown locations seek out main roads). We could, of course, redraw the polygons on the basis of all the outlets to 1980 and see to what extent the Thiessen polygon strategy informs the locational strategy thereafter. When this is done, it is evident that the Thiessen strategy remains very much in evidence, at least as a beginning point to investigate potential new locations. Of course we cannot keep sub-dividing the market; at some point saturation will be reached. Moreover, not all the gaps in the map will be used; some will not be suitable because of factors such as poor access to market or lack of space. This method can be used to identify likely new sites which will then be investigated much more thoroughly. A strategy that has helped this restaurant chain sell billions of its main product!

Figure 9

THIESSEN POLYGONS FOR A CHAIN OF
FAST-FOOD RESTAURANTS

METROPOLITAN TORONTO

Stores located 1969-76 ■
Stores located 1977-80 ●

0   3
miles

LAKE ONTARIO

"What if" scenarios. Since this method is quite easy and fast to apply, it is possible to "try out", at least theoretically, a variety of different scenarios and evaluate their impact on the market areas. This is a powerful use of the model, to actually model and evaluate proposed changes. For instance: What if we located a new store at location X1? What about location X2 instead? X3, X4, X5? By redrawing the polygons for each scenario we could quickly assess and compare the impact of each scenario on the size of market areas and neighbouring stores. Remember that in all cases we would be addressing a base map of census data which provides us with comprehensive details on all of our theoretical market areas.

The next two maps (figures 10 and 11) consider the application of Thiessen polygons to an electronics chain that is expanding in the Toronto area. This is a large chain with large stores that often locate in power centre locations. In figure 10 the solid lines are the polygons drawn on the existing network of stores. If we search for "gaps in the map" we can see two sites worthy of investigation at vertices of polygons, they are labeled West store and North store. Remember the locations on vertices are in relatively poorly serviced areas and are less likely to cannibalize existing stores in the network. Moreover, both sites initially look promising because they are close to main highway intersections.

The next stage is to model the scenarios of opening new stores. In figure 11 the polygons are drawn including the proposed West store, the polygon for this store is shown in dotted lines. We can now see how much territory this new location would get and how much is lost by its neighbours. In another stage we could capture the census data for each of the trade areas with and without the new site. How much market does the new store capture and is it sufficient for it to be viable? How much market is lost by the original stores, will they remain viable? We could follow the same procedure for other prospective sites, e.g. the North site shown on the map, and compare the scenarios. Of course much more rigorous analysis of each prospective site would follow (including land availability, zoning, existing retail, competition etc), but the polygons are a good initial analysis.

Criticisms

- The method is cheap, easy and fast, but:
- See assumptions; does the real world live up to these assumptions? Are centres identical in every respect? Do consumers behave as fully informed, fully-rational decision makers? Are we dealing with the maximizing economic operator or are people partially informed, making decisions within bounded rationality that they find satisfactory, i.e. are they satisficers rather than maximizers? Do consumers live on uniform travel plains?
- It is a theoretical normative (what should be) model rather than identifying what actually is.

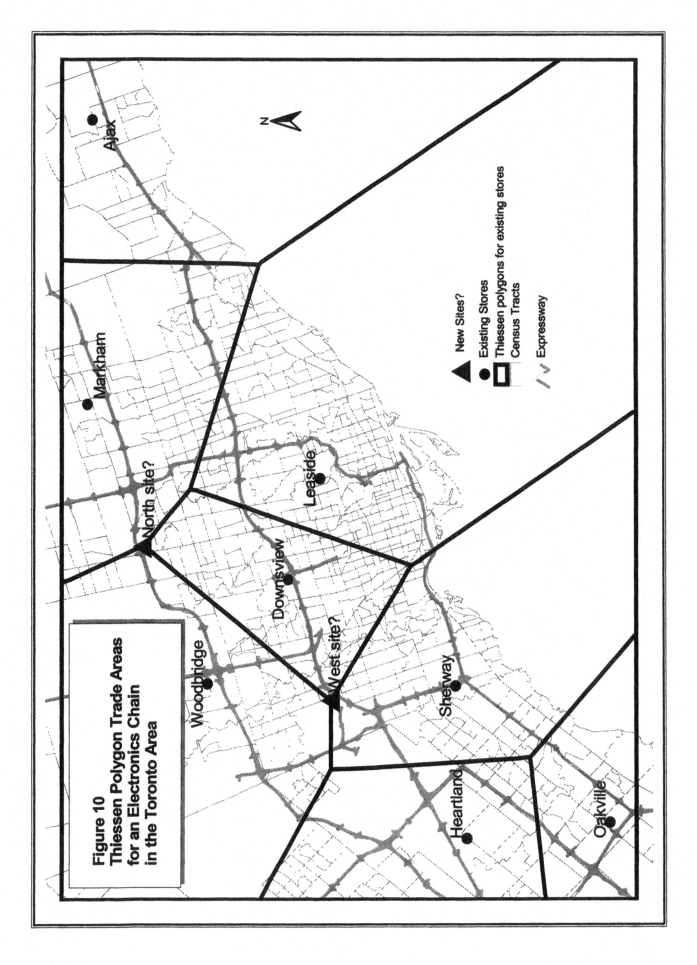

Figure 10
Thiessen Polygon Trade Areas
for an Electronics Chain
in the Toronto Area

New Sites?
Existing Stores
Thiessen polygons for existing stores
Census Tracts
Expressway

Ajax
Markham
North site?
Leaside
Downsview
Woodbridge
West site?
Sherway
Heartland
Oakville

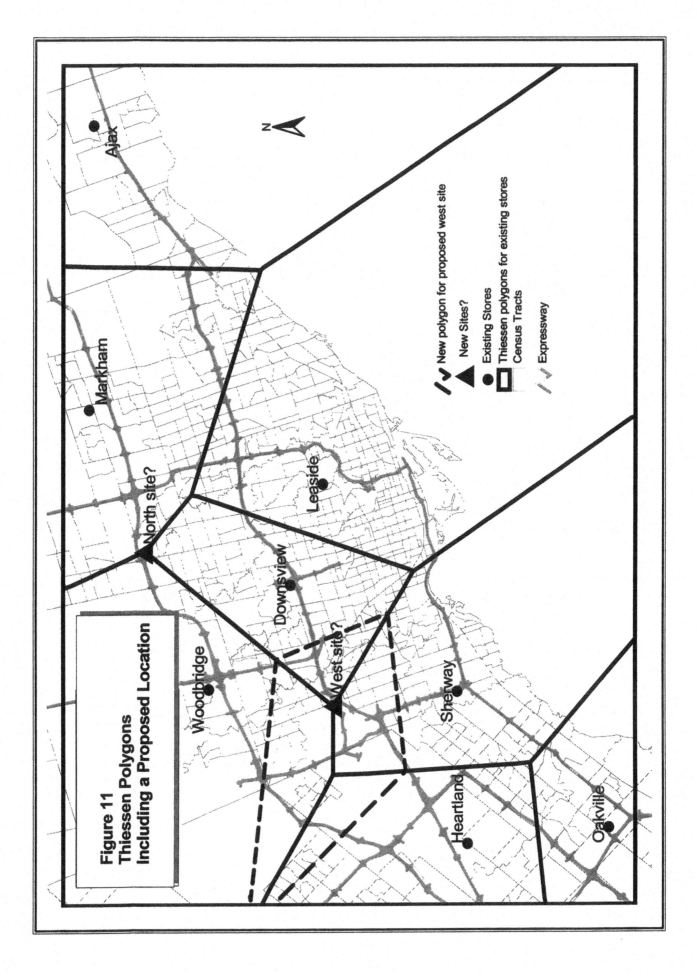

Figure 11
Thiessen Polygons
Including a Proposed Location

New polygon for proposed west site
New Sites?
Existing Stores
Thiessen polygons for existing stores
Census Tracts
Expressway

Ajax
Markham
North site?
Woodbridge
Downsview
Leaside
West site?
Sherway
Heartland
Oakville

N

Converse Breakpoint Method

Introduction

- This simple gravity model is a modification of Reilly's law of retail gravitation.

> **Reilly's Law of Retail Gravitation**
> Two cities attract trade from an intermediate town in the vicinity of the breaking point approximately in direct proportion to the populations of the two cities and in inverse proportion to the squares of the distances from those two cities to the intermediate town (Reilly, 1931).

- The Converse breakpoint method makes it possible to predict the point between two centres (e.g. shopping centres) where the trading influence of each is equal. We can think of this point as the point or line of indifference (i.e. where the utility of the two centres is equal). It is also the market boundary between the centres.

- The method uses distance **and** size to calculate the line of indifference (i.e. the market boundaries).

Technique (see example in diagram below)

- The Converse formula (see below) requires data on distance between centres and size of centres. Together these two variables are thought to adequately measure the relative *utility* of the centres. The formula suggests that the utility of the centre decreases with distance and increases with size.

- Size measures could be: number of stores, square footage of the centre, number of employees, number of parking spaces, etc.

- The formula calculates the distance of the breakpoint (line of indifference) from the subject centre ("Y" in the example). The breakpoint line is extended at a 90 degree angle from a construction line between the centres. The calculation of the breakpoints between the subject centre ("Y") and all the competing centres (X1, X2, etc.) *enables the drawing of a spatial monopoly market area for centre Y.* (See Figure 12.)

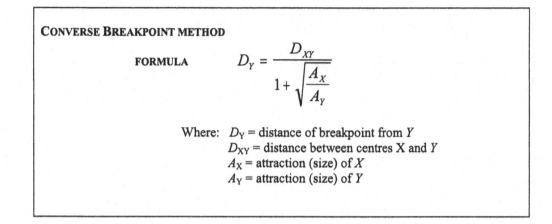

Where: D_Y = distance of breakpoint from Y
D_{XY} = distance between centres X and Y
A_X = attraction (size) of X
A_Y = attraction (size) of Y

Figure 12 Converse Breakpoint Application

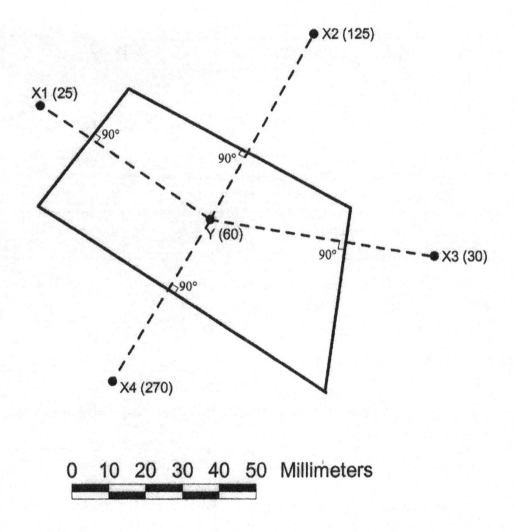

Calculations for the Converse Breakpoint Application

Centre	Distance to Y (mm)	Attraction (No. Stores)	Calculation	Breakpoint from Y (mm)
X_1	55	25	$D_Y, X_1 = \dfrac{55}{1 + \sqrt{\dfrac{25}{60}}}$	33
X_2	57	125	$D_Y, X_2 = \dfrac{57}{1 + \sqrt{\dfrac{125}{60}}}$	23
X_3	62	30	$D_Y, X_3 = \dfrac{62}{1 + \sqrt{\dfrac{30}{60}}}$	36
X_4	50	270	$D_Y, X_4 = \dfrac{50}{1 + \sqrt{\dfrac{270}{60}}}$	16
Y		60		

● The application above has the boundaries drawn for the Converse breakpoint method. You can draw the Thiessen boundaries on the same example to see how the boundaries differ. Intuitively we know that the Converse boundaries will always move closer to the smaller centre giving the larger centre more of the market area.

● Remember that the trade areas will be drawn on a base map of a market area data source such as census tracts (this is evident in the example in the exercise later).

Applications

● Shopping centres, stores and towns that vary in size. If they are much the same in size then the application of this model would produce the same result as the Thiessen polygon method.

Assumptions

● Unlike the Thiessen polygon method the Converse method **does not** assume that all centres are equal in attractiveness (size). It does however have the other unifying assumptions evident in the Thiessen method (fully informed rational maximizers, uniform travel plain, etc.).

● An additional assumption is that some measure of size (e.g. number of stores, number of employees, etc.) is an adequate measure of the attractiveness of centres.

Criticisms

● Again we will find possible weaknesses in the model in it's unifying assumptions. To what extent does the "real world" meet these assumptions? Is a size measurement an effective surrogate measure of all aspects of attraction? Does size effectively measure service and aspects of image in attraction? What about the ambiance and design of the centres?

● In common with the Thiessen method this technique produces spatial monopoly market areas, i.e. once the boundaries are established it is assumed that everybody inside the boundary shops at the subject centre. In reality we are more likely to be dealing with **overlapping** market areas; yes there is a high likelihood that consumers will shop at nearer larger centres but there is always some probability that they will shop at other centres. A more sophisticated gravity model that addresses this concept of overlapping markets in a probability framework is **the Huff model**. We will now address this method in detail.

The Huff Model

The Huff model (see the box below and the application that follows) asks this question of market areas (e.g. census tracts): what is the probability that the consumers in this area will shop at one of a number of centres (e.g. shopping centres) based on the relative utility of centres? There is some probability that consumers will shop at any of the centres in the area. Consumers will more likely shop at a nearer larger centre than a distant smaller centre, but all centres in the area, no matter size or distance, are possible destinations. This is the fundamental difference between this method and the spatial monopoly approaches discussed above. The consumers can be assigned to centres based on calculated probabilities. Note that the variables are still limited to distance and size.

To understand the principle of overlapping markets consider figures 13 and 14. In reality the likelihood of visiting a centre will decrease with distance from the store or centre; this is the distance decay concept. This is shown in figure 13 where probability lines decrease in value with distance. Shoppers are less likely to shop at "a" with distance from it and increasingly likely to shop elsewhere. In the simple example in figure 14 two centres are considered; location "X" (which could be a census tract) is 75% likely to shop at "a" and 25% likely to shop at "b". If "X" were a census tract we could assign 75% of its market to "a" and 25% of its market to "b". Perhaps this is more realistic than the crisp exclusive dividing lines suggested by the spatial monopoly techniques. (See Cadwallader, 1996.)

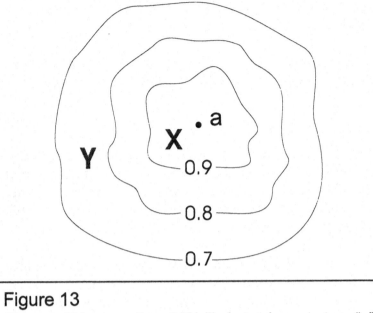

Figure 13
Shopper X is more than 90% likely to shop at store "a";
shopper Y is about 75% likely to shop at store "a".

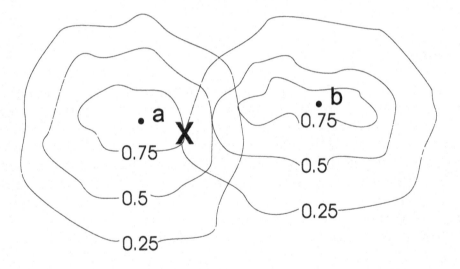

Figure 14
Location X is 75% likely to shop at "a" and 25%
likely to shop at "b".

HUFF MODEL

The Huff model casts Reilly's law of retail gravitation into a probabilistic framework.

Huff postulated that the probability that a consumer at point **"i"** will travel to shopping centre **"j"**, (**Pij**), is a ratio of the *utility of the shopping centre* to the consumer (uij) and the *total utility of all shopping centres* ($\sum$**uij**) that may be considered by the consumer.

$$Pij = \frac{uij}{\sum uij}$$

Components of *utility* are:

    Size of the centre (gravity; attraction of the centre to the consumer)
    Distance (proximity of the centre to the consumer)

In detail:

$$Pij = \frac{\dfrac{Sj}{dij^{b}}}{\sum j \left(\dfrac{Sj}{dij^{b}} \right)}$$

Pij is the proportion of sales from neighbourhood **"i"** that goes to a particular shopping centre **"j"** in the context of all competing facilities.

Where:

i	consumer
j	centre
s	size
d	distance
b	an exponent which is larger for goods associated with greater friction of distance (e.g. is larger for convenience stores than shopping centres)

A HUFF APPLICATION

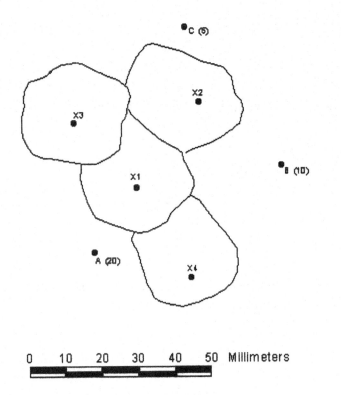

SIZE OF SHOPPING CENTRES   A: 20, B: 10, C: 5

DISTANCES (measured in mm from the map)

Zone	A	B	C
X1	21	40	44
X2	49	28	20
X3	35	58	40
X4	27	39	66

RETAIL EXPENDITURES ($)
X1   10,000,000
X2   5,000,000
X3   15,000,000
X4   20,000,000

EXPONENT b = 1

FORMULA $$Pij = \dfrac{\dfrac{Sj}{dij^{b}}}{\sum j \left(\dfrac{Sj}{dij^{b}} \right)}$$	EACH OF THE MARKET ZONES (X1-X4) CAN BE DIVIDED BETWEEN THE CENTRES A, B, AND C ON THE BASIS OF THE PROBABILITIES CALCULATED USING THE FORMULA. THE PROBABILITIES SUM TO ONE OR 100%

ASSIGNING PROBABILITIES

TO ASSIGN ZONE X1:

PROBABILITY

$$\text{FOR A} = \frac{20/21}{20/21 + 10/40 + 5/44} = 0.72 \times (10{,}000{,}000) = \$7.2\text{m}$$

$$\text{FOR B} = \frac{10/40}{20/21 + 10/40 + 5/44} = 0.19 \times (10{,}000{,}000) = \$1.9\text{m}$$

$$\text{FOR C} = \frac{5/44}{20/21 + 10/40 + 5/44} = 0.09 \times (10{,}000{,}000) = \$0.9\text{m}$$

TO ASSIGN ZONE X2:

PROBABILITY

$$\text{FOR A} = \frac{20/49}{20/49 + 10/28 + 5/20} = 0.40 \times (5{,}000{,}000) = \$2\text{m}$$

$$\text{FOR B} = \frac{10/28}{20/49 + 10/28 + 5/20} = 0.35 \times (5{,}000{,}000) = \$1.75\text{m}$$

$$\text{FOR C} = \text{-- -- -- -- -- -- --} = 0.25 \times (5{,}000{,}000) = \$1.25$$

EACH OF THE OTHER ZONES (X3 and X4) CAN BE ASSIGNED IN THE SAME WAY. THE TOTAL MARKET SHARE FOR ANY CENTRE CAN BE OBTAINED BY ADDING UP THE RETAIL EXPENDITURE ASSIGNED TO IT FROM EACH ZONE. THIS HAS BEEN DONE BELOW.

ZONE X3 PROBABILITIES	ZONE X4 PROBABILITIES
FOR A: 0.66 x $15m = $9.9m	FOR A: 0.69 x $20m = $3.8m
FOR B: 0.20 x $15m = $3.0m	FOR B: 0.24 x $20m = $4.8m
FOR C: 0.14 x $15m = $2.1m	FOR C: 0.07 x $20m = $1.4m
TOTAL 1.00 $15m	TOTAL 1.00 $20m

TOTALS FOR EACH SHOPPING CENTRE

ZONE:	X1	X2	X3	X4	TOTAL
Centre A:	7.2 +	2.0 +	9.9 +	13.8 =	$32.9m
Centre B:	1.9 +	1.75 +	3.0 +	4.8 =	$11.45m
Centre C:	0.9 +	1.25 +	2.1 +	1.4 =	$5.65

The Huff Model as a Predictive Tool

The Huff model can be used to evaluate what the present market should be for centres, but a much more powerful use of the model is to evaluate proposed changes. The model is a very effective tool to assess the likely impact of *proposed* developments such as shopping centres because it can be applied in a diversity of "what if" scenarios. Consider that all the variables in the above example could change; some of the more obvious changes are below:

- What if we introduce a new centre "D" to the N.W. of the existing three? Will this centre be economically viable? Will the original three remain viable? What if we located the proposed centre to the S.E. instead?
- What if we expand one of the existing centres? What are the implications of increasing by different sizes? At what size is it viable and the others remain viable?
- What if the market area expands with the introduction of a new zone of development, X5? What if there is out-migration from some zones, in-migration to others?
- What if the expenditures from the zones change (this can be estimated using census data in conjunction with household expenditure data). Income could increase or decrease. What if the spending habits related to shopping centre goods changes for the zones?
- What if the mobility of the population changes; this could impact the evaluation of exponent 'b", becoming larger with decreased mobility (the population becomes more elderly) and smaller if increased mobility (the population becomes more youthful)? (Note: as observed earlier, strictly speaking the exponent is determined by the type of retail activity rather than the changing mobility of consumers.)

Both the private and public sectors would have much interest in the impact of such changes. For example, a developer considering building a new centre would want to evaluate the viability of the centre. Nearby existing centres would evaluate the proposed new centre to see how much it would impact them. Local authorities would also be interested in the impacts, they may want to see new shopping centre developments but not if they impact existing centres too negatively. Imagine a local planning debate where interested parties use the model to predict changes, supporting their arguments for or against changes.

Critique of normative approaches

Remember that all normative models are theoretical in nature suggesting what should be given certain assumptions about how we think the real world operates. If our assumptions are weak then our model is flawed. If on the other hand the assumptions are reasonably met in our real world application then the models are robust and effective. Normative models are relatively cheap and easy to apply compared to comprehensive surveying and analysis of the real world situation. In some cases, as in predicting future impacts of proposed developments such as shopping centres, the real world scenario does not yet exist so we have little choice but to use predictive normative models.

A PRACTICE EXERCISE
DELIMITING THE TRADE AREA OF A SHOPPING CENTRE

In this exercise you will draw the theoretical market area boundaries for a shopping centre using the Thiessen polygon technique and compare this method to the Converse breakpoint method. Both methods are discussed above.

1.   On Map One delimit the trade area of shopping centre "Y" (Woodbine) using the Thiessen polygon method. Give the map a title.

2.   Using the polygon you generated on Map One indicate (with symbols ▲) theoretically appropriate sites for new shopping centres. Explain why you chose these sites and any possible problems associated with them. Would you locate a shopping centre on an airport runway for example?

3.   If you reside on the market boundary line where will you shop? What is this line called?

4.   Which census tracts (the numbered areas on the map) are *wholly* included in the trade area you have delimited?

5.   See the earlier discussion about how to handle census tracts that only partially fall within the trade area.

6.   Consult Appendix One for the kinds of variables that are available from the census. List some of the variables that you think are relevant in the study of the trade area of a shopping centre.

7.   The shopping centres vary in size as indicated in the following table (the sizes have been modified from the original data).

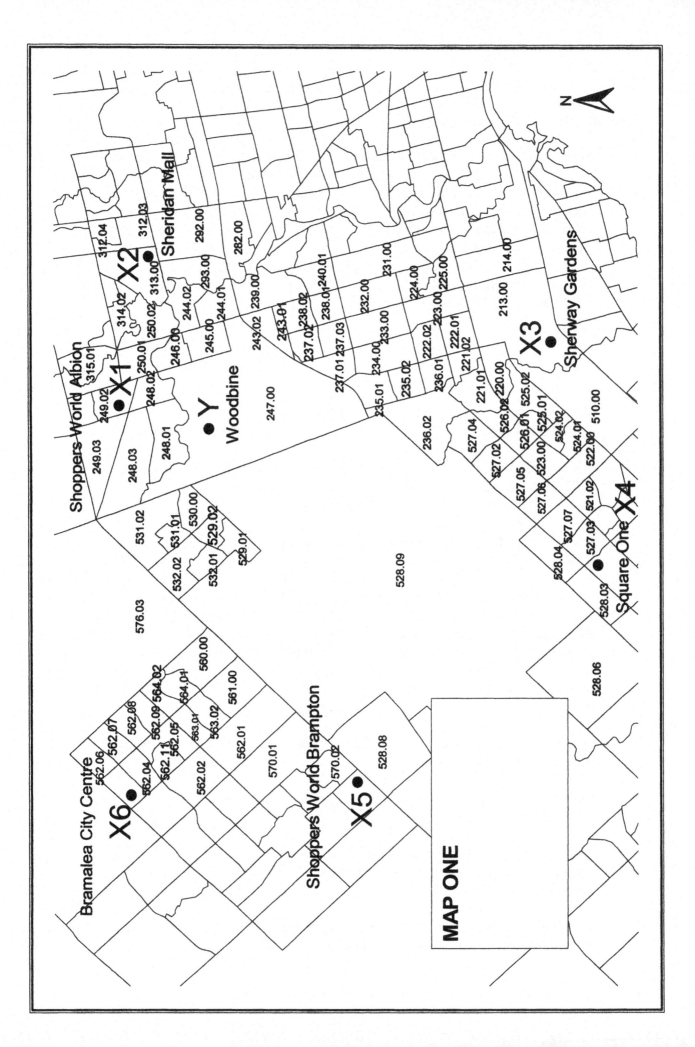

MAP ONE

SHOPPING CENTRE CHARACTERISTICS

Shopping Centres (of >110 stores)	Number of Stores	Gross Leasable area ('000sq.ft.)	Parking Spaces	Date Opened
Woodbine (Y)	185	670	3,420	1985
Shoppers World Albion (X1)	112	301	2,000	1964
Sheridan Mall (X2)	170	300	1,350	1976
Sherway Gardens (X3)	240	967	5,465	1971
Square One (X4)	350	1,400	7,500	1973
Shoppers World Brampton (X5)	225	772	3,900	1969
Bramalea City Centre (X6)	292	1,087	6,000	1973

Source: Directory of Canadian Shopping Centres (1994).

Given that the centres vary in size consider how the market boundaries would change if you were to apply a simple gravity model such as the Converse breakpoint method. Select one of the measures of size in the table above. You need not do the calculations for the method, but for "Y" and each of its competitors indicate if the boundary line would be closer to or further from "Y":

    Y and X1:
    Y and X2:
    Y and X3:
    Y and X4:
    Y and X5:
    Y and X6:

8. Which of the two market area techniques (Thiessen polygon or Converse breakpoint) is best to use for this set of centres and why?

READINGS AND SOURCES

Buckner, B. J. (1998) *Site Selection: New Advancement in Methods and Technology*, New York: Lebhar Friedman.

Cadwallader, M. (1996) *Analytical Urban Geography,* Englewood Cliffs: Prentice Hall.

Chang, K. T. (2002) *Introduction to Geographic Information Systems*, New York McGraw-Hill.

Chrisman, N. (2002) *Exploring Geographic Information Systems*, New York: Wiley.

De Mers, M. N. (2000) *Fundamentals of Geographic Information Systems,* New York: Wiley.

Ghosh, A. and S. McLafferty (1987) *Location Strategies for Retail and Service Firms.* Lexington: D.C. Heath.

Haggett, P. (2001) *Geography, A Global Synthesis* Harlow: McGraw Hill.

Jones, K. G. and D. R. Mock (1984), "Evaluating Retail Trading Performances," in R. L. Davies and D. S. Rogers, *Store Location and Store Assessment Research,* New York: Wiley.

Jones, K. and J. Simmons (1993) *Location, Location, Location: Analyzing the Retail Environment.* (2nd.ed.) Scarborough: Nelson.

Reilly, W. J. (1931) *The Law of Retail Gravitation.* New York: Knickerbocker Press.

Wrigley, N. (1988) *Store Choice, Store Location and Market Analysis*, London: Routledge.

Wrigley, N. and M. Lowe eds. (1996) *Retailing, Consumption and Capital: Towards the New Retail Geography,* Harlow: Longman.

Wrigley, N. and M. Lowe (2002) *Reading Retail: A Geographical Perspective on Retailing and Consumption Spaces*, London: Arnold.

Chapter 5

SITE SELECTION AND EVALUATION
Stephen Swales

Introduction

How do retailers and other service providers identify and evaluate prospective new locations? Imagine a retailer has used a trade area evaluation that suggests a number of new prospective sites for consideration. How are vacant sites evaluated and compared to help inform an expansion of outlets? Alternatively, a retail organization may be arriving to a market for the first time, how do they identify the best set of sites to most effectively service the market they are interested in? A variety of techniques have been developed over the years which range from basic intuition where a seasoned veteran identifies from experience which sites are likely to succeed, to sophisticated statistical approaches which, at least on the face of it, evaluate sites on the basis of statistical verification of the factors associated with good site performance. We will consider a number of these approaches.

The Variety of Site Evaluation Techniques

Originating in the work of Applebaum (1965), site selection methods have been considered by numerous authors including Ghosh and MacLafferty (1987), Jones and Simmons (1987), Lea (1989), Lea and Menger (1990, 1991), Clarke (1998), Hernandez and Bennison (2000), and Birkin, Clarke and Clarke (2002).

Drawing on a survey of U.K. retailers, Hernandez et. al. (1998) identify locational planning techniques and the percentage of companies using them (see Table 1).

Table 1 Use of Locational Planning Techniques
(percentage of responding companies)

Technique	Used (% sample)
Comparative	
Rules of thumb	100
Checklist	63
Analogues	33
Ratio	30
Predictive	
Multiple regression	42
Discriminant analysis	12
Cluster analysis	42
Gravity models	37
Knowledge based	
Expert systems	9
Neural networks	14

Source: T. Hernandez, D. Bennison & S. Cornelius, "The organisational context of retail location planning", *GeoJournal* 45: 299-308, 1998.

Generally the methods increase in sophistication from the top of the table to the bottom. It is noteworthy that the simplest methods are used most often, for example rules of thumb at 100% and checklist at 63%. The newer more sophisticated methods are infrequently used, for example expert systems (9%) and neural networks (14%).

Hernandez and Bennison (2000) have summarized numerous techniques and identified the decision scenarios where each may likely be used; this summary can be found in Table 2.

In our discussion of site selection methods we draw from this list and add others:

- Rules of thumb/ Experience/Gut feeling
- Checklist/Descriptive Inventories/Ranking
- Ratios
- Analogues/Parasitic
- Parasitic
- Ratings
- Regression
- Location allocation
- Neural networks

In part, the omissions from Table 2 are explained by coverage elsewhere. For example, gravity models (or spatial interaction models) are used for estimating consumer behaviour and evaluating trade areas; we consider them in the trade area chapter.

The methods we discuss here are of academic interest, often drawing from classic theories in economic geography and also using leading-edge techniques employed by geographers and others, but throughout we will keep a careful eye on their practical applications. How useful are these methods in retail and other service provision strategies? Are they understood and applied by decision makers in the private and public sectors?

The Diversity of Site Variables

Some retailers, for example small independent operators, do little in terms of rigorous site evaluation, picking a vacant site they like the look of or taking the advice of real estate agents. Jones and Simmons (1993) estimate that fewer than 2% of specialty retailers in Toronto engage in locational research; other retailers, however, consider numerous factors that could impact particular sites, attempting to identify the few key factors that mostly account for site performance. A number of authors, for example Nelson (1958) and Applebaum (1966), have provided lists (checklists) of variables to consider. More recent and comprehensive lists are provided by Ghosh and MacLafferty (1987) and Lea (1989). Table 3 is a simplification of the list provided by Lea (1989). Note that the broad classification is between *situation* variables and *site* variables. Situation variables refer to the characteristics of the surrounding area, for example, the number of households in the area (perhaps within 1km of the site, or within a previously defined trade area). Site variables refer to the character of the actual address being considered and the immediate surroundings, for example, how large is the site, and how many parking spaces are in the immediate vicinity?

Table 2   Decision Scenario by Technique

Technique/s	Decision scenario example	Examples
Experience	A retail property executive is faced with a potential acquisition opportunity (of a minor competitor) and makes an initial judgement based on experience and broad "rules of thumb"	Brown, 1992; Jones and Simmons,1990; Davidson et al. 1988; Beaumont, 1987
Checklists Analogues Ratios	A regional business development manager has been instructed to locate five new sites within his operating area for development. Using an existing formalized set of checklists and basic ratios of potential performance he screens a large number of sites into the top five	Collins, 1992; McGoldrick, 1990; Davies and Rogers, 1984; Rogers and Green, 1979; Applebaum, 1966; Nelson, 1958
Multiple regression Discriminant analysis	A location analyst has been employed to produce a series of sales forecasts for both new and existing stores. He develops a multiple regression model, which is tested and calibrated across a number of different scenarios. The resulting model is used as a bench-marking tool for future development	Rogers, 1997; Greenland, 1994, Morphet, 1991; Wrigley, 1988; Sands and Moore, 1984; Jones and Mock, 1984
Cluster and factor analysis	A marketing team are in the process of developing a strategic blueprint for the company. They are interested in segmenting their existing store portfolio into a number of distinct retail offerings. A combination of factor or cluster analysis is used to group their stores according to a number of key demographic and operation variables	Schaffer and Green, 1998; Green and Kreiger, 1995; Weinstein, 1987
Spatial interaction (i.e. gravity/ location- allocation)	A location analyst is researching the relationship between the location of stores and retail demand by product category. Using a wide spectrum of variables, he produces a model of product class demand, which is used by the merchandising department to tailor the product offering within specific stores	Buckner, 1998; Dugmore, 1997; Lea and Menger, 1991; Berry and Parr, 1988; Ghosh and Rushton, 1987; Ghosh and Craig, 1986
Expert systems Neural networks	The location research department for a major retail organization is interested in automating the screening of a large number of new sites. They train a neural network with information on the existing store portfolio, labeling stores as profitable or non-profitable. The neural algorithm employed is used to support new site development decisions, providing an early indication of the likely performance of new stores	Newing, 1997; Furness, 1997; Murnion, 1996; Coates et al, 1995; Moutinho et al., 1993

Source: Hernandez, T. and Bennison, D. (2000), "The art and science of retail location decisions", *International Journal of Retail & Distribution Management* , *Vol. 28 No. 8. Pp. 357-367.*

Table 3 Key Factors for Site Evaluation

Class of Variable	Some Examples
Situation variables	
Land use measures	• Average daily traffic on routes with direct access to the site • Distance to nearest public transit stop • % of land use retail within 1km of site • Number employed within 10 minute walk of the site • Enrolment in schools within 10 minutes of site • Perceived upscaleness of the general area for retailing • Number of major traffic generators within 300 metres
Socioeconomic & demographic (SED) variables	• Number of households • Average income • % university educated • % households with children • % dwellings owned • % household heads aged 45-54 • % occupations blue collar
Competition variables	• Number of primary competitors within 1 km • Number of secondary competitors within 500 metres • Number of sq. m. competitive space within some distance • Index of competitor marking intensity within the trade area
Site variables	
Site variables	• Type of site (e.g. free standing) • Size of site (e.g., sq. m.) • Visibility of site (or sign) • Number of parking places on site • Years since last renovation • Index of attractiveness of entrance
Store variables	• Index of store management quality • Number of service staff • Average number of cashiers active • Ratio of display space to open space • Index of depth of stock • Probability of "stock outs"

Source: Adapted from A. C. Lea (1989) "An overview of formal methods for retail site evaluation and sales forecasting: Part 1", *The Operational Geographer*, and K. Jones and J. Simmons (1993) *Location, Location, Location: Analyzing the Retail, Environment* 2nd ed. Scarborough: Nelson.

Clearly there are numerous possible variables to be considered. The relevance of each will vary depending on the type of *activity* being considered and also the type of *location* being considered. For example, the variables influencing the success of downtown convenience stores will be different from the variables influencing suburban convenience stores.

The Role of Intuition in Locational Analysis

A cursory glance of the approaches in Tables 1 and 2 will quickly give the impression that the techniques have become more and more sophisticated. Each generation of techniques benefits from new analytical techniques, substantial increases in available data, improved historical perspective, increased computer capability, improvements in analyst expertise, and increased company investment. The temptation is to dismiss the earlier techniques as too simple and subjective in favour of the "more robust" newer methods. But it would be an error to dismiss the importance of intuition which characterizes the earlier methods. We have noted in Table 1 that the intuitive "Rules of thumb" are the most frequently used by companies (albeit that they are rarely the only method used). Lea (1989) notes that the simpler approaches can be used to identify the most feasible sites to be subjected to more rigorous analysis. Furthermore, even the more rigorous statistical methods require some intuitive awareness to identify the variables to be subjected to verification; intuition also come in handy when attempting to identify the weaknesses in the models. The analyst does well to keep common sense and intuition as companions across the whole range of methods. Finally, it is often the case, that senior management mixes intuitive experience with sophisticated analysis when deciding upon location strategies.[1]

The Role of Fieldwork and Sense of Place

Many sophisticated techniques are available to the location analyst today but the role of traditional fieldwork and reading of places is not diminished.

As we will see in many of the methods, including the more sophisticated ones, fieldwork often plays a role in the identification and collection of relevant variables for analysis and also in the final decision on the best site.

Understanding place and people in places is also an intuitive skill. As an analyst for a successful national retail chain in Canada notes:

"If you stop by a Tim Horton's in Bancroft at 11 in the morning on a Wednesday you know the town."

(Quote from an experienced analyst, evaluating the prospective market for a home improvement store.)

The policy of the most successful general goods retailer in the world is that senior executives have to "walk the site" before a decision is made.

Aerial fieldwork is also used. Retail location folklore includes Ray Kroc, the President of McDonalds, flying over prospective market areas to select numerous sites in the early rapid expansion of the chain. Rob Walton, the President of Wal-Mart, pilots his executives in a jet to explore sites. The plane is said to carry Delaware plates, rather than from Arkansas the home of Wal-Mart, such as not to alert people of Wal-Mart interest in prospective sites.

Oblique aerial photos are used by the leading new shopping centre developer in Canada to provide the broad context of sites. Site size, shape, topography, accessibility and visibility characteristics can be quickly evaluated from the air. The industry sometimes refers to such strategies as "Air Attack".

---

[1] Indeed, some work has attempted to model intuition of experts in order to bring it more effectively into the decision-making process; see Clarke, et. al. 2003.

On the ground, location analysts often drive nearby residential areas to get a good sense of their character. One leading analyst routinely drives into nearby neighbourhoods, parks in a randomly selected driveway, and then drives out of the neighbourhood to get a sense if the prospective site would be a natural destination.

Often in the early rapid phases of expansion of a retail chain in new territory there is only limited time to evaluate the sites and also the new chain may want to keep their interest in prospective sites "undercover". They may need to make their decisions "under the enemy's nose" and employ an "element of surprise". The war analogies are real.

"We were selecting many new sites in mid-size towns. We would go to McDonald's, share a McFlurry, look at a map, look at the competition, negotiate a deal ahead of time."

(Quote from a developer associated with the early expansion of one of Canada's leading retailers.)

A leading general merchandise chain in Canada had a significant number of stores in small town Quebec in the early days of expansion partly because the consultant developer had a girlfriend in Montreal. He visited her frequently and they would drive out from Montreal on field trips to evaluate prospective sites. Such factors are difficult to verify and incorporate in quantitative models!

We will now explore each of the techniques. Figure 1 summarizes the key characteristics of the methods making a distinction between older methods such as rules of thumb and newer methods such as location allocation.

Generally speaking the older methods are simple, intuitive, subjective, cheap, data poor, qualitative, requiring low technical expertise and computer use, but are widely used.

By contrast the newer methods are complex, objective, expensive, data rich, quantitative, requiring high technical skill and computer use, and yet are seldom used.

Our discussion will address some of these characteristics drawing out the main differences among the methods. For more technical critiques the interested reader can consult Lea (1989), Lea and Menger (1990, 1991), Birkin et. al. (2002) and Wrigley (1985).

Experience/ Rules of Thumb/ "Gut Feeling"

I have a nose for this from years in the business, show me the sites you are considering and I will pick the winner! (But don't come crying to me if it fails!)

Although essentially subjective, these methods are widely used. An experienced analyst who knows the company, the nature of the stores and likely variables influencing performance may be able to intuitively evaluate sites with a minimum of analysis. This is dependant mostly on trial and error and astute empirical observation. The analyst will have identified from previous experience one or two key factors that seem to be associated with good site performance and will look for these characteristics in the sites under consideration (Jones and Simmons, 1993). In the early days of site selection - when there was a dearth of data, little historical record of successful stores, few developed statistical techniques and limited computer capacity – there was little option but to use simple intuitive approaches. On the positive side these approaches are fast and cheap, but the danger of course is that there is no quantitative evaluation of the characteristics of a site and no demonstrated link between the nature of the site and likely retail performance; this could result in failure at the selected locations. The subjective nature of this and other simple approaches has led one observer to describe them as "degenerate cases of multiple criteria methods" (Lea, 1989, p. 12).

Figure 1 Summary of Characteristics of Site Selection Methods

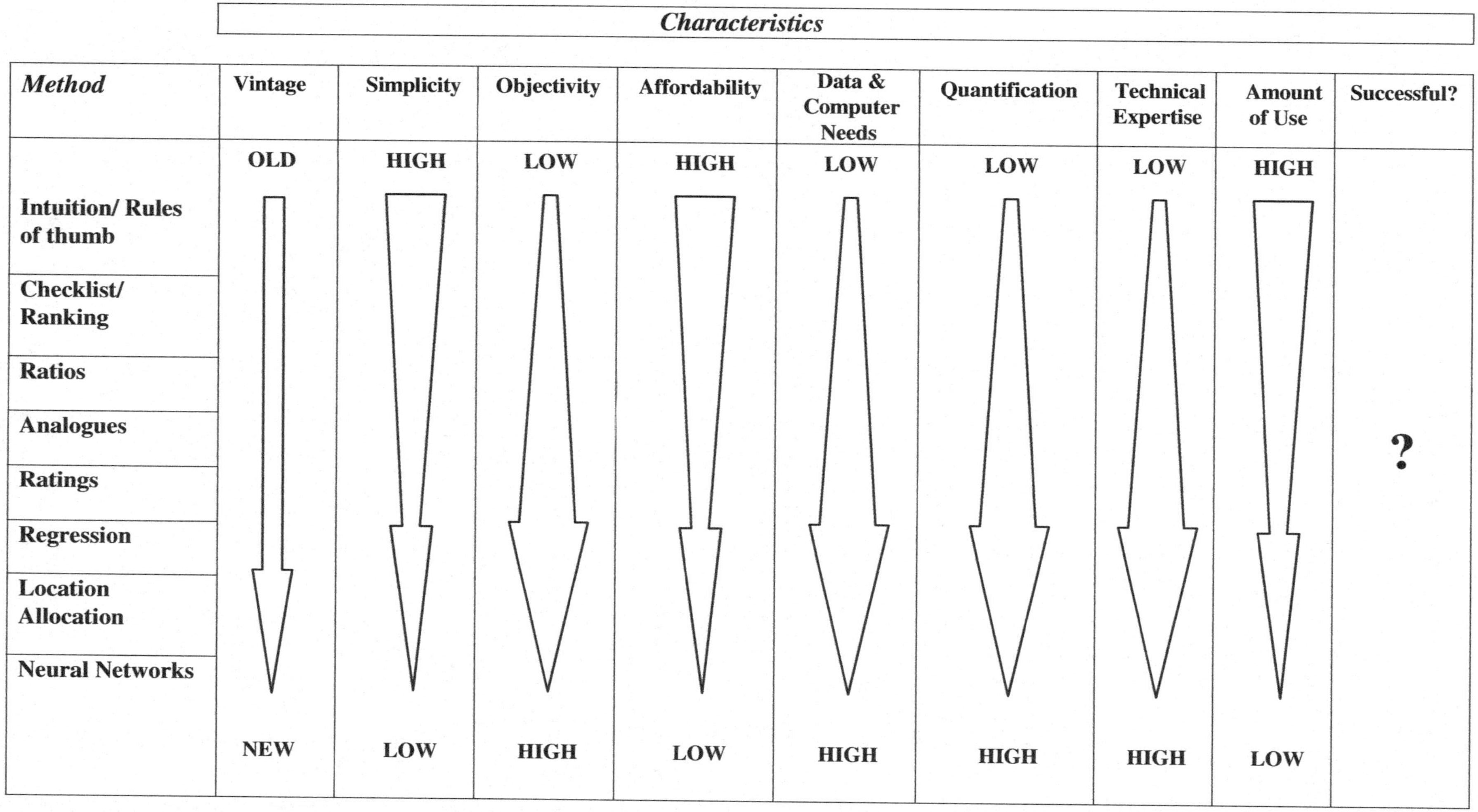

Characteristics

Method	Vintage	Simplicity	Objectivity	Affordability	Data & Computer Needs	Quantification	Technical Expertise	Amount of Use	Successful?
	OLD	HIGH	LOW	HIGH	LOW	LOW	LOW	HIGH	
Intuition/ Rules of thumb									
Checklist/ Ranking									?
Ratios									
Analogues									
Ratings									
Regression									
Location Allocation									
Neural Networks									
	NEW	LOW	HIGH	LOW	HIGH	HIGH	HIGH	LOW	

Checklist/Descriptive Inventories/Ranking

Let's make a list of variables that we think will produce success and rank the prospective sites against this list.

These approaches attempt to identify a list of variables that are thought to be associated with success and quantify the variables for the sites under consideration. Many variables can be considered as we noted in Table 3. In practice it is unlikely that all these variables will be considered, the actual variables on a checklist will depend on the type of retail activity under consideration and the nature of the location being evaluated (e.g. downtown or suburban).

Ghosh and MacLafferty (1987) identify five main categories of variables typically considered on checklists:

- Local Demographics (e.g. population and income of the local area)
- Traffic Flow and Accessibility (e.g. number of vehicles and transit access)
- Nearby Retail Structure (e.g. number of competitors and number of stores)
- Site Characteristics (e.g. size and shape of the lot and visibility of the site)
- Legal and Cost Factors (e.g. zoning and local taxes)

Care must be taken to measure the variables carefully, for example, when counting vehicle traffic it is of little value to include truck traffic.

Ghosh and MacLafferty also note:

> "It is often said that the essence of site evaluation is to find a "100 percent" location - one that has all the desirable characteristics of a good site. It is the one that is located in a good shopping area, has high accessibility and traffic flow, and represents a good retail investment." (Ghosh and MacLafferty, 1987, p72)

Of course finding such a site may be a challenge and if found it likely will be expensive!

With the list the analyst can evaluate the relative strength of potential sites by *ranking* them from best to worst – which site has the most of the variables thought to be important, which has the second most and so on.

In reality the variables identified are not of equal value in ranking the sites so a refinement is to **weight** the variables to reflect what is thought to be their relative importance. Table 4, for example, shows a site evaluation checklist for a bank. Note first that, although there are some similarities to the generic lists of variables that we identified earlier, this list has been tailor made for a bank application. Each of the seven major categories is evaluated using value ratings on the basis of sub-categories, for example the sub-categories for growth trends are: rapid growth, growing, stable and declining with rapid growth receiving the maximum score of 10. But each of the seven major categories is not thought to be equal, and weighted accordingly. Growth trends (with a weighting of 10), income (weighting of 7), competition (weighting of 7) and commercial development (weighting of 7) are thought to be more important than residential development (weighting of 4), office/financial development (weighting 3) and industrial development (weighting 2). Multiplying by the weighting factor will reflect this relative importance of each major category.

Obviously there is a degree of subjectivity in both the identification of the variables and the weighting of them, but this method at least adds some quantification and standardization to the evaluation procedure. Furthermore, this approach is fairly easy to apply, although if a major company is rapidly expanding with 100s or 1,000s of new openings the amount of fieldwork could be exhausting (recall that the founder of McDonald's Restaurants, Ray Kroc, used a plane to speed up the fieldwork in the early days of the fast food chain expansion!).

The major drawback of the method is that there is no *demonstrated* relationship between the checklist variables and store performance (e.g. sales at the store); the variables are selected from experience on the basis of what is thought to be associated with successful sites.

Table 4   A SITE RANKING SCHEME FOR A BANK

Region: _____

Location: _____

	Ranking	Score

	Value Ratings	Weighting Factor	Total Weight
A *Growth trends*			
_____ Rapid Growth	10		
_____ Growing	6–8	☐ x 10	☐
_____ Stable	5		
_____ Declining	0		
B *Family income levels*			
_____ Over $50,000	5		
_____ $36,000–50,000	6–7		
_____ $24,000–36,000	8–10	☐ x 7	☐
_____ $12,000–24,000	2–4		
_____ Under $12,000	0		
C *Competition*			
_____ None established	10		
_____ Established but poorly located	8		
_____ Long established	6	☐ x 7	☐
_____ Well located and long established	4		
_____ Planned and well located	2		
D *Residential development*			
_____ High density, multi-family	7–10		
_____ Medium density, single and		☐ x 4	☐
multi-family	4–6		
_____ Low density, single family	1–3		
E *Commercial development*			
_____ Major concentration (< 600,000 sq.ft.)	7–10		
_____ Medium concentration	4–6		
(400,000–600,000 sq.ft.)		☐ x 7	☐
_____ Minor concentration, scattered, unimportant	1–4		
(100,000–399,999 sq.ft.)			
_____ Next to no concentration	0		
F *Industrial development*			
_____ Major concentration (< 640 acres)	6–10		
_____ Medium concentration (–640 acres)	5		
_____ Minor concentration, scattered, unimportant	1–4	☐ x 2	☐
(> 640 acres)			
_____ Next to no concentration (___ acres)	0		
G *Office/financial development*			
_____ Major downtown core	6–10		
_____ Medium concentration auxiliary core	5	☐ x 3	☐
_____ Minor concentration, scattered, unimportant	1–4		
_____ Negligible development	0		

Source: K. Jones and J. Simmons (1993), Location, Location, Location, Nelson: Scarborough p.311

Nonetheless, as noted, these methods are widely used. Also they may often be used to identify likely sites to be subjected to more rigorous analysis.

Ratios

Ratios differ from the checklist methods above mainly by demonstrating an association between a variable and some measure of performance at actual stores. The variables are measured as ratios relating a performance measure such as sales to a variable such as population. Examples include:

sales/square foot,
sales/employees,
sales/checkout,
sales/capita,
sales/income,
sales/population.

The data can be collected from company records or from fieldwork (Jones and Simmons, 1993).

Since they draw from actual store data these methods can only be used for existing stores so the evaluation of greenfield (undeveloped) sites is not possible.

The methods can be used as a preliminary study to be followed by more sophisticated site analysis.

Analogue Methods

"It works here so it should work in a similar place."

These approaches are based on the simple premise that if stores are successful in one location they will likely be successful in other similar locations. Thus, an existing store, or group of stores, in similar locations are used as analogues.

At its simplest the method identifies the market area around the store through customer spotting[2] and the characteristics of the areas where the customers originated are summarized and then new areas with similar characteristics are searched for. These new areas should be good prospective sites based on the successful experience in the original stores. Sales forecasts can be made for the new store sites on the basis of their market area match with the original store(s).

For the method to work reasonably well the analogue (original) sites and prospective new sites should be alike in physical, locational and trade area circumstances (Clarke, 1998; Birkin et. al. 2002). It can be applied at different scales. For example, perhaps a chain has a successful store in Guelph, Ontario; can a similar market as Guelph be found elsewhere? Perhaps Peterborough or Kingston? At the intra-urban scale, neighbourhoods (e.g. census tracts) from which a successful store draws a disproportionate number of its customers can be identified and summarized and then a search made for similar neighbourhoods in the same urban area or in other cities.

These methods now benefit from more robust and faster analysis using geodemographics and GIS. For example, it may be discovered that existing successful stores have a disproportionate number of the geodemographic group "Affluent Greys" (wealthy retirees) in their trade areas; this geodemographic group can then be searched for elsewhere. This would require the assistance of a commercial geodemographic classification package (e.g. MapInfo *Psyte*) to locate the "Affluent Grey" cluster.

---

[2] Traditionally, customers are "spotted" through in-store surveys or competition entries; much more comprehensive methods are now available via affinity cards, credit cards, digital technology, point-of-sale data, etc.

A similar result can be achieved using simple GIS applications. Imagine that a customer spotting exercise (or simple census tract evaluation around the store) has identified that the home census tracts (where the customers are spotted or in the vicinity of the store) are disproportionately Italian, high income and family oriented. A simple search using GIS can identify *only* the census tract neighbourhoods that have above average values in all three characteristics.

Figure 2 identifies only the neighbourhoods (census tracts) in Toronto that have high income, many singles, high rental values and high incidence of apartment dwellers. This greatly narrows the potential candidate areas; of the possible 932 neighbourhoods only 13 are selected. Most are in central Toronto and these neighbourhoods are seen in the map with commercial land use. In most retail examples most customers are likely to come from nearby so potential commercial sites in the vicinity of selected neighbourhoods can then be identified and evaluated. This can be done by selecting commercial locations that are central to all selected neighbourhoods or by buffering selected neighbourhood points and capturing nearby commercial sites. Commercial areas where we have the market characteristics of interest nearby but no stores can then be investigated in detail.

A similar example is shown in Figure 3, this time for areas with high income and high incidence of family households and Jewish ethnicity. In this case the group has a distinctive linear cluster to the north of downtown Toronto. Only 15 of a possible 932 census tract neighbourhoods are selected.

Figure 2 Target Market and Nearby Commercial Land Use in Central Toronto

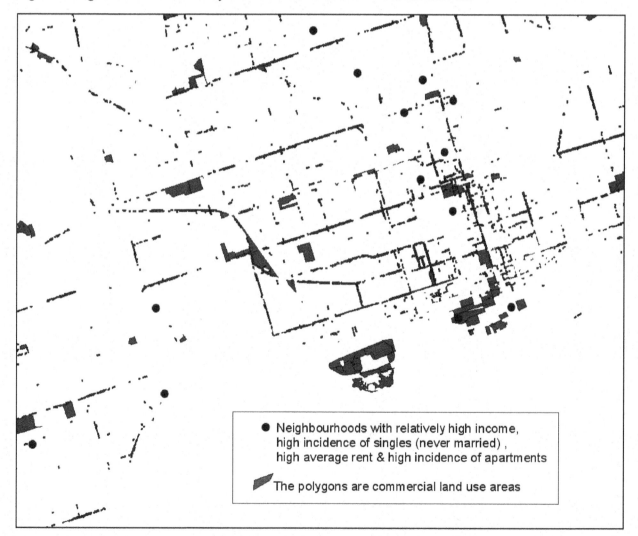

● Neighbourhoods with relatively high income, high incidence of singles (never married), high average rent & high incidence of apartments

The polygons are commercial land use areas

Figure 3: Target Market and Commercial Land Use Areas in North Toronto

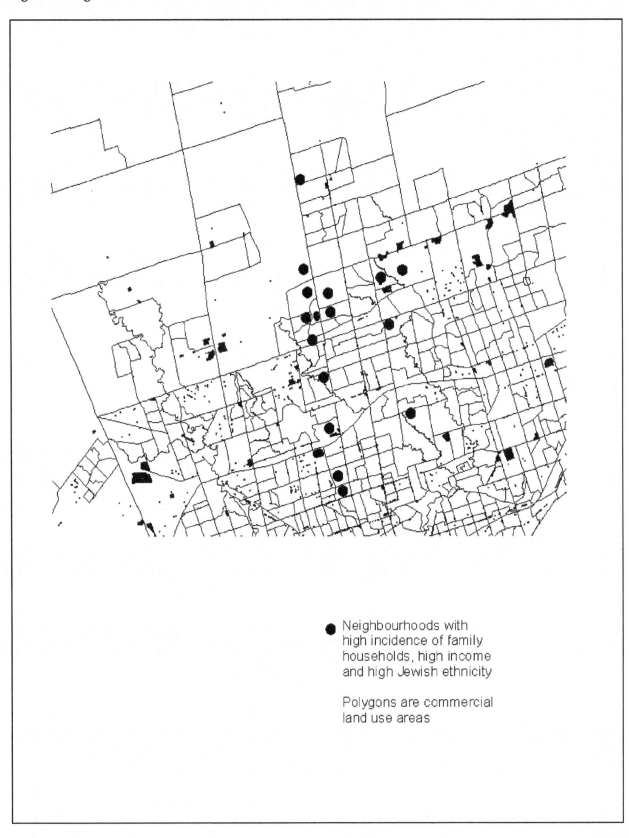

● Neighbourhoods with
high incidence of family
households, high income
and high Jewish ethnicity

Polygons are commercial
land use areas

Clarke (1998) and Birkin et. al. (2002) identify the weaknesses of analogue approaches:

- Can similar sites be found in practice?
- Even within the same retail chain store locations and store performance vary significantly
- Greenfield sites are difficult to evaluate in this way.

Parasitic approach

"That retail chain is successful and has likely done their homework, let's follow them."

Simply, smaller chains will follow the location decisions of bigger more experienced chains. The bigger chains likely use the best locational analysis techniques of the day so why not follow them? Birkin et. al. (2002) note that in the case of British high street retail expansion junior chains would follow the leaders: Marks and Spencer, Woolworth and Boots. Similarly, in the early days of rapid expansion of fast food outlets, McDonald's quickly became the leading chain; the others often mimicked the leader's locational choices. The leading retailer in a sector sometimes has the luxury of selecting something other than the prime (expensive) site, because when it builds it will attract others. "WalMart becomes the best site."

Simplicity and Use

The methods discussed thus far, although relatively simple, are the most widely used. Simkin (1990), drawing from a UK survey, notes that gut feeling, checklist and analogue are the most frequently used methods in a diversity of company types including department stores, variety stores, high street chains and financial outlets. We earlier noted similar findings from Hernandez et. al. (1998).

Ratings Models

"A comprehensive scorecard for sites will enable useful comparisons."

These models are championed by Birkin et. al. (2002) over the traditional checklist and analogue methods and also, in some circumstances, over the more statistically sophisticated models we will discuss later. Shortly we will see that some of the more sophisticated techniques, such as regression analysis, can fail if we cannot find sufficient analogous real-world examples to model on. Birken et. al. (2002), for example, discuss the example of automatic teller machines (ATM's) which are found in a diversity of settings appealing to users from diverse origins such as residential, workplace and recreation. Ratings approaches may work well in these complex market scenarios.

They are similar to the checklist methods in that they identify groups or classes of variables (e.g. market size and nearby retail) that are thought to be associated with performance at sites, but they are more sophisticated in their use of data and verification. The detailed example presented by Birkin et. al. (2002) shows improvements in at least three ways:

a) they benefit from geodemographic data, not just identifying population variables such as number of people, but, drawing from commercial packages, that identify geodemographic clusters (or segments) of the population.

b) distance decay of factors from the site is incorporated into the model thereby accounting for the varying spatial interaction between the customers and the store. Simply put, in reality the impact of variables decreases with distance and this is accounted for by identifying presence of variables within travel time rings (for example, 5 minutes, 10 minutes, 15 minutes) from the site.

c) the rating models are evaluated by verifying predictions against actual performance. For example, in the evaluation of ATM rating models a very close correlation is observed between actual and predicted transactions (Birkin, et. al. 2002).

The Birkin et. al. (2002) example is a commercial application for a client that identifies four major themes for rating:

- **Demand Side:** for example, total population, households, expenditures, affluence index, car ownership, etc.
- **Demographic Mix:** here geodemographic clusters (or neighbourhood types) from a commercial package (Superprofiles) are used. Examples of clusters include: Affluent Achievers, Settled Suburbans, Urban Venturers and Nest Builders. Sub-groups of these include: Young Families, Blue-Collar Families, Retired Workers.
- **Retail Synergies:** are there any nearby generative facilities that will attract complementary market?
- **Supply Ratio:** presence of competitive non complementary retail will be negatively evaluated.

Two of these themes are demand variables; two supply side. The themes vary in their importance and will be weighted accordingly: for example:
Demand Side: 40
Demographic Mix: 20
Retail Synergies: 15
Supply Ratio: 25

Each of the themes will be evaluated for each site producing a scorecard for comparison purposes. For example, a site maybe scored as:
Demand Side: 37
Demographic Mix: 7
Retail Synergies: 10
Supply Ratio: 13
This produces a strong 77 total out of a possible 100 with a useful mix of points coming from both the demand and supply components.

The mixture of diverse market and supply characteristics incorporating distance decay impacts provides a useful mix of relevant factors and related interaction making the approach attractive. Birkin et. al. (2002), however note that there has been little attention to these techniques in the literature. Actual applications include: ATM's, mixed good retailers, banks and convenience stores at petrol (gas) stations (Birkin et. al. 2002, Birkin et. al. 2004). Some problems relate to the dependence on commercial segmentation packages to evaluate the "Demographic Mix".

Regression Methods

"Which variables are statistically associated with performance?"

Regression methods are widely used in retail site selection. The attraction of these methods to many is that they appear to have more statistical rigour than some of the more qualitative methods discussed earlier. Variables thought to be associated with some measure of performance such as sales are only accepted if they are statistically validated. Another attraction of the approach is that, although development of a regression model is costly and time consuming, the actual *application* of the model to prospective sites is very straightforward.

In our discussion we will first briefly discuss **simple regression** to identify key principles then explore a **multiple regression** model. Our objective is not to learn how to apply the actual statistical methods behind the models, but rather to explore the principles of the models and how they would be applied in the real world.

Simple Regression

In simple regression we are looking at the association between two variables. One variable is the **dependant variable** which is thought to depend upon and vary in association with an **independent variable** (sometimes referred to by statisticians as the predictor variable and by others as the explanatory variable). For example, we may be interested in sales performance for stores as the dependent variable, and this is likely to vary in association with an independent variable such as number of households in the vicinity of the store. We can explore this possible relationship for a set of stores using a graph, as in Figure 4. Generally as the number of households increases the sales increase.

Figure 4 Simple Regression: Sales and Number of Competitors

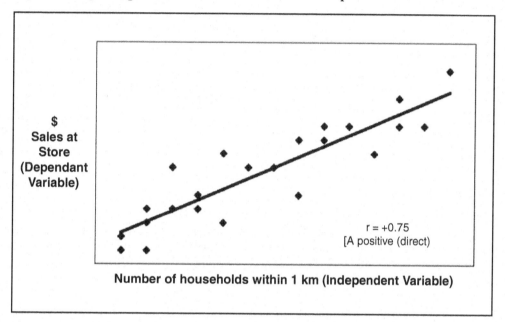

The direction of the relationship is positive (or direct), as the independent variable (households) increases so too does the dependent variable ($ sales). Importantly, we can also measure the strength of this relationship statistically with an r^2 value, which can range from -1 to +1, the closer to 1 (positive or negative) the stronger the relationship. (A value of one (1) would indicate a perfect relationship where every unit of increase in independent variable will be associated with a unit of increase in the dependent variable – all the observations would fall on a straight line.) What is important is that we have statistically validated the independent variable and not just accepted it on an intuitive basis. In the second graph, Figure 5, we consider the likely impact of number of competitors on sales.

In this case the direction of the relationship is negative (or indirect), as the independent variable (number of competitors within 1km) increases the dependent variable ($ sales) decreases. In both these simple examples, the relationships are strong as shown by the r^2 values which are close the value of 1.

Intuitive and Counter-intuitive Variables

You will have noticed that the associations in our two examples are as you would expect them to be. You would think that sales would increase with an increase in number of households and decrease with number of competitors. As such we call these **intuitive** variables. Sometimes the associations between variables, as revealed by the statistical analysis, are not as we would expect them to be, in which case we call them **counter-intuitive** variables. This is an important point and we will return to it later.

Figure 5 Simple Regression: Sales and Number of Competitors

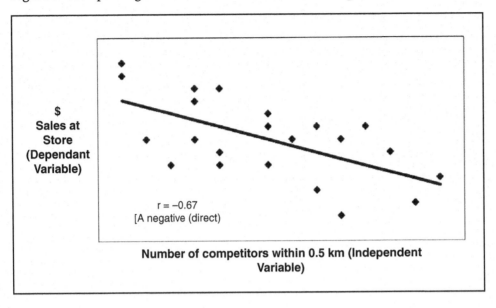

Multiple Regression

As noted, simple regression only explores the relationship between the dependent variable and a single independent variable. It is of course likely that performance at stores will be dependent upon more than one independent variable. In multiple regression we explore the relationship between the dependent variable (usually sales) and several site and situational independent variables. To build a regression model the analyst has to follow these stages:

- For a set of similar stores in a similar type of location collect data on the dependent variable (usually sales) and numerous prospective independent variables (e.g. population, households, age groups, traffic flow, transit access, nearby schools, etc. etc.).
- Isolate key factors that are statistically associated with performance (sales).
- Develop the model by calibrating the constant values of each of the statistically relevant variables.

Note that because the model is based on the experience of an existing set of similar stores that it is a type of analogue model. Although the building of the model is involved and problems can occur at each stage (see later) the model is easy to understand and apply. Consider the following example for downtown convenience stores.

$$Y = 3087 + 3.3X1 + 10.5X2 - 15.1X3 + 0.08X4 - 18.7X5$$
$$R^2 = 0.78$$

The dependent variable Y (weekly sales) is associated with five site and situation variables, X1 – X5:

Y: weekly sales
X1: Number of households within 1km (+)
X2: Number of schools within 1km (+)
X3: Number of competitors within 1km (−)
X4: Number of parking spaces within 500 metres (+)
X5: Distance in metres from nearest public transit (−)

The direction of the relationship (positive or negative) of each independent variable with the dependent variable is shown in brackets. Note that they are all intuitive in nature, i.e. as we would expect them to be. The regression coefficient R^2 shows the amount of variation in the dependent variable (sales) accounted for by the independent variables – the closer to 1 (100%) the better. Note that other variables could be added but a stage is reached whereby the addition of extra variables only improves the model very marginally.

The parts of the model are identified in Figure 6.

Figure 6   Parts of the Regression Model

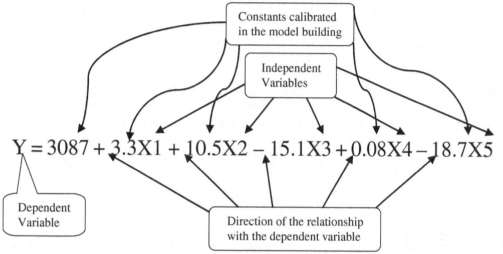

To apply the model is simple. Data for the independent variables for a prospective site are collected and simply plugged into the equation. This can be done for other sites and the predicted weekly sales compared. Site A for example has the following values:

Site A:
X1: Number of households within 1km = 2000
X2: Number of schools within 1km = 10
X3: Number of competitors within 1km = 8
X4: Number of parking spaces within 500 metres = 25
X5: Distance in metres from nearest public transit = 200

If we take the values and plug them into the equation we get predicted weekly sales of $5933.20.

Comparing Prospective Sites

Imagine we collect the independent variable data for three prospective sites and plugged them into the equation. Site A predicts $5933.20 in weekly sales, compared to Site B at $7,567 and Site C at $3,458. Which site do we select? This might seem a silly question, why would it not automatically be Site B with the highest predicted sales?

In applying the model we are only looking at one part of the business decision: how much will we likely get from the site? But what will it cost to occupy each of the sites? Perhaps it is likely that the site with the highest predicted sales would also be the most costly to occupy? We may still select that site, but we have to evaluate the **net** situation at each site: predicted sales relative to the cost of occupying the site.

The following model from Jones and Mock (1984) is for central city sites.

$$Y = 5792 + 34.45X1 - 32.33X2 - 351.11 + 176.29X4$$

Y = Weekly sales
X1: % apartments within half mile (+)
X2: % customers who are pedestrians (−)
X3: car accessibility (−)
X4: number of competitors within 3 blocks (+)

Note that some of these variables could be considered counter-intuitive in their relationship with the dependent variable. Certainly, "number of competitors" was negatively associated with sales in our earlier example, whereas here it is positively associated. See the difference as it *might* appear in simple scatter plots in Figures 7a and 7b.

Figure 7a A Negative Relationship between Sales and Competitors

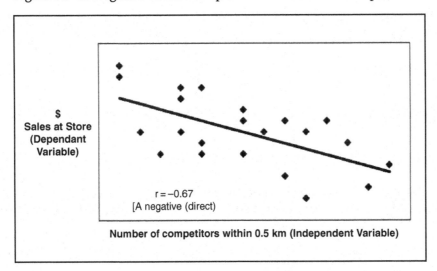

Figure 7b A Positive Relationship between Sales and Competitors

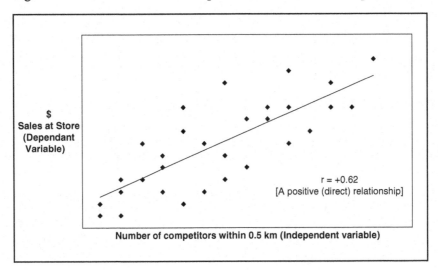

This is an important point. In some of the earlier more intuitive site selection approaches the analyst would very likely have considered competition in a negative light, but in the statistical analysis, in some circumstances at least, the variable is a positive. So the traditional intuitive approaches could routinely be considering some variables in an entirely wrong light. Usually we can explain the counter-intuitive variables in some logical way – explain them "intuitively" if you will. Perhaps the positive aspect of the "number of competitors" reflects that their presence in some circumstances reflects a very good market area – they are all on to a good thing.

Problems and critiques of regression approaches

The weaknesses of these approaches have received attention from Ghosh and MacLafferty (1987), Lea (1989), Clarke (1998), Birkin et. al. (2002), and others. The problems include:

i) Is it possible to find a set of stores sufficiently analogous in character and location? Remember that our model above was for a particular type of store – convenience stores – for a particular kind of location – downtown. It will not work for other types of stores or other kinds of locations. If we wanted a model for suburban sites we would have to start from scratch and different variables would result. If we cannot find sufficient stores of a similar type in a certain kind of location then we run into a dead end and the model cannot be built with any confidence.

ii) Lea (1989) identifies technical problems of three main types:
   (a) Multicollinearity problem. The independent variables should be independent of each other, otherwise they maybe measuring much the same thing. To what extent are the variables truly not associated with each other?
   (b) Nonlinearity. Regression requires relationships between dependent and independent variables to be linear, sometimes they are non linear.
   (c) Heteroscedasticity. "The tendency for the scatter of the dependent variable to increase for larger values of the dependent variable . . ." (Lea, 1989 p.14)

   Note that the technical issues can usually be resolved but they do nonetheless provide problems in the model building.

iii) Sites are considered in isolation as they are evaluated one at a time then later compared. A key strategy of retail chains is that they make interdependent decisions for a set or system of stores that work together relative to each other and relative to the market. Regression methods run counter to this.

iv) For Clarke (1998) and Birkin et. al. (2002) the biggest weakness is that regression models are essentially static, they do not adequately incorporate spatial interaction. What are the customer flows between residential and workplace areas and the retail outlets. How can these processes be incorporated into the models?

Location Allocation Models

"How can a set of facilities be located to best serve a given population?"

Most site selection approaches consider one site at a time. Location allocation models consider multiple sites together asking the question: which set of sites is best, given the population to be serviced? The sites could be, for example, stores in a chain, fire halls or hospitals. In the case of hospitals there is a requirement to service the entire health area population to a minimum level. The minimum level of service is likely to be some measure of distance or travel time, such that everybody within the area jurisdiction is within a required standard travel time or distance of a hospital. Which set of sites most efficiently achieves this? The fire hall example is similar: which set of fire hall locations best facilitates all addresses being within a specified number of minutes drive by a fire truck?

In the case of the retail chain, we are less likely to be looking for a set of sites to best service the *entire* population, but rather a set of sites to service an existing market population or a target population. Clearly, a smaller number of well sited stores have the potential of generating more profit than a larger number of poorly sited stores. The retail chain will consider a balance between the number of stores and the distance the customers have to travel. The fewer the stores the less costly for the chain, but the greater the distance and cost to the consumer to travel to the store thereby decreasing their likelihood of patronizing the stores - Figures 8a, 8b, 8c show the relationships among number of sites, travel distance and costs to the supplier and consumers (see Ghosh and MacLafferty, 1987.)

Another retail application of location application is when two retail chains merge: which set of stores taken from the combined set of stores most efficiently services the combined market of the two chains? Note that in the examples given, the "best sites" are the ones that reduce the travel distance or travel time for the consumer, thereby increasing the "accessibility" of the sites and increasing the propensity of the consumers to visit them.

Figure 8a) Number of Centres and Cost to Supplier

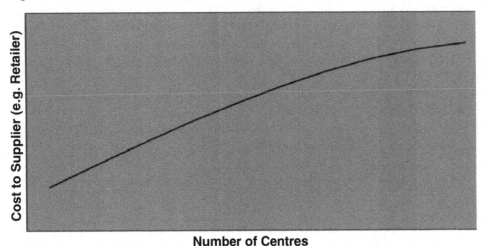

Figure 8b) Number of Centres and Travel Distance for Consumer

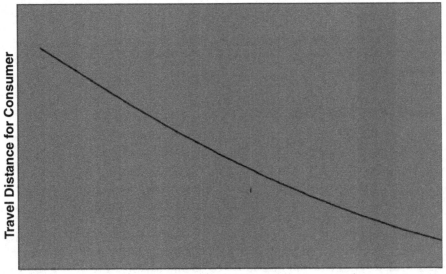

Figure 8c) Number of Centres and Travel Cost to Consumer

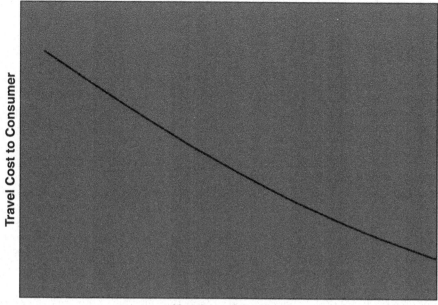

Number of Centres

In the discussion that follows we will work through a simple example of location allocation adapted from Ghosh and McLafferty (1987). Two relatively simple scenarios will be considered: *a) which single site best serves the demand points* and *b) which pair of sites best serve the demand points*. The study area is shown in Figure 9a. We have only three prospective sites and eight demand zones and only two scenarios, but these examples will serve to illustrate the key principles of the model. Real-world examples are likely to be much more complex involving many more demand zones, more prospective sites and more scenarios.

Figure 9a Study Area

a) Three Centres and Eight Demand Points

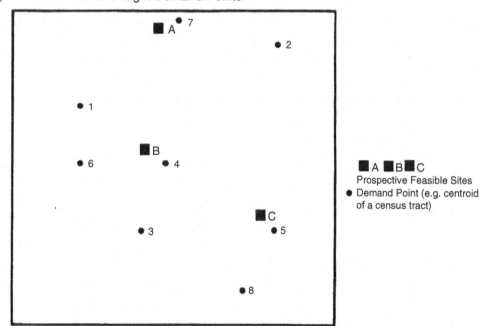

Adapted from Ghosh and McLafferty (1987)

Figure 9a identifies the three feasible sites (A, B, C) under consideration and eight demand points (1-8). The demand points could be, for example, the centroids of census tracts (which provide a source of market area data). Our first objective is to identify the best site to serve all eight demand points efficiently.

To apply the location allocation model we:

- Identify **feasible sites**. The organization will have certain minimum requirements of any site it will use (such as size of site, cost, zoning, access) and will draw up a short list of prospective sites that meet these requirements. In our theoretical example (Figure 9a) there are three prospective sites.
- Identify the **demand points** for the demand zones. These could be, for example, the centroids of census tracts.
- Identify the **objective function**. In deciding on the sites what is the nature of the "efficiency" we are trying to achieve? In the case of the fire halls the objective function might be that all addresses have to be within 8 minutes drive time by a fire truck so that the brigade is saving the building and not just the basement. In most retail applications the objective function is some measure of distance (or drive time) such that the market of interest finds the retail chain accessible. In our example we will use a measure of distance between the demand points and sites to determine the objective function. Which selection of site(s) will minimize this distance for the demand points as a whole? We want to minimize the average distance consumers have to travel to reach the sites (stores); this is our objective function.
- Create a **distance (or time) matrix** between the prospective sites and the demand points (see Table 5)
- Establish an **allocation rule**. How are the users of the facilities likely to decide on which facility they will use? Selecting the closest site is the most obvious allocation rule, but others could be parking at the site, ambience of the store, etc. In our example the allocation rule is proximity; the consumers are assumed to select the nearest site and will be **allocated** to **locations** (sites) accordingly.

The distance matrix in Table 5 shows distances between each site and each demand point. The demand zones vary in their potential to generate business because of differences in population, income etc. and this variation is reflected in the **relative demand weight** shown in the final column of Table 5. Zones 1, 4 and 3 have relatively low levels of demand; zones 5, 8 and 7 high levels of demand and zones 2 and 6 medium levels of demand.

The impacts of the different weightings (or levels of demand of the demand points) are reflected in the weighted distances in Table 6. For example, for site B the consumers from zone 1 will have to travel 3.6 kilometres (see Table 5) which has a relative demand weight of 2, giving a weighted distance of 7.2 (3.6x2)

Table 5   Distances between Three Prospective Sites and Demand Zones

Distance to Site in Kilometres				
Zones (e.g. census tract)	A	B	C	Relative Demand Weight*
1	4.2	3.6	7.2	2
2	3.2	5.0	6.0	5
3	7.1	2.2	4.0	4
4	5.0	0.0	3.6	2
5	7.6	3.6	0.0	8
6	5.8	3.0	6.3	5
7	0.0	5.0	7.6	6
8	9.2	4.5	2.2	7
* Reflects the relative demand of each zone, e.g. zones 1 and 4 have low demand compared to 5 and 8.				

Adapted from Ghosh and McLafferty (1987)

as shown in Table 6. Site A is somewhat less accessible for zone 1 with a weighted value of 8.4, and site C is the least accessible with a weighted value of 14.4. To evaluate which on average is the most accessible site we can sum the columns of weighted values in Table 6. Site B has the lowest total weighted travel distance of 146.3 so this is the site that should be chosen since it is, on average, the most accessible. Site A is the least accessible of all with a high value of 213.0 and site C falls in the middle with a value of 160.1.

Table 6   Weighted Distances* Between Three Prospective Sites and Demand Zones

Zones (e.g. census tract)	Prospective Sites		
	A	B	C
1	8.4	7.2	14.4
2	16.0	25.0	30.0
3	24.4	8.8	16.0
4	10.0	0.0	7.2
5	60.8	28.8	0.0
6	29.0	15.0	31.5
7	0.0	30.0	45.6
8	64.4	31.5	15.4
Total weighted distance (sum of 1-8)	213.0	146.3	160.1

*Weighted distance: distance between site and zone multiplied by relative demand weight. For example, between site A and Zone 1: 4.2 x 2 = 8.4

Adapted from Ghosh and McLafferty (1987)

We will now turn to the more complicated scenario of identifying which pair of sites is the best; that is, given our objective function, which pair of sites is the most accessible overall. So in this scenario, the firm wishes to locate not in one but two sites. Figures 9b, 9c, and 9d below identify three possible pair choices: A and B, A and C, and B and C. For each pair scenario we can create *proximal service areas* by assigning each demand point to the nearest site. For example, in the case of the A and B pair, zones 7 and 2 are assigned to site A and zones 1, 3, 4, 5, 6, and 8 are assigned to site B. These assignments to proximal areas are shown in Table 7. The sums of the pair scenarios will identify the pair that has the least average distance and therefore (given our objective function) the pair that should be chosen. The combination of B and C with a low value of 92.0 is the best.

Table 7   Distances for Pairs of Sites*

Zones (e.g. census tract)	Pairs of Sites		
	A and B	A and C	B and C
1	7.2	8.4	7.2
2	16.0	16.0	25.0
3	8.8	16.0	8.8
4	0.0	7.2	0.0
5	28.8	0.0	0.0
6	15.0	29.0	15.0
7	0.0	0.0	30.0
8	31.5	15.4	15.4
Total	107.3	92.0	101.4

Adapted from Ghosh and McLafferty (1987)

* The zones are assigned to the nearest proximal pair. For example, for zone 1: in the A-B scenario site B is the closest with weighted distance of 7.2 (see Table 6); in the A-C scenario site A is closest with weighted distance of 8.4; and in scenario B-C site B is again the closest with weighted distance of 7.2.

Figure 9a, 9b, 9c, 9d Study Area and Proximal Service Areas for Pairs of Sites

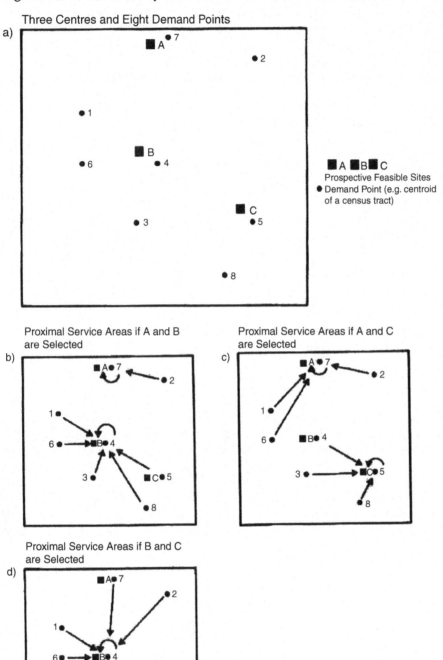

Three Centres and Eight Demand Points

a)

■A ■B■ C
Prospective Feasible Sites
● Demand Point (e.g. centroid of a census tract)

Proximal Service Areas if A and B are Selected

b)

Proximal Service Areas if A and C are Selected

c)

Proximal Service Areas if B and C are Selected

d)

Adapted from A. Ghosh and S.L. McLafferty,
Location Strategies for Retail and Service Firms (1987).

As noted earlier, these are simple applications with just three prospective sites, a limited number of demand zones (eight) and only two scenarios (one site, or a pair of sites). We could be dealing with hundreds of demand zones, numerous prospective sites and many different possible scenarios to evaluate. Moreover, the objective function and allocation rules can be more complex than simply proximity. Nonetheless the examples serve to illustrate the key principles of location allocation.

The main strength of the location allocation approach is that it addresses all the facilities at once with respect to all the demand. This is often the scenario faced by decision makers in the public sector. For example, all the population has to be within reasonable access of a hospital, which set of sites/locations most efficiently meets this goal?

In recent years facility providers in both the public and private sector have moved toward a smaller number of larger facilities relative to the population served. With fewer sites per population unit the location and accessibility of the sites becomes all the more important, even given that the population is more mobile. Planning for these sites can be more effective using the location allocation approach. Which smaller number of sites best services all the prospective hospital patients? Location allocation applications are also very useful ways to evaluate changes across an entire chain of stores. Since the success of the retail chain partly depends on the interdependent systems operation a method that evaluates the entire system at once is attractive. As noted earlier, in the private sector it is less likely that the entire population is being addressed with respect to the sites, but rather that an existing customer base or target market is being assigned. Also in cases where chains merge location allocation can evaluate the best set of locations from the total combined sites.

Given the potential in retail analysis there are surprisingly few retail applications of location allocation, most applications are in public facility location. Lea and Menger (1991) have identified some of the barriers to applying location allocation:

- the approach can be very complex
- there are few retail examples to serve as models
- the computations quickly become complex, and
- little software is available.

Our example above was relatively simple but it is not difficult to see how real-world applications involving numerous sites, hundreds of demand areas, multiple scenarios and varied objective functions could produce an intensely complex array of combinations.

Neural Networks

"Let the computer figure it out."

These methods are very complex, rarefied and rarely used.

They come from a keen interest in artificial intelligence beginning in the early 1990's (Openshaw and Openshaw 1997).

"An **Artificial Neural Network** (ANN) is an information processing paradigm that is inspired by the way biological nervous systems, such as the brain, process information. The key element of this paradigm is the novel structure of the information processing system. It is composed of a large number of highly interconnected processing elements (neurones) working in unison to solve specific problems. ANNs, like people, learn by example. An ANN is configured for a specific application, such as pattern recognition or data classification, through a learning process. Learning in biological systems involves adjustments to the synaptic connections that exist between the neurones. This is true of ANNs as well."

Stergiou, C., and Siganos, D. www.doc.ic.ac.uk/~nd/surprise_96/journal/vol4/cs11/report.html

It is evident from our earlier discussion that location problems can be very complex involving numerous potential sites, many demand zones, a diversity of market variables, various types of spatial interaction and a complexity of scenarios. Neural networks and other knowledge based systems take advantage of recent massive increases in computer power to address complex problems. Not unsurprisingly the technical expertise and understanding and computer requirements are very high. Essentially a multitude of inputs are analysed for pattern and process relationships in a black box environment resulting in a limited number of outputs which, in theory at least, should be easier to apply to real-world problems (see Figure 10).

Figure 10 An Example of a Simple Network

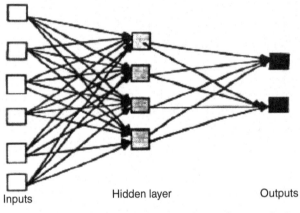

Inputs   Hidden layer   Outputs

Source: Stergiou, C., and Siganos, D., *Neural Networks*. www.doc.ic. ac.uk/~nd/surprise_96/journal/vol4/cs11/report.html

The strength of neural networks is that they should be able to accommodate much complexity compared to other methods, such as regression, which attempt to average out complexities to ensure that the models will "work". Applications include flood prediction in hydrology (Kneale and See, 2004), but relatively little in retail, although Birkin et. al. (2004) note that neural networks can be used with some effect in combination with other techniques.

One method?

We have discussed each of our methods largely in isolation, but there is sometimes overlap where they are used in conjunction. For example, regression methods although robust statistically still benefit from good intuition in the first instance to identify likely variables for investigation. Similarly, regression may be used to identify some variables for consideration in the ratings models.

Likewise, neural networks could be used in some hybrid context with productive effect (Birkin, Boden and Williams 2003).

The capability of the neural networks approach to address complexity is clearly a strength but also probably the key weakness. Is there much point in expending resources on a technique that is so difficult to understand that it cannot be effectively communicated to senior decision makers? Particularly in an industry with a long tradition of intuitive decision making. This brings us nicely to our conclusion.

Conclusion

Researchers of location decision strategies observe that they are a mix of art and science, see for example, Hernandez and Bennison (2000), *The art and science of retail location decisions.*

Even given the more sophisticated methods on offer, traditional intuitive techniques remain popular.

More rigorous techniques appear to add the validity of hard science and quantification, but intuition, even in the more sophisticated techniques, continues to play a significant role.

Likewise, it is important to keep in mind the appeal of the different methods to senior decision makers (Lea, 1989). There is little point pursuing methods if they cause discomfort and puzzlement in senior management. Part of the task of the analyst is to communicate the approach to management in an effective manner.

Many organizations will continue to use a combination of the so-called "retail nose" and the growing suite of rigorous methods.

A number of factors point to increased use of the more rigorous methods:

(a) Organizations have a vast amount of data related to both performance and market to analyse.

(b) Increases in computer data storage and analytical power make the application of the methods more feasible.

(c) More user-friendly software has been developed.

(d) Actual examples of applications serve as models.

(e) The expertise and experience of analysts is significantly higher.

(f) In a keener competitive environment an edge can be gained using these methods.

Even given this trend, armchair mouse-clickers are likely to augment and not replace traditional intuition and fieldwork; ultimately evaluation will take place in the cold light of day:

"At the end of the day, the locational analyst, regional manager and real estate manager will walk the site and sit in the car to observe the site and people before making a final decision."

(Quote from a successful Toronto location analyst for a leading home-improvement retailer.)

References

Applebaum, W. (1965) "Can Store Location Research be a Science?" *Economic Geography* 41: 234–237.

Applebaum, W. (1966), "Methods for determining store trade areas, market penetration and potential sales", *Journal of Marketing Research*, Vol. 3 No.2, pp.127–41.

Applebaum, W. (1968), *Guide to Store Location Research*, Reading, M.A.: Addison-Wesley.

Beaumont, J.R (1987), "Retail location analysis: some management perspectives", *International Journal of Retailing*, Vol. 3 No.2, pp.22–36.

Berry, B.J.L., and Parr, J.B. (1988), *Market Centres and Retail Location*, London: Prentice-Hall.

Birkin, M., Boden , P. and Williams, J. (2003) "Spatial decision support systems for petrol forecourts", in Geertman, S. and Stillwell, J. (eds) *Planning Support Systems in Practice*, Berlin: Springer.

Birkin, M., Clarke, G. and Clarke, M. (2002), *Retail Geography & Intelligent Network Planning*, Chichester: John Wiley & Sons

Birkin, M., Clarke, G. and Clarke, M. and Culf R. (2004), "Using Spatial Models to Solve Difficult Retail Location Problems" in Stillwell, J. and Clarke G. eds. (2004) *Applied GIS and Spatial Analysis* Chichester: Wiley

Brown, S. (1992), *Retail Location: a micro-scale perspective*, Aldershot, Avebury.

Buckner, R.W (1998), *Site Selection: New Advances in Methods and Technology*, New York: Chain Store Publishing Corporation.

Clarke, G. (1998), Changing methods of location planning for retail companies, *GeoJournal* 45: 289–298.

Clarke, I., Mackaness, W., and Ball, B., (2003) "Modelling Intuition in Retail Site Assessment (MIRSA): making sense of retail location using retailers' intuitive judgements as a support for decision making", *The International Review of Retail, Distribution and Consumer Research*, 13:2, April 2003 pp. 175–193.

Coates, D, Doherty, N, French., A., and Kirkup, M. (1995), "Neural networks for store performance forecasting: an empirical comparison with regression techniques", *International Review of Retail Distribution and Consumer Services*, Vol. 5 No.4, pp.415–32.

Collins, A. (1992), *Competitive Retail Marketing: dynamic strategies for winning and keeping customers*, London: McGraw-Hill.

Davidson, W.R., Sweeney, D.J, and Stamp, R.W (1988), *Retailing Management*, Chichester: John Wiley & Sons.

Davies, R.L, and Rogers, D.S. (1984), (eds.) *Store Location and Store Assessment Research*, Chichester: John Wiley & Sons.

Dugmore, K (1997), "A gravity situation", *New Perspectives*, Vol. 5 No.4, pp.18–19.

Furness, D (1997), "Applying data mining to customer relationship management", *Geodemographics: Latest Developments*, London.

Ghosh, A, and Craig, C.S. (1986), "An approach to determining optimal locations for new services", *Journal of Marketing*, Vol. 47 pp.56–68.

Ghosh, A, and Rushton, G (1987), *Spatial Analysis and Location Allocation Models*, New York: Van Nostrand and Reinhold,

Goodchild, M.F. and Noronha, V.T. (1987) "Location-Allocation and Impulsive Shopping: The Case of Gasoline Retailing," in A. Ghosh and G. Rushton (eds. *Spatial Analysis and Location-Allocation Models*. New York: Van Nostrand Reinhold.

Green, P.E, and Kreiger, A.M (1995), "Alternative approaches to cluster-based market segmentation", *Journal of Market Research Society*, Vol. 37 pp.221–38.

Greenland, S (1994), "Branch locations, network strategy and the high street", in McGoldrick, P., Greenland, S (Eds), *Retailing of Financial Services*, London: McGraw-Hill, pp.125–53.

Hernandez, T., Bennison, D. and S. Cornelius, S. "The organisational context of retail location planning", *GeoJournal* 45: 299–308, 1998.

Hernandez, T., Bennison, D. (2000), "The art and science of retail location decisions", *International Journal of Retail & Distribution Management*, Vol. 28 No. 8, pp.357–356.

Jones, K. and Mock, D.R (1984), "Evaluating retail trading performance", in Davies, R.L., Rogers, D.S. (Eds), *Store Location and Store Assessment Research*, Chichester: John Wiley & Sons, pp. 333–60.

Jones, K. and Hernandez, T. (2004) "Retail Applications of Spatial Modelling" in Stillwell, J. and Clarke G. eds. *Applied GIS and Spatial Analysis* Chichester: Wiley.

Jones, K. and Simmons J. (1987), *Location, Location, Location: Analyzing the Retail, Environment* London: Methuen.

Jones, K. and Simmons J. (1993), *Location, Location, Location: Analyzing the Retail, Environment* 2nd ed., Scarborough: Nelson.

Jones, K. and Simmons, J. (1990), *The Retail Environment*, London: Routledge.

Kneale, P. and See, L. (2004) "Forecasting River Stage with Artificial Neural Networks" in Stillwell, J. and Clarke G. eds. *Applied GIS and Spatial Analysis* Chichester: Wiley.

Lea, A. C. (1989), "An Overview of Formal Methods for Retail Site Evaluation and Sales Forecasting: Part 1, *The Operational Geographer,* Vol. 7 No. 2, pp. 8–17.

Lea, A.C., and Menger, G.L (1990), "An overview of formal methods for retail site evaluation and sales forecasting: part two", *The Operational Geographer*, Vol. 8 No.1, pp.17–23.

Lea, A.C., and Menger, G.L (1991), "An overview of formal methods for retail site evaluation and sales forecasting: part three", *The Operational Geographer*, Vol. 9 No.1, pp.17–26.

Lea, A.C. and Simmons, J. (1995), *Location Allocation Models for Retail Site Selection,* Research Report 1995-01, Toronto: Centre for the Study of Commercial Activity.

Mendes, A. B. and Themido, I. H. (2004), "Multi-outlet retail site location assessment", *International Transactions in Operational Research*, 11, 1–18.

McGoldrick, P. (1990), *Retail Marketing,* London: McGraw-Hill.

Morphet, C.S (1991), *International Review of Retail Distribution and Consumer Research*, Vol. 1 No.4, pp.329–53.

Moutinho, L., Curry, B, and Davies, F (1993), "Comparative computer approaches to multi-outlet retail site decisions", *The Services Industries Journal*, Vol. 13 No.4, pp.201–20.

Murnion, S.D (1996), "Spatial analysis using unsupervised neural networks", *Computers and Geosciences*, Vol. 22 pp.1027–31.

Nelson, R.L (1958), *The Selection of Retail Locations,* New York, NY: Dodge,

Newing, R (1997), "Back seat drivers", *New Perspectives*, Vol. 2 No.8, pp.34–6

Openshaw S. and Openshaw S. (1997) *Artificial Intelligence in Geography,* Chichester: Wiley.

Rogers, D (1997), "Site for store buys", *New Perspectives*, Vol. 5 pp.14–17.

Rogers, D., and Green, H.L. (1979), "A new perspective on forecasting store sales: applying statistical models and techniques in the analogue approach", *Geographical Review*, Vol. 69 No.4, pp.449–58.

Sands, S., and Moore, P. (1981), "Store site selection by discriminant analysis", *Journal of the Market Research Society*, Vol. 23 No.1, pp.40–51.

Schaffer, C, and Green, P.E (1998), "Cluster-based market segmentation: some alternative comparisons of alternative approaches", *Journal of Market Research Society*, Vol. 40 pp.155–63.

Simkin, L. P. (1990) "Evaluating a store location", *International Journal of Retail and Distribution Management*, 18, 33–38.

Stergiou C. and Siganos, D., *Neural Networks,* www.doc.ic.ac.uk/~nd/surprise_96/journal/vol4/cs11/report.html. Accessed February 2008.

Stillwell, J. and Clarke G. eds. (2004) *Applied GIS and Spatial Analysis* Chichester: Wiley.

Weinsten, A. (1987), *Market Segmentation,* Chicago, IL.: Prohus,

Wrigley, N. (1985), *Categorical Data Analysis for Geographers and Environmental Scientists,* London: Longman.

Wrigley, N. (1988), (ed.) *Store Choice, Store Location and Market Analysis,* London: Routledge.

Chapter 6

THE CANADIAN MARKET
Jim Simmons and Shizue Kamikihara

The amount and type and location of commercial activity is largely determined by the distribution of the market; but in Canada the market is so widely dispersed in space and so fragmented by topography, language and lifestyle, that the exact parameters of the relationship between market and commercial activities become important. In this section we define the Canadian market, examine its growth over time, and then explore the spatial distribution across the country. The chapter to follow describes the variety of urban markets, and some of the variations within them.

Defining the Market. The size of a market is measured by market income, often defined as the product of the number of households, and the average income per household. At the national or provincial scale we can use the estimates of personal income to measure the market. For various commercial sectors or product groups we may also want to disaggregate the household income into the average expenditures for various products or services, as recorded in the annual report "Spending Patterns in Canada" (Catalogue 62-202). This report uses the survey data from the year 2004. The five-year Census of Canada, complemented by a variety of survey data and massaged by market research firms, provides very detailed information on market income at all spatial scales. It is impossible to summarize all this information; we simply make a few general comments. (To read a more extended discussion of market relationships, see Jones and Simmons, second edition, 1993, Chapter Two.)

The most important segmentation of a given spatial market is the level of household income; first, because of the aggregate impact on purchasing power, and second (very much second!) because of variations in purchasing patterns that occur among income groups. The substantial differences in household income level that occur within cities modify purchasing power and market size from one neighbourhood to another. Average household income in a well to do district may be as much as ten times that of a poorer area. These income differences lead to local concentrations of purchasing power, hence commercial concentrations.

Table 2.1, from "Spending Patterns in Canada", shows the variations in the expenditures among the five income quintiles of Canadian households. Note the range of income levels: the highest income group (average income $146,000) earns more than eight times as much as the lowest income group (average income $17,900). If these higher income families were to spend all their income in stores, this would mean eight times as many stores, sales

and retail employees in the wealthy neighbourhood. These stark differences are partly offset by the varying ratios of store expenditures to income. Poor families allocate much of their income (indeed, go into debt) to buy shelter, while the rich accumulate savings and pay income taxes. As a result there is a substantial decline in the proportion of income actually consumed in stores or on services as income increases, from over 106 per cent of income (going into debt) in the lowest income group to 55 per cent (substantial savings) in the highest quintile. Altogether, then, the high income group receives almost eight times as much money as the poorest group, but spends a smaller proportion: generating only four times as much consumption.

The allocation of consumption to different goods and services is shown in the bottom part of the table. As incomes increase, the proportion allocated to shelter and food declines, releasing money for other activities. Food accounts for 21 per cent of income for the lowest income group, but only 8.3 per cent for the highest. Nonetheless, higher income families spend more than three times as much in actual dollars. Within the consumption expenditures, the car accounts for much of the purchasing power that is released from food and shelter -- increasing from 10.3 per cent to 18.7 per cent of expenditures for the highest income group. The expenditures on various services jump from 19.9 per cent to 22.1 per cent. The share of spending on clothing and recreation also increases, the latter including purchases of cameras, jewellery and sporting goods. Conversely, the shares of personal care goods, and tobacco and alcohol, decline.

As the overall level of household income increases over time, we can expect the overall pattern of expenditure to shift toward the right hand side of the table -- more automobiles, services, and leisure goods such as cameras. And, if the expenditures of the public sector (taxes) decline as well, the net impact of increased income on the commercial sectors will be amplified.

The Growth of the Market. The growth of market income is particularly relevant to firms in the commercial sectors because it provides opportunities for new stores. Recent revisions to the historical estimates of personal income confirm that in recent years the growth has been very modest. Nonetheless, since 1960 the Canadian market has grown at an annual rate of 1.32 per cent in population and 2.29 per cent in real income per capita, for an aggregate growth rate of 3.64 per cent (Table 2.2), which has cumulated over 45 years to support a four or

TABLE 2.1 Household Income and Expenditure, 2004

	Lowest	Second	Third	Fourth	Fifth	National Average
			Quintiles of Income			
Household Size	1.36	2.02	2.55	3.01	3.44	2.53
Avg. Income	$17,905	34,316	54,400	79,158	146,431	64,559
Per Cent Savings[a]	-13.1	-1.0	7.5	10.2	16.3	10.0
Per Cent Taxes	4.2	11.2	15.5	19.0	24.9	19.4
Consumption	$19,140	30,413	41,086	54,826	81,717	45,436
Consumption/ Income	106.9	88.6	75.5	69.3	55.8	68.4
Per Cent of Income						
Shelter	39.6	26.5	22.5	19.2	13.7	19.2
Food	21.4	17.2	13.7	11.6	8.3	11.6
Clothes	4.2	4.3	3.9	3.8	3.5	3.8
Furniture	3.0	3.3	2.8	2.8	2.7	2.8
Auto	11.0	13.6	12.8	12.9	10.4	11.8
Other Retail	6.4	5.7	4.5	3.7	3.3	3.9
Services	21.3	18.1	15.3	15.3	13.8	15.3
Per cent of Consumption						
Shelter	37.1	29.9	29.8	27.7	24.6	28.0
Food	18.5	17.6	16.2	15.0	14.9	15.2
Clothes	3.9	4.9	5.1	5.5	6.3	5.5
Furniture	2.8	3.7	3.7	4.0	4.8	4.1
Auto	10.3	15.4	17.0	18.6	18.7	17.2
Other Retail	6.0	6.4	6.0	5.3	5.9	5.7
Services	19.9	20.4	20.2	22.1	22.1	22.4

[a] Savings includes pension and insurance payments.

Source: adapted from Statistics Canada, "Spending Patterns in Canada, 2004". Catalogue 62-202.

Reproduced with the permission of the Minister responsible for Statistics Canada, 2006.

five-fold increase in the level of commercial activity. While the growth in population and the growth in income per capita both contribute to market growth it is important to note that these two components have different distributions in time and space (See Figure 2.1). Population grows relatively regularly over time but the growth is highly concentrated in space. During the period 1996-2001, for example, over seventy per cent of Canada's population growth occurred in Ontario and British Columbia. Two thirds of this growth occurred in the Toronto and Vancouver CMAs, and most of this is found in a few suburban municipalities such as Mississauga, Brampton, Markham, and Surrey. The very largest urban markets are growing most rapidly, so that the four cities over one million population (Toronto, Montreal, Vancouver, Ottawa) now make up thirty-seven per cent of Canada's population.

Population growth patterns, then, alter spatially defined markets and force retail chains to relocate stores on a continuous basis. Growth rates of income per capita, in contrast, may vary considerably over time, from one year to the next, but affect most locations within the same region in the same way. All provinces, all cities, all neighbourhoods, are now better off, and purchase more goods and services than twenty years ago.

At the same time it is apparent in Figure 2.1 that the rate of growth for both population and income per capita (and especially the latter) is slower now than it was in the 1970s. In constant dollars the total personal income for Canada in 2005 was only 28.4 per cent higher than it was in 1990, compared to 16.5 per cent for the population growth. Income per capita in 2005 (at $31,850) is only ten per cent higher than it was in 1990 ($28,890). Retailers have been doubly hurt because the increasing tax burden has reduced the amount of income available for consumption.

Although by far the most important element of change over the last thirty years has been the long-term growth in

TABLE 2.2 The Canadian Market: 1960-2005

Year	Population[a]	Household[b]	Average Household Size	Personal Income[c]	Income/ Capita	Market growth (annual)	Auto[d]	Auto/ Capita	Female Part'n Rate[e]
1960	17,870	4554	3.9	$205.7	$11,490	...	4,104	.230	...
1965	19,678	5180	3.7	266.7	13,550	7.65	5,279	.268	34.7%
1970	21,324	6035	3.5	357.3	16,760	4.85	6,602	.310	38.3
1975	23,142	7166	3.1	506.4	21,880	4.72	8,693	.376	44.4
1980	24,516	8282	2.9	604.3	24,650	3.47	10,256	.418	50.4
1985	25,843	...	...	675.3	26,130	4.12	11,118	.430	54.7
1990	27,701	...	...	800.3	28,890	2.42	12,622	.456	58.5
1991	28,031	10,018	2.7	782.3	27,910	-2.25	13,061	.466	58.4
1992	28,367	...	...	790.1	27,850	0.99	13,323	.469	57.8
1993	28,682	...	...	791.6	27,600	0.20	13,478	.470	57.7
1994	28,999	...	...	806.7	27,820	1.90	13,639	.470	57.5
1995	29,302	...	...	821.1	28,020	1.79	13,183	.449	57.5
1996	29,611	10,899	2.65	826.1	27,900	0.60	13,217	.445	57.8
1997	29,907	...	...	846.5	28,300	2.47	13,487	.450	57.8
1998	30,157	...	...	877.2	29,090	3.62	13,887	.459	58.4
1999	30,404	...	...	902.1	29,670	2.84	16,538[d]	.542	58.9
2000	30,689	...	...	942.6	30,710	4.48	16,832	.547	59.5
2001	31,021	12,549	2.48	958.5	30,900	1.70	17,055	.549	59.7
2002	31,373	...	...	961.5	30,650	0.31	17,544	.566	60.7
2003	31,669	...	...	970.6	30,650	0.94	17,755	.561	61.6
2004	31,974	...	...	1,000.2	31,280	3.05	17,940	.561	62.0
2005	32,271	...	...	1,027.7	31,850	2.75	18,124	.562	61.8
Growth (%)									
1980-90	13.0	21.0	-6.9	32.5	17.2	...	23.1	9.1	16.1
1990-2005	16.5	n.a.	n.a.	28.4	10.2	...	43.6	23.2	5.6

Source: adapted from Statistics Canada:
[a] In 1000s, "Canadian Economic Observer: Historical Statistics". Catalogue 11-210.
[b] Households (1000s) for Census years only: Census of Canada, 1961, 1966, etc.
[c] Billions of $2005. Catalogue 11-210.
[d] In 1000s. "Road Motor Vehicles: Registrations". Catalogue 53-219. (Defined as passenger automobiles to 1998; less than 4,500 kg. since)
[e] "Historical Statistics of the Labour Force". Catalogue 71-201.

Reproduced with permission of the Minister responsible for Statistics Canada, 2006.

population and income per capita; the Canadian market has also evolved in other ways. Table 2.2 suggests that as personal income increases the population has become steadily more mobile, with a ratio of automobiles per person that is rapidly approaching saturation (if you exclude that part of the population too young or too old to drive). An important aspect of the increased income and mobility has been the entry of women into the labour force, as shown by the increase in the female participation rate from 35 per cent in 1960 to over 60 per cent at present. One result is the growth of commercial services; moving food preparation, for example, outside the home. In recent years, however, these trends have levelled off. Measures of household size, cars per person, and female participation rate have stabilized, in the same way as income levels.

Immigration continues to bring new kinds of consumers into the Canadian market, as well. Although immigrants now come from different countries than before, they continue to locate in the same subset of large cities -- Toronto, Montreal, and Vancouver -- and to concentrate in similar neighbourhoods. The cumulative effect of immigration is the creation of large urban submarkets with different consumption preferences and different travel patterns, that require different marketing approaches.

Finally, the cumulative effect of population aging is beginning to affect the market, especially the smaller urban

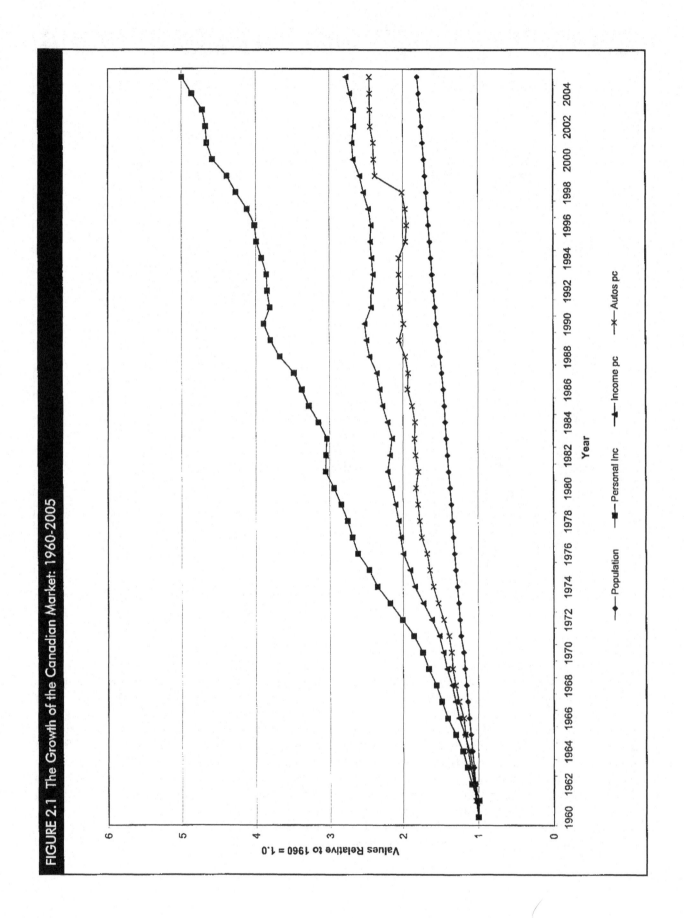

FIGURE 2.1 The Growth of the Canadian Market: 1960-2005

Values Relative to 1960 = 1.0

Year

Population — Personal Inc — Income pc — Autos pc

142

centres. Increasing numbers of consumers are now seniors; a larger proportion of the population is now over fifty years of age. These households are downsizing or thinking about retirement. They are saving, not spending; and their shopping habits are changing. They would sooner shop in nearby pedestrian strips than search for power nodes in distant suburbs (see Simmons, 2005a).

The Spatial Distribution. Although market growth in the long run has been sufficient to support a rapid and almost continuous expansion of commercial activity in every part of the country, there have been marked differences in growth rates among the provinces that have cumulated in a substantial shift in market share. In Figure 2.2a BC has grown most consistently, and Ontario's growth varies with the economic cycle. Alberta has done very well over the last decade. In Figure 2.2b, the Quebec share of the Canadian market has declined regularly since 1961, while that of British Columbia has increased (until 1995). Ontario and Alberta have fluctuated with peaks (declines) in 1970, 1990 and 1999; but Alberta's growth has surged over the last decade and it is about to overtake British Columbia. A negative growth rate over the last five years has left the Eastern Prairies behind the Atlantic region.

By far the most important difference among the provinces is the size of market (Personal Income, in Table 2.3), ranging one hundred-fold from $2.8 billion to $316 billion in 2005. The per capita measures, such as income or automobile use or household size, are quite similar and convergent over time, although some east-west differences

remain. The main reasons that retail and service firms focus on regional markets instead of the national market are the problems of logistics (distance) and language.

Equally important to investors are the prospects for the future. Table 2.4 projects recent population growth trends for regions as far as the year 2031. This seems likely to be a period of declining natural increase as fertility rates decline; so that immigration will account for an increasing share of growth, highly polarized into a few favoured urban areas. The result may be a marked westward shift of the national population, with negative growth east of Quebec, continued growth in Ontario, decline in the eastern prairies and rapid growth in Alberta and B.C. Ontario will provide more than half of the national growth; Alberta and British Columbia will account for the rest. If we add the current levels of income per capita we can extrapolate the market share: by 2031 Ontario may account for 40 per cent of the market, with considerably more of the remainder to the west than to the east. Of course, the unpredictable shifts in future income levels may substantially alter these patterns, especially if annual income per capita growth approaches the population growth rate of 0.74 per cent per year indicated by the demographic forecast.

In interpreting these forecasts of regional growth keep in mind that the growth will be largely concentrated in the extended urban areas or megaregions: Toronto, Montreal, Vancouver, Ottawa, and the Alberta Corridor. They will absorb most of the country's future population growth and investment, and outside these regions their respective

TABLE 2.3 Provincial Markets, 2005

Measure	BC	AB	SK	Province MB	ON	QC	NB	NS	PE	NF
Population[a]	4,255	3,257	994	1,178	12,541	7,598	752	938	138	516
Personal Income[b]	99.3b	93.4	21.8	25.6	316.3	168.1	15.7	20.6	2.8	10.4
Income Growth[c]	11.4%	31.1	8.1	5.0	12.5	11.3	3.4	6.2	7.5	7.8
Income/ Capita[a]	$27.6	33.7	24.8	26.4	31.1	27.8	24.8	26.2	23.9	23.8
Number of Autos[a]	2,238	2,224	657	623	6,776	4,245	451	532	76	253
Autos/ Capita	0.56	0.68	0.66	0.53	0.54	0.56	0.60	0.57	0.55	0.49
Participation Rate[d]	65.6	72.7	68.1	68.6	68.0	65.6	63.6	63.6	68.5	58.8

[a] In 1000s.
[b] Disposable Income in billions of $2005.
[c] 1999-2005, in constant dollars.
[d] Per cent of Population aged 15 years or over in the labour force.

Source: adapted from Statistics Canada: "Canadian Economic Observer: Historical Statistics". Catalogue 11-210, supplemented by the "Provincial Economic Accounts," Catalogue 13-016, and "Road Motor Vehicles: Registrations". Catalogue 53-219.

Reproduced with the permission of the Minister responsible for Statistics Canada, 2006.

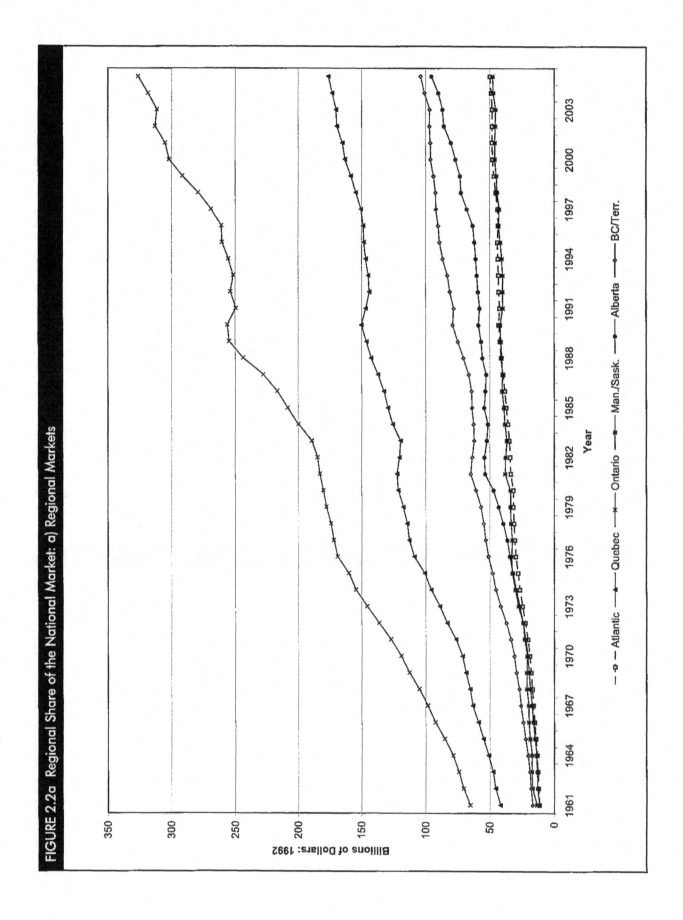

FIGURE 2.2a Regional Share of the National Market: a) Regional Markets

— ɒ — Atlantic —▲— Quebec —✕— Ontario —✱— Man./Sask. —●— Alberta —◇— BC/Terr.

Year

Billions of Dollars: 1992

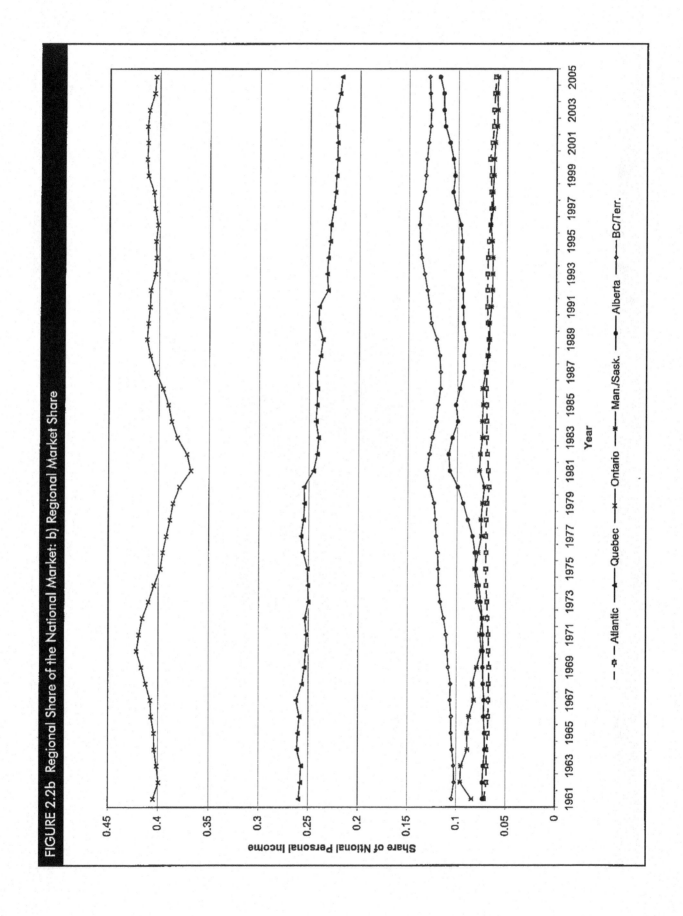

FIGURE 2.2b Regional Share of the National Market: b) Regional Market Share

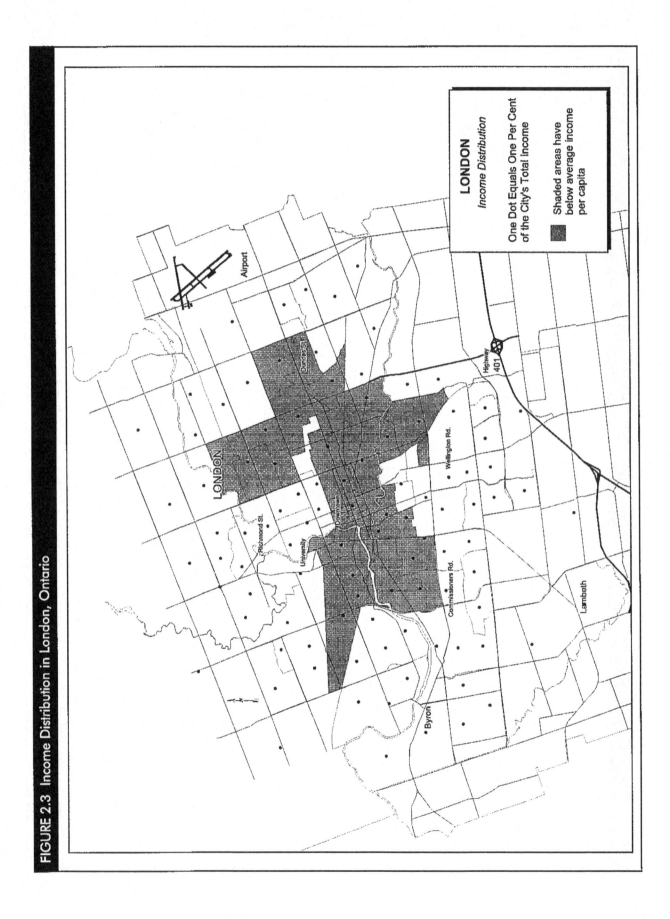

FIGURE 2.3 Income Distribution in London, Ontario

LONDON
Income Distribution

One Dot Equals One Per Cent
of the City's Total Income

Shaded areas have
below average income
per capita

TABLE 2.4   Regional Markets Forecasts to 2031

	B.C.	Prairies	Ontario	Quebec	Atlantic	Canada
Population (1000s)						
2006	4,255	5,429	12,541	7,598	2,344	32,271
2011	4,496	5,637	13,237	7,804	2,357	33,639
2116	4,742	5,853	13,931	7,985	2,372	34,995
2021	4,991	6,066	14,636	8,147	2,388	36,344
2026	5,040	6,265	15,335	8,284	2,400	37,636
2031	5,460	6,444	16,003	8,382	2,403	38,812
Gain	1,101	1,015	3,462	784	59	6,541
Per cent	25.3%	18.7	27.6	10.3	2.5	20.2
Market Share (%)						
2006	13.5	16.8	38.9	23.5	7.3	100.0
2031	14.4	16.6	41.2	21.6	6.2	100.0

Source: "Long-Term Population Projections, Medium Growth Scenario." in Statistics Canada, "Population Projections for Canada, Provinces and Territories, 2005-2031." Catalogue 91-520. Market share is based on income per capita in 2005.

Reproduced with the permission of the Minister responsible for Statistics Canada, 2006.

provinces may not grow any more quickly than Manitoba or Nova Scotia (See Simmons, 2005b).

Finally, Figure 2.3 describes the distribution of the consumer market within a single urban area, using the London, Ontario, example. This is the market that is served by the facilities mapped in Figure 1.2. Each dot represents one percentile of the city's total market income of $8.089 billion in 2001. In London the lowest incomes are found in older areas surrounding downtown and in the traditionally blue-collar sector to the east and south. Household income levels, as shown in Table 2.1, translate directly into retail and service sales.

Chapter 7

URBAN MARKETS
Jim Simmons and Shizue Kamikihara

Firms in the commercial sectors are less concerned with the abstractions such as the national market or even the provinces than with the reality of local markets defined by consumer behaviour: metropolitan and community markets. On the demand side of the commercial relationship it is possible to assemble enormous amounts of market information for very small units indeed. Of particular interest are the characteristics of urban markets, represented by the 140 Census Metropolitan Areas and Census Agglomerations currently defined by Statistics Canada. These markets are defined by commuting patterns -- thus laboursheds (and trade areas).

The Size Variation. Table 3.1 lists the 25 largest urban markets in the country, based on market income in 2001. They vary widely in size, with Toronto more than forty times larger than Sherbrooke; and there is a rough correlation between size of place and average household income. The map in Figure 3.1 confirms the concentration of the market, but also reveals a powerful regional variation in the distribution of these urban areas. That part of central Canada stretching from Windsor to Quebec City has about ten times the density of cities as the rest of the settled part of the country, and includes three of the four largest urban markets. The North is so lightly populated that it is largely irrelevant to a conventional retailer. In addition to the population density differences, there are major physical barriers: the Rockies and the Canadian Shield, and the water barriers that fragment the Atlantic provinces. Given as well, the language barrier that separates francophones and anglophones, it is easy to see why most marketing strategies treat Canada as a series of distinct regional submarkets.

Each of the major regions is served by a major distribution centre that connects the region to Toronto and the goods and services provided by Central Canada: Vancouver, Calgary (the regional centre for the Prairies used to be Winnipeg), Montreal, and Halifax. Regional centres grow as their regional markets grow, while the Ontario region tends to grow with the national market. The lower part of Table 3.1 indicates how the Canadian market is concentrated in a small number of locations. Over 68 per cent of the country's purchasing power can be reached in only 25 markets. The next 75 largest places contribute another 12 per cent, so that eighty per cent of the national market is found in one hundred locations.

Table 3.2 generalizes Canada's urban population distribution in 2001 in another way, by grouping the cities and their population by city size and region. The 140 cities include a population of 23.8 million, about 79.4 per cent of the Canadian population. The four largest cities account for 37.2 per cent of the population, and the 15 urban areas with more than 300,000 population contribute 57.5 per cent of the total. Canada is not only urban, but metropolitan as well! Central Canada (Ontario and Quebec) has 51 per cent of the cities, and 65 per cent of the urban population. The typical Canadian now lives in a large city in Central Canada.

In recent years, the Census concepts of metropolitan area and Census agglomeration have been supplemented by the idea of metropolitan regions (megaregions), as clusters of closely linked metropolitan areas and nearby cities that can be analyzed as single markets -- in many cases larger than most Canadian provinces. Table 3.3 from Simmons and Kamikihara (2005) lists nine megaregions in Canada, that jointly include 64 per cent of the nation's population and 69 per cent of the market.

Recent Growth Trends. These urban markets are not all growing at the same rate (see Table 3.4, and the right hand columns of Table 3.1). The distribution of urban growth over the last decade is far more concentrated than the overall population distribution, helped in part by an influx of immigration and an overall decline in fertility, and in part by the rapid growth of jobs in the commercial sectors. Toronto provides the bulk of the growth, followed by Montreal, Vancouver and Ottawa. Central Canada is the dominant region of growth, followed by Alberta and British Columbia. The four largest cities -- Toronto, Montreal, Vancouver, and Ottawa -- scooped up 60 per cent of the urban population growth, and the fifteen cities with population over 300,000 included 84 per cent of the urban growth. Meanwhile the non-urban areas gained only 200,000 people. Regionally, almost all of the urban growth occurred to the west of the Quebec border, with 87 per cent of the growth in Ontario, the Prairies and BC. Ontario, alone, contributed half of the urban population growth, with 784,000 added residents in Toronto. That is almost 30 per cent of all the population growth in Canada.

When this growth is translated into growth rates, a regular variation in urban growth rates occurs with city size category, ranging from 1.9 per cent for the smallest cities to 17.4 per cent for the largest places. The Census of Canada in 2001 is the third in a row to show this pattern, a pattern that is now stronger than ever (see Simmons and Bourne, 2003). The breakpoint appears around 100,000 popula-

TABLE 3.1 Major Metropolitan Markets: 1991-2001

Market Rank	CMA	2001 Characteristics				Growth Rates, 1991-2001			
		Pop'n	Market Income	H'hlds	H'hld Income	Pop'n	Market Income	H'hlds	H'hld Income
1.	Toronto	4,683	$125.0	1.635	76.5	16.7%	26.3	19.4	5.7
2.	Montreal	3,426	76.1	1,417	53.7	6.3	13.8	11.8	1.8
3.	Vancouver	1,987	47.8	759	63.0	19.3	27.5	24.5	2.4
4.	Ottawa-Hull	1,064	29.5	416	70.9	12.5	26.3	17.8	7.1
5.	Calgary	951	26.4	356	74.0	20.7	49.4	29.1	15.6
6.	Edmonton	938	22.0	357	61.8	10.3	24.8	16.3	7.3
7.	Hamilton	662	16.2	253	64.1	9.5	19.5	14.4	4.5
8.	Quebec	683	14.8	295	50.2	5.4	14.1	16.5	-2.1
9.	Winnipeg	671	14.6	270	54.2	1.6	10.6	5.8	4.5
10.	London	433	10.2	173	58.7	7.8	14.2	12.8	1.2
11.	Kitchener	414	10.1	153	65.7	14.0	29.4	19.6	8.1
12.	St. Catharines	377	8.3	151	55.2	3.3	11.4	10.3	0.9
13.	Halifax	359	8.1	144	56.4	8.0	17.2	18.3	-1.0
14.	Windsor	308	7.8	118	66.1	12.6	42.0	22.3	16.1
15.	Victoria	312	7.5	136	55.5	7.7	13.8	13.6	0.2
16.	Oshawa	296	7.3	104	69.8	19.0	30.0	25.7	3.4
17.	Saskatoon	226	4.7	89	53.0	6.7	16.7	11.8	4.4
18.	Regina	193	4.3	77	56.6	0.6	8.4	7.0	1.3
19.	St. John's	173	3.6	65	54.9	0.6	11.3	17.4	-5.3
20.	Sudbury	156	3.4	63	54.6	-4.5	-1.1	6.3	-7.0
21	Barrie	149	3.4	52	64.7	34.5	56.6	51.7	3.2
22.	Kingston	147	3.4	58	57.7	6.4	13.6	12.9	0.6
23.	Kelowna	148	3.2	60	53.2	24.3	44.7	37.8	4.9
24.	Chicoutimi	155	3.0	62	47.9	-3.8	4.1	9.1	-4.6
25.	Sherbrooke	154	3.0	66	44.7	7.2	17.0	16.6	0.3
	Average	---	---	---	59.3	9.9	21.7	17.9	2.9
	Range	---	---	---	31.8	39.0	57.7	45.9	23.1

	Population	%	Income	%	Income/ Capita	Ratio to Nation
Largest 25 markets	19,064,000	63.5	$463,749m	68.5	$24,330	1.079
Next 25 markets	2,285,000	7.6	48,328	7.1	21,130	0.937
Next 50 markets	1,859,000	6.2	37,489	5.5	20,170	0.895
Largest 100 markets	23,208,000	77.3	549,567	81.2	23,680	1.050
Rest of Canada	6,799,000	22.7	127,001	18.8	18,680	0.828
Canada total	30,007,000	100.0	676,568	100.0	22,547	1.000

Number of households in 1000s
Average household income in $1000s of 2001
Market Income = Aggregate household income in billions of $2001

Source: adapted from Census of Canada, various years. CMAs are defined as of 2001

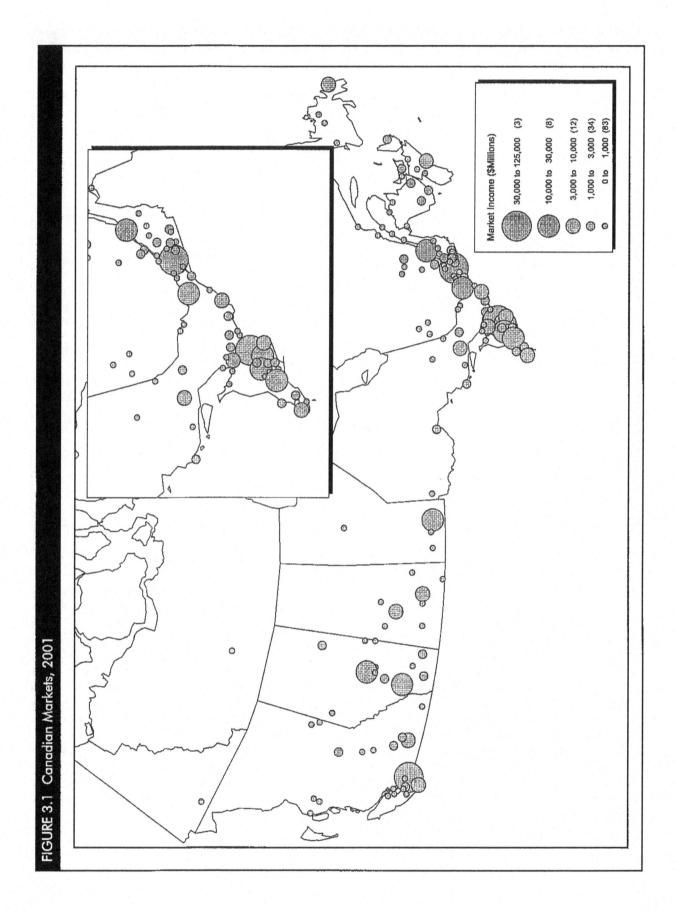

FIGURE 3.1 Canadian Markets, 2001

Market Income ($Millions)

30,000 to 125,000 (3)

10,000 to 30,000 (8)

3,000 to 10,000 (12)

1,000 to 3,000 (34)

0 to 1,000 (83)

TABLE 3.2 Urban Population Growth by City Size and Region, 2001

Number of Cities

Size/Region	BC	Prairies	Ontario	Quebec	Atlantic	Canada
Over 1 m.	1	0	2	1	0	4
300–1,000k	1	3	5	1	1	11
100–300k	2	2	8	3	4	19
30–100k	9	8	15	13	4	49
10–30k	14	11	11	12	9	57
Total	**27**	**24**	**41**	**30**	**18**	**140**

Territories cities grouped with BC.

Urban Population (in 000s)

	BC	Prairies	Ontario	Quebec	Atlantic	Canada
Over 1 m.	1,987	0	5,489*	3,684	0	11,160
300–1,000k	312	2,561	2,194	683	359	6,109
100–300k	295	419	1,197	446	523	2,879
30–100k	540	392	867	619	221	2,638
10–30k	273	184	183	244	170	1,054
Total Urban	3,407	3,556	9,930*	5,676	1,273	23,840
Rural	594	1,518	1,481	1,561	1,013	6,167
Region	**4,001**	**5,074**	**11,411**	**7,237**	**2,286**	**30,007**

*Note that Ontario excludes the 258,000 residents of the Ottawa-Hull CMA who live in Hull. Quebec includes them.

Source: adapted from Census of Canada, various years. CMAs are defined as of 2001

Reproduced with the permission of the Minister responsible for Statistics Canada, 2004.

tion; above that population most Canadian cities grow; below that line the smaller cities are fading away. Only Alberta overcomes this trend, by generating growth for all city sizes, and even rural populations. The Alberta government has maintained a substantial program of transfers to smaller centres for various services, as a spatial redistribution of the oil and gas bonanza.

The maps of market growth, including income variations (Figures 3.2a and 3.2b), present some striking images that elaborate on the Table. In absolute terms the growth is highly concentrated in southern Ontario and Quebec, and to the west of Saskatchewan. Changes in all other locations are very small, whether positive or negative. In terms of growth rates, however, the positive and negative rates differentiate the extensive urban cores in southern Ontario/Quebec, Central Alberta, and the settled parts of southern BC from the peripheral zones to the North. The Canadian frontier is retreating southward at a rapid rate.

The growth in market income (Table 3.1) is particularly important to commercial activities because it provides opportunities for new stores entering a market. Those places that have both grown in number of households and increased the level of household income (e.g. Calgary, Windsor) have substantial advantages over places where neither population nor income levels have grown (Winnipeg, Sudbury). During the 1990s most of the growth in market income resulted from the increase in number of households, as average household size continued to decline. Almost every city increased the number of households by at least ten per cent, but increases in household income were much more variable; with five of the largest CMAs experiencing declines in the level of household income.

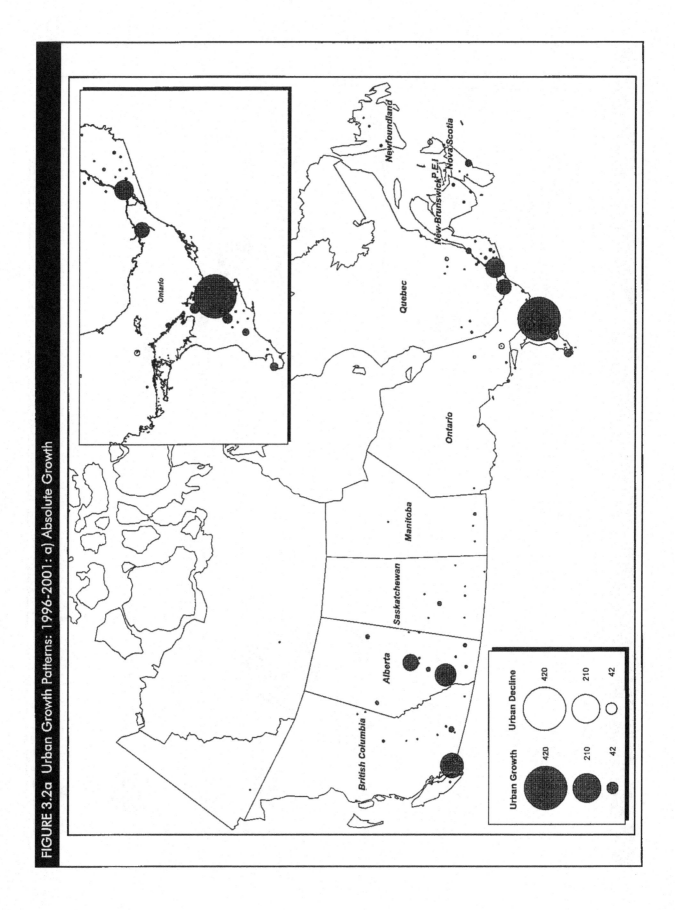

FIGURE 3.2a Urban Growth Patterns: 1996-2001: a) Absolute Growth

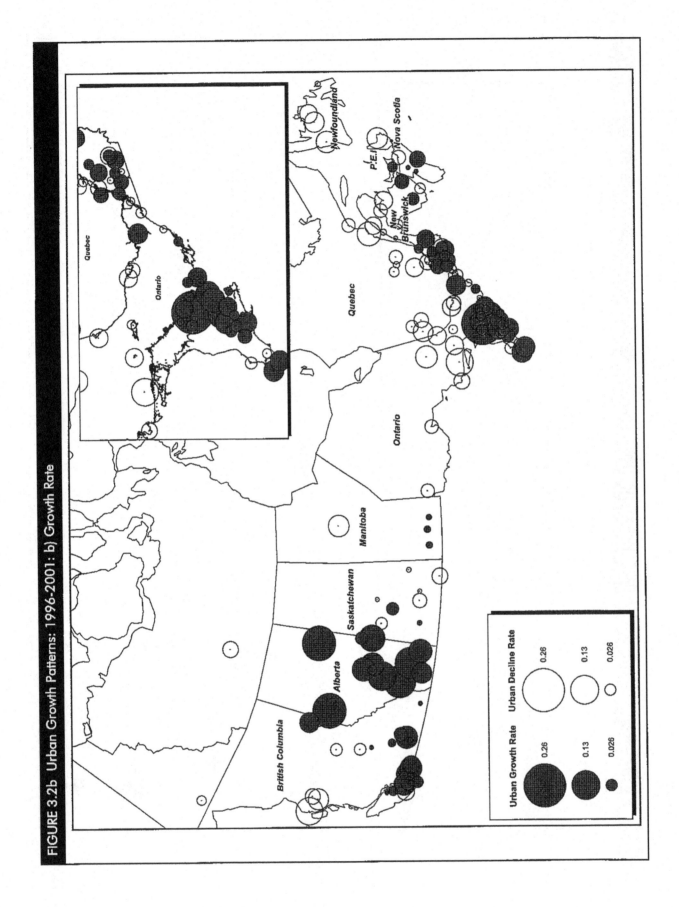

FIGURE 3.2b Urban Growth Patterns: 1996-2001: b) Growth Rate

Urban Growth Rate   Urban Decline Rate

0.26   0.13   0.026   0.26   0.13   0.026

TABLE 3.3 The Size and Growth of Metropolitan Regions

Region	Urban Components	Pop'n, 2001 (000s)	Pop'n Share (%)	Growth 1991-01 (%)	Income/ Capita ($1000s)	Market ($billion)	Market Growth, 1991-2001
Toronto Region	11	6,972	23.1%	17.90	$25.3	179.0	25.4%
Montreal Region	7	3,683	12.3	6.40	22.0	81.1	13.4
Georgia Basin (Vancouver)	8	2,679	8.9	22.20	23.5	62.9	26.0
Alberta Corridor (Calgary/Edmonton)	5	1,983	6.6	18.22	25.5	50.5	36.8
Ottawa-Gatineau	1	1,064	3.5	14.27	27.7	29.5	26.3
Southwestern Ontario (London/Windsor)	8	1,060	3.4	8.29	23.7	25.1	20.8
Quebec City	2	711	2.4	5.98	21.6	15.3	14.6
Winnipeg	2	692	2.3	1.54	21.6	15.0	10.1
Halifax Region	4	465	1.5	6.49	21.6	10.1	15.7
Total Metropolitan Regions	48	19,309	64.2	13.96	24.3	468.4	22.9
Other Urban Centres	92	4,530	15.1	3.26	20.7	93.6	11.9
Rural Areas	0	6,168	20.6	3.39	18.6	114.6	-30.6
Canada	140	30,007	100.0	9.93	22.5	676.6	8.1

Reference: Simmons, J. and Kamikihara, S. 2005. "Canada's Megamarkets." Research Newsletter 2005-10. Toronto: Centre for the Study of Commercial Activity, Ryerson University.

Source: Statistics Canada. Census of Canada, 2001

Reproduced with the permission of the Minister responsible for Statistics Canada, 2006.

The nine megaregions (Table 3.3) have been especially effective in attracting market growth. Between 1991 and 2001 their population increased by almost 14 per cent -- compared to only 3.3 per cent in the rest of the country. This means that more than ninety per cent of Canada's population growth occurred in these nine markets. The concentration of market income is even more dramatic, with these regions increasing by $87billion -- while the rest of the country lost some $35 billion.

The Redistribution of Service Employment. More than three-quarters of the new jobs created in Canada belong to the services, so that changes in the spatial distribution of commercial activity are linked to changes in the market on both the demand side (more people, more services) and the supply side (more services, more jobs). Table 3.5 and Figure 3.3 summarize the patterns of change in commercial employment between 1991 and 2001. Note that the overall growth rate for employment is 15.9 per cent, somewhat lower than the growth of the market at 21.0 per cent. Taxes and savings eat up most of the remainder. The striking feature of the table is the very strong relationship between growth rates and city size -- evident in each region of the country. In the smallest city size group, markets grew at a rate of 12.5 per cent but commercial jobs grew at only 1.6 per cent. In the largest city size category, employment grew at 20 per cent, almost as fast as the market at 22 per cent. Clearly there have been substantial shifts of service activity

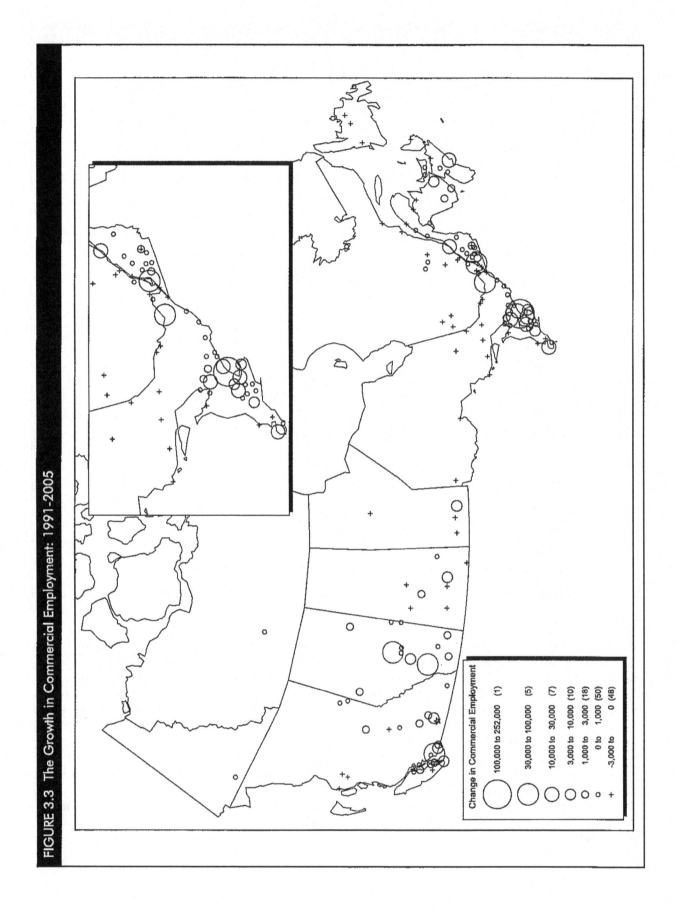

FIGURE 3.3 The Growth in Commercial Employment: 1991-2005

Change in Commercial Employment

100,000 to 252,000 (1)

30,000 to 100,000 (5)

10,000 to 30,000 (7)

3,000 to 10,000 (10)

1,000 to 3,000 (18)

0 to 1,000 (50)

-3,000 to 0 (48)

TABLE 3.4 Urban Growth by City Size and Region: 1991-2001

Urban Population Growth (1000s)

Size/Region	BC	Prairies	Ontario*	Quebec	Atlantic	Canada
Over 1,000,000	384	0	897	238	0	1,519
300,000-1,000,000	24	305	206	37	29	600
100,000-300,000	70	16	127	6	-3	217
30,000-100,000	78	38	14	13	10	153
10,000-30,000	18	8	5	-3	-8	20
Total Urban	574	367	1,249	291	28	2,508
Rural	59	80	76	51	-64	202
Total Region	633	447	1,325	342	-36	2,710

* Ontario excludes the 20,000 population growth that occurred in Hull. It is credited to Quebec.

Population Growth Rate (Per Cent)

Size/Region	BC	Prairies	Ontario	Quebec	Atlantic	Canada
Over 1,000,000	19.3%	...	16.0	6.4	...	17.4
300,000-1,000,000	...	11.9	9.4	5.4	8.0	10.2
100,000-300,000	18.3	3.9	10.6	1.4	-0.5	7.4
30,000-100,000	14.5	9.6	1.6	2.1	4.5	5.6
10,000-30,000	6.5	4.3	2.9	-1.3	-4.8	1.9
Total	20.3	11.5	14.2	5.3	2.2	11.8

Reproduced with the permission of the Minister responsible for Statistics Canada, 2006.

TABLE 3.5 The Growth in Commercial Employment: 1991-2001

Absolute Growth (1000s)

Size/Region	BC	Prairies	Ontario	Quebec	Atlantic	Canada
Over 1,000,000	99.6	...	251.2	80.7	...	431.5
300,000-1,000,000	...	114.8	86.0	12.3	12.0	225.0
100,000-300,000	25.8	4.5	25.7	0.2	4.4	60.7
30,000-100,000	12.7	8.9	19.1	0.0	1.7	42.4
10,000-30,000	1.7	3.8	1.0	-1.2	-2.2	3.1
Total	139.9	132.0	383.0	91.9	16.0	762.7

Growth Rate (Per Cent)

Size/Region	BC	Prairies	Ontario	Quebec	Atlantic	Canada
Over 1,000,000	23.9%	...	24.6	11.2	...	20.0
300,000-1,000,000	...	21.5	15.0	8.6	16.1	17.0
100,000-300,000	24.7	4.9	12.9	0.3	4.4	10.5
30,000-100,000	14.4	13.3	8.7	-0.1	4.1	7.9
10,000-30,000	3.2	9.0	3.0	-3.0	-7.0	1.6
Total	21.1	18.0	18.7	8.3	6.4	15.9

Territories cities are grouped with BC.

Reference: Simmons, Jim. 2005b. "The Changing Pattern of Commercial Specialization." Research Report 2005-8. Toronto: Centre for the Study of Commercial Activity, Ryerson University.

Source: Statistics Canada. Census of Canada, 2001.

TABLE 3.6 The Variations in Specialization, 2001

The Market.

	Population	Income per Capita	Centrality	Wholesale	Recreation
1.	Toronto	Wood Buffalo AB	Wetaskiwin AB	LLoydminster AB	Squamish BC
2.	Montreal	Yellowknife NWT	Grande Prairie AB	Cowansville QC	Orillia ON
3.	Vancouver	Calgary	Camrose AB	Wetaskiwin AB	St. Catharines
4.	Ottawa	Ottawa	Yorkton SK	Fort St. John AB	Stratford ON
5.	Calgary	Toronto	Lloydminster AB	Grande Prairie AB	Collingwood ON
6.	Edmonton	Kitimat BC	Moncton	Moncton	Yorkton SK
7.	Quebec	Whitehorse YK	Red Deer AB	Swift Current SK	Summerside PE
8.	Winnipeg	Windsor	Ft. St. John BC	Truro NS	Kamloops BC
9.	Hamilton	Labrador City NF	Swift Current SK	Yorkton SK	Wetaskiwin AB
10.	London	Guelph	Riviere du Loup	Rouyn-Noranda	Lethbridge AB
131.	Estevan SK	Dolbeau QC	Cape Breton	Squamish BC	Wood Buffalo AB
132.	Elliot Lake ON	Kentville NS	Chatham ON	Prince Rupert BC	Tillsonburg ON
133.	Cowansville QC	Matane QC	Midland ON	Cape Breton	Labrador City NF
134.	Brooks AB	Elliot Lake ON	Campbellton NB	Ottawa	Amos QC
135.	Hawkesbury ON	Cowansville QC	La Tuque QC	Kitimat BC	Leamington ON
136.	Lachute QC	Lachute QC	Shawinigan QC	Courtenay BC	Corner Brook NF
137.	Gander NF	Grand Falls NF	Petawawa ON	La Tuque QC	Petawawa ON
138.	Wetaskiwin AB	Portage la Pr. MB	Elliot Lake ON	Campbellton NB	Grand Falls NF
139.	Kitimat BC	Campbellton NB	Port Alberni BC	Petawawa ON	Baie Comeau QC
140.	Labrador C. NF	Cape Breton NS	Kitimat BC	Elliot Lake ON	Kitimat BC

Reference: Simmons, Jim. 2005b. "The Changing Pattern of Commercial Specialization." Research Report 2005-8. Toronto: Centre for the Study of Commercial Activity, Ryerson University.

Source: Statistics Canada. Census of Canada, 2001

up the commercial hierarchy. In fact, the two largest city size categories absorbed 86 per cent of the employment growth in the commercial sectors. Regionally, the variations more or less reflect the growth of the market -- although the two regions without a city in the largest size category obtained less than their share of growth.

The striking feature of the map (Figure 3.3) is the large number of cities that have actually lost commercial jobs, even where markets have grown (compare to Figure 3.2). Most of the cities that lost employment are small and peripheral, with many of them on the northern frontier -- or otherwise isolated. Only half a dozen are part of the Windsor-Quebec Corridor. A total of 48 cities -- about one third of the total -- lost commercial employment. The largest cities to lose commercial service jobs were Cape Breton, Chatham ON, Trois Rivieres, Greater Sudbury and Saguenay -- each with more than 100,000 population. Most of the extreme values, however, occur in smaller centres. For the most part high growth locations are found near the rapidly growing metropolitan areas: Barrie and Oshawa near Toronto, and Abbotsford and Chilliwack near Vancouver. The slow growth locations are isolated resource-based communities.

Almost eighty per cent of the variation in the growth rate of commercial employment is explained by the growth of the market:

Employment =
-0.0234 + 1.311 Population + 0.233 Income/Capita
$\qquad$ (0.061) $\qquad$ (0.095)
$R^2 = 0.793$

[Please note that the figures under the regression coefficients are standard errors of the corresponding coefficients. The variables are are growth rates in Population and and Per Capita Income.]

and the population parameter suggests that a growing city attracts disproportionate amounts of commercial activity. In fact, a fifty per cent growth rate of population generates a seventy per cent increase in commercial employment, as commercial activity is attracted from nearby competing centres.

Specialization in Services. Research at the CSCA suggests that the various cities within Canada play different roles in the provision of services. Some cities may be strong in recreational activities, while others may specialize in financial services. These patterns of specialization may modify the trade areas of cities – the spatial extent of their markets – as well as affecting their occupational structure, and internal commercial structure. The original paper (Simmons, Jones and Bylov, 2002) measured and mapped a variety of specializations for different services, but the recent version (Simmons, 2005b) focuses on the overall measure of commercial specialization, called centrality, that can be interpreted as the extent to which the city serves markets lying outside its own borders. It asks "which cities reach the largest markets, relative to their own size?" For example, Toronto provides services to all of Canada -- which makes Toronto a major distribution point and attracts all sorts of foreign firms that want to reach the Canadian market. Which smaller cities have similar roles within various regions, and which cities simply buy their goods and services from other places?

Centrality is an important element in the choice of a store or distribution centre to reach a larger market, but how do we evaluate it? We know that population size and income per capita together determine the amount of commercial activity in a city, so we must control for their effects. The usual method is regression analysis, and since the distributions of city size and income per capita are both log-normal, we apply a log-linear regression model. The model estimates the amount of commercial employment that should be generated in a community of given population and income level, and compares the estimate to the observed value. The difference (either positive or negative) can be interpreted as the surplus (or deficit) of facilities, hence a measure of centrality.

This is how it works. Consider the equation for total commercial employment -- wholesale, retail, finance and commercial services:

$$\log \text{Employment} = -2{,}994 + 1.054 \,(\log \text{Population}) + 0.467 \,(\log \text{Income/Capita}) \quad R^2 = 0.992$$

All three variables in the analysis are converted to logarithms so that the intercept A is simply a measure of scale (the size of the commercial sector when the logs of population and income per capita are set to zero). The regression coefficients B1 and B2 indicate the relationship between commercial employment and the two independent variables. The fact that the regression coefficient for

population (1.054) is greater than one indicates that the commercial employment increases disproportionately with population. A city that is ten times larger than another (plus one on a log scale) will have eleven times more employment. In contrast, the regression parameter for income per capita is less than one, which suggests that an increase in income per capita is only partially captured as local consumption. The increase may go to taxes or savings, or spent in larger cities, or for travel.

The coefficient of determination (R^2) indicates what proportion of the variance in employment is explained by the other two variables. In this case the equation predicts 99.2 per cent of the variation in commercial employment, which is a substantial achievement. The variations in commercial specialization among cities are fairly minor deviations within the overall relationships. Conversely, the size of the market explains almost all the variation in commercial activity among cities.

The equation provides an 'all other things being equal' prediction of local commercial employment, to which each urban area can be compared. The city with the largest positive residual (more jobs than expected), hence the greatest relative centrality, is Wetaskiwin AB, an agricultural community serving a prosperous agricultural region half way between Edmonton and Red Deer in Alberta. The residual from a log relationship is actually the logarithm of the ratio of the observed to expected values, and for Wetaskiwin this value translates into a 'surplus' of 15.0 per cent of the predicted commercial employment. This amounts to about 270 jobs more than the expected total of 1815; in other words, Wetaskiwin as a market is 15 per cent larger than it appears to be. At the other end of the list, the largest negative residual occurred in Kitimat BC, which generates 20.2 per cent fewer jobs than predicted, or 1580 jobs instead of 1980. Kitimat sits in the northern wilderness at the dead end of a highway. As a prospective store location, the Kitimat market is substantially smaller than it appears.

Large metropolitan areas are seldom found at either end of the centrality distribution. With their large markets and complex economies, they are most likely to achieve average levels of commercial activity. The places with the greatest centrality (Table 3.6) are mostly agricultural central places in Western Canada, cities that are immersed within a network of smaller settlements (see also Figure 3.3). Those with the lowest values, in contrast, are cities on the frontiers, near the ocean or the northern wilderness. Their trade areas are restricted by the geography, and, because they are positioned at the end of the line, they are unable to pass along goods and services to other places. Low values are also found in the older industrial centres of Central Canada, such as Chatham and Shawinigan. It is important to emphasize the strength of the regional pattern in these analyses. Centrality, like income levels, is not so much the result of local competitive struggles or location advantage, but a reflection of the local economic base (farming or manufacturing or business service). Patterns of centrality will evolve as Canada's space-economy evolves over time.

The overall evaluation of market centrality ignores the diverse specializations among commercial activities. Implicitly it assumes that all cities have the same composition of commercial facilities, and thus the same proportion of wholesaling or financial employment. But we know that this is not so. It is possible to use the same procedure to identify cities that are specialized in wholesaling, recreation, or financial activities; and are therefore especially attractive markets for firms that provide these services, or that share the same pool of customers. The results vary with the sector, as shown in Table 3.6. Wholesale identifies a significant economic specialization that exaggerates the centrality effect. The central places of Western Canada show up strongly, along with regional centres such as Moncton and Truro in the East. The cities that lack wholesaling, however, include the same set of peripheral locations as the commercial activity in general. Recreation shows a quite different pattern, that confirms our intuitive list of 'tourist' towns: Squamish (Whistler), Orillia (Muskoka), St. Catharines (Niagara Falls); as well as identifying the set of places that one would least likely choose for a holiday.

Chapter 8

CANADA'S MEGAMARKETS
Jim Simmons and Shizue Kamikihara

Introduction

The last two Census of Canada confirm that Canada has become a metropolitan nation. Not only do Canadians live in cities; they live in large cities, with 58 per cent of the population now located within only fifteen cities with population greater than 300,000 (Table 1). This spatial concentration of population will increase as long as immigration -- the largest source of population growth -- and service employment -- the major source of new jobs -- continue to be attracted to the largest cities. At the same time, Statistics Canada points out another form of population concentration: the cities that are growing -- in all size groups -- are increasingly clustered around the very largest places: **Toronto, Montreal, Vancouver and Calgary/Edmonton** (Statistics Canada, 2002). This paper takes a look at these metropolitan regions or megamarkets, their characteristics and growth, and speculates about their futures. What are the implications for market analysis?

The report is divided into six sections. The first explores the concept of the megamarkets, and defines nine megamarkets within Canada. The second section compares the markets with each other and against the country as a whole, and the third describes the individual markets. Section four discusses how these metropolitan regions grow, followed by a discussion of the projections to the year 2026. A final section summarizes the findings of the paper.

Defining the Megamarkets

The notion of "city-regions" or metropolitan regions was first raised in a systematic fashion by Bourne (2000), and has been partially operationalized by Statistics Canada (2002). The definition of megamarkets adopted in this report began with Statistics Canada's maps for the four largest metropolitan clusters, and was later extended to include five others (Figure 1 and Table 2): **Ottawa-Gatineau, Quebec City, and Winnipeg** are each large

TABLE 1. The Canadian Urban System, 2001

Number of Cities Size/Region	BC	Prairies	Ontario	Quebec	Atlantic	Canada
Over 1 m.	1	0	2	1	0	4
300-1,000k.	1	3	5	1	1	11
100-300k.	2	2	8	3	4	19
30-100k.	9	8	15	13	4	49
10-30k.	14	11	11	12	9	57
Total	27	24	41	30	18	140

Urban Population (in 000s)	BC	Prairies	Ontario	Quebec	Atlantic	Canada
Over 1 m.	1,987	0	5,489*	3,684	0	11,160
300-1,000k.	312	2,561	2,194	683	359	6,109
100-300k.	295	419	1,197	446	523	2,879
30-100k.	540	392	867	619	221	2,638
10-30k.	273	184	183	244	170	1,054
Total Urban	3,407	3,556	9,929*	5,676	1,272	23,840
Rural	594	1,518	1,481	1,561	1,013	6,167
Region	4,001	5,074	11,410	7,237	2,285	30,007

Territories cities grouped with BC.

*Note that Ontario excludes the 258,000 residents of the Ottawa-Gatineau CMA who live in Gatineau. Quebec includes them.

Source: Statistics Canada, Census of Canada, 2001.

FIGURE 1. The Metropolitan Regions

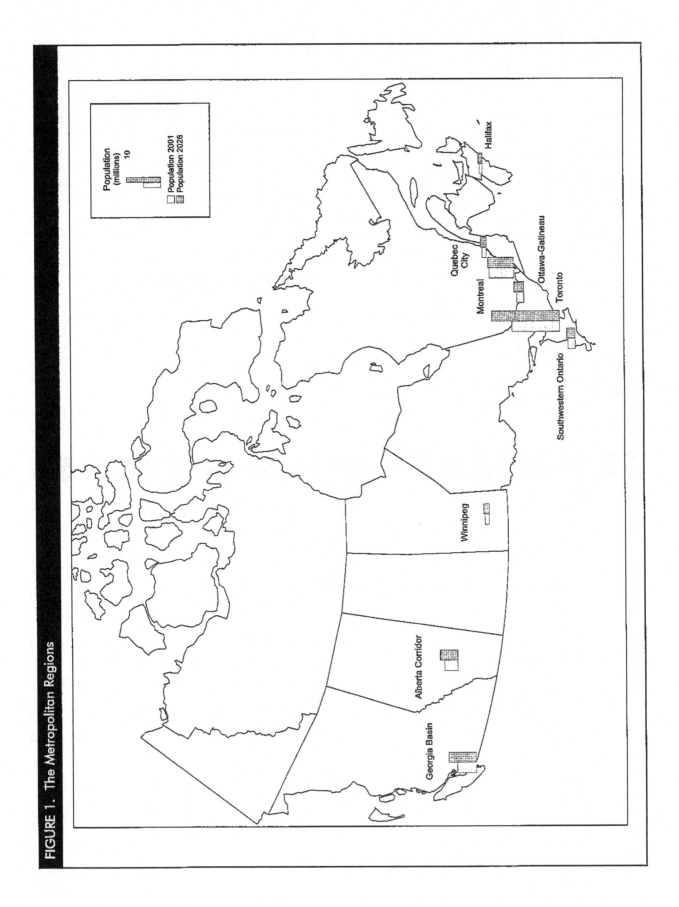

but relatively isolated metropolitan areas, that share a regional market with a larger competitor. Ottawa and Quebec City depend on their specialized political functions to maintain a share of the market. **Halifax** is closely linked to three neighbouring urban areas to form a metropolitan region for the Atlantic region. The Southwestern Ontario region is the most difficult to justify since it includes seven urban areas, widely dispersed. London is the largest place and the traditional regional centre, but it must compete with Toronto (or Kitchener within the Toronto region) to serve the regional market. The next metropolitan region may well emerge in British Columbia's Okanagan area.

Ideally, it would be preferable to define the metropolitan regions as contiguous markets, based on census subdivisions. In practice, it is much simpler to aggregate the component urban areas. Little is lost by excluding nearby rural areas, since the latter are typically small and weakly integrated with the core urban centre. A more serious debate surrounds the outer boundary of the metropolitan region. At what distance does one include or exclude potential urban components? Table 2 indicates considerable variation depending on the local situation. Calgary and Edmonton are almost 300 kilometres apart, but linked by road and air traffic to create a growth corridor. Montreal and Ottawa are only 200 km. apart, but there are no intermediate urban areas and little growth in between them. London and Windsor are 195 kilometres apart, but much of the Southwestern Ontario region is assigned to contiguous urban centres.

Comparing the Megamarkets

The metropolitan regions can be studied in two ways: first, in aggregate, to be compared with the sum of the other urban areas defined by Statistics Canada, and the remaining rural areas; and second, as individual entities (see Table 3). In aggregate the nine study areas, with a total population of 19.3 million within 48 urban areas, represent 64 per cent of the Canadian population, while occupying less than one per cent (0.844) of the land area. The remaining 92 urban areas contribute only 4.5 million population, and there is an additional 6.2 million population in rural areas and communities with less than 10,000 people. Canada is indeed a metropolitan nation. As well, the process of metropolitanization is accelerating. Over the last decade the metropolitan regions have collectively grown at a rate of 14 per cent, compared to only 3.3 per cent for the rest of the country. In contrast to the 1990s, the growth differentials since 1971 are more modest: fifty

per cent versus 23 per cent. Note that there is very little difference between the growth rates of rural areas and the growth rate of other urban centres. The latter range in population from 10,000 to 225,000 (Saskatoon), with many of them located in isolated parts of the periphery (Simmons, 2005).

The individual metropolitan regions represent all parts of Canada and vary in size by more than an order of magnitude. Toronto, including Hamilton, Kitchener, St. Catharines and Oshawa, approached seven million population in 2001, almost one quarter of Canada's population. Montreal was a little more than half of Toronto's population, with Vancouver about 38 per cent, and the other six nodes ranging from 1,983,000 to 465,000. The surprising megamarket on the list is Southwestern Ontario, the region lying between London and Windsor, which approaches Ottawa in total population. In general the densities of the metropolitan regions are related to the population, although Montreal is clearly higher in density than the rest, and Halifax substantially lower.

Although in aggregate the metropolitan regions grow more rapidly than other parts of the country, metropolitan status does not guarantee growth. Vancouver, Calgary/Edmonton, Toronto and Ottawa have grown more rapidly than the country as a whole since 1991 (and 1971), but the others lag behind -- although they may be growth magnets within their own regions. In recent years metropolitan growth has been driven by immigration, as well as the ability of the surrounding region to support services and provide population for the regional centre.

Table 4 describes the metropolitan regions as markets, based on the total household income as reported in the Census 2001. The market size and growth rates simply confirm the overall patterns that were displayed in Table 3. Income per capita increases with the size of the market, although Montreal and Ottawa vary slightly. The final three measures explore the levels of commercial activity. Service employees include all the commercial services: trade, finance, business and personal services. The number of employees per million dollars of market income indicates the degree of commercial specialization. Vancouver and Halifax have the highest values, while Ottawa (government) and Southwestern Ontario (industrial) are the least commercial. Rural areas are the least commercial locations of all. Retail sales and the ratio of sales to the size of the market focus on a particular kind of service activity that contrasts Alberta (high) with Ottawa (low). Calgary has a young and relatively

TABLE 2. Defining the Metropolitan Regions

	Population 2001(000's)	Area (km. sq.)	Growth(%) 1996-2001	Distance to Core (km.)
Toronto	6972.3	16,296.7	17.9	
Toronto CMA	4,682.9	5,902.7	16.7	0
Hamilton CMA	662.4	1,371.2	9.5	74
Kitchener CMA	414.3	827.0	14.0	104
St. Catharines-Niagara CMA	377.0	1,406.4	3.3	110
Oshawa CMA	298.3	903.2	19.0	55
Barrie CA	148.5	897.5	34.5	105
Guelph CA	117.3	378.5	16.3	80
Peterborough CA	102.4	1,199.8	4.1	135
Brantford CA	86.4	71.6	4.9	100
Kawartha Lakes CA	69.2	3,059.2	8.5	135
Port Hope CA	15.6	279.0	3.0	110
Montreal	3,682.9	4,895.7	6.4	
Montreal CMA	3,426.4	4047.4	6.4	0
Saint-Jean CA	79.6	226.3	7.7	40
Saint-Hyacinthe CA	49.5	167.3	0.5	64
Sorel-Tracy CA	41.0	179.6	-8.7	87
Salaberry-de-Valleyfield CA	39.0	106.8	-2.8	61
Joliette CA	35.8	59.6	6.5	75
Lachute CA	11.6	108.7	-1.5	65
Georgia Basin (Vancouver)	2,679.2	7,275.6	22.2	
Vancouver CMA	1987.0	2,878.5	19.3	0
Victoria CMA	311.9	695.3	7.7	67*
Abbotsford CMA	147.4	625.9	22.9	90
Nanaimo CA	85.7	1,279.0	17.1	27*
Chilliwack CA	69.8	1,252.6	21.2	115
Duncan CA	38.8	371.7	14.4	79*
Parksville CA	24.3	81.5	28.2	62*
Squamish CA	14.4	91.1	17.8	60
Alberta Corridor (Calgary-Edmonton)	1,983.0	14,604.3	18.2	
Calgary CMA	951.4	5,083.0	20.8	0
Edmonton CMA	937.8	9,418.6	10.3	294
Red Deer CA	67.7	60.9	14.2	145
Camrose CA	14.9	25.9	9.8	274
Wetaskiwin CA	11.2	15.9	4.1	233
Ottawa-Gatineau	1,063.7	5,318.4	14.3	
Ottawa-Hull	1,063.7	5,318.4	14.3	0
Southwestern Ontario (London)	1,059.9	7,210.4	8.3	
London CMA	432.5	2,333.4	7.8	0
Windsor CMA	307.9	1,022.5	12.6	195
Chatham-Kent CA	107.7	2,470.8	-2.0	110
Sarnia CA	88.3	799.8	-4.3	109
Leamington CA	46.8	509.3	13.9	180
Woodstock CA	33.1	30.4	8.4	46
Stratford CA	29.7	21.9	6.7	60
Tillsonburg CA	14.1	22.3	14.6	70
Quebec City	710.9	3,352.5	6.0	
Quebec CMA	682.8	3,154.3	5.4	0
Saint-Georges CA	28.1	198.2	10.4	102
Winnipeg	691.9	6,181.5	1.5	
Winnipeg CMA	671.3	4,151.5	1.6	0
Portage la Prairie CA	20.6	2,030.0	-1.9	81
Halifax	465.4	10,902.2	6.5	
Halifax CMA	359.2	5,495.5	8.0	0
Truro CA	44.3	2,732.5	3.6	89
New Glasgow CA	36.7	2,066.5	-5.4	151
Kentville CA	25.2	607.7	4.3	110

TABLE 3. The Size and Growth of Metropolitan Regions

Region	Urban Components	Population, 2001 (000s)	Population Share (%)	Population Density (Per Km²)	Growth 1991-2001(%)	Growth 1971-2001(%)
Toronto Region	11	6,972	23.1%	427.8	17.90	60.5
Montreal Region	7	3,683	12.3	752.3	6.40	19.6
Georgia Basin (Vancouver)	8	2,679	8.9	368.3	22.20	86.3
Alberta Corridor (Calgary/Edmonton)	5	1,983	6.6	135.8	18.22	93.1
Ottawa-Gatineau	1	1,064	3.5	200.0	14.27	58.2
Southwestern Ontario (London/Windsor)	8	1,060	3.4	147.0	8.29	22.1
Quebec City	2	711	2.4	212.1	5.98	35.5
Winnipeg	2	692	2.3	111.9	1.54	18.4
Halifax Region	4	465	1.5	42.7	6.49	32.9
Total Metropolitan Regions	48	19,309	64.2	253.9	13.96	49.8
Other Urban Centres	92	4,530	15.1	...	3.26	22.7
Rural Areas	0	6,168	20.6	...	3.39	23.6
Canada	140	30,007	100.0	0.0033	9.93	39.1

TABLE 4. The Metropolitan Regions as Markets

Region	Market ($billion)	Market Growth, 1991-01	Income/ Capita ($000s)	Service Employment/ Market*	Retail Sales ($billion)	Sales/ Market
Toronto Region	179.0	25.3%	$25.3	11.14	$75.0	41.9%
Montreal Region	81.1	13.4	22.0	11.86	37.2	45.9
Georgia Basin (Vancouver)	62.9	26.0	23.5	12.04	28.9	46.0
Alberta Corridor (Calgary/Edmonton)	50.5	36.8	25.5	11.83	26.4	52.2
Ottawa-Gatineau	29.5	26.3	27.7	9.60	11.3	38.4
Southwestern Ontario (London/Windsor)	25.1	20.8	23.7	9.77	12.3	49.2
Quebec City	15.3	14.6	21.6	11.70	7.8	50.6
Winnipeg	15.0	10.1	21.6	11.59	7.2	47.8
Halifax Region	10.1	15.7	21.6	12.39	5.5	55.0
Total Metropolitan Regions	468.4	22.9	24.3	11.35	211.5	45.1
Other Urban Centres	93.6	11.9	20.7	11.07	54.4	58.1
Rural Areas	114.6	-30.6	18.6	5.75	46.7	40.7
Canada	676.6	7.5	22.5	10.37	312.6	46.2

* Employees per $million

affluent population, and a high degree of commercial development (Simmons and Hernandez, 2004). In general, though, the larger the city, the lower the proportion of income that is allocated to retail. Alberta aside, this table may be the spatial expression of the widely noted inverse relationship between income level and the proportion of income allocated to retail.

In addition to size, income and growth, several aspects of lifestyle may affect consumption and marketing (Table 5). The recent history of the regions is recorded in the age structure. High growth regions such as Calgary have younger populations, while slow growth regions such as Winnipeg or Quebec City have older populations. Rural areas are distinguished by high proportions of the very young and the very old cohorts, with lower proportions in the working age population. The metropolitan regions are strongly differentiated from other locations by their access to immigration. One quarter of their population was born outside Canada, and more than twenty per cent grew up speaking a language that was neither French nor English. In smaller cities and rural areas only five or six per cent of the population is foreign-born. But there are striking variations among the metropolitan regions themselves, where the foreign-born proportion ranges from 2.8 per cent in Quebec City to more than thirty per cent in Toronto and Vancouver. Of course, the proportion of francophones also varies widely, from 95 per cent in Quebec City to less than two per cent in Alberta and Vancouver.

Individual Markets

The metropolitan regions also vary widely in their internal spatial structure as shown in Figures 2a to 2e. While Halifax, Quebec City, Ottawa and Winnipeg are essentially unipolar cities, with a few small outliers; the larger and more rapidly growing metropolitan regions display more complex patterns. The five maps show the distribution of the market, based on the household income in each three-digit postal code (FSA). There are more than 1,500 postal codes in Canada, ranging in size up to 30,000 population, and they suggest the pattern of settlement clustering or dispersion within each region. The network of expressways clearly shapes the spatial distribution by reducing the travel time in certain directions. Individual regions are also affected by topographical features (lakes and rivers), or by international boundaries.

TABLE 5. The Metropolitan Regions as Lifestyles

Region	Population (000s)	Age Structure (per cent)				Born Abroad	Mother French	Tongue Other
		0-14	15-44	45-64	65+			
Toronto Region	6,972	19.7	45.2	23.0	12.1	35.3%	1.5%	31.0%
Montreal Region	3,683	18.0	44.1	24.8	13.1	17.0	68.3	8.9
Georgia Basin (Vancouver)	2,679	17/5	44.6	24.5	13.4	32.2	1.3	30.5
Alberta Corridor (Calgary/Edmonton)	1,983	19.7	48.0	22.4	9.9	18.7	1.9	18.1
Ottawa-Gatineau	1,064	19.3	46.0	23.9	10.8	17.4	31.8	15.3
Southwestern Ontario (London/Windsor)	1,060	19.6	43.4	23.3	13.7	15.9	2.5	16.1
Quebec City	711	16.2	43.6	27.2	13.0	2.8	95.0	1.7
Winnipeg	692	19.2	43.7	23.4	13.8	15.9	4.2	19.1
Halifax Region	465	18.4	43.1	24.8	13.4	5.8	2.4	3.7
Total Metropolitan Regions	19,309	18.8	45.0	23.7	12.3	25.1	19.5	21.5
Other Urban Centres	4,530	18.6	42.8	24.9	13.7	6.3	26.7	6.0
Rural Areas	6,168	20.2	40.0	25.5	14.3	5.1	28.6	12.5
Canada	30,007	19.1	43.7	24.3	13.0	18.2	22.5	17.3

The 'Golden Horseshoe', centred on Toronto, now stretches from Peterborough and Barrie to the North, Kitchener to the West, and St. Catharines-Niagara to the South. It was first identified more than sixty years ago when one of the first Expressways in Canada, the Queen Elizabeth Way, linked Toronto and Niagara Falls along the base of the Niagara Escarpment. Although bounded to the South by Lake Ontario and the U.S. border, the Horseshoe continues to incorporate existing settlements to the North and East. As Table 6 indicates, some of the growth in these communities is spillover from Toronto itself. The Toronto CMA has lost more than 55,000 migrants to other cities in the region over the last five years.

Toronto's size and rate of growth affects development (and land prices) throughout Southern Ontario, but especially those places within 200 kilometres. As well, the Horseshoe includes four other major cities: Hamilton, Kitchener, St. Catharines and Oshawa. These are industrial nodes that are linked to the North American market by road and rail. Pearson Airport, the largest in Canada, is located at the very centre of the region. Barrie, Lindsay and Peterborough are the points of entry to 'cottage country', which is increasingly attractive to part-time workers and retirees. The mostly like direction of future growth is the Northwest.

The **Montreal region** is far more compact than the Horseshoe, and the relatively slow rate of growth has not spilled over to adjacent urban areas in the same way as Toronto. To the Northwest the St. Jerome agglomeration has already been integrated into Montreal, and it leads to the Laurentian recreation area. Montreal has long since expanded beyond the original island in the St. Lawrence. Older industrial areas such as Joliette, Sorel, St. Hyacinthe and St. Jean have grown rather slowly, but are gradually being drawn into the metropolitan region by improved transportation facilities. Although the connections to Quebec City to the Northeast are well-developed, there has been very little development into Ontario (toward Ottawa) to the West. Although the region's future growth is projected to be modest, expansion will likely take place around St. Jean and towards Sherbrooke to the East.

The name '**Georgia Basin**' suggests the unique topography of the Vancouver region. The growth of the city of Vancouver has been tightly constrained, initially by the surrounding waterways -- Burrard Inlet and False Creek -- and later by the mountains of the North Shore, the Pacific Ocean to the West, and the U.S. border to the South. Continued rapid growth has been channelled eastward into Abbotsford and Chilliwack. Both places have absorbed out-migrants from the central city.

The other growth frontier for the Georgia Basin is the southern part of Vancouver Island, in Victoria, the oldest city on the west coast, and more recently in Duncan, Nanaimo and Parksville. While these places are two or three hours from Vancouver by ferry, there are frequent air connections to connect spillover businesses and retirees from the big city. Vancouver's airport, shopping, and cultural activities serve the entire region. The projected growth rate for the region is one of the highest in Canada, but the locations for development continue to be limited. Future growth may be vertical, in the form of higher density, as well as eastward along the Fraser Valley, and on Vancouver Island, as growth is diverted away from the central city.

The **Alberta Corridor** is quite different from other metropolitan regions: bi-polar, linear, and more than 300 kilometres in length. The region is more concept than reality; not bounded, but linked together by a transportation corridor (road, rail, air) that links together the two main cities. The concept recognizes the dual growth nodes of Edmonton and Calgary, the carefully balanced growth in the two cities as orchestrated by the province, and the transportation axis. But at the same time, most locations along the corridor are undoubtedly rural, and most future growth will occur in the two nodes at either end. The leading intermediate settlement, Red Deer has only 67,000 people. While Edmonton centres a large farming region that extends east and west, Calgary's urbanization contrasts strongly with the low density ranching country that surrounds it.

Service firms will likely require two outlets to serve the Alberta corridor, located in both major cities. These two metropolitan areas account for more than 95 per cent of the regional population, and will generate almost all the future growth. With the only urban competition in western Canada more than 1000 miles away in Vancouver, the corridor will absorb most of the growth in the Prairies, and especially in the widely distributed energy sectors. In 2001 the Corridor was notably younger and more affluent than other metropolitan regions, and this gap may intensify, as the provincial government continues to redistribute resource revenues into public services.

The **Southwestern Ontario Region** is another dis-

FIGURE 2a. The Largest Markets - Toronto

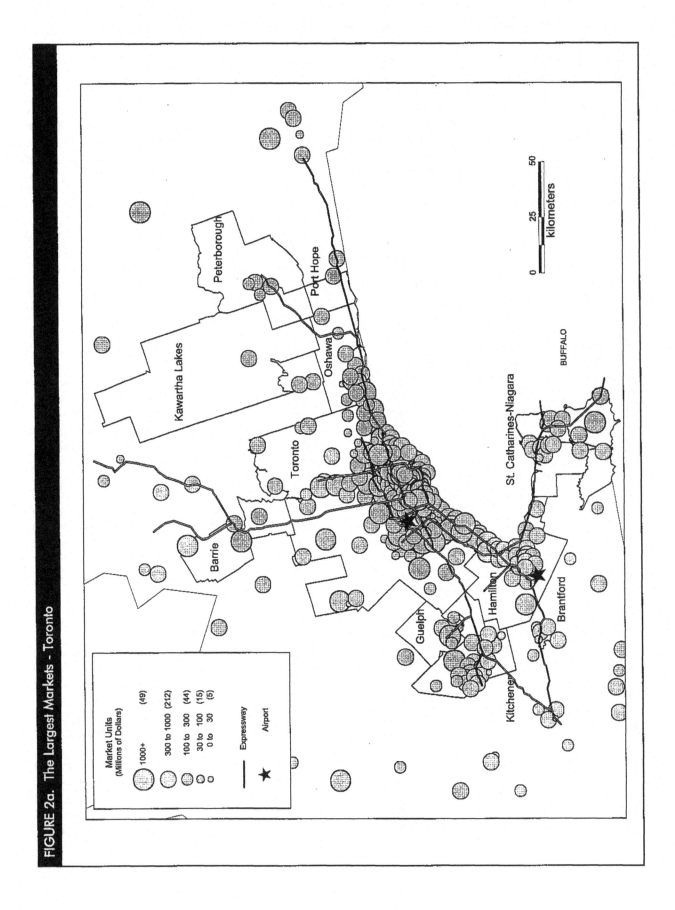

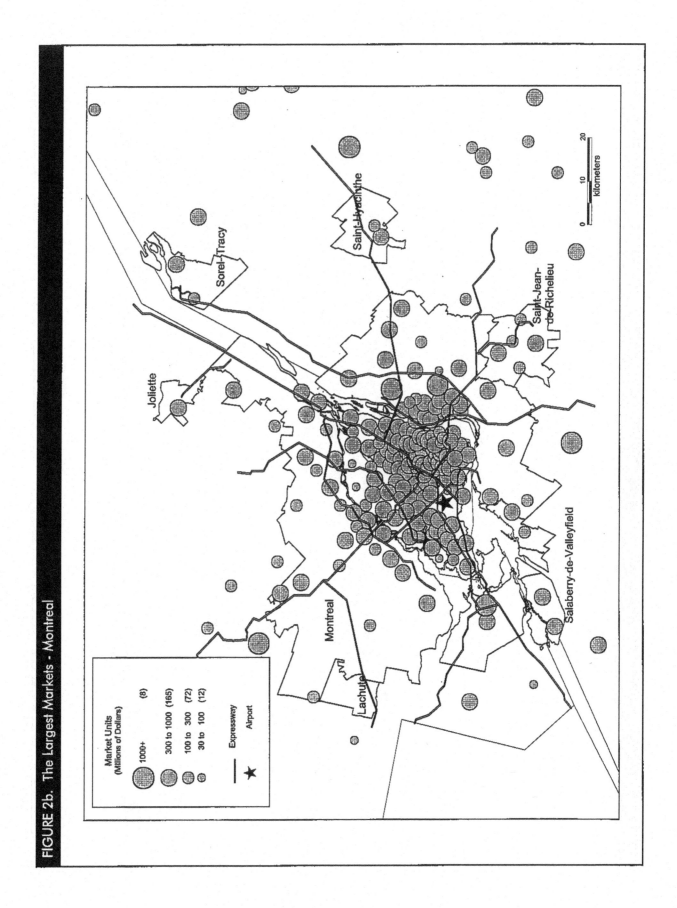

FIGURE 2b. The Largest Markets - Montreal

Market Units
(Millions of Dollars)

1000+ (8)
300 to 1000 (165)
100 to 300 (72)
30 to 100 (12)

— Expressway
★ Airport

Joliette
Sorel-Tracy
Saint-Hyacinthe
Saint-Jean-de-Richelieu
Salaberry-de-Valleyfield
Montreal
Lachute

169

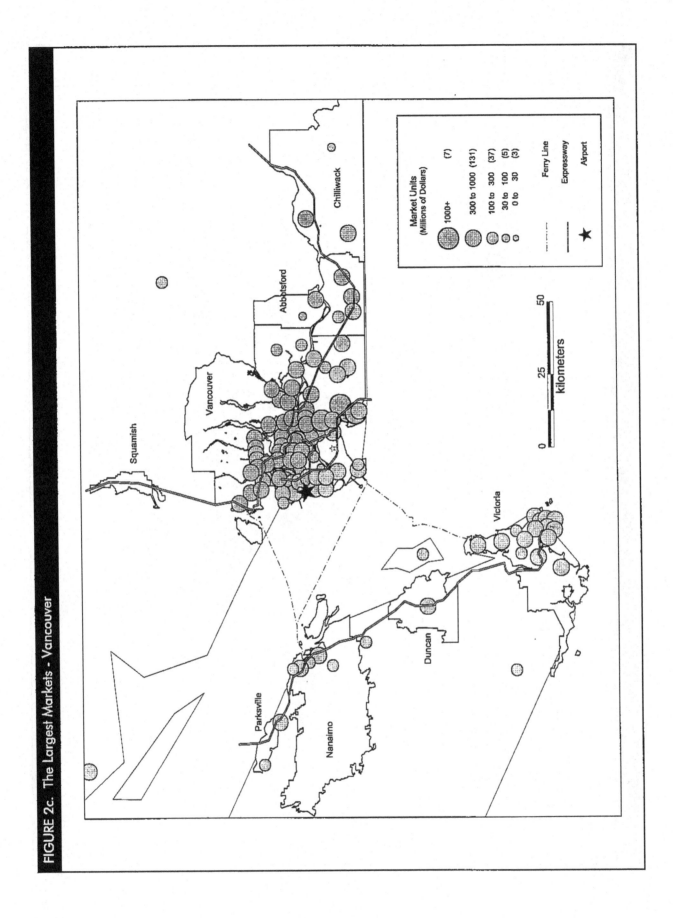

FIGURE 2c. The Largest Markets - Vancouver

FIGURE 2d. The Largest Markets - Alberta

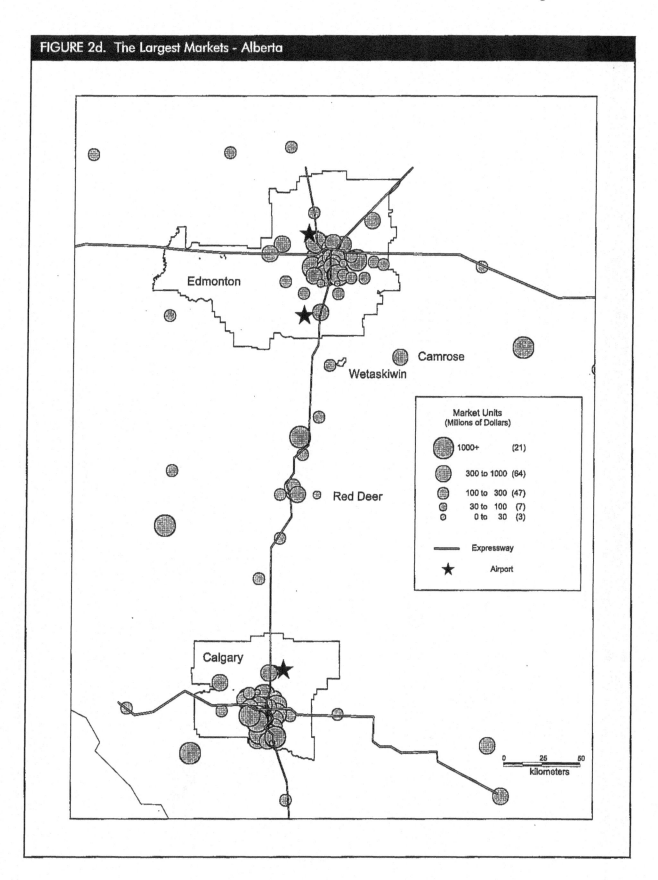

Edmonton

Camrose

Wetaskiwin

Red Deer

Calgary

Market Units
(Millions of Dollars)

1000+	(21)	
300 to 1000	(64)	
100 to 300	(47)	
30 to 100	(7)	
0 to 30	(3)	

—— Expressway

★ Airport

0   25   50
kilometers

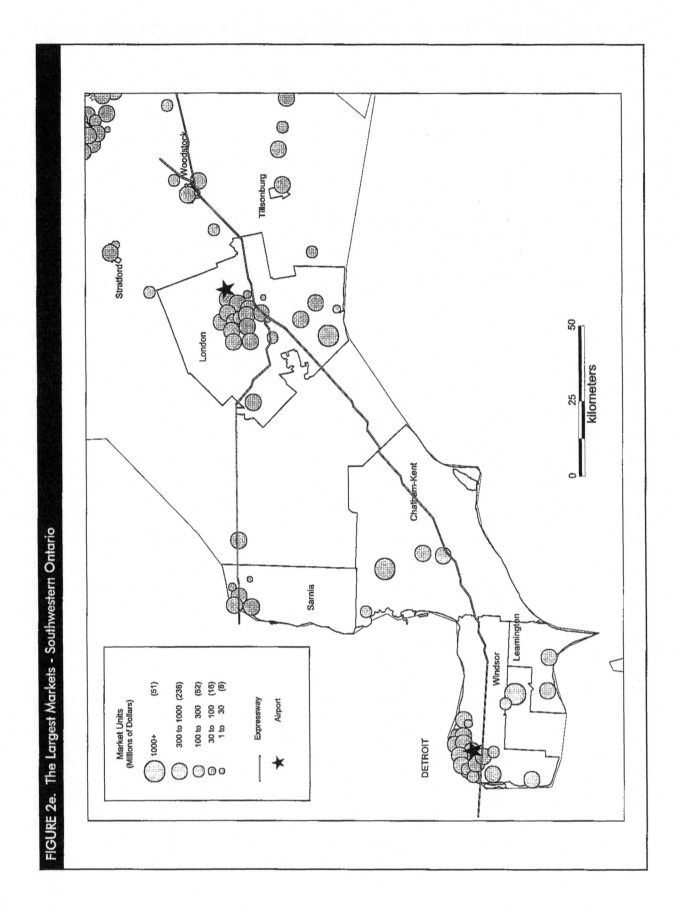

FIGURE 2e. The Largest Markets - Southwestern Ontario

persed market, but the spatial distribution is very different from the Alberta Corridor. Distances are shorter, the settlement pattern operates at a higher density, and most places are linked to a larger centre by commuting patterns; since the CMAs and CAs cover much of the region. People in Sarnia can work or shop in London. People in Chatham may work in the auto plants of either London or Windsor. Universities and specialized hospitals serve the entire region. The region is bounded by the Great Lakes and the U.S. border to the West, and by the Metropolitan region dominated by Toronto to the East. The regional economy depends on manufacturing that now largely serves the U.S. market -- via Windsor, Highway 401 and the rail lines -- but the quality of the service sector will depend on the ability to compete with Toronto. In the past London provided a full set of high order services for the region, but that role is eroding as Toronto expands.

Since London is the centre of the region's distribution system, the other cities are primarily industrial, with high-value jobs and a volatile growth sequence. The region

was badly hurt by the recession in the early 1990s; now it booms and busts according to the decisions about branch plant locations made by multinational firms. The location of future growth is equally unpredictable. Toronto (for services) and Windsor (for exports) provide the two external attractions, but growth could bubble up at any intermediate point. Woodstock, for instance, is rumoured to be the site of a new Toyota plant.

Table 6 suggests that each regional market has a different set of demographic relationships that support its population growth and/or spatial expansion. The table records the number of 'net migrants' (inmovers -outmovers) for each region at various spatial scales during the Census period 1996 to 2001. The immigrants have already been discussed; but they provide a point of comparison for the other magnitudes. Net flows with other regions identify the 'top dogs' in the urban system during this time period. Toronto and Alberta were most successful; Ottawa also gained net migrants. Quebec City, Montreal and Winnipeg lost the most. In contrast, all of the regions gained in exchanges with smaller, non-metropolitan

TABLE 6. Migration Relationships, 1996-2001

| Region | Immigrants | Net Flows within Canada | | | | Flows within Region* | |
		Metro Regions	Other Urban	Rural	Total	Total City**	Net to Core
Toronto Region	463,010	31,550	19,500	-21,050	30,000	215,260	-55,960
Montreal Region	114,930	-23,080	18,590	-7,635	-12,125	26,120	2,905
Georgia Basin (Vancouver)	181,690	-3,585	4,540	-11,665	-10,720	70,060	-7,215
Alberta Corridor (Calgary/Edmonton)	58,730	31,515	42,060	17,295	90,870	38,430	5,510
Ottawa-Gatineau	38,170	8,295	14,730	3,410	26,435	0	0
Southwestern Ontario (London/Windsor)	27,725	-4,670	4,915	3,285	3,530	23,215	1,085
Quebec City	5,350	-23,160	6,370	4,305	-12,485	1,015	-25
Winnipeg	13,515	-12,995	1,780	3,375	-8,115	1,620	380
Halifax Region	4,685	-3,870	6,590	6,085	8,805	5,515	585
Total Metropolitan Regions	907,805	0	119,095	-2,595	116,195	381,235	-52,735

* Among component urban areas.
** Core city is the largest CMA in the region, as identified in Table 2.

Source: Special tabulation of Census data supported by the Social Sciences and Humanities Research Council of Canada, thanks to Prof. Larry Bourne.

cities. Alberta was especially successful, but Montreal, Ottawa, and Toronto also did well.

The relationship with rural areas is more complex. The largest regions, now underbounded, continue to expand spatially and lose migrants to nearby rural areas. Smaller regions, such as Halifax, Winnipeg, and especially Alberta, continue to attract rural migrants from farther away. This expansion into neighbouring places is also apparent in the final column that measures the net shifts among the cities within the regions. The negative values suggest that the Toronto CMA lost 55,000 migrants to other urban areas within the region -- notably Barrie and Oshawa.

The Growth of the Megamarkets

In recent years the growth of Canada's metropolitan regions has depended on a combination of several factors. The first of these, and the simplest to comprehend, has been the ability to attract immigrants. Immigrants have little knowledge of the Canadian labour market, and are increasingly dependent on the assistance of various settlement agencies and compatriots for help in adjusting to the Canadian situation. They are attracted to places that have a previous immigration history, and Toronto, Vancouver, and Montreal have by far the largest concentration of earlier immigrants as we have seen. It has proven to be very difficult to attract newcomers to the Atlantic region or to Quebec outside of Montreal. The cities with immigrants will continue to attract newcomers, achieve population growth, and create jobs.

The second growth factor is the size and growth rate of the regional market in which the metropolitan region is embedded. Halifax depends on the growth of the Atlantic region, Montreal on the growth of Quebec, Toronto looks to Ontario but also to Canada as a whole, while the Alberta Corridor and Vancouver serve the Prairies and British Columbia, respectively. The support of the regional market has two dimensions: economic and demographic. Almost all employment growth now occurs in the services that increasingly prefer to locate in the regional centre, proportional to the overall growth of the regional market. Each dollar earned in British Columbia trickles into Vancouver and creates jobs. Taxes, transfers, and resource revenues support the public sector. But the regional context also places limits on metropolitan growth. The size of the regional centre is proportional to the regional economy, and it cannot grow much faster than the region, as demonstrated by the slow growth of Montreal.

On the demographic side, regional centres have traditionally attracted the in-migration of young people from throughout the region. If the rate of natural increase for the region declines, the potential population growth declines as well, unless the metropolitan region can attract migrants from other regions or from abroad. Montreal and Quebec City have suffered in this respect. Montreal lost anglophone population during the 1970s and early 1980s, and then Quebec as a whole suffered a sharp decline in the fertility rate. Francophone population growth is extremely low. Calgary, in contrast, has been able to attract young people both from Western Canada, and other regions in eastern Canada.

The other element that determines the growth of the megamarket is the latter's competitive strength within the region. In order to take advantage of regional growth -- either economic or demographic -- a city must dominate the market, or at least protect its share. The period 1971 to 2001 witnessed a number of changes in these regional relationships that have affected the growth rates as shown in Table 3. In 1971 the Montreal CMA was larger than Toronto, but the metropolitan regions were more or less equal in size, although Montreal was the historic service centre for the whole country. Thirty years later there can be no doubt about the changed regional roles. Toronto serves the whole country; Montreal the francophone portion. Toronto has grown more rapidly than Canada; Montreal's growth lags behind. A similar eclipse occurred in the Prairies where Calgary has overtaken both Winnipeg and Edmonton to become the leading service centre for this part of Western Canada. In the Atlantic region Halifax has steadily expanded its role as a regional centre, growing more rapidly than potential competitors such as Saint John or St. John's. In Ontario Toronto's growth has been so rapid that it is sucks away service jobs from all parts of the province. Regional sub-centres like London or Kingston have grown much more slowly than Toronto.

One successful weapon in these competitive struggles is the political role. As national capital, the Ottawa region will grow as Canada grows, sharing the spoils with Toronto. Similarly Quebec City benefits as the public sector of Quebec province has expanded over the last thirty years. Edmonton is slowly giving way to Calgary's central role in the service economy, while retaining the political role.

TABLE 7. Population Projections: Metropolitan Regions

Region	Population 2001 (000s)	Income/ Capita ($000s)	Population 2026* (1000s)	Population Growth (000s)	Market Growth ($Billion)	Population Growth Rate 2001-2004**
Toronto Region	6,972	25.3	9,975	3,003	76.0	5.8%
Montreal Region	3,683	22.0	3,821	138	3.0	2.8
Georgia Basin (Vancouver)	2,679	23.5	4,128	1,449	34.1	3.7
Alberta Corridor (Calgary/Edmonton)	1,983	25.5	2,545	562	14.3	5.2
Ottawa-Gatineau	1,064	27.7	1,426	362	10.0	3.6
Southwestern Ontario (London/Windsor)	1,060	23.7	1,212	152	3.6	3.3
Quebec City	711	21.6	793	82	1.8	2.1
Winnipeg	692	21.6	759	67	1.4	1.8
Halifax Region	465	21.6	576	111	2.4	2.9
Total Metropolitan Regions	19,309	24.3	25,234	5,925	146.6	4.3
Other Urban Centres	4,530	20.7	5,086	556	11.5	1.2
Rural Areas	6,168	18.6	5,871	-297	-5.5	
Canada	30,007	22.5	36,191	6,184	150.0	3.0

* Projections begin with the Statistics Canada provincial projections, and assume that each city's share of the provincial population will change over the next 25 years in the same way that it changed during the last 25 years.

** Statistics Canada estimates of annual CMA populations, aggregated for metropolitan regions.

Updates and Projections

Immigration, regional growth, and regional share: these are the key elements in metropolitan growth. What are the prospects for these metropolitan markets in the future? Table 7 shows some simple demographic indicators that extrapolate from current patterns and recent trends. It begins with the population and income per capita in 2001, and projects the population to the year 2026, using provincial population projections prepared by Statistics Canada and the patterns of change within the provinces that have occurred over the last twenty-five years. The Toronto region is projected to reach almost ten million population, with Vancouver passing Montreal to move into second place, at more than four million. The Alberta Corridor should reach 2.5 million; but the other regions will grow only modestly.

The projected population growth over the next 25 years can be multiplied by the current income per capita to project the market growth, a measure of interest to marketers. The results are striking. The metropolitan regions scoop up nearly all the national growth; in fact, Toronto and Vancouver alone will account for more almost three-quarters of the market growth, with Alberta and Ottawa contributing most of the rest. In Montreal, Southwestern Ontario, Winnipeg, Halifax and the smaller cities, marketers will play a zero-sum game, with intense competitive pressure. Rural areas are projected to lose population in aggregate.

The final measure provides a short run confirmation of the projected trends. It is based on the estimated growth rate of census metropolitan areas since 2001. The current growth rates resemble the growth rates of the recent past, and thus the projections into the future.

Summary

For market analysts looking towards the future, the Canadian market may be simpler than it appears. First, more than two thirds of the market is concentrated in nine metropolitan regions that are scattered across the country. Given the high degree of mobility within these regions this market can readily be accessed by a dozen stores or depots.

Second, looking to the future, the growth of the Canadian market will be even more concentrated within half a dozen of these regions. Toronto, Vancouver, the Alberta Corridor, and Ottawa will include almost ninety per cent of the projected growth in the Canadian market. The Toronto region alone is projected to provide more than half of the growth in the national market.

The real complexity in the future will be found within these growing metropolitan regions. In Toronto and Vancouver, one third of the residents were born abroad with a mother tongue that is neither English nor French. Calgary has attracted large numbers of native-born Canadians who are younger and more affluent than residents of other parts of Canada. Each of these markets will require a distinctive approach, and will respond to different brands and media.

As well, each of the largest metropolitan regions has a distinctive spatial structure and pattern of growth that may require a complex network of facilities for some kinds of consumer products. Montreal and Ottawa remain uni-polar, but Toronto's Horseshoe now sprawls more than 200 kilometres from East to West and from North to South. The Alberta Corridor is even more spatially dispersed along a transportation corridor. Each region will require a distinctive spatial strategy to serve a variety of communities that may be differentiated by income, ethnicity and lifestyle.

Although the metropolitan regions will increasingly dominate the Canadian market, almost one-third of Canadians (ten million people) continue to live in small urban centres and rural areas. While these areas are unlikely to provide much future growth they represent a significant opportunity for those firms that are willing to accept the challenge of serving small and dispersed markets.

References

Bourne, Larry S. 2000. "Urban Canada in Transition to the Twenty-first Century: Trends, Issues and Visions." in T. Bunting and P. Filion (eds.) Canadian Cities in Transition. 2nd Edn. Toronto: Oxford University Press pp. 26-51.

Simmons, Jim. 2005."The Changing Pattern, of Commercial Specialization." Research Report 2005-08. Toronto: Ryerson University, Centre for the Study of Commercial Activity.

Simmons, J. and Hernandez, T. 2004. "Power Retail: Close to Saturation?" Research Report 2004-08. Toronto: Ryerson University, Centre for the Study of Commercial Activity.

Statistics Canada. 2002. Census of Canada, 2001. http://geodepot.statcan.ca/Diss/Highlights/

Chapter 9

RECENT CANADIAN URBAN EXPERIENCE: EVIDENCE FROM THE 2006 CENSUS

Stephen Swales

Urban Canada

Although the world as a whole only recently became urban, Canada reached urban status in the 1920's with the proportion of the population urban reaching 80% by 2006 (see Figure 1).

Figure 1 Proportion of the Canadian population living in urban regions since 1901

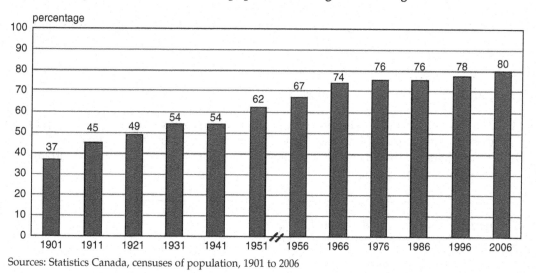

Sources: Statistics Canada, censuses of population, 1901 to 2006

In the next few pages we will use recent data from the 2006 census to evaluate some of the urban characteristics of Canada: the urban spread of large centres, urban change from 2001-2006, and intra-urban patterns of growth.

Canada's Largest Places

Statistics Canada uses a functional definition to identify large urban regions known as Census Metropolitan Areas (CMAs). Essentially they have to be at least 100,000 people in size and include surrounding areas that are functionally linked with the core area through commuting.

CMAs?

A census metropolitan area (CMA) or a census agglomeration (CA) is formed by one or more adjacent munici-palities centred on a large urban area (known as the urban core). **A CMA must have a total population of at least 100,000 of which 50,000 or more must live in the urban core.** A CA must have an urban core population of at least 10,000. To be included in the CMA or CA, other adjacent municipalities must have a **high degree of integration with the central urban area, as measured by commuting flows** derived from census place of work data.

http://www12.statcan.ca/english/census06/reference/dictionary/geo009.cfm

---

There were 33 CMAs in 2006, up from 27 in 2001. The new additions were Saguenay, Peterborough, Brantford, Barrie, Moncton and Guelph. (Note the increase in CMAs was partly due to a relaxing of the minimum core population rule, which had been 100,000 in 2001 and was 50,000 in 2006, although centres were still required to have a minimum population of 100,000.) The 33 CMAs in 2006 are shown in Figure 2. It is evident that Canada is a very southern northern nation; few large centres are distant from the USA border. This "concentrated" population should logistically lend itself to the ease of retail supply, but it has to be tempered with some traditional realities of the Geography of Canada. Although concentrated in the south, the population is stretched out over about 8,000 km. Furthermore, the physical geography of islands and peninsulas in the east, major mountain ranges in the west and the Canadian Shield in northern Ontario and Quebec all serve to inhibit direct and rapid transportation routes. Moreover, the cultural reality of bilingualism can provide opportunities but also barriers for retailers in places like Quebec.

Nonetheless a small number of urban regions command much of the population. Most obviously these are the big four: Toronto, Montreal, Vancouver and Calgary-Edmonton. Add to these Ottawa-Gatineau, Quebec City, Halifax and Winnipeg and the smaller satellite communities near these large cities and you have captured almost all of the population of the country (see data below).

Urban Spread

Statistics Canada has produced an interesting set of animation maps showing the rapid spread of urbaniza-tion for the largest urban regions of Canada. These flash animations show the spread from 1971 to 2006 for each of the six "millionaire" CMAs containing at least one million people: Toronto, Montreal, Vancouver, Ottawa-Gatineau, Calgary and Edmonton.

Flash Animations of Urban Spread

Go to the Statistics Canada web site (www.statcan.ca) and navigate to these flash animations via Census > 2006 Census: Analysis series > Findings >

The direct link is www12.statcan.ca/english/census06/analysis/popdwell/Subprov4.cfm

Note the typical spread from original centres and along major highways. Contrast the confined spread of Vancouver (because of mountains and water) with that of other CMAs.

This rapid spread has had significant implications for distribution of target markets and the growth of new types of retail: suburban malls, suburban strips and more recently power retail.

Canada's Largest Urban Places: Recent Change 2001-2006

Table 1 shows population and dwelling counts for the CMAs of Canada and Figure 3 compares growth rates of the CMAs, 1996 to 2001 and 2001 to 2006. Table 2 identifies the fastest and slowest growing CMAs, between 2001 and 2006.

Figure 2 The Largest Markets in Canada: Thirty Three Census Metropolitan Areas 2006

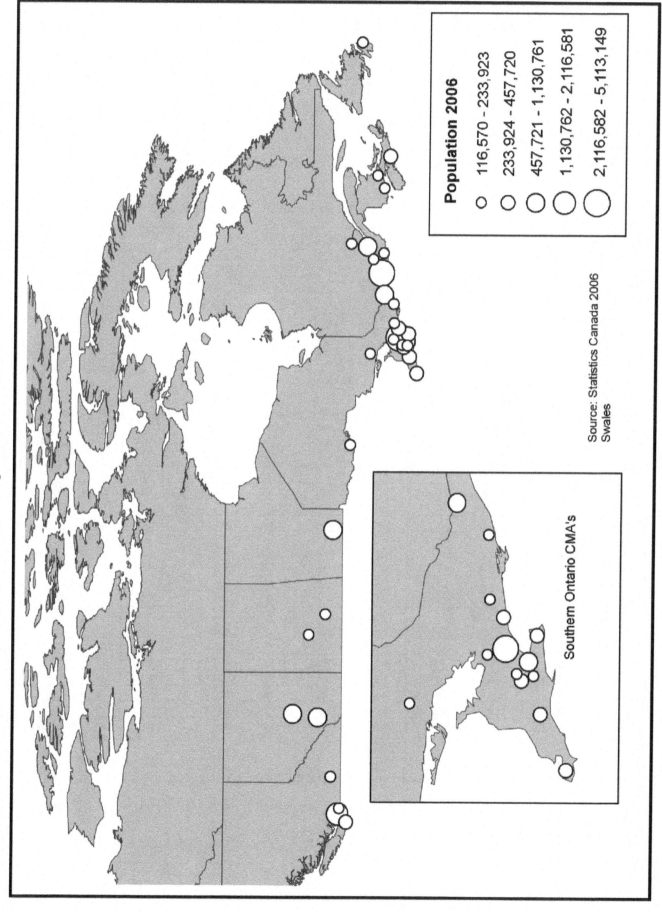

Table 1   Population and dwelling counts, for census metropolitan areas, 2006 and 2001 censuses

Geographic name	Population			Private dwellings, 2006		Land area in square kilometres, 2006	Population density per square kilometre, 2006	Population national rank	
	2006	2001	% change	Total	Occupied by usual residents			2006	2001
Toronto (Ont.)	5,113,149	4,682,897	9.2	1,894,436	1,801,071	5,903.63	866.1	1	1
Montréal (Que.) †	3,635,571	3,451,027 A	5.3	1,593,502	1,525,629	4,258.97	853.6	2	2
Vancouver (B.C.)	2,116,581	1,986,965	6.5	870,992	817,033	2,877.36	735.6	3	3
Ottawa-Gatineau (Ont./Que.)	1,130,761	1,067,800 A	5.9	478,242	449,031	5,716.00	197.8	4	4
Calgary (Alta.) †	1,079,310	951,494 A	13.4	433,616	415,592	5,107.43	211.3	5	5
Edmonton (Alta.)	1,034,945	937,845	10.4	426,132	405,311	9,417.88	109.9	6	6
Québec (Que.) †	715,515	686,569 A	4.2	332,306	316,533	3,276.53	218.4	7	7
Winnipeg (Man.)	694,668	676,594 A	2.7	291,903	281,745	5,302.98	131.0	8	8
Hamilton (Ont.)	692,911	662,401	4.6	279,246	266,377	1,371.89	505.1	9	9
London (Ont.)	457,720	435,600 A	5.1	198,144	184,946	2,665.28	171.7	10	10
Kitchener (Ont.)	451,235	414,284	8.9	177,879	169,063	827.07	545.6	11	11
St. Catharines-Niagara (Ont.)	390,317	377,009	3.5	166,526	156,386	1,397.50	279.3	12	12
Halifax (N.S.)	372,858	359,183	3.8	166,757	155,138	5,495.62	67.8	13	13
Oshawa (Ont.)	330,594	296,298	11.6	123,351	119,028	903.29	366.0	14	16
Victoria (B.C.) †	330,088	311,902	5.8	155,224	145,388	695.35	474.7	15	14
Windsor (Ont.)	323,342	307,877	5.0	134,010	125,848	1,022.84	316.1	16	15
Saskatoon (Sask.)	233,923	225,927	3.5	101,081	95,257	5,206.70	44.9	17	17
Regina (Sask.)	194,971	192,800	1.1	84,998	80,323	3,408.26	57.2	18	18
Sherbrooke (Que.)	186,952	175,950 A	6.3	89,717	82,747	1,231.86	151.8	19	19
St. John's (N.L.)	181,113	172,918	4.7	75,860	70,663	804.64	225.1	20	20
Barrie (Ont.)	177,061	148,480	19.2	67,379	63,877	897.47	197.3	21	23
Kelowna (B.C.)	162,276	147,739	9.8	71,889	66,925	2,904.01	55.9	22	24
Abbotsford (B.C.)	159,020	147,370	7.9	58,099	55,948	625.94	254.1	23	25
Greater Sudbury/ Grand Sudbury (Ont.)	158,258	155,601	1.7	69,669	65,076	3,382.32	46.8	24	21
Kingston (Ont.)	152,358	146,838	3.8	70,003	61,978	1,906.69	79.9	25	26
Saguenay (Que.)	151,643	154,938	−2.1	67,150	64,315	1,753.69	86.5	26	22
Trois-Rivières (Que.)	141,529	137,507	2.9	67,421	63,893	880.36	160.8	27	27
Guelph (Ont.)	127,009	117,344	8.2	52,130	48,775	378.45	335.6	28	32
Moncton (N.B.)	126,424	118,678 A	6.5	55,252	51,593	2,405.91	52.5	29	30
Brantford (Ont.) †	124,607	118,086 A	5.5	49,480	47,847	1,072.90	116.1	30	31
Thunder Bay (Ont.)	122,907	121,986	0.8	55,582	51,426	2,550.40	48.2	31	29
Saint John (N.B.)	122,389	122,678	−0.2	53,583	49,107	3,359.55	36.4	32	28
Peterborough (Ont.)	116,570	110,876 A	5.1	52,165	46,667	1,505.56	77.4	33	33

Symbols

A   adjusted figure due to boundary change

†   excludes census data for one or more incompletely enumerated Indian reserves or Indian settlements

Source: Statistics Canada. 2007. Population and dwelling counts, for census metropolitan areas, 2006 and 2001 censuses - 100% data (table). Population and Dwelling Count Highlight Tables. 2006 Census.
Statistics Canada Catalogue no. 97-550-XWE2006002. Ottawa. Released March 13, 2007.
http://www12.statcan.ca/english/census06/data/popdwell/Table.cfm?T=205&SR=1&S=3&O=D&RPP=33&PR=0&CMA=0 (accessed April 13, 2007)

Study the data in Tables 1 and 2 and Figures 2 and 3 and consider the following ideas and how they might relate to retail market and the logistics of retail supply:

- What is the spatial distribution of large urban places in Canada? We are a very large nation but how many large urban centres are distant from the US border? Which CMA is most distant from the US border (see Figure 2)?
- Although there are 33 CMAs there is a great range in sizes of these places. What is this range?
- How much of the Canadian population is concentrated in the largest six centres?
- What is the geographical pattern of the fastest and slowest growing CMAs?

The six largest CMAs contained 45% of the Canadian population in 2006. Moreover, four large super urban regions, the Golden Horseshoe, Montreal, Vancouver-Victoria and Calgary-Edmonton, contained about 65% of the population. This is remarkable concentration of the population. The only large urban place of any distance from the US border is Edmonton; the vast majority of all other urban places are within 2-3 hours of the border.

As noted, this theme of concentration has to be tempered with the following considerations: the urban centres may cling to the US border, but the east-west spread across the country is more than 5,000 km and the length of the US-Canadian boundary 8,890 km, separating centres considerably; urban regions are separated by physical geography – such as the Rockies in the west and islands and peninsulas in the east; and the two very close urban regions in central Canada are "separated" to some extent by cultural geography – Francophone and Anglophone.

The growth rates of some of the CMAs are quite remarkable given their original size, Calgary for example, already a very large place in 2001, grew by 13.4 % (it had grown by 15.8% between 1996 and 2001). Other rapidly growing large centres included Edmonton (10.45%), Toronto (9.2%) and Vancouver (6.2%) (all grew above the national average). The relative magnitude of absolute growth should be noted. The growth of the Toronto CMA from 2001-2006 (of 430,252) was equivalent to more than two entire Regina CMAs or about an entire London CMA.

Smaller CMAs also growing quickly are arguably within the sphere of influence of the larger centres: Barrie (19.2%), Guelph (8.2%), Oshawa (11.65%) and Kitchener (8.9%) for Toronto and Abbotsford (7.9%) for Vancouver. Still smaller places, not on the list of CMAs but quite close to them, also grew quickly, for example Okotoks, Red Deer and Canmore in Alberta and Chilliwack in B.C. (see Table 3 for the fastest

Table 2   Fastest and slowest growing CMAs in Canada, 2001 to 2006

Fast growing CMAs	% change 2001–2006		Slow growing (declining) CMAs	% change 2001–2006
Barrie	19.2		Saguenay	−2.1
Calgary	13.4		Saint John	−0.2
Oshawa	11.6		Thunder Bay	0.8
Edmonton	10.4		Regina	1.1
Kelowna	9.8		Greater Sudbury	1.7
Toronto	9.2		Winnipeg	2.7
Kitchener	8.9		Trois-Rivieres	2.9
Guelph	8.2		Saskatoon	3.5
Abbotsford	7.9		St Catharines-Niagara	3.5
Vancouver	6.5		Halifax	3.8

Table 3   Mid-size urban centres with the fastest population growth since 2001

Order	Mid-size urban centres	Province	2001	2006	Growth (in percentage)
1	Okotoks	Alberta	11,689	17,145	46.7
2	Wood Buffalo	Alberta	42,581	52,643	23.6
3	Grande Prairie	Alberta	58,787	71,868	22.3
4	Red Deer	Alberta	67,829	82,772	22.0
5	Yellowknife	Northwest Territories	16,541	18,700	13.1
6	Lloydminster	Saskatchewan / Alberta	23,964	27,023	12.8
7	Canmore	Alberta	10,792	12,039	11.6
8	Medicine Hat	Alberta	61,735	68,822	11.5
9	Saint-Jean-sur-Richelieu	Quebec	79,600	87,492	9.9
10	Joliette	Quebec	39,720	43,595	9.8
11	Chilliwack	British Columbia	74,003	80,892	9.3
11	Fort St. John	British Columbia	23,007	25,136	9.3
13	Parksville	British Columbia	24,285	26,518	9.2
14	Lethbridge	Alberta	87,388	95,196	8.9
14	Courtenay	British Columbia	45,205	49,214	8.9
16	Granby	Quebec	63,069	68,352	8.4
17	Nanaimo	British Columbia	85,664	92,361	7.8
17	Collingwood	Ontario	16,039	17,290	7.8
17	Kawartha Lakes	Ontario	69,179	74,561	7.8
20	Vernon	British Columbia	51,530	55,418	7.5
21	Centre Wellington	Ontario	24,260	26,049	7.4
22	Drummondville	Quebec	72,778	78,108	7.3
23	Ingersoll	Ontario	10,977	11,760	7.1
24	Whitehorse	Yukon	21,405	22,898	7.0
25	Woodstock	Ontario	33,269	35,480	6.6

Sources: Statistics Canada, censuses of population, 2001 and 2006
http://www12.statcan.ca/english/census06/analysis/popdwell/Subprov6.cfm

growing CAs). In addition, Statistics Canada notes that municipalities on the periphery of large central municipalities, effectively the outer suburbs of these very large centres, grew at double the national average (2006 Census, Portrait of the Canadian Population, Highlights, March, 2007, www12.statcan.ca/english/census06/analysis/popdwell/highlights.cfm.).

These observations reinforce the theme of urban concentration identified earlier; people may live in relatively small municipalities but they are strongly within the sphere of influence of large urban centres.

Fast growth areas are in southern Ontario, Alberta and B.C.; slow growth areas are in Quebec, Atlantic Canada, the Prairies (outside Alberta) and peripheral regions of Ontario.

Comparing total population and number of dwellings in Table 1 will give you a sense of average household size; note that household size is relatively small for most CMAs. Indeed, the 2001 census showed that approaching 25% of households are composed of just one person. Recent censuses have shown a trend to smaller household size – an important consideration for changing market. Moreover, if you compare the % change of dwellings (in Table 4) with % change of populations (in Table 1) it is apparent that in most CMAs dwellings are growing in number faster than populations; average household size continues to decline.

Figure 3 Population growth of census metropolitan areas, 1996 to 2001 and 2001 to 2006

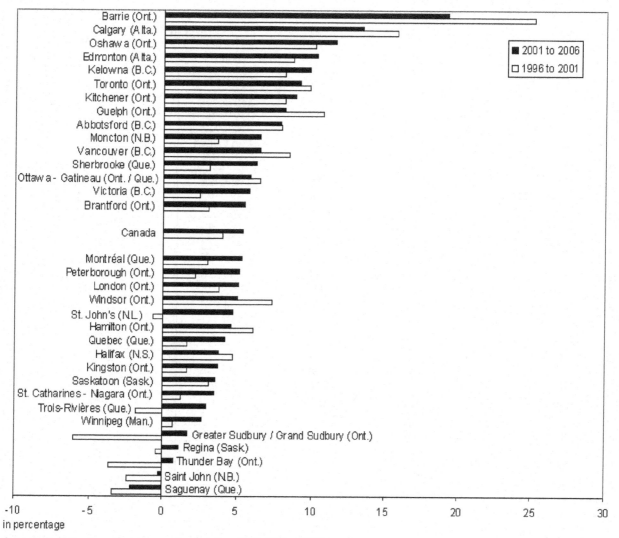

-10 -5 0 5 10 15 20 25 30
in percentage

Sources: Statistics Canada, censuses of population, 1996, 2001 and 2006

"This chart shows the growth rate of Canada's 33 census metropolitan areas between 1996 and 2001 and between 2001 and 2006. The CMAs are listed in decreasing order of 2001 to 2006 growth rate. For each area, the 1996 to 2001 rate is given first, followed by the 2001 to 2006 rate. The rates are 25.1% and 19.7% for Barrie, Ontario; 15.8% and 13.4% for Calgary, Alberta; 10.2% and 11.6% for Oshawa, Ontario; 8.7% and 10.4% for Edmonton, Alberta; 8.2% and 9.8% for Kelowna, British Columbia; 9.8% and 9.2% for Toronto, Ontario; 8.2% and 8.9% for Kitchener, Ontario; 10.7% and 8.2% for Guelph, Ontario; 8.0% and 7.9% for Abbotsford, British Columbia; 3.7% and 6.5% for Moncton, New Brunswick; 8.5% and 6.5% for Vancouver, British Columbia; 3.1% and 6.3% for Sherbrooke, Quebec; 6.5% and 5.9% for Ottawa – Gatineau, Ontario/Quebec; 2.5% and 5.8% for Victoria, British Columbia; and 3.1% and 5.5% for Brantford, Ontario. Then, below Canada's growth rate of 5.4%, the rates are 3.0% and 5.3% for Montréal, Quebec; 2.2% and 5.1% for Peterborough, Ontario; 3.8% and 5.1% for London, Ontario; 7.3% and 5.0% for Windsor, Ontario; −0.7% and 4.7% for St. John's, Newfoundland and Labrador; 6.1% and 4.6% for Hamilton, Ontario; 1.6% and 4.2% for Québec City, Quebec; 4.7% and 3.8% for Halifax, Nova Scotia; 1.6% and 3.8% for Kingston, Ontario; 3.1% and 3.5% for Saskatoon, Saskatchewan; 1.2% and 3.5% for St. Catharines – Niagara, Ontario; −1.7% and 2.9% for Trois-Riviéres, Quebec; 0.7% and 2.7% for Winnipeg, Manitoba; −6.0% and 1.7% for Greater Sudbury/Grand Sudbury, Ontario; −0.4% and 1.1% for Regina, Saskatchewan; −3.7% and 0.8% for Thunder Bay, Ontario; −2.4% and −0.2% for Saint John, New Brunswick; and −3.4% and −2.1% for Saguenay, Quebec."

Source: www12.statcan.ca/english/census06/analysis/popdwell/Subprov3.cfm

Table 4 Dwelling counts, for census metropolitan areas, 2006 and 2001 censuses

Geographic name	Type	Total private dwellings		
		2006	**2001**	**% change**
Toronto (Ont.)	CMA	1,894,436	1,671,087	13.4
Montréal (Que.) †	CMA	1,593,502	1,483,133 A	7.4
Vancouver (B.C.)	CMA	870,992	786,277	10.8
Ottawa - Gatineau (Ont./Que.)	CMA	478,242	432,733 A	10.5
Calgary (Alta.) †	CMA	433,616	368,567 A	17.6
Edmonton (Alta.)	CMA	426,132	371,908	14.6
Québec (Que.) †	CMA	332,306	312,301 A	6.4
Winnipeg (Man.)	CMA	291,903	281,982 A	3.5
Hamilton (Ont.)	CMA	279,246	260,968	7.0
London (Ont.)	CMA	198,144	184,660 A	7.3
Kitchener (Ont.)	CMA	177,879	158,735	12.1
Halifax (N.S.)	CMA	166,757	153,353	8.7
St. Catharines - Niagara (Ont.)	CMA	166,526	159,032	4.7
Victoria (B.C.) †	CMA	155,224	141,985	9.3
Windsor (Ont.)	CMA	134,010	124,097	8.0
Oshawa (Ont.)	CMA	123,351	106,447	15.9
Saskatoon (Sask.)	CMA	101,081	94,688	6.8
Sherbrooke (Que.)	CMA	89,717	83,272 A	7.7
Regina (Sask.)	CMA	84,998	80,772	5.2
St. John's (N.L.)	CMA	75,860	69,118	9.8
Kelowna (B.C.)	CMA	71,889	62,675	14.7
Kingston (Ont.)	CMA	70,003	65,883	6.3
Greater Sudbury / Grand Sudbury (Ont.)	CMA	69,669	68,823	1.2
Trois-Rivières (Que.)	CMA	67,421	64,486	4.6
Barrie (Ont.)	CMA	67,379	56,390	19.5
Saguenay (Que.)	CMA	67,150	65,118	3.1
Abbotsford (B.C.)	CMA	58,099	52,552	10.6
Thunder Bay (Ont.)	CMA	55,582	54,090	2.8
Moncton (N.B.)	CMA	55,252	49,332 A	12.0
Saint John (N.B.)	CMA	53,583	51,775	3.5
Peterborough (Ont.)	CMA	52,165	47,784 A	9.2
Guelph (Ont.)	CMA	52,130	46,254	12.7
Brantford (Ont.) †	CMA	49,480	46,208 A	7.1

Symbols:
 A   adjusted figure due to boundary change
 †   excludes census data for one or more incompletely enumerated Indian reserves or Indian settlements

Source: Statistics Canada. 2007. Dwelling counts, for census metropolitan areas and census agglomerations, 2006 and 2001 censuses - 100% data (table). Population and Dwelling Count Highlight Tables. 2006 Census. Statistics Canada Catalogue no. 97-550-XWE2006002. Ottawa. Released March 13, 2007.
http://www12.statcan.ca/english/census06/data/popdwell/Table.cfm?T=208&SR=1&S=6&O=D&RPP=25&PR=0&CMA=0

Population Change Within Canada's Largest Urban Places

Another perspective on urban and market change is within cities, the intra-urban pattern. Statistics Canada has produced a series of maps showing population change by census tract within each of the largest CMAs. These maps are:

Toronto CMA, Population change, 2001 to 2006 by 2006 Census Tract (CT)

Calgary CMA, Population change, 2001 to 2006 by 2006 Census Tract (CT)

Montreal CMA, Population change, 2001 to 2006 by 2006 Census Tract (CT)

Vancouver CMA, Population change, 2001 to 2006 by 2006 Census Tract (CT)

Edmonton CMA, Population change, 2001 to 2006 by 2006 Census Tract (CT)

Intra-urban Population Change in "Millionaire" CMAs, 2006

Consult each of the census tract maps for the largest CMAs; they can be found at the Statistics Canada web site (www.statcan.ca) at:

Census > 2006 Census: Analysis series > Data tables, figures and maps

The direct link is: www12.statcan.ca/english/census06/analysis/popdwell/tables.cfm#popchange

Where is the population growth taking place in these CMAs?

Outer suburban, inner city or both?

Chapter 10

AGING CONSUMERS AND THE COMMERCIAL STRUCTURE

Jim Simmons, Shizue Kamikihara, and Tony Hernandez

Introduction

Canada's population is aging rapidly, more rapidly than most of us can imagine. By the year 2031, only a quarter of a century from now, almost thirty per cent of the population will be over sixty. As the average age of the population increases, the amount and type of household consumption changes; and the shopping destinations evolve as well. As older consumers retire, their incomes decline -- but not the levels of consumption -- and their expenditures shift towards groceries or pharmacies, and away from furniture, CDs and automobiles.

This paper will explore these changes for Canada as a whole, as well as examining the spatial variations that occur across the country. The aging consumer is much more prominent in slow-growth communities such as Winnipeg or Halifax than in rapidly-growing Calgary or Vancouver. The same is true within the metropolitan area. The older residents are concentrated in older neighbourhoods in the inner city, and will patronize certain kinds of nearby commercial locations. At the same time the rate of expansion of suburban neighbourhoods will slow down.

This paper begins with a discussion of the national demography, and the population forecasts for the next quarter century. At the national level the aging of the population is completely predictable. Today's boomers are tomorrow's seniors. There are very few people entering the Canadian demographic system in these older age groups, and -- barring some kind of national disaster -- the rate of exit is highly predictable. The location of tomorrow's seniors is less predictable, however, since the spatial concentration across the urban system depends in part on overall rates of population growth (hence numbers of young people) in various locations, as well as on the distinctive retirement decisions of seniors. In every region of the country save the far North, selected communities are developing 'retirement' specializations. The list of retirement communities is no longer restricted to Victoria or Kelowna, but now includes places like Elliot Lake and Cobourg, ON; and Camrose, AB. The same phenomenon is occurring within metropolitan areas, as certain neighbourhoods that are perceived to be safe and well-serviced, and have appropriate housing, attract disproportionate numbers of seniors; although for the most part, the age distribution across a community reflects the age of housing.

The second section of the paper evaluates the impact of aging consumers on consumer expenditures, considering, in turn, the potential changes in income, the level of consumption, the kinds of products purchased, and the variety of shopping destinations. The third section will elaborate the discussion of shopping behaviour by focussing on the mobility of seniors, as demonstrated in the Transportation for Tomorrow Survey in the Toronto region. Do seniors travel less, or for different reasons, or do they choose different locations? And how do they respond to major commercial nodes such as downtown, or Yorkdale Shopping Centre and other major malls? Do they patronize the power centres that are emerging around the periphery of the built-up area?

For retailers, targeting seniors as a market is a complex procedure in itself, but it is made more complex in those markets where seniors account for a growing share of the population because the mix of stores and store locations will undoubtedly shift as well. The three sections listed above lead inevitably to a fourth: how do location analysts forecast the impacts of aging consumers on consumer incomes, expenditures and location choices? How large are the effects likely to be? What retail and service sectors will feel the greatest impact? And what are the likely changes within the commercial structure of the city? And finally, one significant side-effect of the aging population is the relative lack of growth in younger age cohorts. This has negative implications for the future growth of suburban housing and consumption, as well as the shopping malls and power centres that typically serve these markets.

This paper begins with the most factual and clear-cut component of the discussion of aging: the recent and projected changes in the age distribution of the Canadian population, followed by a discussion of their spatial preferences, both nationally, and within the city. We emphasize that these changes are massive, involving the net transfer of millions of people among the various age cohorts, and they have significant implications for overall income levels and consumer behaviour.

The Changing Age Structure

Table 1 and Figure 1 summarize the shifts in age groups that Canada has experienced over the last decade (1991-2001). During this period the greatest growth occurred in the age cohort 50 to 55, while the very youngest age group, from 0 to 4, showed a slight decline. All together we witnessed a net shift of about 1.4 million people from the two five-year cohorts aged 45 to 55 into the two cohorts aged 55 to 65. While substantial in magnitude, such shifts in the age structure have only modest implications for the commercial sector. The high growth age groups in their

TABLE 1. Shifts in Age Structure, 1991-2001

Age Group	1991 Number	1991 Share	Change Number	Change Per Cent	2001 Number	2001 Share
0-4	1,907	7.0%	-211	-11.1%	1,696	5.7%
5-9	1,908	7.0	68	3.6	1,976	6.6
10-14	1,878	6.9	175	9.3	2,053	6.8
15-19	1,879	6.8	184	9.8	2,053	6.8
20-24	1,962	7.2	-6	-0.3	1,956	6.5
25-29	2.376	8.7	-478	-20.1	1,898	6.3
30-34	2,491	9.1	-394	-15.8	2,097	7.0
35-39	2.284	8.4	239	10.5	2,523	8.4
40-44	2,087	7.6	492	23.6	2,579	8.6
45-49	1,641	6.0	693	42.2	2,334	7.8
50-54	1,325	4.9	761	57.4	2,086	7.0
55-59	1,223	4.5	371	30.3	1,594	5.3
60-64	1,177	4.3	97	8.2	1,274	4.2
65-69	1,073	3.9	61	5.7	1,134	3.8
70-74	822	3.0	187	22.7	1,009	3.4
75-79	615	2.3	199	32.4	814	2.7
80-84	368	1.3	148	40.2	516	1.7
85-89	189	0.7	93	49.2	282	0.9
90+	94	0.3	40	42.6	134	0.4
Total	27,297	100.0	2,710	9.9	30,007	100.0

Population in 1,000s.

Source: Statistics Canada. Census of Canada, 1991 and 2001.

FIGURE 1. Change in Age Composition, 1991-2001

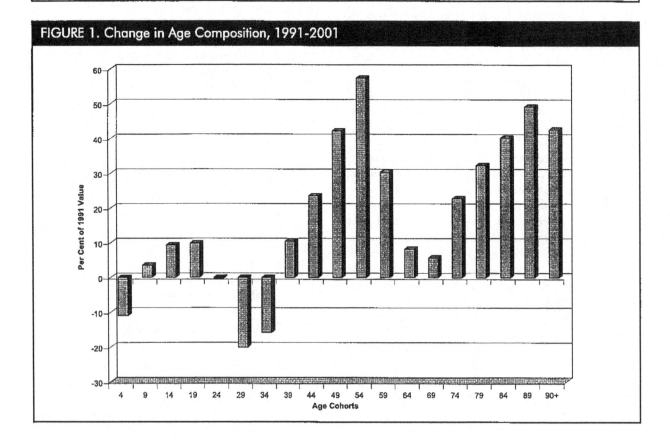

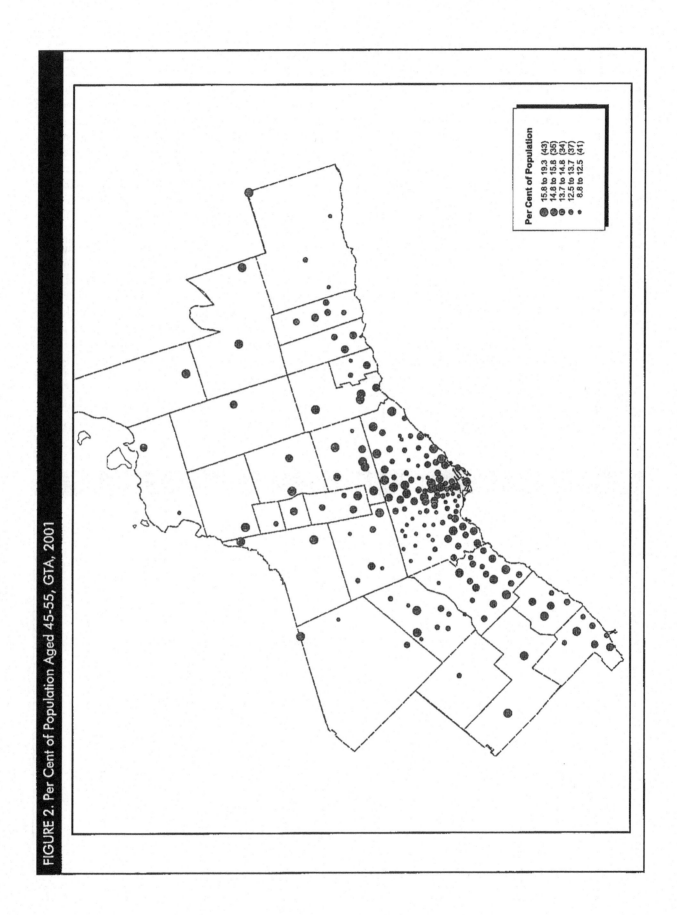

FIGURE 2. Per Cent of Population Aged 45-55, GTA, 2001

Per Cent of Population

15.8 to 19.3 (43)
14.8 to 15.8 (35)
13.7 to 14.8 (34)
12.5 to 13.7 (37)
8.8 to 12.5 (41)

forties and fifties continue to work and to consume, and since many of them are in the periods of peak earnings and savings they consume at high levels. Many of them are also buying houses and relocating within the city, as they upgrade their accommodations while downsizing as family size declines.

Figure 2 maps the current concentration of adults aged 45 to 55 within the Greater Toronto Area. It suggests that although this age cohort is widely dispersed, the highest concentrations are found in the high income sectors of the city -- north along Yonge Street and west along the Lakeshore. This pattern suggests that high income neighbourhoods will be most severely affected by the demographic transition.

The Forecasts for the Future

It is a relatively simple process to project the age distribution for Canada in the years to come. We simply count the current population, multiply by an appropriate factor to account for the well-known rates of survival by age group, add 25 years, and there we are: simple and precise. The unknown procedure is the range of implications that

derive from these projections. Unlike the past decade, the next 25 years will produce unprecedented changes in consumption, as much of the growth takes place in age-groups beyond the retirement age, at the stage of the life cycle when retirement, poor health, and changes in personal mobility have significant impacts on consumption patterns. Figure 3 shows how the age structure is projected to evolve during the period 2001-2031, looking at ten year intervals: 2001, 2011, 2021 and 2031. Each line on the graph shows the age distribution of the Canadian population in one of the study years.

The summary in Table 2 indicates that overall population growth is relatively modest over this time period, increasing from 31 to 39 million, or 25 per cent -- equivalent to an average annual growth rate of 1.01 per cent. The first thing to note on the graph is the dramatic decline in the share of the youngest age cohorts, 0 to 15, during the first decade, a pattern that continues less dramatically through 2031. This is an extension of the pattern observed over the last decade. Each year registers fewer births (or immigrants) in the entry age group than were observed ten, twenty or thirty years ago. Second, we observe that the peak age cohorts (the baby boom of 1955-1965) age regularly, from 35 to 45

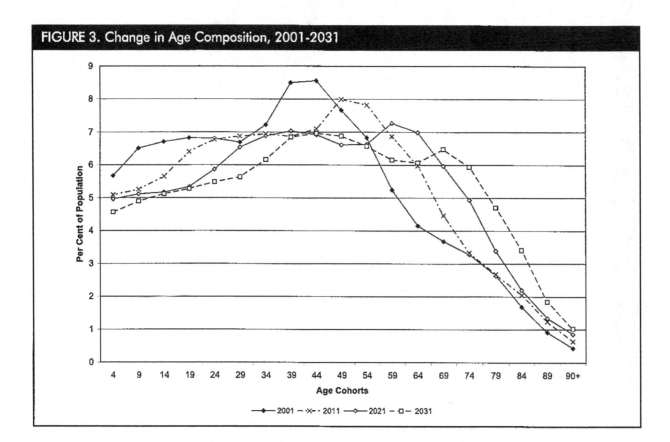

FIGURE 3. Change in Age Composition, 2001-2031

years of age in the year 2001 to the cohorts 75 to 85 by 2031. Finally, the most massive shifts occur in the sequence of age cohorts over age 50 that display regular shifts toward the right side of the graph as each cohort's share of the national population increases by 50 to 100 per cent, or more.

Although it is tempting to think that the overall growth in population will overwhelm the percentile changes in the age cohorts, Table 2 and Figure 4 provide a useful corrective. Virtually all of Canada's population increase will occur in the age cohorts 45 and over. The greatest increases in absolute numbers occur for the age groups between 65 and 74, and the rates of growth are highest for the oldest age groups. The results are inescapable. Every region of the country – no matter how rapid the current growth rate – will age significantly during the next thirty years, and so will every urban area and every neighbourhood. Table 3 shows the current projections for Alberta, the fastest growing province in the country. By 2031 the population over sixty will account for 27 per cent of the population, and 65 per cent of the population growth will have taken place in these cohorts. The largest age cohorts in 2031 will be from 40 to 50 years old – since most of the

current newcomers are in their twenties.

The larger cultural context of the demographic transition will be troubling for many firms and individuals. One would not wish to be a teen-ager in the years to come -- surrounded by disapproval and misunderstanding instead of innovation and experiment. The 2030s will be the antithesis of the 1960s -- more like my youth during the Diefenbaker era. But there will be serious jobs for all those who want a responsible lifestyle. Similar frustrations will face those firms and sectors that currently identify with the youth market: the music industry, Old Navy, Mountain Co-op. On the other hand pharmacies, MDS and nursing homes will thrive.

The Spatial Variation: the Urban System

Although the aging process affects the Canadian population throughout the country, there are substantial variations among urban areas, variations that reflect the growth history of each community – the temporal sequence of booms and busts – as well as the spatial preferences of Canadians as they reach the age of retirement. The 2001 Census provides detailed information on the age

TABLE 2. Shifts in Age Structure, 2001-2031

Age Group	2001 Number	2001 Share	Change Number	Change Per Cent	2031 Number	2031 Share
0-4	1,759	5.7%	22	1.3%	1,781	4.6%
5-9	2,017	6.5	-106	-5.2	1,911	4.9
10-14	2,079	6.7	-80	-3.9	1,999	5.1
15-19	2,117	6.8	-59	-2.8	2,058	5.3
20-24	2,110	6.8	28	1.3	2,138	5.5
25-29	2,074	6.7	125	6.0	2,199	5.6
30-34	2,240	7.2	163	7.3	2,403	6.2
35-39	2,637	8.5	34	1.3	2,671	6.8
40-44	2,655	8.6	62	2.3	2,717	7.0
45-49	2,378	7.7	305	12.8	2,683	6.9
50-54	2,117	6.8	446	21.1	2,563	6.6
55-59	1,628	5.2	773	47.5	2,401	6.2
60-64	1,288	4.2	1,080	83.9	2,368	6.1
65-69	1,142	3.7	1,386	121.4	2,538	6.5
70-74	1,019	3.3	1,299	127.5	2,318	5.9
75-79	819	2.6	1,018	124.3	1,837	4.7
80-84	523	1.7	809	154.7	1,333	3.4
85-89	284	0.9	436	153.5	720	1.8
90+	136	0.4	265	195.9	401	1.0
Total	31,027	100.0	8,008	25.8	39,029	100.0

Population in 1,000s.

Source: Statistics Canada: "Annual Demographic Statistics, 2005" and "Projected Population by Age Groups, 2006-2031."
Note that the 2001 values are estimated populations, and therefore larger (and more accurate) than the actual Census counts that were reported in Table 1.

FIGURE 4. Growth Rate by Age Cohorts, 2001-2031

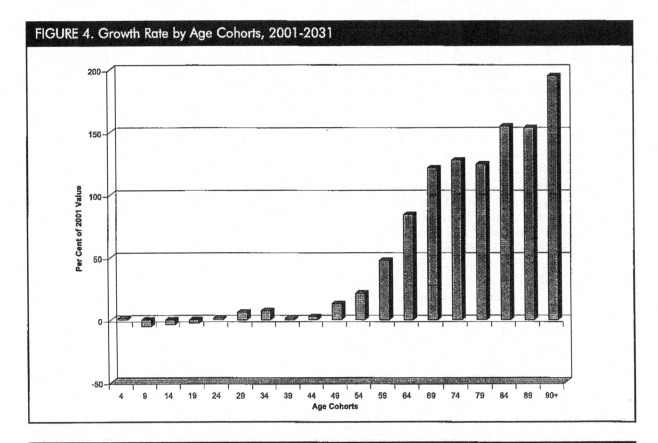

TABLE 3. Shifts in Age Structure, Alberta, 2001-2031

Age Group	2001 Number	2001 Share	Change No.	Change Per Cent	2031 Number	2031 Share
0-4	191	6.2%	22	11.5%	213	5.1%
5-9	211	6.9	10	4.7	221	5.3
10-14	225	7.4	3	1.3	228	5.5
15-19	228	7.5	6	2.6	234	5.6
20-24	230	7.5	10	4.3	240	5.8
25-29	228	7.5	21	9.2	249	6.0
30-34	230	7.5	31	13.5	261	6.3
35-39	261	8.5	21	8.0	282	6.8
40-44	272	8.9	18	6.6	290	7.0
45-49	236	7.7	53	22.5	289	7.0
50-54	191	6.2	80	41.9	271	6.5
55-59	138	4.5	108	78.3	246	5.9
60-64	107	3.5	127	118.7	234	5.6
65-69	93	3.0	153	164.5	246	5.9
70-74	81	2.6	150	185.2	231	5.4
75-79	62	2.0	119	191.9	181	4.4
80-84	41	1.3	84	204.9	125	3.0
85-89	22	0.7	44	200.0	66	1.6
90+	11	0.4	28	195.9	39	0.9
Total	3,057	100.0	1,088	35.6	4,145	100.0

Population in 1,000s.

Source: Statistics Canada: "Annual Demographic Statistics, 2005" and "Projected Population by Age Groups, 2006-2031."

composition of the population at all spatial scales, and on the migration preferences among urban areas for different age groups. This part of the paper examines both of these variations among urban areas, and the part to follow discusses the variations within the Greater Toronto Area.

The distribution of seniors – the proportion of the population aged 60 and over – across the country in 2001 is shown in Figure 5. Although sixty per cent of the urban areas are included within the narrow range from 15 to 20 per cent, there are significant numbers of cities above and below these values. The map suggests that virtually all the resource communities in the north have low proportions of seniors, while the highest proportions occur in small communities in attractive environments on the West Coast, or along the southern edge of the Canadian Shield, or within easy reach of larger metropolitan areas. Table 4 identifies the places with the highest and lowest values, and it includes some of the regional specialized retirement centres such as Tillsonburg, Cobourg and Thetford Mines. Parksville and Elliot Lake each have more than one third of the population over 60. In contrast, the most youthful populations – all found in the North – have fewer then five per cent of the population in this category. Rural areas in all

regions of the country have slightly higher proportions of seniors, a reflection of their lower growth rates.

The map and the table suggest that the extreme values in this spatial distribution reflect conscious choices by seniors about where to live. Although seniors are not highly mobile relative to the population as a whole, the net effect of their movement leads to significant spatial concentrations in the proportions of seniors. For instance, the remaining columns in Table 4 as well as Figure 6 suggest that northern communities suffered substantial outflows of seniors over the period 1996-2001 while selected places across the southern part of the country attracted substantial numbers of in-movers. Interestingly, the highest rates of net out-movement, reflecting the 'push' factor, were twice as large as the highest rates of net in-movement.

Northern Canada aside, it is difficult to generalize the location preferences of seniors in terms of region or city size (Table 5). Seniors are slightly more likely to live in smaller communities than in big cities, and to live in British Columbia and Quebec than in the Prairies (i.e., Alberta). Their recent migration preferences suggest that these values are partly conscious choices and partly the result of

TABLE 4. Where Seniors Live and Move

	Highest Proportion	Rate (%)	Most In-Movers	Number	Highest Rate of Net In-Movement	Rate (%)
1.	Parksville	38.9	Kelowna	2,730	Collingwood	14.5
2.	Elliot Lake	34.4	Barrie	2,095	Parksville	14.2
3.	Penticton	29.8	Hamilton	2,020	Elliot Lake	13.0
4.	Tillsonburg	27.0	Oshawa	1,545	Cobourg	11.3
5.	Cobourg	26.1	Victoria	1,380	Barrie	9.9
6.	Thetford Mines	25.9	Parksville	1,340	Camrose	9.3
7.	Yorkton	25.2	St. Catharines	1,215	Tillsonburg	8.3
8.	Camrose	24.9	London	1,115	Kelowna	7.8
9.	Shawinigan	24.8	Ottawa	1,105	Penticton	7.3
10.	Swift Current	24.4	Edmonton	1,005	Medicine Hat	6.8
131.	Brooks	11.0	Windsor	-310	Brooks	-9.0
132.	Cold Lake	10.9	Wood Buffalo	-415	Whitehorse	-9.1
133.	Petawawa	9.2	Prince George	-465	Terrace	-9.2
134.	Grande Prairie	8.8	Sudbury	-495	Prince Rupert	-10.2
135.	Whitehorse	8.7	Regina	-745	Fort St. John	-12.7
136.	Fort St. John	8.6	Quebec City	-1,290	Kitimat	-13.7
137.	Labrador City	5.4	Winnipeg	-1,390	Yellowknife	-13.8
138.	Thompson	4.8	Vancouver	-4,785	Wood Buffalo	-26.9
139.	Yellowknife	3.9	Montreal	-8,465	Labrador City	-30.5
140.	Wood Buffalo	3.6	Toronto	-20,225	Thompson	-32.0

Seniors are defined as people 60 or more years of age in 2001.

Statistics Canada. Census of Canada, 2001.

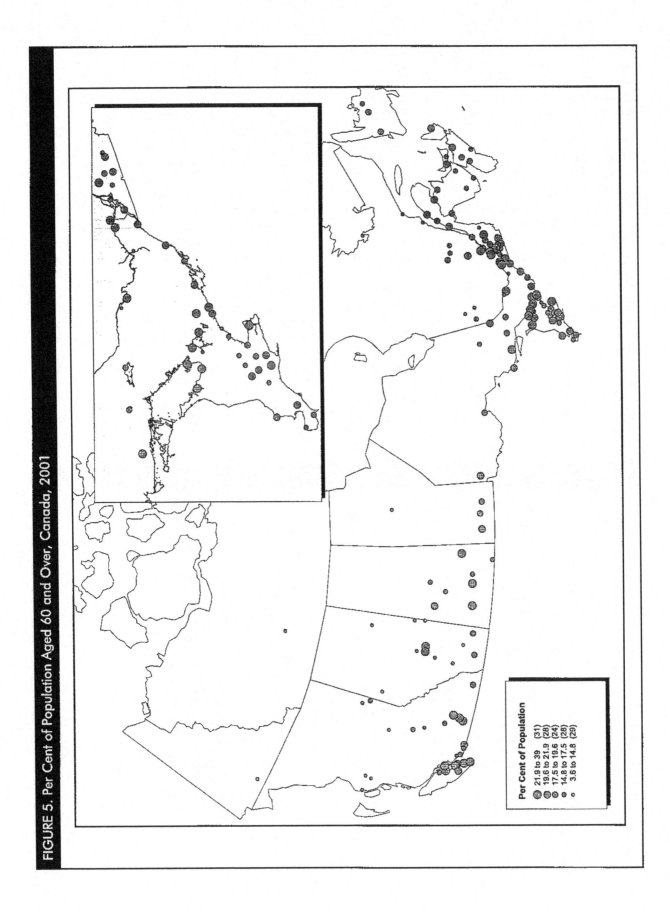

FIGURE 5. Per Cent of Population Aged 60 and Over, Canada, 2001

Per Cent of Population

21.9 to 39   (31)
19.6 to 21.9 (28)
17.5 to 19.6 (24)
14.8 to 17.5 (28)
3.6 to 14.8   (29)

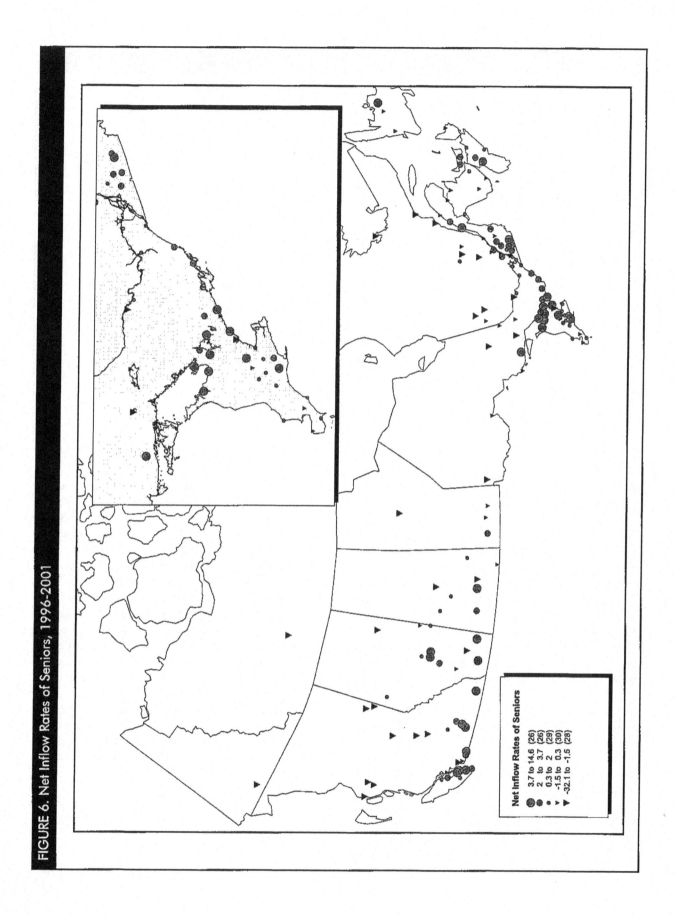

FIGURE 6. Net Inflow Rates of Seniors, 1996-2001

Net Inflow Rates of Seniors

- 3.7 to 14.6 (26)
- 2 to 3.7 (26)
- 0.3 to 2 (29)
- -1.5 to 0.3 (30)
- -32.1 to -1.5 (28)

195

TABLE 5. Seniors by Region and City Size

City Size/Region	BC	Prairies	Ontario	Quebec	Atlantic	Canada
Per Cent Seniors						
Over 1,000,000	16.2	...	15.1	17.3	...	16.0
300,000-1,000,000	22.1	14.4	18.0	17.6	14.8	16.4
100,000-300,000	20.3	15.8	17.2	18.3	17.2	17.5
30,000-100,000	19.6	15.3	20.7	19.2	17.6	19.0
10,000-30,000	16.0	17.2	22.2	18.4	18.2	18.2
Total	17.6	14.8	16.6	17.7	16.7	16.7
Net Migration Rate for Seniors						
Over 1,000,000	-1.49	...	-2.26	-1.43	...	-1.85
300,000-1,000,000	2.00	-0.09	1.07	-1.07	0.93	0.44
100,000-300,000	5.54	-0.92	2.51	1.28	0.17	1.80
30,000-100,000	3.35	2.89	1.77	1.49	1.70	2.17
10,000-30,000	0.22	0.86	4.59	-0.31	0.81	1.22
Total	0.59	0.20	-0.31	-0.74	0.73	-0.001

Seniors are defined as people 60 or more years of age in 2001.
Territories cities grouped with BC.

Statistics Canada. Census of Canada, 2001.

the recent growth history. Big cities have grown more rapidly, thereby adding young people and reducing the overall proportion of seniors. But these places are also losing seniors through net outmigration -- notably to rural areas around growing cities such as Toronto and Vancouver. The regional variations depend on both inmigration by seniors and the overall growth trends in the regions. Thus British Columbia has a high population growth rate, but even higher levels of in-migration by seniors. Quebec has a low growth rate, and loses senior migrants as well. The low proportions of seniors in the Prairies appear to reflect the high levels of in-migration of young people. Other regions show a complex mixture of two processes.

In the future the retirement of the baby boomers that was projected in Figure 4 and Table 2 may add to the uncertainly about urban growth. This transition will affect millions of people. On the demographic side, these seniors are no longer bound to the locations where they work, and are free to relocate wherever they please. As we have seen, they can stay or move to some more attractive location. On the economic side, the firm that once employed them also has a choice; to replace them or not -- and given the slower rate of growth in the labour force (the emerging problem in Alberta) -- it may not be easy to replace workers -- at least not in all locations. Thus we have a variety of possible situations emerging. If the worker ages from 45 to 55, the job, income, and household remain, so the community is unaffected; but the transition out of the labour force at age 65 leads to a variety of different outcomes. The household could leave the community at retirement but the job is maintained (the Grande Prairie solution). Or the household stays, but the job is not replaced (the Elliot Lake solution) or both job and household remain in place (the Collingwood solution) or both disappear (as in Kitimat, BC). Collingwood and Grande Prairie maintain the local income and employment, but the population in Collingwood grows more quickly. Elliot Lake and Kitimat lose jobs and consumer income, but the Elliot Lake population remains, albeit poorer. Kitimat simply declines very quickly in all respects. In future all Canadian cities -- especially smaller ones -- will find themselves somewhere within this spectrum of alternatives.

The Spatial Variation: within the Metropolitan Region (GTA)

For the most part location analysts and retailers are more concerned with locations within the urban areas than with choices among cities. After all, the variations in social characteristics from one neighbourhood to the next tend to be much greater than the same kind of differences between cities. In this spirit we can examine the variations in the proportion of seniors among FSAs (three-digit postal codes) within the Greater Toronto Area (Figure 7). In practice, FSAs include roughly 20,000 people and they are roughly demarcated using municipal boundaries and/or transportation routes, rather than social characteristics. The measure used in Figure 7 differs slightly from Figure 5, in that seniors are defined as those over 65 years of age, rather than 60.

The first surprise is that the range of values is more limited within the GTA, with a ratio of standard deviation to the mean that is less than the value for the national urban system. Secondly, the values show a powerful spatial concentration, in that values for the City of Toronto (13.6 per cent) – roughly settled by 1971 – are fifty per cent higher than the values for the surrounding suburban region (9.2 per cent) that has been largely constructed over the last thirty years. Exceptions within the city include the condominiums around the CBD that were constructed during the last decade or so. Exceptions in the suburbs occur in the old ex-urban developments in Mississauga, Oakville and Burlington along the Lakeshore. For the most part, the proportion of seniors largely reflects the age of the housing. New housing, especially housing in suburban developments, tends to attract young people and young families. Within the city, despite the high rates of mobility overall, the population of the neighbourhood ages as the housing and infrastructure ages. To a considerable degree this makes the spatial structure of aging predictable, although the limited range of variation within Figure 7 reminds us that each household and every neighbourhood, old and new, includes a diversity of age cohorts. Nonetheless, seniors tend to be more highly concentrated in upper income areas -- north along Yonge Street, and west into Central Etobicoke. Well-to-do seniors prefer to live by themselves, while the less well-off are forced to share housing with their children.

The spatial structure suggests that the aging process will generate a sequence of waves of older population cohorts, radiating outwards with all the changes in consumption that this implies. To forecast the demography of Brampton during the decades to come, one examines the recent history of Scarborough. At the same time, the most profound spatial impacts of the aging process may not be visible on the map. Mystery writers sometimes draw our attention to the significance of the dog that didn't bark. In the case of the aging process, the growth of the senior population may be less important than the lack of growth in population cohorts between 0 and age fifty (recall Figure 4). For decades, now, the expansion of the city has been driven by the influx of children (the baby boom), the surge in growth of young adults (the boomers), and the consumption of aging boomers. But now the boomers are approaching retirement, and the future expansion of the suburbs must be based on the impoverished inmigrants from abroad or other parts of Canada. There will be very little net increase in new households, in school-age children, in university students, or entry-level employees. That means that the consumption of housing, of cars, and of major appliances will be restricted to the replacement level. Many small communities in many regions of the country will suffer population declines, but even large and growing cities will experience much slower growth in the suburban zones. Fewer new neighbourhoods translate into fewer opportunities for shopping centres and power malls. Instead, there will be increased competition among existing locations and retail brand names to serve a market that will grow more slowly than in the recent past. And this is the inevitable side-effect of the aging population.

The Impact on Consumption

Given the aging Canadian population, how do we translate the demographic changes into consumption effects? Three kinds of consumption changes accompany the aging process for consumers over sixty: first, reduced income accompanies the withdrawal from the workforce and the gradual decline in household size; second, changes in expenditures are responses to lower incomes as well as the different requirements of older households; and third, changes in the location of consumption reflect changing household requirements and reduced mobility. In these discussions we must remember that the aging occurs in a sequence of stages that may occur at any time from five to forty years. The typical household might experience the aging sequence initially as a modest decline in income at retirement, while consumption patterns continue unchanged. A few years later, expenditures and mobility might decline as medical problems intervene. Eventually, consumption changes more drastically as the survivor is restricted to some kind of care facility. The sequence of change, and the speed of the process, is entirely unpre-

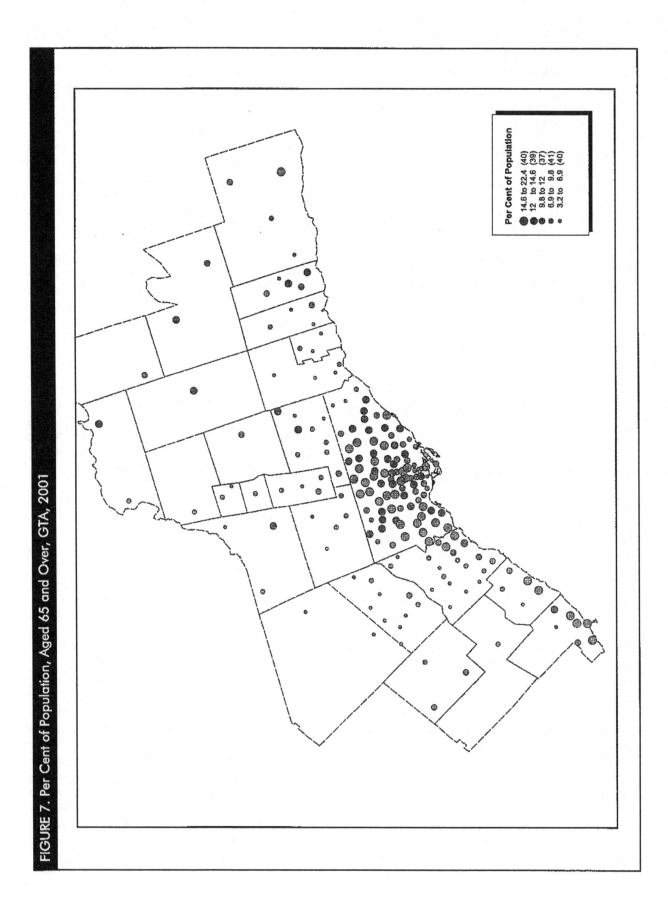

FIGURE 7. Per Cent of Population, Aged 65 and Over, GTA, 2001

Per Cent of Population

● 14.6 to 22.4 (40)
● 12 to 14.6 (39)
● 9.8 to 12 (37)
● 6.9 to 9.8 (41)
· 3.2 to 6.9 (40)

dictable for individuals, but the end result is not. Between retirement and the final curtain, consumption evolves, as we shall see. We can use the average values of cohort income and expenditures as indicators of the changes.

The Changes in Income

As households age, average incomes and expenditures evolve in complex and contradictory ways. This discussion is based on an excellent source of data, the annual survey of household spending by Statistics Canada that includes data on household income. We include two summaries of this information: Table 6 comes directly from a study by Chawla (2005) that compares the survey results for 2003 with data from twenty years before. Chawla's table summarizes the social context of aging and also provides a temporal perspective for the current data. Table 7 summarizes the variations in income and expenditure by age cohort, using the data from the year 2004.

TABLE 6. Profile of Older Households, 1982 and 2003

		1982				2003		
Age Groups	Total	55-64	65-74	75+	Total	55-64	65-74	75+
Households (000's)	2,669	1,203	939	527	4,233	1,881	1,221	1,131
Household type (%)								
Unattached men	7.9	6.6	6.8	12.9	10.6	9.3	9.5	14.1
Unattached women	26.2	16.4	29.3	42.9	24.7	14.3	25.0	41.6
Couples only	36.1	33.6	42.9	29.9	36.8	37.2	43.4	29.0
Households with children								
or relatives	24.5	38.5	15.0	9.1	22.9	35.1	16.8	9.0
Other mixed households	5.3	4.9	6.0	5.2	5.0	4.1	5.3	6.3
Homeownership (%)								
Renter	32.1	27.6	31.7	43.3	27.1	24.2	24.0	35.5
Owner without mortgage	54.4	49.9	60.1	54.6	57.1	49.3	65.4	61.3
Owner with mortgage	13.4	22.5	8.2	2.1	15.7	26.5	10.6	3.2
Income sources (% of Households)								
Earnings	48.8	80.3	29.5	11.3	46.4	76.0	32.4	12.2
Investment income	69.8	66.9	73.2	70.6	35.0	29.1	38.2	41.4
Government transfers	85.4	68.4	99.1	99.9	87.7	73.1	99.4	99.5
Other sources	34.9	26.0	44.1	38.8	47.5	35.5	60.3	53.5
Composition of income (%)								
Earnings	51.0	72.9	22.4	12.4	50.3	71.7	27.7	9.2
Investment income	16.1	10.7	21.8	28.8	5.7	4.1	6.7	10.2
Government transfers	24.0	10.4	42.5	46.3	25.6	10.4	40.8	55.6
Other sources	8.9	6.0	13.3	12.5	18.5	13.8	25.0	24.9
Income from Government Transfers (%)								
None	14.6	31.6	0.9	0.1	12.3	26.9	0.6	0.5
Some	73.2	60.5	84.8	81.6	69.8	63.8	80.5	68.2
Complete	12.2	7.9	14.3	18.3	17.9	9.3	18.9	31.3
Income level (%)								
Under $20,000	31.4	18.1	35.8	53.9	23.7	14.9	23.0	39.1
$20,000 - $34,999	25.8	18.3	34.6	27.4	26.6	17.9	32.3	35.0
$35,000 - $49,999	15.2	18.0	14.5	10.1	16.2	16.4	19.4	12.5
$50,000 or more	27.5	45.6	15.0	8.7	33.5	50.8	25.4	13.4
Expenditure level (%)								
Under $20,000	35.8	18.5	41.9	64.7	24.0	12.8	24.3	42.3
$20,000 - $34,999	26.4	21.3	33.9	24.4	26.2	17.9	31.2	34.7
$35,000 - $49,999	16.3	24.0	12.5	5.7	16.9	17.5	21.1	11.3
$50,000 or more	21.4	36.3	11.6	5.2	33.0	51.9	23.4	11.8

Sources: Family Expenditure Survey, 1982; Survey of Household Spending, 2003.
Compiled by Chawla, 2005.

TABLE 7. Household Income and Expenditures by Age Cohort, 2004

Cohort	Household Income	Household Size	Income per Capita	Taxes	Investment[1]	Expenditure[2]
<25	33,478	2.15	15,571	4,694	-170	32,666
25-30	51,646	2.27	22,751	8,814	4,518	41,540
30-35	70,862	2.86	24,776	15,000	7,981	49,623
35-40	70,698	3.19	22,162	15,238	6,707	50,154
40-45	74,110	3.22	23,015	15,527	8,196	52,856
45-50	82,218	3.03	27,135	17,716	10,818	56,995
50-55	78,892	2.76	28,584	16,480	8,580	55,230
55-60	75,433	2.31	32,655	15,587	11,067	52,272
60-65	54,131	2.01	26,931	10,394	6,511	40,400
65-70	45,336	1.87	24,243	7,191	4,337	37,087
70-75	38,829	1.76	22,062	6,340	792	32,536
75-80	33,338	1.57	21,234	4,425	325	28,505
80-85	32,674	1.46	22,379	5,165	1,652	25,720
>85	25,410	1.27	20,008	2,881	187	22,853
Total	64,393	2.54	24,958	12,650	6,681	46,249

Cohort	Shelter[3]	Clothes	Transport	Health[4]	Recreation[5]	Other[6]
<25	11,495	1,740	5,638	1,391	6,977	885
25-30	15,408	2,231	8,278	1,899	6,485	1,487
30-35	19,434	2,804	9,177	2,311	6,835	2,217
35-40	20,132	2,860	8,270	2,447	6,819	2,087
40-45	19,336	2,962	9,466	2,615	8,148	2,445
45-50	19,835	3,361	10,871	2,937	9,079	2,704
50-55	18,874	2,986	10,456	3,123	8,863	2,943
55-60	18,360	2,824	10,370	2,800	7,698	2,948
60-65	13,136	1,903	8,112	2,796	5,129	3,058
65-70	12,521	1,705	6,866	2,621	4,564	3,129
70-75	11,177	1,294	5,874	2,337	3,579	3,053
75-80	10,637	967	3,748	2,345	2,294	3,969
80-85	9,244	862	2,975	2,096	2,136	4,388
>85	10,055	619	2,585	1,950	1,490	2,983
Total	16,660	2,466	8,479	2,542	6,702	2,630

[1] Net savings, pensions and insurance
[2] Sum of all expenditures
[3] Shelter, furniture, and household operations
[4] Health and personal care
[5] Includes reading, education, tobacco and alcohol and gambling
[6] Miscellaneous and gifts

Source: Statistics Canada, Survey of Household Spending, 2004.

Chawla's table elaborates the aging process: in addition to the decline of income, household size is reduced by including fewer children and relatives, and with more people (especially women) living alone. Income shifts away from earnings towards government transfers. Note that this reliance on government pensions is increasing over time, so that by 2003 31 per cent of households over 75 years of age had no other source of income. Chawla also notes that the ratio of expenditures (including taxes) to income is increasing over time, as consumption and taxation increase, and the level of saving declines.

Table 7 looks at the most recent data on household expenditure as it varies by age group. The first column tracks the regular changes in average household income through the life cycle as it rises gradually to a maximum of

$82,200 between 45 and 49 years of age, declines slowly until age 55 to 59, and then begins to drop more dramatically to end up at less than one-third of the peak income at age 85. At the same time, the decline in household income is partially offset by a parallel decline in household size. This measure peaks with an average of 3.22 persons per household at age 40 to 44, and drops gradually to 2.01 at age 60, and to 1.27 for those over 85. In combination, the income per capita declines more gradually from the maximum value of $32,600 age 55-59, to $21,000 twenty years later. As will be shown later, household income and income per capita decline as households age and decline in size, but the aggregate income per capita for a future community actually increases slightly because there are fewer children.

The sources of income and the changing relationships with consumption and wealth have been throughly explored in a series of Statistics Canada publications by Gower (1998), Harchaoui and Tarkhani, (2004), Myles (2000), and Williams (2003). A review by The Economist (2004), assures us that life expectancy will continue to grow at a regular rate, and for most people, the sooner they retire the better.

Chawla's study suggest that these income variations with age are unlikely to change much overtime (Table 6). First, it is evident that despite the exhortations about retirement savings, investment income is unlikely to replace income from earnings, which leaves transfers from government as the main source of income. Second, the changes over the last two decades suggest a decline in the income from earnings in two of the three age categories, and an increased dependence on government. As defined benefit pension plans (here called other income) are slowly phased out by the private sector, income from investments is supposed to replace them. Government transfers are relatively small, typically $1000 per month from the Old Age pension

(with supplements), and another $1000 per month from the Canada Pension Plan.

It is the withdrawal from employment that accounts for most of the decline in household income, and this fact suggests that the expected aging of the Canadian population may significantly alter income levels – nationally, regionally and locally. For example, the replacement of 1,000 households age 45 to 49 within a community by the equivalent set of households aged 75 to 79 (thirty years later) generates only $33 million compared to $80 million. At the same time, the population also declines, from 3,000 to 1,600; unless replaced by younger in-movers. The actual impact of this aging process will vary from place to place depending on the overall age structure and the level of replacement, but data from the 2001 Census suggest that the initial effects are already observable (Table 8). If we calculate a regression model of income per capita for 140 urban areas, as a function of the per cent seniors in the city, the presence of seniors is more important than either the size of the city or the recent growth rate in determining the level of income per capita. For every percentile of seniors, the average income of the city declines by $226. This, in turn, suggests that the forthcoming demographic transformation may affect retailers by downsizing the income of their customers.

The Changes in Expenditures

Tables 7 and 9 present the latest data on household expenditure broken down by age cohorts, based on the age of the reference person as the 'head of household'. Table 7 presents the actual expenditures, but Table 9 converts the magnitudes into the per cent of income and/or expenditures. Most of the discussion to follow relates to Table 9 as an indication of the choices made by households. At the same time retail analysts expenditures will be interested in

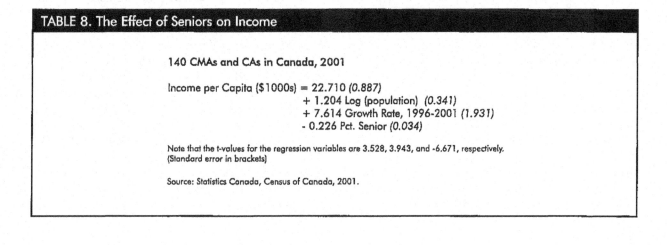

TABLE 8. The Effect of Seniors on Income

140 CMAs and CAs in Canada, 2001

Income per Capita ($1000s) = 22.710 (0.887)
  + 1.204 Log (population) (0.341)
  + 7.614 Growth Rate, 1996-2001 (1.931)
  - 0.226 Pct. Senior (0.034)

Note that the t-values for the regression variables are 3.528, 3.943, and -6.671, respectively.
(Standard error in brackets)

Source: Statistics Canada, Census of Canada, 2001.

TABLE 9. The Allocation of Expenditures by Age Cohort, 2004

| Cohort | PER CENT OF INCOME | | | | PER CENT OF EXPENDITURE | | | | | |
	Taxes	Invest-ment[1]	Expend-iture[2]		Shelter[3]	Clothes	Trans-port	Health[4]	Recrea-tion[5]	Other[6]
<25	13.61	-0.49	94.74		35.19	5.33	17.26	4.26	21.36	2.71
25-30	17.07	8.75	80.43		37.09	5.37	19.93	4.57	15.61	3.58
30-35	21.17	11.26	70.03		39.16	5.65	18.49	4.66	13.77	4.47
35-40	21.55	9.49	70.94		40.14	5.70	16.49	4.88	13.60	4.16
40-45	20.95	11.05	71.32		36.58	5.60	17.91	4.95	15.42	4.63
45-50	21.55	13.16	69.32		34.80	5.90	19.07	5.15	15.93	4.74
50-55	20.89	10.88	70.01		34.17	5.41	18.93	5.65	16.05	5.33
55-60	20.66	14.67	69.30		35.12	5.40	19.84	5.36	14.73	5.64
60-65	19.20	12.03	74.63		32.51	4.71	20.08	6.92	12.70	7.57
65-70	15.86	9.57	81.80		33.76	4.60	18.51	7.07	12.31	8.44
70-75	16.33	2.04	83.79		34.35	3.98	18.05	7.18	11.00	9.38
75-80	13.27	0.97	85.50		37.32	3.39	13.15	8.23	8.05	13.92
80-85	15.81	5.06	78.72		35.94	3.35	11.57	8.15	8.30	17.06
>85	11.34	0.74	89.94		44.00	2.71	11.31	8.53	6.52	13.05
Total	19.64	10.38	71.82		36.02	5.33	18.33	5.50	14.49	5.69

[1] Net savings, pensions and insurance
[2] Sum of all expenditures
[3] Housing, furniture, and household operations
[4] Health and personal care
[5] Includes reading, education, tobacco and alcohol and gambling
[6] Miscellaneous and gifts

Source: Statistics Canada, Survey of Household Spending, 2004.

the magnitudes of expenditures that result, as shown in Table 7. For example, the replacement of a household aged 45 to 54 by one aged 75 or older reduces the expenditures on clothing from $3,174 to $915, and even the amount spent on health care declines from $1,963 to $1,724.

The first portion of each table -- the three left hand columns -- describes the overall allocation of income into taxes, savings and expenditures. In general, the shares of income allocated to taxes and savings decline with age, as the overall income is reduced. This, in turn, implies an increase in the proportion of income that is used for personal consumption. Note how this ratio evolves through the life cycle. In the youngest cohort, consumption is financed by going into debt (implying negative savings), but the recovery is rapid and during the working years the proportion of income for consumption is fairly stable, ranging from 70 to 75 per cent. After retirement, however, the sharp decline in income boosts expenditures to more than eighty per cent of income. As will be evident later, the increase in the expenditure ratio becomes more important than the income decline of aging households in the impact on commercial activities. It is the public sector that suffers most, as lower incomes for households generate fewer taxes

to support a growing demand for health and social services.

The rest of Table 9 (and Table 10 as well) examines the minutiae of consumption (even greater detail is available in the original data source). The close relationship between income and expenditure explains the increased share of expenditures by older age groups that is devoted to the essentials: food (in house!), shelter, and health care; and the declining share of expenditures in such luxuries as clothing, and recreation. Table 10 disaggregates expenditures further to explore some particular issues. If shelter includes household operations and furniture (as in Table 9), the share of expenditures remains reasonably constant into retirement, but if the cost of housing is kept separate seniors appear to spend too much of their income on shelter. Although they cut back on operating costs and furniture, they may be unwilling or unable to adjust to changes in household size by relocating. Personal transportation is another complex issue. As long as the household continues to own a car – for men, until the late 70s – transportation absorbs a high proportion of expenditures. For more rational seniors, especially women living alone, cars are relinquished at some point after age 65 with a corresponding decline in transportation expenditures.

TABLE 10. Age Sensitive Expenditures by Age Cohort, 2004

Cohort	Housing[1]	Private Transport	Health[2]	Prescription Drugs	Reading	Education	Gifts[3]
<25	24.79	15.10	8.75	0.30	0.43	6.68	1.01
25-30	26.53	17.99	8.16	0.28	0.50	2.89	1.91
30-35	27.59	16.49	8.12	0.26	0.52	1.53	2.82
35-40	28.90	14.89	7.98	0.39	0.49	1.67	2.17
40-45	26.02	16.35	8.70	0.32	0.53	2.65	2.62
45-50	25.06	17.46	8.46	0.34	0.60	3.22	2.66
50-55	24.43	17.03	7.92	0.55	0.62	3.51	2.84
55-60	24.02	18.04	7.74	0.58	0.65	2.08	3.26
60-65	23.05	18.66	6.93	1.24	0.71	0.95	4.94
65-70	23.81	16.92	7.08	1.27	0.77	0.60	6.52
70-75	25.53	16.34	6.49	1.44	0.80	0.50	6.39
75-80	27.97	11.33	4.15	1.73	0.82	0.15	11.63
80-85	27.98	10.42	4.54	2.04	0.84	0.24	15.08
<85	35.75	10.32	4.35	1.68	0.82	0.04	10.76
Total	25.85	16.61	7.83	0.59	0.60	2.30	3.55

PER CENT OF EXPENDITURE

[1] Cost of housing alone
[2] Excludes personal care
[3] Family and charities

Source: Statistics Canada, Survey of Household Spending, 2004.

Health care is inevitably expensive for seniors. The share of overall expenditures in this sector drops after retirement (Table 10), but the allocation for prescription drugs increases. Expenditures on reading materials remain high, but education costs are negligible. Finally, we note that the amounts allocated to gifts -- to both family members and charities -- increases sharply in importance. In sum, the choices made by households after retirement are substantially different from those of working households.

The evolution of income and expenditure as the household ages is a complex process, as we have seen. Table 11 attempts to summarize the findings as they relate to households, individuals and markets, in turn. As we saw in Table 7, the impact of aging is most dramatic for households because of the retirement from the labour force. But when we take into account the parallel decline in household size, and the compensatory increase in proportion of household income that is actually spent, most of the apparent income problem disappears. Average expenditure per capita is maintained until very late in the life cycle.

At the regional level we can expect to see spatial variations in the level of income and/or expenditures, largely driven by the variations in population growth. Will the jobs of retirees be maintained within the community? If so, the community will increase in population and income. Will

the neighbourhood attract younger and larger households with higher incomes to replace the seniors who die or relocate? If so, the neighbourhood and the stores and services that depend upon it will thrive. At this point we can return to Table 2 and Figure 4, to evaluate the overall impact on consumption of Canada's aging population. While Canada's population will increase by thirty per cent, seventy per cent of the additional population will be over sixty, and thus characterized by lower levels of household income and different patterns of consumption.

The Changes in Shopping Patterns

The changes in expenditure with age reflect a variety of other life cycle adjustments that may also affect the location of purchases. Table 12 -- also taken from the Survey of Household Spending -- illustrates how these changes accumulate. These data represent average values for a national sample of households in which age is determined by a single reference person in each household. First, note the rapid withdrawal from the labour force, in financial terms, as we have noted; but also in terms of the temporal and spatial involvement with the workplace. The average number of weeks worked per year drops from 35 to six over fifteen years. As a result seniors have much more time to spend on consumption. At the same time, their daily travel patterns are no longer centred on the workplace. Every day

TABLE 11. Aging and Consumption

Households	Individuals	Regions Urban Areas	Neighbourhoods
Income			
Average household incomes decline dramatically with age, dropping more than 50 per cent between age 55 and 75.	The decline in household income with age is partly offset by the decline in household size. Income per capita declines by one-third.	Overall adjustments in age composition to 2031 result in a modest decline of 0.7 per cent in income per capita of adults across Canada; but the income increases by 4.5 per cent when the decline of the number of children is included.	
		Income growth in urban areas depends on the ability to replace the jobs of retirees.	Income growth in older neighbour-hoods depends on the ability to attract younger households
Expenditures			
The decline in household income is partially offset by the increase in the proportion that is spent, from 69% to 85% between age 55 and 75.	On a per capita basis expenditures is higher for seniors than for younger households, and remains high until death.	Expenditures are maintained, and even increase as people age. It is the allocation among various goods and services that changes.	

TABLE 12. The Aging Process, 2004

Cohort	Income	Employment Weeks Worked	Single Family Housing (Per Cent)			Cars per Household			Shopping by Car	As Driver (Per Cent)
			Male	Female	Total	Male	Female	Total		
50-54	$39,088	35.7	70.0	62.6	66.6	1.56	1.52	1.54	88.4	74.0
55-59	31,979	28.4	66.0	59.6	63.0	1.46	1.38	1.42	89.2	71.0
60-64	17,269	16.7	66.4	55.5	61.0	1.34	1.22	1.28	89.3	65.9
65-69	7,458	5.9	65.8	53.7	59.7	1.34	0.99	1.17	86.8	62.2
70-74	2,657	2.5	58.8	55.7	57.1	1.21	0.92	1.05	86.4	61.8
75-79	726	1.3	65.1	41.3	51.6	1.10	0.68	0.86	87.9	61.9
80-84	1,305	1.1	55.9	42.0	48.0	0.96	0.47	0.69	83.7	61.2
85+	306	0.5	35.2	35.6	35.5	0.79	0.29	0.45	86.4	52.4

Source: Statistics Canada, Survey of Household Spending, 2004.
Shopping Trips from Transportation for Tomorrow Survey, 2001.

is Sunday: a stroll to the local retail strip may replace a hurried stop at a convenience store on the way home from work. Different stores are patronized, in different locations.

Second, aging encourages a gradual disengagement from the single-family dwelling. The change is slightly delayed if there is a man in the house, but even so seniors slowly reduce their expenditures on renovations and maintenance, and many of them eventually downsize their dwellings. Multifamily units are more likely to be located in higher density neighbourhoods with nearby shopping and public transit (to downtown). There is less need to travel longer distances to shop. Third, the household may gradually reduce the use of the automobile, and eventually give it up. As the final columns in the table indicates, the proportion of shopping trips that take place in cars gradually declines over time; and the role of the senior is increasingly that of passenger instead of driver. This final stage in the aging process restricts the shopping trip to the neighbourhood strip mall or transit accessible locations. And with a smaller household and dwelling unit, there is less need to travel long distances to the big mall or power centre.

All of the changes listed above affect the shopping location. If electronics, home furnishings, and clothes rank low on your shopping priorities there is less reason to seek out power centres. And power centres and power nodes, with their confusion of entrances, stores, and walkways, are too stressful for many senior shoppers -- although a Wal-Mart will attract them with lower prices for basics. Instead, senior households will frequent the traditional and familiar shopping locations: nearby stores or an older mall or downtown that is on the bus route. Their world is centred on the home: they are less likely than younger households to explore new commercial facilities.

These patterns are unlikely to reverse the current trends toward bigger stores and power retail locations, since the households that buy heavily are still young and mobile. Over time, however, we will see an erosion of certain kinds of retail activity as the proportion of young and active households declines. Senior households are significantly less well-off than middle-aged households, and they behave that way. These are people who are aware of the change in their income level. They spend their money cautiously, looking for bargains in stores that offer value rather than glitz. The households are smaller in size; so that both consumers and retailers lose economies of scale. As seniors grow in number, fashions will trend towards the downscale and the individual, and away from innovation.

The Changes in Mobility

It is evident from the discussion above that our present knowledge of the travel patterns and shopping behaviour of seniors is quite limited. This section of the paper explores the trip data from the Transportation for Tomorrow Survey (or TTS) (http://www.jpint.utoronto.ca/ttshome/) to see in what ways seniors' travel patterns in general, and shopping patterns in particular, differ from the rest of the population. We will begin with an overview of the TTS project and its data base, and then explore the data in two ways: first, to develop some aggregate measures of age differences in mobility, and second, to evaluate how seniors respond to a variety of commercial concentrations within Toronto such as downtown, Yorkdale, or major power centres on the periphery.

The Transportation for Tomorrow Survey

This project, sponsored jointly by the Government of Ontario, the regional governments in the study area, and the Toronto Transportation Commission, involves in-depth interviews of 150,000 households about their household characteristics and daily travel patterns. The data have been gathered in 1986, 1991, 1996, and 2001, and the 2006 survey is currently in preparation. We will work with the 2001 data. Each household is asked a series of questions about demography, housing, etc. and each individual over the age of 11 is asked about workplace, driver's licence, Metropass, etc. The distinctive contribution of the survey is the collection of travel information, in which each individual person trip is coded by start time, purpose, origin, travel mode, and destination (Table 13).

Over the years the TTS has expanded its spatial coverage until it now extends from Peterborough to Simcoe County to Wellington to Niagara, including 6.5 million people and

TABLE 13. The Transportation for Tomorrow Survey Data Base

Geography	Households	Persons	Trips
Regions,	Geography	Age/gender	Start time
Municipalities,	Dwelling unit	Occupation	Purpose
Traffic zones.	Household data	Car, transit pass	Geography
for Census data, and	Vehicles,	Employed	Origin
TTS summary data	Drivers,	School	Geography
(households,	Workers,	Workplace	Destination
persons, trips, etc.)	Trips, etc.	Trips	Mode of travel
			Trip length

Source: Transportation for Tomorrow Survey, 2001

TABLE 14. Trips by Trip Purpose, 2001

				Destinations (Per Cent)						
Origins	Other[1]	Sub-work[2]	School	Sub-school[3]	Daycare	Deliver[4]	Work	House	Shop	Total Trips[5]
Deliver	7.22	0.76	1.01	0.04	0.38	10.75	15.71	58.87	5.26	888.8
Work	7.43	9.97	0.29	0.01	0.59	3.18	0.03	74.90	3.59	3,013.7
Other	15.97	2.29	0.68	0.19	0.10	2.24	2.63	68.93	6.96	2,138.6
Home	22.72	1.23	14.06	0.25	0.64	10.32	38.97	0.11	11.69	6,001.5
School	5.06	0.06	0	0.66	0.10	0.74	2.11	90.18	1.09	903.6
Daycare	5.73	0.65	1.70	0.04	2.47	4.94	32.54	47.58	4.40	65.7
Shop	9.09	1.27	0.09	0.06	0.11	2.13	0.89	72.03	14.33	1,186.8
Total Destinations[5]	2,150.9	446.1	878.0	26.6	65.9	894.2	2,586.6	5,962.4	1,188.2	14,198.7

[1]   Destinations that are neither work, nor school, nor shopping, nor home: typically social events.
[2]   A second work place destination.
[3]   A second school destination.
[4]   A trip to deliver or pick-up a passenger.
[5]   In 1000's.

Source: Transportation for Tomorrow Survey, 2001.

2.4 million households. On average, each person over the age of 11 makes 2.5 trips per day for a total of 14.2 million trips. Table 14 describes the flow of trips among different activities among nine kinds of destinations, for the region as a whole. Trips beginning at home are the most frequent, generating 42 per cent of all trips. Other important origins are the workplace (21 per cent) and 'other' (mostly social) trips (15 per cent). More than 1.1 million trips (8.3 per cent) originate at stores. The destinations are ranked in roughly the same order as the origins. One issue of importance for the analysis of shopping patterns is the origin of the 1.19 million shopping trips. About 59 per cent of the trips come directly from home, and another 9.1 per cent come from work, while 12.5 per cent and 14.3 per cent come from social locations or other shopping places, respectively. Thus the location or spatial concentration of these alternative locations that are away from the home also affects the choice of store.

For this analysis we have extracted all those trips made by seniors (60 years of age or more) and we can compare them with the population as a whole. Note that in this section we study individual seniors rather than senior households. We can examine the mobility of seniors in general, and for the subset of trips that target shopping destinations. It will be evident that seniors display significantly different patterns of shopping behaviour from the younger cohorts.

Overall Patterns of Mobility for Seniors

The comparisons between seniors and non-seniors were carried out in two stages. This part of the paper compares the overall movement patterns such as the numbers of trips of various kinds, and the distance travelled, while the section to follow will focus on the shopping trips to various retail locations within the City of Toronto. Once again, we find incredible detail in the TTS data.

Table 15 provides an overview of the effects of aging on mobility across the TTS study area. We observe that seniors make up about 16 per cent of the population but generate only 14 per cent of all trips because, among other things, trips to work or school are no longer part of the daily routine. On the other hand, the time available to seniors permits them to take far more shopping trips -- amounting to an amazing 32 per cent of all shopping trips. Twenty per cent of all trips taken by seniors go to shopping destinations. The result is more trips to spend less money: seniors fill the malls, sitting on benches, sipping coffee in the food court, cruising the corridors, thus creating the illusion of retail activity without filling the cash registers.

Shopping trips by seniors tend to more oriented to the home (65 per cent) compared to younger cohorts (55 per cent) and the destinations are also closer to the home; with

TABLE 15. The Mobility of Seniors, Toronto Region			
Activity	Age 1-59	Age 60-98	All Age Groups
Number of Persons	5,459,600	1,070,000 (16.6%)	6,529,600
Number of Trips	12,254,700	1,944,000 (13.7%)	14,198,700
Number of Shopping Trips	799,300	387,400 (32.6%)	1,186,700
Trips per Person	2.26	1.82	2.17
Shopping Trips per Person	0.148	0.362	0.182
Per Cent Trips for Shopping (%)	6.35	19.9	8.4
Shopping Trips from Home	446,800	253,700	701,800
Per Cent from Home (%)	55.9	65.5	59.1
Average Distance: All Trips (Km.)	5.95	4.95	5.81
Average Distance: Shopping Trips (Km.)	3.65	3.45	3.58
Per Cent Shopping Trips within same Ward (Toronto)	28.8	35.6	31.1
Mode of Travel (Shopping Trips) (%)			
Auto	84.5	87.1	85.4
Transit	12.7	11.6	12.3
Other	1.5	0.6	1.2
Walk	1.3	0.7	1.1

Source: Transportation for Tomorrow Survey, 2001

35 per cent of all trips within the home ward compared to only 29 per cent for younger cohorts. (Note that the City of Toronto contains 44 wards with an average population of just over 50,000 people.) If we measure the average distance travelled we find that seniors make shorter trips as well (since they exclude the journey-to-work), at 4.95 km. on average, compared to 5.95 km. for younger people -- a difference of twenty per cent. Their shopping trips are also shorter than those of younger people on average, at 3.45 km. compared to 3.65. Finally, the data on the mode of travel destroys any illusions about seniors' use of transit, or a return to the pedestrian lifestyle. Instead, we find that seniors are more likely than young people to use a car on a shopping trip, and the probability of a walk to the shop is negligible. In summary, seniors shop much more frequently than younger households, but shop closer to home; and chances are they drive or ride in the car to make their trips.

Comparing Commercial Locations

The TTS also permits the analysis of trade areas for specific shopping locations; including the variations in trade areas for different kinds of travellers, according to age cohort, occupation, workplace location; or mode of travel -- be it car or transit or bicycle. We have examined the distribution of shopping trips among the 481 traffic zones within the City of Toronto (with an average population of

about 5,000 people); for seniors and for the rest of the population. Figure 8 presents the spatial context for the analysis, as the distribution of seniors by residence and by shopping destination, as derived from the TTS. The map of residence suggests that seniors are actually much more dispersed than the pattern in Figure 7 suggested. The fact that there were higher proportions of seniors in higher income areas simply means that well-to-do seniors can afford to live by themselves instead of sharing a dwelling with the younger generation. The map of the destinations of all shopping trips undertaken by seniors shows that shopping trips are highly clustered at shopping centres and other commercial nodes, but the clusters, in turn, are dispersed in an orderly fashion across the urban landscape. Each neighbourhood has access to a variety of commercial locations of varying sizes. Note that the regions displayed on the map are political units -- the wards defined by the municipal government (and referred to in Table 15).

Table 16 lists the leading commercial destinations for all age groups. Scarborough Town Centre leads the way, generating more than 15,000 trips per day, followed by the other large regional shopping centres: Yorkdale, Sherway, and the Eaton Centre. Cloverdale and Fairview Mall are smaller shopping centres that manage to attract more visitors than the larger ones. Note that downtown, as represented by the Eaton Centre, ranks six on the list, but

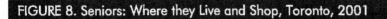

FIGURE 8. Seniors: Where they Live and Shop, Toronto, 2001

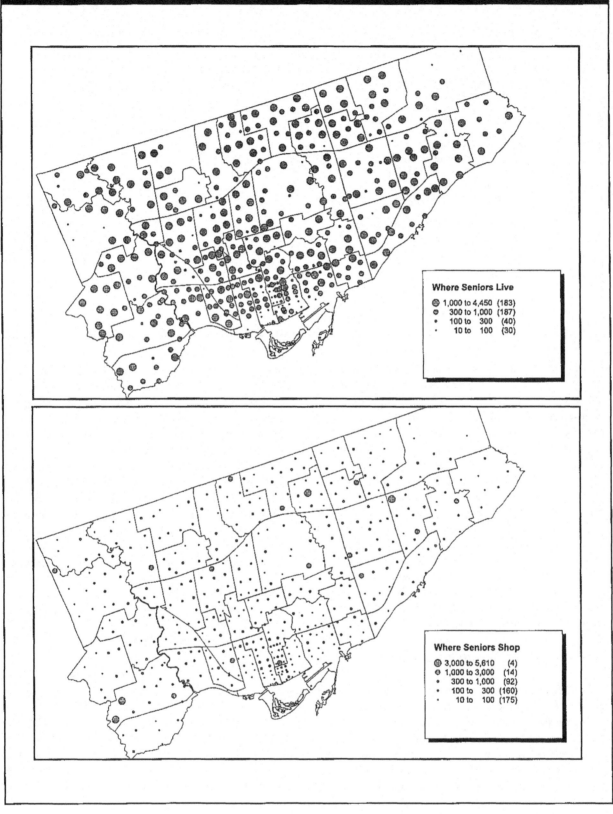

TABLE 16. Leading Shopping Destinations, Toronto, 2001

Rank	Shopping Trips	Name	Rank Seniors[1]	Rank Non-Seniors[2]	Per Cent Visitors who are Seniors[3]
1.	15,105	Scarborough T. C.	2	1	29.4%
2.	13,178	Yorkdale S. C.	5	2	21.8
3.	11,615	Cloverdale Mall	1	7	48.3
4.	10,870	Sherway Gardens	3	4	33.7
5.	9,361	Fairview Mall	4	5	32.1
6.	9,192	Eaton Centre	11	3	19.7
7.	7,508	Dufferin Mall	14	6	19.2
8.	7,374	Eglinton Square	6	8	37.3
9.	5,460	Bayview Village	9	9	34.8
10.	5,251	Centrepoint Mall	8	11	44.4
11.	4,710	Cedarbrae Mall	10	12	39.8
12.	4,631	Gerrard Square	7	17	57.7
13.	4,486	Woodbine Centre	15	10	28.2
14.	3,831	Morningside Mall	12	16	41.6
15.	3,797	Sheridan Mall	13	15	40.8
16.	3,364	Queensway/Kipling	17	13	31.3
17.	3,060	Ellesmere/Warden	26	14	24.9
18.	2,826	Agincourt Mall	16	23	43.4
19.	2,737	Shoppers World	19	19	34.9
20.	2,668	Woodside Square	20	20	35.0

Source: Transportation for Tomorrow Survey, 2001.

if nearby traffic zones were included (south of Queen, Yonge and Bloor) downtown would rank first, although not by much; and largely due to the downtown employment. Virtually all the leading destinations within the City of Toronto are traditional shopping centres; neither retail strips nor power centres make the list. In part this reflects the way traffic zones are delineated as small neighbourhood units that break up retail strips or clusters of power retail; but the importance of the malls also reflects the reality of commercial attractions. Malls draw customers, and especially seniors.

The generation gap is demonstrated by the differential ranking assigned to the various malls by different age groups. For seniors the top attraction is Cloverdale Mall, a shopping centre with about 300,000 square feet of floor area on the far West end of the city, about a mile north of Sherway Gardens. Other places that rank high for seniors include Fairview Mall, Eglinton Square, and Gerrard Square. The Eaton Centre ranks relatively low, as do Yorkdale and Dufferin Mall. Another measure of the attractiveness of various locations is the ratio of seniors to the total number of visitors. The overall seniors ratio for the City of Toronto is exactly one third, but at Gerrard Square the ratio is over 57 per cent seniors, and several other malls attract more than 40 per cent. Conversely, the ratio of seniors in the Eaton Centre, Yorkdale, or Dufferin Mall is only twenty per cent. Further analysis of special attractions or "Seniors' Days" would probably elaborate the pattern of specialization.

A quick inspection of the patterns suggests that seniors prefer smaller, more accessible community scale malls over the larger regional malls along the expressways. A supermarket and a Zellers, a bank and a drug store, and a variety of other inexpensive shops is sufficient. The Eaton Centre attracted 1.45 per cent of senior trips, but 2.96 -- more than twice much -- of non-seniors. The three regional malls drew 8.8 per cent of seniors, but 11.3 per cent of younger people. On the other hand, the 14 malls at the next smaller size level generated 23.3 per cent of senior trips but only 18.9 per cent of younger shoppers.

The maps of trade areas for seniors and non-seniors show another aspect of the location preferences of seniors: because they place more emphasis on nearness than variety, they are less likely to travel long distances to large malls and they generate compact trade areas around the shopping

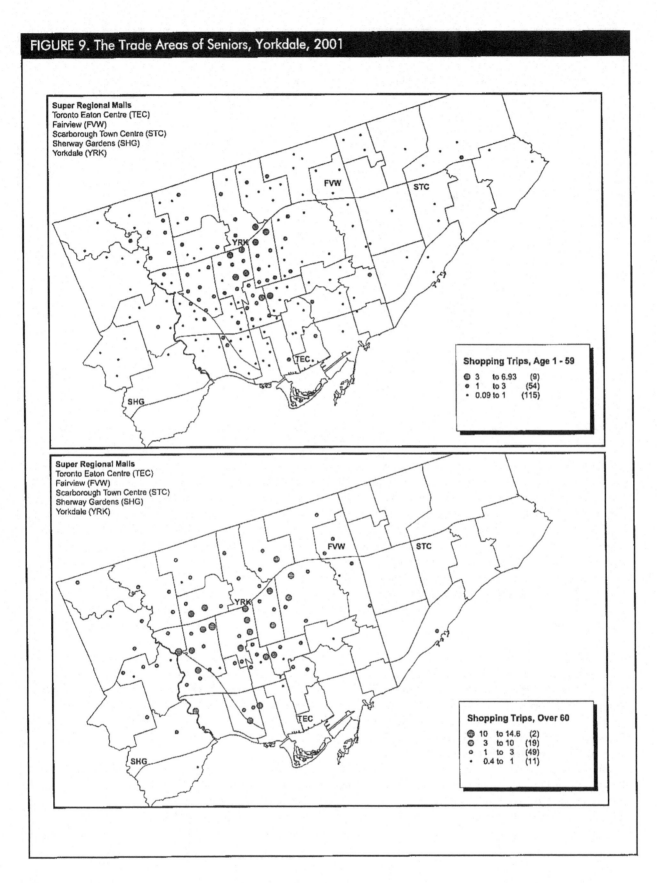

FIGURE 9. The Trade Areas of Seniors, Yorkdale, 2001

Super Regional Malls
Toronto Eaton Centre (TEC)
Fairview (FVW)
Scarborough Town Centre (STC)
Sherway Gardens (SHG)
Yorkdale (YRK)

Shopping Trips, Age 1 - 59
3 to 6.93 (9)
1 to 3 (54)
0.09 to 1 (115)

Super Regional Malls
Toronto Eaton Centre (TEC)
Fairview (FVW)
Scarborough Town Centre (STC)
Sherway Gardens (SHG)
Yorkdale (YRK)

Shopping Trips, Over 60
10 to 14.6 (2)
3 to 10 (19)
1 to 3 (49)
0.4 to 1 (11)

centres. Figure 9 contrasts the trade area for Yorkdale for younger adults (above) and for seniors (below). Younger adults from all over the city visit Yorkdale occasionally; but the seniors come in larger numbers from nearby residential areas. The same is true of Scarborough Town Centre or Sherway. Seniors come from smaller but well-defined trade areas that have higher penetration rates.

The study of shopping behaviour reveals that seniors are already a significant factor in the traffic to shopping centres, because of their propensity to 'go to the mall' -- even if it does not involve a significant purchase. Doubling the population of seniors may overwhelm the parking lots and washrooms of shopping centres. The analysis of destinations indicates that their choices may not match those of younger populations. Propinquity, combined with the availability of some basic services, appears to be more important than variety or sophistication.

Connecting the Dots

An overview of the aging process as it affects commercial activity involves a variety of academic disciplines: the demographers contribute their forecasts of future population, the economists probe the expected changes in income and expenditure, transportation engineers explore the travel patterns of seniors, and location analysts attempt to disaggregate this information for specific destinations. The problem at this stage in the paper is to summarize all these bits of information to make a coherent whole. We begin the discussion with a simulation model that explores the differences between high growth and slow growth

regions of the country, in order to see the range of consumption effects that derive from the aging population. This is followed by another exercise that applies the results from the TTS analysis to one of the conventional location models. The final part of the paper summarizes the results of the entire report.

Simulating the Effects of the Aging Population

In an attempt to evaluate the impact of the aging population on consumption, we have carried out an experiment in simulation, with the results reported in Table 17.

First, it is apparent that the impact of aging on consumption will depend on the local growth rate. Nowadays, most population growth takes place through migration, and migration is largely driven by young people – aged 15 to 35. While we have documented the modest patterns of relocation by seniors, these numbers are small relative to migration levels as a whole; so that the net addition or loss of young people becomes the major factor in modifying the ration of seniors -- in addition to the aging process. While this paper refers to the projected changes in the national population that incorporate an overall growth rate of twenty-five per cent, those locations that grow more rapidly add more younger households; while places that grow more slowly will lose these households and feel the impact of the aging process more strongly. Our simulation experiment compares six regions of Canada: the Atlantic provinces, Quebec, Ontario, the Eastern Prairies (Manitoba and Saskatchewan), Alberta and BC. As the 2031 populations suggest, these regions include a wide

---

TABLE 17. Simulating the Impact of the Aging Process by Region: Demographics

	BC	AB	SK/MB	ON	QC	ATL.	CANADA
Population, 2001	4,177	3,057	2,151	11,898	7,397	2,341	31,021
Population, 2031	5,616	4,145	2,332	16,130	8,396	2,402	39,021
Change	1,439	1,088	181	4232	999	61	8,000
Growth Rate (%)	34.5	35.6	8.4	35.6	13.5	2.6	25.8
Change in Seniors	977	705	282	2,569	1,334	433	6,300
Growth Rate Seniors (%)	135.8	169.1	72.5	130.1	102.7	104.8	120.9
Change in Seniors/Total Change	67.9	64.8	155.8	60.7	133.5	709.8	78.8
Per Cent Seniors, 2031 (%)	30.2	27.1	28.8	28.2	31.6	35.2	29.5

Population in 1000's

Source: Statistics Canada: "Annual Demographic Statistics, 2005" and "Projected Population by Age Groups, 2006-2031."

TABLE 18. Simulating the Impact of the Aging Process by Region: Income and Expenditures

	BC	AB	SK/MB	ON	QC	ATL.	CANADA
Population, 2001	4,177	3,057	2,151	11,898	7,397	2,341	31,021
Population, 2031	5,616	4,145	2,332	16,130	8,396	2,402	39,021
Growth Rate (%)	34.5	35.6	8.4	35.6	13.5	2.6	25.8
Regional Factor	1.056	0.961	0.929	1.067	0.941	0.870	1.000
Income per Capita							
2001	$28,850	25,970	24,700	29,130	23,250	23,740	27,280
2031	$28,510	25,740	24,560	28,750	26,920	23,340	27,090
Growth Rate (%)	3.63	4.76	4.55	4.12	2.60	4.45	4.34
Growth Rate (%)							
Total Income	39.3	42.1	13.4	41.16	16.5	7.2	31.5
Total Expenditure	68.7	72.0	37.3	70.9	41.0	29.8	59.2

Source: Statistics Canada: "Annual Demographic Statistics, 2005";
"Projected Population by Age Groups, 2006-2031"; "Census of Canada, 2001";
Survey of Household Spending, 2004".

range of projected growth rates, from 2.6 per cent in the Atlantic region to 35 per cent in Ontario, Alberta, and British Columbia. Furthermore, the lower the growth rate of population, the more accelerated the aging process, as indicated by the per cent of the regional growth that is contributed by seniors: between 60 and 70 per cent of the total in the high growth regions, but more than one hundred per cent in the slow growth areas. The bottom line of the demographic analysis is the per cent of population aged over 60 in the year 2031 by region, ranging from 27 per cent in Alberta to 35 per cent in the Atlantic region.

The demographic analysis projects the population by age cohort for each region, and if we multiply each cohort by the average income per capita for the age cohort, as derived from the Census of Canada, 2001, we can estimate the overall income per capita for each region. The same income vector for cohorts is applied to the 2031 populations in order to estimate regional incomes per capita in 2031. The income estimates for both years are further modified by multiplying by the regional factor, again derived from the Census, 2001 that compares the regional income per capita in 2001 to the national average. Finally we compute the growth rates of income per capita by region, as determined by the cohort population shifts. As noted earlier, the decline in household income with age is partly offset by the corresponding decline in household size that moderates the effect on income per capita. As well, Canada in 2031 will have a substantially smaller population under fifteen years of age. The result, as shown in Table 18, is a slight increase in income per capita at the regional scale due to the demo-

graphic shifts. It amounts to 4.34 per cent nationwide, and ranges from 2.60 per cent in Quebec to 4.76 per cent in Alberta. This effect, combined with the 25 per cent increase in population, produces an overall income growth of more than thirty per cent. Most of the income growth is due to the population growth, as indicated by the pattern of regional variation.

The final stage in the simulation sequence evaluates the expenditure effect. As households age and incomes decline, the share of income devoted to taxes and savings is reduced, so that consumption increases. Based on the changes in cohorts, the overall ratio of expenditures to income increases from 0.743 in 2001 to 0.899 in 2031; and this shift has a substantial impact on consumption, almost doubling the impact of the overall growth in income. Nationally, expenditures increase by 59 per cent, compared to 31 per cent for income, and even the Atlantic region can expect a thirty per cent increase in consumer expenditure. At the same time, this increased share of income devoted to consumption takes place within households that are smaller and poorer, as well as older. The consumption process is fragmented.

It will not escape the attentive reader that we have ignored the potential growth in the national income, as well as any additional regional variations that may take place over thirty years. Will Alberta become richer? Will Newfoundland find prosperity? To be blunt, economists simply avoid income forecasts that extend beyond the current business cycle, and we must do the same. At the same time it is probably realistic to estimate a modest rate of average annual growth in income each year – perhaps of the order of one per cent (since the overall labour force is unlikely to grow substantially, this improvement must come from the increase in productivity) and this growth may also help to soften the impact of aging on expenditures, both nationally and locally, just as it has diffused the impact of other recent retail innovations such as big box stores (Simmons, 2001).

Note that the simulation permits a variety of other experiments, in that the less reliable steps in the model can be evaluated systematically in a form of risk analysis. For example, Statistics Canada provides a range of population projections that reflect different population scenarios. To apply each of them in turn, and to examine the results, would give a sense of the variance in outcomes that can occur in various regions over different time periods. Similarly, we could suggest alternatives scenarios of regional economic growth (by changing the regional adjustment factors), or changes in the relative incomes of senior cohorts in expectation of the introduction of various social programmes.

Allocating the Growth to Locations

At this point we can return to the question, "Where do they shop? If we can forecast the redistribution of income as a result of the aging process, and we assume that the current distribution of retail facilities remains unchanged (a major assumption!), what can we say about the impact of aging on the location of retail sales? Consider a community within the city where the proportion of seniors has doubled, but the households are smaller and automobile use is in decline -- but shopping trips are increasing.

Suppose that we apply some form of the Huff model to explain shopping behaviour (see Hernandez et al., 2004):

Mall Shopper Utility Function

Mall Patronage Probability Function

$$U_{ij} = A_j^\alpha D_{ij}^\beta \qquad P_{ij} = \frac{A_j^\alpha}{D_{ij}^\beta} \bigg/ \sum_j \frac{A_j^\alpha}{D_{ij}^\beta}$$

U_{ij} is the utility of mall j to consumer at location i

P_{ij} is the probability that a consumer at location i will patronize mall j

A_j is the attractiveness of mall j

D_{ij} is the distance between i and j

α is the attractiveness parameter
β is the distance decay parameter

The model simple states that the utility (i.e., a surrogate for sales) of a given mall will be a function of the 'attractiveness' of the mall in relation to the distance of the mall from the consumers in neighbourhoods i. The attraction of the mall could be measured in terms of square footage, the number of tenants, retail quality or a combination of factors. The α and β parameters reflect how consumers react to 'attraction' and 'distance', e.g., a large β value would reflect that mall patronage declines sharply as distance from the mall increases (i.e., being close to the mall is important).

In applying the model, we can make some assumptions about a world in which there are twice as many seniors as present. First, the expenditures in neighbourhood i will change, as the neighbourhood ages. If the number of households (dwelling units) remains the same, overall income and expenditure will decline (as in upper income areas). If the housing is adjusted to permit an increased number of senior households, income and expenditure may well increase. At any rate the household units will be smaller and more numerous; with more seniors living alone, notably women.

Second, the trips to shopping facilities will be more numerous than before, and more of them will begin at the home. Thus the attractiveness of nearby malls will be greater (β will be larger, a steeper distance decay curve), although the sales per trip will decline. Figure 10 shows how the number of shopping trips varies with distance for seniors and nonseniors. Seniors take more short distance trips, especially less than two kilometres; but beyond that point, non-seniors dominate. Seniors are less likely to drive, and more likely to shop near the house. Since they buy fewer 'big-ticket' items, and more food and pharmacy products, they are less attracted to large malls, downtown, or power centres. There may be a non-linear relationship between the number of trips and floor area, as the attraction is reduced above a certain size of mall. The result may be seen declining sales in the larger commercial concentrations that are located farther away from consumers. Meanwhile, smaller centres that are closer to households should compete more successfully. The increased friction of distance (β) should reduce the amount of competition, as each commercial location intensifies its hold on a trade area that is reduced in size, thus strengthening spatial monopolies. Exceptions to these generalizations may include those downtowns (positive) that benefit from good service by public transit, and power retail centres in general (negative) since they are less attractive to senior shoppers. Upscale shopping destinations may also be threatened as aging consumers resolve the income changes by bargain-hunting.

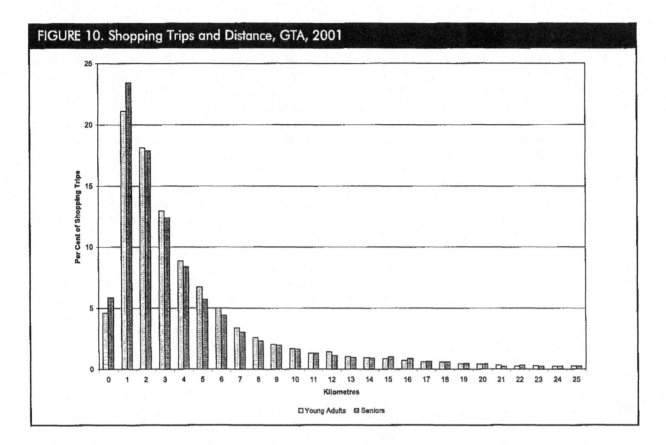

FIGURE 10. Shopping Trips and Distance, GTA, 2001

Summary

This research report has highlighted:

- The next thirty years will witness substantial changes in Canada's age distribution, as the baby boomers retire, the birth rate declines, and immigration cannot keep pace with the aging. We estimate that more than two thirds of Canada's population growth will take place in cohorts that are sixty years or older. Only one third of the growth occurs in the cohorts that are active in the labour force.

- The process of aging will affect every part of the country, but certain locations are more vulnerable. The distribution of seniors in 2001 shows substantial variations at the scale of the urban system and also within the city. These variations are linked to historical growth rates, and also to the preference of retirees for warmer and high amenity places. The elderly are also concentrated in the older parts of the metropolitan region, and in neighbourhoods where the housing is more appropriate to their needs.

- Worldwide data support the continuation and even the extension of these patterns. Life expectancy is everywhere increasing at a regular rate, and early retirement has a universal appeal. Only the most draconian social policies can overcome these trends.

- An important impact of aging on consumption is the substantial loss of household income – as much as fifty per cent – that occurs with retirement. If the retiree population grows at the expense of the working population significant declines in local income can result. For example, at the urban system scale each percentile increase in the proportion of seniors reduces income per capita by $226.

- Paradoxically, this decline in household income is off-set by the decline in household size, and the declining share of population under fifteen. The most important contribution of the aging population to consumption is the increased share of income that is diverted from taxes and savings into expenditures. As a result expenditures per capita are higher for seniors than for younger households.

- These modest increases in expenditures are accompanied by changes in the types of purchases, reflecting the decline in household size and lifestyle changes. Seniors continue to buy the necessities of food, shelter and health care, but cut back sharply on luxury items such as clothing and furniture.

- Evidence from the Transportation for Tomorrow Survey suggests that seniors -- with more time available -- are twice as likely to go shopping as non-seniors, and more likely to travel directly from home. On average their shopping trips are shorter, and more often remain within the same city ward.

- This shopping behaviour results in a different set of location preferences that downgrade the largest commercial concentrations (downtown and the regional malls) in favour of community scale shopping centres with supermarkets and discount department stores. The seniors that will make up a growing proportion of the Canadian population in the years to come are different kinds of consumers than their younger counterparts in a variety of ways. Inevitably, some -- if not all -- of the commercial fabric will have to respond.

References

Chawla, R. K. 2005. "Shifts in Spending Patterns of Older Canadians." Perspectives on Labour and Income. (Statistics Canada, Catalogue 75-001), December 2005, pp. 17-28.

Gauthier, A. and Smeeding, T. 2000. "Time Use at Older Ages: Cross-National Differences," OECD.

Gower, D. 1998. "Income Transition upon Retirement." Perspectives on Labour and Income. (Statistics Canada, Catalogue 75-001), 10, 4 (Winter), pp. 18-23.

Harchaoui, T.M. and Tarkhani, F. 2004. "Shifts in Consumer Spending." Perspectives on Labour and Income. (Statistics Canada, Catalogue 75-001), 15, 2 (summer), on-line.

Hernandez, T., Lea, T. and Bermingham, P. (2004) What's in a Trade Area?, Research Report 2004-03. Toronto: Centre for the Study of Commercial Activity, Ryerson University.

Myles, J. 2000. "Incomes of Seniors." Perspectives on Labour and Income. (Statistics Canada, Catalogue 75-001), 12, 4, pp. 23-30.

Sauve, R. 2005. The Current State of Canadian Family Finances - 2004 Report. Ottawa: The Vanier Institute of the Family.

Simmons, J. 2001. "The Economic Impact of Wal-Mart Stores". Newsletter 2001-12. Toronto: Centre for the Study of Commercial Activity, Ryerson University.

Simmons, J. and Kamikihara, S. "Commercial Activity in Canada: 2006." Research Report 2007-03. Toronto: Centre for the Study of Commercial Activity, Ryerson University.

The Economist. 2004. "Forever Young; a Survey of Retirement." March 27, 18 pp.

Turcotte, M. and Schnellenburg, G. 2007. A Portrait of Seniors in Canada, 2007. Ottawa:(Statistics Canada, Catalogue 89-519).

Williams, C. 2003. "Finances in the Golden Years." Perspectives on Labour and Income. (Statistics Canada, Catalogue 75-001), November, on-line.

Chapter 11

CANADA'S LEADING RETAILERS
Christopher Daniel and Tony Hernandez

Introduction

This paper is the fourth edition of the CSCA's Canada's Leading Retailers report, a series analyzing the strategies of growth carried out by Canada's leading retailers during fiscal 2004. It addresses the reorganization of retail capital emerging from ongoing processes of consolidation and organic growth in Canada's top 95 retail conglomerates. Although the popularity of the merger process as a corporate growth strategy reached its height in the1990s and has since slowed, it continues to be an important component of Canada's retail economy. In order to shed some light on the reorganization of retailing in Canada during fiscal 2004, this report will focus on three aspects of the country's leading retailers: their economic profiles, market concentration, and the major events in each of the major retail categories throughout the year.

Definitions, Reporting Periods, and the transition to NAICS

The classification of firms as Canada's leading retailers is based primarily on the total sales of the retail conglomerates. The CSCA considers a conglomerate or business to be one of Canada's leading retailers when the total retail sales of that company within Canada are greater than 100 million dollars. A series of financial and locational information on each company has been systematically collected for these companies since 2000 using a variety of sources ranging from corporate annual filings, industry reports, company rankings, and newspaper articles[1]. The information contained in this report pertains to the fiscal 2004 year, being the year beginning on January 1st 2004 and ending on December 31st 2004. This distinction is an important one to make because many companies use varying definitions for their fiscal year. Some companies will refer to their information as belonging to the year in which it is reported, whereas other companies will report the information as belonging to the year in which the majority of their reporting period takes place.

Information stated in this report that was taken from annual reports is included where the majority of the reporting period occurs during the January 1st 2004 to December 31st 2004 time period. For private companies, the most recent information available from industry reports, company rankings, and newspaper articles are used where the

majority of the year preceding the publication date of the information source lies within the indicated reporting period. For example, if a company released an annual report which they referred to as their 2005 annual report, but the reporting period was from February 1st 2004 to January 31st 2005, then the information found in that report could be used to determine the numbers included in this 2004 report. Similarly, if a company ranking was published in one of the major business industry magazines containing yearly information on one of the private retail companies, and the article was released in October of 2004, then the information found in that article could be used to update the numbers for that company in this report. Conversely, an annual report that covered the June 1st 2003 to May 31st 2004 time period, or a newspaper article published in February 2004, would not be used to determine the information contained in this report.

Another important distinction to make in this report is the use of a different industrial classification system. In 1997, Canada, the United States, and Mexico developed a common industrial classification system called NAICS (North American Industrial Classification System) that was designed to simplify industrial comparisons of the three countries after they signed the North American free trade agreement. In the previous edition of this report, retail conglomerates were reported with SIC(1980) codes (Standard Industrial Classification) whereas this edition reports conglomerates based on NAICS codes.

In the SIC system, the retail categories are split between wholesale and retail trade based on the class of the customer. This meant that businesses that sold products to the public for personal or household use were considered "Retail". Those businesses that primarily sold products to retailers, manufacturers, dealers, public institutions, farmers, professionals and other wholesalers were considered to be "Wholesale" under the SIC system. With the NAICS codes, wholesale and retail are defined based on whether or not the products are sold in a store. As a result of this fundamental difference between the two systems, some stores have experienced a change in sector from wholesale in the SIC system to retail in the NAICS system. For example, computer stores, sellers of building materials (including home centres) and office supply and stationery stores, which were wholesalers under SIC, have become retailers under NAICS. Establishments whose principal activity is installation and repair, which belonged under retail trade in

---

[1] The data warehouse of the Centre for the Study of Commercial Activity (CSCA) holds all information used in this analysis.

SIC, are now part of the service sector in NAICS. This results in a crossover of approximately 6% of businesses from the wholesale sector to the retail sector under NAICS.

The switch in the use of classification systems in this report was made necessary by the fact that Statistics Canada began releasing retail trade data only under the NAICS system beginning in March of 2004, meaning that information related to this report such as total retail sales figures and retail sales by trade groupings are only released in the NAICS format. Although the NAICS system is not comparable with the SIC system as was explained previously, retail trade figures for NAICS have been released as far back as January 1991. This means that although the previous edition of the leading retailers report is not directly comparable to this edition, it is possible to recalculate some of the key figures in this report for the purpose of comparison.

Leading Retailers' Profiles & Strategies

The data for 2004 retail sales indicate that 95 corporations, controlling approximately 373 chains, contribute to over 68% of the non-automotive total sales as is shown in Table 1. Canada's leading retailers do the bulk of the retail activity and serve a variety of regional markets and social niches. Most of their networks continue to focus on the country's major markets where innovative and more efficient store formats can easily reach their critical mass of customers. Canada's leading retailers tend to concentrate their operations in the four provinces that include the largest cities: Ontario, Quebec, British Columbia and Alberta (Simmons and Kamikihara, 2005)[2].

The list of the 95 leading retailers, shown in Table 2, illustrates that the top three corporations in Canada control approximately 23% of the retail market, or 52.7 billion dollars, with over 3,100 retail locations between the three combined. There are 29 different companies operating in

[2] Simmons, J. and Kamikihara, S. 2005 *Commercial Activity in Canada*, 2004. CSCA Research Report 2005-04. Toronto, Ryerson University.

TABLE 1. Distribution of Retail Sales (NAICS): 2003 and 2004

2003

Sector	Sales		
Automotive	112,532.0		
All Others	218,615.0		
Top 95 retailers		149,202.0	68.25%
Other retailers		69,413.0	31.75%
Total	331,147.0		

2004

Sector	Sales		
Automotive	116,064.0		
All Others	230,657.0		
Top 95 retailers		158,862.73	68.87%
Other retailers		71,794.27	31.13%
Total	346,721.0		

Source: Data obtained from Statistics Canada, Retail Trade 63-005-XIE

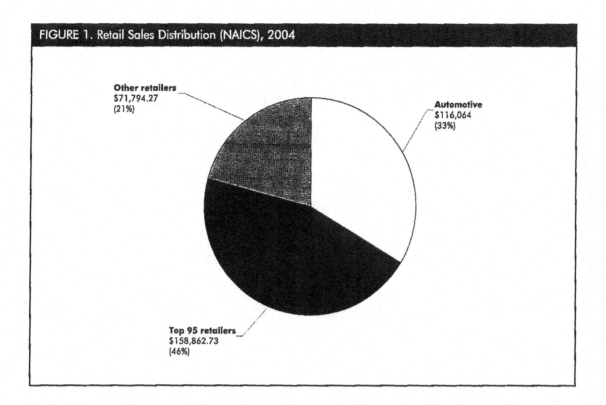

FIGURE 1. Retail Sales Distribution (NAICS), 2004

Other retailers
$71,794.27
(21%)

Automotive
$116,064
(33%)

Top 95 retailers
$158,862.73
(46%)

Canada that have at least one-billion dollars in total retail sales, controlling a combined 14,718 store locations and approximately $140 billion in total retail sales - representing 88.1% of total sales by the retailers covered in this report, 60.7% of total non-automotive retail sales in Canada, and 40.4% of total retail sales in the Canadian market.

In comparison with previous years, the most noticeable changes in the ranking of the top retailers that are not attributable to new information sources can be seen in American Eagle Outfitters, Spiegel Holdings Inc. (Eddie Bauer), 2963876 Canada Inc. (Boutique Marie Claire), Groupe Les Ailes de la Mode (formerly Les Boutiques San Francisco), and Gendis Inc. (SAAN). American Eagle Outfitters dropped to number 72 on the list, down 19 spots from number 53, largely due to the sale of the 107 store Bluenotes/Thriftys chain. Spiegel Holdings dropped 9 spots to number 84 after going bankrupt following several consecutive missed quarterly filings and experiencing a slew of store closures in the U.S. Groupe Les Ailes de la Mode fell nine spots to number 82 after selling off its flagship San Francisco banner in addition to its Victoire Delage and Moments Intimes lingerie stores, all while recovering from a lengthy round of bankruptcy proceedings. Sales at the SAAN junior

department store chain plummeted during fiscal 2004, resulting in a drop of 8 spots to number 59 for Gendis Inc, who sold its slumping retail business to SAAN Acquisition Corp in December of 2004. Boutique Marie Claire (2963876 Canada Inc.) was the only company to significantly increase its ranking position, largely due to their purchase of the San Francisco banner from Groupe Les Ailes de la Mode.

Rona, YM, The Brick, and Wal-Mart did not change much in their ranking among the top retailers, but these companies are notable for having a significant percentage increase in total sales from the previous year. YM increased their sales by approximately 31% over the previous year, mainly resulting from their increased number of stores after purchasing the Bluenotes/Thriftys chain from American Eagle Outfitters. Wal-Mart continued to be a leader in the Canadian retail sector with an estimated 21% increase in total sales over the previous year due to increases in the number of stores, average store size, and sales per square foot. The Brick Warehouse Corporation grew their total sales by approximately 23%, mainly on the strength of their United Furniture Warehouse acquisition in early 2004, which more than doubled their store count overnight.

TABLE 2. Profile of Canada's Leading Retail Corporations: 2004-2005

Corporate Ownership	Selected Chains/Banners	Capital Control	Retail Sales ($ Millions)	Cum %. Sales	No. Chains	Footage Sq.ft.(000s)	Employees Total No.	Activity (NAICS)	No. of Stores	HQs Loc.
Weston Group	Loblaw, No Frills, Real Canadian Superstore	CAN	26,209	11.36%	17	51,343	130,000	445, 452	1,577	ON
Wal-Mart Inc.	Wal-Mart, Sam's Club	USA	14,335	17.58%	2	30,554	54,554	452	262	ON
The Sobeys Group	Sobeys, Price Chopper, IGA	CAN	12,189	22.86%	13	25,047	34,652	445, 446	1,310	NS
Costco Co. Inc.	Costco	USA	7,918	26.30%	1	9,765	12,000	452	63	ON
Hudson's Bay Co.	The Bay, Zellers, Home Outfitters	CAN	7,070	29.36%	6	47,351	69,694	442, 448, 452	547	ON
Metro Inc.	Metro, Super C, Loeb	CAN	5,999	34.46%	10	10,434	28,644	445, 446	629	QC
Sears-Roebuck & Co.	Sears, Sears Whole Home, Sears Outlet	USA	5,815	31.88%	4	20,600	41,962	442, 452, 454	187	ON
Safeway Inc.	Safeway	USA	5,247	36.76%	1	9,919	30,677	445	218	AB
Canadian Tire Corp. Ltd.	Canadian Tire, Mark's Work Wearhouse, Work World	CAN	5,164	39.00%	3	16,582	48,000	448, 452	790	ON
The Home Depot Inc.	The Home Depot	USA	4,752	41.06%	1	12,402	20,004	444	117	ON
Shoppers Drug Mart Inc.	Shoppers Drug Mart, Home Health Care	CAN	4,723	43.10%	2	7,000	38,779	446	964	ON
Home Hardware Stores Ltd.	Home Hardware, Home Furniture, Home Building Centre	CAN	4,263	44.95%	3	8,871	27,378	442, 444	1,159	ON
Tengelmann Warenhandelsgesells	Food Basics, A&P, Dominion	GER	4,210	46.78%	5	9,452	23,778	445	250	QC
Rona Inc.	Rona, Reno Depot, Botanix	CAN	3,680	48.37%	13	12,790	21,487	444	550	QC
Katz Group Canada Ltd.	IDA, Pharma Plus, Rexall Drug Store	CAN	3,531	49.90%	7	4,270	9,945	446	1,086	AB
Best Buy Enterprise	Best Buy, Future Shop	USA	3,225	51.30%	2	3,147	9,822	443	144	BC
Holding 29527 Canada Ltee.	Jean Coutu Pharmacy, PJC Sante Beaute, PJC Clinic	CAN	2,735	52.49%	3	2,821	12,813	446	320	QC
The Jim Pattison Group	Save On Foods & Drugs, Overwaitea Foods, AG Foods	CAN	2,681	53.65%	13	5,206	15,619	445	163	BC
McKesson Corp.	Clinique Sante, A&P Pharmacy, Health Care Pharmacy	USA	2,198	54.60%	5	2,657	6,397	446	498	AB
Tim-Br Marts Ltd.	Tim-Br Mart, BMR	CAN	1,869	55.41%	3	4,340	10,107	444	434	AB
TJX Companies Inc.	Winners, HomeSense	USA	1,593	56.10%	2	5,872	7,568	442, 448	208	ON
The Brick Warehouse Corporation	The Brick, United Furniture Warehouse, HomeShow	CAN	1,549	56.78%	3	4,965	6,200	442	168	AB
Pharmasave Drugs Ltd.	Pharmasave	CAN	1,509	57.43%	1	2,012	3,997	446	323	BC
Staples Inc.	Staples/Business Depot	USA	1,508	58.08%	1	5,712	7,750	453	238	ON
Developments Orano Inc.	Mac's, Couche-Tard, Becker Milk	CAN	1,461	58.72%	10	4,610	13,389	445	1,844	QC
London Drugs Ltd.	London Drugs	CAN	1,210	59.24%	7	1,475	5,605	446	59	BC
Uniprix Inc	Uniprix, Unipharm	CAN	1,200	59.76%	3	1,538	4,000	446	210	QC
The Forzani Group Ltd.	Sport Mart, Sports Experts, Sport Check	CAN	1,108	60.24%	10	4,844	8,855	448, 451	389	AB
IKEA AB	Ikea	SWE	1,070	60.71%	1	2,786	4,500	442	11	ON
GAP Inc.	The Gap, Old Navy, Bananna Republic	USA	960	61.12%	6	2,145	5,522	448	227	QC
The Reitman Group	Reitmans, Penningtons, Smart Set	CAN	912	61.52%	11	3,788	10,295	448	873	QC
BMTC Group Inc.	BMTC Bicault & Martineau, Tanguay Ameublements	CAN	802	61.87%	4	1,313	2,082	442	25	QC
Indigo Books & Music Inc.	Chapters, Coles The Book People, Indigo Books & Music	CAN	787	62.21%	6	2,583	6,448	451	258	ON
The Hart Group	CompuSmart, Hart Stores, Compucentre	CAN	763	62.54%	5	2,001	2,334	443, 452	176	QC
Toys "R" Us Inc.	Toys "R" Us	USA	758	62.87%	1	2,331	2,794	451	63	ON
Leon's Furniture Ltd.	Leon's Furniture	CAN	670	63.16%	1	3,990	1,969	442	57	ON
North West Co. Fund	Northern Stores, North Mart	CAN	605	63.42%	4	1,096	5,361	445, 452	148	MB
The Beta Industries	Athlete's World, Bata Shoe Store, Athlete's World Outlet	CAN	574	63.67%	3	1,450	5,220	448, 451	340	ON
InterTAN Inc.	Radio Shack, Battery Plus, Rogers Plus	USA	559	63.91%	3	1,625	3,521	443	966	ON
Davaldou Holdings Inc.	Aldo, Globo Shoes, Transit	CAN	505	64.13%	13	1,232	4,926	448	464	QC
YM Inc.	Suzy Shier, Stitches, Bluenotes	CAN	494	64.34%	11	1,462	5,284	448	480	ON
Groupe Sodisco-Howden Inc.	Pro Hardware, Ace Hardware	CAN	477	64.55%	2	3,297	9,842	444	750	QC
Groupe Jacob	Boutique Jacob, Jacob Annexe, Jacob Jr.	CAN	427	64.73%	8	1,008	2,430	448	212	QC
International Clothiers Inc.	Fairweather, International Clothiers, Randy River	CAN	406	64.91%	13	1,217	2,182	448	300	ON
HMV Inc	HMV Canada, HMV Canada Outlet	GBR	370	65.07%	2	430	1,902	451	102	ON
Jace Holdings	Thrifty Foods	CAN	359	65.23%	1	630	3,200	445	18	BC
La Senza Corp.	La Senza, La Senza Girl, Silk & Satin	CAN	355	65.38%	3	966	3,623	448	296	QC
Truserv Corp.	V&S Department Stores, True Value Hardware	CAN	352	65.53%	5	2,798	2,945	444, 452, 453	567	MB

TABLE 2. Profile of Canada's Leading Retail Corporations: 2004-2005 (cont.)

Corporate Ownership	Selected Chains/Banners	Capital Control	Retail Sales ($ Millions)	Cum. % Sales	No. Chains	Footage Sq.ft.(000s)	Employees Total No.	Activity (NAICS)	No. of Stores	HQs Loc.
Wittington Investment Ltd.	Holt Renfrew, Holt Renfrew Last Call	GBR	337	65.68%	2	572	2,034	452	11	ON
Giant Tiger Stores Ltd.	Giant Tiger	CAN	331	65.82%	1	2,489	4,338	452	131	ON
York Management Serv. Inc	Northern Reflections, Northern Getaway	USA	312	65.96%	2	738	3,726	448	249	ON
Office Depot Inc.	Office Depot/The Office Place	USA	278	66.08%	1	925	1,650	453	33	ON
Sony Corporation	The Sony Store	JPN	276	66.20%	1	227	1,233	443	72	ON
Roots Canada Ltd.	Roots, Roots Factory Outlet, Roots Kids	CAN	259	66.31%	4	612	1,283	442, 448	147	ON
Grafton-Fraser Inc.	Tip Top, Jack Fraser, George Richards Mr Big & Tall	CAN	259	66.42%	7	772	2,245	448	191	ON
Men's Wearhouse Inc.	Moore's The Suit People	USA	256	66.53%	1	684	1,200	448	114	ON
Zale Corp.	Peoples Jewellers, Mappins Jewellers	USA	249	66.64%	2	264	1,731	448	166	ON
Foot Locker Inc.	Foot Locker, Champs Sports	USA	249	66.75%	2	553	1,127	451	169	ON
Gendis Inc.	Saan, Red Apple Clearance Centre	CAN	244	66.86%	2	3021	3,136	448	239	MB
Denninghouse Inc.	Buck or Two	CAN	238	66.96%	1	1,523	2,546	452	331	ON
Le Chateau Inc.	Le Chateau, Le Chateau Outlet	CAN	233	67.06%	2	671	2,823	448	170	QC
Lagardere SCA	UCS, Maison de la Presse Internationale, Piccadilly Place	FRA	229	67.16%	12	211	1,530	451, 453	270	ON
Payless ShoeSource Inc.	Payless ShoeSource	USA	225	67.26%	1	976	1,900	448	305	ON
Le Groupe de la Famille Pelletier	Metro GP, Supermarche GP	CAN	212	67.35%	2	363	1,300	445	14	QC
Boise Cascade Corp.	Grand & Toy	USA	202	67.44%	1	300	2,700	453	70	ON
2963876 Canada Inc.	Mode Le Grenier, Boutique Marie Claire, Claire France	CAN	199	67.52%	9	822	2,387	448	290	QC
Saunders Karp & Magrue	Bootlegger, Ricki's, Cleo	USA	184	67.60%	4	1,220	2,831	448	283	ON
Hy & Zel's Inc.	Hy & Zel's The Supermarket Drug Store	CAN	182	67.68%	1	374	850	446	17	ON
Mountain Equipment Co-op	Mountain Equipment Co-op	CAN	178	67.76%	1	369	346	451	9	BC
Danier Leather Inc.	Danier Leather, Danier Leather Factory Outlet	CAN	166	67.83%	2	372	1,286	448	95	ON
Sports Excellence Corp.	Sports Excellence, Propac, Andre Lalonde Sports	CAN	162	67.90%	3	875	897	451	175	QC
American Eagle Outfitters Inc	American Eagle Outfitters, AE Outlet	USA	160	67.97%	2	330	1,262	448	69	ON
Nygard Co.	Jay Set, Tan Jay, Alia	CAN	160	68.04%	7	425	1,959	448	194	ON
Liquidation World Inc.	Liquidation World, Liquidation World Factory Outlet	CAN	159	68.11%	2	1,664	1,720	452	86	AB
Pet Valu Inc	Pet Valu	USA	147	68.17%	1	557	813	453	253	ON
EvelynHarry Enterprises Inc.	Harry Rosen, Harry Rosen Factory Outlet	CAN	143	68.23%	2	189	498	448	16	ON
Polo Ralph Lauren Corp.	Club Monaco, Caban, Club Monaco Factory Outlet	USA	133	68.29%	4	311	1,535	442, 448	44	ON
Fuji Photo Film Co. Ltd.	Black's Photography, Astral Photo	JPN	130	68.35%	2	203	1,655	443	156	ON
6149286 Canada Inc.	Pantorama, Levis 1850, Original Levis Store	CAN	128	68.40%	8	327	1,974	448	160	QC
Continental Saxon Group	Cotton Ginney, Cotton Ginney Factory Outlet	CAN	124	68.46%	2	482	1,232	448	137	ON
The Children's Place Retail Stores Inc	The Children's Place, The Disney Store	USA	118	68.51%	3	317	2,218	448, 453	69	ON
Groupe Les Ailes de la Mode	Les Ailes de la Mode, Bikini Village	CAN	110	68.56%	3	343	1,140	448, 452	68	QC
Petsmart Inc.	PetSmart	USA	109	68.60%	1	497	1,043	453	25	ON
Spiegel Holdings Inc.	Eddie Bauer	USA	108	68.65%	1	270	851	448	37	ON
The Body Shop International Plc	The Body Shop, The Body Shop Outlet	GBR	75	68.68%	2	109	849	446	109	ON
Laura Canada Inc.	Laura, Melanie Lyne, Finds	CAN	67	68.71%	6	300	980	448	54	QC
Blinds-to-Go Inc.	Blinds to Go	CAN	67	68.74%	1	230	1,200	442	46	QC
AEON Co. Ltd.	Talbots, Talbots Factory Outlet	JPN	63	68.77%	2	126	525	448	28	ON
Inditex Group	Zara	SPN	55	68.79%	1	122	218	448	12	ON
Long & McQuade Ltd.	Long & McQuade	CAN	48	68.81%	1	120	480	451	24	ON
Williams-Sonoma Inc.	Pottery Barn, Williams Sonoma, Pottery Barn Kids	USA	42	68.83%	3	90	400	442	11	ON
Tabi International Corp.	Tabi International, Tabi International Factory Outlet	CAN	35	68.85%	2	135	383	448	89	ON
H & M Hennes & Mauritz AB	H & M	SWE	34	68.86%	1	114	182	448	6	ON
French Connection Group plc	Fcuk	GBR	22	68.87%	1	55	175	448	12	ON
Edizione Holding SPA	United Colors of Benetton/Benetton, Benetton012	ITA	9	68.87%	3	30	196	448	17	USA

Market Control and Concentration

Canadian capital remained a strong influence in the Canadian retail sector as a whole during 2004. As can be seen in Table 3, Canadian retailers controlled approximately 20,000 stores and 63% of total retail sales of the major corporate chains. The influence of American retailers was reduced to 5177 stores and 32% of total retail sales. An important development that significantly influences the distribution of retail sales in this table is the Capital Control assignment given to Shoppers Drug Mart Inc. In late 2003, the American investor group led by Kholberg, Kravis, Roberts Co. that bought Shoppers Drug Mart in 1999 sold their majority stake in the company on the Toronto Stock Exchange (TSX), making Shoppers Drug Mart a widely held public company. The investor relations department at Shoppers Drug Mart Inc. believes that approximately 90% of the investors holding Shoppers Drug Mart shares are Canadian investors and it is for this reason that the capital control designation for Shoppers Drug

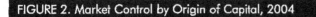

TABLE 3. Top 95 Leading Retailers' Market Control by Origin of Capital, 2004

Origin	2004 Sales (Millions)	%	Number of Stores	%	Millions/Store
Canada	100,308.19	63.14	19,968	76.21	5.02
Foreign	58,554.55	36.86	6,233	23.79	9.39
USA	51,675.38	32.53	5,177	19.76	9.98
Other Foreign	6,879.16	4.33	1,056	4.03	6.51
Total	158,862.74		26,201		

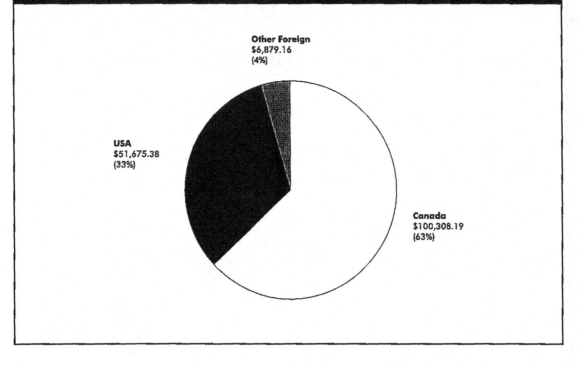

FIGURE 2. Market Control by Origin of Capital, 2004

Other Foreign
$6,879.16
(4%)

USA
$51,675.38
(33%)

Canada
$100,308.19
(63%)

Mart has been switched to Canadian in this report. The total sales per store of Canadian retailers continued to be lower than those of foreign retailers, with Canadian stores averaging just 5 million dollars per store compared with 10 million and 6.5 million per store in American and other foreign retailers respectively.

The concentration ratio (CR4), shown here for each of the major retail trade categories, depicts the sum of the market shares of the four largest corporations in a given industry. The CR4 is an important measure of market concentration as it gives a good indication of the relative size of the four largest corporations in relation to the market as a whole. For example, if the top four companies in a given sector each produced ten percent of the total sales for that sector, the CR4 would be 40%. In most nations, when the CR4

TABLE 4. Market Concentration (CR4) by NAICS, 2004

NAICS Sector		2004 Sales (Millions)	%	First	%	Second	%	Third	%	Fourth	CR4
442	Furniture & Home Furn.	12,945.40	11.97	The Brick	8.26	IKEA AB	7.20	Sears Co.	6.19	BMTC Gr.	33.62
443	Electronics & Appliances	11,024.90	29.25	Best Buy	5.70	Hart Group	5.07	InterTAN Inc.	2.50	Sony Corp.	42.53
444	Home Improvement	20,970.60	22.66	HomeDepot	19.17	Home Hard.	17.55	Rona Inc.	8.91	Tim-Br Mart	68.29
445	Grocery	82,357.60	31.82	Weston Gr.	14.59	Sobeys Gr.	6.69	Metro Inc.	6.37	Safeway Inc.	59.47
446	Pharmacy & Personal Care	22,769.30	20.74	Shop. D.M.	15.51	Katz Gr.	12.01	Jean Coutu	9.65	McKesson	57.92
448	Clothing & Footwear	20,188.40	6.55	TJX Co.	4.76	GAP Inc.	4.52	Reitman Gr.	3.26	Cdn Tire	19.08
452	General Merchandise	42,123.70	34.03	Wal-Mart	18.80	Costco	16.18	Hud. Bay Co.	11.59	Sears Co.	80.60
451	Hobby Stores	8,831.40	12.45	Forzani Gr.	8.92	Indigo Inc.	8.58	Toys 'R' Us	4.34	Bata Ind.	34.28
453	Miscellaneous	9,446.10	15.96	Staples	2.94	Office Depot	2.14	Grand & Toy	1.56	Pet Valu	22.59

Top 4 Retail Conglomerates/Corporations

FIGURE 3. Concentration Ratio (CR4) by NAICS, 2004

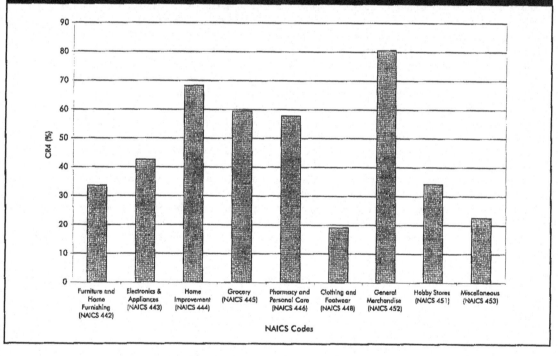

for a particular industry reaches 40%, oligopolistic behavior becomes likely in the marketplace[3].   The Canadian market typically experiences higher levels of market concentration than other nations in many sectors due to the somewhat more relaxed approach to the merger and acquisition process taken in the Canadian regulatory environment as is evidenced by the Canadian Competition Act enacted by the Federal government in 1986.   The Competition Act introduces the idea that efficiency gains can outweigh the costs of a reduction in competition because the smaller Canadian economy requires greater market concentration in order to achieve economies of scale and to be competitive in the world economy. The end result of this policy can be seen in Table 4, where concentration ratios of 40% or more can be seen in five out of the nine retail sectors covered in this report. The NAICS sector with the highest CR4 continues to be the General Merchandise sector with a CR4 of 80.6%, followed by Home Improvement (68.2%), Grocery (59.4%), Pharmacy (57.9%), and Electronics & Appliances (42.5%).

Retail Sector Analysis

Fiscal 2004 was an interesting year for the Canadian retail industry.   Acquisitions in several of the major sectors altered the retail landscape while competition in the Grocery sector was especially fierce.   The Grocery and General Merchandise sector saw big changes in 2004, mainly caused by the pending arrival of the super centre format of Wal-Mart Stores Inc. that sells a full line of general merchandise in addition to a full line of grocery items. Many of the major retail conglomerates added either general merchandise or prescription drug offerings to their existing grocery operations, or increased grocery items to their existing general merchandise and pharmacy offerings, effectively blurring the lines between some of the retail sectors. Examples of this phenomenon include Loblaw Cos. that has increased the number of Real Canadian Superstore locations, particularly in Ontario, offering both groceries and general merchandise, and Shoppers Drug Mart that began increasing the number of food and high end cosmetics items at its larger stores. Despite this blurring of retail sectors by some of the larger conglomerates, it is still possible to examine differences within the retail sectors based on the dominant retail function performed by these retail chains. Maps of selected retail conglomerates are provided for each of the retail sectors discussed here to provide some background on the spatial distribution of retail activities in each of these sectors.

442 – Furniture & Home Furnishings

The biggest event in the furniture and home furnishings sector in 2004 was, by far, the initial public offering of The Brick Warehouse Corporation, which would become The Brick Group Income Fund on July 20th for gross proceeds of $272 million dollars. In June of 2004, The Brick Warehouse Corporation announced that it was planning an income trust public offering, ending months of speculation about the future of the company. In addition to the public offering, The Brick announced plans to add approximately 60 more stores to its existing network of Brick, United Furniture Warehouse, and Homeshow locations, including new ventures into the Quebec and Atlantic markets[4]. An important component of the offering was that it would involve the sale of a sixty per-cent stake in the company as William Comrie, who started The Brick 33 years prior, divested his stake in the chain after stepping down as CEO in March of 2004.

443 – Electronics and Appliances

On March 31st 2004, Circuit City Stores Inc. announced its acquisition offer for the outstanding shares of InterTan Canada Ltd., which operated approximately 990 stores in Canada under the Radioshack, Rogers Plus, and Battery Plus banners, at the cost of US $286 million or $14 per share[5]. Shortly after the announcement, RadioShack Corp. announced that it would be terminating its advertising contract with InterTan citing a non-payment of a US $55,000 annual fee under the companies' branding agreement as the grounds for the termination[6]. The attempt to terminate the advertising contract was widely seen as an indicator that the stores operating under InterTan as RadioShack would have to be rebranded to another name within a year of RadioShack's legal action.   Circuit City's purchase of InterTan was speculated to be the first step in their attempt to compete with Best Buy Co. who had recently entered the Canadian market with its own big box stores and with its purchase of the Future Shop brand.

---

[3] Scherer, F.M. & D. Ross 1990 *Industrial Market Structure and Economic Performance*. 3rd Edition. (Houghton Mifflin Co, Boston) in Gomez-Insausti, R. 2003 Canada's Leading Retailers: Characteristics, Strategies, & Dominance. Research Report 2003-08 CSCA, Ryerson University.

[4] Strauss, M. 2004 *"Brick launches income trust offering"* Globe and Mail, June 1 2004.

[5] Lexpert 2004 *"Circuit City Stores acquires InterTAN"* National Post, July 7, 2004.

[6] Reuters 2004 *"RadioShack says its pulling the plug on branding deal with InterTan"* Toronto Star, April 7, 2004.

444 – Home Improvement

The majority of the movement in this sector in 2004 came from Rona Inc. In their bid to increase market share Canada-wide to 22% by 2007, Rona announced an aggressive strategy in 2004 that would see them spend up to $300 million on expansion in Ontario and Western Canada over three years[7]. Robert Dutton, CEO of Rona Inc., stated that acquisitions of smaller regional chains, recruitment of dealers from other banners, and the construction of additional big box stores would play an important part in this expansion[8]. However, the main objective of Rona for 2004 was to complete the integration of their 2003 acquisitions of the 20 Reno-Depot stores that included 6 The Building Box stores in Ontario and they stated that another acquisition would not be likely until 2005. In April of 2004, Rona announced that it would be re-branding The Building Box banner to Rona Home & Garden as part of its push westwards. In their second quarter report, Rona indicated that the benefits of their 2003 acquisitions had been far better than expected and that sales had increased in the second quarter by approximately 53 percent[9]. As was expected based on their announced expansion strategy, Rona declared another acquisition at the very end of 2004, purchasing the 14 store Alberta based Totem Building Supplies Inc. for $100 million on December 21st. At the time of the acquisition, Rona indicated that the Totem brand would likely survive after the acquisition, with Robert Dutton stating that "you pay $100-million for a concept, and people"[10].

445 – Grocery

Fear generated by the pending arrival of the grocery selling super-centre format of Wal-Mart Stores Inc. was the dominant influence on the Canadian grocery sector in 2004. Price competition between the major grocery conglomerates of Loblaw Cos., Metro Inc. and Sobeys Inc. was fierce, causing drastic reductions in profit for both Metro and Sobeys. Largely the result of Loblaws Cos. attempt to make the Canadian market as unpalatable as possible for the entry of Wal-Mart super-centres, these competitive pressures were only expected to become more acute in the years ahead. The future for the Canadian grocery sector was so bleak in 2004 that in February, major European discount grocer Lidl cancelled their planned Canadian expansion of up to 200 stores, citing intense domestic competition[11], abandoning months of investment in head office staff and real-estate research. By the end of 2004, Loblaw Cos. was continuing with its 'Real Canadian Superstore as a preemptive strike' strategy for dealing with the arrival of Wal-Mart and was committed to lowering food prices while increasing the number of non-food items in its stores. Considering the amount of competition facing Canadian grocery conglomerates in 2004, and the fact that almost all of the major players were still consolidating operations from earlier acquisitions, merger and acquisition activity in this sector was understandably quiet. Sobeys Inc. completed its acquisition of the 15 Commisso's and 6 Cash & Carry stores in February of 2004, an acquisition that strengthened the Atlantic based grocery conglomerate's presence in the Ontario market considerably, mainly in the Niagara peninsula region.

446 – Pharmacy and Personal Care

The biggest changes in the pharmacy and personal care sector in 2004 were the acquisition of Body Shop Canada by its United Kingdom parent Body Shop International PLC, the Jean Coutu move into the U.S. market with the acquisition of the Eckerd pharmacy chain, and the entry of Paris based cosmetics chain Sephora. Body Shop International PLC announced plans to acquire the operations of their Canadian and Hong Kong operations in June as part of a consolidation program aimed at achieving greater efficiencies[12]. The deal for the 108 store Canadian business, including 69 franchise and 39 corporately owned stores, was closed on July 22 for $26 million[13], a surprisingly small acquisition price compared to the Hong Kong acquisition that included just 26 stores for $27 million. However, the acquisition price may have been indicative of ailing fortunes at Body Shop Canada as they reported a pre-tax loss of $4 million in the previous year[14].

---

[7] Tomesco, F 2004 *"Rona in a push to boost market share: Will spend $300M on Ontario, Western Canada expansion"* National Post, February 4, 2004.

[8] Carr, N. 2004 *"Major expansion in Rona's game plan: Strategy includes acquisitions, more big-box stores"* National Post, April 7, 2004.

[9] Bell, K. 2004 *"Acquisitions help double Q2 earnings: 'Awesome Results'"* National Post, August 12, 2004.

[10] Brethour, P. 2004 *"Rona builds up Alberta business; $100-million cash deal for Totem nearly doubles number of outlets in province"* The Globe and Mail, December 21, 2004.

[11] Strauss, M. 2004 *"Lidl halts plans for Canadian grocery chain"* The Globe and Mail, February 10, 2004.

[12] Flavelle, D. 2004 *"Body Shop owners sell to U.K. parent"* The Toronto Star, June 25, 2004.

[13] Lexpert 2004. *"Body Shop's $26M acquisition"* National Post, September 22, 2004.

[14] Jarvis, P. 2004 *"Body Shop buys out lead Canada franchisee"* National Post, July 24, 2004.

The Jean Coutu Group (PJC) acquisition of the Eckerd pharmacy chain in the US was perhaps the most publicized event in the pharmacy and personal care sector. The acquisition of 1,539 Eckerd bannered stores was finalized on July 31st at a cost of approximately $2.5 billion[15], making Jean Coutu the fourth largest drugstore operator in North America. The deal was not without its downside though, as many analysts predicted that Jean Coutu would face an uphill battle in returning the Eckerd chain to profitability. It was also predicted that other Canadian drugstore chains would take the acquisition as an opportunity to gain market share in Quebec where Coutu commands 40% of the market. In September of 2004, Shoppers Drug Mart Corp. announced that it was making plans for a major expansion in Quebec with the Pharmaprix chain of drug stores.

One of the biggest entries into the Canadian market in 2004 was the Paris based Sephora chain of cosmetics stores. Sephora opened its first store in the Toronto Eaton Centre on November 4th, coming into a market that is already witnessing an increase in competition between stores selling fine beauty and fragrance products. Although The Bay is the leading Canadian retailer of high-end cosmetics, they faced stiffer competition from Shoppers Drug Mart Inc. and Loblaw Cos. who have added pressure by increasing their selections of premium cosmetics and have increased the floor space devoted to these products in their new and remodeled stores. Sephora did not speculate on the number of stores it had planned for Canada, only stating that it planned at least one more store in Toronto for the spring of 2005, but some analysts speculated that Sephora would be in most of the better Canadian regional malls within a couple of years[16].

448 – Clothing and Footwear

The Canadian clothing and footwear sector experienced several big changes in 2004. San Francisco Inc. sold its flagship San Francisco banner to Boutiques Marie Claire, American Eagle Outfitters completed the sale of the Bluenotes chain to YM Inc., Gendis announced the sale of

the Saan/Red Apple stores, and Swedish retailer H&M entered the Canadian market. Late in 2003, San Francisco Inc. entered bankruptcy protection and on January 27th of 2004 announced the sale of its 36 store flagship banner San Francisco to Groupe Marie Claire for $3.2 million as part of its restructuring program in addition to the sale of its Victoire Delage and Moments Intimes lingerie chains[17]. San Francisco Inc. later emerged from bankruptcy protection as Groupe Les Ailes de la Mode and announced that they would be focusing their efforts on the Bikini Village banner and the Les Ailes de la Mode department store banner.

American Eagle Outfitters entered the Canadian Market in December of 2000 with the acquisition of the Thriftys/Bluenotes banner from Dylex Ltd. of Canada for $74 million US[18]. While under the control of American Eagle, some of the Bluenotes locations were converted to American Eagle stores and the Thriftys stores were converted to the Bluenotes banner. Unfortunately, the 107 store Bluenotes chain was a drag on the performance of American Eagle for several years as they unsuccessfully attempted to turn the chain around. Bluenotes was sold to Canadian clothing conglomerate YM Inc. in December of 2004, a company that "has a reputation for acquiring unloved and unwanted retail banners"[19].

Gendis Inc., owner of the junior department store chain Saan and the Red Apple clearance centres, ended years of unsuccessful turn around attempts for the small town retailer with its sale to Saan Acquisition Corp. of Toronto. Squeezed by competition from bigger discount chains like Wal-Mart, Zellers, and Giant Tiger, the Saan Stores division of Gendis saw sales plummet to $243 million in 2004, down 21% from $311 million in 2003[20]. Saan Acquisition Corp. sought bankruptcy protection soon after the acquisition and initial reports indicated that a significant number of stores would have to close, resulting in significant job losses[21].

[15] Lexpert 2004 *"Jean Coutu Group obtains Eckerd bannered stores"* National Post, September 8, 2004.

[16] Grace Marr, L. 2004 *"Shoppers Expansion Spree; National drugstore chain has opened three stores in Hamilton area since October"* Hamilton Spectator November 24, 2004.

[17] Canadian Press 2004 *"Marie Claire buys insolvent LesBoutiques for $3.2M"* National Post, January 27th, 2004.

[18] Yeomans, M. 2004 *"American Eagle Outfitters selling Bluenotes"* Pittsburgh Tribune-Review, November 24, 2004.

[19] Covert, J. and Georgiades, A. 2004 *"American Eagle sells Canadian chain Bluenotes to YM: Stiffer competition: Retailer's buyer called a 'marketing powerhouse"* National Post, November 24, 2004.21

[20] Gendis Inc. Annual Report January 29, 2005

[21] Strauss, M. 2004 *"Saan chain gets creditor protection; 'Significant' number of stores must close"* The Globe and Mail, January 7, 2005.

227

Another large company to enter the Canadian market in 2004 was Swedish retailer H&M. H&M had started acquiring Canadian real estate late in 2002 and in March of 2004 opened their first Canadian store at Fairview Mall in Toronto. H&M is often compared with Swedish Furniture chain IKEA because the two Swedish companies both incorporate a philosophy of providing stylish, yet affordable products. By the end of 2004, H&M had opened 6 new stores in Canada.

451 – Hobby Stores

Two major transactions took place in the Canadian Hobby sector in 2004, the acquisition of Nevada Bob's Golf stores by the Forzani Group and the Children's Place Retail Stores Inc. acquisition of The Disney Store chain from Walt Disney Co. In August of 2004, Forzani Group Ltd. agreed to buy the Canadian interests of golf equipment Chain Nevada Bob's International Inc. for an undisclosed amount. Although Forzani did not release financial details of the transaction, they did indicate that the acquisition cost was so small as to be "immaterial" and that they expected the deal to immediately increase total sales with a cumulative effect of adding $30 million in yearly sales to Forzani. Forzani stated that it intended to expand the chain by opening more of the popular golfing stores, and that they believed that Nevada Bob's was a banner with tremendous potential, but would not comment on where or when this expansion would take place. The acquisition of Nevada Bob's 26 Canadian stores puts Forzani in competition with the Golf Town banner based out of Markham, Ontario that has 21 stores across the country[22].

Children's Place Retail Stores Inc. agreed to purchase 313 North American retail stores from Walt Disney Co. in October of 2004, including 13 Disney stores in Canada. Financial terms of the deal were not disclosed but the transaction involved a royalty agreement that was to begin giving Disney royalty payments in 2006 for the use of the names of its characters and its own brand, which is unheard of for Disney as it is typically known as being highly protective of its brands[23]. The Disney store has been underperforming for years though and in an industry with a long list of corporate casualties, typically blamed on the low-price emphasis of Wal-Mart Stores Inc., many saw the acquisition as a risky one for Children's Place.

452 – General Merchandise

The biggest event in the general merchandise sector in 2004 was, considering the amount of press it received, the announced merger of US retailing giants K-Mart Holding Corp. and Sears Roebuck & Co in November. Although the announced merger of these two American companies did not have an immediate impact on the operations of Sears Canada Inc., the deal did cause a significant amount of speculation on the possibility of a take over bid by the new US parent company that already owned 54% of Sears Canada Inc. The result of these buyout speculations and rumors was a six percent increase in the share price of Sears Canada Inc. to $18.50, but were valued by some investors as high as $21 per share[24].

Both Sears Canada Inc. and Hudson's Bay Co made headlines with their announcements of new off-mall and power centre store concepts that would be tested during 2004. Although both Sears Canada and Hudson's Bay already had some power centre stores in the form of Sears Whole Home and Home Outfitters respectively, the announcements of these new formats marked a significant change in strategy within the two companies. Sears had announced a strategy early in 2004 to test two to four specialty power-centre outlets under the names Sears Wellness (health & fitness), Sears Sleep (mattresses), Sears Coverings (windows and floors), and Sears Tech (electronics)[25]. At the end of 2004, Sears had opened four Sears Appliances and Mattresses stores and two Sears Coverings stores along with announcements for the opening of several free standing department stores in 2005. Hudson's Bay Co. announced the introduction of a Winners style discount chain under the banner of Designer Depot, offering merchandise at markdowns of between 40% and 70%. Hudson's Bay Co. opened the first self contained Designer Depot store in the Vaughn Mills shopping centre on November 3rd of 2004 and had announced the construction of up to 10 more in the following year[26].

[22] Carr, N. 2004 *"Sporting retailer Forzani Group to buy golf equipment chain Nevada Bob's"* The Canadian Press, August 19 2004.

[23] Sikora M. 2004 *"Disney Finds a Buyer for Its Toy Stores: Uniquely crafted deal thrusts Children's Place into the fiercely competitive toy retailing field"* Mergers and Acquisitions: The Dealmakers Journal, December 1, 2004.

[24] Shaw, H. 2004 *"Will New U.S. Retail Giant Look North?"* National Post, November 19, 2004.

[25] Strauss, M. 2004 *"Big chains now chasing even bigger markets"* Globe and Mail, February 9, 2004.

[26] Baird, A 2004 *"Hudson's Bay Co – Hudson's Bay store likens buying to "practically stealing"* Canada Stockwatch, November 3rd, 2004.

In the dollar store end of the general merchandise sector, Montreal based Dollarama was sold to Boston based Bain Capital LLC for approximately $885 million and included the sale of approximately 360 stores across Canada[27]. Meanwhile, Denninghouse Inc. was forced to close 80 of its 92 corporately owned 'Buck or Two' bannered dollar stores when it sought bankruptcy protection in August following the purchase of 33 failed franchise locations in Atlantic Canada[28]. In December of 2004, Denninghouse announced that it would sell the remaining 200 store franchise portion of the business to Buck or Two Extreme Retail Inc. and Buck or Two (2004) Inc[29].

453 – Miscellaneous

The 'Miscellaneous' NAICS category is made up of establishments primarily engaged in retailing a specialized line of merchandise that is not covered by any of the other NAICS retail categories. Miscellaneous covers stores such as Florists, office supplies stores, stationery stores, gift, novelty and souvenir stores, used merchandise stores, pet and pet supplies stores, art dealers and manufactured (mobile) home dealers. There was very little major corporate movement in this sector in 2004, with no major mergers or acquisition activity taking place between the major players. The market leader in this diverse category is Staples\Business Depot, who opened 14 new Canadian stores Canada wide and increased their total sales by $107 million, bringing their store count to 238 and $1.5 billion total sales.

Summary

- The concentration of non-automotive retail sales by Canada's leading retailers increased by 0.62% over 2003.

- Canadian retailers continue to be a strong influence in the Canadian retail economy with 63% of non-automotive retail sales.

- Five out of the nine NAICS sectors exhibited CR4 values of higher than 40%

- Mergers and Acquisitions continue to play an important role in reshaping the structure of Canada's leading retailers, with large acquisitions taking place in 6 of the 9 retail sectors.

- Competition increased dramatically in the Grocery sector in advance of the arrival of the Wal-Mart Supercentre general merchandise/grocery format.

[27] Bloomberg News 2004 "Bain buys retailer Dollarama in reported $885M deal" National Post, November 25, 2004
[28] Carr, N. 2004 "Dollar store chain up for sale; Denninghouse seeks protection for 80 of 93 corporate stores to be closed" Toronto Star, August 17, 2004.
[29] Canadian Press 2004 "Denninghouse selling dollar stores" Toronto Star, December 9, 2004.

Chapter 12

THE CHANGING CHARACTER OF THE RETAIL STRIPS IN THE CITY OF TORONTO: 1996–2005

Tony Hernandez, Jim Helik, and Peter Moore

INTRODUCTION

Retail strips form a significant part of Toronto's retail landscape. They can be found across the City from the downtown to the outer suburbs, varying in size, form and function; and can be broadly defined as clusters of store-front commercial activities: pedestrian-scale, with stores linked together by the flows of consumers (Simmons *et al.*, 1996). The diversity of retail strips in Toronto reflects the waves of economic and urban development that the City has experienced along with its multi-cultural heritage. Many of Toronto's distinctive neighbourhoods are charac-terized by the mix of commercial activity located along their major streets, such as *'Old Chinatown'* (Spadina) *'Greektown'* (Danforth), *'Little Italy'* (College), *'The India Bazaar'* (Gerrard), the *'Mink Mile'* (Bloor Street West). However, as new forms of retail have developed (e.g., major malls and power centres) and many retail functions have suburbanized, how have Toronto's retail strips changed? What role do they play in the retail landscape today? How might this change in the future? This research report specifically addresses these questions by assessing the changing character of retail strips in the City of Toronto between 1996 and 2005. The three primary research objectives are as follows:

1. To analyse the changing character of retail strips with reference to numerous metrics, including, mix of tenants, employment, presence of major corporate chains and vacancy rates

2. To generate a functional classification of retail strips to provide an objective means to differentiate between types of retail strip environment

3. To assess the role of retail strips with specific reference to the 'Avenues' planning concept

RESEARCH CONTEXT

The retail landscapes of urban Canada reflect the immense diversity of social classes, incomes, ethnicity, lifestyles, and business formats that comprise our cities. Retail strips, suburban plazas, major suburban malls, power centres, downtown shopping areas, and revitalized boutique districts are some of the most visible elements of the metropolitan landscape. Retail strips are one part of an increasingly complex retail system – planned and unplanned. Traditionally chain stores have tended to dominate the planned shopping centres while the independents have normally been restricted to unplanned central city or retail strip locations. Indeed, an important aspect of retail strips is their functional specialization (Leigh, 1965; Jones, 1984). Strips of all sizes often specialize in economic activity or to serve a distinctive market. A major source of variation is the size of strip, measured either in number of stores or floor area. The smaller strips typically vary their economic function in predictable fashion, gathering additional retail and service activities as they grow in size and extend their market areas. They often start-out as convenience centres, then expand to serve more extensive markets, and perhaps to specialize in a lifestyle market that may extend across the metropolitan region. The larger strips have developed an impressive degree of specialization, in both function and ethnicity. Retail strips, then, are a distinctive commercial form and part of the urban landscape.

In a North American context, many cities have witnessed a steady erosion of the traditional urban retail strips. While they are found in some larger and older US cities, they have virtually disappeared from many other places in the US. As is the case with all forms of commercial structure, over time the role, form and function of retail strips can change dramatically: some maintain or even strengthen their position while others spiral into decline. For example, many of the older retail strips are left over from an era of street cars or other transit modes that defined linear patterns of accessibility within a (relatively) high-density residential environment. These traditional strips are not automobile-oriented; parking lots and turning cars disrupt the pedestrian flow. By contrast, the most recent retail strips are typically located in the suburbs, geared towards the auto-dependent suburban shopper, with parking a key consideration. However, to fully understand the changing character and role of retail strips it is important to place their development within the context of theories relating to the retail system. This section provides: (i) an overview of existing classifications of retail structures; (ii) a brief history of the evolution of the Canadian retail system with specific reference to retail strips: and, (iii) the positioning of retail strips as specialized retail areas.

Classification of Retail Structures

The development of systematic classifications of retail structures can be traced back to the pioneering works of Proudfoot (1937) and Berry (1963). These studies differentiated shopping environments on the basis of their locational and functional characteristics and provided a framework for interpreting the retail structure. Proudfoot's work described the existing retail pattern for the pre-1945 city and identified five types of retail structure - the CBD, outlying business centre, principal shopping thoroughfare, neighbourhood shopping street and isolated store clusters. Berry's well-known classification of the retail hierarchy summarized the early post-war city. Here, the dominant business elements of centres, ribbons and specialized areas are interpreted in terms of central place postulates. Davies (1976) developed an integrated model of urban retail form that was based on the simultaneous overlapping of nucleations, ribbons and specialty retail area characteristics. According to Davies, the retail pattern of the city centre can be viewed in broad terms as a nucleation that is structured in a series of zonal belts of retail activity. Jones (1984) provided a reworking of the Berry model,

dividing the urban retail system into two structural forms - strips and centres, with each differentiated according to its location in either inner-city or suburban environments. Finally, Jones and Simmons (1990) classified retail types as either unplanned nodes, linear strips or planned shopping centres by the size of market they serve ranging from metropolitan to neighbourhood (see Figure 1)[n.b., with 'planned' referring to managed shopping environments]. It is interesting to note that, despite the significant structural transformation that has occurred in the Canadian retail landscape in recent years, the systematic classification of retail structures in a holistic manner has not been an active area of academic research for more than a decade. From a planning perspective, the concept of retail hierarchy is well established and widely operationalised.

FIGURE 1. Retail Classification

	Unplanned Nodes	Linear Strips	Planned Shopping Centres
Metropolitan	a) Downtown		a) Super-Regional Mall
	b) Specialized Product District: e.g. entertainent design	b) Specialty Strip e.g fashion	b) Specialty Mall e.g. fashion, discount, outlet mall
	b) Industrial Zone: cluster of diverse and unrelated commercial activities	b) Ethnic Strip	b) Theme Mall
Regional	a) Power Node, (big box stores)	b) Specialty Strips e.g. automobile furniture, antiques	a) Regional Mall
	a) Suburban Downtown		a) Power Centre (big box stores)
	b) Produce Markets		
Community	a) Major Intersection in central city	a) Pedestrian Strip	a) Community Plaza
		a) Arterial Strip a) Supercentre	
		b) Specialty Strips, e.g. automotive, fast-food	b) Specialty Mall e.g. airport, university
Neighbourhood	a) Corner Cluster	a) Pedestrian Strip	a) Neighbourhood Plaza a) Suburban Strip Mall b) Malls within Office Bldg., Hotels

a) denotes spatial market
b) denotes specialty market

Source: based on Jones and Simmons (1993)

Retail structural analysis has had a long tradition in urban geography. In the 1950s and 1960s, North American studies of retail structure dominated the literature (Simmons, 1964, 1966). These studies explored suburban retail strip development, retail mix and usage patterns, inner-city retail decline, the emergence of the shopping centre and the specialty retail phenomenon. In the 1970s and 1980s, the interest in retail studies shifted to the United Kingdom (Shaw, 1978; Sibley, 1976). British geographers, in an attempt to formulate responsive retail planning policies, studied a wide variety of urban retail issues (Bromley and Thomas, 1993). These included inner-city blight, retail decentralization, the quality of inner city retail areas, the impact of hypermarkets and future role of planned regional shopping centres. More recently, structural analysis has focused on the impact of major retail chains and new formats on the retail system, often with an emphasis on corporate locational strategies (Hernandez, 2001; Graff, 1998; Laulajainen, 1987). In Canada, the CSCA's research mandate has focused on the evolution of the Canadian retail system. The final disposition of the retail system is viewed as the outcome of the spatial strategies of, and interplay between, developers, retailers, planners and consumers - the actors that ultimately shape the future form of the urban retail landscape.

Evolution of the Canadian Urban Retail System

The contemporary retail landscape of urban Canada is the product of a series of complex structural changes. Retail structure is perhaps the most responsive element in the urban landscape. The entry and exit rate of retailers into the system is highly volatile. Very minor shifts in the income, demographic, lifestyle and/or competitive characteristics of an area can lead to quite rapid changes in both form and structure of the retail environment. Conceptually, the retail fabric of our cities has been created in response to demographic, technological, behavioural, and entrepreneurial change. At the most basic level, retailers locate in response to market conditions. If the population/income mix or market potential is appropriate, retail development will be in demand.

The spatial pattern of these retail groupings relates to the technology of the time. When mobility is low, retail activities concentrate; when mobility increases, retail activities disperse. At a finer level, consumer and entrepreneurial decisions can determine which retail areas grow and which areas decline. Consumer preferences for

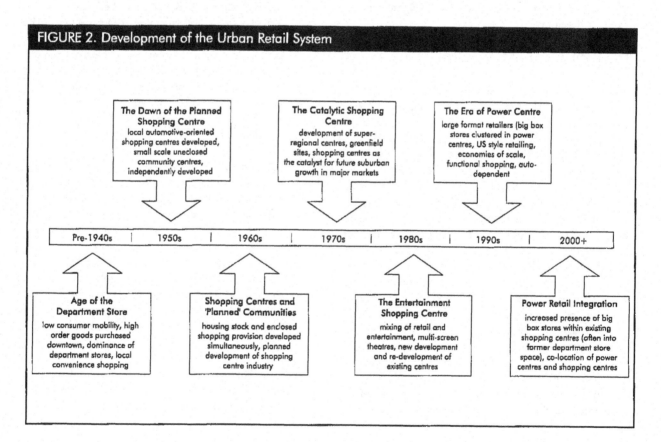

FIGURE 2. Development of the Urban Retail System

both retail goods and destinations can reflect a whole set of considerations that can be broadly defined as lifestyle-related. Certain urban shopping areas move in and out of fashion for particular consumer groups. On the supply side, investment decisions are based on the entrepreneur's assessment of the prospects of market over time.

The urban retail system has experienced several transformations in the last sixty years. These transformations were tied to successions in types of urban structure and transportation: the compact pre-automobile city; the dispersed automobile city; and the emerging information city. Figure 2 shows the major phases of evolution of the Canadian retail systems tracing development from the pre-World War II era through to present day. Retail strips have been part of the urban retail system throughout the various eras of retail development. Many of the smaller unenclosed shopping centres and plazas developed through the 1950s to 1970s remain a key element of the retail strip environment. The most recent developments have taken place in the newer suburbs, with clusters of large format (big box) retailers. The community-based shopping development style of the 1950s has gone full circle to form part of the new suburban retail developments of present day, as seen with food and pharmacy-anchored community and neighbourhood shopping developments.

The Positioning of Specialized Retail Areas

There have always been specialized retail clusters within metropolitan areas. These retail districts attract weekend shoppers from all over the region. The pattern of specialty retailing can be either dispersed or concentrated. The former includes merchants who offer a highly specialized product (e.g., model trains, comic books, and historical documents) and who rely on consumer motivations that can be best described as esoteric. These retailers have no need to form specialty clusters since they offer one-of-a-kind merchandise and their customers will travel long distances to purchase the product. The other group of specialty retailers cluster in order to reach a certain set of consumers. These comprise clusters of antique and art dealers, furniture stores, high fashion retailers, suppliers of electronic equipment, restaurants and automobile show-rooms. Jones and Simmons (1993) have identified five distinct types of specialty clusters. These include specialty product areas, fashion centres, factory outlets/off-price centres, historic or theme developments and ethnic strips. In addition to these five clusters, lifestyle centres geared to the higher-income shopper can be added as a new variant of

speciality retail. These areas can be either planned or unplanned and serve four distinct sets of consumer demands. First, they may cater to individuals who have a preference for high-quality, status-oriented, brand labels and tend to demand high cost, exclusive goods. In other cases, they may serve consumers who are bargain conscious and have a propensity to shop for discount merchandise. Third, they may be associated with lifestyle purchases that can be linked to cultural heritage, peer-pressure or age. Finally, they may satisfy certain shopping needs that are purely esoteric and are predicated on the need to acquire or collect a particular item.

A number of retail strip environments can be identified within these specialty clusters:

- The neighbourhood speciality strip is typically found in older residentials areas that have experienced gentrification (e.g., The Beaches, Toronto; Rue St-Denis, Montréal; Old Strathcona, Edmonton). These strips typically have a mix of retail and service that cater to the local cosmopolitan and tourist markets.

- Fashion streets are often the most expensive and visible shopping locations within the metropolis (e.g., Bay-Bloor/Yorkville; Rue St-Denis, Montreal) with close links to the high-income sectors and/or executive employment locations. These high-fashion streets have been particularly attractive to European chains and in a number of instances these retail environments have been incorporated into mixed-use projects that integrate offices, hotels, and entertainment.

- Ethnic strips are normally associated with the point of entry of an immigrant group in the city. At first, the retail component expands to serve the needs of the immediate neighbourhood. In this phase certain types of products dominate, in particular food and fashion retailers, restaurants and personal services that are linked to the cultural heritage of the community. Eventually, the strip evolves to cater to members of the ethnic group throughout the metropolitan area. In time, these areas may also become tourist attractions as is the case with Kensington Market and Chinatown in Toronto.

Finally, within this system the downtown constitutes a distinct retail environment. This district, previously the unchallenged centre of high-order retail activity, has had to adapt to successive retail transitions over a century. The CBD's high density built environment also distinguishes it from other parts of the metropolitan region. This places a premium on downtown space and forces all establishments, including retail, to be parsimonious with their use of land. Downtown's accessibility potential sets it apart from suburban locales. It enjoys unparalleled transit accessibility, while being less accommodating to cars than the suburbs where parking is free and plentiful. The central business district of a city combines almost all the retail clusters described above: it is the highest order unplanned centre and it serves the entire metropolitan region. Usually, it incorporates a series of diverse retail areas. These can include skid row retailing that features bars, cheap restaurants and adult entertainment; high-fashion streets; major inner-city shopping centres; entertainment districts; traditional shopping streets; underground retail concourses; ancillary malls associated with mixed-use developments; and historic redeveloped specialty retail areas.

In summary, retail strips are found across the entire retail system in a variety of forms. They can be found, for example, within the downtown as the main shopping streets, clustered in the inner-urban areas, often serving specialized functions, and dispersed throughout the suburbs along major arterial routes. The strips are part of a larger retail system that has and continues to evolve as a result of waves of economic, social and urban development.

METHODOLOGY

The research utilized a geomatics-based approach to manage and analyse the changing character of retail strips in Toronto. The temporal data sets used were all georeferenced to custom defined retail strips. A large part of the research involved collating, fusing and preparing time sequenced analysis and visualization of the data sets. This section provides: (i) a description of the study area and delineation of the retail strips; (ii) details on the data sets used within the study; and, (iii) a comparison of the Toronto Employment Survey (TES) and CSCA Retail Database (CRD).

The 'Avenues' Study Area

Managing population and employment growth that the City of Toronto expects over the next 25 years is a key concept behind the City's new Official Plan. The City sees this growth occurring in three major areas: the Downtown

and Central Waterfront, the four Centres in the City (at Yonge and Eglinton and in the former North York, Etobicoke and Scarborough) and along the Avenues. The Avenues are important corridors along major streets where reurbanization is both anticipated and encouraged to create new housing and job opportunities. This study addresses the changing character of retail activities on the Avenues identified in the Official Plan (see http://www.toronto.ca/planning/official_plan/introduction.htm). The study area includes all the major retail strips that are located along designated Avenues.

There is great variation among the Avenues in existing local conditions, including presence of retail, lot sizes, ownership patterns, other land uses on the Avenues, and adjacent land uses. Thus, there is no "one size fits all" program for reurbanizing the Avenues. Similarly, not all lands that fall within the Avenues are designated for growth. The Avenues are identified at a broad scale, while reurbanization will be achieved through the preparation of Avenue Studies for strategic mixed use segments of these areas. Thus, change will occur incrementally along the Avenues over a number of years. It is therefore very important for the City to understand not only how retailing is changing on the Avenues, but also the role that commercial activity may play in reurbanization on the Avenues.

The precise boundaries of the retail strips used within this study were defined through manual inspection of customized land parcel maps categorized by land use, official plan 'Avenue' maps and CSCA retail strip boundary maps. The operational problem is how to define their boundaries. Along the major arterial streets retail strips go on for mile after mile. The decision to end one here and begin another can be quite arbitrary. The strips were laboriously defined through team meetings and detailed discussion on a strip-by-strip basis. It should be noted that the study area strips are a subset of the CSCA's existing retail boundaries and a subset of the designated Avenue boundaries. In addition, some 'Avenue' – like areas in the Downtown are also included in the study. In order to better understand how local strips function, a number of the longer avenues were split into several sections. In total, 95 strips (avenue sections) were identified and mapped (with custom polygons generated for subsequent analysis) – see Map 1.

As already noted some Avenue locations are not included in the study. This is either due to: (i) the absence of retail establishments along the Avenues; or, (ii) the result of the exclusion of sections of the Avenues that contain large

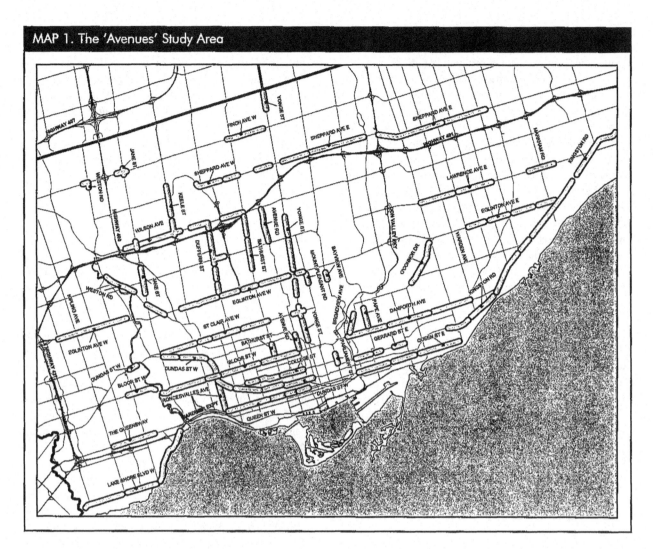

MAP 1. The 'Avenues' Study Area

shopping malls or power centres (which do not function as strips, e.g., Sherway Gardens, Cloverdale Mall, Yorkdale Shopping Centre, Fairview Mall, and the Eglinton Town Centre area).

Data Sets

Two major data sets are used in this study: employment survey data from the City of Toronto and retail structural data from the CSCA. These data are both obtained from field surveys conducted annually but at different times of the year and by different survey teams. Data for every year from 1996 to 2005 was available:

The Toronto Employment Survey (TES)

The City of Toronto Employment Survey is a unique resource in Canada. Conducted on an annual basis since 1983, the survey records the number of full-and part-time employees as well as the nature of employment activities for every employment establishment across the City. The survey covers all businesses as well as other employment locations, such as schools, hospitals, community centres, construction sites. It does not survey people who work at home. This amounts to over 71,500 establishments in 2005. A team of 25 individuals gather employment information over four months, and personally visit every establishment in the City. When necessary, phone follow-ups are performed in order to obtain complete information. The data is used to:

- monitor employment activity
- provide background data for economic and transportation studies
- classify all non-residential land uses
- perform economic development sector analysis
- aid in forecasting future urban structure scenarios

The employment data by individual work place is not released to the public, and is treated as confidential information. It is only made available to the public in an aggregate form. More information (including reports of past surveys) can be found online at: http://www. toronto.ca/demographics/surveys.htm.

In this study it provides two functions. Since the data covers all areas in the City, it is the only source for tenant information on the Avenues that are not included in the CSCA's retail database. The second function comes from the fact that the data covers all employment operations in the City, not just retail and service establishments. Thus, it provides a comprehensive data set to analyse other employment activities (such as office, institutional, and industrial) that may also be found along the City's Avenues. Appendix A provides a list of the core data fields maintained within the TES.

CSCA Retail Data (CRD)

The CSCA has collected data on the type and location of retail and service establishments within the Greater Toronto Area since 1993 – over time having built and maintained large, digital, geographically-referenced databases of commercial activity. The Centre undertakes annual surveys to update data on over 55,000 retail and commercial service store location - along retail streetfronts (strips), within shopping centres, power centres and free standing. The database is a resource for describing and analyzing changes in the retail system. Appendix B provides a list of the core data fields maintained within the CSCA Retail Database. More details on the CSCA's proprietary database can be found online at http://www.csca. ryerson.ca/Databases.html. The data is used to:

- provide an inventory of all major retail and consumer service activities in Toronto
- track changes in the location, size and function of retail and service establishments
- identify new areas of development
- support decision making related to the retail and consumer service landscape

Comparison of Data Sources

The TES provides a comprehensive annual record of all the places of employment in the City, across the full range of employment activities, including retail-related employment. The CRD, in contrast, focuses exclusively on consumer service-related type activities, capturing the vast majority of retail and service activities within the GTA (including the City). The CRD omits smaller retail areas (typically less than 30,000 sq. ft.) and primarily captures street-level establishments (except in the case of multi-level shopping centres). In addition, the CRD includes units that are not occupied at the survey time ('vacant' properties), while the TES does not include any information about vacant units.

Geographical Boundaries

The combination of TES and CRD result in two geographical definitions for each strip: (i) the area covered by the CRD (which is also covered by the TES), which we call the 'CSCA Strips'; and, (ii) a larger area covered by the TES, but not fully covered by the CRD, which we call the 'Extended Strips'. Essentially, the CRD strip geography was used as the basis for delineating the strips used within this study, however, each strip was extended where necessary to conform with existing 'Avenues' boundaries.

Activity Categories

A key data element in each survey is the classification of the establishment's land use or activity – the NAICS/SIC (North American Industrial Classification System / Standard Industrial Classification) codes in the CRD (as defined by Statistics Canada) and the Activity Code in the TES. Both are hierarchical classifications, whereby major categories are progressively subdivided into smaller and more precise categories. This means that both can be used for unique user defined classifications or aggregations. Generally, the TES Activity Code has fewer categories than the SIC; i.e., it has more aggregation at the level of field observation. To facilitate comparison of the surveys a look-up table was generated to match CRD NAICS/SICs and the TES Activity codes. The matching process was undertaken on a code-by-code basis, and while an identical match was not always possible, every effort was made to join categories in a logically consistent manner. For this study, a 24 category classification (see Table 1) was developed.

Establishments in TES and CRD

A summary of the establishment counts in the CRD and the TES is presented in Table 2. In 2005, the TES identified 21,655 establishments on the 95 extended strips. In the area covered by the CSCA, the CRD recorded 14,196 establishments for the 95 strips, including 1,255 vacant units which were not recorded by the TES. As

TABLE 1. Activity Categories

Cat.	Activity Description	Cat.	Activity Description
1	Manufacturing & Distribution Services	13	Liquor
2	Household & Appliance Stores	14	Drug Stores
3	Automotive	15	Shoe Stores
4	General Merch.	16	Clothing & Fabric Stores
5	Financial & Insurance Industries	17	Book & Stationery Stores
6	Business Services	18	Florists Lawn & Garden Centres
7	Health Services	19	Hardware Stores
8	Food & Beverage Services	20	Sporting Goods and Toys
9	Recreational Services	21	Watches, Jewellery, Camera and Music Stores
10	Personal & Household Services	22	Other Retail
11	Hair & Beauty Services	23	Others
12	Food	24	Vacant

TABLE 2. Establishments on the Strips, TES and CRD 2005

Data Sets	No. of Establishments	
	CSCA Strips	Extended Strips
CRD Counts	14,196	-
CRD Vacant Counts	1,255	-
TES Counts	19,040	21,611
TES minus CRD Counts (inc. Vacant)	4,844	-
TES minus CRD (exc. Vacant)	7,415	-

would be expected the TES includes more service-related establishments, as the CRD does not survey most establishments above the ground floor, or within retail areas of less than 30,000 sq. ft. Some differences can also be expected because the two surveys are conducted at different times of the year.

Table 3 lists establishment counts on the CSCA strips by category, and highlights the differences between the two data sources. In the 'Difference' column in Table 3 positive numbers show categories with a higher count in the CRD data, while negative shows categories with a higher count in the TES data. Generally, the counts of retail stores in both surveys are relatively comparable while the counts for services (i.e., Financial & Insurance Services, Business Services, Health Services, and Personal & household services) are significantly different. In relative terms, the CRD identifies a comparatively larger number of General Merchandise stores and Florist, Lawn & Garden Stores – these differences are mainly due to the mismatch problems in the categories mentioned previously (e.g., Florists are included as 'Other Retailers' within the TES). In sum, on most strips the TES counts more establishments than the CRD. On the ten strips where the CRD counts more, the differences are generally small (less than 10 per cent).

Extended 'Avenue' Strips

In total, the TES recorded 2,571 establishments on the extended strips but outside of the CSCA strips. Service categories accounted for the largest shares of these establishments: Health Services 21.4%, Personal & Household Services 17.2%, Business Services 14.2%, and Food & Beverage Services 10.9%. Overall, the TES data for

Category	TES	CRD	Difference	% Difference	# of TES outside of CRD strips	% TES outside of CRD strips
Financial & Insurance Services	957	557	-400	-41.8	126	11.6
Business Services	2,171	660	-1,511	-69.6	364	14.4
Health Services	2,236	713	-1,523	-68.1	549	19.7
Food & Beverage Services	2,735	2,464	-271	-9.9	281	9.3
Recreational Services	461	393	-68	-14.8	57	11.0
Personal & Household Services	2,554	1,260	-1,294	-50.7	443	14.8
Hair & Beauty Services	1,304	1,000	-304	-23.3	107	7.6
Automotive	514	312	-202	-39.3	146	22.1
Household & Appliance Stores	549	675	126	23.0	36	6.2
General Merch.	40	255	215	537.5	1	2.4
Food	1,695	1,258	-437	-25.8	155	8.4
Liquor	72	70	-2	-2.8	5	6.5
Drug Stores	262	263	1	0.4	35	11.8
Shoe Stores	116	125	9	7.8	3	2.5
Clothing & Fabric Stores	895	960	65	7.3	48	5.1
Book & Stationery Stores	117	112	-5	-4.3	12	9.3
Florists Lawn & Garden Centres	31	142	111	358.1	3	8.8
Hardware Stores	114	116	2	1.8	9	7.3
Sporting Goods and Toys	83	182	99	119.3	5	5.7
Watches, Jewellery, Camera and Music Stores	356	347	-9	-2.5	16	4.3
Other Retail	1,523	909	-614	-40.3	112	6.9
Manufacturing & Distribution Industries	247	168	-79	-32.0	57	18.8
Others	8	0	-8	.	1	11.1
Vacant	0	1,255	1,255			
Total	19,040	14,196	-4,844			

TABLE 3. Number of Establishments by Category: Comparison of TES and CRD 2005

the CSCA strips included 88.1% of the establishments identified by the TES on the extended strips (i.e., 11.9% of the establishments were outside the CSCA strip geography). The commercial categories with over 10% of their establishments outside of the CSCA strips were all 'service' categories, except for drug stores. In sum, the CRD captures the vast majority of retailing activity on the strips when compared with the TES (as would be expected due to the differing aims of the CRD and TES data collections).

THE CHANGING CHARACTER OF RETAIL STRIPS

This section presents three perspectives on the changing character of the retail strips: (i) the employment perspective, based on analysis of TES data for the extended strip boundaries; (ii) the built form perspective, based on TES surveys; and, (iii) the retail perspective, based on analysis of CRD for CSCA strips.

The Employment Perspective

Establishments and Employment

In 2005, 21,611 establishments were located on the 95 extended strips, representing 30.2% of the total establishments within the City. The number of jobs on the strips in 2005 increased by 3,467 (1.9%) against a city wide increase of more than 100,000 (9.4%). This is against a decrease in the number of establishments, with 566 less establishments on the strips (-2.6%) and nearly 2,700 less establishments across the entire city (-3.6%). Overall, however, the strips' share of the city's employment market remained stable, at about 30% of total establishments and decreased by 1.05% to 14.4% of total jobs. In total the strips provided over 180,000 jobs, against a city-wide employment count of 1.26 million.

The overall stability of the strips within the city's employment picture masks considerable change on the individual strips. Fifty-one strips saw a decline in establishments between 1996 and 2005, while 40 strips saw

TABLE 4. Total Number of Establishments and Employment: Strips vs. City, TES 1985, 1996 and 2005

	Establishments			Employment		
Year	City	Strips	% on Strips	City	Strips	% on Strips
1985	73,096	22,352	30.6%	1,181,663	182,186	15.4%
1996	74,203	22,177	29.9%	1,154,205	178,349	15.5%
2005	71,509	21,611	30.2%	1,262,653	181,816	14.4%
Change, 1996-2005	-2,694	-566	21.0%	108,448	3,467	3.2%
% Change	-3.6	-2.6	n.a.	9.40	1.94	n.a.

an increase - one strip added over 100 establishments and two lost over 100. In relative terms, however, twelve strips added or lost more than 20% of their establishments between 1996 and 2005. As Maps 2 and 3 show, the strips that grew the most tended to be in the northern and eastern post-war suburbs, while many of the older strips declined, particularly those to the west and north of the downtown.

Average Establishment Size

In 2005, the average size (as measured by number of employees) of all establishments on the strips was 8.4, with average size ranging from 3 to 25 on the 95 strips. The majority of strips have a smaller average establishment size than the overall average establishment size of the strips. Fourteen strips have an average establishment size of 10 or more. As a group, their main distinguishing characteristic is that they have a high proportion of financial, business and health service establishments and office buildings – they contain nearly half of all the office buildings on the strips. The overall average size of the establishments on the strips has increased marginally since 1996 (8.0 in 1996 and 8.4 in 2005; an increase of 5%).

Share of Establishments on the Strips

As highlighted in Table 4 the strips maintained a steady share of the city's employment between 1996 and 2005 (30% of establishments and 15% of employees). Variations by category are presented in Figure 3. In comparison to the City, the strips have a relatively higher share in retail categories (except general merchandise), with over 40% of the establishments. In contrast, the strips have a very low share of the City's non-commercial establishments (Manufacturing & Distribution Services, Other). The most noticeable change between 1996 and 2005 is that the strips lost share in General Merchandise Stores, Household &

Appliance services and Automotive but gained more in 'Others' establishments.

Average Establishment Size by Category

Most sectors ranged fairly close to the overall average establishment size of about 8 employees per establishment. The biggest category was general merchandise (45 in 2005), such as Zellers and Wal-Mart. Figure 4 shows average size by category and changes between 1996 and 2005. It highlights the small growth in most retail categories, partly reflecting the impact of new formats and big boxes over the past decade.

The average establishment size on the strips is much smaller compared to all establishments across the rest of the city – eight employees per establishment versus twenty one. Generally, all types of establishments were bigger in the rest of city than on the strips, except general merchandise stores (with an overall decrease in the total number of general merchandise stores). For most retail stores, such as Drug stores, Hair and Beauty services, Food stores, Shoe stores, Clothing & Fabric stores, Florists lawn & garden centers, there were only very small differences in average establishment size between the strips and the rest of the city. The overall difference between average establishment size on the strips versus the rest of the city is likely a reflection of the increased presence of large format retailers in non-strip locations.

Establishments by Category

Strips are gradually becoming more service oriented, with the service categories increasing from 67% of establishments in 1996 to 69% in 2005. On the other hand, retailing declined from 31% to 29%. Table 5 shows a 1% increase in service establishments between 1996 and 2005, but a 9% decrease in retailing. As shown in Figure 5, among service categories, health services and food & beverage

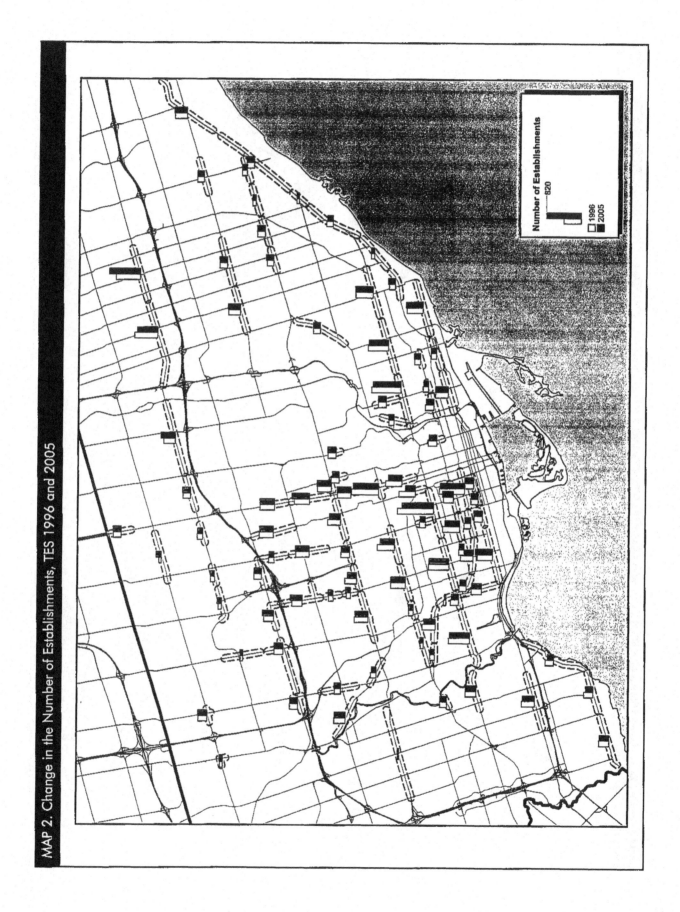

MAP 2. Change in the Number of Establishments, TES 1996 and 2005

Number of Establishments

820

□ 1996
■ 2005

239

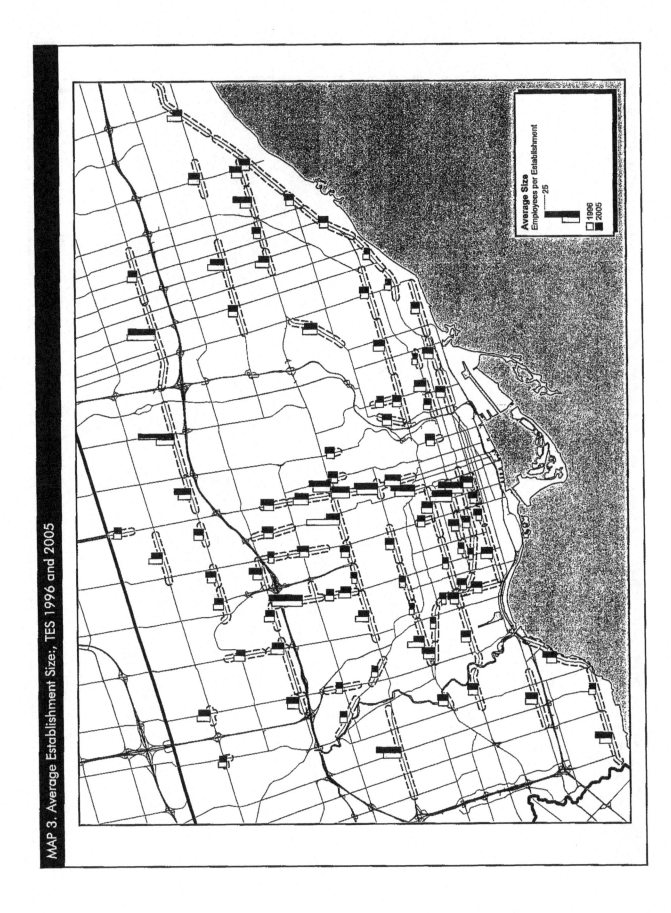

MAP 3. Average Establishment Size:, TES 1996 and 2005

Average Size
Employees per Establishment
25

1996
2005

240

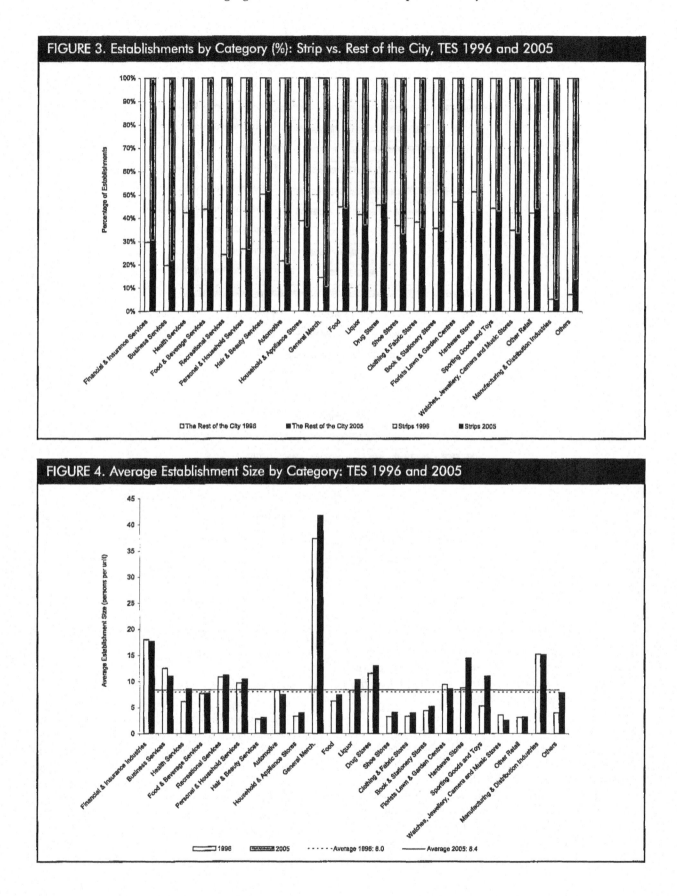

FIGURE 3. Establishments by Category (%): Strip vs. Rest of the City, TES 1996 and 2005

FIGURE 4. Average Establishment Size by Category: TES 1996 and 2005

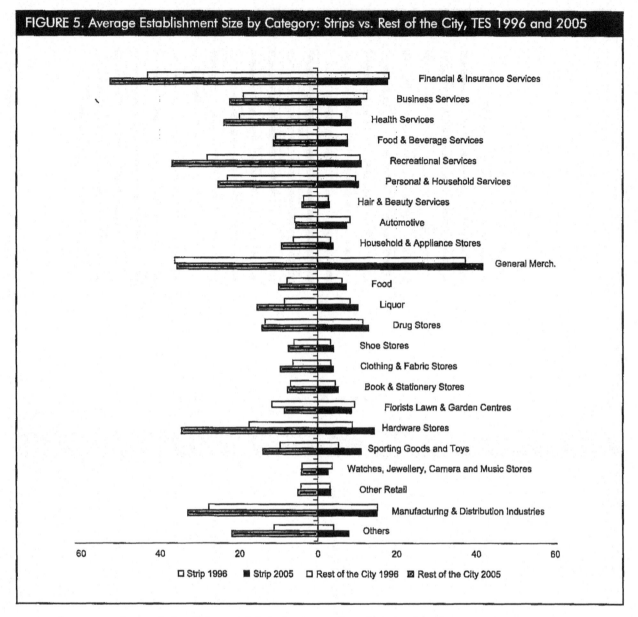

FIGURE 5. Average Establishment Size by Category: Strips vs. Rest of the City, TES 1996 and 2005

□ Strip 1996   ■ Strip 2005   □ Rest of the City 1996   ☒ Rest of the City 2005

services (restaurants, bars, etc) sharply increased their share of total establishments, and along with business services and personal and household services they account for the bulk of the service establishments.

Food stores and clothing and fabric stores are the largest retailing categories (except for 'Other Retail'), though most relative growth was in drug stores and 'other retail' stores. The number of establishments in most of the categories changed significantly over the 1996 to 2005 period. While the total number of establishments declined by 2.6% (566 establishments) over this period.The relatively small overall change masked much more drastic adjustments in the individual sectors.

Employees by Category

The service categories, together accounted for 77.4% of the jobs on the strips in 2005, up from 76.4% in 1996 (see Table 6 and Figure 7). The jobs related to manufacturing & distribution services dropped to only 2.5% in 2005 from 3.5% in 1996. Retailing accounts for a relatively small proportion of employees, with food stores being the largest category at about 7.5%. While establishments declined overall, employment increased - especially in health services. This however masks divergent sector-by-sector experiences: most sectors were much higher or lower than the overall average.

TABLE 5. Establishments by Category, TES 1996 and 2005

Category	Establishments				% of Total			% of Sub-Group		
	1996	2005	Chg	%Chg	1996	2005	Chg	1996	2005	Chg
Financial & Insurance Services	1,112	1,083	-29	-2.6	5.01	5.01	0.00	7.49	7.22	-0.28
Business Services	2,493	2,535	42	1.7	11.24	11.73	0.49	16.80	16.89	0.10
Health Services	2,710	2,785	75	2.8	12.22	12.89	0.67	18.26	18.56	0.30
Food & Beverage Services	2,801	3,016	215	7.7	12.63	13.96	1.33	18.87	20.10	1.23
Recreational Services	558	518	-40	-7.2	2.52	2.40	-0.12	3.76	3.45	-0.31
Personal & Household Services	3,199	2,997	-202	-6.3	14.42	13.87	-0.56	21.56	19.97	-1.58
Hair & Beauty Services	1,254	1,411	157	12.5	5.65	6.53	0.87	8.45	9.40	0.95
Automotive	713	660	-53	-7.4	3.22	3.05	-0.16	4.80	4.40	-0.41
Total Services	14,840	15,005	165	1.1	66.92	69.43	2.52	100	100	
Household & Appliance Stores	659	585	-74	-11.2	2.97	2.71	-0.26	9.53	9.30	-0.23
General Merch.	69	41	-28	-40.6	0.31	0.19	-0.12	1.00	0.65	-0.35
Food	2,096	1,850	-246	-11.7	9.45	8.56	-0.89	30.31	29.40	-0.91
Liquor	91	77	-14	-15.4	0.41	0.36	-0.05	1.32	1.22	-0.09
Drug Stores	281	297	16	5.7	1.27	1.37	0.11	4.06	4.72	0.66
Shoe Stores	164	119	-45	-27.4	0.74	0.55	-0.19	2.37	1.89	-0.48
Clothing & Fabric Stores	1,133	943	-190	-16.8	5.11	4.36	-0.75	16.38	14.98	-1.40
Book & Stationery Stores	153	129	-24	-15.7	0.69	0.60	-0.09	2.21	2.05	-0.16
Florists Lawn & Garden Centres	39	34	-5	-12.8	0.18	0.16	-0.02	0.56	0.54	-0.02
Hardware Stores	207	123	-84	-40.6	0.93	0.57	-0.36	2.99	1.95	-1.04
Sporting Goods and Toys	109	88	-21	-19.3	0.49	0.41	-0.08	1.58	1.40	-0.18
Watches, Jewel., Cam.,Music Stores	397	372	-25	-6.3	1.79	1.72	-0.07	5.74	5.91	0.17
Other Retail	1,517	1,635	118	7.8	6.84	7.57	0.73	21.94	25.98	4.04
Total Retail	6,915	6,293	-622	-9.0	31.18	29.12	-2.06	100	100	
Manufacturing & Distribution Ind.	414	304	-110	-26.6	1.87	1.41	-0.46	98.10	97.12	-0.98
Others	8	9	1	12.5	0.04	0.04	0.01	1.90	2.88	0.98
Other	422	313	-109	-25.8	1.90	1.45	-0.45	100	100	
Grand Total	22,177	21,611	-566	-2.6	100	100				

FIGURE 6. Total Establishments by Category (%), TES 1996 and 2005

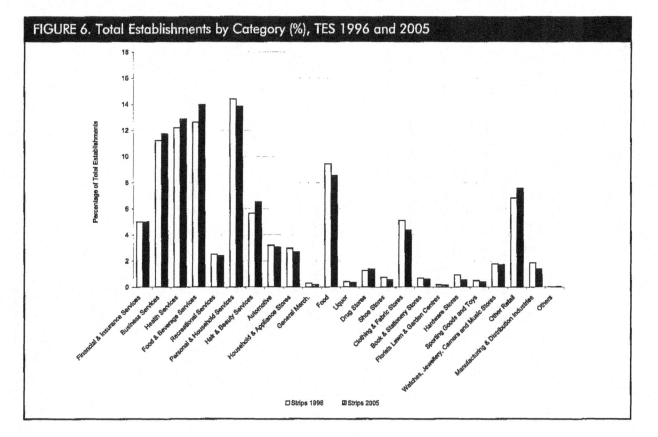

Table 6. Employment by Category, TES 1996 and 2005

Category	Employment				% of Total			% of Sub-Group		
	1996	2005	Chg	%Chg	1996	2005	Chg	1996	2005	Chg
Financial & Insurance Services	20,065	19,184	-881	-4.4	11.25	10.55	-0.70	14.73	13.64	-1.09
Business Services	31,232	27,919	-3,313	-10.6	17.51	15.36	-2.16	22.93	19.85	-3.08
Health Services	16,709	24,021	7,312	43.8	9.37	13.21	3.84	12.27	17.07	4.81
Food & Beverage Services	21,607	23,267	1,660	7.7	12.12	12.80	0.68	15.86	16.54	0.68
Recreational Services	6,053	5,786	-267	-4.4	3.39	3.18	-0.21	4.44	4.11	-0.33
Personal & Household Services	31,172	31,292	120	0.4	17.48	17.21	-0.27	22.88	22.24	-0.64
Hair & Beauty Services	3,465	4,296	831	24.0	1.94	2.36	0.42	2.54	3.05	0.51
Automotive	5,930	4,920	-1,010	-17.0	3.32	2.71	-0.62	4.35	3.50	-0.86
Total Services	136,233	140,685	4,452	3.3	76.39	77.38	0.99	100	100	
Household & Appliance Stores	2,194	2,312	118	5.4	1.23	1.27	0.04	6.13	6.34	0.21
General Merch.	2,576	1,712	-864	-33.5	1.44	0.94	-0.50	7.20	4.70	-2.50
Food	13,096	13,666	570	4.4	7.34	7.52	0.17	36.60	37.48	0.88
Liquor	757	794	37	4.9	0.42	0.44	0.01	2.12	2.18	0.06
Drug Stores	3,252	3,862	610	18.8	1.82	2.12	0.30	9.09	10.59	1.50
Shoe Stores	531	481	-50	-9.4	0.30	0.26	-0.03	1.48	1.32	-0.16
Clothing & Fabric Stores	3,800	3,719	-81	-2.1	2.13	2.05	-0.09	10.62	10.20	-0.42
Book & Stationery Stores	676	670	-6	-0.9	0.38	0.37	-0.01	1.89	1.84	-0.05
Florists Lawn & Garden Centres	368	292	-76	-20.7	0.21	0.16	-0.05	1.03	0.80	-0.23
Hardware Stores	1,821	1,776	-45	-2.5	1.02	0.98	-0.04	5.09	4.87	-0.22
Sporting Goods and Toys	581	970	389	67.0	0.33	0.53	0.21	1.62	2.66	1.04
Watches, Jewel., Cam., Music Stores	1,439	956	-483	-33.6	0.81	0.53	-0.28	4.02	2.62	-1.40
Other Retail	4,686	5,248	562	12.0	2.63	2.89	0.26	13.10	14.39	1.30
Total Retail	35,777	36,458	681	1.9	20.06	20.05	-0.01	100	100	
Manufacturing & Distribution Ind.	6,307	4,602	-1,705	-27.0	3.54	2.53	-1.01	99.50	98.48	-1.01
Others	32	71	39	121.9	0.02	0.04	0.02	0.50	1.52	1.01
Other	6,339	4,673	-1,666	-26.3	3.55	2.57	-0.98	100	100	
Grand Total	178,349	181,816	3,467	1.9	100	100				

FIGURE 7. Employment by Category (%), TES 1996 and 2005

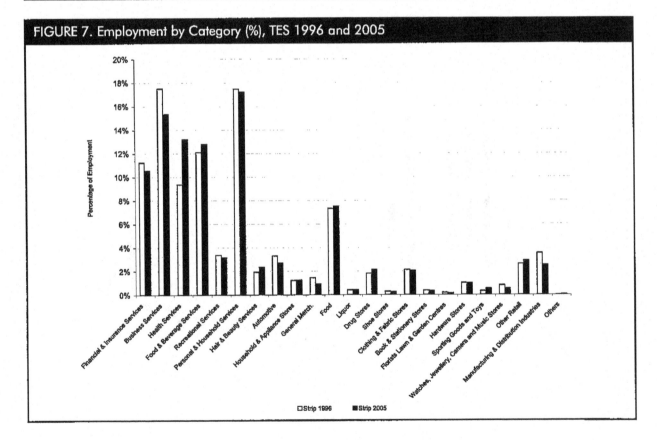

The Built Form Perspective

Built Form on the Strips

Although a store with apartments above is usually thought of as typical, there is actually a variety of building forms on the strips. The brief analysis that follows looks at the built form of each land parcel and each establishment. The data for land parcels are only available for 2005, because of inconsistencies in the parcel mapping for 1996; whereas the data for establishments are available for both 1996 and 2005.

The Parcels

The TES recorded employment on just over 10,000 parcels on the strips in 2005, representing about 40% of the parcels in the City on which the TES recorded employment. The typical attached/row retail building with offices or apartments above dominates the strips' built form. 71% of such parcels in the City are on the strips and they account for 66% of the strips' parcels with employment in 2005 (Table 7). All other types account for relatively small proportions (6% or less) of the commercial buildings on the strips. Note, however, that over 40% of the City's shopping centre parcels are on the strips, reflecting the strips overall importance in the City's employment make-up .

The Establishments

Table 8 is a summary of establishments by built form for 1996 and 2005. Both in 1996 and 2005, over 80% of establishments on the strips were found in three types of buildings: attached/row retail with another use, shopping centers and office buildings. Note that while 'attached row retail with another use' accounted for 66% of parcels, they only accommodated 47% of establishments. On the other hand, not surprisingly, shopping centres and office buildings accounted for a much higher proportion of establishments than parcels.

When comparing 1996 and 2005 (see Table 9), we see the increasing role of shopping centres and residential buildings in accommodating establishments on the strips, and a decline in the number of establishments in stand alone buildings. The increase in residential buildings results partly from employment in new mixed use buildings, as well as the conversion of existing houses or parts of houses to employment activities. Some stand-alone businesses closed and the property was no longer used for employment by 2005 (vacant, new housing). Note also a decline of nearly 400 establishments in the typical row building with another use. Their overall importance changed little however – declining only from 47.4% of establishments in 1996 to 46.8% in 2005 (Table 8).

TABLE 7. Parcels by Built Form: Strips vs. Rest of the City, TES 2005

Built form	Number City	Strips	R.O.C	% of Each Location City	Strips	R.O.C	% of Each Built Form Type Strips	R.O.C
Stand alone (detached) retail / commercial	1,708	618	1,090	6.8	6.1	7.2	36.2	63.8
Attached / Row retail – single use	1,106	596	510	4.4	5.9	3.4	53.9	46.1
Attached / Row retail with another use	9,343	6,606	2,737	37.0	65.7	18.0	70.7	29.3
Shopping Centre[1]	938	392	546	3.7	3.9	3.6	41.8	58.2
Automotive	1,497	440	1,057	5.9	4.4	7.0	29.4	70.6
Office Building	2,702	589	2,113	10.7	5.9	13.9	21.8	78.2
Residential	1,224	292	932	4.8	2.9	6.1	23.9	76.1
Community Facilities (public and private)	1,567	276	1,291	6.2	2.7	8.5	17.6	82.4
Other[2]	5,173	243	4,930	20.5	2.4	32.4	4.7	95.3
Total	25,258	10,052	15,206	100.0	100.0	100.0	39.8	60.2

R.O.C. Rest of City

[1] These data are for parcels. Some shopping centres have more than one parcel. We estimate there are 732 shopping centres in the City, with 259 (or 35.4%) on the strips.

[2] 'Other' includes a variety of building forms not typically found on the strips, such as industrial buildings, and utilities, transportation, communications and education buildings.

TABLE 8. Establishments by Built Form, TES 1996 and 2005

Built Form	1996				2005			
	City	Strips	% of City	% of Strips	City	Strips	% of City	% of Strips
Stand alone (detached) retail / commercial	3,122	1,108	4.2	5.0	2,397	798	3.4	3.7
Attached / Row retail – single use	2,837	1,134	3.8	5.1	2,548	1,133	3.6	5.2
Attached / Row retail with another use	16,118	10,518	21.7	47.4	15,277	10,123	21.4	46.8
Shopping Centre	10,138	2,716	13.7	12.2	11,052	3,036	15.5	14
Automotive	2,283	686	3.1	3.1	2,274	639	3.2	3.0
Office Building	22,503	4,907	30.3	22.1	21,095	4,716	29.5	21.8
Residential	534	138	0.7	0.6	2,061	486	2.9	2.2
Community Facilities (public and private)	2,005	418	2.7	1.9	2,190	401	3.1	1.9
Other	14,663	563	19.8	2.5	12,615	279	17.6	1.3
Total	74,203	22,188	100%	100%	71,509	21,611	100%	100%

TABLE 9. Change in Establishments by Built Form, TES 1996-2005

Built form	No. of establishments		% Chg in No. of Establishments		Change in % of Establishments	
	City	Strips	City	Strips	City	Strips
Stand alone (detached) retail / commercial	-725	-310	-23.2	-28.0	-0.9	-1.3
Attached / Row retail – single use	-289	-1	-10.2	-0.1	-0.3	0.1
Attached / Row retail with another use	-841	-395	-5.2	-3.8	-0.4	-0.6
Shopping Centre	914	320	9.0	11.8	1.8	1.8
Automotive	-9	-47	-0.4	-6.9	0.1	-0.1
Office Building	-1,408	-191	-6.3	-3.9	-0.8	-0.3
Residential	1,527	348	286.0	252.2	2.2	1.6
Community Facilities (public and private)	185	-17	9.2	-4.1	0.4	0.0
Other	-2,048	-284	-14.0	-50.4	-2.1	-1.2
Total	-2,694	-577	-3.6	-2.6	0.0	0.0

The Retail Perspective

Overview

Table 10 provides summary data for the 95 CSCA retail strips (a subset of the Extended Strips). Between 1996 and 2005 the number of stores increased from 12,873 to 14,196 (see Map 4), an increase of more than 1,300 stores (10.3 %) [this increase is in contrast to the TES findings, reflecting the street-level focus of the CRD data collection]. The estimated square footage of these strips increased from 19.1 million to 20.2 million (an increase of 6.2%), with the average square footage per store remaining relatively unchanged at just over 1,400 square feet (albeit with the median estimated size less than 1,000 sq. ft.). The overall vacancy rates for these strips has remained relatively stable decreasing slightly (-0.1%) to 8.8% vacant. In terms of

ethnicity the total number of stores classified as 'ethnic' has declined by 21.0% (-462 stores). This is against an overall increase in the total number of stores along the strips. In 1996, 18.7% of the stores along the strips were classified as ethnic, by 2005 this had declined to 13.4%. From the perspective of corporate ownership of stores, there has been a small increase in the number of corporate chains between 1996 and 2005, however, in relative terms the percentage of chain stores has decreased from 17.2% to 15.4%, with the percentage of Top Retail Chains, as defined by the CSCA (corporations with over $100 million in annual sales, see Daniel and Hernandez, 2006), declining from 2.8% in 1996 to 2.4% in 2005 (note: the top retail chains do not include restaurant chains). These summary statistics mask substantial variation at the strip level. This section provides details on the spatial and temporal variation by strip, focusing on the changing: sector activities, vacancy levels, number and size of stores, chain ownership and ethnicity.

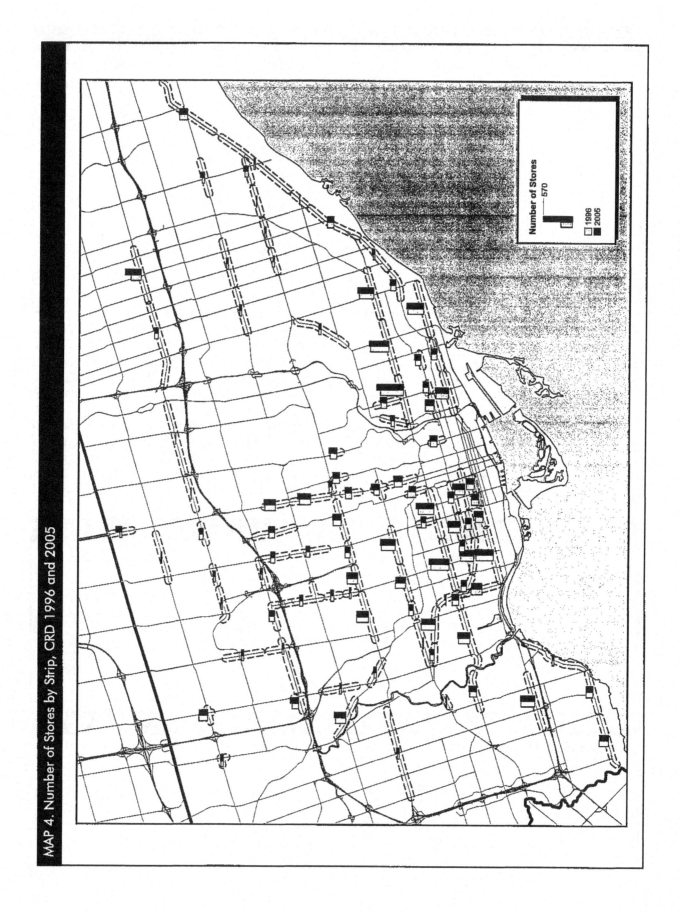

MAP 4. Number of Stores by Strip, CRD 1996 and 2005

Number of Stores
570
1996
2005

TABLE 10. Retail Change on the Strips, CRD 1996 and 2005

	1996	2005	Chg	Chg %
Stores	12,873	14,196	1,323	10.3%
Vacant	1,140	1,255	115	10.1%
% Vacant	8.9%	8.8%	-0.0	
Ethnic	2,196	1,734	-462	-21.0%
% Ethnic	18.7%	13.4%	-5.3	
Chain	2,023	1,995	-28	-1.4%
% Chain	17.2%	15.4%	-1.8	
Top Retail	324	314	-10	-3.1%
% Top Retail	2.8%	2.4%	-0.3	
Total Floor Area	19.1	20.2	1.2	6.2%
Average Floor Area Per Store	1,480.7	1,425.7	-55.0	-3.7%

Size and Distribution of Stores by Strip

The retail strips varied in terms of the number of stores and size of retail units. The numbers of stores ranged from ten to over five hundred across the two study periods, with the mean number of stores increasing from 143 in 1996 to 165 in 2005 (the median increased from 120 to 145 stores). Table 11 shows the distribution of the number of stores on the selected strips. It can be seen that in 2005 that 40.0 percent of the strips were comprised of 100 stores or less, with just under one-fifth ranging from 101 to 150 stores.

The aggregate growth in retail stores across the sample is illustrated with the shift toward larger retail strips in 2005. The number of strips with less than 50 stores decreased from 24.2 percent in 1996 to 18.9 percent in 2005. Table 12 highlights the relative stability of the strips in terms of the size of stores operated. Sixty seven stores of over 3,000 square feet (a 15 percent increase) were added to the strips between 1996 and 2005. This can be seen within the broader 'boxing' of retail formats over the study period, that is, integration of large format retailers across a range of location types (in power centres, malls and along retail

TABLE 11. Number of Stores by Strip, CRD 1996 and 2005

No. of Stores	1996	%	2005	%	Chg	Chg %
<=50	23	24.2%	18	18.9%	-5	-21.7%
51 - 100	16	16.8%	20	21.1%	4	25.0%
101 - 150	24	25.3%	18	18.9%	-6	-25.0%
151 - 200	8	8.4%	16	16.8%	8	100.0%
201 - 250	11	11.6%	5	5.3%	-6	-54.5%
251 - 300	6	6.3%	7	7.4%	1	16.7%
301 - 350	3	3.2%	5	5.3%	2	66.7%
351+	4	4.2%	6	6.3%	2	50.0%

TABLE 12. Change in Retail Strips Store Size, CRD 1996 and 2005

Size of Stores (sq. ft.)	Stores 1996	%	Stores 2005	%	Chg % Share
<1,000	10,539	81.9%	11,705	82.5%	0.6
1,000-3,000	1,769	13.7%	1,859	13.1%	-0.6
3,000-10,000	414	3.2%	476	3.4%	0.1
>10,000	151	1.2%	156	1.1%	-0.1

strips or free standing in the extended strips). In sum, the data highlights a move toward larger retail strips, with evidence of increased numbers of large format retailers along certain strips.

Stores by Category

Table 13 provides a listing of the total store count for the strips in 1996 and 2005. The categories that have gained the most in absolute terms include Food and Beverage Services (+305), Personal and Household Services (+239), Hair and Beauty Services (+198) and Health Services (+200) – all service categories. In contrast, the categories that have decreased the most in terms of the total number of stores are primarily retail categories, including, Food

(-115), Clothing Stores (-68) and Hardware Stores (-58). In relative terms (see percentage change), Manufacturing and Distributive Services (comprising postal, courier and telecommunication services) grew by over 270 percent, along with gains in Health Services (+39%), Business Services (+26.2%), Hair and Beauty Services (+24.7%) and Personal and Household Service (+23.4%). The data highlights a steady transition across many of Toronto's strips away from the traditional retail functions towards service (personal, business, household, distributive and health). With 'services' in 2005 accounting for 56.9% of all the non-vacant stores, increasing from 52.7% in 1996. Compared to the 'retail' sub-category witnessing a 5.1% decrease in store share from 47.0% in 1996 to 41.8% in 2005.

TABLE 13. Retail Strips by Category, CRD 1996 and 2005

Category	Stores 1996	2005	Chg	% Chg	% of Total (exc. vacant) 1996	2005	Chg	% of Sub-Group 1996	2005	Chg
Financial & Insurance Industries	501	557	56	11.2%	4.3	4.3	0.0	8.1	7.6	-0.5
Business Services	523	660	137	26.2%	4.5	5.1	0.6	8.5	9.0	0.5
Health Services	513	713	200	39.0%	4.4	5.5	1.1	8.3	9.7	1.4
Food & Beverage Services	2,159	2,464	305	14.1%	18.4	19.0	0.6	34.9	33.5	-1.5
Recreational Services	330	393	63	19.1%	2.8	3.0	0.2	5.3	5.3	0.0
Hair & Beauty Services	802	1,000	198	24.7%	6.8	7.7	0.9	13.0	13.6	0.6
Personal & Household Services	1,021	1,260	239	23.4%	8.7	9.7	1.0	16.5	17.1	0.6
Automotive	330	312	-18	-5.5%	2.8	2.4	-0.4	5.3	4.2	-1.1
Total Services	**6,179**	**7,359**	**1,180**	**19.1%**	**52.7**	**56.9**	**4.2**	**100**	**100**	
Household & Appliance Stores	574	675	101	17.6%	4.9	5.2	0.3	10.4	12.5	2.0
General Merch.	266	255	-11	-4.1%	2.3	2.0	-0.3	4.8	4.7	-0.1
Food	1,373	1,258	-115	-8.4%	11.7	9.7	-2.0	24.9	23.2	-1.7
Liquor	68	70	2	2.9%	0.6	0.5	0.0	1.2	1.3	0.1
Drug Stores	242	263	21	8.7%	2.1	2.0	0.0	4.4	4.9	0.5
Shoe Stores	147	125	-22	-15.0%	1.3	1.0	-0.3	2.7	2.3	-0.4
Clothing & Fabric Stores	1,028	960	-68	-6.6%	8.8	7.4	-1.3	18.7	17.7	-0.9
Book & Stationery Stores	132	112	-20	-15.2%	1.1	0.9	-0.3	2.4	2.1	-0.3
Florists Lawn & Garden Centres	177	142	-35	-19.8%	1.5	1.1	-0.4	3.2	2.6	-0.6
Hardware Stores	173	116	-57	-32.9%	1.5	0.9	-0.6	3.1	2.1	-1.0
Sporting Goods & Toys	180	182	2	1.1%	1.5	1.4	-0.1	3.3	3.4	0.1
Watches, Jewellery, Cam. and Music	366	347	-19	-5.2%	3.1	2.7	-0.4	6.6	6.4	-0.2
Other Retail	783	909	126	16.1%	6.7	7.0	0.4	14.2	16.8	2.6
Total Retail	**5,509**	**5,414**	**-95**	**-1.7%**	**47.0**	**41.8**	**-5.1**	**100**	**100**	
Manufacturing & Distribution Services	45	168	123	273.3%	0.4	1.3	0.9			
Total Other	**45**	**168**	**123**	**273.3%**	**0.4**	**1.3**	**0.9**			
Vacant	1,140	1,255	115	10.1%	9.7	9.7	0.0			
Total Stores	**12,873**	**14,196**	**1,323**	**10.3%**						

TABLE 14. Change in Ethnic Retail on the Strips, CRD 1996 and 2005

Ethnicity	1996	% of Ethnic	2005	% of Ethnic	Chg	% Chg	Chg in %
Chinese	588	26.8	458	26.4	-130	-22.1	-0.4
East European	30	1.4	17	1.0	-13	-43.3	-0.4
Greek	163	7.4	110	6.3	-53	-32.5	-1.1
Indian	128	5.8	124	7.2	-4	-3.1	1.3
Italian	433	19.7	234	13.5	-199	-46.0	-6.2
Jewish	46	2.1	39	2.2	-7	-15.2	0.2
Korean/Japanese	96	4.4	148	8.5	52	54.2	4.2
Latin American	43	2.0	38	2.2	-5	-11.6	0.2
Other	180	8.2	197	11.4	17	9.4	3.2
Polish	70	3.2	48	2.8	-22	-31.4	-0.4
Portuguese	207	9.4	154	8.9	-53	-25.6	-0.5
Vietnamese	78	3.6	71	4.1	-7	-9.0	0.5
West Indian	134	6.1	96	5.5	-38	-28.4	-0.6
Total Ethnic	**2196**	**18.7**	**1734**	**13.4**	**-462**	**-21.0**	**-5.3**

Stores by Ethnicity

The ethnic mosaic of retail strips is arguably one of the most distinctive elements of Toronto's retail structure. The growth of ethnic retail has been closely linked with the flow of immigrants to the City, as a result, Toronto houses a number of ethnic retail strips, including, Greektown, Little Italy, The Indian Bazaar and Chinatown/s (see Map 5 for the location of a subset of the ethnic stores in 2005 by major ethnic group). For an establishment to be defined as ethnic within the CRD, it has to have a distinctive signage that caters to a specific ethnic group. As shown in Table 14, the number of ethnic establishments decreased between 1996 and 2005, from 18.7 to 13.4 percent of all establishments on the strips. The most significant decline was in the number of Italian businesses, and the largest growth in Korean & Japanese and 'Other Ethnic'. The distinctive spatial pattern of ethnic retail is shown in Map 6 with the percentage of ethnic establishments in 2005 mapped by strip. The largest decreases in ethnic retail have been taking place along the traditional ethnic strips. Table 15 provides a breakdown of ethnic stores by major categories.

Vacancy Rates

In 2005, the CRD recorded 1,255 vacant units on the 95 strips (14,196 total units), for an overall vacancy rate of 8.8% (note: the CSCA definition of vacancy is based on a store being vacant at the time of data collection, i.e., vacancy from a consumer perspective. This differs from real estate definitions of vacancy that are based on active lease agreements, that is, if a tenant is paying a lease on a property it is not vacant, regardless of whether or not the store is in actual operation [e.g., a store may close but may be liable for a given number of months of lease payments]). Sixty-five strips had less than 10% of their retail units vacant while 5 strips had more than 20% of their retail units vacant in 2005 (see Table 16). The vacancy rate has declined slightly from 1996 to 2005, however, there is significant variation across the strips, as can be seen in Map 7. Table 17 compares the vacancy rate for the selected strips against the Rest of the City. It should be noted that the selected strips consist of strip locations and community and neighbourhood centres (i.e., plazas). The vacancy rate for the shopping centres on the selected strips is higher than for the Rest of the City. This reflects the mix of larger shopping centres included in the Rest of the City: typically, larger centres have lower vacancy rates (see Table 18). Comparing the strips, the stability of vacancy on the selected strips can be contrasted to a significant decrease in strip vacancy for the Rest of the City, decreasing from 11.4% in 1996 to 7.9% in 2005.

Retail Chains

The CRD identifies retail and service establishments that are part of chains, that is, businesses with at least four or more locations (as defined by Statistics Canada). In addition, the CSCA also tracks store openings and closures of major retail chains, defined broadly as corporations with over $100 million dollars in total retail sales. The presence of chains, or lack thereof, on retail strips can be used in part

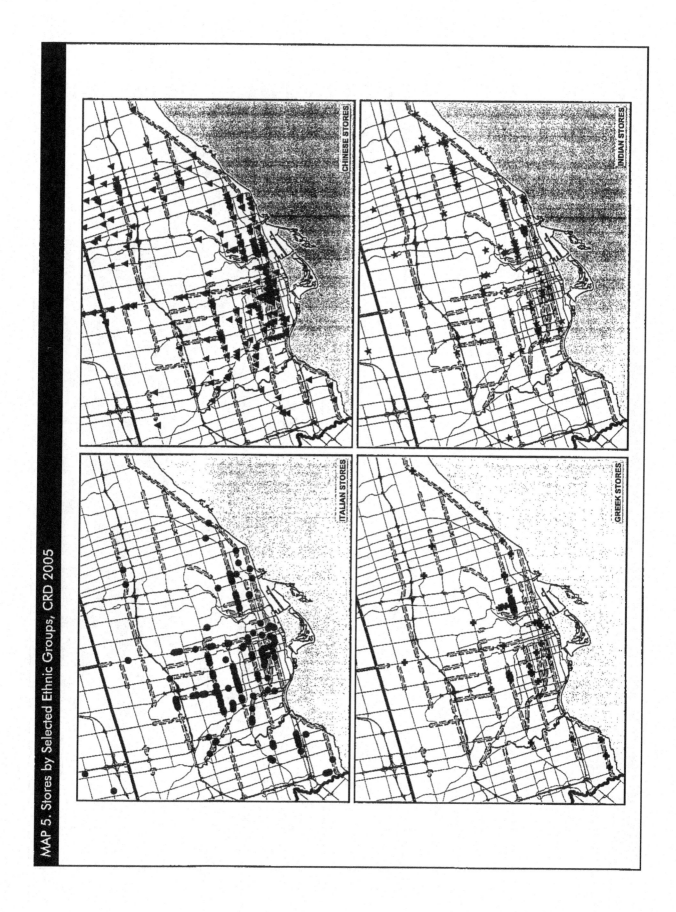

MAP 5. Stores by Selected Ethnic Groups, CRD 2005

CHINESE STORES

INDIAN STORES

ITALIAN STORES

GREEK STORES

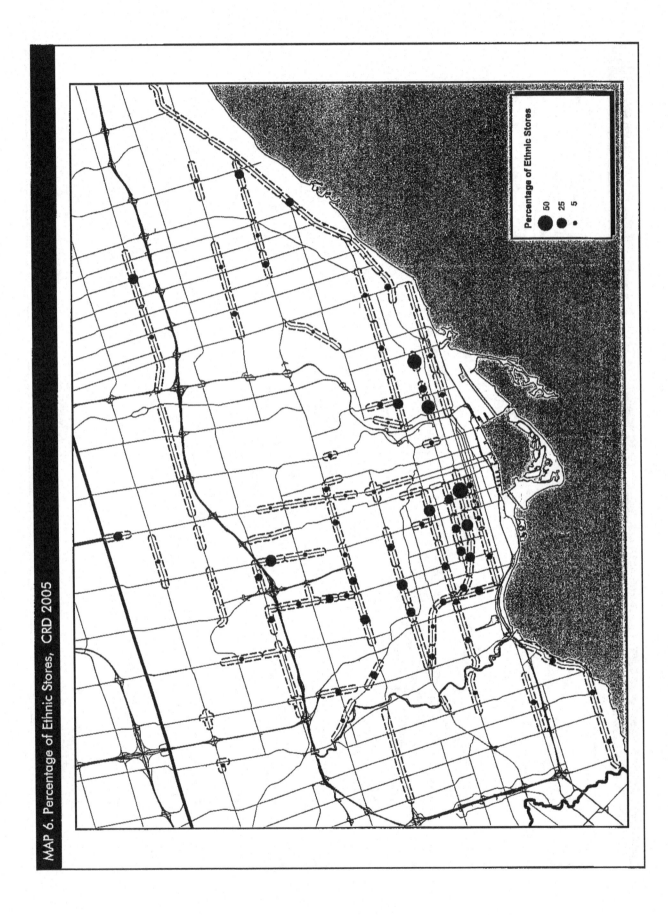

MAP 6. Percentage of Ethnic Stores, CRD 2005

Percentage of Ethnic Stores

50
25
5

TABLE 15. Ethnic Retail by Category, CRD 1996 and 2005

Ethnicity	Fashion 1996	Fashion 2005	Fashion Chg	Food 1996	Food 2005	Food Chg	Food & Beverage Services 1996	Food & Beverage Services 2005	Food & Beverage Services Chg	Services 1996	Services 2005	Services Chg	Other 1996	Other 2005	Other Chg
Chinese	35	13	-22	145	106	-39	163	118	-45	134	139	5	111	82	-29
East European	10	8	-2	5	1	-4	5	5	0	6	3	-3	4	0	-4
Greek	13	5	-8	27	17	-10	71	54	-17	36	25	-11	16	9	-7
Indian	29	27	-2	33	27	-6	32	35	3	9	11	2	25	24	-1
Italian	78	40	-38	71	30	-41	152	96	-56	85	46	-39	47	22	-25
Jewish	1	1	0	21	13	-8	5	7	2	11	14	3	8	4	-4
Korean/Japanese	9	8	-1	16	12	-4	29	59	30	28	49	21	14	20	6
Latin American	1	0	-1	6	5	-1	19	19	0	12	7	-5	5	7	2
Other	15	8	-7	57	50	-7	62	87	25	25	39	14	21	13	-8
Polish	1	1	0	25	19	-6	9	5	-4	23	16	-7	12	7	-5
Portuguese	18	9	-9	39	24	-15	52	51	-1	71	54	-17	27	16	-11
Vietnamese	2	1	-1	14	14	0	32	30	-2	24	18	-6	6	8	2
West Indian	14	8	-6	40	29	-11	48	44	-4	20	12	-8	12	3	-9
Ethnic	226	129	-97	499	347	-152	679	610	-69	484	433	-51	308	215	-93
% Ethnic	19.23	11.89	-7.34	29.65	21.81	-7.84	31.45	24.76	-6.69	13.12	9.45	-3.67	10.18	6.68	-3.50
Non-Ethnic	949	956	7	1184	1244	60	1480	1854	374	3206	4150	944	2718	3003	285
Total	1175	1085	-90	1683	1591	-92	2159	2464	305	3690	4583	893	3026	3218	192

% Ethnic by Category

Ethnicity	Fashion 1996	Fashion 2005	Fashion Chg	Food 1996	Food 2005	Food Chg	Food & Beverage Services 1996	Food & Beverage Services 2005	Food & Beverage Services Chg	Services 1996	Services 2005	Services Chg	Other 1996	Other 2005	Other Chg
Chinese	15.5	10.1	-5.4	29.1	30.5	1.5	24.0	19.3	-4.7	27.7	32.1	4.4	36.0	38.1	2.1
East European	4.4	6.2	1.8	1.0	0.3	-0.7	0.7	0.8	0.1	1.2	0.7	-0.5	1.3	0.0	-1.3
Greek	5.8	3.9	-1.9	5.4	4.9	-0.5	10.5	8.9	-1.6	7.4	5.8	-1.7	5.2	4.2	-1.0
Indian	12.8	20.9	8.1	6.6	7.8	1.2	4.7	5.7	1.0	1.9	2.5	0.7	8.1	11.2	3.0
Italian	34.5	31.0	-3.5	14.2	8.6	-5.6	22.4	15.7	-6.6	17.6	10.6	-6.9	15.3	10.2	-5.0
Jewish	0.4	0.8	0.3	4.2	3.7	-0.5	0.7	1.1	0.4	2.3	3.2	1.0	2.6	1.9	-0.7
Korean/Japanese	4.0	6.2	2.2	3.2	3.5	0.3	4.3	9.7	5.4	5.8	11.3	5.5	4.5	9.3	4.8
Latin American	0.4	0.0	-0.4	1.2	1.4	0.2	2.8	3.1	0.3	2.5	1.6	-0.9	1.6	3.3	1.6
Other	6.6	6.2	-0.4	11.4	14.4	3.0	9.1	14.3	5.1	5.2	9.0	3.8	6.8	6.0	-0.8
Polish	0.4	0.8	0.3	5.0	5.5	0.5	1.3	0.8	-0.5	4.8	3.7	-1.1	3.9	3.3	-0.6
Portuguese	8.0	7.0	-1.0	7.8	6.9	-0.9	7.7	8.4	0.7	14.7	12.5	-2.2	8.8	7.4	-1.3
Vietnamese	0.9	0.8	-0.1	2.8	4.0	1.2	4.7	4.9	0.2	5.0	4.2	-0.8	1.9	3.7	1.8
West Indian	6.2	6.2	0.0	8.0	8.4	0.3	7.1	7.2	0.1	4.1	2.8	-1.4	3.9	1.4	-2.5
Ethnic	100.0	100.0	0.0	100.0	100.0	0.0	100.0	100.0	0.0	100.0	100.0	0.0	100.0	100.0	0.0

253

TABLE 16. Vacancy Rate by Strip , CRD 1996 and 2005

	<10%	10-15%	15-20%	20-25%	>25%
1996	68	15	7	3	2
2005	65	19	6	1	4

TABLE 17. Vacancy Rates: Strips vs. Rest of the City, 1996 and 2005

	Strips		Rest of City	
	1996	2005	1996	2005
Shopping Centre	10.2	11.3	9.4	6.2
Strip	8.6	8.5	11.4	7.9
Combined	8.9	8.8	9.9	6.5

TABLE 18. Shopping Centre Vacancy: Strips vs. Rest of City, CRD 1996 and 2005

	Strips		Rest of City	
Shopping Centre Size	1996	2005	1996	2005
more than 750,000 sqft	-	-	5.4	4.0
between 400,000 and 750,000 sqft	-	-	8.8	7.0
between 100,000 and 399,999 sqft	13.4	15.3	9.7	6.0
between 30,000 and 99,999 sqft	6.4	6.8	11.4	7.2

to describe the 'uniqueness' of retail environments. Traditionally, retail strips have been characterised as unplanned retail environments, comprised of a large proportion of independent, often family run businesses. Between 1996 and 2005 the number of chain retailers decreased by -1.4% percent, from 2,023 to 1,995, and top chains decreased by -3.1 percent, from 324 to 314. When set against the base growth of the retail strips, the percentage of establishments on the strips that are part of a chain decreased since 1996, from 17.2% to 15.4%, with the percentage of top chains decreasing -0.3% to 2.4%. When the selected strips are compared against major planned elements of the retail environment, such as super-regional and regional shopping centres, with often more than 75 percent chain retail, the independent business orientation of the strips is even more evident and a defining element of the retail strips. Simply, while chains are present, the strips remain the domain of the independent trader (the 'shop-keeper'). However, if the selected strips included more of the downtown core then the renewed interest amongst chains in the downtown retail environment would likely be apparent. Conversely, the most recent suburban neighbourhood and convenience type centres (food and pharmacy anchored) would also be more likely to comprise a larger share of chain operators as opposed to traditional independent retail businesses.

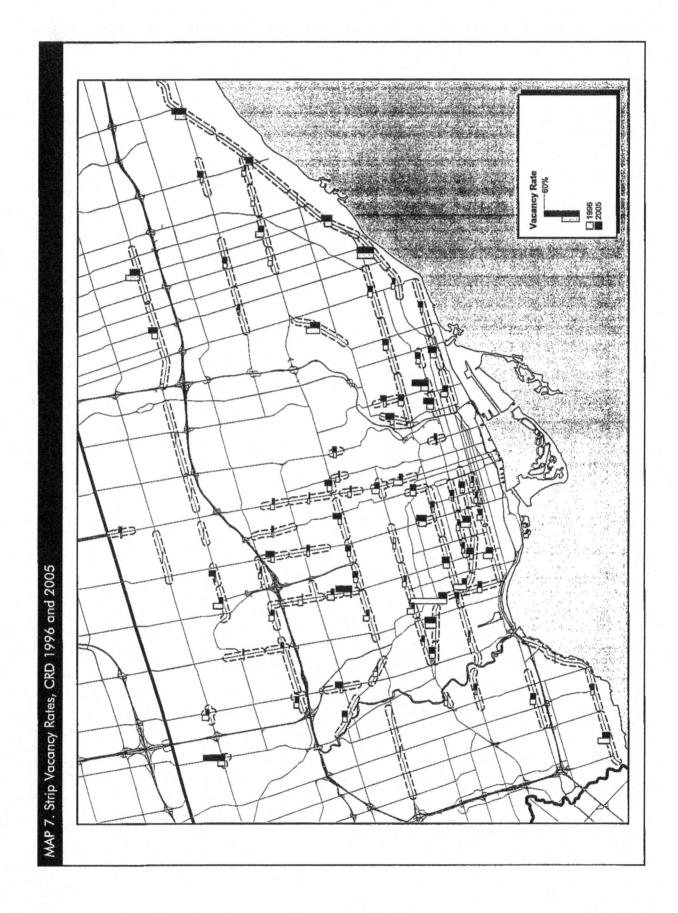

MAP 7. Strip Vacancy Rates, CRD 1996 and 2005

TABLE 19. Retail Chain Stores by Category, CRD 1996 and 2005						
	1996			**2005**		
Category	Non-Chain	Chain	% Chain	Non-Chain	Chain	% Chain
Financial & Insurance Industries	133	368	73.5	210	347	62.3
Business Services	487	36	6.9	624	36	5.5
Health Services	513	0	0.0	713	0	0.0
Food & Beverage Services	1,718	441	20.4	1,977	487	19.8
Recreational Services	261	69	20.9	328	65	16.5
Personal & Household Services	614	60	8.9	836	91	9.8
Cleaners	289	58	16.7	299	34	10.2
Hair & Beauty Services	754	48	6.0	956	44	4.4
Automotive	241	89	27.0	239	73	23.4
Total Services	**5,010**	**1,169**	**18.9**	**6,182**	**1,177**	**16.0**
Household & Appliance Stores	520	54	9.4	605	70	10.4
General Merch.	194	72	27.1	203	52	20.4
Food	1,202	171	12.5	1,104	154	12.2
Liquor	14	54	79.4	18	52	74.3
Drug Stores	139	103	42.6	140	123	46.8
Shoe Stores	113	34	23.1	90	35	28.0
Women's Clothing	437	54	11.0	433	36	7.7
Men's Clothing	134	6	4.3	102	6	5.6
Other Clothing & Fabric Stores	341	56	14.1	342	41	10.7
Book & Stationery Stores	111	21	15.9	97	15	13.4
Florists Lawn & Garden Centres	172	5	2.8	138	4	2.8
Hardware Stores	129	44	25.4	85	31	26.7
Sporting Goods	102	13	11.3	92	15	14.0
Jewellery Stores	170	7	4.0	190	3	1.6
Musics Stores	78	8	9.3	71	5	6.6
Other Retail (inc. Toy Stores)	823	128	13.5	936	126	11.9
Total Retail	**4,679**	**830**	**15.1**	**4,646**	**768**	**14.2**
Manufacturing & Distribution Services	21	24	53.3	118	50	29.8
Total Other	**21**	**24**	**53.3**	**118**	**50**	**29.8**

FUNCTIONAL CLASSIFICATION OF RETAIL STRIPS

The heritage in the classification of retail function can be traced back to the work of, for example, Simmons (1964, 1966) and Jones (1984). Over recent years, the CSCA has undertaken a number of studies on the retail structure of Toronto, with specific reference to retail strips (see Sinopoli, 1996,; Simmons & Simmons, 1997; Simmons *et al.* 1998; Yeates, 2000); and, more broadly, categorized retail activity across Canada (for example, see Simmons & Kamikihara, 2005). Sinopoli (1996) devised a ten cluster group classification of retail strips for Toronto, ranging from office service centre strips to mixed ethnic specialization strips. Yeates (2000) provided a three tier hierarchy of retail strips, basing classification primarily on size and draw,

with regional, community and neighbourhood nodes identified. There is not a universally agreed way in which to classify retail function or a commonly used set of variables to choose from. Each classification is a product of the focus of the respective study, and the availability of data to capture functional components.

Functional Classification Methods

This section outlines a cluster analysis based approach to retail functional classification. Data from 2005 for the selected strips in this study were used. The multivariate approach essentially defines the retail strips in Toronto across a number of dimensions: size, retail and service function and vitality. A number of what are regarded as key variables were selected to reflect underlying 'functional' elements of the strips. Specifically, both hierarchical and non-hierarchical cluster analysis were used. These heuristic methods were used in combination to assess the best number of classes (clusters) to select, along with descriptive statistics to determine the most appropriate mix of variables. Clustering software developed at the CSCA was used during the exploratory cluster building phase, using an implementation of the k-means algorithm. More details on cluster analysis as applied in segmentation type studies is provided by Chakrapani *et al.* (2006) or see Everitt for a more technical perspective (2004).

In total, 93 strips were used in the cluster analysis. Two strips were omitted due to total store counts of less than 10 (Sheppard Ave. E. & Burbank Drive and Kingston Rd. & St. Clair Ave. E).The main variables used were: % Ethnic, % Chain, % Retail (by various categories), % Service (by various categories) and a number of variables related to the number of stores and size of retail square footage.

Results

The final results are based on a hierarchical cluster analysis. In total, 9 retail strip cluster groups were identified across Toronto. Table 20 provides a summary of the characteristics of these groups, along with a basic descriptor for each of the strip clusters. The terms 'high', 'mid' and 'low', etc.. refer to the mean value for the given variables for the cluster relative to the group of 93 strips used within the study.

Due to the complex mix of functions along retail strips, the following classification is forwarded as one of many possible views of 'function'. A number of the clusters could have been easily aggregated to reduce the total number of clusters, however, our aim was to attempt to pick out some of the nuances of the retail strip environments in Toronto. Map 8 shows the clustering of the strips, for example, the ethnic clusters along Spadina, Bathurst, College and Gerrard (clusters 2 and 9); and the restaurant clusters along Queen St. W (cluster 7). The classification highlights the functional mix of retail strips that are located adjacent to one another. Strips that may appear to be long stretches of homogeneous commercial activity can be split into a number of functional sections, providing different types of retail and service, and potential serving different groups of consumers. The ease of entry and exit for businesses along the retail strips in part explains their highly dynamic character. The classification is based on data from 2005, however, the evolution of retail strip function over time has been underlined in the earlier sections of this report (e.g., transition towards more service, less retail) - replicating the same method for data in 1996 will result in a different set of retail strip cluster groups. It should also be noted that the classification is based on a selection of the strips, i.e., those that fall within the boundaries of the 'Avenues'. In undertaking a Toronto-wide classification, that is, including all the strips, other types of cluster will be evident, for example, automotive strips (Golden Mile, Eglinton Ave.) and furniture / home electronics strips (Kennedy Rd.).

TABLE 20. Functional Retail Strip Classification Summary

	Strip Cluster	No. of Strips within Cluster	Ethnic	Chain	Fashion	Food/ Restaurants	Personal & Business Services
1	Suburban Strip	11	High	High	Very High	Mid	Mid
2	Ethnic Service	8	High	Very Low	Very Low	Mid	High
3	The Average Strip (non-fashion)	14	Mid	Mid	Low	Mid	Mid
4	The Average Strip (with fashion)	16	Mid	Mid	Mid	Mid	Mid
5	Personal Service Strips	9	Mid/Low	Mid/Low	Mid	Low	Very High
6	Non Ethnic Mixed	7	Very Low	Mid/Low	Mid/High	Low	Mid
7	Restaurant Strips	9	Mid/Low	Mid	Very Low	Very High	Low
8	Chain Destinations	15	Mid/Low	High	Low	Very High	Mid/High
9	Urban Ethnic Food Specialization	4	Very High	Very Low	Very Low	High/Very High	Low

MAP 8. Functional Classification of Retail Strips

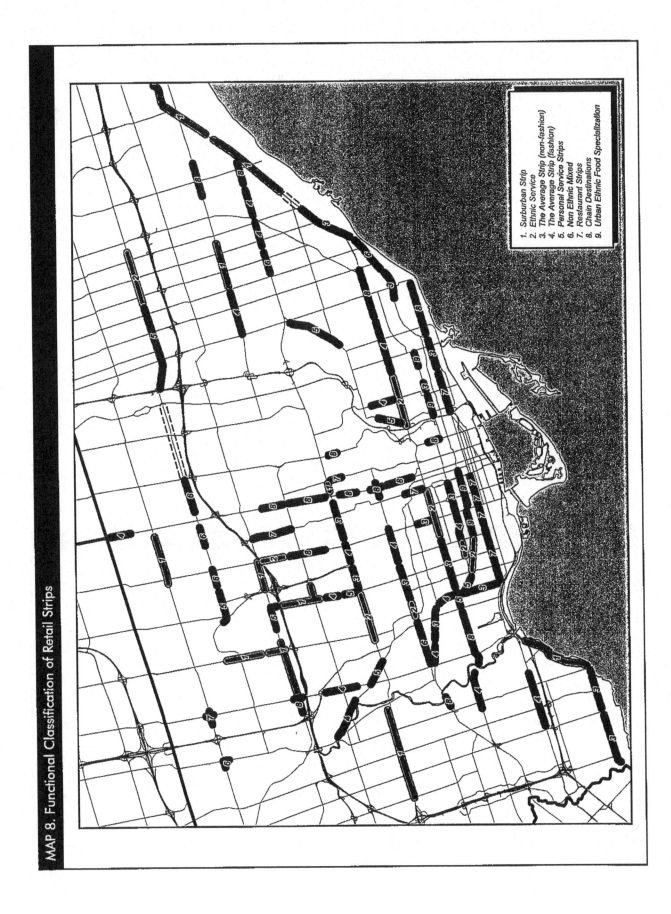

Legend:
1. Surburban Strip
2. Ethnic Service
3. The Average Strip (non-fashion)
4. The Average Strip (fashion)
5. Personal Service Strips
6. Non Ethnic Mixed
7. Restaurant Strips
8. Chain Destinations
9. Urban Ethnic Food Specialization

SUMMARY

This report has highlighted the diversity of Toronto's retail strips. They are home to a variety of retail types and built forms, partly reflecting when they were originally developed: the 'streetcar strips' in the older parts of the city with their typical rows of stores often with offices or apartments above; the mixed strips in the older suburbs, with rows of stores, small plazas, old service stations; and the auto-oriented strips with their strip plazas and shopping centres, drive-through restaurants and services, service stations, and large stores.

They are also home to a wide variety of commercial and retail functions: about 70% of the establishments are services and 30% are retail stores. The strips show a diverse mix of functions leading to distinctive strips, often serving a market beyond their local neighbourhood; for example, ethnic strips, restaurant strips, and fashion strips. Many strips, however, are 'average,' providing a variety of stores and services to their local neighbourhoods.

The total amount of activity on the strips has not changed much over the past 20 years: they are home to about 22,000 establishments and 180,000 employees, or 30% of Toronto's establishments and 15% of its employment. But this masks a great deal of change within the strips. Service functions such as health services, restaurants and bars, and hair and beauty services are becoming more important. On the other hand traditional retailing is declining, especially household and appliance stores, department stores, fashion (clothing and shoes), food stores, and hardware stores.

The strips appear to provide flexible locations that accommodate many of the broader changes in the service economy and the retail sector. As places that help to meet the retail and service needs of the City, they have persisted while their local character has constantly evolved. The decline in retail on the strips is partly a result of the growth of 'new format' retailing – big boxes, power centres, category killers and the like. In fact the new formats tended to avoid many of the strips, with their smaller lots and more pedestrian-oriented built form. As the non-strip market areas have become almost 'saturated' with the new formats, however, they are now turning their attention more and more to the strips.

The 'Avenues' in Toronto's Official Plan provide a coherent approach to redevelopment on the strips, particularly to accommodate population growth. They are expected to change and redevelop 'incrementally' over a number of years. Commercial activity will have a key role in their redevelopment, providing shops and services for the residents, and supporting their role as focal points for the local community. Commercial activity on the ground floor of mid-rise apartment buildings is often seen as the ideal form for much of this development. But we need to understand how the commercial sector 'works' in these environments. How big should the stores be? How much parking do they need? Should they be 'independent' units or 'planned' centres? Is there a place for new format stores?

This report provides the essential context for addressing such questions. It highlights the strips' variety and adaptability, and the need for planning that recognizes the dynamic, diverse and changing nature of their environments and the communities that they serve.

References

Berry, B.J.L. (1963) Commercial Structure and Commercial Blight, Department of Geography, Research Paper No.85, University Of Chicago, Chicago.

Bromley, R.D.F. And Thomas, C.J. Eds (1993) Retail Change: Contemporary Issues, UCL Press Ltd., London.

Daniels, C. and Hernandez, T. (2006) Canada's Leading Retailers, CSCA Research Report 2006-09, Centre for the Study of Commercial Activity, Ryerson University, Toronto

Chakrapani, C., Lea, T. and Hernandez, T. (2006) Market Segmentation, CSCA Research Report 2006-06, Centre for the Study of Commercial Activity, Ryerson University, Toronto

Davies, R.L. (1976) Marketing Geography: with Special Reference to Retailing, Methuen, London.

Everitt, B. (2004) Cluster Analysis, 4th Edition, Oxford University Press, London.

Graff, T.O. (1998) 'The Locations of Wal-Mart and Kmart Supercenters: Contrasting Corporate Strategies', The Professional Geographer 50 (1), 46–57.

Hernandez, T. (2001) 'The Impact of Big Box Internationalisation on a National Market: A Case Study of Home Depot in Canada", The International Review of Retail, Distribution and Consumer Research, 13(1), 77-98.

Jones, K.G. (1984) Specialty Retailing in the Inner City , Department of Geography, Monograph 15, York University, Toronto.

Jones, K.G. And Simmons, J. (1993) Location, Location, Location: Analyzing the Retail Environment, 2nd Edition, Nelson Canada, Toronto.

Laulajainen, R. (1987) Spatial Strategies in Retailing, D. Reidel, Dordrecht, Holland.

Leigh, R. (1965). Specialty-Retailing: A Geographic Analysis. B.C. Geographical Series No. 6. ,Tantalus Research, Vancouver.

Proudfoot, M.J. (1937) 'City Retail Structure', Economic Geography 13, 425-28.

Shaw, G. (1978) Process And Pattern in the Geography of Retail Change, Occasional Papers in Geography, No. 24, University Of Hull, Hull.

Sibley, D. (1976) The Small Shop in the City, Occasional Papers In Geography, No. 22, University of Hull, Hull.

Simmons, J.W. (1964). The Changing Pattern of Retail Location, Department of Geography, Research Paper No. 104., University of Chicago, Chicago.

Simmons, J.W. (1966) Toronto's Changing Retail Complex, Department of Geography, Research Paper No. 104, Univeristy of Chicago, Chicago.

Simmons, J.W. and Simmons, S. (1997) Change in Toronto Retail Strips: Metro Toronto 1993-1996, CSCA Research Report 1997-12, Centre for the Study of Commercial Activity, Ryerson University, Toronto.

Simmons, J.W., Montgomery, D. and Simmons, S. (1998) The Retail Structure of the Greater Toronto Area, CSCA Research Report 1998-02, Centre for the Study of Commercial Activity, Ryerson University, Toronto.

Simmons, J.W. and Kamikihara, S. (2005) Commercial Activity in Canada: 2004, CSCA Research Report 2005-04, Centre for the Study of Commercial Activity, Ryerson University, Toronto.

Sinopoli, T. (1996) The Diversity of Retail Strips in Metropolitan Toronto, CSCA Research Report 1996-11, Centre for the Study of Commercial Activity, Ryerson University, Toronto.

Yeates, M. (2000) The GTA @ Y2K: The Dynamics of Change in the Commercial Structure of the Greater Toronto Area, CSCA Research Report 2000-01, Centre for the Study of Commercial Activity, Ryerson University, Toronto.

APPENDIX A: TES Data Structure

The following lists the data elements in TES.

ESTABLISHMENT AND EMPLOYMENT
Address of establishment
Primary Roll number
Sub roll number
Sequence number
Unit number
Occupant's name
Contact name
Contact phone number
Current full time employees
Current part time employees
Total current employees
Fulltime employees of last year
Part time employees of last year
Activity code (3 digits)
The year since the establishment was at current location
The year the establishment was surveyed
Building's name if applicable
Parcel code
The number of stories
Which employment district if applicable
Whether in regional centers if applicable

APPENDIX B: CRD Data Structure

The following lists the data elements in CRD.

STRIP BOUNDARY / STRIP TENANTS
Strip_name – name given to each unique strip
Desc_ – description of each strip giving boundary definition
Municipality – name of Municipality
Num_Of_Stores – number of stores collected on strip
Num_of_Vacant – number of stores that were vacant on the strip
Vacancy_Rate – vacancy rate
Company_name – store name of retailer or commercial service located on retail strip
Ethnicity – ethnicity of consumer that retailer or commercial service is targeting
Size_sqft – size categories
Actual_Est_size – actual or estimated size of retailer in square feet
BB_Desc - type of Big Box store (superstore / category killer / membership club, etc..)
SIC – Statistics Canada Standard Industrial Classification code used to determine type of retailer
SIC_Description – code description
NAICS – North American Industry Classification Code used to determine type of retailer
NAICS_Description – code description

SHOPPING CENTRES / SHOPPING CENTRE TENANTS
Mall_Name - name of Shopping Centre
Address – address of Shopping Centre
Intersection – closest major intersection
Municipality – name of Municipality Power Centre is located
Parking_space – the number of parking spaces the shopping center has
Floor_Space_Sqft – size of Shopping Centre measured in square feet
Mall_Type – format of Shopping Centre (enclosed / island / strip)
Levels – number of levels in the mall
Num_of_Stores – number of Shopping Centre tenants
Num_of_Vacant – number of Shopping Centre vacancies
Vacancy_Rate – Shopping Centre vacancy rate
Company_Name – store name of retailer or commercial service located in Centre
SIC – Statistics Canada Standard Industrial Classification code used to determine type of retailer
SIC_Description – code description
NAICS – North American Industry Classification Code used to determine type of retailer
NAICS_Description – code description
Ethnicity – ethnicity of consumer that retailer or commercial service is targeting
Size_Sqft – size ID description
Actual_Est_Size – actual or estimated size of retailer or commercial service in square feet

Chapter 13

THE MALL
Neil Wrigley and Michelle Lowe

In his 1960 publication *Shopping towns USA* Victor Gruen, acknowledged as a pioneering architect of the shopping mall in North America, looks to ancient Greece with its *stoa* (merchants' building) centrally placed within the *agora* or city square for the basic principles of town square design. According to Gruen, the growth of suburban America in the 1950s (encouraged by the automobile) led to the rapid movement away from this framework. In the absence of alternatives, planned shopping centres provided:

> the needed place and opportunity for participation in modern community life that the ancient Greek *agora*, the medieval market place and ... town squares provided in the past. That the shopping centre can fulfil this ... urgent need of suburbanites for the amenities of urban living, is convincingly proved in a large number of centres. In such centres, pedestrian areas are filled with teeming life not only during normal shopping hours, but on Sundays and holidays when people windowshop, promenade, relax in the garden courts, view exhibits and patronize the restaurants (Gruen and Smith, 1960: 22).

Fascinatingly, over four decades on, one of the leading examples of shopping mall design in contemporary USA, 'The Forum Shops' in Las Vegas, also looks to ancient Greece and Rome for its design principles. A recreation of the streets of Rome from 300 BC to AD 300, The Forum Shops has as its centrepiece a spectacular fountain which features four Greek and Roman gods which regularly come to life and perform an eight-minute production of the 'Gods of Olympus'. The star attraction at the Forum is the painted ceiling or 'sky' which is lit in such a way that a 24-hour cycle – sunrise to sunset – takes just three hours. The ultimate in fashioning 'the mall as street' – bringing the exterior (the sky) to the interior of the mall – the Forum is, like Gruen's early shopping centres, also 'filled with teeming life' and is providing a model for future mall development in North America and elsewhere.

This chapter begins by examining the history and development of the shopping mall; it then considers North America's 'mega-malls' followed by their counterparts in the UK the regional shopping centres. Attention is paid to the people who inhabit these new consumption environments. Finally, the chapter charts the emergence of a number of new landscapes of consumption – from speciality centres and festival marketplaces to factory outlet centres and airport shopping malls.

Constructing suburban utopias – history and development of the shopping mall

Planned shopping districts existed in the United States from the early decades of the twentieth century. Market Square, which opened in 1916 in the Chicago suburb of Lake Forest, was the first and was followed by Highland Park Shopping Village completed in 1931 in Dallas, where importantly 'storefronts were turned away from the public street and inward around a central area – a special courtyard where cars couldn't go' (Kowinski, 1985: 105). But it was not until the 1950s that shopping centres – classically constructed with a large department store at one end, two parallel rows of shops, and a pedestrian area in the middle – developed rapidly. Victor Gruen Associates as architects were responsible for a large number of America's shopping centres or *malls* as they became known. From the outset Gruen's centres were designed to serve the civic, cultural and social needs of new suburban communities and were intended to be developed alongside apartments, office buildings, theatres, etc.

Southdale, Minneapolis, which opened in 1956, was the world's first enclosed (fully covered) mall. Air-conditioned and temperature-controlled, Southdale avoided the vagaries of the Minnesota climate (very cold winters, very hot summers) in which Victor Gruen, its architect, had calculated that there were only 126 'ideal weather shopping days' per annum. In this context, 1950s advertisements for the centre promised 'Tomorrow's Main Street Today' and Southdale was marketed as 'A whole new shopping world in itself'. Located at Edina, Minneapolis, the centre provided the prototype for the majority of malls built since. Reading 12.1 by Wilbur Kowinski, an American journalist, recounts the story of the Southdale Mall and demonstrates how the centre provided an important model for subsequent mall development.

Reading 12.1 – The invention of the mall

Southdale ... is where the mall was invented. Although it now seems to be a superior but not unusual mall – with its soaring Garden Court, its Interior Systems furniture shop, B. Dalton Booksellers, Berman Buckskin, Children's Barber, Chrome Concepts, Fanny Farmer and Eat & Run – in 1956 Southdale represented innovation, creative problem-solving, and aesthetic daring, as well as shopping-center heresy.

When Southdale was being planned, the normal shopping center was a long strip, all on one level, with at best one department store. Gospel was that nobody was going to walk or even ride up to a second level in a drive-in shopping center; if they couldn't reach a store by practically parking in front of it, car-dependent people wouldn't go.

Finally a few daring developers tried a two-level center, and it worked. The Rouse Company did it with the Mordawmin Shopping Center in Baltimore and the Dayton-Hudson Company with Northland in Detroit ... At Northland, the two-level open mall proved itself. By a handy coincidence, one chain store had a shop on each level and they did identical business, which seemed to mean that people weren't entirely averse to getting out of their cars and walking around a shopping center, or riding an escalator to see what was going on upstairs. But while others contemplated what exactly this might mean, Northland's designer was hurrying on to the next step, the truly fateful one, at Southdale. His name was Victor Gruen ...

[The] problem, in Edina, Minnesota, was the weather. It not only got very cold and snowy in the winter ... it also got baking hot in the summer. Gruen's answer to the problem turned out to be the most fateful advance made at Southdale.

The solution was, of course, complete enclosure. Gruen saw it immediately and went to the Dayton-Hudson hierarchy with his proposal. He told them about the covered pedestrian arcades in Europe, especially the Galleria Vittorio Emanuele in Milan, Italy, with its arcades rising four storeys to a glass barrel vault and a central glass cupola 160 feet high ... Enclosure could also make the central court a much more dramatic place, as became apparent in the planning stages of Southdale ... For the first time a shopping center would have a real vertical dimension, with the Central Garden Court soaring to a high ceiling, and the two levels of the mall visible to each other.

Extracted from: Wilbur Kowinski (1985): *The malling of America: an inside look at the great consumer paradise.* New York: Morrow, 117–19.

The Southdale 'model' was adapted and utilized for shopping centres throughout America. Significantly, however, Gruen and his associates became disillusioned with the way in which their ideas were diluted by other developers. As Cesar Pelli, a design partner, lamented, 'Malls have not become true community centers. At Southdale it was realised that people will come in great numbers with just a few public activities' (Kowinski, 1985: 123). Notwithstanding this, however, advances made at Southdale still form the basic framework of shopping centre design. Importantly, the concept of enclosure gave mall architects the possibility of fashioning an interior space sheltered from the outside world and its elements. Forty years later, in the 1990s, the Mall of America, also in Minnesota, and reputedly the world's largest mall, extended on a gigantic scale some of the concepts pioneered at Southdale.

North America's mega-malls

During what Margaret Crawford (1992: 7) refers to as the 'golden years' of the 'malling of America' – the period 1960 to 1980 – when 'the basic regional mall paradigm was perfected and systematically replicated, [and] developers methodically surveyed, divided and appropriated suburban cornfields and orange groves to create a new landscape of consumption', almost 30,000 malls were constructed. In time, as regional malls approached saturation point, super-regional malls began to appear 'at freeway interchanges – such as the Galleria outside Houston, South Coast Plaza in Orange County, and Tyson's Corner near Washington, DC – [and] became catalysts for new suburban mini cities' (Crawford, 1992: 24 – see also Garreau, 1991). Ed Soja (1996: 11) paints a fascinating picture of such a mini city in Orange Country with at its heart what he describes as the 'curiously insubstantial' South Coast Plaza, 'California's largest and most profitable shopping mall, with nearly three million square feet of space and almost ten thousand parking places, Nordstrom's, May Co., Sears, Bullocks, Saks Fifth Avenue, Robinson's, the Broadway, over two hundred other stores and boutiques, and nearly half a billion dollars of taxable retail sales in 1986'. However, it is two 'mega-malls' completed in the late 1980s and early 1990s that have attracted increasing amounts of attention. The largest of these, the Mall of America, is located on the former site of the Met Stadium – home of Minnesota's professional baseball and football teams in Bloomington, Minneapolis. Built by Melvin Simon Associates, one of the largest developers of shopping centres in the USA, the mall opened in August 1992 and includes four nationally recognized department stores – Bloomingdale's, Macy's, Nordstrom and Sears, over 400 other stores and a seven-acre amusement park (Goss, 1999). But it is another giant North American mall development – West Edmonton Mall constructed in the 1980s – that has so far attracted the greatest degree of attention by geographers (Hopkins, 1990; Johnson, 1991). The importance of West Edmonton Mall was that it was explicitly 'the shopping mall as entertainment centre (and) tourist attraction' (Jones and Simmons, 1990: 223). Figure 12.1 shows the major magnets within the mall (department stores and leisure facilities) in its early years.

Reading 12.2 by Jeffrey Hopkins, a Canadian geographer, provides a picture of the West Edmonton 'Mega'-Mall (WEM) and hints at the way in which geographers have explored this pioneering consumption space. Hopkins' intention in the broader article from which this reading is extracted is to provide a 'reading' of WEM which emphasizes the various ways in which the mall stimulates a sense of 'elsewhereness' – 'the overt manipulation of time and/or space to simulate or evoke experiences of other places' (Hopkins, 1990: 2) – in its clientele. As such Hopkins' article should be read alongside those of Shields (1989) and Goss (1993) who also focus on the manipulation of space within the retail built environment, a theme which has been explored in detail in Chapter 9.

Reading 12.2 – The West Edmonton mega-mall

A novel mixture of retail, commercial, recreational and entertainment facilities literally under one 950-million-dollar roof . . . Occupying a 110-acre site about six miles west of the centre of Edmonton, Alberta, this two-storey 5,200,000-square-foot structure, completed in 1986, contains over six hundred stores and services . . . including four major department stores, four junior department stores, two auto showrooms and 11,775 parking stalls . . . WEM employs approximately 18,000 people . . . contains almost 23 per cent of Edmonton's total retail space, takes in 42 per cent of all consumer dollars spent in

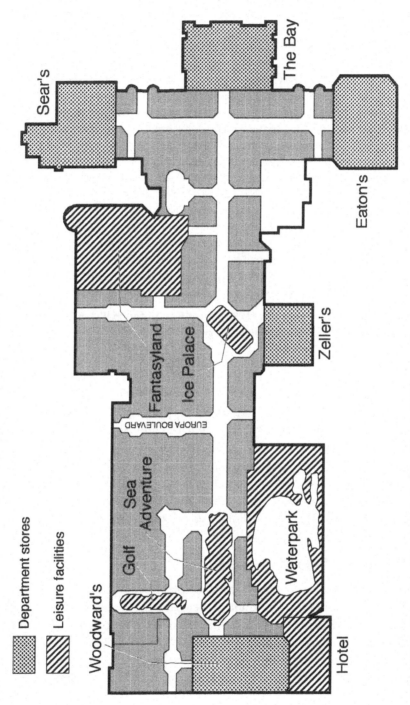

Figure 12.1: *The retail and leisure mix in the West Edmonton Mall – main floor*
Source: Redrawn from Jones and Simmons (1990).

shopping centres in the Edmonton area ... and accounts for more than 1 per cent of *all* retail sales in Canada ...

While the exterior of WEM is a standard frame structure of brick with flat and galleria roofs surrounded by four-lane roads and two-level parking garages, the interior is distinct. Mall attractions include a seven-acre waterpark, a National Hockey League-size skating rink, an 18-hole miniature golf course, a Fantasyland with a triple-loop roller coaster, a four-acre sea aquarium with four Atlantic bottlenose dolphins, four fully operational submarines, and a scaled replica of Christopher Columbus's *Santa Maria*. There are also numerous exotic flora, fauna and fountains, a 'New Orleans' – themed streetscape, eight statues, 19 movie theatres and a Fantasyland Hotel with 360 rooms, 120 of which are modelled according to one of six themes: Arabian, Coach, Hollywood, Polynesian, Roman or Truck ...

This mega-mall typifies 'disneyfication' and 'imagineering', and reflects the trend in North America towards specialized, self-contained built environments. The annexation of much of a city's retail/social life into a corporate, self-contained, 'disneyfied' built environment, however, is unparalleled. Disney's parks are isolated entities, world's fairs are temporary and amusement parks tend to be seasonal. The mega-mall is 'spectacle' integrated into the everyday and open year round ... but a statement that WEM is merely a 'disneyfied' or 'imagineered' shopping mall is a static analogy, one that is metaphorically correct but reveals nothing about process(es). Built environments which provide such 'specialised experiences' go beyond two-dimensional illusion by providing three-dimensional theatre in which patrons are both spectators and actors (sightseers themselves are part of the show). WEM is neither merely disneyfied, nor Disneyland simply imagineered, both are part of a much larger set of processes, one of which is simulated elsewhereness.

Extracted from: Jeffrey Hopkins (1990): West Edmonton Mall: landscape of myths and elsewhereness. *Canadian Geographer*, 34, 2–17.

But it is not only the North American 'mega-malls' which have attracted this kind of critical attention. Britain's regional shopping centres, in particular the Metrocentre in the north-east, Meadowhall outside Sheffield, Lakeside at Thurrock, east of London, and Merry Hill in the West Midlands – all 1980s centres – have been the subject of research, and Brent Cross – Britain's first regional shopping centre constructed in the 1970s – has also been examined in detail by Miller et al. (1998). It is to these smaller British equivalents of the North American centres that we will now turn (Lowe, 2000b).

Britain's regional shopping centres

In the UK, in the context of more restricted planning regulation and higher land values (see Chapter 7), mall development, at least on anything approaching the scale and type of those at Mall of America or West Edmonton, has been much more circumspect. Indeed, it was not until 1976 that Brent Cross, Britain's first purpose-built regional shopping centre was opened, and it was another decade before there were any more such centres. Brent Cross was unusual at the time in that it was the only shopping centre to have been built on a previously undeveloped site outside of an established shopping area and not being part of a new town. When it opened . . . [it] had 82 tenants with 800,000 square feet of retail space on a site of 52 acres. There were 3500 free car parking spaces and over 4000 employees. Besides two anchor stores (John Lewis and Fenwick), the centre included a Waitrose supermarket and branches of Boots, C&A, Marks & Spencer and W.H. Smith (Miller et al., 1998: 32).

Significantly, Brent Cross was built in an area without major existing shopping facilities and with the approval of local authorities (Guy, 1994b: 300).

In the early 1980s, in the first term of the Thatcher administration, a deregulationist stance led to a relatively favourable environment for proposed regional shopping centres and a wave of planning applications were submitted (Schiller, 1986). More specifically, the enterprise zone experiment created the possibility of large tracts of land on which unencumbered development could take place. The Metrocentre in Gateshead (opened in 1986) was constructed on part of the Tyneside enterprise zone, whilst Merry Hill in the West Midlands was sited on two adjoining enterprise zones (Dudley and Round Oak). In both of these cases early developments on the enterprise zones comprised retail warehousing and these were later supplemented by more 'up-market' enclosed regional malls. At Meadowhall in Sheffield a regional shopping centre was planned at the outset and this was also the case at Lakeside (these centres both opened in 1990).

Much of the literature on Britain's regional shopping centres has concentrated on planning dimensions (Guy, 1994a and b), specifically their impact on neighbouring towns and cities. But regional shopping centres have also provided foci for two other types of research: first, work emphasizing the crucial role of the regional entrepreneur in the development of these centres; and, second, research which has examined the experience of shoppers within them. Here we focus on three readings on Britain's regional shopping centres which deal with these issues.

Reading 12.3 is a composite of extracts from a study of the retail impact of Meadowhall – a regional shopping centre of more than 1,250,000 square feet three miles north-east of the centre of Sheffield – by Jonathan Reynolds and Elizabeth Howard of the Oxford Institute of Retail Management (OXIRM), and a paper by Gwyn Rowley which examines the decay in Sheffield's CBD following the opening of the Meadowhall complex. Both of these studies were undertaken in the early 1990s, in the preliminary stages of Meadowhall's development.

Reading 12.3 – The early impact of Meadowhall on Sheffield

Any assessment of Meadowhall inevitably involves consideration of its effects, both economic and social, on the city centre. However, this analysis should be seen in the context of the combined, and to some extent complementary roles which the city centre and Meadowhall perform . . . The changes in Sheffield's role have not been straightforward, however, and the 'impact' of Meadowhall in the conventional sense of trade diversion is difficult to quantify . . .

Sheffield's role began to change long before Meadowhall was developed, even though the pace of change has accelerated rapidly in the last five years . . . The limitations of Sheffield's [shopping centre] layout – its very elongated nature which unusually is weak at or near the central point . . . offering the dual focus points of The Moor and Fargate [which] present a confusing shopping 'offer' for shoppers and retailers – and the failure to create strength and retail depth at the core have meant the city has failed to improve as others have done . . .

Our survey shows Sheffield's share of non-food shopping trips has fallen by 38 per cent . . . Therefore, in terms of its relative decline, Sheffield appears to have lost substantially more of its market share than originally forecast in planning for Meadowhall. Of course, not all this decline will be directly attributable to Meadowhall itself . . . competing centres, including retail parks [have also] increased their market share . . .

However, given its size, proximity and the degree of overlap between the centres, together with the corresponding decline of the city centre . . . We consider Meadowhall to have been a significant factor in Sheffield's further decline between 1990–1994. Meadowhall's 'impact' appears to have been higher than that predicted [because] . . . regional household expenditure has not continued to grow as it did in the 1980s: thus there has been no 'cushion' for existing centres. Meadowhall has opened in a static or slow growing market. [In addition] the relative attraction of Meadowhall over Sheffield is greater than that of the Metrocentre over Newcastle. The latter was – and is – a much stronger centre than Sheffield, with a much better range of modern shopping including significant new additions during the 1970s (Eldon Square) and subsequently.[1]

Since Meadowhall opened in 1990, trade in the city centre appears to have fallen by more than one third, and the entire northern third of the CBD, the Haymarket/ CastleMarkets area, has been devastated. Streets are lined with boarded-up shops, whitewashed windows and down-market discounters. Several charity shops now occupy what were prime retail sites until the late 1980s . . . While the central section of the CBD around Fargate retains a certain ebullience there are signs of decay there as well. The Marks & Spencer store is running a definite second to the company's Meadowhall branch and ranges of goods are consequently relatively limited. The local John Lewis Store, Cole Brothers, still survived in 1992 but a number of smaller retailers . . . had closed down and moved to Meadowhall . . . The southern section of the CBD, around the Moor, is seeking a specific market niche in what can be termed a bazaar economy with cheap street-market stalls along the pedestrianized Moor . . . the general air is of a non-CBD local shopping district . . . Marks & Spencer closed its store on the Moor when it opened its Meadowhall branch.[2]

Extracted from: [1] **OXIRM (1994):** *Sheffield retail study.* **Oxford: Oxford Institute of Retail Management);** [2] **Gwyn Rowley (1993): Prospects for the central business district. Chapter 6 in Rosemary Bromley and Colin Thomas (eds)** *Retail change: contemporary issues.* **London: UCL Press, 110–25.**

Reading 12.4 by Michelle Lowe discusses the 'regional entrepreneurs' behind the Metrocentre and Meadowhall before focusing explicitly on the Richardson brothers' activities at Merry Hill. This extract, from the early 1990s, hints at substantial leisure developments due to be constructed alongside the retail centres at Meadowhall and Merry Hill. Such a mixture of retail and leisure was modelled on the success of parallel developments in North America, but, in reality, as Reynolds (1993: 80) notes, 'Planning the leisure component within the UK regional centres ... in line with US principles was ... fraught with difficulty.' Indeed, at the Metrocentre, the leisure element was substantially scaled down 'and leisure as such failed to appear at all in Sheffield's Meadowhall Centre or Thurrock's Lakeside'. Figure 12.2 shows the layout of the Meadowhall Centre and illustrates how leisure was largely omitted from this scheme. At Merry Hill, 'waterfront' developments currently comprise office buildings, a hotel and some restaurants, pubs and a nightclub but other leisure facilities have yet to materialize (Lowe, 1998).

Reading 12.4 – Regional entrepreneurs and regional shopping centres in the 1980s

Regional entrepreneurs became flag bearers for Mrs Thatcher's vision of regional regeneration. Not surprisingly, they have become the targets for a great deal of media attention. John Hall, for example, the most famous of these characters, the man behind the massive Metrocentre at Gateshead, played a pivotal role in Mrs Thatcher's cleverly managed 1987 election campaign. His centre, situated on a site on the banks of the River Tyne, provided an image of a Britain – and perhaps more significantly from the point of view of vote-winning, a view of a North-East – pulling itself up by its bootstraps. Hall is currently developing a major leisure/living complex around his home, Wynyard Hall, near Billingham in Cleveland.

John Hall, albeit the best known, is only one of an increasing number of individuals who have emerged in some of Britain's regions as leaders of a new form of regional regeneration. Within the same retailing/leisure framework Eddie Healey has instigated the development of Meadowhall, a new shopping and leisure experience close to the M1 on Sheffield's outskirts ... At Merry Hill in the West Midlands ... Don and Roy Richardson, twin brothers, have developed an out-of-town regional shopping centre ... The Merry Hill development rose like a phoenix from the ashes of industrial decline and is currently into Phase Five of its operations.

The Richardson family background is in heavy truck distribution in the West Midlands region. Their business bought and sold trucks and lorries nationwide, and was very successful. In addition, the family had also been involved in the acquisition and redevelopment of steelworks sites in the Black Country area. In many ways, then, these brothers were and still are archetypal 'local heroes'.

As well-known local characters and businessmen, the brothers were approached by Dudley Metropolitan Borough Council who wanted them to become involved in the Dudley enterprise zone in order to 'create activity' ... The centrepiece of the Richardsons' involvement in the ... enterprise zone ... is the Merry Hill Centre. By 1989 Merry Hill retail

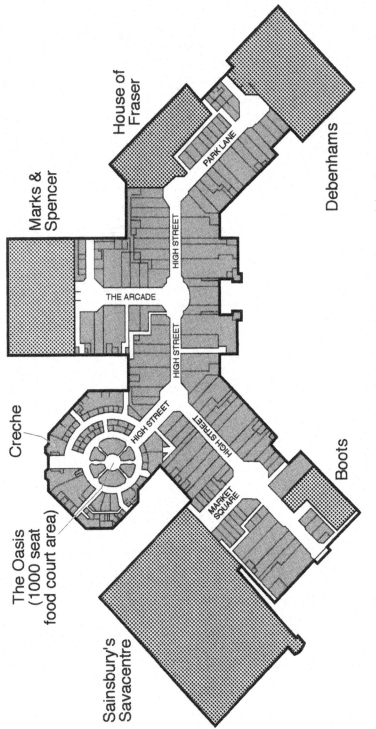

Figure 12.2: *The Meadowhall Centre, Sheffield, illustrating how leisure was largely omitted from Britain's regional shopping centres* Source: *Redrawn from Guy (1994).*

had reached Phase Five. Phases One, Two and Three respectively comprised retail warehousing ... MFI, Toys R Us, Comet, Macdonalds and Children's World ... In later stages ... there was a shift in the style of development ... Phase Four was the first phase of upmarket retail, a double-story connecting mall, and this has subsequently been followed by Phase Five, a retail fashion-based mall of over one million square feet incorporating ... major stores ... Sainsburys, Debenhams, Next, BHS [and Marks & Spencer] ...

Not content with their success in the retail field ... the Richardson brothers have topped the whole Merry Hill Scheme with a monorail system threading through the current complex and scheduled to link Merry Hill retail with further Richardson developments currently under construction in the vicinity ... There is a planned waterfront leisure and business scheme on an adjoining site ... 'Merry Hill: The Waterfront' will be a major leisure complex. The latest proposals include at 'Waterfront East' office development, and at 'Waterfront West' two hotels, conference and exhibition centre, a fun park, waterworld, ice rink and other sporting facilities ...

The Richardsons will not rest with the transformation of the West Midlands region which they have orchestrated by their Merry Hill Scheme. Their latest project involves one of Britain's most famous industrial landmarks. The former tyre factory, Fort Dunlop, alongside the M6 in Birmingham, is to become the centrepiece of a multi-million pound scheme creating thousands of new jobs ... It is clearly the case that the Richardson brothers ... [are] 'regional entrepreneurs' ... these individuals are exemplary of the curious intermingling of regional culture, regional identity and regional regeneration which is occurring during an era largely dominated by increased globalisation.

Extracted from: Michelle Lowe (1993): Local hero! An examination of the role of the regional entrepreneur in the regeneration of Britain's regions. Chapter 10 in Gerry Kearns and Chris Philo (eds) *Selling places: the city as cultural capital, past and present*. Oxford: Pergamon Press, 214–21.

Reading 12.5 is taken from research by Daniel Miller, Peter Jackson, Nigel Thrift, Michael Rowlands (like Miller an anthropologist) and Beverley Holbrook which explores the experience of shopping at Brent Cross from the perspective of 'ordinary consumers' and uses a variety of methodological approaches (from a questionnaire survey to focus groups and ethnography). Here we take an extract which places their work in context and suggests that shopping (in such malls and elsewhere) provides an active and independent component of identity construction.

Reading 12.5 – The mother of UK shopping malls: shopping and identity

In 1997, Brent Cross Shopping Centre celebrated its twenty-first birthday; it had officially come of age. Described in *The Independent* newspaper as 'the mother of malls' ... Brent Cross was Britain's first purpose-built regional shopping centre. Since its opening in 1976, Brent Cross has been overtaken by several bigger and more spectacular malls (Merry Hill,

Meadowhall and Lakeside among them), but its claims to have been in some sense 'the first' have rarely been challenged. As such, it has attracted both praise and blame. Accused of destroying the traditional English high street, wrecking the environment and replacing freely accessible public places with sanitised and tightly controlled private space, shopping centres such as Brent Cross (and their latter-day successor, shopping malls) have nonetheless proved extremely popular and financially successful places. At £300 a square foot, rents in Brent Cross are as high as in London's West End, offering consumers a safe and climate-controlled alternative to the perceived dangers and unpredictability of city-centre shopping. Over the years, Brent Cross has become an accepted part of many consumers' weekly (and in some cases daily) routine, no longer seen as a spectacular symbol of modernity and progress. Brent Cross has responded to the competition from more recent developments undertaking a multi-million pound face lift, letting in more daylight, increasing the amount of free parking space and generally sprucing up its appearance, aiming to attract a younger generation of shoppers as well as those who grew up with the centre . . .

What we were seeking to establish through this research was less the 'meaning of the mall' and rather more the diverse and often contested meaning of . . . shopping places and their relationship to the identity of those who shopped there. Rejecting the ungrounded theorising that has tended to dominate recent work on consumption . . . we ground . . . our understanding of contemporary consumption in the lives of 'ordinary consumers' and let . . . their voices be heard through transcriptions from our focus groups and ethnographic observations . . .

[We argue] that shopping does not merely reproduce identities that are forged elsewhere but provides an active and independent component of identity construction . . . One of our key findings [is] that shopping is an investment in social relationships, often within a relatively narrowly defined household or domestic context, as much as it is an economic activity, devoted to the acquisition of particular commodities. While our respondents rarely shopped as whole families . . . we found social relations within the family to be the dominant context of contemporary consumption . . .

The carefully controlled environment of shopping centres and malls provides consumers with a haven from the perceived dangers of high street shopping and the risk of unplanned encounters with various (often racialised) others. As such, the privatisation of space within shopping centres and malls provides a solution to the now widespread fear of public space, with closed circuit television and other visible means of improved personal security adding to the sense of risk-free shopping . . .

Consumers' fears about the increasingly 'artificial' nature of contemporary shopping represents the other side of their desire for a carefully managed and crime-free shopping environment. Again, we argue that these feelings are as much about the social context of shopping as they are about the physical setting of the shopping centre or mall. When people yearn for a return to 'personal service' or support current trends for opening up enclosed shopping centres to 'natural light', we suggest that they are at least as concerned about the increasing artificiality of their social relationships (and in particular the perceived materialism of their children) as they are about the physical environment itself.

Extracted from: Daniel Miller et al. (1998): *Shopping, place and identity*. London: Routledge, viii–xi.

The work of Miller, Thrift, Jackson, Rowlands and Holbrook is considered to be novel to the extent that it pays attention to the *people* who shop in malls – 'what shoppers do and what they understand as shopping'. Whilst earlier studies of malls have given a good deal of attention to the people within these shopping places, these literatures have concentrated primarily on the public's use of these spaces but have ignored 'the cultural practices of shopping' per se. It is to an assessment of this work that we will now turn.

Peopling the mall

Our starting point in this section is the fact that suburban malls have often been somewhat romantically viewed as new egalitarian public spaces. As Langman (1991, quoted in Shields, 1992: 5) suggests,

> whatever one's status or job in the world of work or even without job, there is an equality of just being there and looking at the shows of decor, goods and other people. Malls appear democratic and open to all, rich or poor, young or old . . . This is the realm where the goods of the good life promised in the magazine ads and television commercials can be found.

In this framework, there has been considerable attention paid to the activities of mall-rats – 'people who seem to do nothing else but hang out at the mall, all day, everyday' (Kowinski, 1985: 33). Mall-rats are usually (but not exclusively) adolescents for whom 'malls have become a primary hang out and site of such truly significant life events as first use of a charge card, driving a car (to the mall) and losing one's virginity in the parking lot' (Langman, 1992: 58). Like 'the street' discussed in Chapter 10, the mall is viewed in these accounts as offering people 'a third place beyond home and work/school, a venue where . . . [they] can congregate, commune and "see and be seen"' (Goss, 1993: 25). The mega-malls of North America and Britain's regional shopping centres specifically market themselves as 'open to all' and provide a range of activities from old-age pensioners' tea dances to teenage school break activities in order to support this image. Indeed, in North America many malls even throw open their doors early in the morning in order to give space to the multitude of 'mall walkers' who like to practise their keep-fit activities in the safety and security of these centres (Goss, 1993). Customers at the mall then – of all ages – 'become performers in their own drama' (Chaney, 1990: 63) as a new indoor *flânerie* – reminiscent of the 'sociality of the street' (see Chapter 10) takes shapes.

In reality, of course, the key word here is *customers* and any *flânerie* that does happen is strictly controlled. As Chaney (1990: 64) notes 'people walk here . . . as if their conduct might be called into question at any moment'. Malls are effectively spaces for the white middle classes – 'they reclaim, for the middle-class imagination, "The Street" – an idealized social space free, by virtue of private property, planning and strict control, from the inconvenience of the weather and the danger and pollution of the automobile, but most importantly from the terror of crime associated with today's urban environment' (Goss, 1993: 24) (see Chapter 9).

Reading 12.6 by Rob Shields, a sociologist whose pioneering work on consumption spaces (Shields, 1992) is well known in geography, is taken from *Environment and Planning D: Society and Space*, a leading journal of critical social and cultural geography. In this extract Shields contrasts the spaces of the mall – and the activities these allow – with those of the street. But Shields also draws attention to the fact that not all users of malls are 'passive dupes', rather 'post-shoppers' at malls play at being consumers and are thus able to exploit the possibilities of these places for their own purposes.

Reading 12.6 – Malls, *flânerie* and post-shoppers

Being in the tightly policed, semiprivate interior of a mall is quite different from being 'on the street'. 'No loitering', as the signs in the mall say. Certain types of comportment are expected ... in malls, business deals are struck and social relationships made as they are in the street cafés of continental Europe ...

The shopping centre and its practices – a new indoor *flânerie* (strolling), the habit of window shopping as much as 'hanging out' or being an onlooker enjoying the crowds – have become established features of contemporary urban life ... *Flânerie* has acquired a less gendered character to become an almost universal diversion amongst new middle-mass consumers ... Thus, in the United States, for example, the most frequented public spaces are shopping malls ... The large regional centres ... have a sizeable group of users who visit simply for enjoyment and to observe the world ...

[But] unlike the street-life of the European tradition, the surrounding environment in the centre is carefully and consciously managed ... To congregate in such spaces ... requires that one observe bourgeois norms of social docility and conservatism both in dress and action. The displays of 'peacock clothing ' or 'punk spectacle' common in the United Kingdom or USA are relegated to just outside the doors of ... [the] mall. Instead, the clothing adopted is a fashion industry edition of punk or gothic style ... One must always look as if one has bought something or is about to buy. Hence their uniform, classless appearance. Also, there are thus no hangouts. The greatest rebellion is the act of sitting down on the floor, ignoring benches ... Movement after a few minutes is often essential to avoid the security guards patrolling for loiterers ...

Why patronize such a place? The key to the success of the mall appears to lie in the manner of appropriation by its users, the *flâneurs* ... The carnivalization of the mall by its users provides the only means at hand to balance its 'commercial terror' ... Like Urry's 'post-tourist' who knows that mass tourism is a game played for status, the mall has its 'post-shoppers' who, as *flâneurs*, play at being consumers in complex, self-conscious mockery ... This tinges the complicitous self-implication and apathy of the *flâneurs* ... with parody. The effect is to disrupt the pretentiousness of [the] mall ... The users, both young and old, are not just resigned victims, but actively subvert the ambitions of the mall developers by developing the insulation value of the stance of the jaded, world-weary *flâneurs*; asserting their independence in a multitude of ways apart from consuming ... It is this practice ... which is the heart of the postmodern experience of the mall.

Extracted from: Rob Shields (1989): Social spatialization and the built environment: the West Edmonton Mall. *Environment and Planning D: Society and Space*, 7, 147–64.

Shields' work discussed above places emphasis on the mall as part and parcel of 'post-modernism' (Harvey, 1989a) but, as other authors have recognized, the 'post-modern retail environment' (Goss, 1992) comprises far more than the suburban mega-mall or regional shopping centre. Indeed, as we noted in our 1996 review of the new retail geography, 'the differentiation of shopping malls is far more advanced than a reading of the literature to date would suggest' (Lowe and Wrigley, 1996: 26). And there are many examples of 'malls' which have not been covered so far in this chapter. It is to these alternative consumption spaces that we will now turn.

The malling of retail space: new landscapes of consumption

From the 1980s onwards malls in North America approached saturation point. The serial reproduction of mall formats across the United States – 'the malling of America' – had proceeded apace throughout the previous quarter of a century and in this climate the concept of differentiation became important. However, as Crawford (1992: 10) suggests, 'the system demonstrated a surprising adaptability [and] in spite of its history of rigidly programmed uniformity, new economic and locational opportunities prompted new prototypes'. Speciality centres – an anchorless collection of upmarket shops and restaurants pursuing a specific retail and architectural theme – were joined by downtown 'mega-structures' and 'festival marketplaces'.

Reading 12.7 by John Goss, captures the range of these new mall types in North America. Such new landscapes of consumption often became important vehicles of 'civic boosterism' in conditions of heightened interregional competition in the 1980s (Harvey, 1989b).

Reading 12.7 – The post-modern retail environment

The essential forms of the post-modern retail environment – the speciality centre and the downtown 'megastructure' – reflect the vernacular and high forms of post-modernism respectively, while a hybrid form – the festival marketplace – combines elements of both. The speciality centre is an 'anchorless' collection of upmarket shops pursuing a specific retail and architectural theme. It is prone to quaintification. Typical designs in North America include New England villages (Pickering Wharf, Salem, Massachusetts); French provincial towns (The Continent, Columbus, Ohio); Spanish–American haciendas (The

Pruneyard, San Jose); Mediterranean villages (Atrium Court, Newport Beach, California); and timber mining camps (Jack London Village, Oakland, California). Pride of place must, however, go to the Borgota in Scottsdale, Arizona, a mock thirteenth-century walled Italian village, with bricks imported from Rome and shop signs in Italian ... and to the Mercado in nearby Phoenix, Arizona, modelled on traditional hillside villages of Mexico, with original components imported from Guadalajara and buildings given Hispanic names ...

The downtown megastructure, on the other hand, is a self-contained complex including retail functions, hotel, offices, restaurants, entertainment, health centres and luxury apartments. Typical examples include Water Tower Place in Chicago, the Tower City Centre in Cleveland and Town Square in St Paul ... These small worlds ensure that the needs of affluent residents, office workers, conference attenders and tourists can be met entirely within a single hermetically sealed space. Several features distinguish the downtown megastructure from the suburban shopping mall, although by now many of these have been extensively 'retrofitted' in the post-modern style ... Daylight [has been returned] in glazed malls reminiscent of nineteenth-century European arcades ... natural light allows the planting of ficus, bamboos and 'interiorised' palms to simulate the tropical environments of tourism ... elaborate watercourses and waterfalls simulate nature, rather than urban fountains ... Pure and perfected nature ... is ironically found indoors within the city, and no longer in the deteriorating environments of the suburbs ...

The downtown malls are also no longer primarily 'machines for shopping', although the aesthetics of movement are retained in the sweep of huge escalators and the trajectory of 'bubble' elevators. Now passage through the mall is an interactive experience, an adventure in winding alleys resembling the Arabian Souk or medieval town, with the unpredictability of 'pop-out' shop fronts – glass display cases which jut out into the mall – and mobile vendors ...

The festival market combines [shopping and entertainment] with an idealised version of historical urban community and the street market, typically in a restored waterfront district after the model of Faneuil Hall Marketplace in Boston. These environments reflect a nostalgia for manual labour, public gatherings and the age of commerce. Buildings and vessels are restored, and there is usually a historic museum on site. The marketplace is typically decorated with antique signage and props which casually suggest an authentic stage upon which the modern consumer can act out a little bit of history. The street entertainers, barrow vendors and costume staff often support this image.

Extracted from: John Goss (1992): Modernity and postmodernity in the retail landscape. In Kay Anderson and Fay Gale (eds) *Inventing places: studies in cultural geography.* **Melbourne: Longman Cheshire, 158–77.**

Meanwhile, in the UK, different economic and political imperatives – specifically the shifting nature of government policy towards out-of-town retail developments (see Chapter 7; also Guy, 1994b, 1998b, 1998c, 1998d; Wrigley, 1998a) – has led to a similar duplication of new retail formats. Indeed, by the 1990s a 'fourth wave' of innovative retail developments comprising 'more specialised, up market formats, such as warehouse clubs, airport retailing and factory outlets centres' was identified (Fernie, 1995, 1998).

Table 12.1: *Existing and proposed factory outlet centres in the UK, December 1995*

Operator	Trading name	Location of factory outlet	Date of opening	Square footage
Existing				
BAA/MacArthur Glenn	Cheshire Oaks	Chester	Open	110,000
Brighton Marina Co.	Brighton Marina	Brighton	Open	40,000
C & J Clark	Clarks Village	Street, Somerset	Open	72,000
	K Village	Kendal, Cumbria	Open	19,000
Freeport Leisure	Hornsea Freeport	Hornsea, East Yorkshire	Open	40,000
	Freeport Village	Fleetwood	Open	60,000
Schroders Property	Jacksons Landing	Hartlepool	Open	60,000
(formerly the Guinea Group)				
Lightwater Holdings	Lightwater Valley	Yorkshire	Open	19,000
Value Retail	Bicester Village	Bicester	Open	107,000
Proposed				
BAA/MacArthur Glenn–	Great Western	Swindon	1997	180,000
Tarmac/Richardson	Bridgend	Bridgend	1997	175,000
	Junction 28	Mansfield	1998	200,000
BAA/MacArthur Glenn	Western Links	Weston-super-Mare	NA	150,000
	NA	York	1997	300,000
	NA	Bathgate	1998	110,000
Bisley Properties	Tobacco Dock	London	NA	160,000
European Outlet Markets Ltd	Killarney Company Stores	Killarney	1996	79,000
Fairclough Homes	NA	Dover	NA	130,000
Freeport Leisure	NA	Westwood, Scotland	NA	50,000
The Guinea Group	Clacton Common	Clacton-on-Sea	NA	116,000
	Leven Fields	Kinross	1997	80,000
Lansfastigheter Prop	The Galleria	Hatfield	NA	300,000
Lister & Co.	Manningham Mills	Bradford	1996	100,000
Morrison Construction Group	Royal Quays	North Shields	1996	100,000
Oldway Property Group	New House Village	Chepstow	NA	50,000
Oldrids	NA	Grantham	1996	55,000
PSIT	Rolling Stock	Haydock	1996	160,000
Ram Euro-Centres	Cotswold Village	Tewkesbury	NA	155,000
Ram Euro-Centres/C & J Clark	Yorkshire Outlet	Doncaster	1996	155,000
Rockeagle Developments	Festival Shopping	Ebbw Vale	1996	90,000
Schroder Property	Chorley Mills	Chorley	1997	46,000
Sea Containers/Ellison Harte	Harwich Europort F/O Centre	Harwich	1996	150,000
Value Retail	Sandbach Village	Sandbach	NA	100,000
Walton Commercial	NA	Liverpool	NA	150,000

Source: Adapted from Fernie (1996), 17–18.

Warehouse clubs, which sell food and non-food items to club members at low prices in 'no frills' surroundings, and factory outlet centres, which sell cut-price merchandise direct from manufacturers in purpose-built centres, both have their origins in the US where they have enjoyed considerable success (Guy, 1994b). In the UK, warehouse clubs such as the US chain Costco met with more limited fortunes in the wider context of the severe mid-1990s shake-out in the discount food retail sector (Wrigley and Clarke, 1999). In contrast, factory outlet centres initially performed more strongly. In 1993 there were two such centres – at Hornsea and Street; by 1995 there were nine and proposals for a further 25 (Fernie, 1998). Table 12.1 illustrates existing and proposed factory outlet centres in the UK in December 1995. Several of the factory outlet centres, particularly the designer outlet mall at Bicester Village in Oxfordshire, are modelled on the New England village design which Goss in Reading 12.7 describes as 'quaintification'. More recently, due to tightening land use planning regulation, there is evidence of a slowing of this trend. For example, Fernie (1998) shows that by mid-1997 only 15 such centres were trading, that the scale of some of the developments planned may be downgraded, and that their format is likely to be more 'downmarket' than in the USA.

Airport retailing has expanded from its original duty/tax-free orientation (wines and spirits, perfumes and tobacco) to encompass a broad range of merchandise tailored to the lifestyles of various passenger groups. As a result, many high-street retailers are now trading successfully in airports (Freathy and O'Connell, 1998) and the interiors of airport terminals present the traveller with an array of consumption possibilities in mall-type settings. In 1994 Chesterton calculated that Britain's 15 largest airports had a total of 248 speciality shops occupying 323,792 square feet of retail floorspace (Chesterton, 1994) and there has been considerable expansion since that date.

New landscapes of consumption such as the factory outlet centre or airport mall have developed rapidly in the past decade and have joined new purchasing opportunities at the railway station, petrol/service station and hospital in widening the retail offering. This is not to suggest, of course, that other kinds of retail development present in North America have been absent from the UK. In particular, speciality centres and festival marketplaces – such as those found in London (Covent Garden or Whiteleys, a former department store), Glasgow (Princes Square), Leeds (Corn Exchange) or Southampton (Canute's Pavilion) (Guy, 1994b) have become familiar sites in many of Britain's towns and cities. But it is the 'home' the traditional site of reproduction/consumption – which has been recast as a new consumption landscape of the most considerable potential. Our next (and final) chapter addresses this alternative consumption space in detail.

Chapter 14

POWER RETAIL GROWTH IN CANADA AND THE GTA: 2006

Tony Hernandez, Tansel Erguden, and Magnus Svindal

The evolution of power retailing has been the focus of numerous CSCA reports over the last decade. The development and clustering of large format or 'big box' retailers into a variety of functional forms continues to account for a significant proportion of retail change in Canada. This 'Americanisation" of the retail landscape has provided Canadian consumers with an increased selection of retail venues at which to shop and spend their valuable leisure time. The purpose of this research letter is to provide an update on the growth of big boxes, power centres and power nodes in Canada, with particular focus on the Greater Toronto Area (GTA). It should be noted that due to the rapid development of the big box format across Canada the definition and classification of power retail developments are subject to periodic updating to reflect their role and function in the retail economy. This research letter provides a snap-shot of power retailing across Canada at the end of 2006 based on in-house data collected by the CSCA in partnership with Rogers Media who publish, on an annual basis, 'The Directory of Power Centres'. Further information on ordering the directory is available online - www.mondayreport.ca (for information on the CSCA - www.csca.ryerson.ca).

Big Boxes, Power Centres and Power Nodes

Big box, power centre and power node developments since the early 1990s have transformed the retail environment across urban Canada. Table 1 provides definitions of big box retail, power centres and power nodes - the term 'power retail' is used broadly to refer to the clustering of big box retailers. In a relatively short period of time, just over a decade, power retail developments have grown to form a key element of the retail fabric. Research by the CSCA has highlighted the national importance of power retail veneus, with many of Canada's major hotspots of retail activity defined by the presence of power centres and power nodes (see for example CSCA Research Letter 2006-03 'Hotspots in Canadian Retailing). The CSCA, through field survey, identified 2,886 big box tenants within 389 power centres and 174 power nodes across Canada at the end of 2006.

The reasons for big box and associated power retail development growth can be traced to a number of factors, including: the influx of US 'big box' retailers to Canada through the 1990s (e.g., Home Depot entering Canada in 1992, Wal-Mart in 1994); the re-zoning of industrial sites for retail development; the suburbanization of retail functions and availability of large development sites; planning regimes across much of Canada since the 1990s that placed few barriers in the way of major big box retailers / developers; and, a slowdown in mall development (albeit with substantial re-development and re-configuration of existing shopping centre space). Stated simply, big box retail stores have been a relatively low-cost form of retail development, meeting the needs of retailers to acrue economies of scale in their operations and Canadian consumers' demands for price, product selection and service.

The impact of large format retailers on retail structure has been the focus of a number of recent CSCA studies. These impacts can be measured in a number of ways, for example, closure rates, vacancy rates, retail turnover, market share, penetration, saturation, and so forth. The extent of their impact is debatable, however, the rate of power retail growth and diffusion represents a fundamental shift in the retail structure of Canada. For example, the City of Toronto's Planning Department amended their Official Plan to accommodate the growth of power developments. They state that these new format developments are 'eclipsing shopping malls', and have supported a move to abandon the traditional retail hierarchy within their planning strategy. While the term 'eclipsing' may slightly overstate the structural transformation that is taking place, it does signal a move on the part of policy-makers in accepting power retail developments as an integral element of the contemporary retail landscape (see CSCA Research Report 2005-02 for a discussion of the role of planning within retail development - the findings from the research highlight the wide variance in definition and development patterns of power retailing across the GTA).

TABLE 1. Definitions of 'Power Retail'	
Retail Structure	**Typical Configuration**
Big Box	Big box retailers are retail outlets that are typically at least three or more times larger than other comparable stores. The definition of big box varies by sector and is determined by gross leasable area
Power Centre	Three or more big box retailers with shared parking lot and typically ancillary commercial services
Power Node	One power centre with additional big boxes or other power centres / major malls within a one kilometre radius, typically centred on a major intersection

Power Retail: Canada

The CSCA, in partnership with Rogers Media, has collected tenant data and mapped the location of power centres and power nodes across Canada since 2001. This national database of power retail provides a unique source of field-surveyed data on the nature and extent of these retail developments. The database contains information on the location and number of power centres and power nodes, the number and mix of retail tenants, along with the locations of the new 'emerging' power centres that are currently under development. The Directory of Power Centres, available from Rogers Media provides site plans for these power retail venues.

In 2006, the CSCA identified 389 power centres across Canada with 2,886 big box retail tenants accounting for 107.3 million square feet of retail space. The power retail locations also have a sizeable number of non-big box retail tenants, for example, ancillary services (restaurants, personal and business services) and smaller retail stores. There were 6,060 non-big box tenants located within power centres across Canada (22.1 million square feet). In total, there were 8,946 retail tenants in the 389 power centres, accounting for 129.5 million square feet of retail space. (an estimated 15 percent of all retail space in Canada, accounting for over 20 to 25 percent of total non-automotive retail sales). Many power centres were clustered into power nodes, with 174 power nodes identified with 3,041 big box retail tenants, equating to 110.9 million square feet of retail space; and 17,724 non-big box tenants(67.1 million square feet).

It is interesting to note the continued regional variation in power retail development across Canada. As in previous years, Ontario led the way on the basis of total power retail square footage, followed by Alberta, Quebec and British Columbia. In absolute terms, Ontario housed more than double the power retail of Alberta and Quebec, three times the value of British Columbia,

and more than remaining Provinces combined. However, on a per capita basis, Alberta (essentially the retail markets of Calgary and Edmonton) was the most developed in 2006. At the national level, Saskatchewan and Prince Edward Island both indexed highly on a per captia basis. British Columbia and Quebec experienced growth in the number of power centres, whilst New Brunswick and Nova Scotia with their smaller and relatively stagnant retail markets have, unsurprisingly, not seen extensive development. The fastest growth has taken place in the major metropolitan markets of Canada; these metropolitan markets have provided developers with prime sites and as a result experienced the highest ratio of power retail square footage per capita growth. Toronto unsurprisingly housed the largest number of power retailers, and Calgary the most power retail when measured against total market size. The reasons for the variation in power retail development are subject to debate, including, restricted land availability and associated development costs, land-use planning issues, the existing retail infrastructure and cultural-competitive concerns of US and other international retailers with regard to entering French-speaking Canada.

Table 3 provides a selected listing of major retailers operating stores within power centres and/or power nodes in Canada in 2006. For example, Business Depot / Staples operated 140 of their 252 store portfolio within power retail location, and were located in approximately three-fifths of all of the power centres in Canada. Of these stores, 116 were located in power node locations, with stores present in two-thirds of all Canadian power nodes. Table 3 also details the type of power retail location, either a store located in a power centre, a free-standing store in a power node, a store in a power centre within a larger power node, or a store within a mall within a power node. In the example of Business Depot / Staples it can be seen that of the 116 stores located in power nodes, 17 were located free-standing in power nodes, 18 within malls in power nodes and the remaining 81 stores in power centres within power nodes.

TABLE 2. Power Retail By Province, 2006

	POWER CENTRES							POWER NODES						
Province*	No. of PC's	No. of Big Boxes	Retail Sq. Ft. (000s)	No. of Non Big Boxes	Retail Sq. Ft. (000s)	Total No. of PC Tenants	Total Retail Sq. Ft (000's)	No. of PN's	No. of Big Boxes**	Retail Sq. Ft. (000's)	No. of Non Big Boxes***	Retail Sq. Ft. (000's)	Total No. of PN Tenants	Total Retail Sq. Ft. (000's)
AB	57	536	18,637	1,608	5,241	2,144	23,878	20	525	17,579	2,596	8,893	3,121	26,472
BC	52	330	12,001	987	3,187	1,317	15,188	23	353	13,368	2,210	7,369	2,563	20,736
MB	12	101	4,125	167	642	268	4,767	8	166	6,804	1063	4,882	1,229	11,687
NB	3	29	1,240	31	181	60	1,421	3	51	2,193	371	1,511	422	3,704
NF	4	31	1,678	100	212	131	1,890	1	5	326	44	158	49	484
NS	9	60	2,495	100	653	160	3,148	7	94	3,672	622	2,613	716	6,286
ON	171	1,205	42,439	2,245	8,094	3,450	50,533	78	1,296	44,619	6,826	24,844	8,122	69,463
PE	2	17	716	39	96	56	812	1	13	673	77	197	90	870
QC	62	482	18,683	651	3,371	1,133	22,054	23	420	16,054	2,887	12,873	3,307	28,926
SK	17	95	5,354	132	496	227	5,850	10	118	5,636	1028	3,785	1146	9,421
Total	389	2,886	107,367	6,060	22,173	8,946	129,540	174	3,041	110,924	17,724	67,125	20,765	178,049

* does not include Yukon, Northwest Territories or Nunavut.
** within power node, excluding mall.
*** including mall and power centre tenants.

TABLE 3. Selected Retailers - Stores Operated by Location Type, 2006

Banner (Ownership)	Sector	Total No. of Stores Operated	of which located in						PC	PR of which located in			
			FS*	%	Mall*	%	PR	%		FS in PN	PC in PN	Mall in PN	Total in PN
Chapters	Book & Stationery	71	7	9.9%	16	22.5%	48	67.6%	36	4	29	8	41
The Real Canadian Superstore	Other General Merch.	114	42	36.8%	10	8.8%	62	54.4%	45	15	32	2	49
Sears Whole Home Furniture	Household Furniture	48	1	2.1%	4	8.3%	43	89.6%	34	7	27	2	36
BouClair	Fabric & Yarns	33	0	0.0%	3	9.1%	30	90.9%	24	3	17	3	23
Canadian Tire	Home & Autoparts	468	249	53.2%	62	13.2%	157	33.5%	113	35	69	9	113
Costco	Other General Merch.	68	14	20.6%	0	0.0%	54	79.4%	35	18	23	1	42
Future Shop	Consumer Electronics	121	16	13.2%	15	12.4%	90	74.4%	73	12	56	5	73
Home Depot	Hardware Stores	145	26	17.9%	3	2.1%	116	80.0%	92	24	62	0	86
Ikea	Household Furniture	12	3	25.0%	0	0.0%	9	75.0%	8	1	3	0	4
Loblaws	Supermarkets	91	44	48.4%	26	28.6%	21	23.1%	16	3	10	2	15
Mark's Work Wearhouse	Men's Clothing	322	68	21.1%	85	26.4%	169	52.5%	143	9	83	17	109
Michaels	Hobby & Toys	55	0	0.0%	1	1.8%	54	98.2%	50	4	40	0	44
Moores The Suit People	Men's Clothing	116	33	28.4%	18	15.5%	65	56.0%	53	1	44	11	56
Penningtons	Women's Clothing	144	14	9.7%	44	30.6%	86	59.7%	61	9	39	16	64
PetSmart	Pets	33	1	3.0%	0	0.0%	32	97.0%	29	3	27	0	30
Pier 1 Imports	Household Furniture	68	4	5.9%	1	1.5%	63	92.6%	57	5	44	1	50
Reitmans	Women's Clothing	367	18	4.9%	204	55.6%	145	39.5%	103	2	66	40	108
The Brick	Household Furniture	112	58	51.8%	9	8.0%	45	40.2%	31	9	24	5	38
Business Depot/Staples	Book & Stationery	252	53	21.0%	47	18.7%	152	60.3%	117	17	81	18	116
The Shoe Company	Shoes	54	2	3.7%	6	11.1%	46	85.2%	44	1	38	1	40
Toys "R" Us	Hobby & Toys	64	6	9.4%	23	35.9%	35	54.7%	19	6	19	10	35
Wal-Mart	General Merch.	269	65	24.2%	46	17.1%	158	58.7%	137	8	75	13	96
Winners	Other Clothing	185	11	5.9%	68	36.8%	106	57.3%	79	5	59	22	86
Zellers	General Merch.	280	9	3.2%	197	70.4%	74	26.4%	24	1	17	49	67
Indigo Books & Music	Book & Stationery	15	2	13.3%	6	40.0%	7	46.7%	6	0	4	1	5
Old Navy	Other Clothing	61	2	3.3%	22	36.1%	37	60.7%	23	4	18	10	32
Home Outfitters	Household Furniture	56	1	1.8%	6	10.7%	49	87.5%	41	2	31	6	39
HomeSense	Household Furniture	58	1	1.7%	11	19.0%	46	79.3%	38	2	34	6	42
Best Buy	Consumer Electronics	47	3	6.4%	7	14.9%	37	78.7%	30	5	28	2	35
Sam's Club	General Merch.	6	0	0.0%	0	0.0%	6	ſ00.0%	4	2	4	0	6

* not in Power Retail Location

FS = Free Standing; PC = Power Centre; PN = Power Node; PR = Power Retail

Power Retail: GTA

The GTA has experienced a rapid growth of big box format retailers since 1999 (see Table 4), increasing 50.2 percent to 1,278 big box stores in 2006. The retail square footage of these stores totaled an estimated 41.7 million retail square feet. The development of big boxes has been largely focused in and around power centre and power node developments. The GTA has witnessed the development of 32 additional power centres between 1999 and 2006, a growth of approximately 60 percent, to bring the total to 79 power centres (of which, 9 are part-developed). The number of power nodes has increased from 24 to 28 over the same period, for example, Oakville Town Centre Power Node and Highway 2 & Harwood Avenue Power Node.

The growth of power retail is also reflected in the increasing proportion of big box stores located in power centres and power nodes. For example, in 1999, 36.4 percent of big boxes were located in power centres, by 2006 this figure increased by nearly one-third to 46.6 percent. Simply, fewer retailers are opening free-standing boxes and are instead opting to take advantage of the benefits of clustering with other power retailers. Although over the last couple of years a counter- power centre trend is emerging with a small number of power retailers favouring freestanding locations. The average number of big boxes per power centre and power node has steadily increased, from 6.6 to 7.5 and 14.7 to 21.6 respectively. The average number of non-big box tenants within power centres and nodes has also increased, reflecting an evolution of the power retail concept. This clustering of big box and non-big box retail has provided consumers in the GTA with a number of major retail venues. For example, the power node at Warden and Eglinton (see Figure 1) houses 119 big box and non-big box tenants (totaling an estimated 1.5 million square feet of retail space). Of which, 32 tenants are big boxes, accounting for 74 percent of the retail square footage. The power node is currently under further development with the recent addition of new tenants and an expansion of the existing node to the north of Eglinton Avenue, with the opening of a Wal-Mart Supercenter store, and a number of smaller stores. It is interesting to note that the power node has developed along 'The Golden Mile' auto-dealer strip, next to Eglinton Square (a community-sized mall).

The mix of big box retail tenants has changed significantly since 1999 (see Table 5). There has been a clear movement on the part of fashion retailers to develop big box formats. The power centres five years ago were anchored by large grocery, general merchandise, hardware and electrical retailers - increasingly, the growth of fashion retail and ancillary service, what has been termed the mini-box phenomenon (see Table 6). The growth of restaurants and entertainment within power centres also highlights the move from functional discount 'category' killing shopping to cross-shopping leisure behaviours. It is also worth noting the growth of financial and business services within power centre venues (with a trend towards flagship bank branches).

TABLE 4. Big Box Growth in the GTA, 1999 to 2006

	1999	2000	2001	2002	2003	2004	2005	2006	Change No.	Change %
Total No. of Big Boxes (BB)	851	925	1011	1073	1123	1185	1227	1278	427	50.2%
Freestanding (No)	116	131	145	147	140	132	135	137	21	18.1%
Freestanding (%)	13.6%	14.2%	14.3%	13.7%	12.5%	11.1%	11.0%	10.7%	-2.9%	na
In Malls (No)	425	434	459	480	497	511	524	545	120	28.2%
In Malls (%)	49.9%	46.9%	45.4%	44.7%	44.3%	43.1%	42.7%	42.6%	-7.3%	na
In Power Centres (No)	310	360	407	446	486	542	568	596	286	92.3%
In Power Centres (%)	36.4%	38.9%	40.3%	41.6%	43.3%	45.7%	46.3%	46.6%	10.2%	na
In Power Nodes (No)	353	397	451	489	513	563	583	606	253	71.7%
In Power Nodes (%)	41.5%	42.9%	44.6%	45.6%	45.7%	47.5%	47.5%	47.4%	5.9%	na
Total No. of PC's	47	50	60	67	70	76	78	79	32	68.1%
(of which part developed)	(16)	(16)	(18)	(20)	(15)	(14)	(12)	(9)	-7	-43.8%
Total No. of PN's	24	24	27	27	28	28	28	28	4	16.7%
Avg No. of BB per PC	6.6	7.2	6.8	6.7	6.9	7.1	7.3	7.5	0.9	na
Avg No. of BB per PN	14.7	16.5	16.7	18.1	18.3	20.1	20.8	21.6	6.9	na
Avg No. of Non BB per PC	7.6	8.6	8.6	8.4	10.8	12.4	13.8	14.8	7.3	na
Avg No. of Non BB per PN	79.7	82.8	77.2	77.9	81.2	86.8	90.4	95.7	16.0	na

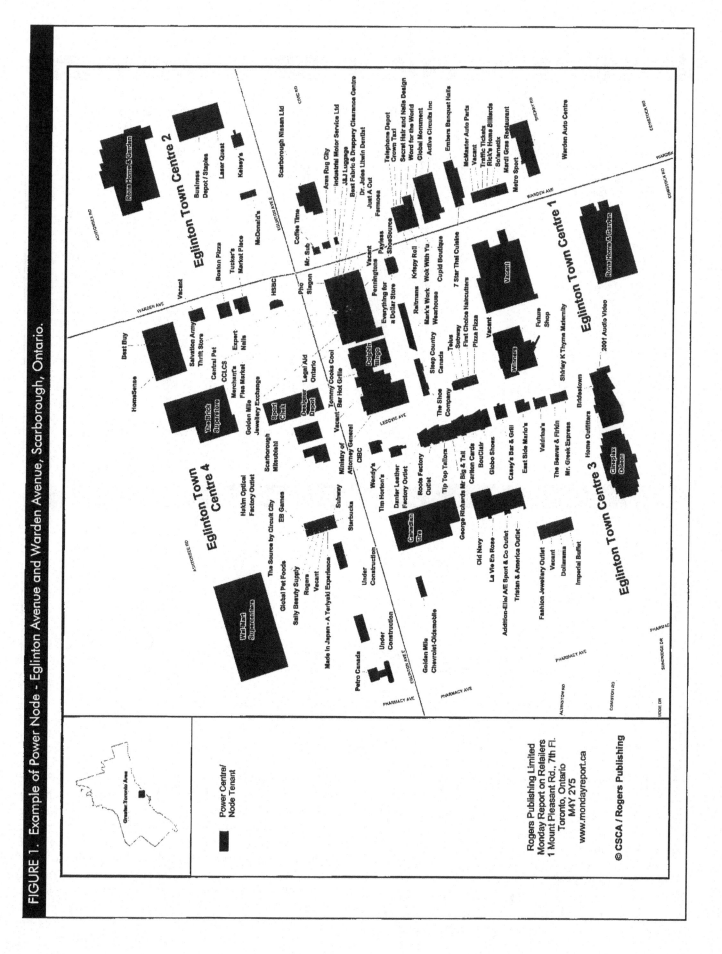

FIGURE 1. Example of Power Node - Eglinton Avenue and Warden Avenue, Scarborough, Ontario.

Power Centre/
Node Tenant

Rogers Publishing Limited
Monday Report on Retailers
1 Mount Pleasant Rd., 7th. Fl.
Toronto, Ontario
M4Y 2Y5
www.mondayreport.ca

© CSCA / Rogers Publishing

285

TABLE 5. Big Box Growth in the GTA by Sector, 1999 to 2006

Sector	1999	2000	2001	2002	2003	2004	2005	2006	Change No.	Change %
Other Clothing & Fabric Stores	118	127	149	165	174	184	194	206	88	74.6%
Household & Appliance Stores	108	117	123	151	161	166	177	186	78	72.2%
Food & Beverage Services	78	84	94	95	103	114	120	132	54	69.2%
Women's Clothing	55	71	68	72	73	93	93	102	47	85.5%
General Merch.	58	63	70	71	80	84	89	96	38	65.5%
Other Retail	77	81	85	82	77	82	87	86	9	11.7%
Book & Stationery Stores	66	72	72	75	72	74	73	72	6	9.1%
Men's Clothing	46	50	54	56	61	61	62	65	19	41.3%
Food	50	47	55	58	61	60	59	60	10	20.0%
Recreational Services	33	39	46	48	50	53	54	56	23	69.7%
Sporting Goods	33	33	39	45	51	55	56	55	22	66.7%
Hardware Stores	21	26	35	37	37	39	41	41	20	95.2%
Drug Stores	25	26	28	29	34	39	39	39	14	56.0%
Automotive	20	23	28	30	32	32	33	34	14	70.0%
Shoe Stores	32	34	35	35	34	33	34	31	-1	-3.1%
Music Stores	8	8	7	7	7	7	7	7	-1	-12.5%
Liquor	4	4	4	4	4	4	4	4	0	0.0%
Jewellery Stores	1	2	2	1	1	2	2	2	1	100.0%
Florists, Lawn & Garden Centres	14	14	14	10	9	1	1	1	-13	-92.9%
Miscellaneous	4	4	3	2	2	2	2	3	-1	-25.0%
Total	851	925	1011	1073	1123	1185	1227	1278	427	50.2%

TABLE 6. Average Retail Square Footage by Big Box Location Type in the GTA, 1999 to 2006

Big Box Location Type	1999	2006	Change No.	Change %
Freestanding	47,268	56,113	8,845	18.7%
Located in a Mall	31,145	29,675	-1,470	-4.7%
Located in a Power Centre	33,370	33,875	506	1.5%
Located in a Power Node	30,853	32,687	1,835	5.9%
All Big Boxes	34,153	34,468	315	0.9%

The Evolution of Power Retailing

Today there exists a wide range of power development configurations, from power centres to regional power nodes. Some of these developments have been planned, others have evolved over time, in conjunction with *ad hoc* planning approvals and as a result formed diffused ribbon type developments (i.e., power strips). Table 7 provides examples of a number of the 'emerging' power retail structures. For example, a number of malls have now developed big box space on their own pads, with the big boxes located exterior to the mall. The 'boxing of the mall' (interior big box tenants) is now well established, with boxes now anchoring or multi-anchoring many malls across Canada (e.g., utilizing retail space once occupied by the traditional department stores). The clustering of power centres has resulted in the forming of regional power nodes, with a retail draw comparable to major regional shopping malls. Simply, big box retail is no longer confined to freestanding arterial locations, but instead the format continues to be integrated across a range of new and existing retail structures (see CSCA RL 2007-07 for an update on lifesytle centres and associated mixed-use developments).

TABLE 7. Evolving Retail Structures

Development	Configuration	Example Development
Shopping Mall with Exterior Power Tenants	Shopping mall with big box retail tenants located on property, free-standing from the mall.	Scarborough Town Centre Scarborough, Ontario
Shopping Mall with Interior Power Anchor Tenants	Shopping mall with big box retail tenants located within complex. Typically situated in mall where former traditional anchor tenants (i.e., department stores) were located.	Markville Shopping Centre Markham, Ontario
Power Strip	Three or more free-standing big boxes located contiguously along arterial routes within 500 metres, not apparently sharing the same parking facilities or part of the same development. May include other ancillary smaller commercial services.	Calgary Trail & 34th Avenue, Edmonton, Alberta
Regional Power Node	Two or more power centres and/or power strips with a minimum of 20 big box retailers. These nodes have a large retail draw, with sizeable trade areas.	Highway 7 and Highway 400, Toronto, Ontario
Power Mall	Shopping mall with power retailers. Walk-through between power tenants limited, i.e., access to some of the power retailers only available via parking lot.	Country Club Centre, Nanaimo, British Columbia

Summary

This research letter has highlighted:

- the continued growth and evolution of power retail across Canada

- the majority of major retail development in Canada during the late 1990s / early 2000s was focused on big box and power centre formats

- power retail development has been uneven across Canada, with the most developed markets including, the Greater Toronto Area and Calgary

- big boxes are found in a variety of retail environments

- the integration of big box retailers into major shopping malls, and the move to locations on out-pads. These changes (the move to multi-anchors) have altered the traditional flow of customers within the malls, and on the mall property (e.g., boxes now occupy former parking lot space)

- the diversification of the retail tenant mix of power developments, as illustrated by the increased presence of fashion and ancillary services (e.g. restaurants, financial institutions)

- the development of a new set of retail destinations across urban Canada (and increasingly within smaller town markets located on the fringe of major metropolitan areas)

Chapter 15

HOT SPOTS IN CANADIAN RETAILING: 2002–2003

Tony Hernandez, Tansel Erguden, and Philip Bermingham

This report is the sixth in our series of updates that identify and interpret changes in the major concentrations of retail sales activity across Canada. (see Hot Spots in Canadian Retailing, CSCA Research Letters, 1998-02, 2002-09, 2004-1, 2005-03 and 2006-03). Using the SARTRE (Small Area Retail Trade Estimates) database provided by Statistics Canada, this update examines changes in the ranking of major retail areas in Canada for the 2002-2003 period. In the research, the hot spots of Canadian retailing are identified and evaluated for three major retail categories: (i) total retail sales (excluding automotive); (ii) fashion retailing, and; (iii) general merchandise goods. With the release and interpretation of this information, a more precise view of the dynamics of the Canadian retail economy as of 2003 (the most recent date for which data are available) is made possible.

The SARTRE Data

The SARTRE database links retail trade sales to store locations at a fine level of geographical detail -- the Forward Sortation Area(FSA)[1]. It combines data from survey and taxation information for all incorporated retailers in Canada. The data then can be grouped, if the rules of suppression are not broken, according to the 2, 3, or 4 digit North American Industrial Classification System (NAICS) codes. The resulting database allows for an assessment of retail performance by major retail category for relatively small geographical areas. The SARTRE database provides longitudinal small area retail sales estimates for the years 1989-2003. The 2003 database provides retail sales for 1,456 geographical areas (FSAs). In total, the database incorporates approximately 125,500 retail locations. These retail locations accounted for $251 billion in retail sales (excluding the automotive sector) in 2003. To comply with data release agreements with Statistics Canada, the data are expressed in index form (referred to as Sales Scores) that relate to the national average[2]. For more detailed analysis, in some cases it is possible to disaggregate the data into the major two digit retail NAICS codes. To provide a more realistic interpretation of the distribution of retail sales, the automotive sector (including the sale of gasoline) has been removed from the analysis.

The 20 Retail Hot Spots

When the FSAs within the SARTRE database are ranked by their reported retail sales figures for 2003, it is possible to identify major shopping nodes that exist within the Top 20 Canadian markets (see Table 1). The Markville/Pacific Mall and Woodside Power Centre retail cluster in Markham/Unionville, Ontario (L3R) that reported sales 12.3 times the national average was the dominant retail node in Canada. This area captures the concentration of 19 shopping centres and one power centre that served this relatively high income suburban area. Between 2002 and 2003, there was substantial movement in the ranks of major retail nodes as measured by their total non-automotive retail sales. Two retail areas entered our Top 20 listing for the first time: the Carrefour Laval retail cluster in Laval, Quebec and, Woodbine Centre in Etobicoke, Ontario. Four areas re-entered the list in 2003: Kildonan Place in Winnipeg, Manitoba; Place Laurier in Quebec City, Quebec; Strawberry Hill in Surrey and Lansdowne Centre in Richmond, British Columbia. Conversely, six retail areas that were previously in the Top 20 were removed from our list, these included: South Common Mall/Erin Mills Centre, Missausauga, Ontario; Metro Centre, Burnaby and Coquitlam Centre, Coquitlam, British Columbia; Southgate Centre, Edmonton, Alberta; Fairview

---

[1] The FSA is a combination of the first three characters of a postal code (alpha – numeric – alpha). It identifies a major geographic area in an urban or a rural location, with the full six character postal code identifying the smallest delivery area (local delivery unit) within a given FSA. In 2001, there were approximately 1,600 FSAs across Canada, serving on average 7,000 households (see *www.statscan.ca* and *www.canadapost.ca*).

[2] Sales Scores are derived by dividing the individual FSA value by the category average. Due to suppression, in 2003, there were 172 FSAs with no figures for overall retail sales, 1,012 FSAs with no figures for fashion retail sales, and 545 FSAs with no figures for general merchandise retailing. These FSAs were dropped from the analysis in their respective categories.

Table 1. Top 20 Canadian Retail Hot Spots: 2003

Rank 2003	Rank 2002	Rank 2001	FSA	Market	Sales Score	Sales/ Location ($000)	Power Centre	Major Shopping Destination	Shopping Centres (No. of)	Power Centres (No. of)
1	2	1	L3R	Markham/Unionville Ont	12.32	2264.5	Woodside Centre	Markville S.C./Pacific Mall	19	1
2	1	14	L4L	Woodbridge Ont	9.56	3227.2	Seven & 400 Power Ctr/Colossus Power Ent Ctr/Westridge Power Centre	Langstaff Place S.C.	13	3
3	4	2	T2H	MacLeod Trail, Calgary	7.74	3758.3	Heritage Towne Cnt/Chinook Crossing	Chinook S.C.	11	2
4	3	4	S7K	Saskatoon, CBD	6.95	2712.5	River City Centre	Midtown S.C.	6	1
5			H7T	Laval, Que	6.54	3780.3	Hwy 15 & Hwy 148 NW	Carrefour Laval	5	1
6		7	R2C	Winnipeg, Man	5.66	5490.6	Kildonan Place	Kildonan Place	7	1
7	15	10	L3Y	Newmarket	5.58	2746.0	Woodland Hills Centre/Trinity RioCan Newmarket/Yonge St and Green Lane/RioCan Centre Newmarket	Upper Canada Mall	10	4
8	11	13	T1Y	Calgary, Alta	5.33	3884.3	Sunridge Towne Centre 1 & 2	Sundridge S.C.	8	2
9	8	9	H3A, H3B	Montreal, CBD	5.26	1623.3		Place Ville Marie/Eaton Centre/ Place Montreal Trust	11	
10	5	6	L4M	Barrie, Ont	5.19	3037.3	Bayfield St & Livingstone St	Bayfield Mall/Georgian Mall	7	1
11	10	5	M6A	Toronto (North York)	5.06	2355.1		Yorkdale S.C.	4	
12	9	12	M5B, M5C	Toronto,CBD	4.97	2385.3		Eaton Centre/The Bay	8	
13	14	11	N8X	Windsor, Ont	4.92	3244.4	Devonshire Power Centre	Devonshire Mall	7	1
14		19	G1V	Quebec City, CBD	4.85	2043.9		Place Laurier	3	
15	13		V5X	Vancouver, B.C.	4.84	7748.4				
16		20	V3W	Surrey	4.67	2986.3	Strawberry Hill/Nordel Way Power Centre	Kings Cross S.C.	5	2
17	17	16	T5T	West Edmonton, Alta	4.61	2028.6	Terra Losa Power Centre	West Edmonton Mall	6	1
18	6	3	M1P	Toronto (Scarborough)	4.60	2396.7	Kennedy Commons	Scarborough Town Centre	8	1
19		17	V6X	Richmond, B.C.	4.58	1701.5	Hwy 99 & Bridgeport Rd	Lansdowne S.C.	10	1
20			M9W	Toronto (Etobicoke)	4.53	2458.9		Woodbine Shopping Centre	10	1

* Sales/Location calculated as retail sales in FSA/# of locations in FSA.

Pointe-Claire, Pointe Claire and, Jean Talon & Hwy 15 centre in Montreal-St Laurent, Quebec. As in previous years, the areas that experienced relative increases in their rankings were associated with large super regional shopping centres and/or power centre combinations. Examples of these high growth areas included Carrefour Laval, Laval, Quebec (H7T); Kildonan Place, Winnipeg, Manitoba (R2C); and the Upper Canada Mall retail cluster in Newmarket (L Y); and Place Laurier, Quebec City, Quebec (G1V).

As of 2003, the Greater Toronto Area (GTA) accounted for seven of the Top 20 shopping concentrations in Canada and, not unexpectedly, these areas included Markham/Unionville, Hwy 7 and 400 (Woodbridge), Newmarket, Yorkdale, Scarborough Town Centre, the Toronto Eaton Centre and Woodbine Centre (Etobicoke). Greater Vancouver was home to three, Greater Montreal and Calgary home to two of the Top 20 retail concentrations. Other dominant retail locations were found in Edmonton, Winnipeg, Saskatoon, Quebec City, Windsor, and Barrie. In comparing the 2002 and 2003 rankings, what continues to surprise is the degree of change in the ranking of retail hot spots across the country, with two hot spots new entries on the list, and four re-entries. This change underlines the dynamic nature of the retail economy and reinforces a number of elements – the ubiquitous supply of big box (large format) retailing; the changing role of the traditional department stores, and, the fluidity of locational strategies of major retail chains. Yet, despite the movement in the rankings in 2003, 9 out of Top 10 areas in 2002 remained in the list in 2003.

Top 20 Fashion Retail Hot Spots

The Canadian Fashion Retail Hot Spots measure the distribution of shoe, apparel and fabric retail sales across the country (see Table 2). Just less than half of the entries (9 FSAs) from the Retail Hot Spots also appear as Fashion Hot Spots, decreasing from 10 in 2002.

However, between 2002 and 2003, the key fashion concentrations remained relatively stable with 16 of the Top 20 entries and 14 of the Top 15 entries found in both years. Pacific Centre in Vancouver, British Columbia; Hwy 7 & 400 in Woodbridge, Ontario; Bayshore Shopping Centre in Nepean, Ottawa, Ontario; and, Polo Park Centre in Winnipeg, Manitoba were new entries. The four areas exiting the list in 2003 included, surprisingly, Markville/Pacific Mall and Woodside Power Centre retail cluster in Markham/Unionville, Ontario (L3R), Marche Central Power Centre in Montreal(H2N), Kennedy Commons/Scarborough Town Centre (M1P), and Bloor St. West in Toronto (M5S).

Canada's dominant fashions areas included: (i) the major super-regional malls (e.g., Yorkdale, West Edmonton Mall, Chinook Centre, Square One, Carrefour Laval, Sherway Gardens); and, (ii) the major downtown areas of Montreal (2), Toronto (2), Quebec City, Ottawa, and Calgary. The fact that 7 of the fash-

ion concentrations are located in CBDs confirms the continuing specialized importance of downtown retailing in Canada's major urban markets, and the importance of business employees and tourists to the fashion market. The fashion orientation of Toronto's Bay/Bloor area (M4W) and its corresponding status as Canada's Fifth Avenue has again been highlighted, with an average fashion store sales in this area of approximately $4.8 million per retail location in 2003. As in 2002, both the sales scores and sales/location ratio show a greater range across this group, with the range increasing over the 2002 to 2003 period.

Top 20 General Merchandise Hot Spots

Table 3 presents the highest ranking FSAs with respect to the general merchandise (i.e., NAICS group 45) category. This complex grouping includes department stores, warehouse clubs and superstores, sporting goods, books, record and tapes, office supplies, pet stores and miscellaneous retailers. The category tends to capture major retail destinations that provide a combination of: (i) major freestanding stores; (ii) a major regional mall; and, (iii) power centres. As a result, the sales per location is high; but what is most obvious is the fact that 18 out of the 20 FSAs contain at least one power centre (unchanged from 2002). As one would expect, the ranking of dominant general merchandise hot spots has a distinct suburban orientation. The list captures the emerging power centre/shopping centre clusters that are re-shaping the retail landscape across Canada. These hot spots include retail clusters associated with the Chinook area in Calgary (at the top of the ranking in 2003); the Bayfield Strip in Barrie, Ontario; White Oaks in London; Upper Canada Mall in Newmarket (climbing ten positions in the ranking); Lansdowne Centre in Richmond; the Mississauga Square One retail complex; the Fairview Pointe Claire power node; and, the Hwy 7 & 400 power node in suburban Toronto, and the Abbotsford retail concentration in British Columbia. Seventeen of the Top 20 areas in 2002 remained on the list in 2003. New entries include South Point Shopping Centre in Edmonton, Alberta; Place Laurier in Quebec City, Quebec; and, Intercity Shopping Centre in Thunder Bay, Ontario. With Yonge-Eglinton Centre in Toronto and the Vision Centre power cluster in St. Catherines, Ontario; and Macleod Trail/Southcentre Mall in Calgary, Alberta exiting the Top 20 in 2003.

Provincial Analysis: Ontario

The SARTRE data also can be used to examine the distribution of retail hot spots at a variety of spatial scales. To illustrate this application, Maps 1 and 2 present the location of the Top 100 retail concentrations in Ontario in 2003. Superimposed on these maps are the locations of power centres and major regional shopping centres for 2003, respectively. The retail sales in these dominant FSAs (including automotive sales) ranged from a high of $2.2 billion to a low of $640 million. Moreover, 20 FSAs reported sales of over $1 billion for 2003. These included the retail concentrations of Macleod Trail, Calgary, Alberta; Markham/Unionville, Woodbridge, Newmarket and Barrie, Ontario. The

Table 2. Top 20 Canadian Fashion Retail Hot Spots: 2003

Rank 2003	Rank 2002	Rank 2001	FSA	Market	Sales Score	Sales/ Location ($000)	Power Centre	Major Shopping Destination	Shopping Centres (No. of)	Power Centres (No. of)
1	1	1	H3A,H3B	Montreal, CBD	14.77	1339.5		Place Ville Marie/Eaton Centre/ Place Montreal Trust	11	
2	2	2	M6A	Toronto (North York)	12.98	2141.5		Yorkdale S.C.	4	
3	3	3	M5B,M5C	Toronto,CBD	10.81	1566.6		Eaton Centre/The Bay	8	
4	4	4	G1V	Quebec City, CBD	9.94	1295.6		Place Laurier	3	
5	5	6	T5T	West Edmonton, Alta	8.63	1349.9	Terra Losa Power Centre	West Edmonton Mall	6	1
6	6	5	M4W	Toronto, CBD	7.73	4810.3		The Hudson Bay Centre/Bloor St.	7	
7	8	13	T2H	MacLeod Trail, Calgary	7.42	1829.5	Heritage Towne Cnt/Chinook Crossing	Chinook S.C.	11	2
8	7	9	L5B	Mississauga City Centre	6.86	1370.4	Square One Power Ent. Cnt/ RioCan Grand Park	Square One	9	2
9	11	10	H7T	Laval, Que	6.47	1188.5	Hwy 15 & Hwy 148 NW	Carrefour Laval	5	1
10	9	7	M9C	Toronto (Etobicoke)	6.44	1837.6	Hwy 427 & The Queensway 1 & 2	Sherway Gardens	10	2
11			V7Y	Vancouver	6.11	2789.7		Pacific Centre (6 Towers)	1	
12	10	11	H3G	Montreal	6.03	1965.9		La Maison Ogilvy	1	
13	14	18	V5H	Burnaby, B.C.	5.92	1126.5		Metrotown Centre	6	
14			L4L	Woodbridge Ont	5.28	1070.8	Seven & 400 Power Ctr/Colossus Power Ent Ctr/Westridge Power Centre	Langstaff Place S.C.	13	3
15	12	15	NBX	Windsor, Ont	5.11	1426.9	Devonshire Power Centre	Devonshire Mall	7	1
16			K2B	Ottawa: Nepean	5.06	1731.4		Bayshore Shopping Centre	2	
17	15	12	T2P	Calgary, CBD	5.04	1326.8		Eaton Centre/TD Square	9	
18	19	14	J3V	St-Bruno	4.97	945.3	Hwy 116 & Hwy 30 Power Centre	Les Promenades St-Bruno	2	1
19	20	16	K1N	Ottawa, CBD	4.84	1380.5		Rideau Centre	2	
20			R3G	Winnipeg	4.82	1449.2	Polo Park Power Centre	Polo Park Shopping Centre	3	1

* Sales/Location calculated as retail sales in FSA/# of locations in FSA.

Table 3. Top 20 Canadian General Merchandise Retail Hot Spots: 2003

Rank 2003	Rank 2002	Rank 2001	FSA	Market	Sales Score	Sales/Location ($000)	Power Centre	Major Shopping Destination	Shopping Centres (No. of)	Power Centres (No. of)
1	1	3	T2H	MacLeod Trail, Calgary	9.57	5527.3	Heritage Towne Cnt/Chinook Crossing	Chinook S.C.	11	2
2	3	1	L4M	Barrie, Ont	9.12	5264.7	Bayfield St & Livingstone St	Bayfield Mall/Georgian Mall	7	1
3	13	17	L3Y	Newmarket	7.05	3631.1	Woodland Hills Centre/Trinity RioCan Newmarket/Yonge St and Green Lane/RioCan Centre Newmarket	Upper Canada Mall	10	4
4	4	6	H9R	Pointe Claire, Que	6.96	5953.5	Trans Canadienne & Boul St-Jean Power Centre/Hwy 40 and Boul Des Sources	Fairview Pointe-Claire	6	2
5	5	5	V6X	Richmond, B.C.	6.68	2736.5	Hwy 99 & Bridgeport Rd	Lansdowne S.C.	16	1
6	6	8	T1Y	Calgary, Alta	6.59	5543.6	Sunridge Towne Centre 1 & 2	Sunridge S.C.	8	2
7	7	4	V2S	Abbotsford	6.27	5566.5	Abbotsford Power Centre/Marshall Rd & Sumas Way	Seven Oaks S.C.	7	2
8	10	14	N6E	S. London, Ont	6.24	5154.1	Wellington Southdale Plaza/Crossroads Centre/London Wellington	White Oaks S.C.	9	3
9	9	11	R2C	Winnipeg	6.11	7325.5	Kildonan Place	Kildonan Place	7	1
10	8	16	L5B	Mississauga City Centre	6.10	4790.3	Square One Power Ent. Cnt/RioCan Grand Park	Square One	9	2
11	12	12	P3A	Sudbury	6.04	4993.4	Notre Dame Ave & Lasalle Blvd	New Sudbury Centre	6	1
12	2	2	L3R	Markham/Unionville Ont	6.00	1375.5	Woodside Centre	Markville S.C./Pacific Mall	19	1
13	11	10	K2G	Ottawa (Nepean)	5.79	5778.6	RioCan Merivale Place/College Square/Merivale Rd & Hunt Club Rd PC	Merivale Mall	9	3
14	17	19	L4L	Woodbridge Ont	5.58	2701.3	Seven & 400 Power Ctr/Colossus Power Ent Ctr/Westridge Power Centre	Langstaff Place S.C.	13	3
15	16		T8V	Grande Prairie	5.47	3914.3	Gateway Power Centre 1 & 2	Prairie Mall	6	2
16			T6E	Edmonton	5.43	2244.0	South Point Shopping Centre II	Merchant's Row S.C.	10	1
17			G1V	Quebec City, CBD	5.30	2885.3		Place Laurier	3	1
18	14	13	V3B	Coquitlam	5.26	4849.2	Lougheed Hwy And Ottawa St	Coquitlam Centre	9	1
19	19	18	L1S	Ajax	5.24	6439.1	Harwood Place	Harwood Place	12	1
20			P7B	Thunder Bay	5.13	3195.4	Thunder Bay Power Centre	Intercity Shopping Centre	4	1

* Sales/Location calculated as retail sales in FSA/# of locations in FSA.

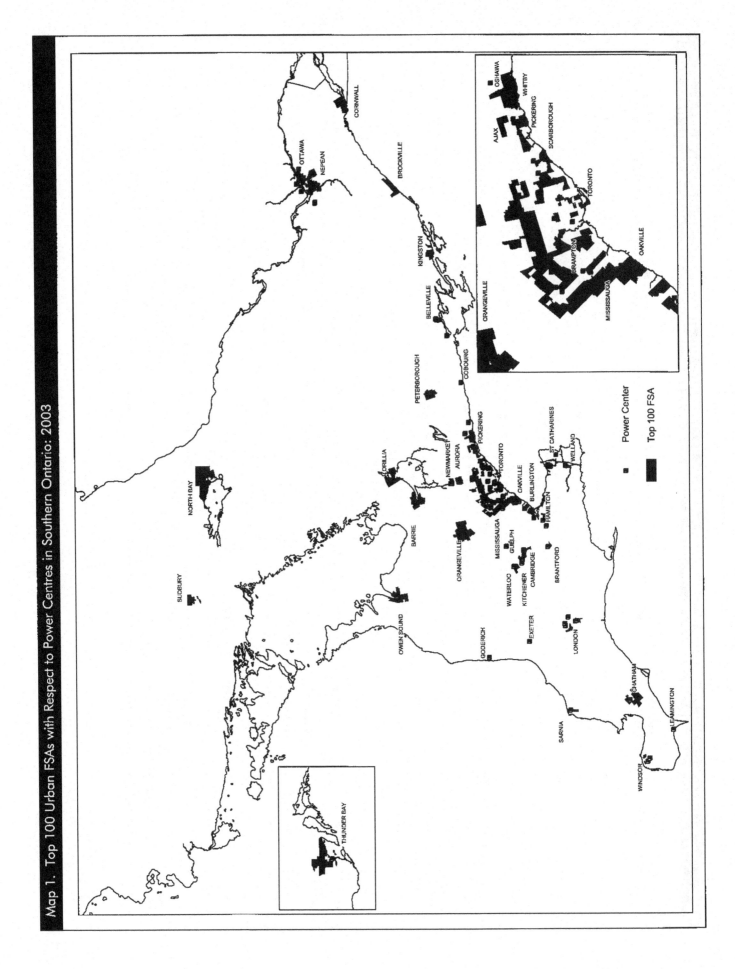

Map 1. Top 100 Urban FSAs with Respect to Power Centres in Southern Ontario: 2003

Power Center

Top 100 FSA

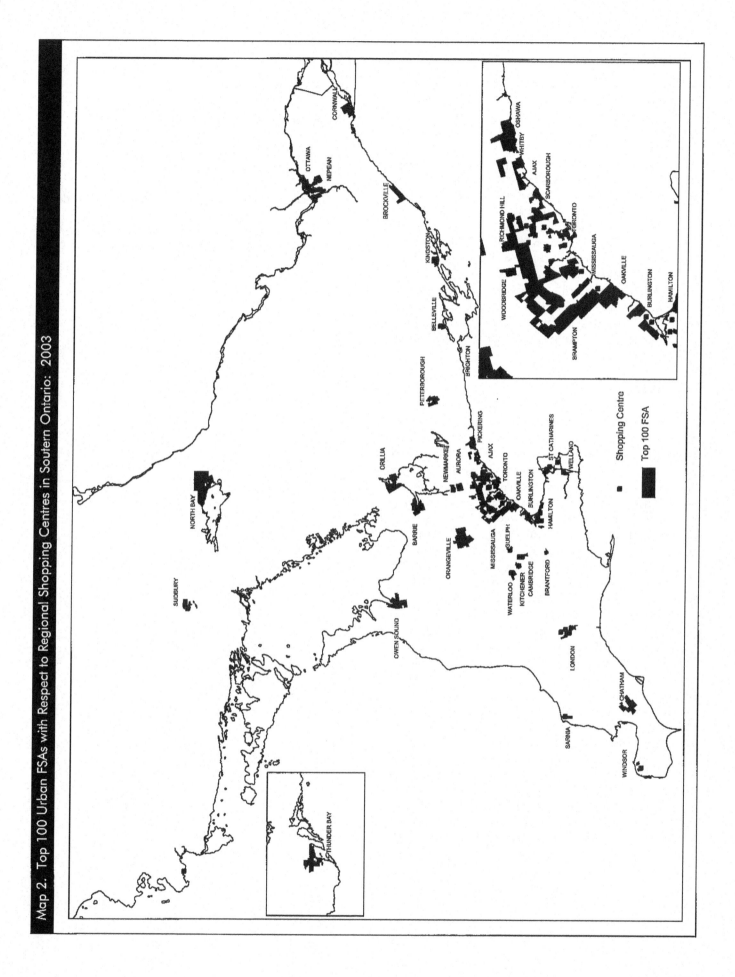

Map 2. Top 100 Urban FSAs with Respect to Regional Shopping Centres in Soutern Ontario: 2003

Shopping Centre

Top 100 FSA

map patterns clearly reflect the major urban concentrations in the province and as expected these are highly correlated with the location of the major regional shopping centres, power centres in the suburbs and downtown cores in the province.

Map 1 shows the association between power centre locations and the Top 100 retail hot spots across southern Ontario. With few exceptions the power centre network and the dominant retail concentrations in the province are closely aligned. Map 2 provides a similar assessment for the major regional shopping centre network (defined as centres in excess of 500,000 square feet). Again, only a few of the retail hot spots are lacking a major mall. In both instances the dominance of the GTA market is illustrated. When compared with previous updates the newly emerging retail markets can be identified - with these markets increasingly characterised with combinations of major mall and power centres. The patterns identified in 2002 remain largely unchanged.

Conclusion

The SARTRE database allows the analysis of yearly sales and location numbers at the FSA level for a variety of retailing designations. If one examines the data spatially and across retail types (e.g., total retail, fashion retail, and general merchandising) a diversity of locations and patterns appear. Even though the absolute sales figures have remained hidden, the set of benchmarks that have been created provide a means of viewing the performance of the Canadian retail economy at a micro-geographic level. The complex nature of the retail system can be clearly identified by such an analysis. As one would expect, there is some obvious stability in the ranking of Canadian retail hot spots. Both total retail sales and fashion hot spots exhibited relatively stability with relatively minor adjustments in the rankings of the Top 10 to 15 positions (with a few exceptions). A steady structural change was found in the general merchandise category that reflects the emergence of the power node concept, combining shopping centres and power centres, as major destinations for non-food and fashion expenditures. The SARTRE data permits the retail analyst to evaluate the pattern of dominant retail locations in Canada at a point in time and to comment on the shifting patterns of retail sales. As of 2003, and in-line with the findings in 2002, the Canadian retail economy was characterized by a mix of major fashion-oriented downtowns, large regional malls and a maturing system of power centres that has now saturated the system. The retail landscape continues to respond quickly to new retail formats and concepts, changes in the distribution of the market, and shifts in consumer preferences.

Summary

This research letter has highlighted:

- the evolving pattern and relative stability of retail concentrations across Canada

- the role of power centres in the suburban retail landscape

- the dominance of retail destinations with combinations of power retail and major mall developments

Chapter 16

CONSUMER BEHAVIOUR AND POWER RETAILING

Brian Lorch

The retail landscape of Canadian cities has been dramatically altered over the past 15 years by the rapid expansion of big box store and power centre developments. Research of this phenomenon has been disproportionately directed towards the supply side of the shopping equation through analysis of aspects such as corporate locational decision-making and tenant mix selection. In this research letter, attention is focused on the demand side of power retail shopping. The letter reports on a case study conducted in Winnipeg that explores dimensions of trips made by residents of a suburban neighbourhood to a nearby power retail node as well opinions held about power retail shopping.

Power Retail: A Different Shopping Experience

The advent of the power centre retailing in Canada in the 1990s offered consumers a radically different type of shopping experience from that of traditional enclosed regional and super-regional shopping centres. A trip to an enclosed centre typically involves parking one's vehicle in a parking lot surrounding the mall, making one's way to the nearest of a limited number of entry points, walking through a climate-controlled pedestrian-dedicated corridor to access a variety of stores. In many regards, the designers of power centres have taken the geography of the mall and turned it inside out. Instead of one centrally-sited structure, power centres utilize a campus style of development that places multiple buildings around the perimeter of the site leaving the interior for parking. To move from one store to another, consumers must go outdoors where a combination of factors such as inclement weather, ready access to vehicles and the sheer distance involved in walking to their next intended destination within the power centre entice shoppers to move about power centres by car rather than by foot.

In this report, the extent to which consumers have embraced this new style of shopping is explored by presenting the results of a case study undertaken in Winnipeg, Manitoba. One objective of the study was to determine how frequently consumers from one residential subdivision made use of a nearby power centre and how they behaved once at the centre.

Another was to gauge how the opening of the power centre had altered their patronage habits with regard to some of Winnipeg's major enclosed shopping centres as well as their general opinions about the type of shopping experience offered by power centres.

Case Study Background

Whyte Ridge is a residential subdivision located in the southwest quadrant of Winnipeg. Lots in the subdivision were first made available in the late 1980s and since then over 2,000 single family homes have been constructed. Table 1 summarizes some of the attributes of area as captured by the 2001 Census. Husband-wife families with children at home predominate. Income levels are also high, the neighbourhood average being $93,000.

Prior to 1999, shopping within close proximity to Whyte Ridge was restricted to a gas station / convenience store and a small un-anchored strip plaza located at the corner of Scurfield and Kenaston Boulevards. To access higher order goods in an enclosed mall environment, residents had three options: Grant Park, St. Vital or Polo Park shopping centres. Distances to these malls ranged from 6.5 to 8.5 kilometers (see Map 1).

In 1999, Wal-Mart was the first store to open in a newly created power centre at the intersection of Kenaston and McGillivray Boulevard directly adjacent to Whyte Ridge.

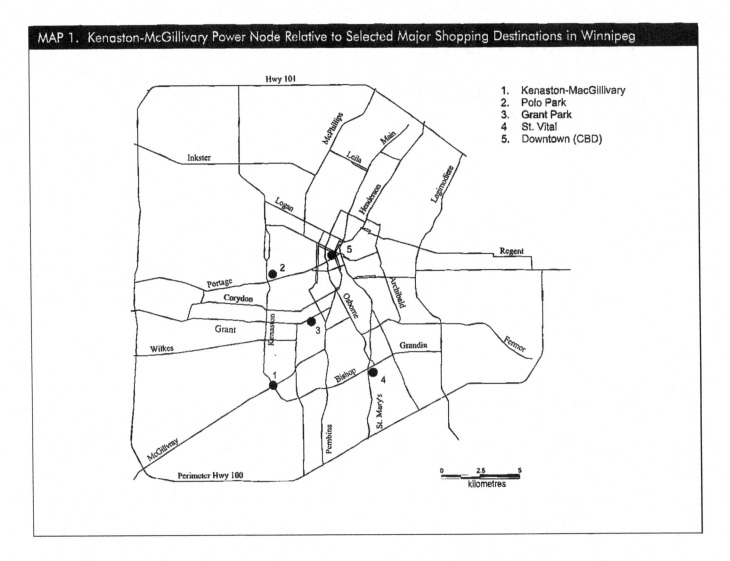

MAP 1.   Kenaston-McGillivary Power Node Relative to Selected Major Shopping Destinations in Winnipeg

1. Kenaston-MacGillivary
2. Polo Park
3. Grant Park
4   St. Vital
5. Downtown (CBD)

Subsequently, an additional 300,000 square feet of retail space has been added to the power centre to house tenants such as Safeway, Home Outfitters, Bombay, Urban Barn, Tommy Hifiger and Home Sense and a Home Depot outlet is currently under construction. Neighbouring properties also now house two planned open air format shopping developments, one anchored by a Canadian Tire and the other by Sobey's. All told, the Kenaston-McGillivray (K-M) node now contains 750,000 square feet of retail space (see Map 2).

In the late Fall, 2003, questionnaires were hand delivered to a systematically selected sample of 400 homes in Whyte Ridge with instructions that the person responsible for most of the household's shopping complete the survey. The questionnaire asked for details of the shopper's most recent trip to the K-M power node and how frequently he / she patronized the power node compared to other shopping destinations. In addition, respondents were asked to indicate their level of agreement with a series of statements reflecting various aspects of shopping within power and enclosed shopping centres. Of the questionnaires returned, 150 were deemed usable for the purposes of the study. Females completed 75% of the surveys.

Two-thirds of the respondents were from double-income households and 56% were from husband-wife families with children at home.

TABLE 1. Profile of Whyte Ridge Subdivision

Population	6,400
Population 65 & over (%)	3.5
Occupied Dwellings	1,950
Owner Occupied (%)	98.5
Census families	1,845
Average children per census family	1.4
Population 20 & over with university degree	35.7
Average household Income ($)	92,350
Females 25 & Over Employed (%)	73.1

Source: 2001 Census of Canada, Census Tract Profile Data

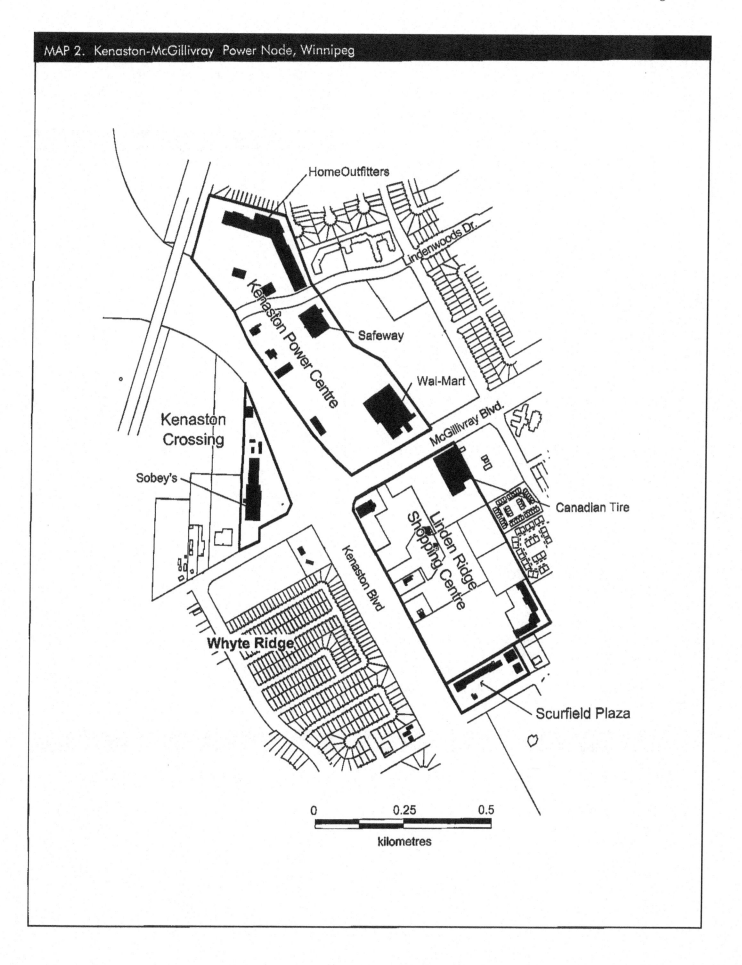

MAP 2.   Kenaston-McGillivray Power Node, Winnipeg

Attributes of a Power Retail Shopping Trip

Table 2 summarizes some of the attributes of the last trip made by respondents to the K-M node. Nearly all trips were made by car and had a specific store or stores as a destination. As with enclosed centres, these destination stores tend to be anchor-type tenants. The draw of Wal-Mart is especially strong as it was named as a destination on over one-half of the surveys. The purposeful nature of most trips is further indicated by relatively low volume of spillover store visits. One-half indicated that they visited no other stores other than the ones they intended to visit before they left on their trip while another one-quarter visited just one additional store. This pattern marks a significant departure from what is hoped for by developers of enclosed centres when they place anchor tenants at opposite ends of a mall to generate traffic through the interior corridor thereby encouraging impulse shopping. At the K-M node, it would appear that many of the smaller stores must rely more on their own ability to generate traffic than rely on spill-over from the big anchors like Wal-Mart. To a degree, this reliance is reflected in the 46 different stores named by respondents as intended destinations.

As anticipated, shoppers frequently use vehicles to move between stores within the power node. Two or more stores were visited on 109 of the trips. Of these, just under 90 percent involved a car being parked more than once. Of all 150 trips analyzed, one-third involved parking a vehicle three or more times.

Frequency of Power Retail Shopping Trips

Table 3 provides a glimpse of how frequently Whyte Ridge residents patronize the K-M node relative to other major shopping destinations in Winnipeg. On the whole, residents appear to be taking advantage of the convenience offered by the K-M node as 95% indicated that they shop there at least once a week. The corollary to this is the large percentage of

respondents who now claim to visit regional shopping nodes such as Polo Park, St. Vital and Grant Park less than once a month when before the development of the K-M node, such malls were prime destinations for Whyte Ridge shoppers.

TABLE 2. Attributes of Most Recent Shopping Trip to KPN	
Travel by car (%)	98.7
Intention to visit specific store (%)	96.0
Number of destination stores named (%)	
one	30.7
two	35.8
three or more	31.8
Most commonly mentioned destination stores (%)	
Wal-Mart	53.4
Sobey's	32.2
Safeway	28.1
Canadian Tire	17.1
Home Outfitters	7.5
Number of additional stores visited (%)	
none	49.7
one	24.8
two or more	25.5
Times vehicle was parked at K-M when two or more stores were visited (%)	
once	11.0
twice	54.1
three or more	34.9
Visits to other shopping districts on same trip (%)	
none	72.7
one	23.3
two or more	4.0
Combined trip to K-M with other activity (%)	
no other activity	12.0
one or more activities	88.0
Activities combined with power centre trip (%)	
a household errand	66.7
journey to/from work	30.6
journey to sports/recreation activity	7.3
Money spent at K-M on this trip ($)	
Average	116
Standard Deviation	91

TABLE 3. Frequency of Shopping Trips to Selected Destinations (%)					
Frequency of Trips	K-M PN	Polo Park	St. Vital Centre	Grant Park	Downtown
2+ times / week	75.8	2.7	5.4	2.0	2.1
1 / week	20.1	6.8	13.5	3.4	2.7
2-3 / month	2.7	16.3	26.4	11.6	3.4
1 / month	1.3	20.4	28.4	17.0	7.5
Less than 1/Month	0.0	32.0	19.6	30.6	8.9
Hardly Ever	0.0	20.4	6.8	33.3	43.2
Never	0.0	1.4	0.0	2.0	32.2

TABLE 4. Anticipated Frequency of Visits to Selected Nodes as the K-M Node Expands (%)

Frequency of Trips	K-M PN	Polo Park	St. Vital Centre	Grant Park	Downtown
No Change	50.7	63.3	65.8	64.9	70.7
Visit Less Often	3.4	27.3	26.2	21.6	21.1
Visit More Often	36.5	0.7	1.3	0.7	0.0
Not sure	9.5	8.7	6.7	12.8	8.2

TABLE 5. Opinions of Respondents about Power Centre and Enclosed Centre Shopping Environments

Behavioural Statement	Disagree or Strongly Disagree	Agree or Strongly Agree	Average Rating [1]
Shopping at a retail area such as K-M is more convenient than shopping at an enclosed mall	33.6	47.6	3.2
When I go to the K-M, I usually have a specific purpose for doing so.	4.7	92.6	4.2
I am just as likely to walk to the K-M as take my automobile	91.3	4.0	1.6
I sometimes go to the K-M to just browse in the stores with no specific purpose in mind	68.0	22.0	2.4
I sometimes go to Polo Park or St. Vital Shopping Centres just to browse in the stores with no specific purpose in mind	33.3	59.3	3.3
Big box stores offer more variety than conventionally-sized stores found in enclosed malls.	34.7	37.0	2.97
Big box stores offer lower prices than smaller stores offering similar merchandise	25.4	34.6	3.06
I get more value for my shopping dollar at big box stores	32.0	25.3	2.87
I get better service at big box stores than I do at smaller stores offering the same merchandise	54.6	4.0	2.32
I don't mind walking outdoors to get from store to store in an open-air shopping mall	40.0	32.7	2.9
The K-M is a safe place for pedestrians	41.6	37.6	2.9
The K-M is more visually appealing than the indoor environment of an enclosed mall such as Polo Park	55.3	11.7	2.4

[1] Respondents rated each opinion on a scale of 1 (strongly disagree) to 5 (strongly agree). The average is the mean score of the ratings on a given statement.

At the time of survey, several new stores had just opened at K-M and others were under construction. With these openings, the K-M node tenant mix acquired a significant focus on fashion and home decor. Given that several stores now duplicate functions as well as banners present at Polo Park and St. Vital the issue of whether K-M will begin to cannibalize sales at these regional centres is raised. Some evidence of this possibility is found in Table 4. About one in three respondents thought the new stores at K-M would increase their frequency of visits to that node while one in four believed they would visit Polo Park and St. Vital less often.

Opinions about Power Retailing

Table 5 provides an overall summary of the respondent's rating of various aspects of the power retail shopping experience. Some of the opinions offered are consistent with actual shopping behaviour. For example, close to one-half agreed that shopping at a power node like K-M is more convenient than going to an enclosed mall and almost all agreed that their trips to K-M usually involve taking a vehicle. Moreover, the low frequency of spill-over purchases observed in actual trip behaviour falls in line with the large majority who stated trips to K-M usually have a specific purpose and the small minority who agreed that they sometimes go to K-M just to browse. The latter is much more associated with the trips to Polo Park and St. Vital.

While Whyte Ridge residents are on the whole pleased by the convenience the K-M development offers, they are not entirely enamoured with the big box store and power centre shopping experience. Only about one-third agreed that big box stores offer more variety than conventional stores found in enclosed malls or that big box stores have lower prices than smaller stores offering similar merchandise while just one in four thought they received more value for their shopping dollar at big box stores. As for the shopping environment itself, only one in ten believed the visual appeal of K-M is superior to that provided by an enclosed mall. That vehicles are often used to move between stores is also consistent with the plurality who don't particularly like having to walk outdoors to reach other stores and perceive that K-M is not a particularly safe place for pedestrians.

Summary

Through a case study of consumers in Winnipeg, the following characteristics of and opinions about power retail shopping have been highlighted:

Trip Characteristics

- a large majority visited a neighbouring power centre on a weekly basis

- most trips had a specific purpose

- the most popular destinations were major anchor tenants

- few trips included visits to stores other than those shoppers intended to visit prior to leaving on the trip

- visits to the power centre are more frequent than to the closest regional indoor malls

- expansion of the power centre's fashion and home decor offerings are likely to reduce the number of trips made to region malls

Opinions

- consumers like the convenience provided by power centre shopping

- big box stores are not perceived by many as having price, variety and value advantages over conventionally-sized stores

- the power centre is not seen as a place to browse

- the power centre environment is not as visually appealing

Future Trend?

- increased consumer demand for more visually appealing and pedestrian-friendly open air format shopping

Chapter 17

LIFESTYLE CENTRES IN CANADA: 2007

Tony Hernandez

The 'lifestyle centre' label is regarded by many practitioners in the retail development and planning industry as an over-used misnomer that is increasingly being adopted to describe a wide range of retail developments. Yet, in spite of such over-use (and some would argue mis-use), the core defining principles of the lifestyle concept are generally agreed to and characterised as a form of open-air retail development that houses a mix of more upscale specialty retail tenants (albeit with many variations on this theme). In the US, lifestyle centres (and their hybrids) have been developed since the late 1980s through to present day. By contrast, the Canadian market has not experienced a parallel growth of the lifestyle concept (as is often the case with US retail innovations). Over the last few years however there have been signs of change in the Canadian marketplace, with a small number of emerging retail development projects being designed with 'lifestyle' components (and in some cases, labeled as 'lifestyle centres'). This research letter aims to provide a context for what may be a changing tide in Canadian retail real estate development. The letter first addresses issues relating to the definition of 'lifestyle centres' then tracks the development of the lifestyle concept in the US. The Canadian experience is then presented, with a number of existing and in-development projects detailed. The letter concludes by discussing the growing trend towards mixed-use and the associated challenges this creates for retail developers in partnering with other property class developers (residential, office, hotel, etc..). As these trends play out, the CSCA will continue to monitor these lifestyle concept developments, and in future studies will report on their impact.

The author would like to thank the industry practitioners (who will remain anonymous) that offered their views and insights on the nature, extent, scale and potential of lifestyle retailing in Canada. Any errors or omissions are, of course, those of the author alone.

Introduction

The lifestyle centre concept, essentially characterized as upscale open-air retail, has been a popular form of development in the US since the late 1980s. As of March 2007, the International Council of Shopping Centres (ICSC) identified approaching 160 lifestyle centres operating in the US, accounting for over 45 million square feet of retail space - with more centres with lifestyle components in the development pipeline (see ICSC (2003) and Chain Store Age (2006) for examples of lifestyle centres in the US). In Canada, during the same period, only a small handful of 'lifestyle' centre type developments have been proposed or are currently under development, and an even smaller number completed (e.g., Park Royal in West Vancouver and Centropolis in Montreal). But, why hasn't the Canadian retail development industry followed the lead from the US? It is often noted that the US and Canada are inextricably linked, with trends (economic, technological, and some would even argue social and cultural) in the US filtering into Canada over a number of years. You only need to look at the profile of the Top

retailers operating in Canada to see that many are head-quartered south of the border (Daniel and Hernandez, 2006). Over the last decade these US retailers pioneered and rolled-out the large-format concept across Canada – fundamentally changing the structure of retailing in Canada. If you track the history of shopping centre growth in the US and Canada, it is relatively straightforward to identify 'shopping development' eras. With the dawning of the shopping centre in the 1950s and 1960s, predominantly plaza and neighbourhood type centres; the widespread development of enclosed regional and super-regional malls from the mid- 1960s to 1980s; to the growth of outlet and power centre formats in the late 1980s and 1990s. While, as one would expect, the scale and extent of retail development in the US has outstripped the Canadian market, the mix of retail has had a certain level of ubiquity. The only significant difference in walking through a super-regional sized mall in the US and Canada would be in the names of the retailers, and not necessarily the variety of stores or overall retail offer (sure enough, there are always Canadian consumers looking for that particular US retailer that you can't find in

Canada, and you may find comparatively more restaurants in the US malls). Certainly, there are types of retail development in the US that have been more widely rolled-out, such as entertainment centres and outlet centres, reflecting scale differences between the US and Canada. The length of development trends has also varied, for example, the continued development of large enclosed malls in the US through the late 1990s to present day (albeit at a reduced rate) versus the virtual moratorium on regional scaled centres in Canada over the same period - with the exception of the opening of Vaughan Mills in 2004 (a 1.2 million square foot enclosed mall), and the in-development projects of Cross Iron Mills in Calgary (www.crossironmills.com) and Lac Mirabel in Montreal (www.lacmirabel.com).

Lifestyle centres represent a point of divergence in what has otherwise been a relatively parallel path of shopping centre development in the US and Canada. Is this simply a case of an extended period of lag in the development process due to a relatively risk-averse (compared to the US) property investment industry in Canada (with the Canadian retail system now at the stage of 'catch-up')? Does the lack of lifestyle centre development in Canada reflect an underlying mismatch between this type of centre and the Canadian marketplace (e.g., the often expressed view that Canada lacks the upscale demographics in the numbers needed to make the lifestyle concept viable). Or, has the lifestyle concept in Canada been eclipsed by the most recent 'mixed-use', 'town center' and other 'hybrid'

developments? Is Canada destined to experience a new wave of lifestyle retail development, as it did with the power centre transformation through the mid-1990s to present-day? Has the rapid rate of power centre growth left any room for 'lifestyle' retail? These key questions among a number of others related to the functional form of lifestyle centres and their potential growth in Canada are discussed in this research letter.

Defining Lifestyle Centres

While definitions vary as to what constitutes a lifestyle centre, they are generally defined on two core attributes: (i) they are **open-air**, at least in part; and (ii) they house **a mix of more upscale retailers and services**. As Terry McEwen, President of Poag and McEwen Lifestyle Centres highlights, *'the real core is based upon having a significant critical mass of the better national specialty stores and restaurants'* (ICSC, 2005, p.1). Table 1 details a number of existing definitions of lifestyle centres. In 2001, the ICSC set up a special committee to look into the issues of defining these centres, leading to a number of position papers (see Baker, 2001, 2002, 2004; Baker and Chapman, 2003; ICSC, 2003, 2005; Powers, 2007; Turbidy and Uiberall, 2004). It is of note that the ICSC has generated both a US and Canadian set of retail development type (RDT) definitions, basically subdividing RDTs into either *mall* or *open-air* categories. While distinctions are made between the US and Canada across many of the subgroup RDTs - the lifestyle centre definitions are identical. As the lifestyle centre concept

Table 1. Definitions of 'Lifestyle Centres'

Lifestyle Centre Definition	Source (Year)
Most often located near affluent residential neighborhoods, this center type caters to the retail needs and "lifestyle" pursuits of consumers in its trading area. It has an open-air configuration and typically includes at least 50,000 square feet of retail space occupied by upscale national chain specialty stores. Other elements differentiate the lifestyle center in its role as a multi-purpose leisure-time destination, including restaurants, entertainment, and design ambience and amenities such as fountains and street furniture that are conducive to casual browsing. These centers may be anchored by one or more conventional or fashion specialty department stores.	ICSC (2007) http://icsc.org/srch/lib/ USDefinitions.pdf
Typically offer open-air, amenity-rich shopping with extensive landscaping, outdoor music playing and convenient parking located close to the stores. They target affluent neighborhoods and include upscale specialty retail, trendy restaurants and theatres or other entertainment features. With a gross leasing area (GLA) ranging between 300,000 and 500,000 square feet, lifestyle centers typically do not include traditional retail anchor stores	Co-Star (2006) (formerly NRB) http://www.costar.com/News/ Advisor/Archive/Article.aspx?id= EC00A7DC785D1AB22C28 E13658A17904
An open-air shopping center offering the finest of national specialty shops and restaurants...a shopping experience geared towards today's busy lifestyle. Easy access, convenient parking, a safe environment, superior architecture, and an inviting atmosphere are some of its features.	Poag and McEwen Lifestyle Centers (2007) http://www.pm-lifestyle.com/ media_center/fact_sheet/ index.html

has evolved, a new class of 'lifestyle mall', essentially spanning both the open-air and mall categories defined by the ICSC, has also become used within the industry (to describe both redevelopment of existing malls and new mall development with lifestyle components). The end result is that despite best efforts to define 'lifestyle centres' there still exists considerably variation in the specific attributes that are required to meet lifestyle centre status. As Gunning (2006, p.60) notes *lifestyle centers do not necessarily subscribe to a prototype for the location they call home, the tenants they house, and the uses they mix*. The difficulty of neatly compartmentalizing retail developments into one type or another is discussed in detail by DeLisle (2005) and Guy (1998).

Within this definitional quagmire it is possible to identify a number of the retailers that have favoured lifestyle-focused developments in the US, these include; in Fashion - Ann Taylor, Banana Republic, Talbots, Victoria's Secrets, Chico's, J.Jill, J. Crew, Coldwater Creek, Coach; in Home Décor & Design – Crate & Barrel, Pottery Barn, Restoration Hardware, Williams Sonoma; and in other sectors; Apple, Barnes & Nobles, Borders, Starbucks, P.F. Chang's, Ben & Jerry's, The Cheesecake Factory and Wholefoods. While this list of tenants (see Table 2) is far from comprehensive it does reflect the types of retailer that have been attracted to lifestyle developments, with the ICSC noting

a tenant mix shift within US lifestyle centres towards more women's fashion and restaurants in recent years (see Powers, 2007). It is also interesting to note how many of these retailers currently operate in both the US and Canada. Of the 64 retailers listed in Table 2, only approximately two-fifths already operate in Canada. The potential development (and ultimate success) of lifestyle developments in Canada will be largely conditioned by the ability to create the 'right' mix of tenants (and uses) to provide the necessary retail, service and 'sense of place' differentiation for consumers to engage with the concept - this may well involve attracting more US and other international retailers to Canada.

Opportunities and Challenges

Despite efforts to pin down the terminology, the 'lifestyle centre' has become a concept that for many practitioners precise definition is not really worth the effort - you somehow know one when you see one. This probably points to the fact that lifestyle centres are about design, ambience, and experience, as much as function or routine (Kim, 2003). So why not in Canada? The points that are most often raised in response to this question include:

Table 2. Selection of Retailers found in Lifestyle Centres in the US (Excluding US Department Stores)				
Sector	**Retailer (✳ already operates in Canada)**	**Sector**	**Retailer (✳ already operates in Canada)**	
Fashion	Abercrombie & Fitch ✳	Home Décor / Design	Bombay Company ✳	
	Aeropostale ✳		Crate & Barrel	
	American Eagle Outfitters ✳		Kirklands	
	Ann Taylor / Ann Taylor Loft		Pier 1 ✳	
	Anthropologie		Pottery Barn ✳	
	Banana Republic ✳		Restoration Hardware ✳	
	Gap / Gap Kids ✳		Smith & Hawken	
	Chico's		Storehouse	
	Coach ✳		Sur La Table	
	Coldwater Creek		Williams Sonoma ✳	
	Eddie Bauer ✳		Z Gallerie	
	Express	Food / Restaurants	Ben & Jerry's ✳	
	Gymboree ✳		Biaggi's	
	Hollister ✳		Bravo / Brio	
	Janie and Jack		California Pizza Kitchen	
	J.Jill		Champps Americana	
	J. Crew		The Cheesecake Factory	
	Joseph A Bank		Cold Stone Creamery	
	Limited Too		Dean & DeLuca	
	Talbots ✳		Johnny Rockets ✳	
	Tommy Bahama ✳		Noodles & Co.	
	Victoria's Secret		On the Border	
	White House / Black Market		Panera Bread	
Other Retail	Apple ✳		P.F. Chang's	
	Bang & Olufsen		Olive Garden ✳	
	Barnes & Nobles		Red Robin ✳	
	Bath and Body Works		Starbucks ✳	
	Borders		Ted's Montana Grill	
	Bose ✳		TGI Fridays ✳	
	The Sharper Image		Wholefoods ✳	
	Yankee Candle		Wild Oats	

(i) the *cold climate* through the long-winter means shoppers will not want to walk around lifestyle streetscapes;

(ii) the *lack of upscale suburban neighbourhoods* (as epitomized by higher-income 'gated' suburban communities foundin the US), and therefore the lack of interest on the part of upscale retailers to enter or expand within the Canadian marketplace, and;

(iii) the comparative *conservatism of Canadian retail development* compared to what takes place south of the border, with a resulting reluctance to enter , into perceived higher risk development (i.e., the inertia associated with navigating unchartered waters).

In answer to the first point re. the climate, over the last fifteen years, Canada has witnessed the widespread growth of open-air retail in the form of highly functional and auto-dependent retail locations - the power centre. The long-standing success of these 'open-to-the-elements' centres probably indicates that Canadian shopper may be somewhat more hardy when it comes to dealing with the cold (frankly, if you live in Canada you are not shocked by the thermometer dipping below the freezing mark). If you look at the evidence from the US you find lifestyle centres located across thenorthern snowbelt region – with design and technology offering shelter-from-the-storm, such as using winterizing sidewalk technology (Chain Store Age, 2007) and building design to shield and shelter consumers from icy wind chills. That said, on certain 'extreme cold alert' days or during and immediately following heavy snowfall, the winter weather will likely present a significant deterrent to even the most ardent shopaholic.

The limited development of lifestyle centres in Canada may have more to do with market fundamentals. Are Canadian consumers simply not discerning enough? Do they need to be educated to become more sophisticated shoppers, as opposed to price-driven consumers? Does Canada simply lack the echelons of middle- to upper-income shoppers? In the major Canadian markets wealth concentrations are often found within existing downtown/inner urban and older suburban areas, e.g., the Rosedale and Forest Hill neighbourhoods of Toronto. These established markets are served with existing retail and service that caters to middle- and upper-income consumers (e.g., Bayview Village, Yorkville/Bloor Street). Unlike the US, Canada has not witnessed the same degree of suburbanization of affluence, instead Canadian suburbs are immersed in the 'middle-ground'. This is not to say that there are not affluent suburban areas in Canada, just that in comparison to the US, the no-brainer markets for lifestyle type developments may be harder to meaningfully identify and thus harder to justify in terms of attracting the right mix of retailers (and developers/investors to the table).

A major theme of research at the CSCA has involved tracking the widespread development, clustering and integration of large format (big box) retailers across Canada (typically within power centre locations). Power retail has dominated the development

of new retail space in Canada over the last decade (Hernandez, Erguden and Svindal, 2007). However, the impetus to develop new alternate types of retail venue has grown as the power centre RDT has entered the mature stage of its lifecycle, and concerns mount over the level of big box retail saturation, consumer fatigue with the concept and the availability of development sites (i.e., that are in the right place for the right cost at the right time– with appropriate planning permissions).

Lifestyle Developments in Canada

With these caveats noted, a straw-poll of industry practitioners identified clear evidence of new forms of retail development with 'lifestyle' components in Canada. For example, *The Village at Park Royal* located adjacent to the Park Royal Regional Shopping Mall on North Shore, Vancouver is marketed as a lifestyle centre. The 238,000 square foot centre houses 33 tenants, with a number of major big box stores including The Home Depot, Urban Barn, Old Navy and Michaels. Opened in the Fall of 2004, it provides a winding streetscape in an architecturally themed coastal environment. Parking is provided directly in front of the stores, and limited to one-hour only along the main street which is lined with trees, street furniture and ornate lighting. Located next to the 1.2 million square foot Park Royal Shopping Mall, one of Canada's first major regional centres developed in the 1950s, the Village at Park Royal provides an up-market unenclosed retail spur to the existing mall, serving the relatively high income demographic of North Shore. *The Shops at Don Mills*, originally developed in the 1950s/60s as a community centre in the suburbs of Toronto, is undergoing a major redevelopment and repositioning with lifestyle components. With construction currently underway, the site will house a mix of retail, residential and office uses planned around a central square, fountain and clock tower. *Centropolis* in Montreal, marketed as an 'open-air commercial village' aims to deliver not only an exclusive fashion shopping experience, but a wide selection of restaurants, bars and other attractions for lively evenings and well-spent leisure time. The centre houses 56 retail tenants with a total retail GLA of just over six hundred thousand square feet. Appendix A lists a selection of other developments in Canada with lifestyle and mixed-use components. Some of these developments are essentially more sophisticated power centres with design features to soften the functional form of the centres (such upgraded power centres have been termed 'Power Plus Centres' (Field, 2007) and 'Omni-Centres' (Hazel, 2005)), e.g., they incorporate 'Main Streets' and winding retail strips, tree-lined walkways between parking lots, along with the addition of street-furniture and design elements to promote pedestrian flows (Field, 2005). A number are best described as major renovations and re-positioning or re-badging of existing retail space, with the addition of new lifestyle-focused space to existing sites. Others resemble more mixed-use developments with integrated retail, office, hotel and residential uses.

Retail in the Mix

The bottom-line is that the potential for widespread development of 'traditional' lifestyle centres, in a similar fashion as to what has occurred in the US, is unlikely within Canada. As opposed to a game of catch-up, the existing evidence points towards a future that will see more varied development utilising lifestyle components: redevelopment of existing retail venues with lifestyle components (particularly older malls); the evolution of power centres with increased design ambience; and, the move towards mixed-use developments where developers that are well-versed in building retail, office and residential will join forces to create entire new communities with integrated retail. As the ICSC broadly define: *'mixed-use development is a real estate project with planned integration of some combination of retail, office, residential, hotel, recreation or other functions. It is pedestrian-oriented and contains elements of a live-work-play environment. It maximizes space usage, has amenities and architectural expression and tends to mitigate traffic and sprawl'* (http://icsc.org/srch/lib/Mixed-use_Definition.pdf). Many of these new urbanist developments (often part of master-planned communities) are being labelled as 'Urban Villages', 'Town Centers', 'Town Squares' and 'Main Streets'. With smart growth the prevailing wisdom in planning circles in Canada, the mixing of uses (including retail) and the remit to intensify land-uses and increase urban density (reducing sprawl) will likely result in more of these types of mixed-use development being proposed and ultimately built-out across urban Canada.

Regardless of the terminology used, market fundamentals will drive these changes – that is, the strength of the Canadian economy (including the propensity for risk-taking within the retail development/ property investment industry) along with the demographic composition of the country. With a large cohort of aging baby-boomers (some affluent) moving their way up the age pyramid, the opportunities for niche lifestyle developments catering to the more senior consumer will become more viable; and conversely, the mass middle-ground consumer may start to expect more from their shopping experience, beyond the sterile functionality offered by traditional power centres. Through the CSCA's annual field survey of power centres across Canada, it is becoming increasingly apparent that a number of existing power centres are now developing fashion-focused extensions and the new power centres under development are incorporating more fashion and restaurants than in the past, for example, Mega Centre Notre-Dame in Laval, Carrefour De La Rive Sud in Boucherville, and Marche Central in Montreal. As these changes take place it will be increasingly difficult to pigeon-hole retail developments into neatly arranged compartments, the boundaries between RDTs will become increasingly fuzzy. As Terry McEwen points out *'the lines are becoming a little blurry as strip centers and malls are taking on some of the characteristics of a lifestyle center. It seems that everyone is calling their center a lifestyle center today when formerly many would have been called a 'mall without a roof' or a*

'strip center with higher-quality architecture" (ICSC, 2005, p.1). With the integration and morphing of lifestyle components across mixed-use, power centre, major mall, downtown and suburban strip developments the new breed of retail locations are likely to be some form of hybrid. As Fickes (2007,p.135) notes: *'the lifestyle concept has blossomed into something much larger than a shopping center format. It has become a vehicle that has freed developers from the constraints of traditional formats and enabled them to tailor a design to the style, architecture and retail needs of individual communities'.* This flexibility in design will provide the development industry with a multitude of strategic and operational opportunities and challenges – and present retailers with an even more complex environment in which to make their location decisions.

Summary

This research letter has highlighted:

- the core defining elements of lifestyle centres

- the widespread development of lifestyle centres in the US, during a period in which power retail development dominated the construction of new retail space in Canada

- the emergence of retail developments in Canada with 'lifestyle' components

- the movement toward mixed-use developments (increasing interest in integrating retail with residential)

- the difficulty in compartmentalizing retail into neatly defined categories, essentially the boundaries between development types are becoming more blurred

- the jury remains out on the scale, extent and potential for 'traditional' lifestyle centre development in Canada (i.e., following the early lifestyle model in US)

- the Canadian variant of the lifestyle-focused retail development is a format in the making, and will likely include a mix of redeveloping existing properties (e.g., upgrading of power centres, re-positioning and renovations of malls, along with main street initiatives) and new developments (e.g., lifestyle components within mixed-use developments, lifestyle-power centre hybrids, smaller niche lifestyle centres in selected markets)

References

Baker, M. (2001) 'Lifestyle Centers – A Defining Moment', *ICSC Research Review*, 8(4), pp 1-6, International Council of Shopping Centers, New York.

Baker, M. (2002) 'Lifestyle Centers Part II: The Shopper's Verdict', *ICSC Research Review*, 9(4), pp 1-7, International Council of Shopping Centers, New York.

Baker, M. and Chapman, J. (2003) *Lifestyle Centers: An ICSC Consumer Research Report*, International Council of Shopping Centers, New York.

Baker, M. (2004) 'Lifestyle Centers – What's New in Development and Performance', *ICSC Research Review*, 10(4), pp 1-5, International Council of Shopping Centers, New York.

Chain Store Age (2006) 'Project Profiles: Fifteen Fabulous Lifestyle Centres', *Chain Store Age*, April, pp. 109-118.

Chain Store Age (2007) 'Winterizing the Walkways: A Snow-Melting System Keeps Sidewalks Clear', *Chain Store Age*, July, pp. 107-108.

Daniel, C. and Hernandez, T. (2006) 'Canada's Leading Retailers: 4th Edition', *CSCA Research Report 2006-10*, Centre for the Study of Commercial Activity, Ryerson University, Toronto.

DeLisle, J.R. (2005) *Shopping Center Classifications: Challenges and Opportunities*, ICSC Working Paper Series, International Council of Shopping Centers, New York.

Fickes, M. (2007) 'Everything's Coming Up Lifestyle: Extending the Wildy Successful Lifestyle Center Concept', *Chain Store Age*, March, pp. 130-135.

Field, K. (2005) 'Hybrid Hype: Mix-and-Match Retail Destinations Merge Big Box and Lifestyle to Drive Traffic', *Chain Store Age*, July, pp. 125-128.

Field, K. (2007) 'Power-Plus: A New-and-Improved Power Center Adds More Amenities to the Mix', *Chain Store Age*, April, p. 80.

Gunning, J. (2006) 'The Life in Lifestyle Centers', *Urban Land*, August, pp. 58-64.

Guy, C. (1998) 'Classifications of Retail Stores and Shopping Centres: Some Methodological Issues', *Geojournal*, 45(255-264).

Hazel, D. (2005) 'Three in One: Omnicenters Blend Aspects of Malls and Power and Lifestyle Centers', *Shopping Centers Today*, March, International Council of Shopping Centers, New York.

Hernandez, T., Erguden, T. and Svindal, M. (2007) 'Power Retail Growth in Canada and the GTA: 2006', *CSCA Research Letter 2007-06*, Centre for the Study of Commercial Activity, Ryerson University, Toronto.

ICSC (2003) *Leisure and Lifestyle Retailing*, International Council of Shopping Centers, New York.

ICSC (2005) 'At the Center of Lifestyle Centers', *ICSC Research Review*, 12(1), pp 1-3, International Council of Shopping Centers, New York.

Powers, H.E. (2007) 'The Remaking of Lifestyle Center: The Ascendency of Women's Apparel and Restaurants', *ICSC Research Review*, 14(3), pp 12-15, International Council of Shopping Centers, New York.

Turbidy, M. and Uiberall, J. (2004) 'Lifestyle Center Tenant Space Allocation: a Look Inside the Tenant Mix of Lifestyle Centers', *ICSC Research Review*, 11(2), pp 1-6, International Council of Shopping Centers, New York.

Kim Y.K., Sullivan, P., Trotter, C. and Forney, J. (2003) 'Lifestyle Shopping Center: A Retail Evolution of the 21st Century', *Journal of Shopping Center Research*, 10(2), pp. 61-94, International Council of Shopping Centers, New York.

Appendix A. Selection of Canadian Retail Developments with 'Lifestyle' and/or 'Mixed-Use' Components
(collated from public domain information on company web sites and site/leasing plans)

Project:	**The Village at Park Royal**
Location:	Vancouver, British Columbia
Uses:	RETAIL
Retail Sq. Ft. (No. of Retail Units):	238,000 (33)
Major Retail Tenants:	Home Depot, Whole Foods, Michaels, Homesense, Old Navy
Developer/s:	Larco Investments Ltd.
Developer Status:	Completed 2004
Web Link:	http://www.shopparkroyal.com/thevillage/index.php

Description (abridged from developer, architect, constructor, press release/media):

The Village at Park Royal is located on an 18-acre parcel adjacent to West Vancouver's Park Royal Shopping Centre. Planned by F&A Architects of California and Musson Cattell Mackey Partnership, the development is a complex of nine distinct buildings ranging in size from 9,600 to 72,000 sq. ft. The Village is pedestrian friendly featuring a "Main Street", front-of-store parking and wide landscaped sidewalks. The architecture of the Village is designed to honour the cultural history of the Westcoast and recall the turn of the century fishing villages that dotted the shores of BC's coastline. (http://www.mcmparchitects.com/retail.cfm?ProjectID=133)

Project:	**Centropolis**
Location:	Laval, Quebec
Uses (Planned Uses):	RETAIL, ENTERTAINMENT, OFFICE (HOTEL)
Retail Sq. Ft. (No. of Retail Units):	612,756 (56)
Major Retail Tenants:	Colosus, La Cordee, Arte Pelle Inc., Energie Cardio, Bernard Trottier Sports, SAQ Selection, Clement + Mad Max + Mady
Developer/s:	Ivanhoe-Cambridge
Developer Status:	Part Completed (Opened 2000)
Web Link:	http://www.centropolis.ca/

Description (abridged from developer, architect, constructor, press release/media):

An immense lifestyle centre, Centropolis is the hub for several banners with innovative and attractive concepts. It is located in downtown Laval, on one of its most strategic sites just off the Laurentian Autoroute, and near several major thoroughfares. Since it was first opened, this city within a city continues to welcome prestigious tenants such as Colossus Famous Players, La Cordée and L'Académie. A new development phase provided for the addition of retail and office space particularly around the central place, on la Promenade. Furthermore, depending on the season, a beautiful skating rink and fountain can be found at the central place. An open air-commercial village, with retail, entertainment, office and planned hotel uses. (http://www2.icleasing.ca/EN/PropertyProfile.aspx?PropertyID=8)

Project:	**Faubourg Boisbriand**
Location:	Montreal, Quebec
Uses (Planned Uses):	RETAIL (RESIDENTIAL, OFFICE)
Retail Sq. Ft. (No. of Retail Units):	550,000 (22)
Major Retail Tenants:	Costco, Toys R Us, JYSK, Golf Town, Zellers, The Brick, HomeSense, Bureau en Gros, Deco Decouverte
Developer/s:	Cherokee Investment Partners, Kimco Realty Corporation, North American, Sterling Centrecorp
Developer Status:	Part Completed (Opened 2006)
Web Link:	http://www.faubourgboisbriand.com/index_flash_e.html

Description (abridged from developer, architect, constructor, press release/media):

Faubourg Boisbriand – an integrated community. Its residential sector, commercial shopping area and business park offer a lifestyle where anything and everything is possible; a place to live, work, shop and also enjoy leisure time. As a brownfield redevelopment, Faubourg Boisbriand is a harmonious blend of architecture and urban development, in a spacious area with a lake, walking trails and bicycle paths. The Big Box retail store outlets are close at hand and the Village (opening August 2008) offers restaurants, boutiques and other services in a friendly, pedestrian-friendly atmosphere. Faubourg Boisbriand provides a lifestyle for people of all ages. The development consists of townhouses, triplexes, condos, apartments and seniors' residences. (http://www.faubourgboisbriand.com/index_flash_e.html)

Project:	**Dartmouth Crossing**
Location:	Halifax, Nova Scotia
Uses (Planned Uses):	RETAIL, ENTERTAINMENT (OFFICE, HOTEL)
Retail Sq. Ft. (No. of Retail Units):	600,000 (35) (as of August 2007)
Major Retail Tenants:	Wal-Mart, Canadian Tire, Home Depot, Best Buy, Home Outfiters, JYSK, Linens 'n Things
Developer/s:	North American
Developer Status:	Part Completed (Opened 2007)
Web Link:	http://www.dartmouthcrossing.com/

Description (abridged from developer, architect, constructor, press release/media):

Halifax's newest and most anticipated retail and commercial development is here. Dartmouth Crossing is a destination unlike any other in the region. It brings together the best elements of any shopping experience. A prime location that offers consumers value and convenience in an exciting and unique environment. Shopping comes to life like never before at Dartmouth Crossing. Major growth potential in a major market. Phase One of Dartmouth Crossing offers 220 acres and 1.6 million square feet of retail and commercial space and will be one of the region's premiere shopping locations. It serves a broad market comprised of a large population of daily commuters from Halifax, tourists and visitors from across the Maritimes. Dartmouth Crossing features the value of large and mid-size retail, the intimacy of village-style shops and boutiques and the convenience of such amenities as restaurants, future hotels and theatres. It's a complete shopping destination with something for everyone. (http://www.dartmouthcrossing.com/development/)

Project:	**Carrefour Champêtre**
Location:	Bromont, Quebec
Uses (Planned Uses):	RETAIL
Retail Sq. Ft. (No. of Retail Units):	180,000 (~20)
Major Retail Tenants:	Mix of Fashion Retail & Restaurant
Developer/s:	Devimco
Developer Status:	Part Completed (Opened 2007)
Web Link:	http://www.carrefourchampetrebromont.com/

Description (abridged from developer, architect, constructor, press release/media):

Le Carrefour Champêtre will reconstitute a traditional village of the Eastern Townships. The architecture of each building will respect the forms and details of the past, namely the City Hall, the Bank, the General Store or Post Office. The layout of the stores will include a Town Square with parking on sides, public gazebos and benches. Located in Bromont, Le Carrefour Champêtre is 45 minutes south of Montreal on Hwy. #10, in the Eastern Townships, Quebec's summer and winter playground. The economic growth in Bromont is impressive. The population within a 30 minute drive is over 210,000 and there are 167,000 visitors from the U.S. which is only a 20 minute drive from the Vermont border. There has been a substantial increase in all the activities related to tourism, residential development and commercial business. There are currently three residential projects under development all on Mont Brome and a hotel and residential condominium are adjacent to the site. (http://www.marino.ca/active.htm)

Project:	**Deerfoot Meadows**
Location:	Calgary, Alberta
Uses (Planned Uses):	RETAIL, ENTERTAINMENT (HOTEL, RESIDENTIAL)
Retail Sq. Ft. (No. of Retail Units):	~1,000,000 [~2,250,000 when built out](Not listed)
Major Retail Tenants:	Ikea, Real Canadian Superstore, (Wal-Mart)
Developer/s:	Heritage Partners Limited Partnership
Developer Status:	Part Completed (first big box stores opened in 2005)
Web Link:	http://www.deerfootmeadows.com/

Description (abridged from developer, architect, constructor, press release/media):

The 360-acre Deerfoot Meadows is the largest infill retail project in North America surrounded by affluent residences at the nexus of two of Western Canada's largest freeways. Heritage Partners' $80 million freeway interchange development investment taps into these conduits. The Deerfoot Meadows project currently draws more than 60,000 visitors per day to more than 1.7 million sq. ft. of existing big box retailers.. The project is consists of a number of components; big-box/power centre, 'Meadows Collection' - a proposed 500,000 sq. ft. urban lifestyle village, a luxury auto mall, and 'The Bluffs' (residential and retail community). (http://www.deerfootmeadows.com/Corporate/Site1/)

Project:	**Quartier/DIX30**
Location:	Brossard, Quebec
Uses (Planned Uses):	RETAIL, ENTERTAINMENT, HOTEL (RESIDENTIAL)
Retail Sq. Ft. (No. of Retail Units):	1,930,000 (~200+)
Major Retail Tenants:	Future Shop, Winners, Homesense, Urban Planet, Business en Gros, JYSK, Indigo, Rona
Developer/s:	Devimco
Developer Status:	Part Completed (Phase I - Opened 2006)
Web Link:	http://www.quartierdix30.com/

Description (abridged from developer, architect, constructor, press release/media):

A spectacular new urban lifestyle centre located at the intesection of Highway 10 and Highway 30
Upon completion, the centre will comprise of over 1.9 million square feet of retail space and boast over 200 stores and services. This centre will be home to a variety of anchors including Maxi, RONA (both retailer owned), Canadian Tire, Cineplex Odeon, Winners, HomeSense, Staples/Business Depot and Indigo as well as Hotel Alt, an avant grande boutique hotel designed by the Germain Group, a 900-seat live theatre and concert hall, a spa and a gym. (https://riocan.com/property/property.cfm?property_id=199)

Project:	**The Shops at Don Mills**
Location:	Toronto, Ontario
Uses (Planned Uses):	(RETAIL, RESIDENTIAL, OFFICE)
Retail Sq. Ft. (No. of Retail Units):	450,000 (Not listed)
Major Retail Tenants:	Not listed
Developer/s:	Cadillac-Fairview
Developer Status:	Under Construction (Phase 1 – Retail projected to open Autumn 2008)
Web Link:	http://www.shopsatdonmills.ca/

Description (abridged from developer, architect, constructor, press release/media):

A new urban village is being created in the heart of Don Mills . An open-air neighbourhood setting where thousands will choose to live, work, play and shop just minutes away from one of Toronto's most affluent neighbourhoods. Shops at Don Mills will combine more than 450,000 GLA of premium national retailers and local merchants on 30 acres of land, tied together by office buildings, pedestrian-friendly streets and a central town square. Up to 1,200 condominiums will be built on an additional 8.5 acres to seamlessly fit within this urban community. Shops at Don Mills will create a revitalized shopping destination that includes a central square, a fountain and clock tower surrounded by retail, residential and office space. There is also a planned parkade that will ultimately accommodate over 1,300 vehicles. The first phase - retail lifestyle centre, the second - addition of residential units. Our long term vision is to recreate Shops at Don Mills as a truly integral part of the community. The new lifestyle centre will be an open-air concept with the goal of providing unique one-of-a-kind experiences.(http://www.cfspace.com/notesdata/leasing/cf_space.nsf/PropInfoFlash!OpenForm&ID=DONNEW8)

Project:	**Park Place**
Location:	Barrie, Ontario
Uses (Planned Uses):	(RETAIL, ENTERTAINMENT, HOTEL, OFFICE)
Retail Sq. Ft. (No. of Retail Units):	880,730 (Not listed)
Major Retail Tenants:	Not listed
Developer/s:	North American
Developer Status:	Planning / Under Construction – Phase 1 completion by 2009, build-out by 2012
Web Link:	http://www.parkplacebarrie.com/

Description (abridged from developer, architect, constructor, press release/media):

Park Place will be unlike anything Ontario has seen before. It is a up-scale, attractive development with a wide range of amenities and features. There is something for everyone at Park Place. The Retail Village is beautifully landscaped, featuring water fountains choreographed to music, an outdoor fireplace and attractive pedestrian- friendly streetscapes. Visitors to the village will enjoy up-scale retail shopping, fashionable restaurants, hotels and trendy bars with stylish outdoor patios, and additional attractions, such as a fitness centre and spa, a comedy club, children's entertainment, live and film theatre, and much more. Second floor medical/professional office space will have a balcony view of the main street. People will enjoy the nature paths that wind through Barrie's largest new park. Space has been offered for a south-central library branch and bus depot – a great location for both of these amenities. Plans are being made for a shuttle service to introduce visitors to downtown Barrie. A campus-like, prestige business park for corporate head offices is also part of the plan. This development will enhance retail and business offerings for the entire community. (http://www.parkplacebarrie.com/html/life-features.html)

Project:	**Windermere**
Location:	Edmonton, Alberta
Uses (Planned Uses):	(RETAIL, ENTERTAINMENT, HOTEL, RESIDENTIAL)
Retail Sq. Ft. (No. of Retail Units):	Not listed
Major Retail Tenants:	Not listed
Developer/s:	Windermere Commercial Lands Ltd.
Developer Status:	Planning / Under Construction
Web Link:	http://www.windermereedmonton.com/

Description (abridged from developer, architect, constructor, press release/media):

Putting a little city in the suburbs. Revolutionary design incorporating residential, hotel, retail and entertainment facilities in a master planned concept. Will encompass one million leasable square feet of comprehensive commercial development on 111 acres in Edmonton's fastest growing market. Ideal access directly off major ring road. Adjacent to 500+ acres of prime residential land which is now under construction and will house over 60,000 additional people at full build-out in 2010. Windermere Edmonton is a master planned urban village community that is assembled, designed, zoned and built from the ground up. Featuring a total land assembly of over 650 acres (117+ acres commercial, 533+ acres residential) nestled in the Southwest corner of Edmonton, Alberta. Big box retail perimeter around an urban village core.(http://www.windermereedmonton.com/content/view/26/38/)

Project:	**Morgan Crossing**
Location:	Surrey, British Columbia
Uses (Planned Uses):	(RETAIL, RESIDENTIAL)
Retail Sq. Ft. (No. of Retail Units):	450,000 (~50+)
Major Retail Tenants:	Not listed
Developer/s:	Larco Investments Ltd.
Developer Status:	Planning
Web Link:	http://www.morgancrossing.ca/

Description (abridged from developer, architect, constructor, press release/media):

Experience the main street promenade in this vibrant town centre with intimate public squares, plazas and gathering places. Everyday shopping becomes a pleasant part of your daily routine at Morgan Crossing. With over 50 fashion, grocery, houseware and electronics shops, as well as essential services like banking, aesthetics, medical and dental care just a few minutes stroll from any of the charming residences, Morgan Crossing truly does have it all! British Columbia's newest, most sophisticated lifestyle environment, will offer offer approximately 450,000 sq. ft. of retail space and 400,000 sq. ft. of residential space. (http://www.morgancrossing.ca/[click on Shop])

Project:	**The Village**
Location:	Surrey, British Columbia
Uses (Planned Uses):	(RETAIL, RESIDENTIAL)
Retail Sq. Ft. (No. of Retail Units):	500,000
Major Retail Tenants:	Not listed
Developer/s:	Grosvenor
Developer Status:	Planning
Web Link:	http://www.grosvenor.com/Portfolio/The+Village.htm

Description (abridged from developer, architect, constructor, press release/media):

The Village is a proposed projected located at 32nd Avenue and 152nd Street in South Surrey, BC. The vision behind The Village will be an attractive place to live, shop and socialize in the heart of Rosemary Heights in South Surrey. It will provide an aesthetically pleasing environment that embraces the principles of sustainability and smart growth. The Village will consist of street-front retail along with approximately 400 condominium homes located above and around the retail mix. (http://www.grosvenor.com/Portfolio/The+Village.htm)

Project: **Lac Mirabel**
Location: Montreal, Quebec
Uses (Planned Uses):   (RETAIL, RESIDENTIAL, ENTERTAINMENT, HOTEL)
Retail Sq. Ft. (No. of Retail Units):   ~2,600,000 (~300)
Major Retail Tenants: Cabela, Others not listed
Developer/s: Gordon Group Holdings
Developer Status: Planning / Under Construction (Opening planned for 2009)
Web Link: http://www.lacmirabel.com/

Description (abridged from developer, architect, constructor, press release/media):

Introducing Lac Mirabel, designed to be the first true "green retail destination" in Canada. Lac Mirabel is a state-of-the-art retail-shopping complex constructed in harmony with its surrounding, creating a retail destination of a new generation. Located off of Highway 15, Lac Mirabel will be the first newly developed indoor/outdoor retail entertainment destination in over 25 years in Quebec. Anchored by Cabela's, the World's Foremost Outfitter of Outdoor Gear, this 14 Million Square Foot mixed use property will offer an unsurpassed selection of the world's finest regional and specialty retailers, restaurants, a European-inspired spa, luxury hotels and a multi-sports complex. (http://www.lacmirabel.com/home.php?language=en)

Project: **The Commons at Niagara on the Green**
Location: Niagara, Ontario
Uses (Planned Uses):   (RETAIL, ENTERTAINMENT, HOTEL, RESIDENTIAL, OFFICE)
Retail Sq. Ft. (No. of Retail Units):   720,350
Major Retail Tenants: Not Listed
Developer/s: First Gulf Corporation
Developer Status: Planning (Construction in 2009)
Web Link: http://www.firstgulf.com/development/niagara.php

Description (abridged from developer, architect, constructor, press release/media):

Shoppers and tourists will soon have a new destination to visit. The Commons at Niagara on the Green located in charming Niagara on the Lake will be a regional shopping destination. The Commons has the distinction of being one of Ontario's first mixed use developments. The 75 acre site will boast over 700,000 sq.ft. of retail, residential and office space with construction slated to begin in 2009. The picturesque Niagara Region will provide a most attractive back drop for The Commons, making location and draw to both Canadian and American shoppers. The beautiful setting is in addition to the many desirable shops and services that will open their doors in this lifestyle shopping and entertainment destination. The Commons will offer a viable alternative to those that make the trip to Buffalo to visit unique stores and to seek one of a kind deals; doing away with the inconvenience of border crossing, while encouraging shoppers to spend their money in Ontario. Hotel and other entertainment venues scheduled to open on site.
(http://www.firstgulf.com/development/niagara.php)

Project: **Town & Country**
Location: Saanich, British Columbia
Uses (Planned Uses):   (RETAIL, RESIDENTIAL, OFFICE)
Retail Sq. Ft. (No. of Retail Units):   683,941
Major Retail Tenants: Wal-Mart, Others not listed
Developer/s: Morguard
Developer Status: Planning
Web Link: http://www.morguard.com/portal/portfolio.cfm?
                                            fuseaction=property.portfolioFacts&property_PK=711

Description (abridged from developer, architect, constructor, press release/media):

Town & Country Shopping Centre is a single level, strip retail shopping centre located in Saanich, a suburb of Victoria, British Columbia. The Centre was constructed in 1961 and is anchored by Wal-Mart. Plans for the redevelopment include a mixed-use lifestyle centre comprised of approximately 700,000 s.f. of retail and office plus approximately 500,000 s.f. of residential to be built on air space parcels to be sold to a residential developer.
(http://www.morguard.com/portal/portfolio.cfm?fuseaction=property.portfolioFacts&property_PK=711)

Chapter 18

SOME DATA AND OBSERVATIONS ON THE DIGITAL DIVIDE AND INTERNET SHOPPING

Stephen Swales

Internet access and use of it for online shopping have grown rapidly in recent years but it is evident that a digital divide remains. The use of the Internet in general, and for online shopping in particular, varies significantly by demographic composition and region. Furthermore, some types or goods and services are much more likely to be purchased online than others. Although online purchases are growing quickly barriers remain and online shopping remains a tiny proportion of total expenditures.

These ideas are explored in some of the data and observations below.

The Digital Divide

Despite early optimistic statements, access to the Internet shows remarkable variations by income, education, employment, age and ethnicity. Consider the relatively early data on the digital divide for the US in the table below.

In 2000, to be well-educated, employed, of high income, relatively young and white (or Asian American) meant to have relatively high access to the Internet.

To be poor, of limited education, unemployed, old and African American (or Hispanic) meant to have low levels of access to the Internet.

Some Digital Divide Data for the USA (all data are for August 2000)

POPULATION CHARACTERISTIC	% INTERNET ACCESS (Home or work. 51% of households had computers at home)
All Households	41.5
All Individuals (all following are for individuals)	44.4
Income	
>$75,000	70
<$15,000	18.9
$15,000–24,999	18.4
25,000–34,999	25.3
Education	
Bachelor's degree or higher	74.5
High school graduate	30.6
Not graduated high school	21.7
Employed	56.7
Unemployed	29
Age	
50 yrs +	29.6
25–49	55.4
18–24	56.8
9–17	53.4
Ethnic	
White	50.3
Asian Americans	49.4
African Americans	29.3
Hispanic	23.7

(Source: M. Castells, 2001 *The Internet Galaxy,* Oxford: Oxford. Based on a survey conducted by the US Commerce Department's National Telecommunications and Information Administration)

Canadian Internet experience has similarities. In 2004 approximately 68% of households had regular access to the Internet up from 51% in 2000.

Accessibility in 2000 varied as follows:

Canadian Internet Access, 2000

Higher Internet Access	Lower Internet Access
High Income	Low Income
Young	Old
Families with Children	Families Without Children
University Degree	Less than High School
Urban	Rural

Source: Statistics Canada, Catalogue no. 56F0009XIE

Women also had slightly lower levels of Internet access than men. More notably, females had different intensity of use and reasons for use.

Regional Variation in Internet Access in Canada

More recent data, for large cities, small towns and rural areas are shown in the table below. The source of data for the following tables is the Canadian Internet Use Survey (CIUS) conducted regularly by Statistics Canada. Note that the larger cities tend to have higher Internet access than "other urban areas" and substantially higher levels than "rural and small town areas".

Percent of adult Canadians using Internet during 2005	
	%
Halifax	75
Montréal	68
Ottawa–Gatineau	77
Toronto	75
Winnipeg	70
Calgary	77
Edmonton	69
Vancouver	71
Other urban areas	68
Rural and small town areas	58

Source: http://www.statcan.ca/Daily/English/060815/d060815b.htm

Reasons for Internet Use

Note that in the table below communication and information collection type uses predominate. Also note that "Window shopping" (57%) is more significant than "Ordering personal goods or services" (43%).

Reasons for adult home users to go on-line during 2005 (Canada)	
	%
E-mail	91
General browsing	84
Weather or road conditions	67
Travel information or making travel arrangements	63
View news or sports	62
Search for medical or health related information	58
Electronic banking	58
Window shopping	57
Pay bills	55
Search for information about governments	52
Ordering personal goods or services	43
Education, training or school work	43
Research community events	42
Play games	39
Chat or to use a messenger	38

Obtain or save music (free or paid downloads)	37
Obtain or save software (free or paid downloads)	32
Research investments	26
Listen to the radio over the Internet	26
Communicate with governments	23
Download or watch TV or a movie over the Internet	12
Any other personal non-business reason	11

Source: http://www.statcan.ca/Daily/English/060815/d060815b.htm

Characteristics of Internet Users, Canada, 2005

The following table shows variation in Internet use for people 18 years and over in Canada for 2005. It is evident that some of the patterns observed in the 2000 data above persist. Internet use clearly varies by age, education and income. Presence of children in the household is also important. The patterns are discussed in the box following the table.

Characteristics of individuals using the Internet in Canada 2005		
	Location of Internet access	
	Any location[1]	**Home**
	% of all individuals aged 18 years and over[2]	
All Internet users	67.9	60.9
Household type		
Single family households with unmarried children under age 18	80.9	74.1
Single family households without unmarried children under age 18	62.5	56.9
One-person households	48.7	38.2
Multi-family households	78.8	67.5
Sex		
Males	68.0	61.5
Females	67.8	60.3
Age		
18 to 34 years	88.9	77.3
35 to 54 years	75.0	68.3
55 to 64 years	53.8	49.3
65 years and over	23.8	22.5
Level of education		
Less than high school	31.2	26.5
High school or college	72.0	63.9
University degree	89.4	83.4
Personal income quartile[3]		
Lowest quartile	58.7	52.3
Second quartile	56.9	50.2
Third quartile	71.3	63.4
Highest quartile	83.2	77.7

Note: The Canadian Internet use survey (CIUS) tables beginning with 2005 replace the Household Internet survey (HIUS) tables from 1997 to 2003. The unit surveyed is now the individual rather than the household. Only adults aged 18 years and over were surveyed.

1. Internet access from **any location** includes use from home, school, work, public library or other location, and counts an individual only once, regardless of use from multiple locations.
2. Percentage of all individuals, aged 18 years and over, who responded that they had used the Internet in the previous 12 months for personal non-business use from any location.
3. The survey respondents are divided into four equal groups based on their annual personal income, each group representing 25% of the income spectrum from highest to lowest. The lowest quartile is $13,000 or less, the second quartile is from $13,001 to $26,999, the third quartile is from $27,000 to $45,999 and the highest quartile is $46,000 and higher.

Source: Statistics Canada, CANSIM, tables (for fee) 358-0123, 358-0124, 358-0125 and 358-0126.

Last modified: 2006-08-15.

Drawing on the data above, the findings of the Statistics Canada 2005 Canadian Internet Use Survey (CIUS), still identify significant digital divide:

Digital divide persists among certain groups

Canada's digital divide (the gap in the rate of Internet use among certain groups of people) still exists, according to CIUS data. Income, education, age and the presence of children in the household all influence Internet use.

About 88% of adults with household incomes of $86,000 or more used the Internet last year, well above the proportion of 61% among adults living in households with incomes below $86,000.

Similarly, 80% of adults with at least some post-secondary education used the Internet, compared with just under one half (49%) of adults with less education.

Canadians between the ages of 18 and 44 (85%) were over one and a half times more likely to use the Internet than those 45 years of age and older (50%).

The presence of children under 18 years in the household is also associated with a higher rate of Internet use among adults. About 81% of persons in households with children used the Internet, compared to only 61% of persons in households without children.

While there was no clear pattern between the proportion of men and women using the Internet, there are differences in their intensity and types of use.

Source: http://www.statcan.ca/Daily/English/060815/d060815b.htm Accessed April 15, 2007

Summary Observations on Internet Access and Online Shopping

Drawing from the tables above and the Statistics Canada article below (Box One), we can draw the following summary observations:

- Despite a growth in use, a digital divide persists.
- This digital divide is evident along the following lines: age, income, education, ethnicity, region and urban v. rural. (In some cases gender is also important.)
- A tiny fraction of total Canadian expenditures take place on the Internet, only $3bn of $688bn in 2003. If purchases of retail goods alone are considered it still only amounts to about 1%.
- Nonetheless, Internet shopping is growing quickly.
- The potential is immense; approximately 70% of Canadian households had regular Internet access in 2004. (This is a similar level as other western nations.)

- The bias in composition of Internet users represents a very attractive target market: disproportionately young, high income, well educated and urban.

- A clear distinction is between virtual "window shopping" and actual online purchases. For many, the Internet represents a source of information on goods and services to be followed by traditional physical shopping – this "click and mortar" activity partly explains why many retailers have a major online presence despite online sales being a small proportion of total sales.

- In Canada in 2003 about a third of online purchases were from foreign Internet sites.

- Quality of Internet access (speed) and shopping use of the Internet varies by region with relatively high levels in B.C., Alberta and Ontario and relatively low levels in Quebec. Atlantic Canada is interesting in that it has relatively low levels of access but quite high levels of shopping use – perhaps a reflection of more limited traditional shopping opportunities in some sectors.

- In 2003, Ontario accounted for almost half of total online shopping; B.C. was second most important.

- Books and magazines remain the most popular purchases. Digital products (e.g. software and music) and travel arrangements are also important.

- Much more important than household Internet shopping in purely economic terms are Business to Business (B2B) transactions (in Canada about 75% of total).

Barriers to Online Shopping

Despite its rapid growth, barriers to online shopping remain explaining its small share of total sales:

- **Fulfilment** is expensive for the retailer. It is costly to deliver goods to individual households, not just in the actual physical delivery but also other logistical elements such as ordering and warehousing. Unlike traditional physical shopping where the shopper carries the cost of the distance between the store and home, online shopping requires at least some of the cost to be carried by the retailer. The fact that it usually has to be quick delivery increases this cost of fulfilment.

- Most people have access to traditional shopping venues, but **there is not universal access to the Internet.** Some market segments are still excluded.

- Online shopping, in most cases, **lacks instant gratification**. For many, part of the pleasure of shopping is the immediate acquisition of the good at the store. Online items are typically delivered taking at least one day even with today's efficient delivery systems. Notably, goods that do provide instant gratification, such as downloaded music and software, do reasonably well on the 'net.

- There is still a **security concern** for users paying over the Internet; paradoxically this is even the case for people who regularly pay online.

- Part of shopping pleasure for many is the **tactile experience** - shoppers like to see and interact physically with the goods before they purchase them.

- The most important reason why online shopping is unlikely to usurp traditional shopping relates to **the entertainment, social and cultural significance of shopping.** For better or worse, many consumers thoroughly enjoy shopping, and the virtual version does not come close to matching the real thing!

Similar observations were made in the early days of another "remote" mode of shopping:

"... in the short term, ... teleshopping seems likely to complement rather than replace the vast majority of face-to-face shopping in malls and city centres. This is because shopping has emerged as a key leisure activity, where the *whole point* is to leave the confines of the home to explore physically new consumer spaces in cities. As Judy Hillman (1993; 3) argues 'the telestore may be too remote, except for the housebound, the isolated and the hyperactive. For most people, shopping is likely to remain a social, visual, tactile, stimulating, if sometimes exhausting, acquisitive experience, which brings particular pleasure in the unexpected bargain or encounter'." –Graham, S. and Marvin, S. (1996), *Telecommunications and the City: Electronic Spaces, Urban Places*, London: Routledge. P.156.

Box One: Statistics Canada Article on Internet Shopping, 2003 Data

(http://www.statcan.ca/Daily/English/040923/d040923a.htm)

E-commerce: Household Shopping on the Internet, 2003

Canadian households spent just over $3.0 billion shopping on the Internet on everything from airplane tickets to books, according to the 2003 Household Internet Use Survey (HIUS).

An estimated 3.2 million Canadian households actively participated in e-commerce in 2003, up from 2.8 million the year before. These households accessed the Internet from various locations, not just home. In total, they placed 21.1 million orders, up from 16.6 million the previous year.

The $3.0 billion in orders placed over the Internet represents a 25% increase from $2.4 billion spent online in 2002. This growth rate far exceeds the 5% increase in the number of households that accessed the Internet from any location in 2003.

Total electronic commerce spending represents only a fraction of the $688 billion in total personal expenditure in Canada last year. However, the new figures confirm that households are increasingly using the Internet as a method of purchasing goods from both Canadian and foreign vendors.

The electronic commerce components of the HIUS from 2001 to 2003 were redesigned to capture Internet shopping from households that regularly used the Internet from various locations, solely for household purposes. **Note to readers**

Data in this report are from the 2003 Household Internet Use Survey (HIUS), from which estimates for Internet use were released on July 8th. The HIUS was administered to a sub-sample of the households included in the Labour Force Survey (LFS).

The respondent provides a proxy response to questions for all members of the household. Of households indicating that they regularly use the Internet, about 89% of the individuals answering the survey for their household were one of the members that regularly used the Internet from various locations.

Residents of Yukon, the Northwest Territories and Nunavut, persons living on Indian reserves, full-time members of the Canadian Armed Forces and inmates of institutions were excluded from the coverage.

In 2003, 34,674 households were eligible for the HIUS. Interviews were completed for 23,113 of these households, for a response rate of 67%. Results were weighted to the entire count of households, excluding those listed above.

Regular-use households are those who responded "yes" to the question, "In a typical month does anyone in your household use the Internet (from any location)?"

Unlike the LFS, in which information is collected on each eligible household member individually, the HIUS collected information on the household as a whole. A designated member of the household enumerated the online shopping characteristics made by all members of the household in the previous 12 months.

The Household Internet Use Survey will not be conducted for the 2004 reference year and is targeted to be replaced by an individual level survey for reference year 2005.

Previously, household e-commerce data were collected only if the Internet shopping was conducted from home. This constituted a break in the data series.

One-third of online purchases made on foreign Web sites

For every $10 spent by households on Internet purchases last year, $6.90 was spent on Canadian Web sites. On the other hand, Canadians spent almost $1 billion of their e-commerce dollars at foreign Web sites.

This constituted a 6% gain from a year earlier and was much lower than the 27% growth in foreign orders placed between 2001 and 2002. The number of orders coming across the border however increased 27%.

During the year, an estimated 4.9 million households, or 40% of the total, were Internet shoppers. That is, they had at least one member who used the Internet to support purchasing decisions, either by window-shopping or by placing online orders.

Of these 4.9 million households, an estimated 3.2 million, or 65%, went beyond window-shopping and placed orders online. More than five out of six households paid for their purchases online, a 52% increase from the reference year 2001.

About 1.7 million households reported that they used the Internet only to window-shop, virtually unchanged from 2001. This group browsed online catalogues to narrow their purchasing decisions, but did not place orders or make purchases online. They represented 14% of all Canadian households.

Of these window-shoppers, almost one-half indicated that they later made purchases directly from vendors, indicating that online catalogues are an effective means of obtaining walk-in or telephone orders.

Concerns still high, but online credit card use rises

More Canadian households were paying for their goods and services online in 2003. Paradoxically, many shoppers indicated concerns about security aspects of the Internet, but they were still willing to use their credit cards online.

More than three-quarters of the 2.7 million households that paid online indicated that they were concerned, or very concerned, about financial transactions conducted over the Internet.

In fact, the proportion of electronic commerce households that paid for their Internet orders online rose from 79% in 2001 to 85% last year. This contributed to increased growth in the number of orders paid online.

Books, magazines still most popular purchase

Reading materials such as books, magazines and newspapers were still the most popular online purchases in 2003. About 30% of e-commerce households reported purchasing these items.

However, consumers are increasingly using the Internet to make travel arrangements. In 2003, 22% of households reported making travel arrangements over the Internet, up from 18% the year before.

Growth in the number of households purchasing commodities was highest for consumer electronics (+86%) and videos and DVDs (+68%). The number of households that ordered music online increased 36%, while the number downloading free music declined.

Household growth of commodity categories where members only window-shopped was greatest for health, beauty items and vitamins; consumer electronics; clothing, jewelry and accessories; and housewares and appliances.

Digital products

One bundle of goods and services purchased over the Internet by Canadian households for personal non-business use is referred to as "digital products."

This group of orders includes products purchased online that are delivered in a digital format from the vendors' computer to the purchasers' computer. Almost 20% of electronic commerce households bought digital products in 2003, up from 16% a year earlier.

On average, these households purchased $180 of these products, which were comprised mostly of software, software licenses and music.

An estimated $113 million of these products were purchased by Canadian households, almost double that of the previous year. Venders outside Canada accounted for more than half the dollar value.

High-speed access at home gateway to online purchases

Households with a high-speed connection are more likely to be electronic commerce households. Over 7 of 10 electronic commerce households have a high-speed connection.

Speed of household connection by region			
2003			
	Proportion of total households using regularly from home	**High speed from home**	**Low speed from home**
Atlantic Canada	47%	56%	44%
Quebec	45%	59%	41%
Ontario	60%	62%	38%
Manitoba and Saskatchewan	52%	70%	30%
Alberta	58%	74%	26%
British Columbia	62%	77%	23%
Total	**54%**	**65%**	**35%**

Access speed of electronic commerce household by region			
2003			
	Proportion of regular use households purchasing from home	**High speed from home**	**Low speed from home**
Atlantic Canada	49%	65%	35%
Quebec	39%	68%	32%
Ontario	49%	69%	31%
Manitoba and Saskatchewan	49%	76%	24%
Alberta	50%	80%	20%
British Columbia	50%	80%	20%
Total	**47%**	**72%**	**28%**

Of the households that pay for their purchases online, 73% access the Internet at home using a high-speed connection.

Those households west of Ontario with a high speed connection are slightly more likely than national average to purchase goods from home.

Ontario households account for almost half of total e-commerce spending

On average, e-commerce households spent $956 annually online, with an average dollar value per order of $144 in 2003. The average expenditure per household and the average dollar value per order were above the national average for Alberta, British Columbia and Ontario.

Households in Ontario contributed one-third of the increase in purchases last year, and represented nearly one-half of the $3.0 billion total e-commerce spending. They also placed 46% of all orders made online. Nearly 30% of Ontario spending was conducted with foreign vendors.

Alberta recorded the highest provincial growth in e-commerce spending (+43%), followed by Quebec (+41%) with the Atlantic provinces close behind at 36% growth.

Households in British Columbia were Canada's second largest market for electronic commerce. They spent over half a billion dollars on Internet purchases, almost 17% of the national total.

Available on CANSIM: tables 358-0018 to 358-0023. Definitions, data sources and methods: survey number 4432.

Additional data tables related to the information presented in this series are available online in the publication *Internet use in Canada* (56F0003XIE, free).

Data from the 2003 Household Internet Use Survey, conducted in January 2004, for January to December 2003, is now available on the CD-ROM *Household Internet Use Survey—Public Use Microdata File*, 2003 (56M0002XCB, $2,140). The survey provides information on the use of the Internet by Canadian households within the 10 provinces. This is the seventh cross-sectional microdata file to be released in the series beginning with the Household Internet Use Survey for 1997.

Appendix A

PROFILE OF CENSUS DATA FOR TORONTO CMA AND CENSUS TRACTS 0001–0006, 2001

Table 1. Selected Characteristics for Census Tracts, 2001 Census – 100% Data and 20% Sample Data

No.	Characteristics	Toronto A CMA/RMR	Toronto 0001	Toronto 0002	Toronto 0004	Toronto 0005	Toronto 0006
	POPULATION CHARACTERISTICS						
1	Population, 1996 (1)	4,263,759	695	563	6,940	5,374	247
2	Population, 2001 (2)	4,682,897	626	658	7,417	5,438	262
3	Population percentage change, 1996-2001	9.8	-9.9	16.9	6.9	1.2	6.1
4	Land area in square kilometres, 2001	5,902.74	6.10	3.16	0.34	0.38	0.01
5	Total population – 100% Data (3)	4,682,895	625	660	7,420	5,440	260
	by sex and age groups						
6	Male	2,282,665	345	320	3,960	2,605	125
7	0-4 years	148,010	15	10	230	170	-
8	5-9 years	163,370	25	20	170	160	-
9	10-14 years	159,360	20	40	140	120	-
10	15-19 years	156,355	20	30	145	120	-
11	20-24 years	152,420	30	10	285	195	-
12	25-29 years	161,270	40	10	440	270	5
13	30-34 years	185,295	40	15	520	270	10
14	35-39 years	212,215	40	15	450	300	10
15	40-44 years	197,685	30	25	385	220	10
16	45-49 years	169,510	35	35	320	175	10
17	50-54 years	152,290	15	50	280	140	10
18	55-59 years	110,355	15	30	160	110	5
19	60-64 years	87,955	10	10	135	90	10
20	65-69 years	76,220	5	5	110	75	10
21	70-74 years	63,560	10	10	85	80	10
22	75-79 years	45,610	-	10	55	65	15
23	80-84 years	24,930	-	-	30	25	5
24	85 years and over	16,255	-	-	20	10	5
25	Female	2,400,230	280	340	3,455	2,835	135
26	0-4 years	140,650	10	15	210	160	-
27	5-9 years	154,175	20	30	190	180	-
28	10-14 years	150,590	10	20	135	155	-
29	15-19 years	147,580	10	25	140	140	-
30	20-24 years	154,190	25	15	310	195	5
31	25-29 years	173,420	30	10	420	240	-
32	30-34 years	198,160	25	15	395	280	5
33	35-39 years	218,570	25	20	320	260	10
34	40-44 years	207,070	25	35	305	220	5
35	45-49 years	182,220	30	45	230	175	10
36	50-54 years	160,690	20	50	195	165	5
37	55-59 years	115,200	5	30	135	125	10
38	60-64 years	95,605	15	5	110	130	10
39	65-69 years	84,655	15	10	80	140	10
40	70-74 years	76,525	5	10	85	100	20
41	75-79 years	64,955	10	10	90	90	20
42	80-84 years	39,710	5	-	50	40	10
43	85 years and over	36,275	-	5	55	55	25
44	Total population 15 years and over	3,766,745	525	525	6,340	4,495	260
	by legal marital status						
45	Never married (single)	1,225,500	245	205	3,290	2,135	90
46	Legally married (and not separated)	1,994,235	165	210	2,095	1,425	90
47	Separated, but still legally married	117,840	30	20	265	230	10
48	Divorced	220,760	60	65	430	385	20
49	Widowed	208,410	30	20	270	325	55
	by common-law status						
50	Not in a common-law relationship	3,579,710	480	450	5,890	4,170	265
51	In a common-law relationship	187,030	50	80	455	330	-
52	Total population – 20% Sample Data (4)	4,647,955	625	660	7,170	5,305	...
	by mother tongue						
53	Single responses	4,556,475	610	655	6,995	5,175	...
54	English	2,684,200	460	635	3,295	2,405	...
55	French	57,485	-	-	140	85	...
56	Non-official languages (5)	1,814,795	145	20	3,560	2,690	...
57	Italian	195,960	-	-	35	20	...
58	Chinese, n.o.s.	165,125	10	-	45	75	...
59	Cantonese	145,490	35	-	30	25	...
60	Portuguese	108,935	15	-	65	135	...
61	Punjabi	95,945	-	-	15	20	...
62	Other languages (6)	1,103,335	75	20	3,375	2,410	...
63	Multiple responses	91,480	20	-	175	130	...
64	English and French	7,810	10	-	40	30	...
65	English and non-official language	77,430	-	-	110	90	...
66	French and non-official language	4,590	-	-	20	10	...
67	English, French and non-official language	1,655	-	-	-	-	...

See reference material at the end of the publication. – Voir les documents de référence à la fin de la publication.

Table 1. Selected Characteristics for Census Tracts, 2001 Census – 100% Data and 20% Sample Data

No.	Characteristics	Toronto A CMA/RMR	Toronto 0001	Toronto 0002	Toronto 0004	Toronto 0005	Toronto 0006
	POPULATION CHARACTERISTICS						
	by home language						
68	Single responses	3,605,875	600	640	5,260	3,730	...
69	English	2,902,975	475	640	3,690	2,695	...
70	French	9,875	-	-	15	-	...
71	Non-official languages (5)	693,025	125	-	1,555	1,040	...
72	Cantonese	88,970	25	-	-	20	...
73	Chinese, n.o.s.	81,940	15	-	15	75	...
74	Italian	51,800	-	-	-	-	...
75	Punjabi	49,180	-	-	10	20	...
76	Portuguese	37,055	10	-	-	35	...
77	Other languages (6)	384,075	75	-	1,530	885	...
78	Multiple responses	1,042,080	25	15	1,910	1,570	...
79	English and French	49,550	-	-	100	95	...
80	English and non-official language	970,100	15	10	1,785	1,465	...
81	French and non-official language	4,780	-	-	10	15	...
82	English, French and non-official language	17,655	-	10	25	-	...
	by knowledge of official languages						
83	English only	4,069,010	560	560	6,065	4,645	...
84	French only	4,070	-	-	10	60	...
85	English and French	393,415	40	100	805	420	...
86	Neither English nor French	181,455	25	-	295	175	...
	by knowledge of non-official languages (5) (7)						
87	Italian	277,560	-	-	100	120	...
88	Cantonese	178,675	35	-	50	45	...
89	Chinese, n.o.s.	161,150	10	-	60	115	...
90	Spanish	142,635	15	10	380	425	...
91	Portuguese	129,945	15	-	70	170	...
92	Punjabi	125,475	-	-	30	20	...
93	Tagalog (Pilipino)	106,590	55	-	520	450	...
	by first official language spoken						
94	English	4,366,370	610	655	6,645	4,945	...
95	French	61,075	-	10	160	145	...
96	English and French	43,460	-	-	75	45	...
97	Neither English nor French	177,055	20	-	295	170	...
98	Official language minority - (number) (8)	82,800	-	10	195	170	...
99	Official language minority - (percentage) (8)	1.8	-	1.5	2.7	3.2	...
	by ethnic origin (9)						
100	Canadian	861,945	165	300	1,075	815	...
101	English	783,770	105	270	555	465	...
102	Scottish	517,115	75	255	510	265	...
103	Irish	487,215	75	145	525	320	...
104	Chinese	435,690	90	-	255	245	...
105	Italian	429,385	10	30	145	95	...
106	East Indian	345,855	-	-	400	355	...
107	French	220,540	40	50	315	220	...
108	German	220,140	30	120	220	130	...
109	Portuguese	171,545	25	-	110	130	...
110	Polish	166,695	10	10	565	365	...
111	Jewish	161,215	-	50	30	15	...
112	Jamaican	150,840	10	-	175	115	...
113	Filipino	140,405	60	-	555	540	...
114	Ukrainian	104,490	-	-	190	125	...
	by Aboriginal identity						
115	Total Aboriginal identity population (10)	20,305	10	-	80	75	...
116	Total non-Aboriginal population	4,627,655	615	660	7,085	5,230	...
	by Aboriginal origin						
117	Total Aboriginal origins population (11)	44,400	-	-	100	100	...
118	Total non-Aboriginal population	4,603,555	620	660	7,075	5,205	...
	by Registered Indian status						
119	Registered Indian (12)	8,705	10	-	55	45	...
120	Not a Registered Indian	4,639,250	615	655	7,115	5,260	...

Table 1.   Selected Characteristics for Census Tracts, 2001 Census – 100% Data and 20% Sample Data

No.	Characteristics	Toronto A CMA/RMR	Toronto 0001	Toronto 0002	Toronto 0004	Toronto 0005	Toronto 0006
	POPULATION CHARACTERISTICS						
	by visible minority groups						
121	Total visible minority population	1,712,530	220	-	3,540	3,035	...
122	Chinese	409,530	75	-	195	250	...
123	South Asian	473,805	-	-	1,020	590	...
124	Black	310,500	25	-	555	725	...
125	Filipino	133,675	40	-	545	535	...
126	Latin American	75,910	20	-	160	265	...
127	Southeast Asian	53,565	25	-	250	355	...
128	Arab	42,830	-	-	75	40	...
129	West Asian	52,985	-	-	135	60	...
130	Korean	42,620	10	-	25	20	...
131	Japanese	17,420	-	-	-	10	...
132	Visible minority, n.i.e. (13)	66,450	15	-	550	165	...
133	Multiple visible minorities (14)	33,245	20	-	20	20	...
	by citizenship						
134	Canadian citizenship (15)	4,036,445	585	650	5,290	4,110	...
135	Citizenship other than Canadian	611,510	40	10	1,875	1,195	...
	by place of birth of respondent						
136	Non-immigrant population	2,556,860	450	585	3,050	2,270	...
137	Born in province of residence	2,224,905	405	500	2,350	1,865	...
138	Immigrant population (16)	2,032,960	170	75	3,770	2,845	...
139	United States	37,795	-	20	80	40	...
140	Central and South America	135,720	10	-	375	285	...
141	Caribbean and Bermuda	167,420	10	-	315	315	...
142	United Kingdom	142,985	-	30	135	85	...
143	Other Europe (17)	573,255	20	20	1,030	605	...
144	Africa	98,975	10	-	150	215	...
145	Asia and the Middle East	869,515	125	-	1,670	1,290	...
146	Oceania and other (18)	7,295	-	-	15	10	...
147	Non-permanent residents (19)	58,140	10	-	345	190	...
148	**Total immigrant population**	2,032,960	165	75	3,770	2,850	...
	by period of immigration						
149	Before 1961	223,520	10	45	225	150	...
150	1961-1970	251,390	-	-	240	235	...
151	1971-1980	343,130	35	20	380	375	...
152	1981-1990	422,890	70	-	950	600	...
153	1991-2001 (20)	792,030	55	-	1,975	1,480	...
154	1991-1995	376,530	20	-	740	780	...
155	1996-2001 (20)	415,505	30	-	1,235	700	...
	by age at immigration						
156	0-4 years	163,310	-	30	300	175	...
157	5-19 years	556,015	80	20	950	715	...
158	20 years and over	1,313,635	85	25	2,525	1,960	...
159	**Total population**	4,647,960	625	655	7,170	5,305	...
	by religion						
160	Catholic (21)	1,578,875	75	35	2,320	1,810	...
161	Protestant	1,131,055	110	270	1,005	660	...
162	Christian Orthodox	178,695	10	-	190	210	...
163	Christian, n.i.e. (22)	160,420	95	-	355	300	...
164	Muslim	-254,115	10	-	530	315	...
165	Jewish	164,510	10	15	70	40	...
166	Buddhist	97,165	-	10	615	395	...
167	Hindu	191,305	-	-	600	385	...
168	Sikh	90,595	-	-	20	20	...
169	Eastern religions (23)	10,990	-	10	20	70	...
170	Other religions (24)	5,540	-	-	15	25	...
171	No religious affiliation (25)	784,695	310	305	1,435	1,070	...
172	**Total population 15 years and over**	3,728,985	535	540	6,095	4,365	...
	by generation status						
173	1st generation (26)	1,964,320	180	75	3,825	2,840	...
174	2nd generation (27)	806,625	85	140	865	545	...
175	3rd generation and over (28)	958,035	270	325	1,405	975	...
176	**Total population 1 year and over (29)**	4,590,795	625	655	7,035	5,245	...
	by place of residence 1 year ago (mobility)						
177	Non-movers	3,942,615	540	615	5,610	4,240	...
178	Movers	648,180	90	35	1,425	1,000	...
179	Non-migrants	368,055	75	20	810	600	...
180	Migrants	280,130	10	15	620	405	...
181	Internal migrants	176,490	-	-	230	85	...
182	Intraprovincial migrants	152,265	10	-	165	55	...
183	Interprovincial migrants	24,220	-	-	65	35	...
184	External migrants	103,640	10	15	390	315	...

Table 1. Selected Characteristics for Census Tracts, 2001 Census – 100% Data and 20% Sample Data

No.	Characteristics	Toronto A CMA/RMR	Toronto 0001	Toronto 0002	Toronto 0004	Toronto 0005	Toronto 0006
	POPULATION CHARACTERISTICS						
185	Total population 5 years and over (30)	4,356,845	595	635	6,725	4,975	...
	by place of residence 5 years ago (mobility)						
186	Non-movers	2,377,470	315	495	2,675	2,350	...
187	Movers	1,979,375	280	140	4,050	2,625	...
188	Non-migrants	1,051,720	225	130	2,010	1,640	...
189	Migrants	927,655	55	10	2,045	980	...
190	Internal migrants	553,470	25	10	680	220	...
191	Intraprovincial migrants	466,970	20	-	415	165	...
192	Interprovincial migrants	86,500	10	-	265	55	...
193	External migrants	374,185	35	10	1,370	760	...
194	Total population 15 to 24 years	607,665	95	70	865	655	...
	by school attendance						
195	Not attending school	195,360	50	15	460	265	...
196	Attending school full time	379,000	40	50	375	345	...
197	Attending school part time	33,300	-	10	25	45	...
198	Total population 15 years and over	3,728,980	535	540	6,095	4,360	...
	by highest level of schooling						
199	Less than grade 9 (31)	319,055	50	10	610	495	...
200	Grades 9-13 without high school graduation certificate	693,720	180	115	1,120	825	...
201	Grades 9-13 with high school graduation certificate	494,990	95	60	800	760	...
202	Some postsecondary without degree, certificate or diploma (32)	442,275	40	65	855	605	...
203	Trades certificate or diploma (33)	278,975	30	25	400	245	...
204	College certificate or diploma (34)	542,090	75	110	760	580	...
205	University certificate below bachelor's degree	103,845	10	25	125	110	...
206	University with bachelor's degree or higher	854,035	45	135	1,425	740	...
	by combinations of unpaid work						
207	Males 15 years and over	1,797,065	305	270	3,250	2,100	...
208	Reported unpaid work (35)	1,569,655	220	225	2,855	1,895	...
209	Housework and child care and care or assistance to seniors	137,620	10	25	85	50	...
210	Housework and child care only	455,250	55	70	430	370	...
211	Housework and care or assistance to seniors only	114,105	-	45	100	40	...
212	Child care and care or assistance to seniors only	3,675	-	-	-	-	...
213	Housework only	826,680	140	85	2,130	1,375	...
214	Child care only	23,555	10	-	105	55	...
215	Care or assistance to seniors only	8,780	-	-	10	-	...
216	Females 15 years and over	1,931,915	235	270	2,845	2,265	...
217	Reported unpaid work (35)	1,778,265	220	245	2,645	2,125	...
218	Housework and child care and care or assistance to seniors	209,100	15	75	130	100	...
219	Housework and child care only	574,090	75	60	670	725	...
220	Housework and care or assistance to seniors only	149,040	10	30	105	55	...
221	Child care and care or assistance to seniors only	2,220	-	-	-	-	...
222	Housework only	823,945	120	80	1,695	1,230	...
223	Child care only	13,345	-	-	35	10	...
224	Care or assistance to seniors only	6,520	-	-	-	15	...
	by labour force activity						
225	Males 15 years and over	1,797,065	300	270	3,250	2,095	...
226	In the labour force	1,344,785	140	195	2,265	1,400	...
227	Employed	1,272,115	125	190	2,025	1,280	...
228	Unemployed	72,665	10	10	240	125	...
229	Not in the labour force	452,285	165	75	985	695	...
230	Participation rate	74.8	46.7	72.2	69.7	66.8	...
231	Employment rate	70.8	41.7	70.4	62.3	61.1	...
232	Unemployment rate	5.4	7.1	5.1	10.6	8.9	...
233	Females 15 years and over	1,931,915	235	270	2,845	2,265	...
234	In the labour force	1,219,805	155	190	1,785	1,235	...
235	Employed	1,140,985	150	180	1,575	1,115	...
236	Unemployed	78,820	-	10	205	125	...
237	Not in the labour force	712,110	80	80	1,060	1,030	...
238	Participation rate	63.1	66.0	70.4	62.7	54.5	...
239	Employment rate	59.1	63.8	66.7	55.4	49.2	...
240	Unemployment rate	6.5	-	5.3	11.5	10.1	...

No.	Characteristics	Toronto A CMA/RMR	Toronto 0001	Toronto 0002	Toronto 0004	Toronto 0005	Toronto 0006
	POPULATION CHARACTERISTICS						
	by labour force activity – concluded						
241	Both sexes - Participation rate	68.8	54.2	72.2	66.4	60.5	...
242	15-24 years	62.1	47.4	33.3	67.4	52.7	...
243	25 years and over	70.1	55.1	77.4	66.2	61.9	...
244	Both sexes - Employment rate	64.7	51.4	68.5	59.1	54.8	...
245	15-24 years	54.6	42.1	33.3	54.9	45.8	...
246	25 years and over	66.7	52.8	74.2	59.8	56.5	...
247	Both sexes - Unemployment rate	5.9	3.5	5.1	11.0	9.5	...
248	15-24 years	12.0	22.2	-	19.0	13.0	...
249	25 years and over	4.9	4.2	5.6	9.7	9.0	...
250	Total labour force 15 years and over	2,564,590	290	385	4,050	2,640	...
	by industry based on the 1997 NAICS						
251	Industry - Not applicable (36)	42,565	10	-	190	105	...
252	All industries (37)	2,522,025	285	390	3,855	2,540	...
253	11 Agriculture, forestry, fishing and hunting	9,425	-	-	-	-	...
254	21 Mining and oil and gas extraction	2,665	-	-	-	-	...
255	22 Utilities	15,765	-	-	10	10	...
256	23 Construction	124,395	-	20	145	95	...
257	31-33 Manufacturing	395,975	30	30	635	400	...
258	41 Wholesale trade	151,870	-	10	165	45	...
259	44-45 Retail trade	272,680	40	10	320	240	...
260	48-49 Transportation and warehousing	123,135	-	15	155	85	...
261	51 Information and cultural industries	100,755	25	30	260	165	...
262	52 Finance and insurance	177,210	40	25	200	120	...
263	53 Real estate and rental and leasing	56,890	-	10	95	40	...
264	54 Professional, scientific and technical services	246,655	20	70	360	185	...
265	55 Management of companies and enterprises	4,840	-	-	-	-	...
266	56 Administrative and support, waste management and remediation services	121,490	30	-	305	185	...
267	61 Educational services	143,990	10	60	155	80	...
268	62 Health care and social assistance	189,450	25	25	195	245	...
269	71 Arts, entertainment and recreation	47,875	-	45	155	90	...
270	72 Accommodation and food services	141,560	20	15	405	320	...
271	81 Other services (except public administration)	110,750	15	15	185	125	...
272	91 Public administration	84,660	20	15	105	105	...
	by class of worker						
273	Class of worker - Not applicable (36)	42,560	-	-	190	105	...
274	All classes of worker (37)	2,522,020	285	390	3,850	2,535	...
275	Paid workers	2,324,255	275	295	3,595	2,375	...
276	Employees	2,220,370	270	250	3,535	2,350	...
277	Self-employed (incorporated)	103,885	-	45	65	20	...
278	Self-employed (unincorporated)	191,105	10	90	260	160	...
279	Unpaid family workers	6,670	-	-	-	-	...
	by occupation based on the 2001 NOC-S						
280	Male labour force 15 years and over	1,344,785	135	195	2,265	1,400	...
281	Occupation - Not applicable (36)	18,665	-	-	85	55	...
282	All occupations (37)	1,326,120	130	195	2,175	1,345	...
283	A Management occupations	207,875	-	40	135	45	...
284	B Business, finance and administration occupations	171,540	10	10	250	215	...
285	C Natural and applied sciences and related occupations	158,545	-	15	270	135	...
286	D Health occupations	25,560	-	-	25	25	...
287	E Occupations in social science, education, government service and religion	63,035	10	30	95	55	...
288	F Occupations in art, culture, recreation and sport	45,715	10	45	155	120	...
289	G Sales and service occupations	251,335	65	25	505	390	...
290	H Trades, transport and equipment operators and related occupations	269,765	25	25	410	275	...
291	I Occupations unique to primary industry	17,430	-	-	25	-	...
292	J Occupations unique to processing, manufacturing and utilities	115,320	15	-	315	80	...
293	Female labour force 15 years and over	1,219,805	150	190	1,785	1,240	...
294	Occupation - Not applicable (36)	23,900	-	-	105	45	...
295	All occupations (37)	1,195,910	150	195	1,675	1,195	...
296	A Management occupations	120,415	-	20	80	50	...
297	B Business, finance and administration occupations	376,190	80	55	380	255	...
298	C Natural and applied sciences and related occupations	48,725	-	-	55	40	...
299	D Health occupations	78,460	-	10	70	105	...

No.	Characteristics	Toronto A CMA/RMR	Toronto 0001	Toronto 0002	Toronto 0004	Toronto 0005	Toronto 0006
	POPULATION CHARACTERISTICS						
	by occupation based on the 2001 NOC-S – concluded						
	E Occupations in social science, education,						
300	government service and religion	126,225	-	45	165	70	...
301	F Occupations in art, culture, recreation and sport ...	47,445	10	45	60	100	...
302	G Sales and service occupations	285,645	45	10	635	430	...
	H Trades, transport and equipment						
303	operators and related occupations	24,940	-	10	65	30	...
304	I Occupations unique to primary industry	4,615	-	-	10	-	...
	J Occupations unique to processing,						
305	manufacturing and utilities	83,245	15	-	155	110	...
306	Total employed labour force 15 years and over	2,413,100	280	370	3,605	2,395	...
	by place of work						
307	Males	1,272,115	125	185	2,020	1,275	...
308	Usual place of work	1,038,285	100	120	1,635	1,050	...
309	At home	74,105	-	20	145	60	...
310	Outside Canada	8,985	-	15	10	10	...
311	No fixed workplace address	150,740	30	35	240	165	...
312	Females	1,140,985	150	180	1,575	1,115	...
313	Usual place of work	1,008,320	130	130	1,385	960	...
314	At home	78,185	10	55	60	70	...
315	Outside Canada	3,770	-	-	-	-	...
316	No fixed workplace address	50,715	10	-	125	80	...
	Total employed labour force 15 years and over with usual place of work or no fixed						
317	workplace address	2,248,060	265	285	3,385	2,250	...
	by mode of transportation						
318	Males	1,189,025	125	150	1,875	1,210	...
319	Car, truck, van, as driver...........................	873,095	70	55	670	440	...
320	Car, truck, van, as passenger	50,270	-	10	55	40	...
321	Public transit	201,505	30	25	900	590	...
322	Walked	43,300	10	25	180	90	...
323	Other method	20,845	20	40	70	45	...
324	Females	1,059,035	140	130	1,515	1,035	...
325	Car, truck, van, as driver...........................	591,845	25	25	270	145	...
326	Car, truck, van, as passenger	90,585	10	-	60	65	...
327	Public transit	302,290	95	45	965	705	...
328	Walked	59,065	10	15	175	85	...
329	Other method	15,250	-	35	45	40	...
	Total population 15 years and over who worked						
330	since January 1, 2000	2,741,935	305	415	4,030	2,720	...
	by language used at work						
331	Single responses	2,462,700	290	410	3,495	2,345	...
332	English	2,413,940	275	410	3,460	2,295	...
333	French	2,650	-	-	-	-	...
334	Non-official languages (5)	46,105	10	-	30	50	...
335	Chinese, n.o.s.	12,940	10	-	10	-	...
336	Cantonese	10,490	10	-	-	-	...
337	Other languages (6)	22,670	-	-	25	50	...
338	Multiple responses	279,235	10	10	540	375	...
339	English and French	59,330	-	-	130	75	...
340	English and non-official language	211,735	15	10	385	295	...
341	French and non-official language	295	-	-	-	-	...
342	English, French and non-official language	7,880	-	-	25	-	...
	DWELLING AND HOUSEHOLD CHARACTERISTICS						
343	Total number of occupied private dwellings	1,634,755	245	260	3,530	2,545	...
	by tenure						
344	Owned	1,033,465	130	260	235	235	...
345	Rented	601,280	110	-	3,295	2,310	...
346	Band housing	10	-	-	-	-	...
	by structural type of dwelling						
347	Single-detached house	737,325	20	250	380	160	...
348	Semi-detached house	147,985	155	10	155	125	...
349	Row house	124,640	55	-	10	70	...
350	Apartment, detached duplex	31,865	-	-	25	25	...
351	Apartment, building that has five or more storeys	447,245	-	-	1,935	1,400	...
	Apartment, building that has fewer than						
352	five storeys (38)	141,040	-	-	990	745	...
353	Other single-attached house	3,890	-	-	30	15	...
354	Movable dwelling (39)	775	-	10	-	-	...

Table 1. Selected Characteristics for Census Tracts, 2001 Census – 100% Data and 20% Sample Data

No.	Characteristics	Toronto A CMA/RMR	Toronto 0001	Toronto 0002	Toronto 0004	Toronto 0005	Toronto 0006
	DWELLING AND HOUSEHOLD CHARACTERISTICS						
	by condition of dwelling						
355	Regular maintenance only	1,116,105	105	150	2,235	1,655	...
356	Minor repairs	402,760	80	90	1,040	610	...
357	Major repairs	115,890	60	25	255	275	...
	by period of construction						
358	Before 1946	213,350	185	155	1,585	975	...
359	1946-1960	264,760	55	65	955	395	...
360	1961-1970	287,340	-	-	600	325	...
361	1971-1980	304,020	-	-	165	200	...
362	1981-1990	312,650	-	-	155	425	...
363	1991-2001 (20)	252,635	-	30	65	225	...
364	Average number of rooms per dwelling	6.1	5.8	5.8	3.6	3.7	...
365	Average number of bedrooms per dwelling	2.6	2.4	2.4	1.2	1.3	...
366	Average value of dwelling $	273,397	158,514	148,678	334,092	258,914	...
367	**Total number of private households**	**1,634,755**	**240**	**260**	**3,525**	**2,540**	...
	by household size						
368	1 person	359,595	75	70	1,620	1,150	...
369	2 persons	448,195	70	70	995	665	...
370	3 persons	287,690	40	45	455	365	...
371	4-5 persons	452,500	55	75	405	290	...
372	6 or more persons	86,775	10	-	50	70	...
	by household type						
373	One-family households	1,141,790	120	165	1,470	1,125	...
374	Multiple-family households	66,930	10	10	45	55	...
375	Non-family households	426,035	115	90	2,015	1,370	...
376	Number of persons in private households	4,637,215	610	660	7,045	5,280	...
377	Average number of persons in private households	2.8	2.5	2.5	2.0	2.1	...
378	Average number of persons per room	0.5	0.4	0.4	0.6	0.6	...
379	Tenant households in non-farm, non-reserve private dwellings (40)	595,320	105	-	3,255	2,290	...
380	Average gross rent $ (40)	870	809	-	696	644	...
381	Tenant households spending 30% or more of household income on gross rent (40) (41)	251,100	60	-	1,570	1,070	...
382	Tenant households spending from 30% to 99% of household income on gross rent (40) (41)	201,620	40	-	1,355	885	...
383	Owner households in non-farm, non-reserve private dwellings (42)	1,030,660	130	255	235	235	...
384	Average owner's major payments $ (42)	1,171	843	697	1,447	1,034	...
385	Owner households spending 30% or more of household income on owner's major payments (41) (42)	221,790	35	55	110	70	...
386	Owner households spending from 30% to 99% of household income on owner's major payments (41) (42)	193,340	30	50	85	50	...
	CENSUS FAMILY CHARACTERISTICS						
387	**Total number of census families in private households**	**1,280,955**	**135**	**175**	**1,555**	**1,220**	...
	by census family structure and size						
388	Total couple families	1,070,960	90	155	1,205	805	...
389	Total families of married couples	974,350	65	105	965	645	...
390	Without children at home	320,725	30	30	345	225	...
391	With children at home	653,620	40	75	620	415	...
392	1 child	227,680	20	30	320	175	...
393	2 children	292,915	10	35	195	170	...
394	3 or more children	133,025	10	10	100	75	...
395	Total families of common-law couples	96,610	30	45	235	165	...
396	Without children at home	60,985	15	30	195	115	...
397	With children at home	35,630	10	-	45	50	...
398	1 child	17,995	-	10	50	40	...
399	2 children	12,445	-	-	-	-	...
400	3 or more children	5,190	-	-	-	10	...
401	Total lone-parent families	210,000	45	25	350	420	...
402	Female parent	175,650	45	20	315	395	...
403	1 child	102,455	25	10	205	230	...
404	2 children	51,510	10	-	80	135	...
405	3 or more children	21,685	10	15	35	30	...

No.	Characteristics	Toronto A CMA/RMR	Toronto 0001	Toronto 0002	Toronto 0004	Toronto 0005	Toronto 0006
	CENSUS FAMILY CHARACTERISTICS						
	by census family structure and size – concluded						
406	Male parent	34,350	-	-	30	25	...
407	1 child	21,665	-	-	25	10	...
408	2 children	9,410	-	-	-	10	...
409	3 or more children	3,275	-	-	-	-	...
410	Total number of children at home	1,641,660	165	190	1,625	1,495	...
	by age groups						
411	Under 6 years	351,595	45	40	520	365	...
412	6-14 years	560,230	35	75	550	570	...
413	15-17 years	178,705	15	35	140	130	...
414	18-24 years	326,785	30	40	275	265	...
415	25 years and over	224,345	45	-	130	155	...
416	Average number of children at home per census family (43)	1.3	1.3	1.1	1.0	1.2	...
417	Total number of persons in private households	4,637,215	610	655	7,045	5,275	...
	by census family status and living arrangements						
418	Number of non-family persons	643,640	215	140	2,665	1,760	...
419	Living with relatives (44)	128,310	30	15	315	185	...
420	Living with non-relatives only	155,730	115	55	725	425	...
421	Living alone	359,595	70	70	1,620	1,150	...
422	Number of family persons	3,993,575	395	515	4,385	3,520	...
423	Average number of persons per census family	3.1	2.8	2.9	2.8	2.9	...
424	Total number of persons 65 years and over	502,575	45	25	595	570	...
425	Number of non-family persons 65 years and over	173,655	20	20	400	355	...
426	Living with relatives (44)	47,575	-	15	20	25	...
427	Living with non-relatives only	8,510	-	-	50	10	...
428	Living alone	117,570	10	-	335	315	...
429	Number of family persons 65 years and over	328,930	25	10	190	215	...
	ECONOMIC FAMILY CHARACTERISTICS						
430	Total number of economic families in private households	1,231,225	135	170	1,635	1,210	...
	by size of family						
431	2 persons	429,865	60	65	815	545	...
432	3 persons	278,900	30	35	410	315	...
433	4 persons	307,715	25	55	270	200	...
434	5 or more persons	214,740	20	20	140	155	...
435	Total number of persons in economic families	4,121,890	425	535	4,700	3,705	...
436	Average number of persons per economic family	3.3	3.1	3.1	2.9	3.0	...
437	Total number of unattached individuals	515,320	185	125	2,345	1,570	...
	2000 INCOME CHARACTERISTICS						
	Population 15 years and over by sex and total income groups in 2000						
438	Total - Both sexes	3,728,980	535	540	6,095	4,360	...
439	Without income	214,230	45	40	360	275	...
440	With income	3,514,750	490	500	5,730	4,085	...
441	Under $1,000 (45)	168,025	25	20	265	235	...
442	$ 1,000 - $ 2,999	159,170	40	25	295	155	...
443	$ 3,000 - $ 4,999	132,710	30	25	225	150	...
444	$ 5,000 - $ 6,999	136,835	10	15	290	290	...
445	$ 7,000 - $ 9,999	188,715	75	25	475	420	...
446	$10,000 - $11,999	142,605	25	25	345	210	...
447	$12,000 - $14,999	223,650	50	25	520	375	...
448	$15,000 - $19,999	288,290	55	60	695	540	...
449	$20,000 - $24,999	262,390	25	20	635	455	...
450	$25,000 - $29,999	247,090	30	20	415	310	...
451	$30,000 - $34,999	267,745	10	35	500	250	...
452	$35,000 - $39,999	217,705	35	25	275	220	...
453	$40,000 - $44,999	198,250	35	30	215	110	...
454	$45,000 - $49,999	141,795	20	-	135	75	...
455	$50,000 - $59,999	228,750	15	50	170	140	...
456	$60,000 and over	511,015	20	95	260	160	...
457	Average income $ (46)	35,618	20,426	96,488	21,817	20,456	...
458	Median income $ (46)	25,593	14,440	25,674	17,355	16,772	...
459	Standard error of average income $ (46)	84	1,676	53,738	443	536	...

No.	Characteristics	Toronto A	Toronto 0001	Toronto 0002	Toronto 0004	Toronto 0005	Toronto 0006
		CMA/RMR					
	2000 INCOME CHARACTERISTICS						
	Population 15 years and over by sex and total income groups in 2000 – concluded						
460	Total - Males	1,797,065	305	270	3,250	2,100	...
461	Without income	80,800	20	30	155	130	...
462	With income	1,716,260	285	240	3,090	1,965	...
463	Under $1,000 (45)	77,370	10	15	170	125	...
464	$ 1,000 - $ 2,999	63,825	30	15	140	70	...
465	$ 3,000 - $ 4,999	50,025	30	10	80	45	...
466	$ 5,000 - $ 6,999	51,105	-	-	145	145	...
467	$ 7,000 - $ 9,999	69,220	55	10	280	165	...
468	$10,000 - $11,999	61,600	20	10	155	110	...
469	$12,000 - $14,999	78,540	15	-	230	80	...
470	$15,000 - $19,999	119,150	25	20	380	245	...
471	$20,000 - $24,999	117,635	15	-	345	250	...
472	$25,000 - $29,999	112,675	-	-	190	175	...
473	$30,000 - $34,999	127,815	10	10	320	150	...
474	$35,000 - $39,999	108,245	20	25	140	95	...
475	$40,000 - $44,999	108,095	20	10	155	70	...
476	$45,000 - $49,999	80,050	10	-	85	30	...
477	$50,000 - $59,999	139,440	10	25	105	80	...
478	$60,000 and over	351,475	20	65	170	120	...
479	Average income $ (46)	44,126	19,455	171,226	23,121	22,909	...
480	Median income $ (46)	31,160	10,026	36,046	19,208	19,767	...
481	Standard error of average income $ (46)	162	2,542	106,460	616	867	...
482	Total - Females	1,931,915	230	270	2,845	2,265	...
483	Without income	133,430	30	10	210	150	...
484	With income	1,798,485	210	260	2,635	2,120	...
485	Under $1,000 (45)	90,650	15	10	90	110	...
486	$ 1,000 - $ 2,999	95,350	15	-	160	80	...
487	$ 3,000 - $ 4,999	82,685	-	15	145	105	...
488	$ 5,000 - $ 6,999	85,730	-	10	145	150	...
489	$ 7,000 - $ 9,999	119,490	20	15	195	260	...
490	$10,000 - $11,999	81,010	-	15	195	105	...
491	$12,000 - $14,999	145,115	35	20	290	290	...
492	$15,000 - $19,999	169,135	25	40	310	290	...
493	$20,000 - $24,999	144,755	15	20	290	205	...
494	$25,000 - $29,999	134,420	25	10	220	135	...
495	$30,000 - $34,999	139,930	-	20	180	95	...
496	$35,000 - $39,999	109,465	15	10	130	115	...
497	$40,000 - $44,999	90,155	-	15	60	40	...
498	$45,000 - $49,999	61,745	20	10	50	40	...
499	$50,000 - $59,999	89,315	10	20	70	55	...
500	$60,000 and over	159,540	-	30	95	40	...
501	Average income $ (46)	27,498	21,755	27,844	20,287	18,178	...
502	Median income $ (46)	20,523	15,360	22,541	15,489	14,092	...
503	Standard error of average income $ (46)	53	2,018	2,719	629	635	...
	by composition of total income						
504	Total - Composition of income in 2000 % (47)	100.0	100.0	100.0	100.0	100.0	...
505	Employment income %	82.0	72.3	88.8	77.4	73.4	...
506	Government transfer payments %	7.9	20.5	2.3	16.8	21.2	...
507	Other %	10.1	7.3	8.3	5.8	5.5	...
	Population 15 years and over with employment income in 2000 by sex and work activity						
508	Both sexes with employment income (48)	2,659,220	325	410	3,905	2,615	...
509	Average employment income $	38,598	22,347	105,831	24,772	23,436	...
510	Standard error of average employment income $	95	2,237	60,972	554	703	...
511	Worked full year, full time (49)	1,508,125	150	165	2,055	1,415	...
512	Average employment income $	51,112	31,209	230,797	30,519	29,210	...
513	Standard error of average employment income $	145	2,741	156,494	729	932	...
514	Worked part year or part time (50)	1,083,230	145	230	1,805	1,100	...
515	Average employment income $	22,655	17,477	25,422	18,684	17,491	...
516	Standard error of average employment income $	106	3,426	3,009	766	989	...
517	Males with employment income (48)	1,382,055	165	205	2,185	1,340	...
518	Average employment income $	46,613	22,179	184,261	25,932	26,981	...
519	Standard error of average employment income $	172	3,563	115,667	756	1,095	...
520	Worked full year, full time (49)	857,885	40	95	1,195	765	...
521	Average employment income $	58,789	36,791	364,249	31,281	33,227	...
522	Standard error of average employment income $	242	6,732	247,495	961	1,407	...
523	Worked part year or part time (50)	494,115	100	105	960	530	...
524	Average employment income $	27,287	20,148	28,899	19,726	19,613	...
525	Standard error of average employment income $	218	4,424	5,183	1,101	1,589	...

Table 1. Selected Characteristics for Census Tracts, 2001 Census – 100% Data and 20% Sample Data

No.	Characteristics	Toronto A CMA/RMR	Toronto 0001	Toronto 0002	Toronto 0004	Toronto 0005	Toront 0006
	2000 INCOME CHARACTERISTICS						
	Population 15 years and over with employment income in 2000 by sex and work activity – concluded						
526	Females with employment income (48)	1,277,170	160	200	1,720	1,270	.
527	Average employment income $	29,924	22,523	26,792	23,302	19,703	.
528	Standard error of average employment income $	64	2,707	3,037	805	827	.
529	Worked full year, full time (49)	650,240	105	70	855	650	.
530	Average employment income $	40,984	29,009	38,032	29,453	24,506	.
531	Standard error of average employment income $	100	2,534	6,223	1,112	1,098	.
532	Worked part year or part time (50)	589,125	45	125	840	570	..
533	Average employment income $	18,769	11,384	22,426	17,497	15,505	..
534	Standard error of average employment income $	69	4,899	3,181	1,039	1,185	..
	Census families by structure and family income groups in 2000						
535	Total - All census families	1,280,955	135	175	1,555	1,225	..
536	Under $10,000	64,185	-	-	120	125	..
537	$ 10,000 - $19,999	66,640	15	10	290	215	..
538	$ 20,000 - $29,999	112,350	30	10	215	205	..
539	$ 30,000 - $39,999	120,075	30	30	270	185	..
540	$ 40,000 - $49,999	118,995	40	-	190	130	..
541	$ 50,000 - $59,999	113,210	10	15	130	120	..
542	$ 60,000 - $69,999	111,850	-	15	95	70	..
543	$ 70,000 - $79,999	100,165	10	10	95	40	..
544	$ 80,000 - $89,999	86,695	-	15	35	50	..
545	$ 90,000 - $99,999	73,065	-	-	30	20	...
546	$100,000 and over	313,720	-	55	85	50	...
547	Average family income $	81,245	37,530	249,877	41,851	39,641	...
548	Median family income $	63,700	37,442	60,119	34,046	32,493	...
549	Standard error of average family income $	232	2,798	146,717	1,574	1,757	...
550	Total - All couple census families (51)	1,070,955	90	150	1,205	805	...
551	Under $10,000	38,815	-	-	100	50	...
552	$ 10,000 - $19,999	36,860	10	10	185	70	...
553	$ 20,000 - $29,999	83,410	25	10	150	135	...
554	$ 30,000 - $39,999	88,295	15	25	190	125	...
555	$ 40,000 - $49,999	93,430	20	10	175	120	...
556	$ 50,000 - $59,999	94,805	10	15	100	90	...
557	$ 60,000 - $69,999	97,425	10	20	85	70	...
558	$ 70,000 - $79,999	89,905	-	-	85	40	...
559	$ 80,000 - $89,999	79,590	-	15	35	50	...
560	$ 90,000 - $99,999	67,900	-	-	30	20	...
561	$100,000 and over	300,530	-	55	85	50	...
562	Average family income $	88,436	37,285	282,332	45,280	48,251	...
563	Median family income $	70,079	30,797	65,495	37,972	44,166	...
564	Standard error of average family income $	271	4,250	165,815	1,916	2,271	...
	Incidence of low income in 2000						
565	Total - Economic families	1,231,145	130	170	1,635	1,215	...
566	Low income	176,710	35	20	600	500	...
567	Incidence of low income in 2000 % (52)	14.4	29.0	12.4	36.7	40.9	...
568	Total - Unattached individuals 15 years and over	511,770	185	125	2,345	1,575	...
569	Low income	179,840	115	35	1,155	875	...
570	Incidence of low income in 2000 % (52)	35.1	61.7	25.2	49.2	55.7	...
571	Total - Population in private households	4,633,415	610	655	7,040	5,280	...
572	Low income	771,535	260	95	3,005	2,355	...
573	Incidence of low income in 2000 % (52)	16.7	42.6	14.3	42.6	44.6	...
	Private households by household income groups in 2000						
574	Total - All private households	1,634,755	240	260	3,530	2,545	...
575	Under $10,000	87,030	25	10	425	465	...
576	$ 10,000 - $19,999	145,415	30	30	790	640	...
577	$ 20,000 - $29,999	146,420	40	25	610	410	...
578	$ 30,000 - $39,999	155,395	40	30	585	270	...
579	$ 40,000 - $49,999	150,040	35	15	355	195	...
580	$ 50,000 - $59,999	138,200	20	30	200	170	...
581	$ 60,000 - $69,999	133,130	15	20	135	125	...
582	$ 70,000 - $79,999	117,065	25	20	165	65	...
583	$ 80,000 - $89,999	100,945	-	30	90	70	...
584	$ 90,000 - $99,999	84,700	-	-	40	35	...
585	$100,000 and over	376,420	15	50	125	105	...
586	Average household income $	76,454	39,562	186,805	34,968	32,700	...
587	Median household income $	59,502	35,654	56,442	28,382	23,070	...
588	Standard error of average household income $	192	3,451	105,807	953	1,167	...

Appendix B

AVERAGE HOUSEHOLD EXPENDITURES BY PROVINCE AND TERRITORY

Source: Statistics Canada, CANSIM, table 203-0001.

AVERAGE HOUSEHOLD EXPENDITURES BY METROPOLITAN AREAS

Source: Statistics Canada, CANSIM, table 203-0001 and Catalogue no. 62F0026MIE.

Average household expenditures, by province and territory (Newfoundland and Labrador)				
	2005			
	Canada		**N.L.**	
	Average expenditure per household	Households reporting expenditures	Average expenditure per household	Households reporting expenditures
	$	%	$	%
Total expenditures	**66,857**	**100.0**	**52,612**	**100.0**
Total current consumption	47,484	100.0	38,250	100.0
Food	7,135	100.0	6,270	100.0
Shelter	12,614	99.8	8,415	99.8
Household operation	3,091	100.0	2,742	100.0
Household furnishings and equipment	1,969	93.7	1,810	94.3
Clothing	2,588	99.1	2,330	99.1
Transportation	9,073	98.1	7,635	95.6
Health care	1,799	97.7	1,524	98.4
Personal care	1,094	99.6	994	100.0
Recreation	3,918	98.0	3,263	97.8
Reading materials and other printed matter	284	82.2	199	79.3
Education	1,219	44.3	867	40.8
Tobacco products and alcoholic beverages	1,422	83.6	1,332	84.0
Games of chance (net amount)	278	69.4	270	68.5
Miscellaneous	1,001	91.2	599	83.6
Personal income taxes	13,698	92.7	10,123	83.1
Personal insurance payments and pension contributions	3,921	81.9	3,106	76.1
Gifts of money and contributions	1,753	75.2	1,133	87.8

Source: Statistics Canada, CANSIM, table (for fee) 203-0001.

Average household expenditures, by province and territory (Prince Edward Island, Nova Scotia) 2005				
	P.E.I.		N.S.	
	Average expenditure per household	Households reporting expenditures	Average expenditure per household	Households reporting expenditures
	$	%	$	%
Total expenditures	**53,007**	**100.0**	**56,105**	**100.0**
Total current consumption	38,887	100.0	41,038	100.0
Food	6,230	100.0	6,403	100.0
Shelter	9,652	100.0	10,097	99.9
Household operation	2,887	99.8	3,081	100.0
Household furnishings and equipment	1,619	95.8	1,607	95.6
Clothing	2,068	98.7	2,087	99.2
Transportation	7,209	97.4	7,922	97.0
Health care	1,820	98.3	1,693	98.5
Personal care	957	100.0	965	99.5
Recreation	2,794	98.2	3,219	98.5
Reading materials and other printed matter	269	87.2	263	84.3
Education	983	42.4	1,012	39.1
Tobacco products and alcoholic beverages	1,453	82.0	1,468	82.4
Games of chance (net amount)	273	71.1	320	74.6
Miscellaneous	672	88.8	901	88.2
Personal income taxes	9,356	92.4	10,207	87.5
Personal insurance payments and pension contributions	3,339	83.6	3,388	78.4
Gifts of money and contributions	1,424	84.0	1,471	80.3

Source: Statistics Canada, CANSIM, table (for fee) 203-0001.

Average household expenditures, by province and territory (New Brunswick, Quebec)				
2005				
	N.B.		Que.	
	Average expenditure per household	Households reporting expenditures	Average expenditure per household	Households reporting expenditures
	$	%	$	%
Total expenditures	53,714	100.0	55,348	100.0
Total current consumption	39,370	100.0	39,418	100.0
Food	6,135	100.0	6,900	100.0
Shelter	9,074	99.7	9,715	99.8
Household operation	2,931	100.0	2,420	100.0
Household furnishings and equipment	1,632	93.6	1,623	91.1
Clothing	2,034	98.7	2,189	98.3
Transportation	8,335	97.5	7,132	98.0
Health care	1,772	98.6	1,861	97.8
Personal care	916	99.7	1,022	99.3
Recreation	3,279	97.2	3,235	97.4
Reading materials and other printed matter	232	81.3	232	77.5
Education	755	38.1	650	43.3
Tobacco products and alcoholic beverages	1,350	78.1	1,365	86.7
Games of chance (net amount)	239	70.4	230	72.9
Miscellaneous	688	90.5	845	90.4
Personal income taxes	9,865	89.1	11,464	90.1
Personal insurance payments and pension contributions	3,314	82.3	3,634	81.6
Gifts of money and contributions	1,165	79.6	831	64.1

Source: Statistics Canada, CANSIM, table (for fee) 203-0001.

Average household expenditures, by province and territory (Ontario, Manitoba)				
2005				
	Ont.		Man.	
	Average expenditure per household	Households reporting expenditures	Average expenditure per household	Households reporting expenditures
	$	%	$	%
Total expenditures	**75,920**	**100.0**	**60,181**	**100.0**
Total current consumption	52,926	100.0	41,579	100.0
Food	7,431	100.0	6,351	100.0
Shelter	15,135	99.9	9,997	99.5
Household operation	3,452	100.0	2,810	99.7
Household furnishings and equipment	2,160	95.5	1,705	91.9
Clothing	2,936	99.5	2,179	98.5
Transportation	10,351	98.0	8,253	98.1
Health care	1,587	98.0	1,558	96.6
Personal care	1,167	99.6	977	99.3
Recreation	4,089	98.1	3,859	97.9
Reading materials and other printed matter	325	83.2	279	83.8
Education	1,620	46.4	964	41.8
Tobacco products and alcoholic beverages	1,288	82.6	1,298	79.1
Games of chance (net amount)	301	67.7	360	69.0
Miscellaneous	1,083	92.2	989	91.2
Personal income taxes	16,308	95.9	12,571	93.7
Personal insurance payments and pension contributions	4,388	82.4	3,819	78.8
Gifts of money and contributions	2,299	79.8	2,211	80.3

Source: Statistics Canada, CANSIM, table (for fee) 203-0001.

Average household expenditures, by province and territory (Saskatchewan and Alberta)				
	2005			
	Sask.		Alta.	
	Average expenditure per household	Households reporting expenditures	Average expenditure per household	Households reporting expenditures
	$	%	$	%
Total expenditures	**57,734**	**100.0**	**75,346**	**100.0**
Total current consumption	41,337	100.0	53,019	100.0
Food	5,854	100.0	7,390	100.0
Shelter	9,924	99.8	13,137	99.9
Household operation	2,879	99.9	3,569	100.0
Household furnishings and equipment	1,772	92.5	2,432	94.1
Clothing	2,231	98.8	2,889	99.5
Transportation	8,387	98.0	10,301	98.9
Health care	1,712	97.9	2,130	97.5
Personal care	989	99.9	1,236	99.9
Recreation	3,998	97.7	5,100	99.2
Reading materials and other printed matter	244	88.6	303	86.4
Education	843	39.2	1,348	45.3
Tobacco products and alcoholic beverages	1,330	82.4	1,759	84.9
Games of chance (net amount)	252	73.3	295	66.8
Miscellaneous	919	90.7	1,132	93.3
Personal income taxes	10,792	88.9	16,094	93.7
Personal insurance payments and pension contributions	3,742	78.7	4,043	87.5
Gifts of money and contributions	1,863	85.8	2,190	79.2

Source: Statistics Canada, CANSIM, table (for fee) 203-0001.

Average household expenditures, by province and territory (British Columbia, Yukon Territory)				
2005				
	B.C.		Y.T.	
	Average expenditure per household	Households reporting expenditures	Average expenditure per household	Households reporting expenditures
	$	%	$	%
Total expenditures	**68,231**	**100.0**	**64,477**	**100.0**
Total current consumption	51,002	100.0	45,660	100.0
Food	7,502	100.0	7,350	100.0
Shelter	13,899	99.8	11,428	100.0
Household operation	3,228	100.0	3,010	100.0
Household furnishings and equipment	2,057	93.2	1,559	93.3
Clothing	2,611	99.6	2,120	100.0
Transportation	9,366	98.5	9,390	97.3
Health care	2,185	96.9	949	95.3
Personal care	1,058	99.5	877	100.0
Recreation	4,246	98.1	4,905	99.1
Reading materials and other printed matter	288	83.7	362	88.0
Education	1,453	44.9	477	38.0
Tobacco products and alcoholic beverages	1,693	82.5	2,185	83.2
Games of chance (net amount)	274	67.9	327	60.9
Miscellaneous	1,143	90.5	720	83.1
Personal income taxes	11,921	91.6	13,411	91.0
Personal insurance payments and pension contributions	3,492	79.7	3,850	88.1
Gifts of money and contributions	1,816	73.4	1,557	73.0

Source: Statistics Canada, CANSIM, table (for fee) 203-0001.

Average household expenditures, by province and territory (Northwest Territories, Nunavut)				
2005				
	N.W.T.		**Nvt.**	
	Average expenditure per household	Households reporting expenditures	Average expenditure per household	Households reporting expenditures
	$	%	$	%
Total expenditures	**89,729**	**100.0**	**64,225**	**100.0**
Total current consumption	62,201	100.0	46,327	100.0
Food	10,002	100.0	12,819	100.0
Shelter	17,692	99.1	10,027	98.6
Household operation	3,820	99.7	3,082	100.0
Household furnishings and equipment	1,944	86.7	1,916	86.3
Clothing	3,564	98.8	2,739	95.8
Transportation	10,503	94.9	4,607	81.8
Health care	1,373	90.0	735	74.8
Personal care	1,277	98.0	902	99.5
Recreation	6,166	96.4	5,347	94.9
Reading materials and other printed matter	327	79.3	136	49.5
Education	591	34.6	235	19.3
Tobacco products and alcoholic beverages	3,182	89.2	2,771	89.4
Games of chance (net amount)	638	63.6	407	48.6
Miscellaneous	1,121	87.6	606	49.5
Personal income taxes	20,949	94.8	13,467	83.5
Personal insurance payments and pension contributions	5,299	92.4	3,246	85.0
Gifts of money and contributions	1,279	65.3	1,186	45.2

Source: Statistics Canada, CANSIM, table (for fee) 203-0001.

Average household expenditures, by selected metropolitan area (St. John's, Charlottetown-Summerside)				
2005				
	St. John's		Charlottetown-Summerside	
	Average expenditure per household	Households reporting expenditures	Average expenditure per household	Households reporting expenditures
	$	%	$	%
Total expenditure	62,474	100.0	54,536	100.0
Total current consumption	43,455	100.0	39,235	100.0
Food	6,577	100.0	6,111	100.0
Shelter	10,876	99.6	10,591	100.0
Household operation	2,994	100.0	2,953	99.7
Household furnishings and equipment	2,256	94.6	1,592	96.2
Clothing	2,684	99.5	2,140	98.3
Transportation	7,798	97.5	6,357	97.0
Health care	1,676	97.9	1,767	97.9
Personal care	1,144	100.0	998	100.0
Recreation	3,466	98.4	2,916	98.0
Reading materials and other printed matter	294	85.6	280	86.9
Education	1,178	44.1	1,086	45.5
Tobacco products and alcoholic beverages	1,515	88.9	1,432	85.1
Games of chance (net amount)	249	69.8	249	68.1
Miscellaneous	748	89.6	763	88.7
Personal income taxes	13,722	88.3	10,277	92.3
Personal insurance payments and pension contributions	4,101	77.9	3,611	82.8
Gifts of money and contributions	1,195	84.3	1,413	79.7

Note: Metropolitan area: the overall concept for delineating metropolitan areas is one of a large urban area together with adjacent urban and rural areas that have a high degree of social and economic integration with this urban area.

Source: Statistics Canada, CANSIM, table (for fee) 203-0001 and Catalogue no. 62F0026MIE.

Average household expenditures, by selected metropolitan area (Halifax, Saint John)				
	2005			
	Halifax		**Saint John**	
	Average expenditure per household	Households reporting expenditures	Average expenditure per household	Households reporting expenditures
	$	%	$	%
Total expenditure	**67,891**	**100.0**	**62,313**	**100.0**
Total current consumption	47,161	100.0	43,596	100.0
Food	6,917	100.0	6,553	100.0
Shelter	12,661	99.8	10,481	99.0
Household operation	3,367	100.0	3,265	100.0
Household furnishings and equipment	1,833	95.7	1,674	92.4
Clothing	2,492	99.5	2,562	99.7
Transportation	8,394	98.4	9,016	99.5
Health care	1,894	98.4	1,735	98.2
Personal care	1,087	99.4	1,055	99.5
Recreation	3,866	98.4	3,485	99.1
Reading materials and other printed matter	331	87.3	276	81.7
Education	1,310	43.2	1,120	38.4
Tobacco products and alcoholic beverages	1,506	88.8	1,459	81.4
Games of chance (net amount)	418	74.9	223	71.7
Miscellaneous	1,083	90.3	691	88.7
Personal income taxes	14,891	93.4	13,769	93.8
Personal insurance payments and pension contributions	4,160	82.4	3,460	82.4
Gifts of money and contributions	1,678	77.4	1,487	80.6

Note: Metropolitan area: the overall concept for delineating metropolitan areas is one of a large urban area together with adjacent urban and rural areas that have a high degree of social and economic integration with this urban area.

Source: Statistics Canada, CANSIM, table (for fee) 203-0001 and Catalogue no. 62F0026MIE.

Average household expenditures, by selected metropolitan area (Quebec, Montreal)				
2005				
	Québec		Montréal	
	Average expenditure per household	Households reporting expenditures	Average expenditure per household	Households reporting expenditures
	$	%	$	%
Total expenditure	**56,789**	**100.0**	**57,659**	**100.0**
Total current consumption	39,916	100.0	40,138	100.0
Food	7,017	100.0	6,988	100.0
Shelter	9,567	100.0	10,605	99.7
Household operation	2,082	100.0	2,459	100.0
Household furnishings and equipment	1,639	93.8	1,683	89.2
Clothing	2,127	99.5	2,330	98.3
Transportation	7,571	99.6	6,651	97.5
Health care	1,920	99.1	1,829	97.4
Personal care	1,039	98.9	1,061	99.5
Recreation	3,844	97.7	3,108	96.3
Reading materials and other printed matter	255	87.4	239	75.9
Education	736	50.6	801	45.4
Tobacco products and alcoholic beverages	1,259	92.4	1,257	83.4
Games of chance (net amount)	125	72.4	241	68.2
Miscellaneous	734	91.8	884	90.2
Personal income taxes	11,718	90.7	13,123	89.5
Personal insurance payments and pension contributions	4,092	88.3	3,557	78.8
Gifts of money and contributions	1,063	65.4	842	60.2

Note: Metropolitan area: the overall concept for delineating metropolitan areas is one of a large urban area together with adjacent urban and rural areas that have a high degree of social and economic integration with this urban area.

Source: Statistics Canada, CANSIM, table (for fee) 203-0001 and Catalogue no. 62F0026MIE.

Average household expenditures, by selected metropolitan area (Ottawa–Gatineau (Ontario part), Toronto)				
	2005			
	Ottawa–Gatineau (Ontario part)		Toronto	
	Average expenditure per household	Households reporting expenditures	Average expenditure per household	Households reporting expenditures
	$	%	$	%
Total expenditure	86,788	100.0	85,123	100.0
Total current consumption	59,813	100.0	57,693	100.0
Food	7,732	100.0	8,035	100.0
Shelter	16,081	100.0	17,771	99.9
Household operation	3,909	100.0	3,586	100.0
Household furnishings and equipment	2,775	97.1	2,160	96.6
Clothing	3,005	100.0	3,420	99.4
Transportation	11,494	100.0	10,842	99.1
Health care	2,076	100.0	1,688	98.3
Personal care	1,279	100.0	1,308	99.9
Recreation	5,092	98.8	3,982	98.4
Reading materials and other printed matter	422	94.3	316	80.2
Education	2,447	60.1	1,924	47.9
Tobacco products and alcoholic beverages	1,533	89.6	1,177	78.0
Games of chance (net amount)	194	65.3	299	65.1
Miscellaneous	1,775	97.2	1,185	92.5
Personal income taxes	18,396	99.0	20,105	96.3
Personal insurance payments and pension contributions	5,788	87.1	4,476	86.3
Gifts of money and contributions	2,791	78.6	2,849	79.4

Note: Metropolitan area: the overall concept for delineating metropolitan areas is one of a large urban area together with adjacent urban and rural areas that have a high degree of social and economic integration with this urban area.

Source: Statistics Canada, CANSIM, table (for fee) 203-0001 and Catalogue no. 62F0026MIE.

Average household expenditures, by selected metropolitan area (Winnipeg, Regina)				
2005				
	Winnipeg		Regina	
	Average expenditure per household	Households reporting expenditures	Average expenditure per household	Households reporting expenditures
	$	%	$	%
Total expenditure	**64,250**	**100.0**	**63,525**	**100.0**
Total current consumption	43,479	100.0	45,371	100.0
Food	6,608	100.0	6,428	100.0
Shelter	10,882	99.4	11,865	100.0
Household operation	2,797	99.5	3,039	100.0
Household furnishings and equipment	1,759	91.4	2,031	96.7
Clothing	2,390	98.5	2,568	98.7
Transportation	8,349	98.5	8,995	97.5
Health care	1,560	95.5	1,559	99.5
Personal care	1,052	99.2	1,198	100.0
Recreation	3,858	97.9	3,883	99.1
Reading materials and other printed matter	307	83.3	288	91.0
Education	1,237	46.1	1,023	42.9
Tobacco products and alcoholic beverages	1,273	80.5	1,433	86.5
Games of chance (net amount)	380	66.8	264	77.9
Miscellaneous	1,025	89.8	796	91.2
Personal income taxes	14,569	93.7	12,174	91.7
Personal insurance payments and pension contributions	4,061	78.6	4,447	82.2
Gifts of money and contributions	2,141	79.5	1,533	88.4

Note: Metropolitan area: the overall concept for delineating metropolitan areas is one of a large urban area together with adjacent urban and rural areas that have a high degree of social and economic integration with this urban area.
Source: Statistics Canada, CANSIM, table (for fee) 203-0001 and Catalogue no. 62F0026MIE.

Average household expenditures, by selected metropolitan area (Saskatoon, Calgary)				
2005				
	Saskatoon		Calgary	
	Average expenditure per household	Households reporting expenditures	Average expenditure per household	Households reporting expenditures
	$	%	$	%
Total expenditure	**65,203**	**100.0**	**85,553**	**100.0**
Total current consumption	45,097	100.0	58,345	100.0
Food	6,109	100.0	8,097	100.0
Shelter	11,847	100.0	15,270	100.0
Household operation	3,214	99.7	3,763	100.0
Household furnishings and equipment	1,961	94.1	3,063	93.7
Clothing	2,513	99.5	3,471	99.3
Transportation	8,275	99.6	10,090	98.8
Health care	1,737	97.9	2,260	98.2
Personal care	1,145	100.0	1,393	99.6
Recreation	4,190	98.0	5,359	99.2
Reading materials and other printed matter	318	88.4	338	84.9
Education	1,261	49.5	1,746	49.6
Tobacco products and alcoholic beverages	1,234	80.7	1,887	84.3
Games of chance (net amount)	182	59.8	283	67.0
Miscellaneous	1,110	93.8	1,326	94.1
Personal income taxes	13,894	93.6	20,344	97.4
Personal insurance payments and pension contributions	4,354	84.1	4,517	91.4
Gifts of money and contributions	1,859	83.1	2,347	81.6

Note: Metropolitan area: the overall concept for delineating metropolitan areas is one of a large urban area together with adjacent urban and rural areas that have a high degree of social and economic integration with this urban area.

Source: Statistics Canada, CANSIM, table (for fee) 203-0001 and Catalogue no. 62F0026MIE.

Average household expenditures, by selected metropolitan area (Edmonton, Vancouver)				
2005				
	Edmonton		Vancouver	
	Average expenditure per household	Households reporting expenditures	Average expenditure per household	Households reporting expenditures
	$	%	$	%
Total expenditure	**72,215**	**100.0**	**72,782**	**100.0**
Total current consumption	50,672	100.0	54,145	100.0
Food	7,575	100.0	8,004	100.0
Shelter	12,662	99.9	15,250	99.9
Household operation	3,390	100.0	3,303	100.0
Household furnishings and equipment	2,040	93.5	1,947	91.4
Clothing	2,888	99.6	2,950	99.5
Transportation	9,813	99.3	9,414	99.3
Health care	1,932	96.4	2,311	95.8
Personal care	1,187	99.9	1,152	99.4
Recreation	4,561	98.8	4,169	97.2
Reading materials and other printed matter	317	86.4	312	79.5
Education	1,471	49.3	2,027	48.7
Tobacco products and alcoholic beverages	1,534	85.8	1,764	78.7
Games of chance (net amount)	278	68.3	326	61.9
Miscellaneous	1,023	91.1	1,216	88.9
Personal income taxes	15,587	91.7	13,487	90.9
Personal insurance payments and pension contributions	4,236	85.1	3,695	83.3
Gifts of money and contributions	1,720	74.4	1,454	69.1

Note: Metropolitan area: the overall concept for delineating metropolitan areas is one of a large urban area together with adjacent urban and rural areas that have a high degree of social and economic integration with this urban area.

Source: Statistics Canada, CANSIM, table (for fee) 203-0001 and Catalogue no. 62F0026MIE.

Average household expenditures, by selected metropolitan area (Victoria, Whitehorse)				
2005				
	Victoria		Whitehorse	
	Average expenditure per household	Households reporting expenditures	Average expenditure per household	Households reporting expenditures
	$	%	$	%
Total expenditure	61,896	100.0	67,219	100.0
Total current consumption	47,162	100.0	47,961	100.0
Food	6,746	100.0	7,616	100.0
Shelter	13,463	100.0	12,990	100.0
Household operation	3,317	100.0	3,075	100.0
Household furnishings and equipment	2,235	91.7	1,698	93.0
Clothing	2,368	100.0	2,112	100.0
Transportation	8,230	95.6	9,791	99.3
Health care	1,742	99.1	1,008	96.9
Personal care	1,052	100.0	886	100.0
Recreation	4,111	99.2	4,945	100.0
Reading materials and other printed matter	282	94.0	374	89.9
Education	1,132	46.2	583	41.4
Tobacco products and alcoholic beverages	1,383	91.7	1,876	83.8
Games of chance (net amount)	164	81.1	297	61.8
Miscellaneous	940	91.2	710	82.7
Personal income taxes	10,002	89.9	14,098	90.4
Personal insurance payments and pension contributions	3,357	83.3	3,804	87.9
Gifts of money and contributions	1,375	79.4	1,356	78.1

Note: Metropolitan area: the overall concept for delineating metropolitan areas is one of a large urban area together with adjacent urban and rural areas that have a high degree of social and economic integration with this urban area.

Source: Statistics Canada, CANSIM, table (for fee) 203-0001 and Catalogue no. 62F0026MIE.